THE BIRTH LITANY

1. I DESIRE BIRTH.

2. I AM READY TO BE BURNED AND CONSUMED; FOR THAT IS WHAT BIRTH IS.

3. I AM READY TO BE NAKED AND UNPROTECTED, AND TO SUFFER FROM MY NAKEDNESS, FOR THAT IS WHAT LIFE IS.

4. I AM READY TO MAKE THE PILGRIMAGE THROUGH MATTER IN DARKNESS AND IN FIRE, SO THAT THE CIRCLE OF THE UNCREATE SHALL BECOME ONE WITH THE CIRCLE OF THE CREATE.

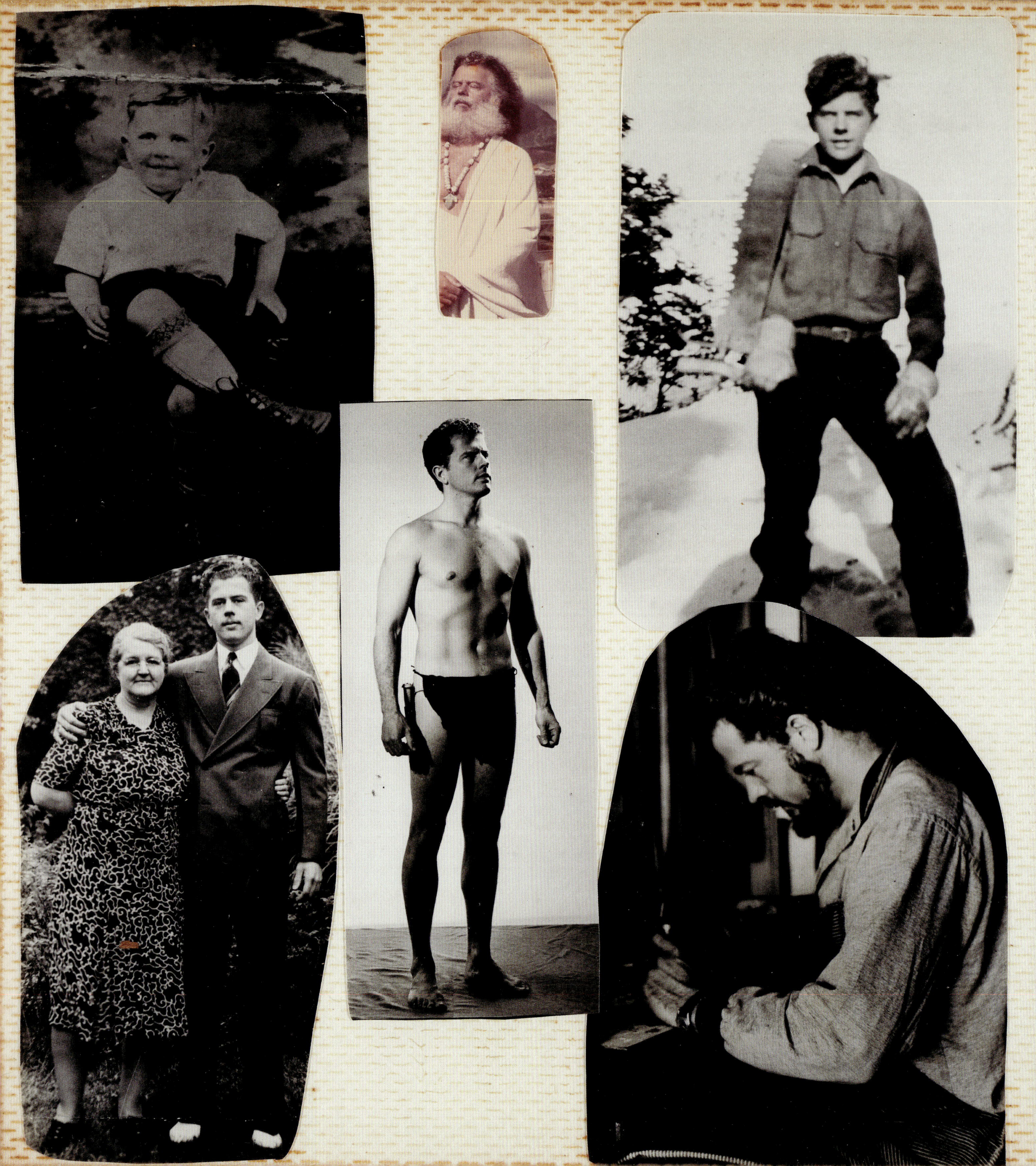

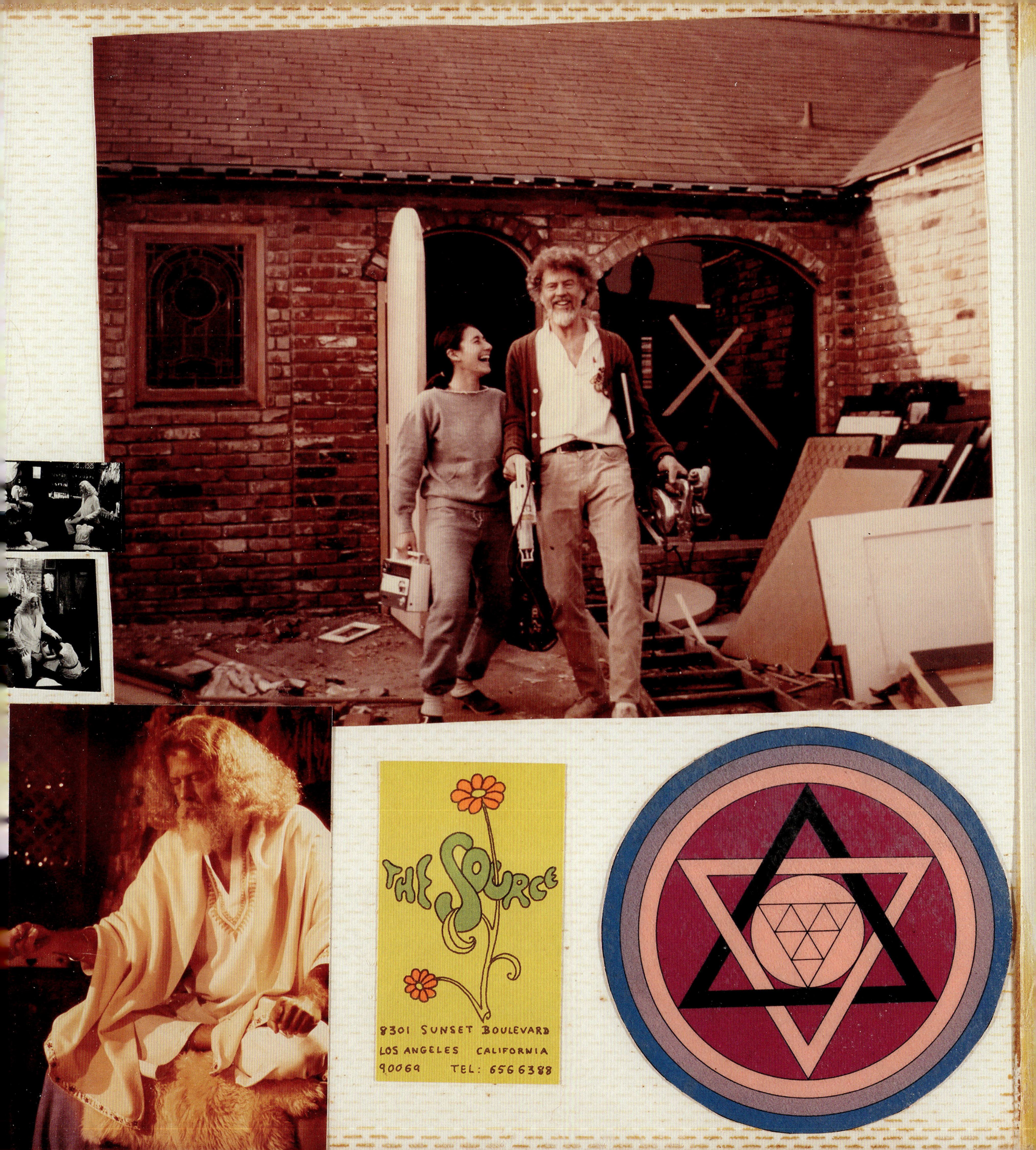

THE SOURCE
8301 SUNSET BOULEVARD
LOS ANGELES CALIFORNIA
90069   TEL: 656 6388

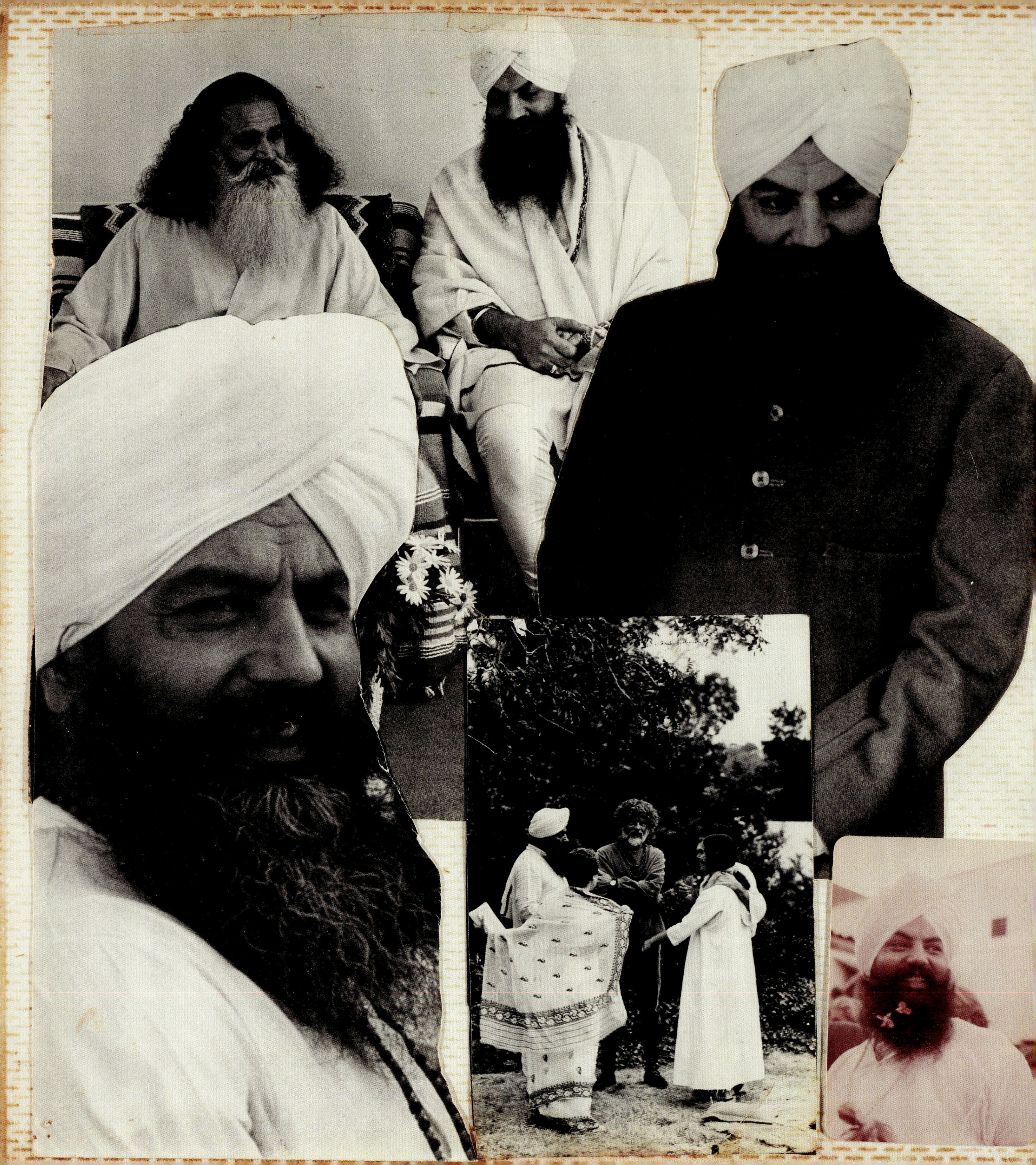

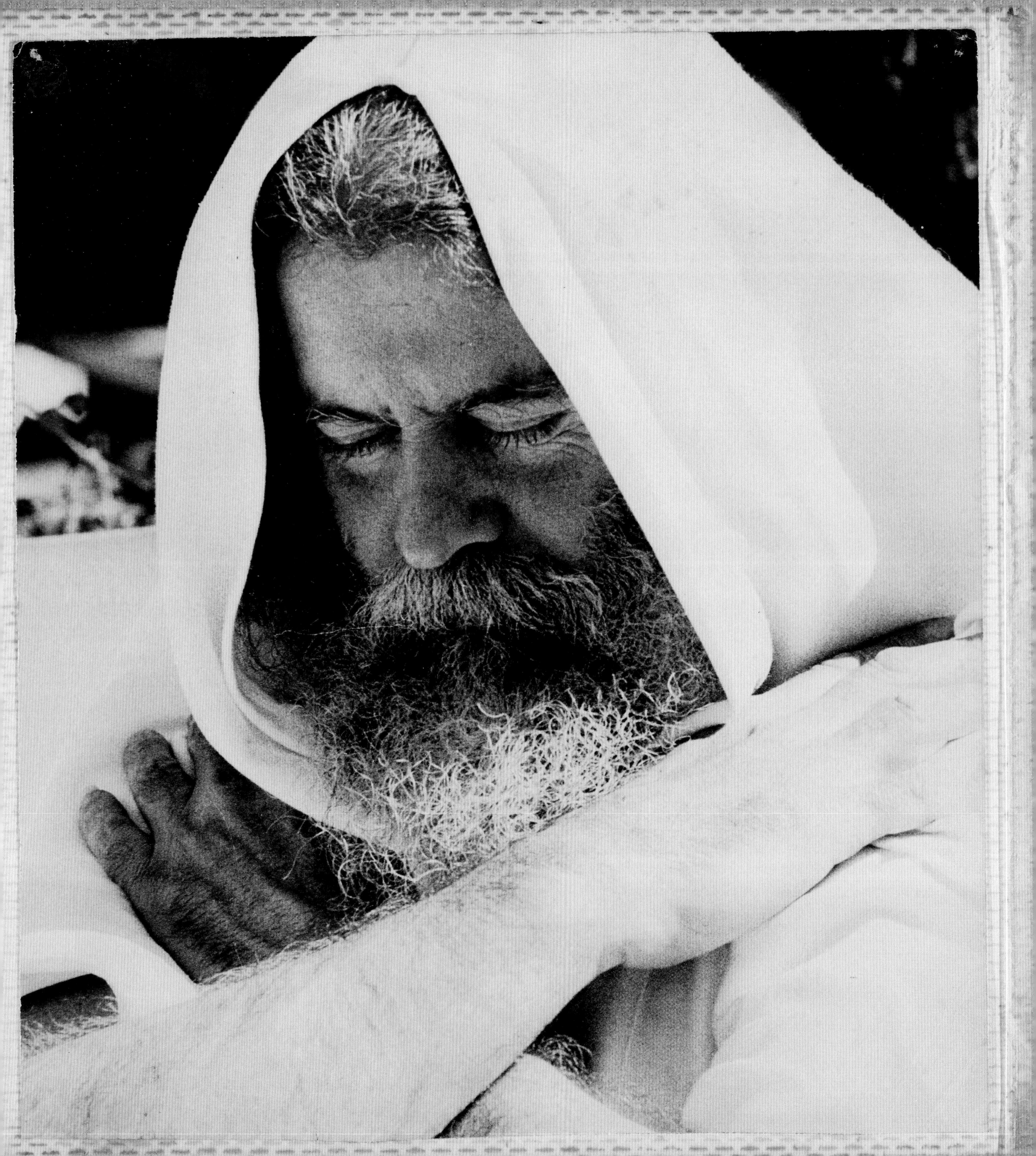

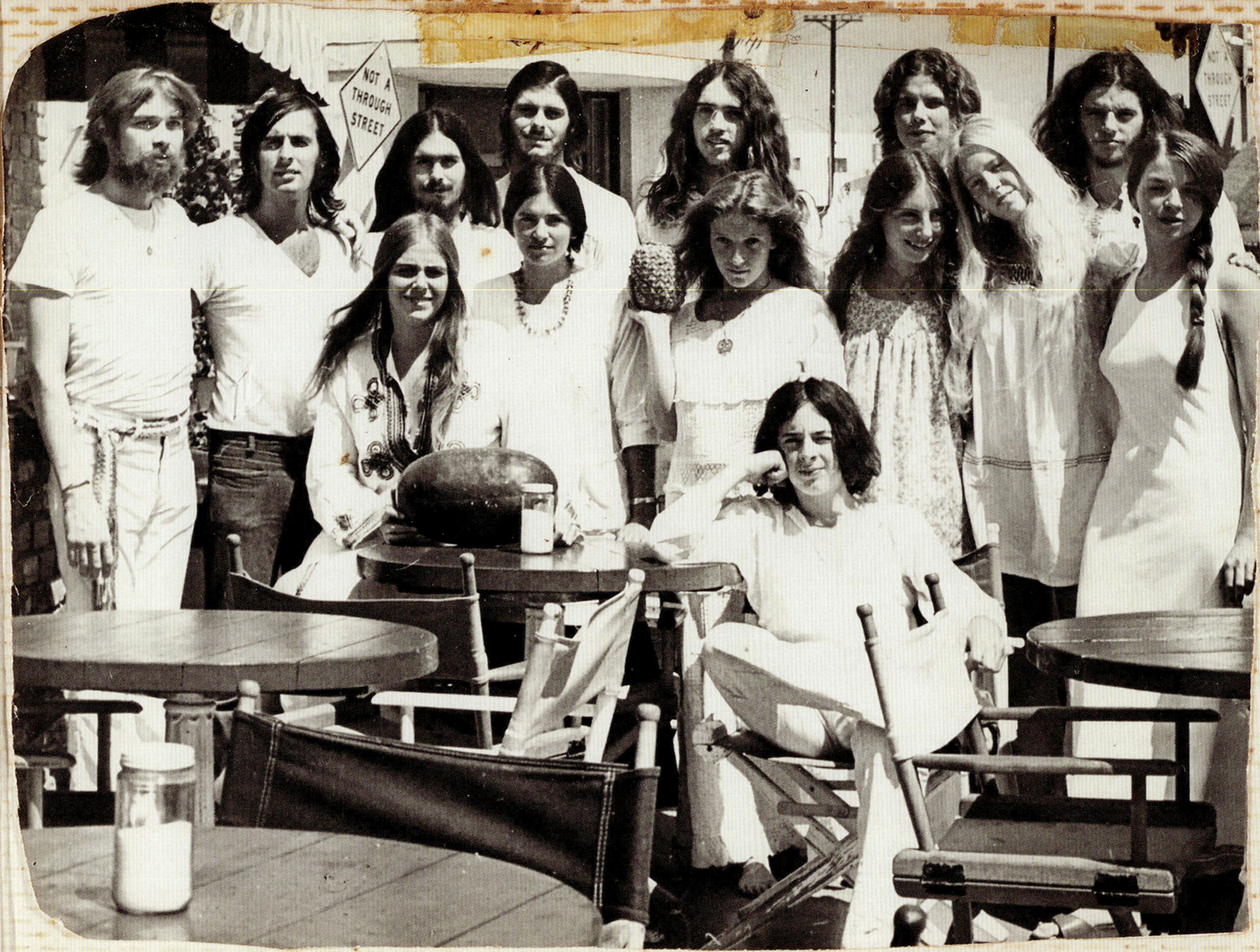

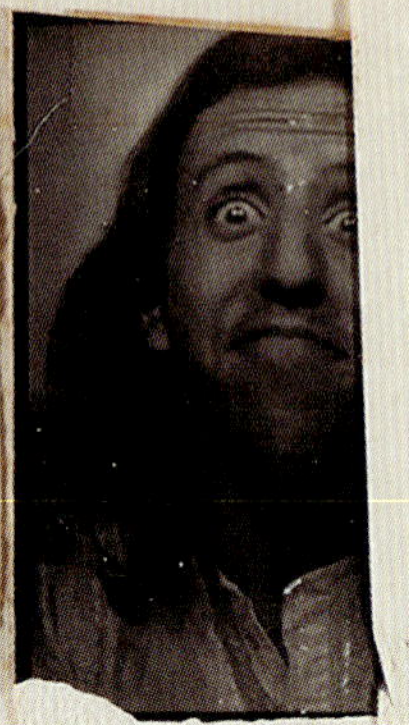

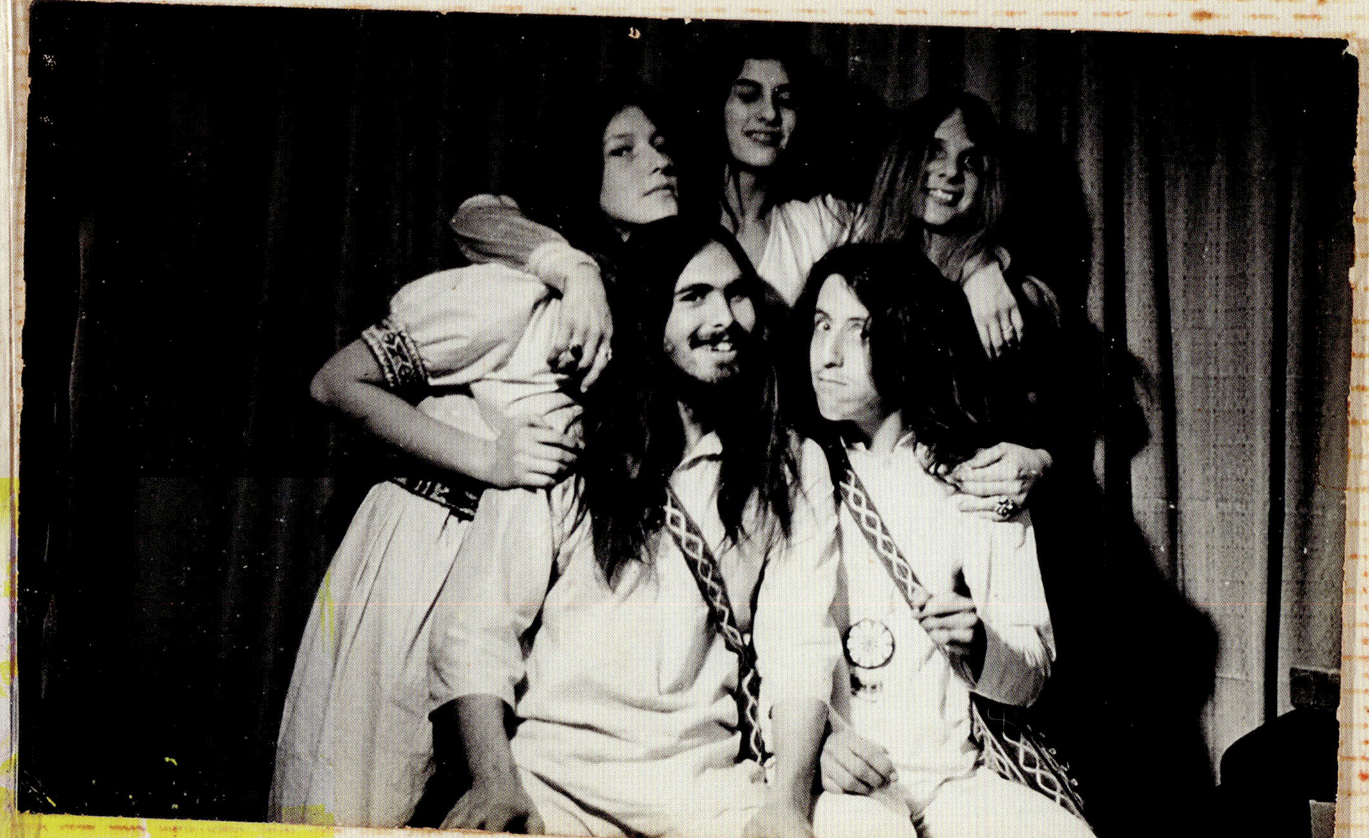
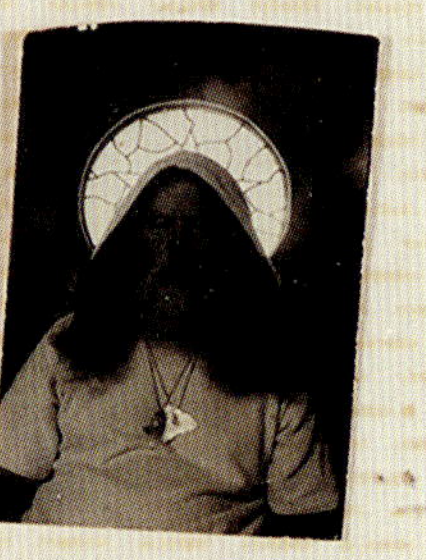

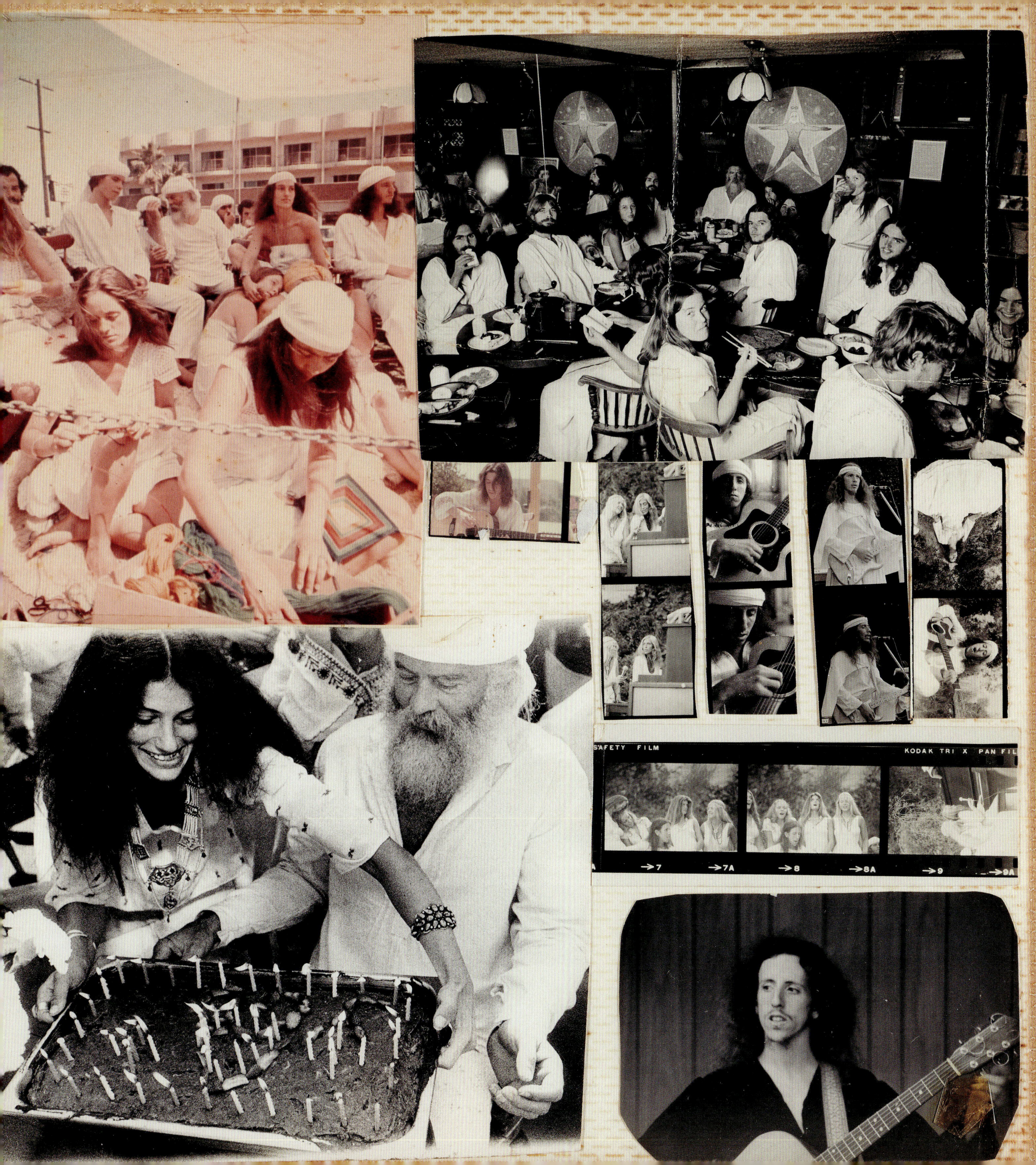

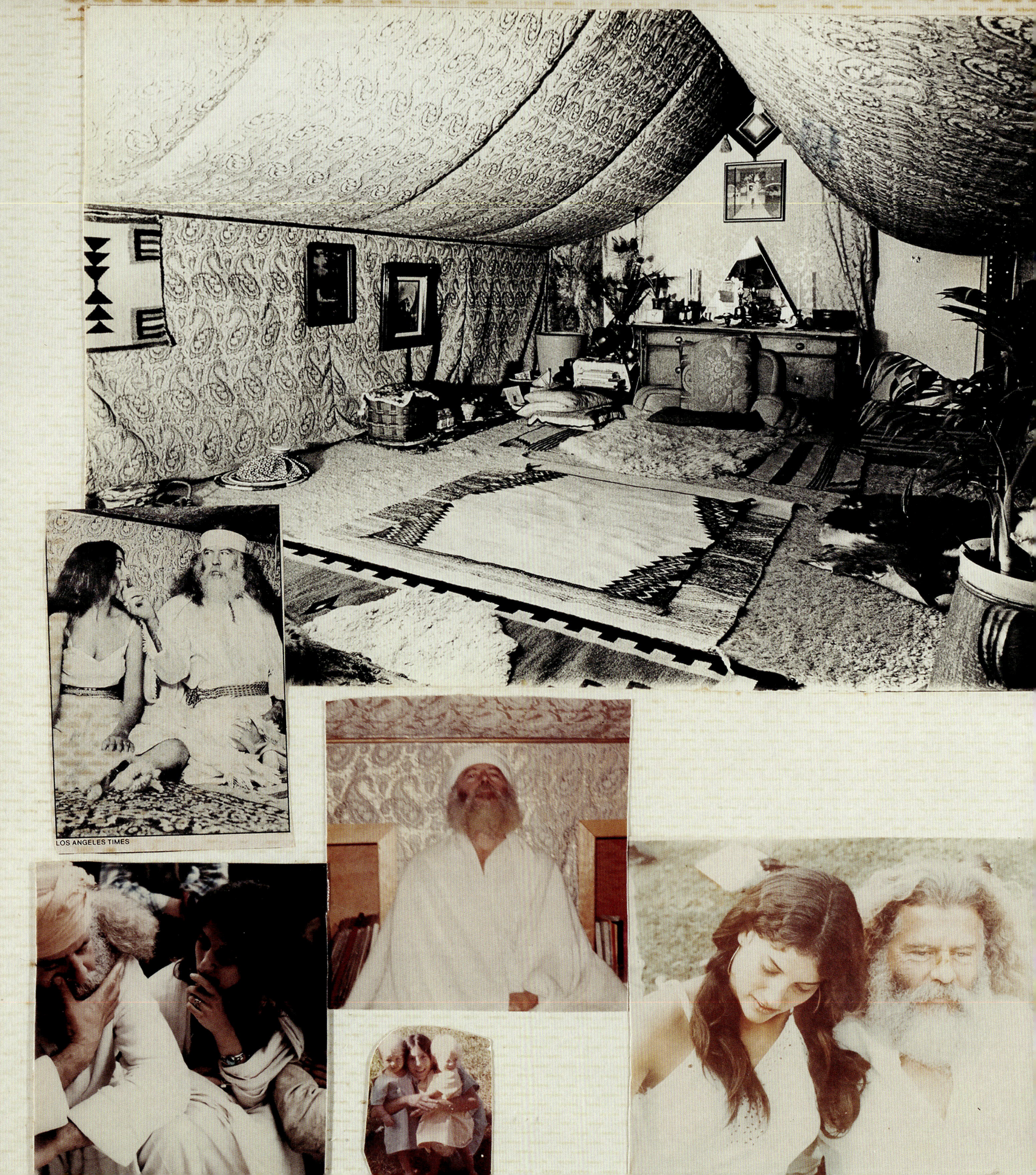

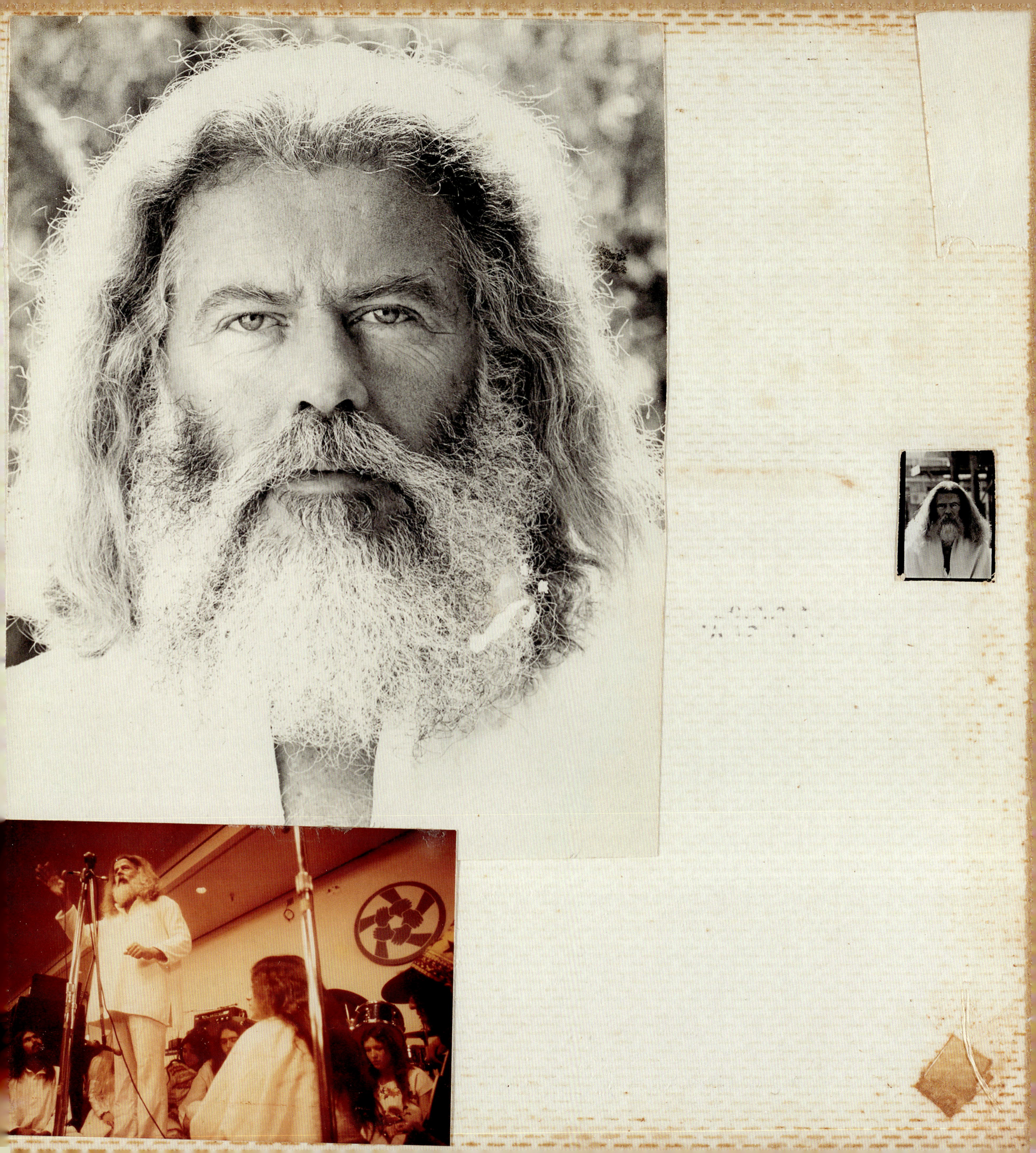

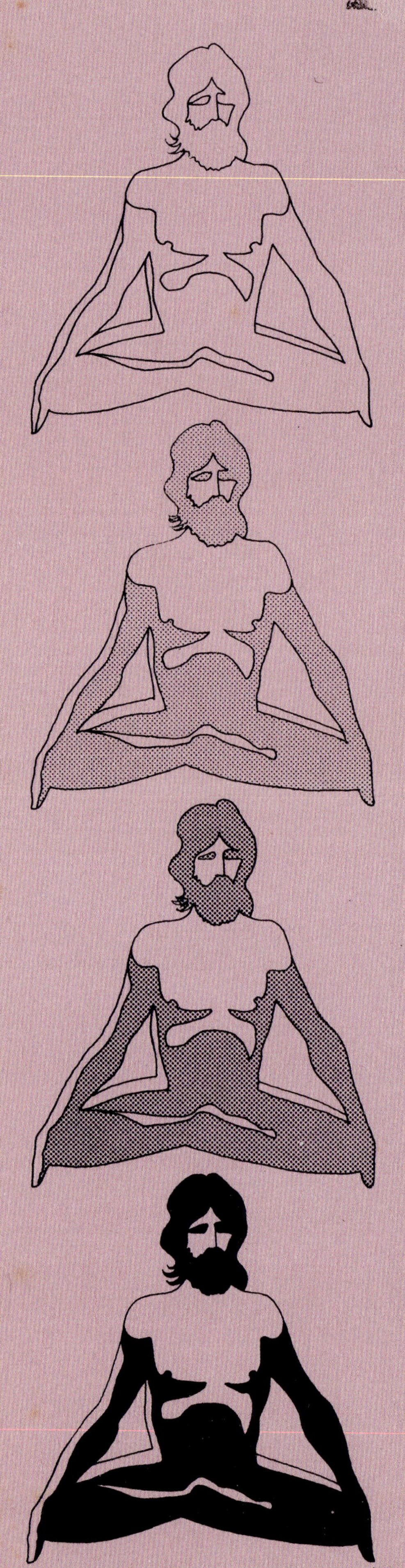

the family that meditates together

levitates together

Join in our rise to liberation
through the knowledge of meditation.

It gives us great joy to share
the temple we love with those
who seek spiritual realization.

Classes will be taught by our family
everyday between 9 a.m. and 8 p.m.
(every hour on the hour)
at 8301 Sunset boulevard at Sweetzer
next to The Source restaurant.

And they are price-less.

THE SOURCE BROTHERHOOD

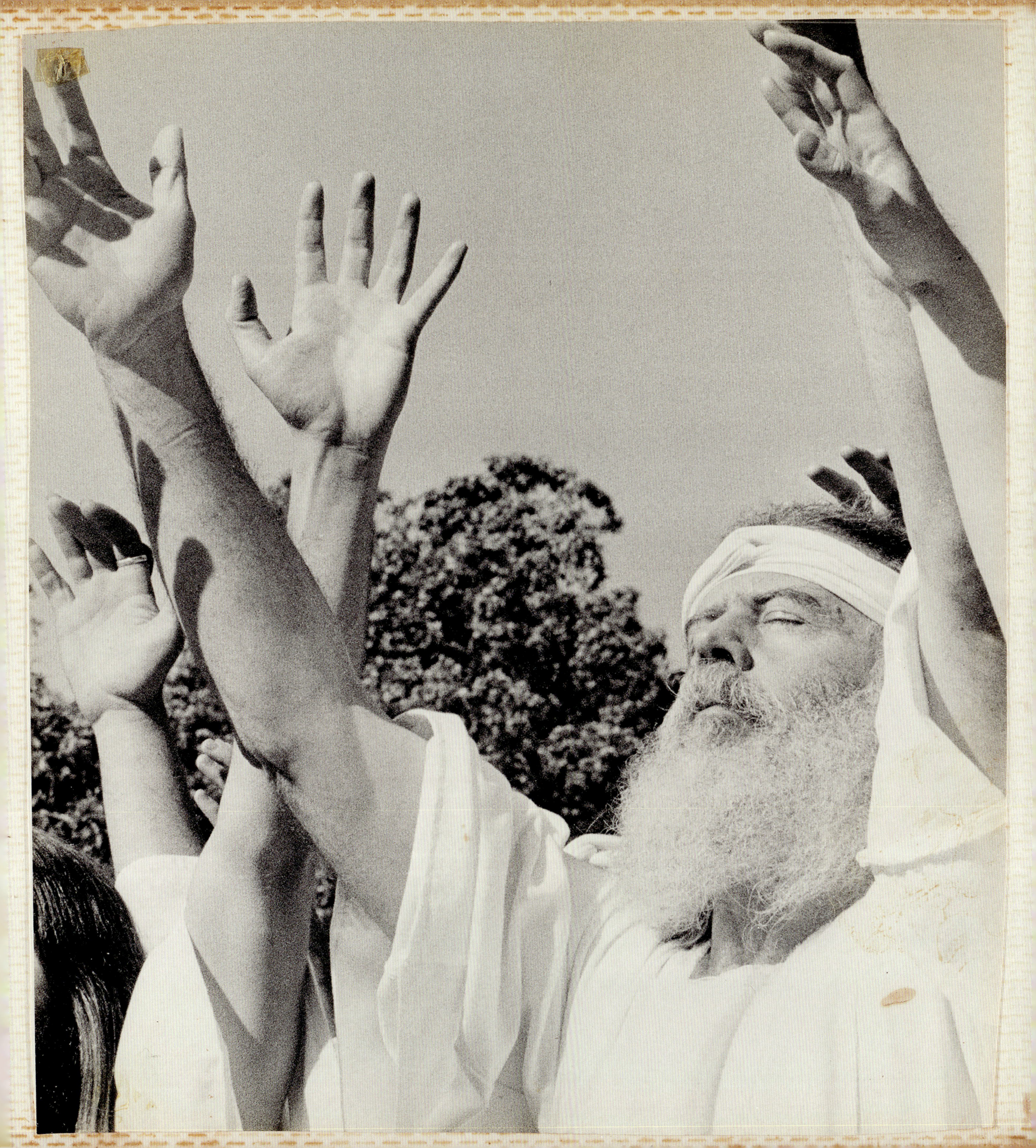

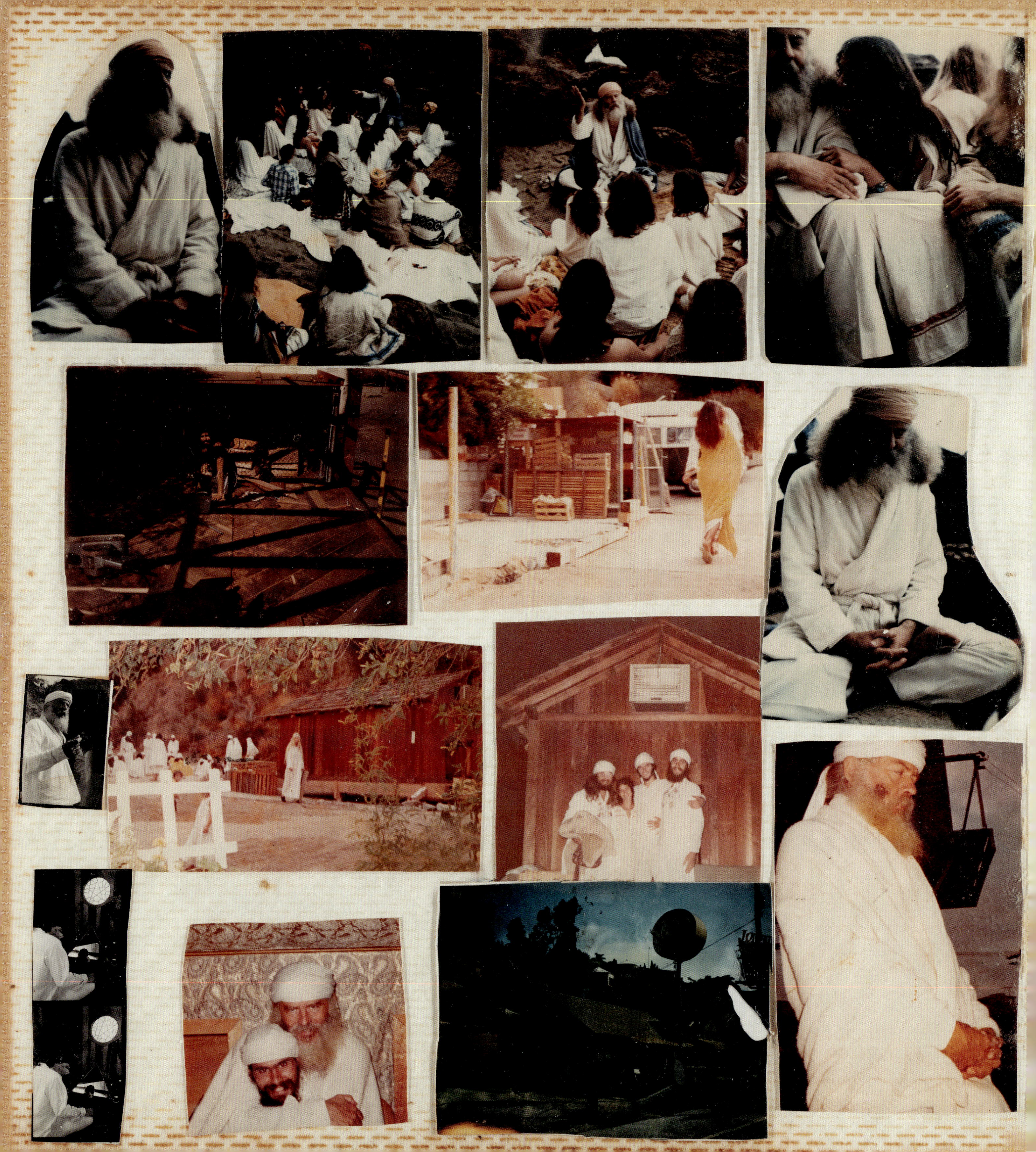

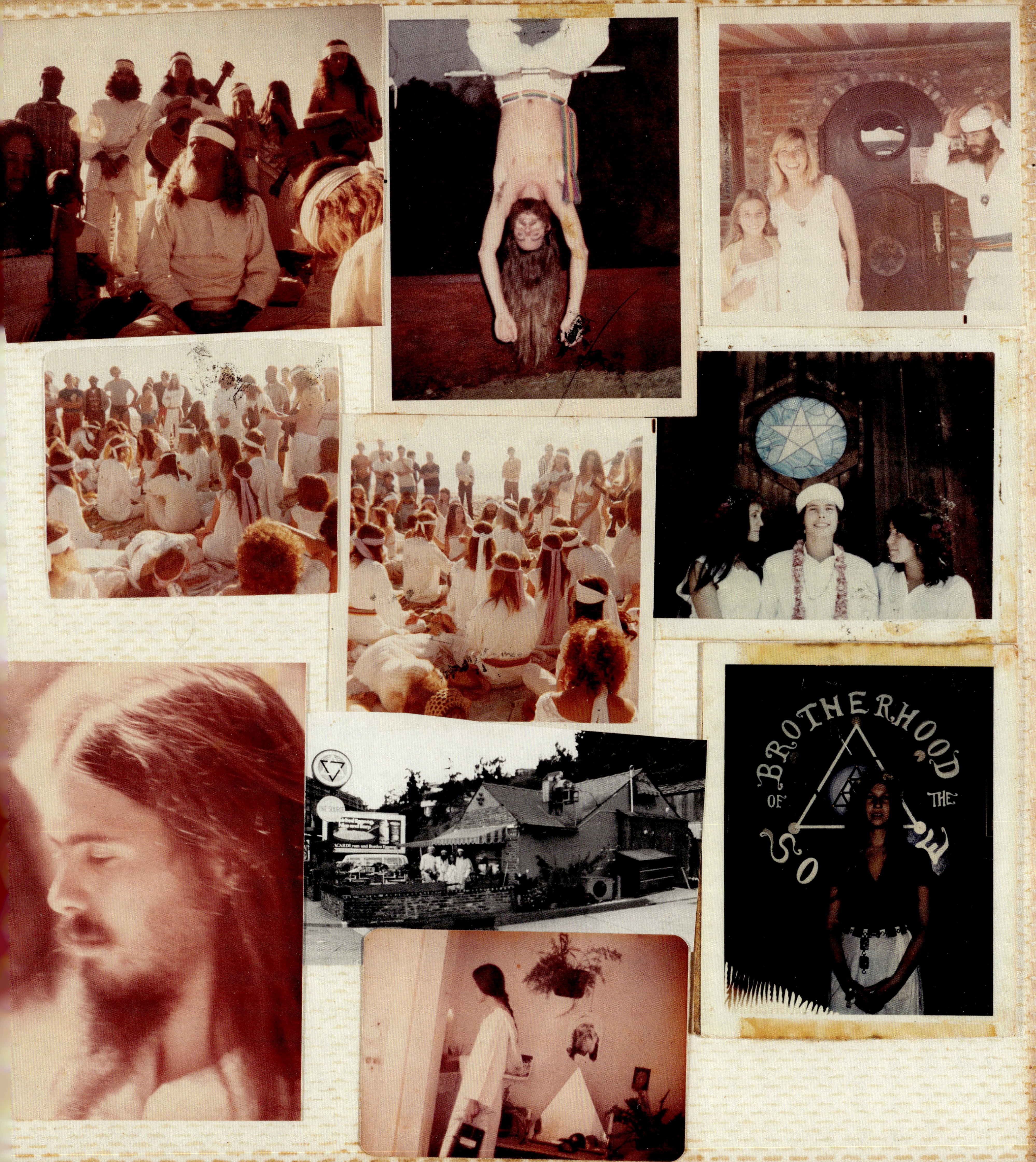
BROTHERHOOD
OF
THE
SO

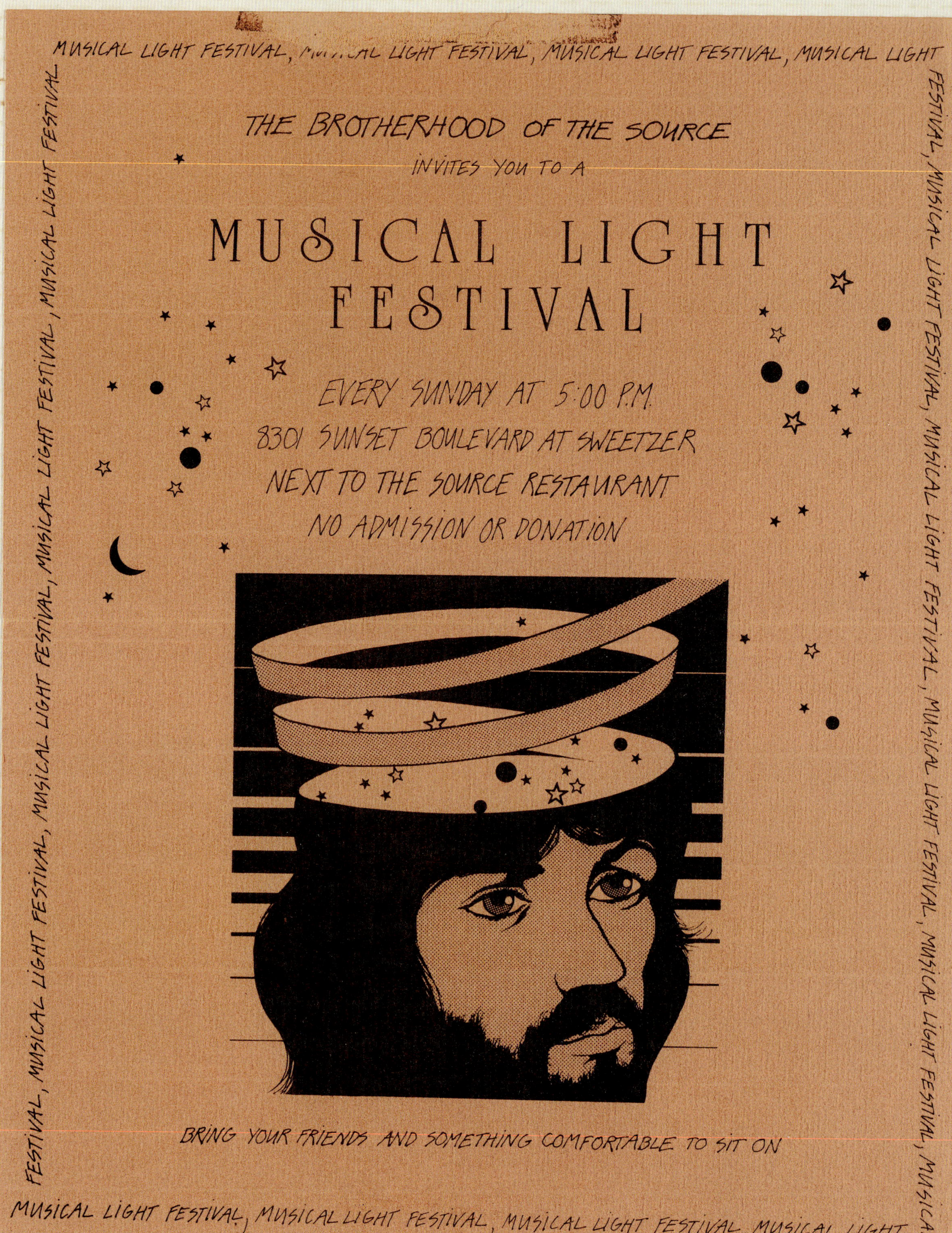

MUSICAL LIGHT FESTIVAL, MUSICAL LIGHT FESTIVAL, MUSICAL LIGHT FESTIVAL, MUSICAL LIGHT
THE BROTHERHOOD OF THE SOURCE
INVITES YOU TO A
MUSICAL LIGHT FESTIVAL
EVERY SUNDAY AT 5:00 P.M.
8301 SUNSET BOULEVARD AT SWEETZER
NEXT TO THE SOURCE RESTAURANT
NO ADMISSION OR DONATION
BRING YOUR FRIENDS AND SOMETHING COMFORTABLE TO SIT ON
MUSICAL LIGHT FESTIVAL, MUSICAL LIGHT FESTIVAL, MUSICAL LIGHT FESTIVAL, MUSICAL LIGHT
FESTIVAL, MUSICAL LIGHT FESTIVAL, MUSICAL LIGHT FESTIVAL, MUSICAL LIGHT FESTIVAL, MUSICAL LIGHT FESTIVAL, MUSICAL LIGHT FESTIVAL, MUSICAL
FESTIVAL, MUSICAL LIGHT FESTIVAL, MUSICAL LIGHT FESTIVAL, MUSICAL LIGHT FESTIVAL, MUSICAL LIGHT FESTIVAL, MUSICAL LIGHT FESTIVAL, MUSICAL

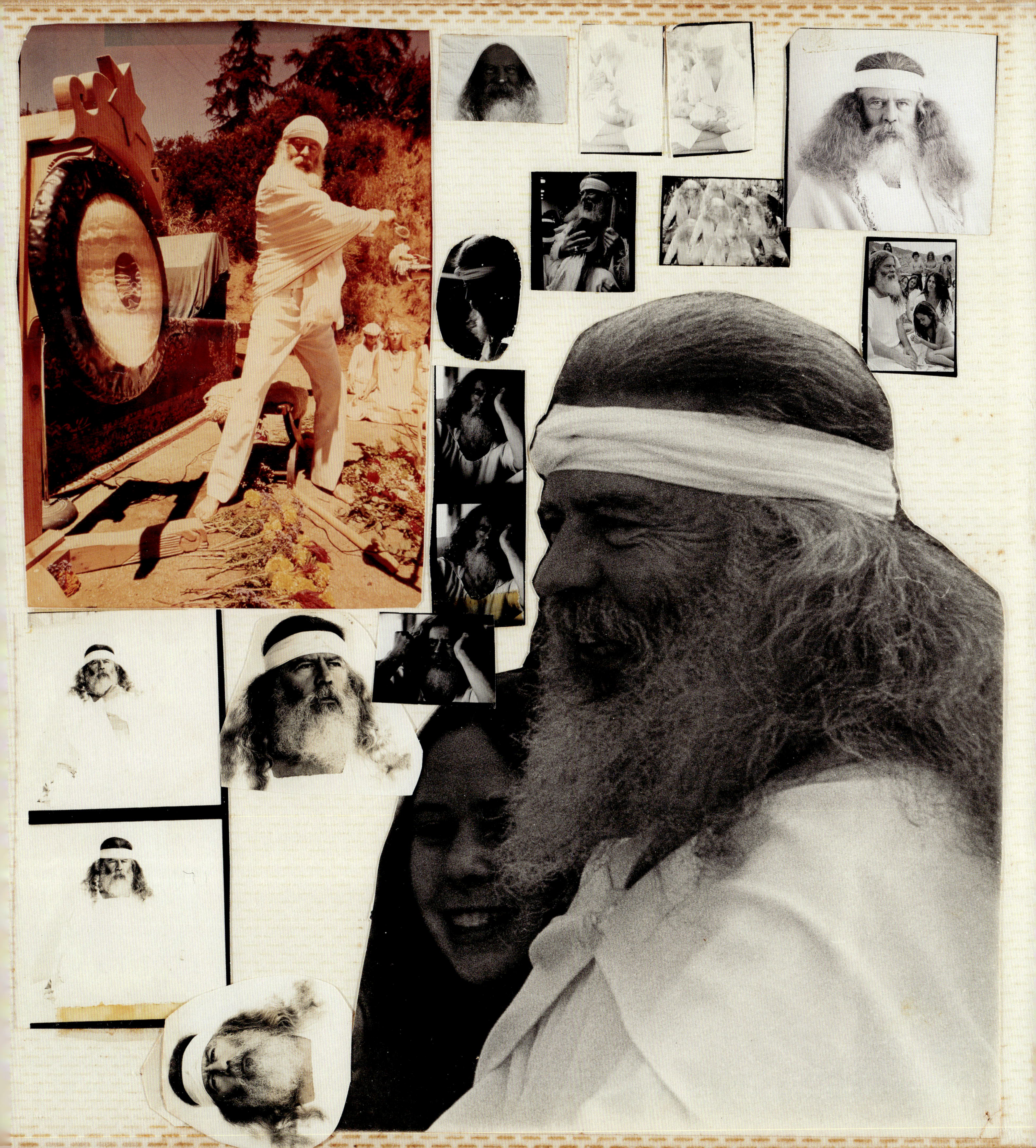

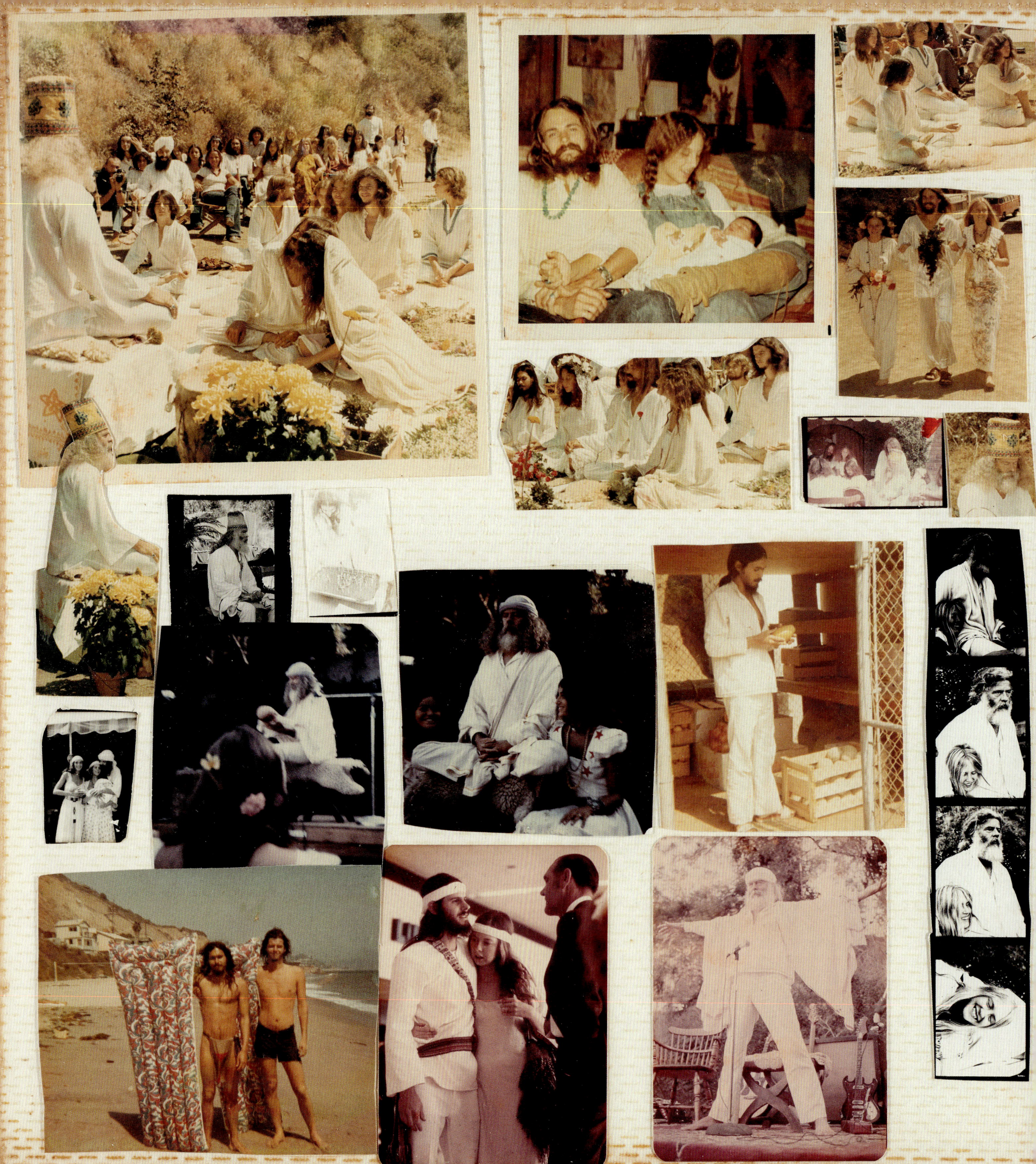

ASTROLOGY of the ETERNAL NOW

As the light grows in the heart within, as the taste for pure life grows stronger, the consciousness opens towards the great, secret places within, where all life is one, where all lives are one. Thereafter, this outer, manifested life loses its attraction, and we seek rather the deep infinitudes. Instead of the outer form and surroundings of our lives, we long for their inner, everlasting essence. We yearn for that quiet communion in the inner chamber of the soul, where spirit speaks to spirit. Astrology of the Eternal Now is one means of opening, from without, the way to the heart within...

BROTHERHOOD OF THE SOURCE
8301 SUNSET BLVD., L.A.
656-6388

PVT. JIM BAKER

By GORD

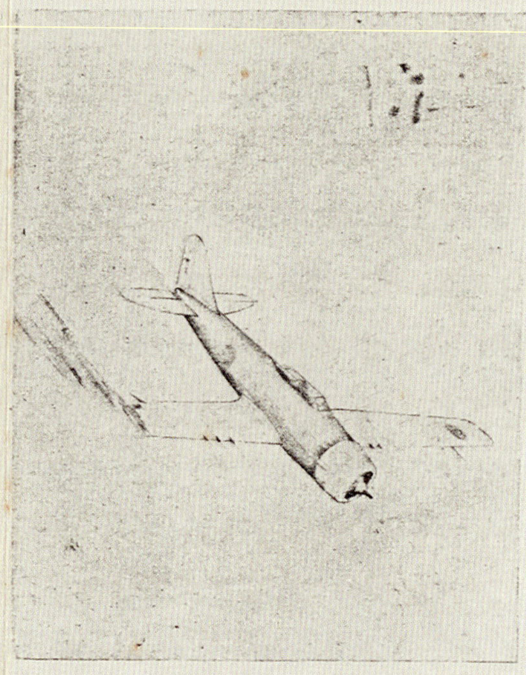

BEING a loader at a National weightlifting championship is no fun. They say the loader does all the work and the lifter gets all the glory. I guess that's the way it was with Jim Baker at the Nationals last year in Cincinnati. I'll bet more than half the competitors don't remember Jim. But it was Jim who changed the plates and loaded the barbell every time. A lifter seldom pays any attention to the chap who puts the weights on the bar; he just goes out there and lifts . . . if he makes the lift—fine—he gets a big hand . . . while the loader makes the bar heavier for the next man.

Jim was a fair lifter, not ready yet for National competition but he wanted first hand information on the champs and the best way to get it was to offer his services as a loader. Jim was tall, he stood 6′ 2″ and could make the light heavyweight class. He could total over 600 and make most lifters step on the one hand clean and jerk, for Jim could hoist over 170 in this fashion. . . . What's all this got to do with 13 dead Japs? . . . give me time, Bud, I'll get there. . . .

A few weeks after the Nationals Jim walked into the Cincinnati Central Y and buttonholed Emmett Faris, Ohio weightlifting chairman. Jim said he was going to join the Marines and it was necessary to have a couple of signatures of American citizens to help fix

things. Howard Bond, a Cinncy policeman, and Emmett put their John Henrys on Jim's character.

Being a bar bell man Jim passed "like a top" for the Marine Corps and in no time he was in training at San Diego. It didn't take Jim long to win medals for marksmanship and be classed as an Expert Marksman. Jim was assigned to the *U. S. S. Chicago*. Everything was peaceful—quite routine work until January 29th.

It was getting dark and night comes quick in the tropics. The *Chicago* is a heavy battle cruiser and she was plowing through a flat sea 30 miles off Guadalcanal. She was returning from convoying troops to the South Seas with every man of her crew itching for a go at the Japs and a little disappointed at not having it. . . . Suddenly from overhead comes a whining scream . . . a fast plane diving with motor off . . . it's a Zero!

Before any guns could be brought into action, even before anyone knew what was happening there was a deafening crash . . . the Zero had suicide crashed into the superstructure of the *Chicago* . . . instantly it burst into flames. The flames were much brighter than a plane normally makes. This one must have been loaded with inflammables . . . it was now apparent to every man of the *Chicago* what had happened. The Zero was in advance of a larger force; it had glided in from a high altitude with motor cut and suicide crashed into the *Chicago* and with its bright flames making a perfect beacon for the oncoming Japs. . . .

The men of the *Chicago* didn't have to wait long. A swarm of Jap torpedo planes came racing in 10 feet over the water . . . it's dark now but the Japs aim their lethal tin fish at the bright light of the burning Zero wreckage.

The Marines who man the anti-aircraft batteries of the *Chicago* go to work . . . this is what they've been waiting for . . . they let go with everything aiming at the flashes from the Jap's exhaust vents . . . the first batch of torpedoes go wild.

The second wave of Jap planes come in incredibly close and launch their torpedoes . . . the *Chicago* gets one . . . the explosion is so violent it throws the men sprawling on the deck . . . flames roll over the side of the ship . . . another and another torpedo find their mark . . . at midnight the *Chicago* is a

dead ship but every plane of that last wave a dead duck too . . . at 4 A. M. the torpedo planes stop coming in.

The *Chicago* had a respite of four hours. She was listing badly and all headway was lost. At 8 A. M. Jap bombers roared in to administer the death blow but their marksmanship was poor . . . the entire morning went by and no bomb hit the gallant ship . . . then came more Zeros.

Marine Pvt. Jim Baker and three others comprise the forward gun crew. They have the best spot for shooting, also the best spot to be shot at. Plane after planes dives in—first on one side—then on the other. Baker's shooting is very effective, the Jap Zeros pick up plenty of his lead. Pretty soon he learns just how much lead-off to give and he can see his tracers hitting home . . . he starts chalking up his score . . . one . . . two . . . three

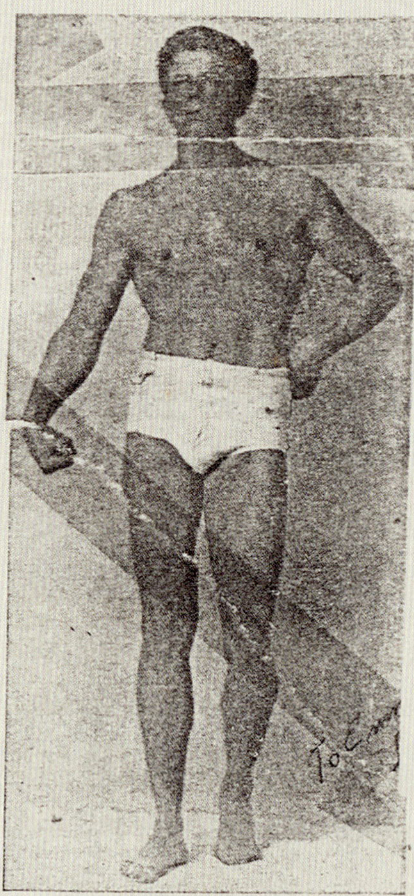

PVT. JIM BAKER *of Cincinnati, hero of the* U. S. S. Chicago. *When this picture was taken* JIM *weighed 185 pounds, stood 6′ 2″ tall and was 19 years old. He was particularly good on the One Hand Clean and Jerk, having done over 170.*

AND 13 DEAD JAPS

VENABLES

. . . five . . . ten . . . a violent lurch of the ship . . . some internal explosion wrenches Baker from his machine-gun harness. He hits the deck hard. Looking off to one side he sees a Zero roaring in with all guns spitting . . . he rolled over just in time—the spot on the deck he vacated gets all chewed up by Jap machine-gun slugs . . . Baker gets back in his harness, singles out an oncoming Zero and steps on the trigger . . . he is dispatched to a more peaceful and less transitory world.

A new type of two place combat job sweeps in close, its rear gunner strafing the men on the *Chicago's* deck . . . as it nears the fore part of the ship the Jap gunner runs out of ammunition . . . he is quite visible to all the men though clipping off better than 200 per . . . he waves to the *Chicago* and gives a thumb and nose salute. Pvt. Baker picks him up in his spiderweb sight . . . gives him the right amount of lead-off and lets him have it . . . he never got back home to brag to his pals about his contempt for Americans. Baker's score stands at 12 enemy planes down.

All through the hot day enemy planes roared in. There was no hope for the *Chicago*. She was a dead ship; taking in water fast and listing treacherously. At any moment she might roll over. Still the Jap planes come in —like hounds harrying a crippled stag. In the mid-afternoon a bomber scores a direct hit. At 5 P. M. orders are given to abandon ship. The sea is thick with the *Chicago's* men. The gun crew have already gone overboard and Baker is ready to go when he sese a lone Zero diving in to strafe the men struggling in the water. Baker gets back in the machine-gun harness. There are only 10 shots in the big drum. He cuts loose . . . the Zero is too far away and nothing happens . . . but the Zero pilot sees Baker and swings toward him. There is no one left to fit another drum of ammunition in place. A loaded drum weighs 60 pounds . . . Baker grasps one in one hand . . . releases the empty one with the other and slaps the full one into place . . . the Zero is almost on him and machine gun bullets are spitting past his head. He steps on the trigger . . . there is a burst of flame and the Zero hurtles past 20 yards away to crash in the sea.

The *Chicago* is sinking fast. Baker's work is done. He gets overboard and swims madly to escape the suction of the sinking ship. He can feel the pull but he makes it. The

Chicago goes under in six minutes!

Pvt. Jim Baker was in the water several hours when a destroyer picked him up. Two days later he was ashore.

Pvt. Jim Baker was officially credited with shooting down 13 Jap planes.

Pvt. Jim Baker went home to Cincinnati on his fourteen day furlough sporting a decoration for conspicuous gallantry. Emmett Faris was planning a demonstration of weightlifting at the National War Physical Fitness Convention. He asked hero Baker if he could possibly take time out from the numerous social functions showered on him to appear at the lifting. Baker instantly agreed—once a weightlifter always a weightlifter.

And Jim is a real patriotic American. He got married on his birthday. I don't mean that getting married on one's birhday is a patriotic gesture but Jim happened to be born on the 4th of July.

In April Baker reported to Mare Island, Calif. for further training. They have a lot of weights down there at Mare Island and you can bet that Jim Baker is getting in shape for anything that comes along. He wants to be assigned to another ship and get another crack at the Japs, particularly the ones that like to shoot seamen struggling in the water.

We feel proud and thrilled to know that Jim Baker was a weightlifter like one of us. To build his strength and fine physique he used bar bells and dumbells. Bar bells and dumbells come from York and when Jim gets his next crack at the Japs he may be using another well known product of our city (York has to horn in on some of the credit, you know, Cincinnati can't have it all) for the new type of machine gun, the one that may well win the war on the seas, is made in York—so, happy hunting, Pvt. Jim Baker, and lots of luck.

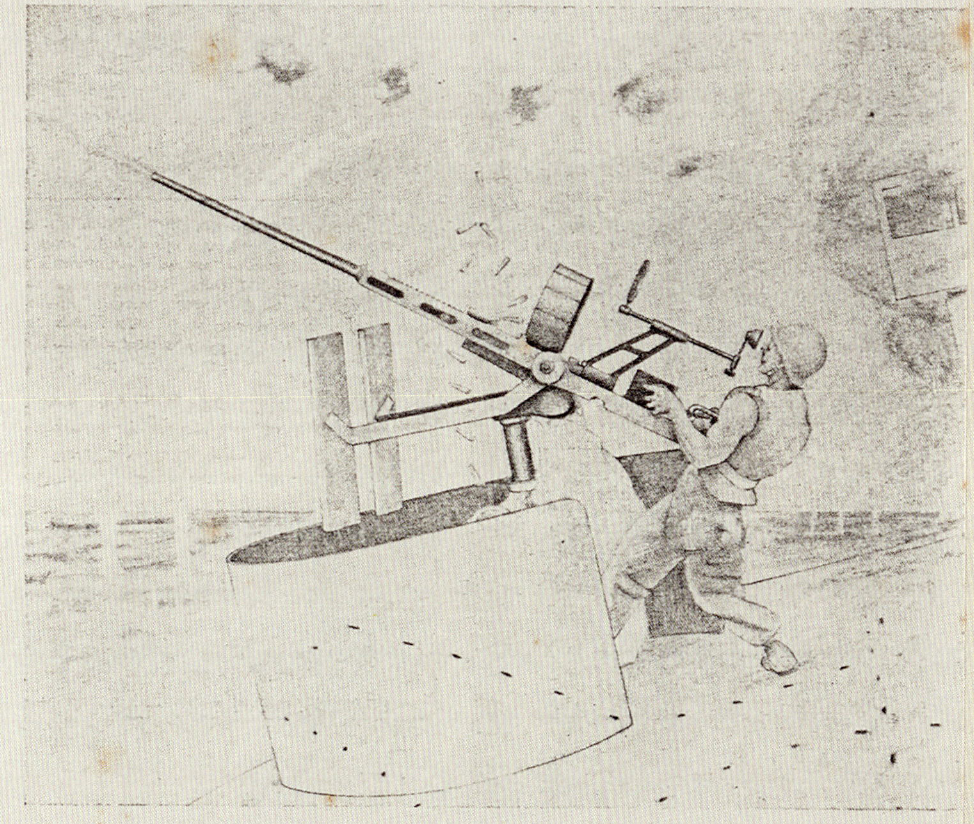

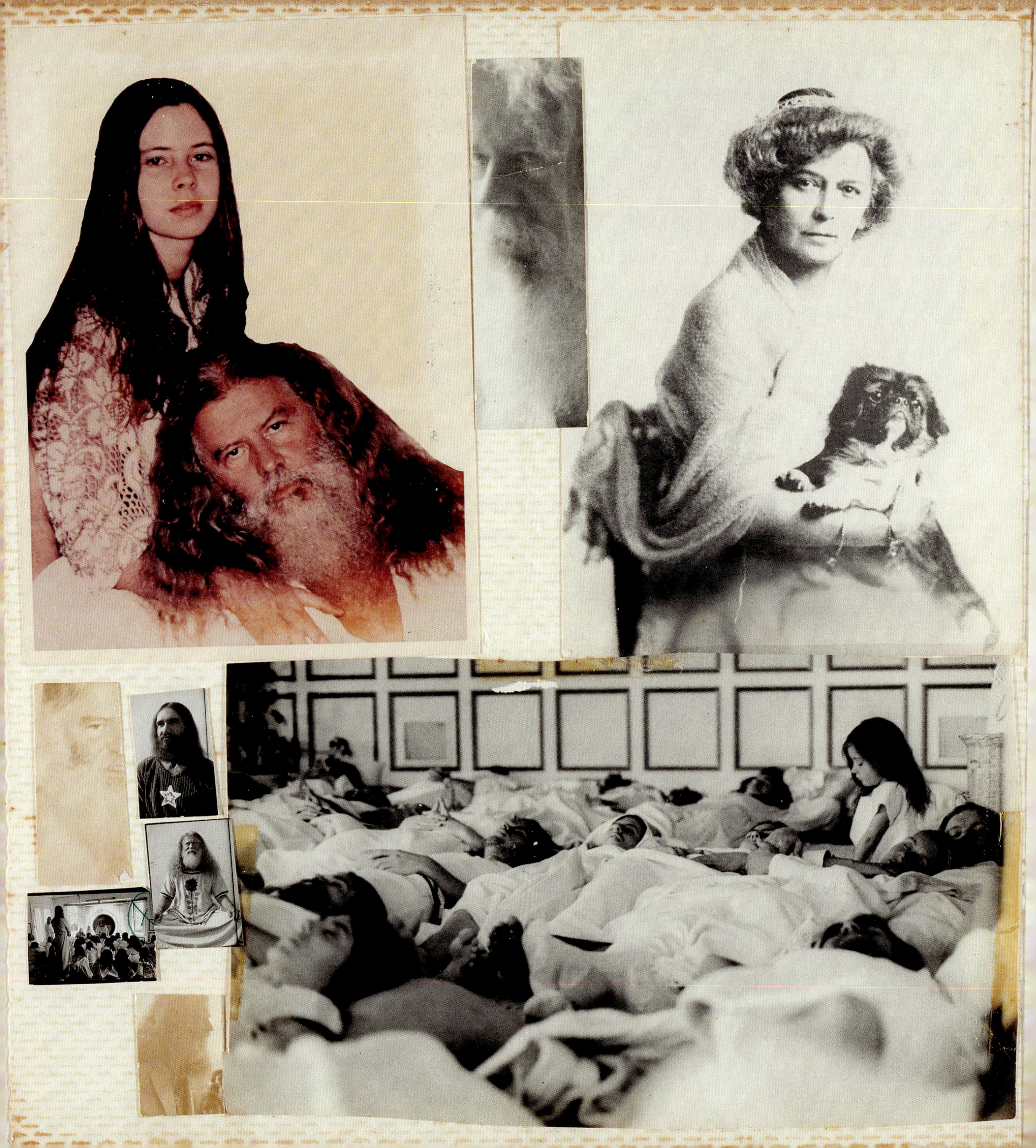

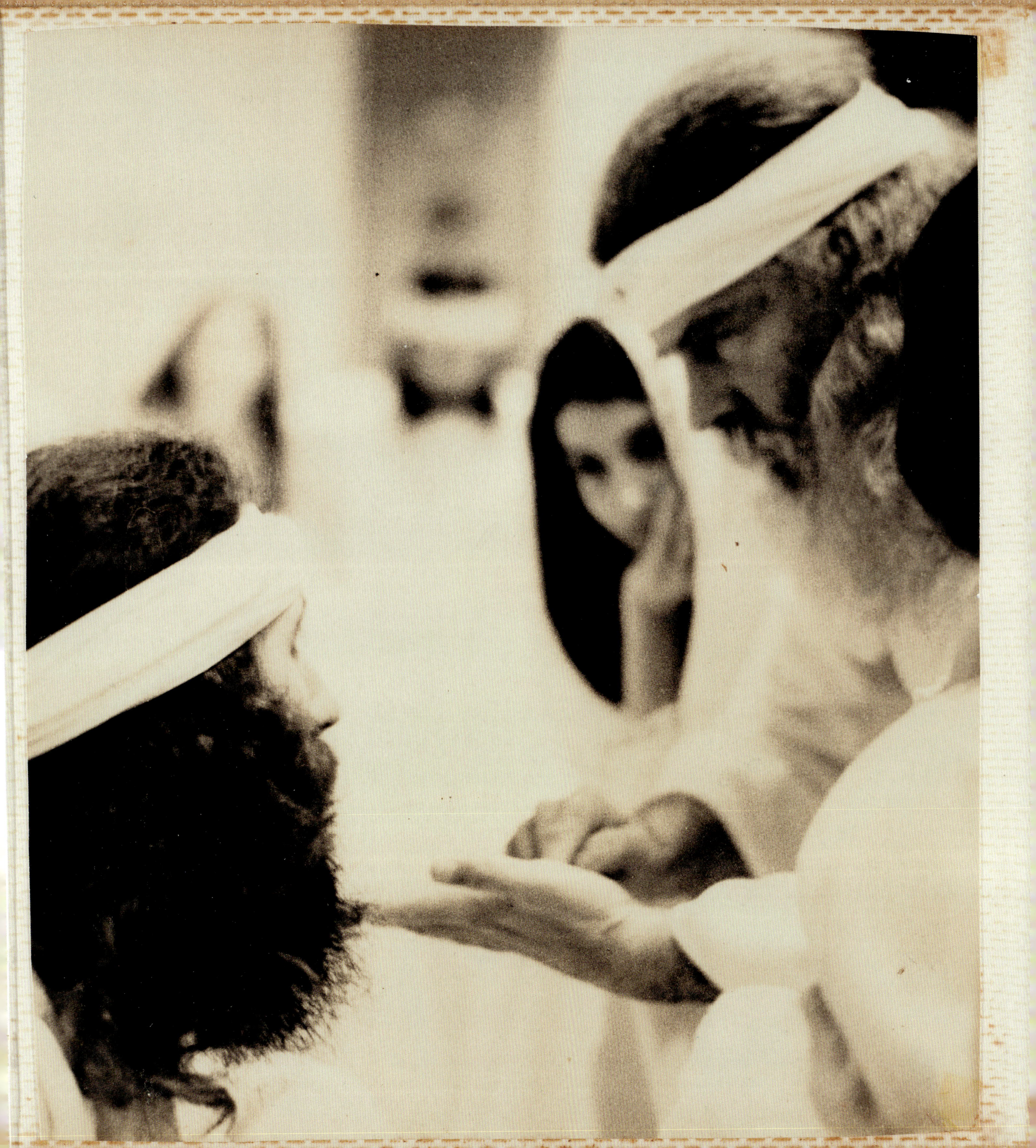

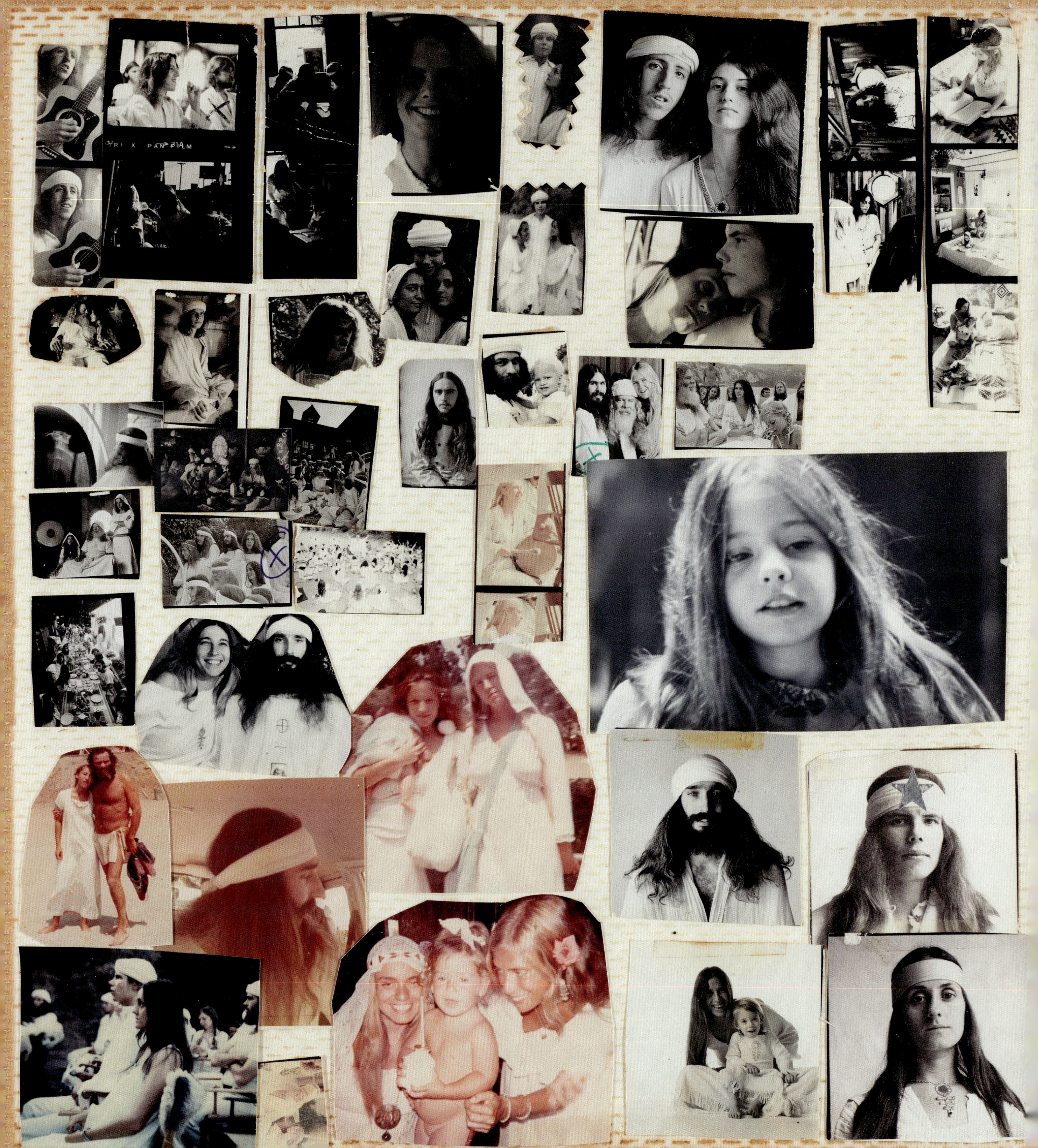

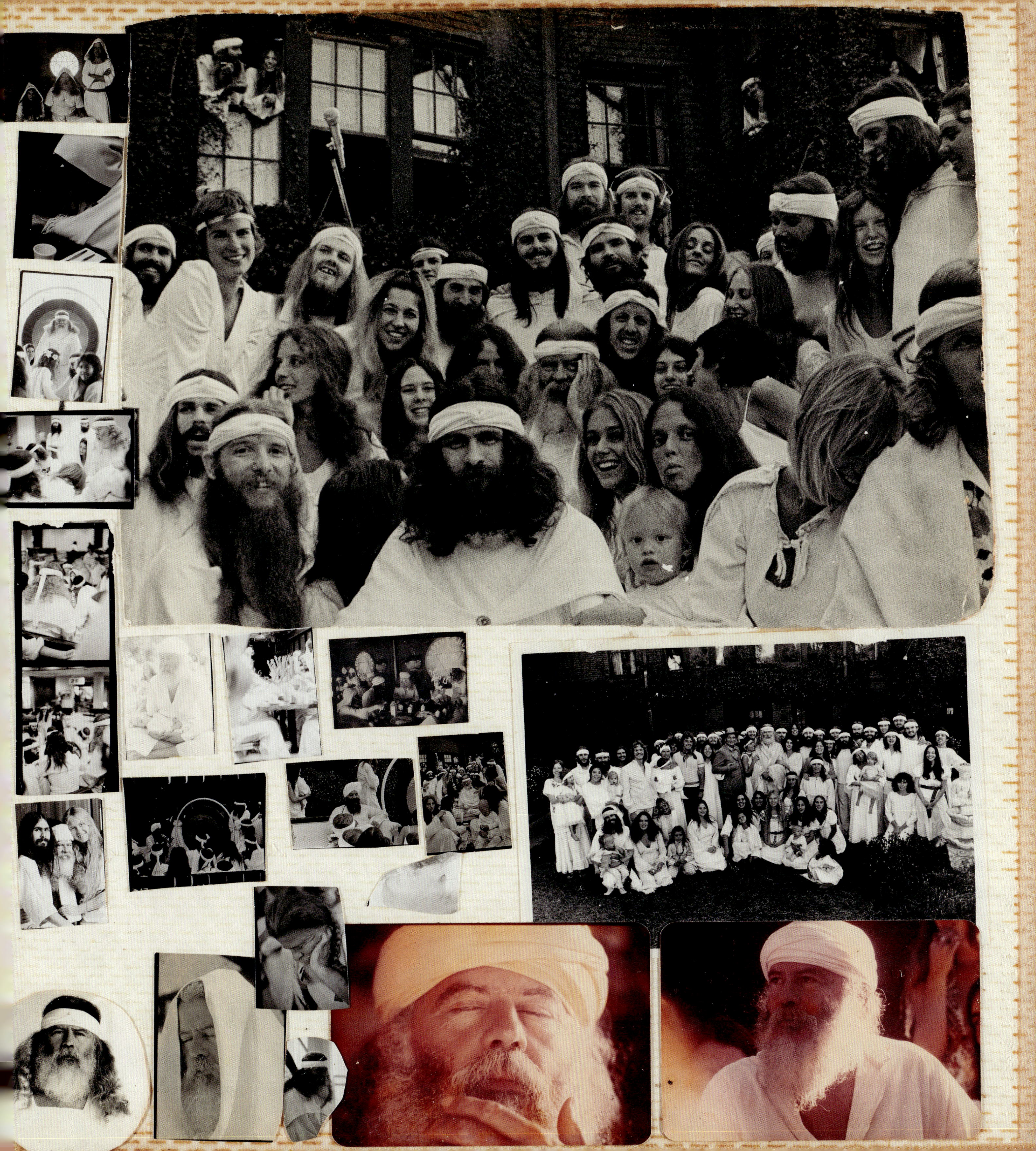

YAHOWHA'S DAILY MENU

"The reason Thoth became great is because he used the keys."

Father

1. As you awaken, exhale YAHOWHA for your first breath.

2. After exhaling say either aloud or to yourself; BE STILL AND KNOW I AM GOD.

3. Dip into our Mother Ocean (or a swimming pool) to rinse your body of all sleep and negativity. TAU!

4. Follow the physical exercise program every morning.

5. Do the Star Exercise to tune yourself into the Universal Life Energy Currents of the morning.

6. Practice the pineal wave to eliminate any trace of negativity within.

7. Take a cold shower to clean and rinse your body.

8. Instruct your Tahuti Water and coffee or tea.

9. Lose yourself to find yourself.

10. Use the power of silence. It is the Golden Key of Love and Wisdom.

11. Use the Sacred Breath to bring yourself into a central balance point to be used all day, especially after the sacred herb.

12. Use the key of laughter.

13. Stretch the sciatic nerve.

14. Do the Mystic Road together before class.

15. Instruct the fire of the Sacred Herb, pumping your stomach seven times and exhaling YAHOWHA. Roll your neck

16. Visualize your vehicle for your next lifetime. See it in perfect equilibrium.

17. Meditate on the Tarot Card of the day.

18. Never react to any situation. Always act or speak consciously, after reflecting for three seconds, saying YAHOWHA.

19. If there is a thought you do not want to have, exhale
     forcefully and say, GO GET OUT!

20. If anything knocks you out of your center, use the key of
     the calming breath.

21. Implant your subconscious mind, using your God and Fire
     fingers on the bridge of your nose, take a deep breath,
     visualize it while repeating what it is you want to remember.

22. Chant YAHOWHA'S NAME throughout the entire day.

23. Never miss the rising of the Sun.

24. Get into the ocean after class, rinse your pineal.

25. Eat twice a day, and chew untill liquid, consciously di-
     recting every bite. Always sit down and eat with a relaxed
     vibration and stay seated untill digested. Never snack
     between meals.

26. When dealing with anyone outside the family, ask yourself
     "What can I do to help this one?"

27. Use the key of discretion.

28. When returning home in the evening after a day in the maya,
     rinse your body with the power of the ocean.

29. Always remember the power of I AM.

30. Reread the Ten Commandments.

31. Visualize our Dome Community, see our paradise.

32. Review your day before going to sleep, correctly visualizing
     that which was not perfect.

33. Program your subconscious mind before going to sleep with the
     Mystic Road of the day.

34. Exhale YAHOWHA your last breath before falling asleep.

35. Receive the proper amount of sleep-five hours.

36. Hang upside down.

37. Sneeze through your nose with your mouth shut.

38. Laugh internally.

39. Drink no coffee after noon.

40. Respect time. Always be fifteen minutes early.

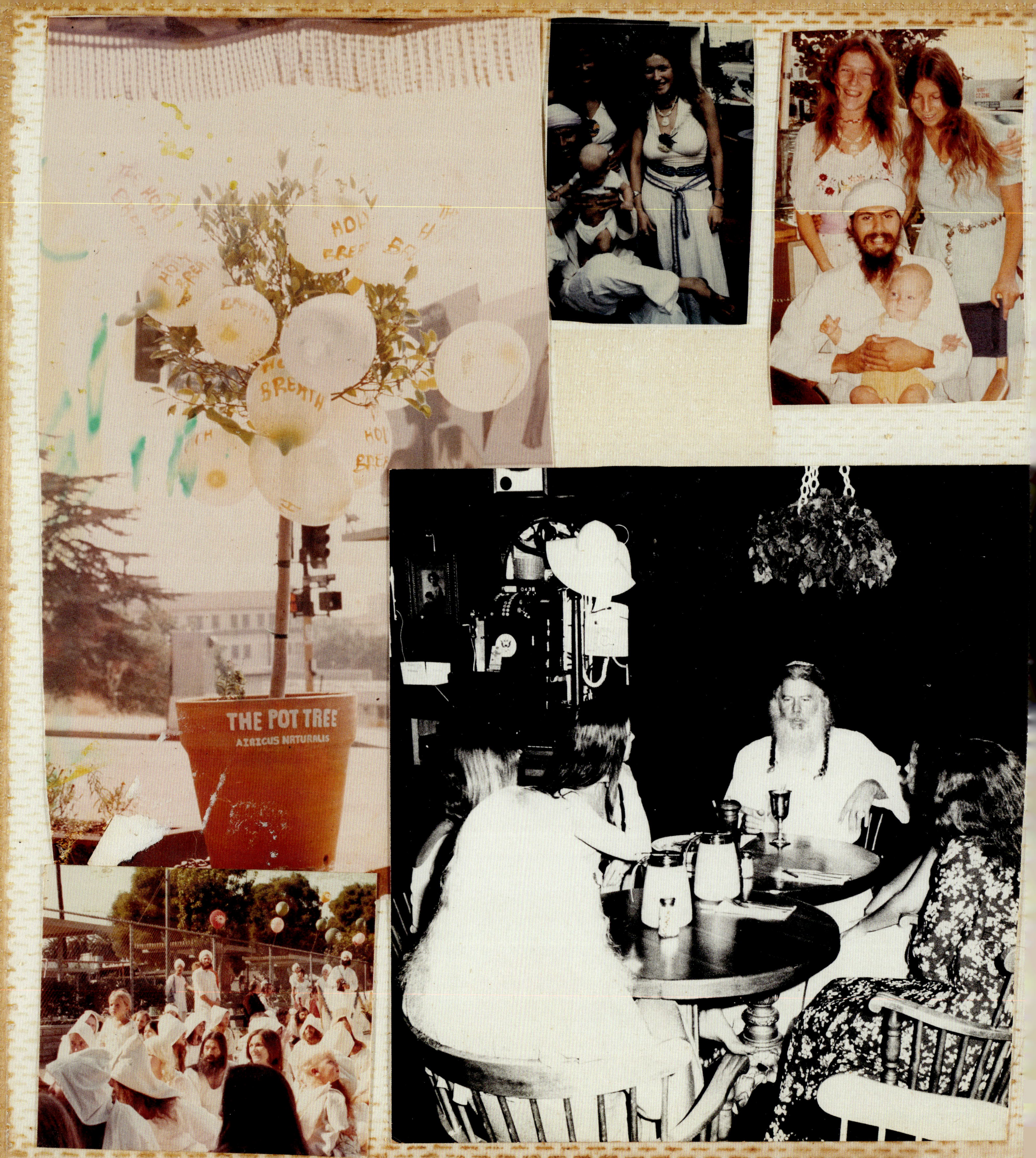
THE POT TREE
AZRICUS NATURALIS

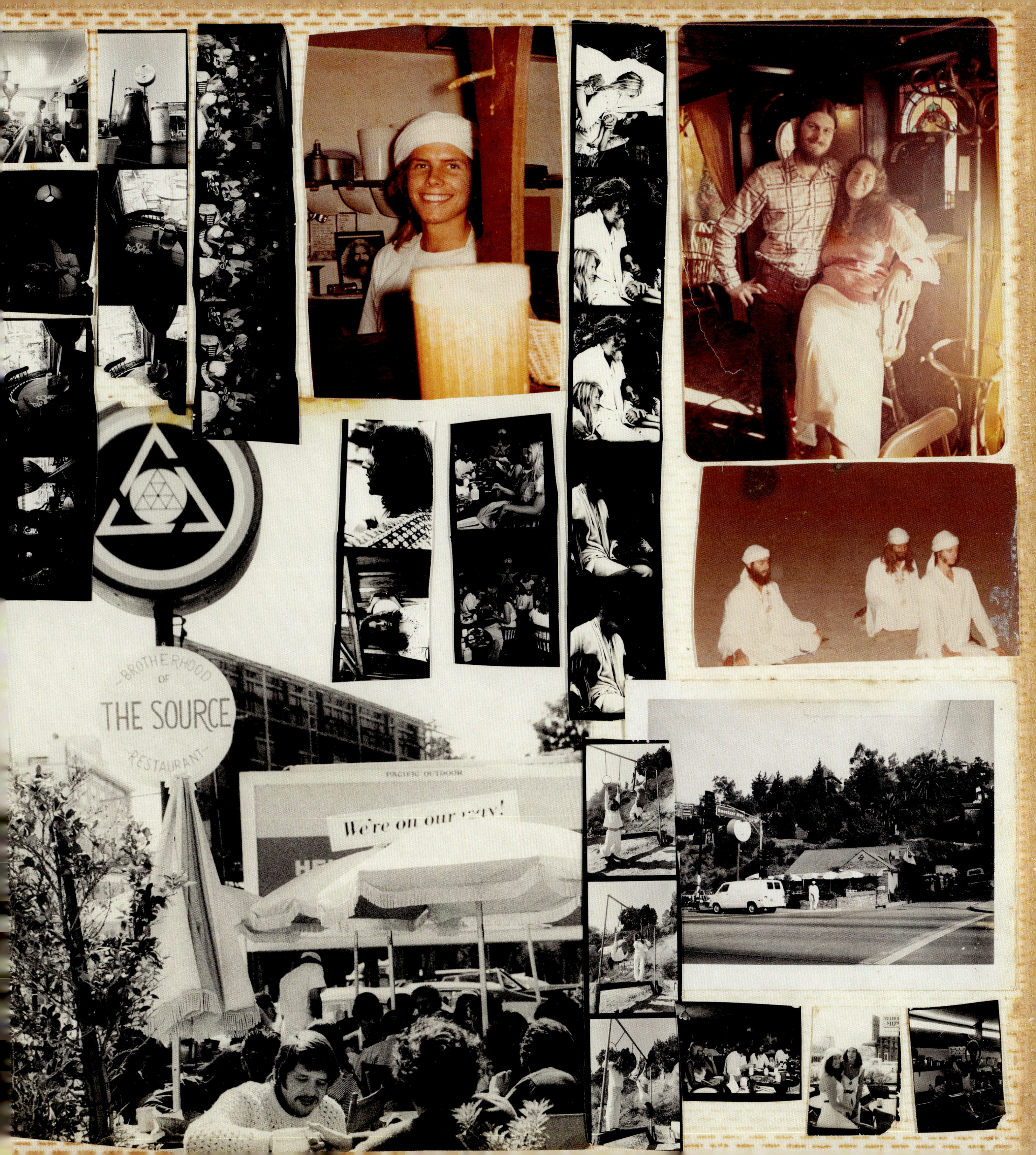
~BROTHERHOOD~ OF THE SOURCE ~RESTAURANT~
PACIFIC OUTDOOR
We're on our way!

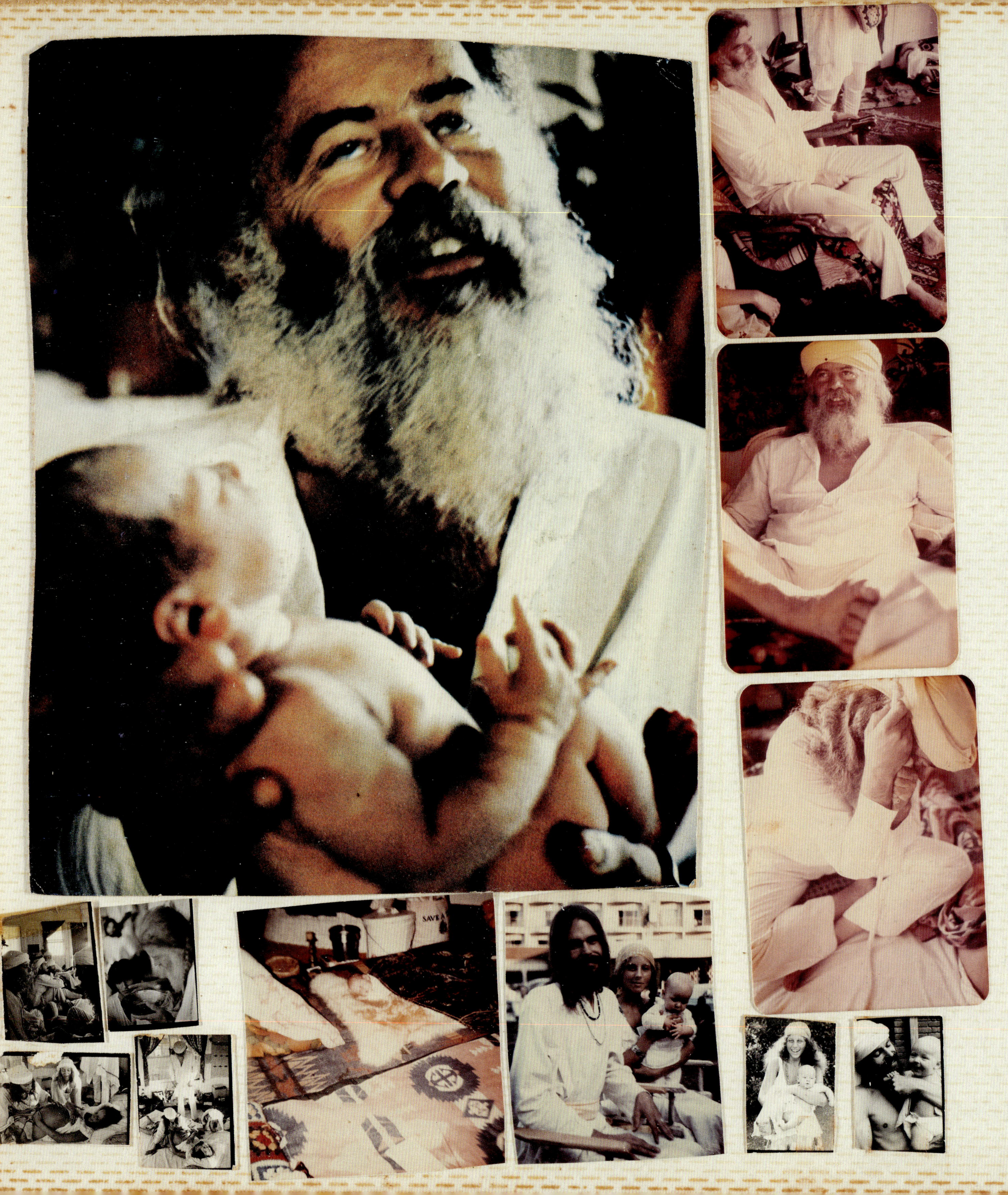

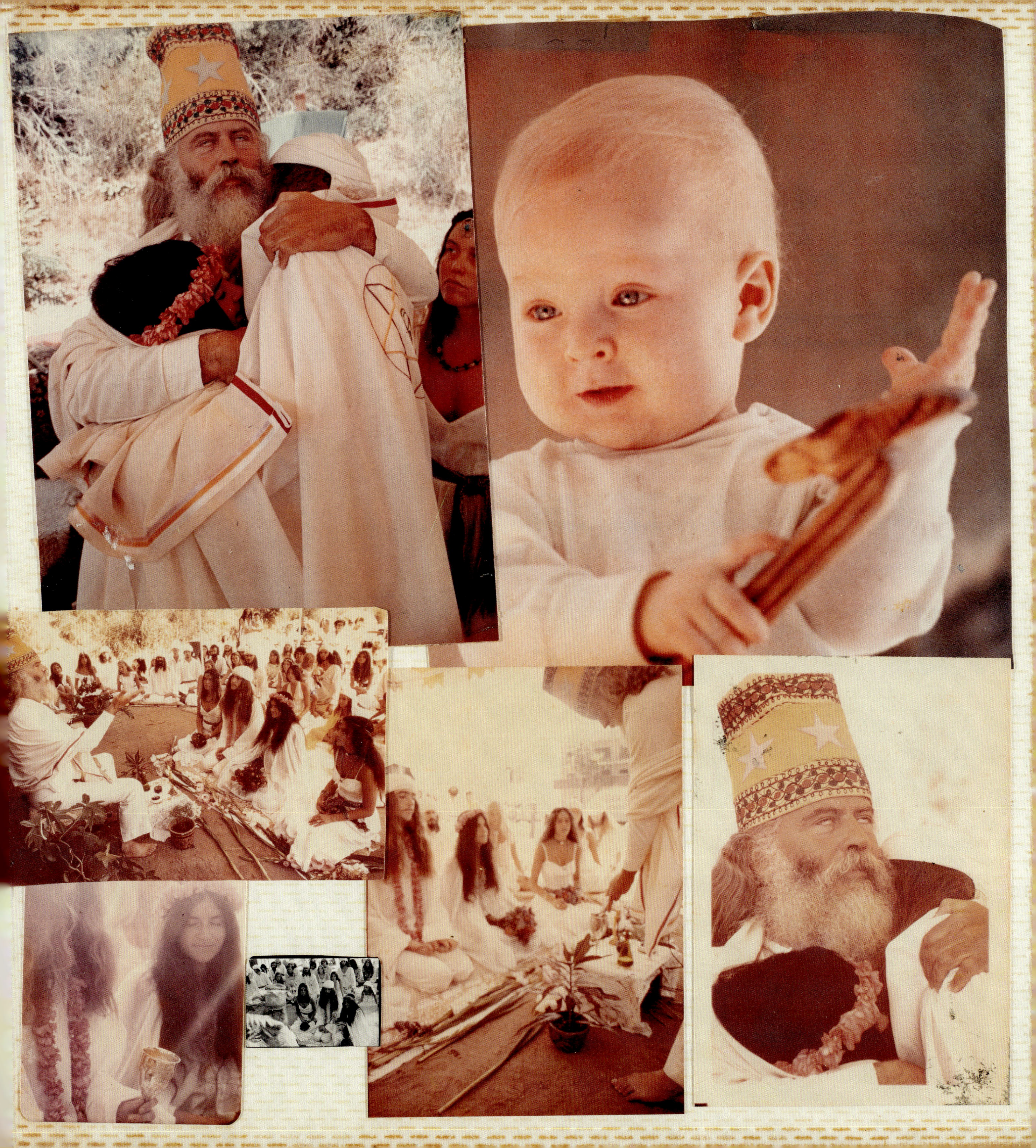

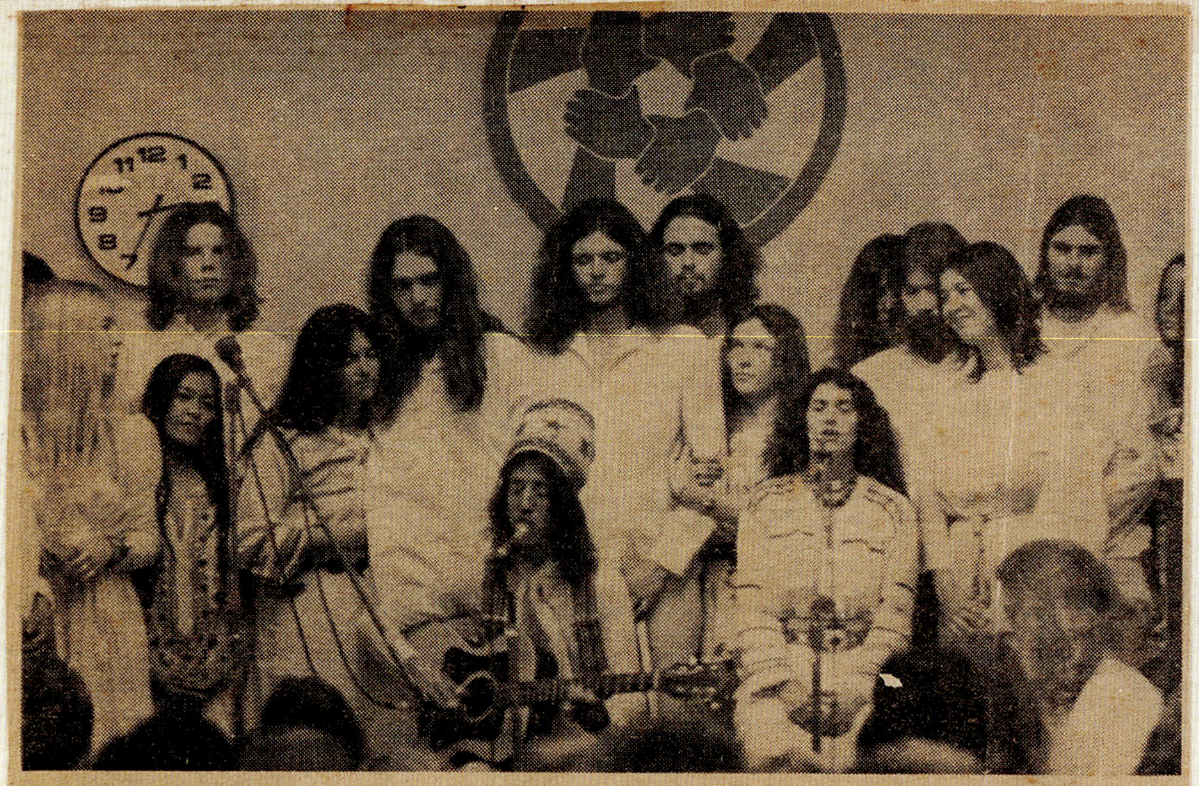

The Aquarian Ceremonies of the festival attracted a large number of young people. Providing Mediational and acoustical music, as seen above, was "The Source." Many of these musicians can be seen hanging around Jim Baker's *Source* health food restaurant on Sunset Strip. This group rocked the festival with their rendition of "Honkey Tonk Holy Man."

All photos by Art Kunkin.

BARN HÄNGANDE I ETT REP

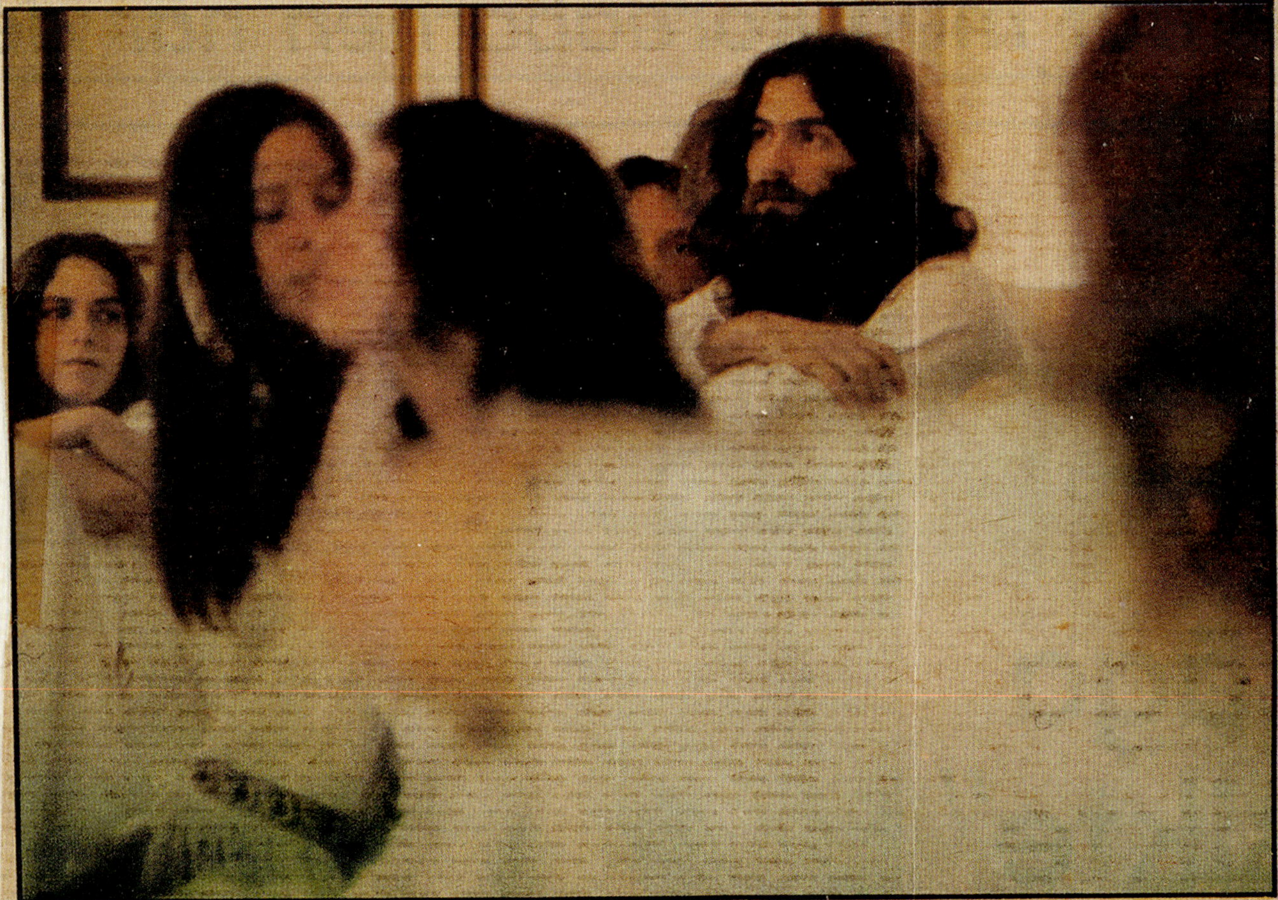

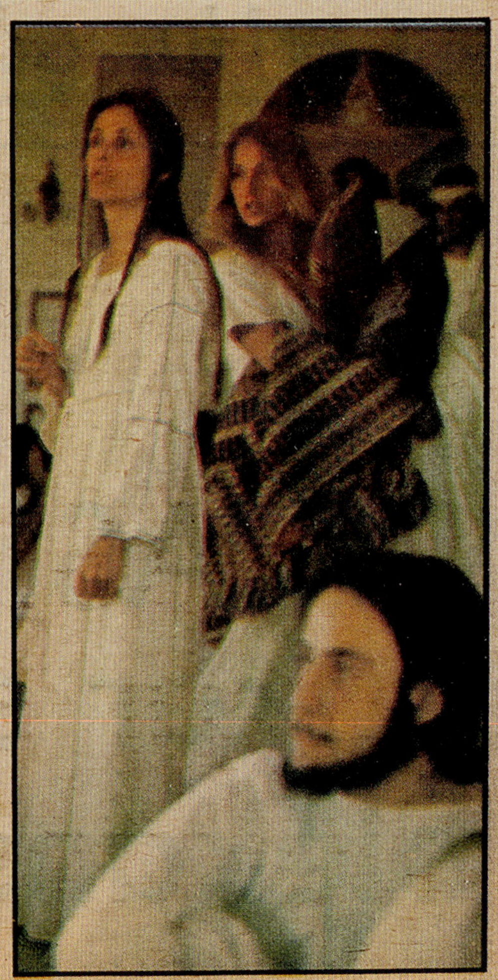

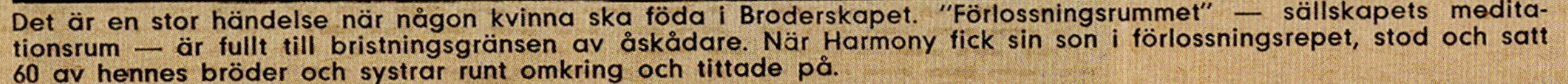

Det är en stor händelse när någon kvinna ska föda i Broderskapet. "Förlossningsrummet" — sällskapets meditationsrum — är fullt till bristningsgränsen av åskådare. När Harmony fick sin son i förlossningsrepet, stod och satt 60 av hennes bröder och systrar runt omkring och tittade på.

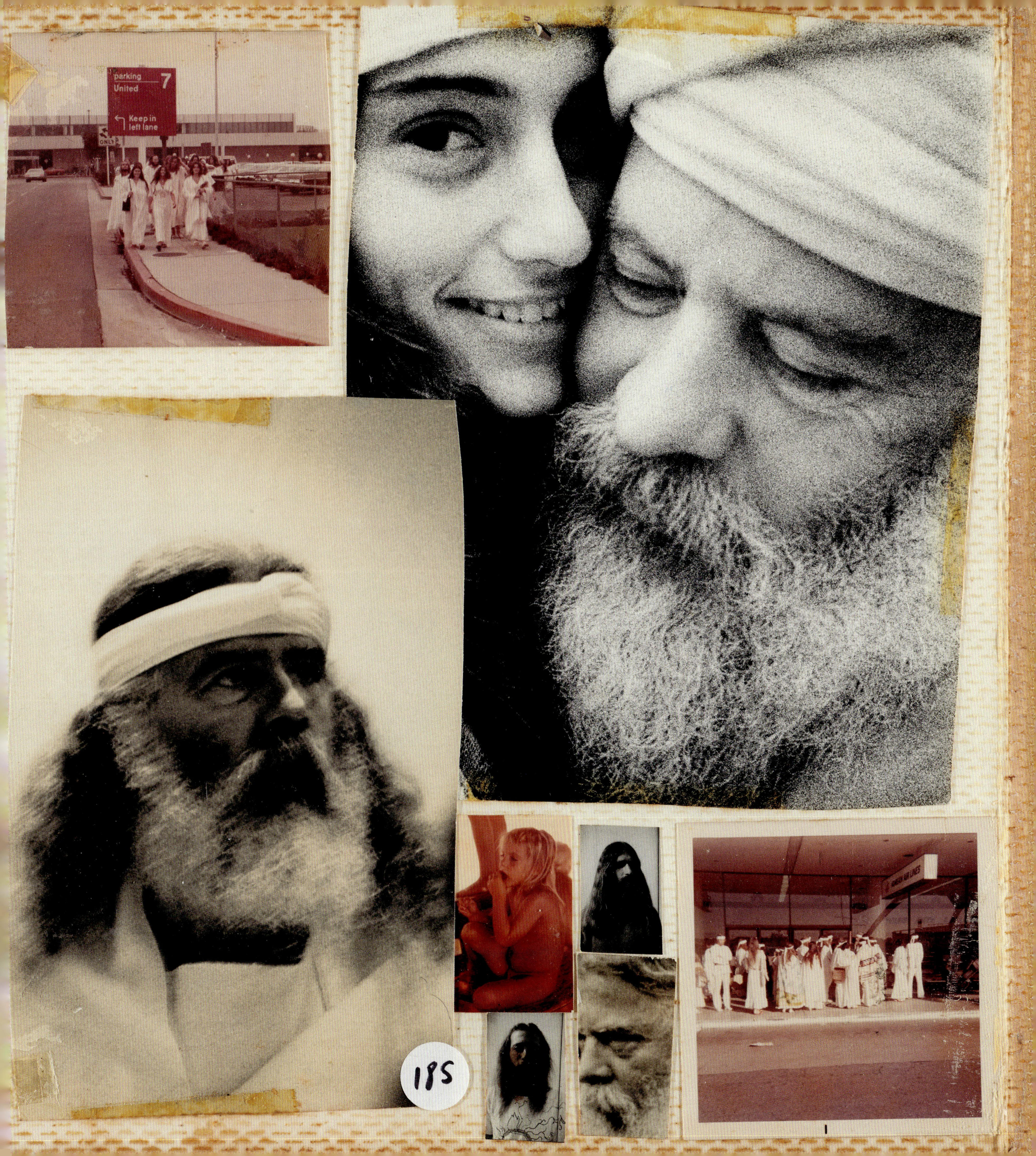

185

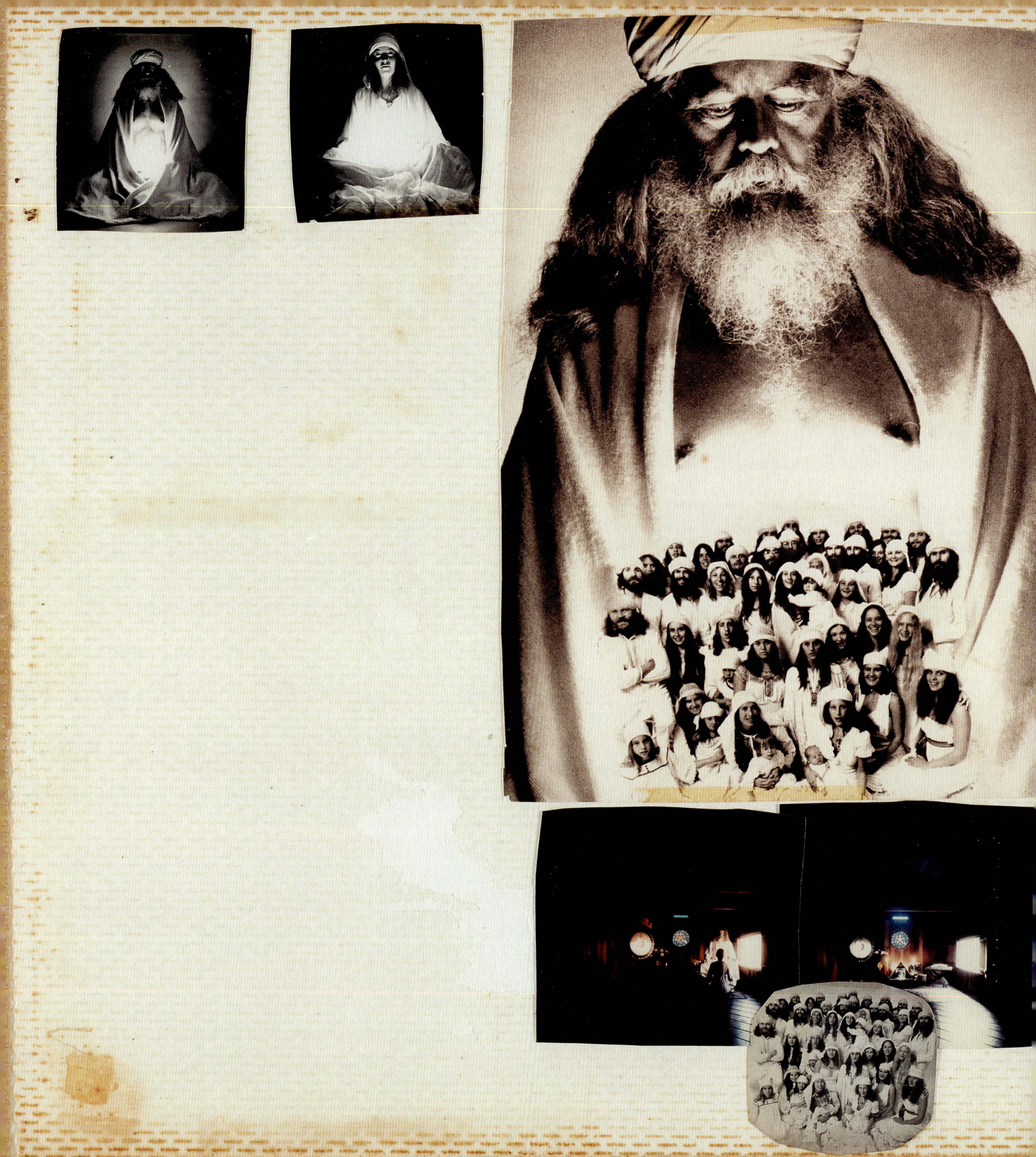

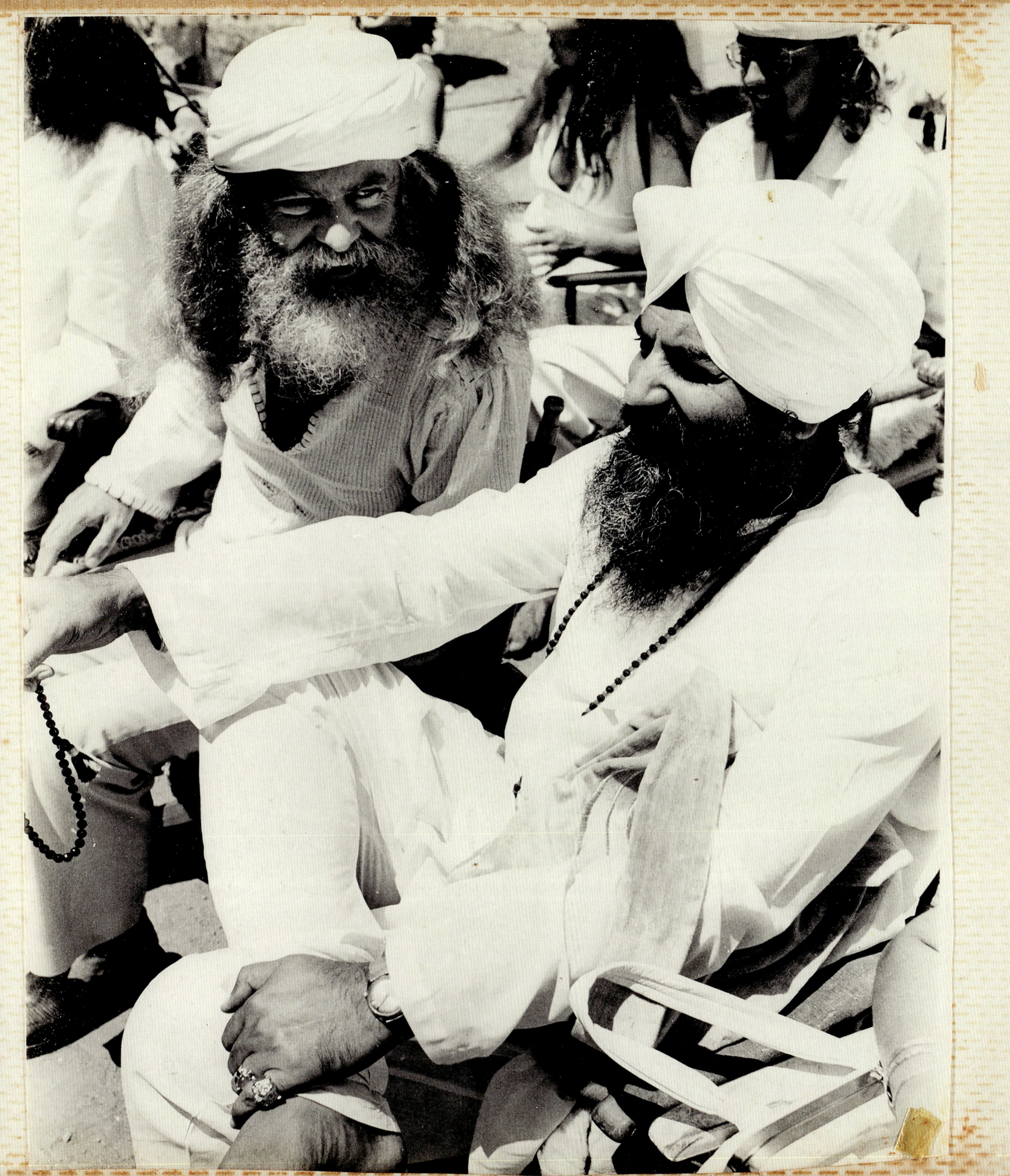

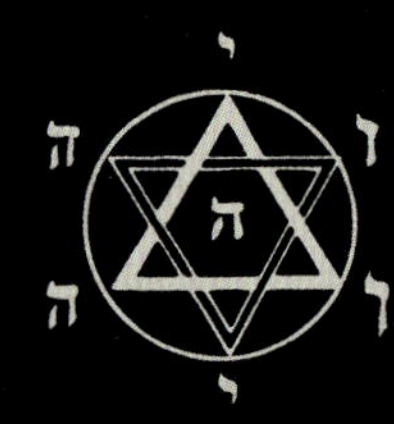

The Brotherhood of the Source
presents

THE FATHER OF AQUARIUS

on

God and Hair

The Brotherhood of the Source Presents

★ Father of Aquarius on God and Hair

★ Natural Child-Birth Film on the Birth of Sol-Amon

★ Bonadea - High Priestess of Astrology

★ Mother Ahom Singing Celestial Songs with a New Age Sound

Wilshire Ebell Theatre

Sun-day May 28, 1972

7:30

The Source is a growing center where the practical aspects
of Spirit are lived and experienced first-hand. One master
from the East said, "The Source will be a source of light for
many." The men and women you see about you who staff and maintain
this temple(in this age a restaurant can be a temple, for all is
spirit) compose a spiritual body, the Brotherhood of the Source.

The great seal of Sol-Amon, on the north wall of the dining
room,says that this is indeed the sixth day spoken of in the Bible,
the magic talisman of Hermes offers protection to all those who
have found the harmony of the balanced pairs of opposites. They
become the star, the embodiment of Cosmic Order.

The key to attain this Cosmic Conciousness is totally outlined
in the Ten Commandments for the Age of Aquarius, recognized by
the Brotherhood as the Highest code of Ethics to date, and
in fact a key to Liberation.

We are your servants, we are your teachers. As it says in
the Bhagavad Gita, "For the protection of the innocent I AM
reborn from age to age."

In this city of the angels, by the setting sun, the light
that illumines has come again.

Every evening Monday thru Saturday, in the redwood temple
classes are given covering the varied subjects of Cosmic
Conciousness, Astrology, the Ten Commandments for the New Age,
Techniques of Meditation and long concealed secrets of
channeling Universal Life Energy

YOD HE VAU HE

IS THE OLDEST AND MOST ESOTERIC NAME OF GOD. THE WORD GIVES THE KEY TO ALL WISDOM TO THE MORTAL WHO CAN DISCOVER THE CORRECT WAY OF PRONOUNCING IT, (THROUGH THE OPENING OF THE SIX SUN CENTERS AND SIX MOON CENTERS.)

YOD = THE PRINCIPLE AND ORIGIN OF ALL THINGS, THE I, THE ACTIVE PRINCIPLE, THE IMAGE OF MASCULINITY.

HE = THE IMAGE OF FEMININITY, THE PASSIVE PRINCIPLE, THE WOMAN RELATIVE TO THE MAN, THE SUBSTANCE RELATIVE TO THE ESSENCE.

VAU = UNITING OF THE ACTIVE WITH THE PASSIVE SIGNIFYING LINK OR ANALOGY, THE MEETING IN A MUTUAL ZONE WHICH IS THE LINK WHICH UNITES ALL ANTAGONISMS IN THE WHOLE OF NATURE.

HE = THE FORGOTTEN 4TH LETTER IN THE NAME OF GOD IS HEREBY RESTORED TO ITS ORIGINAL INTEGRITY BY THE SECOND **HE**. THE REPETITION OF THE SECOND **HE** REPRESENTS THE PASSAGE OF THE TRINITARIAN LAW INTO A NEW APPLICATION. IN OTHER WORDS, A TRANSITION FROM THE PHYSICAL WORLD TO THE SPIRITUAL WORLD, OR ACTUALLY ANY WORLD TO THE WORLD IMMEDIATELY FOLLOWING IT. THE SECOND **HE** THEN BECOMES A **YOD** IN GERM, OR **YOD** IN MINIATURE (MICROCOSM) IN TRANSITION; THE GRAIN OF WHEAT RELATIVE TO THE EAR, ETC.

IF YOU WILL OPEN YOURSELF TO THE VIBRATION OF **YOD-HE-VAU-HE** A RESPONSIVE CHORD WILL BE STRUCK WITHIN YOU WHICH WILL RESTORE YOU TO YOUR LOST HERITAGE.

SO MOTE IT BE, **FATHER**

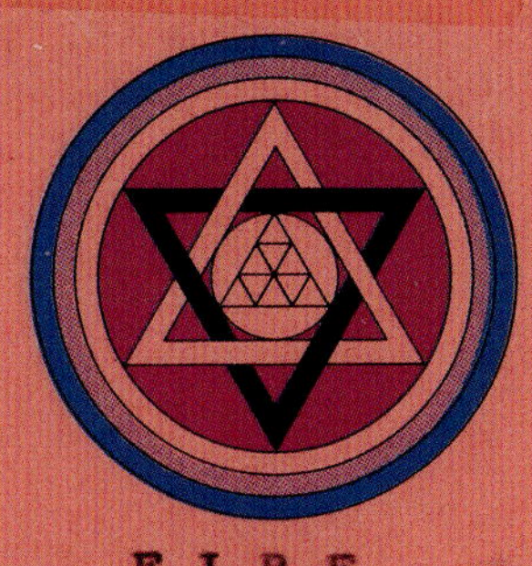

F I R E

JEALOUSY, HATRED, VINDICTIVENESS, IRRASCIBILITY, ANGER.

A I R

FRIVOLITY, SELF-PRESUMPTION, BOASTING, SQUANDERING, GOSSIPPING.

W A T E R

INDIFFERENCE, FRIGIDITY, COMPLIANCE, NEGLIGENCE, SHYNESS,
INSOLENCE, INSTABILITY.

E A R T H

LAZINESS, CONSCIENCELESS, MELANCHOLY, IRREGULARITY, ANOMALY,
DULLNESS.

****

F I R E

ACTIVITY, ENTHUSIASM, FIRMNESS, COURAGE, DARING.

A I R

DILIGENCE, JOY, DEXTERITY, KINDNESS, LUST, OPTIMISM.

W A T E R

MODESTY, ABSTEMIOUSNESS, FERVENCY, COMPASSION, TRANQUILITY,
TENDERNESS, FORGIVENESS.

E A R T H

RESPECT, ENDURANCE, CONSCIENTIOUNESS, THOROUGHNESS, SOBRIETY,
PUNCTUALITY, RESPONSIBILITY.

The Source

8301 Sunset Boulevard, Los Angeles, California 90069
(213) 656-6388

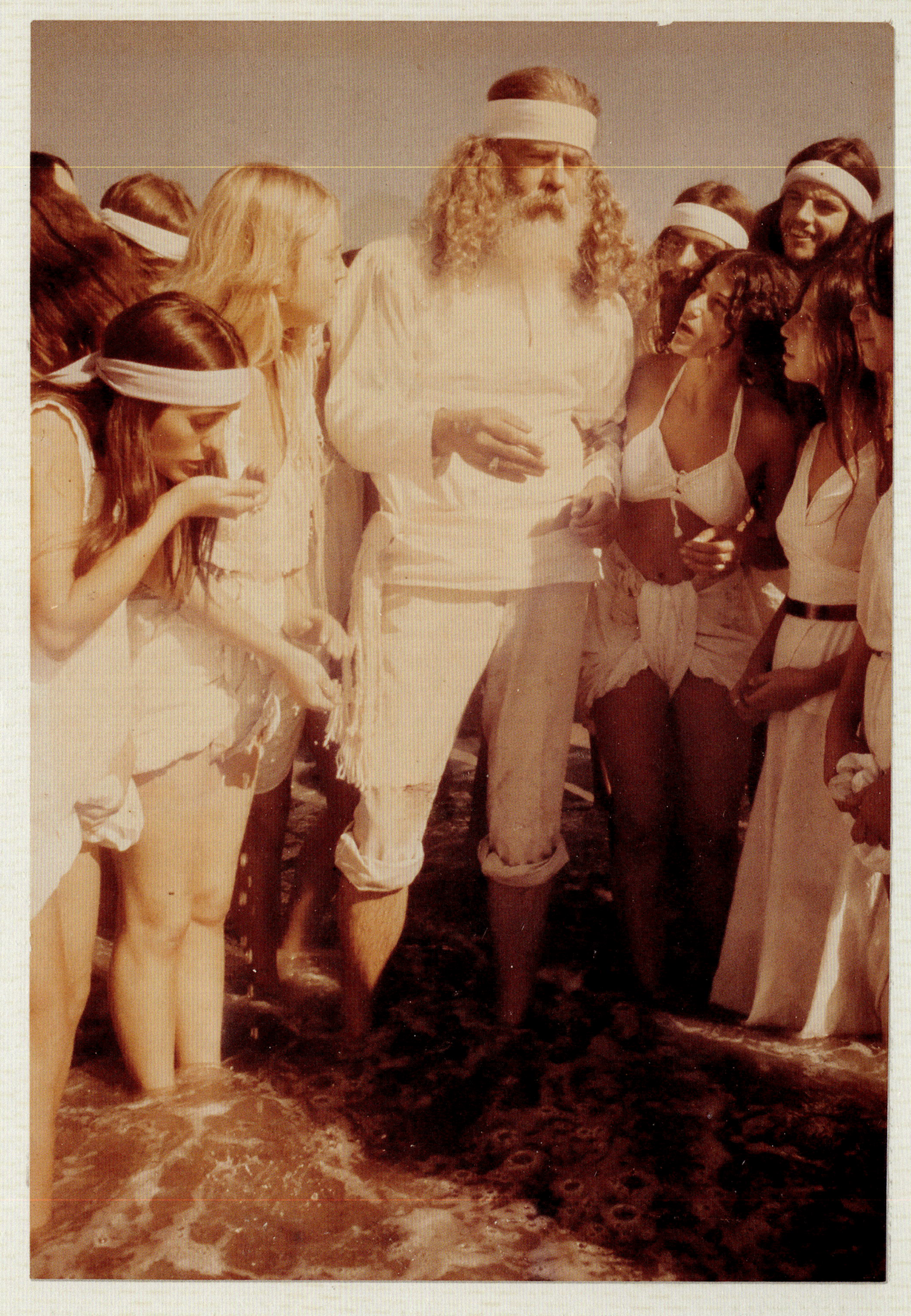

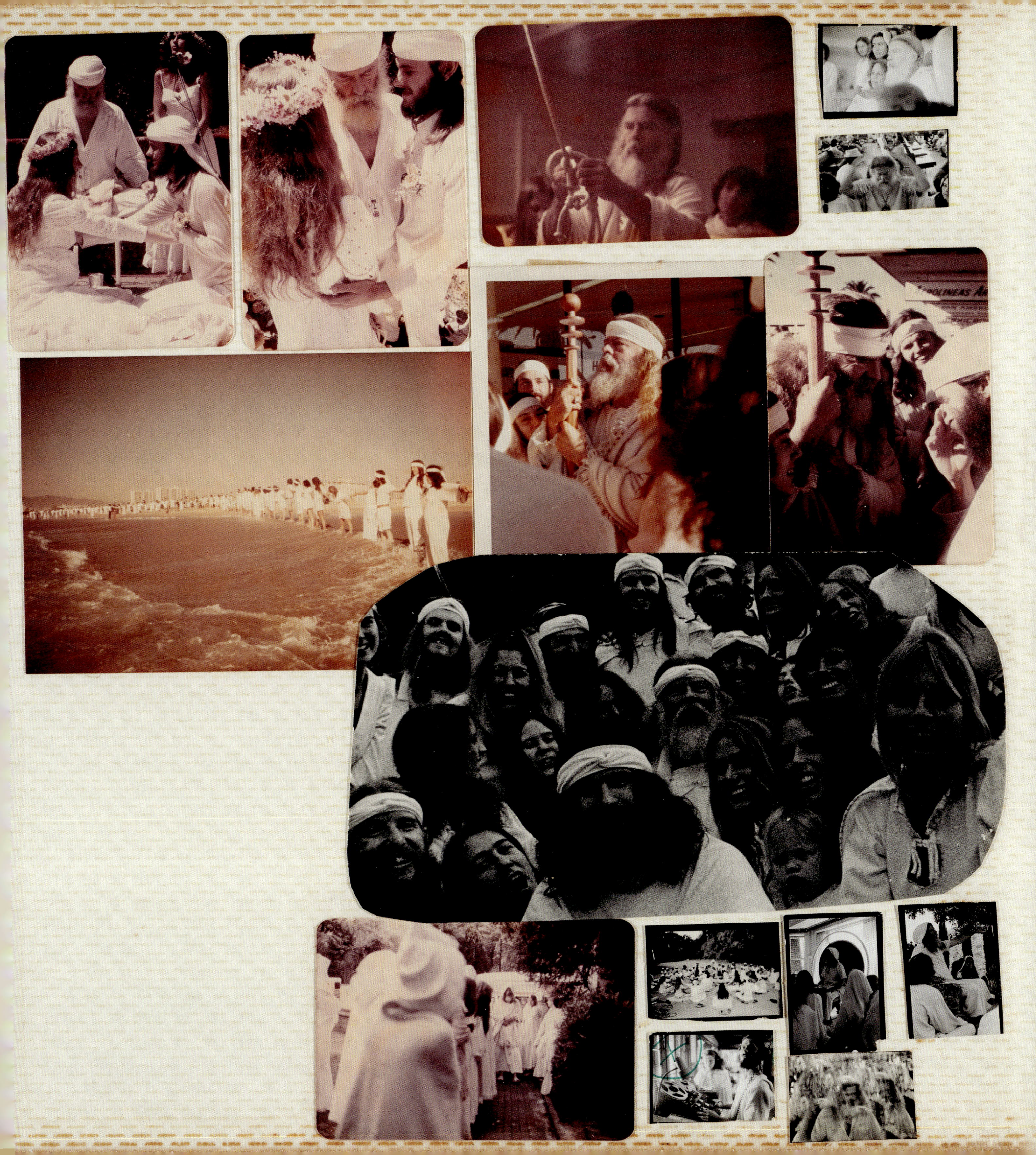

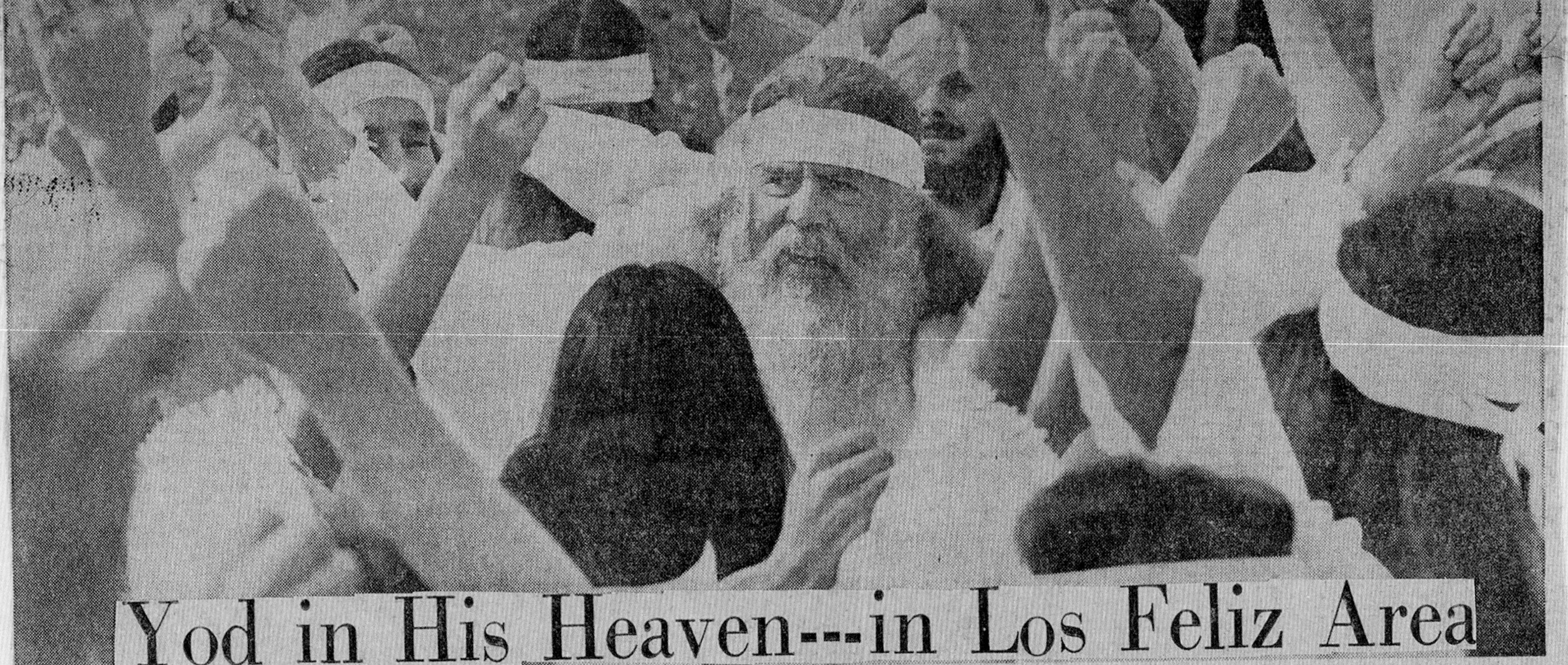

Yod in His Heaven---in Los Feliz Area

FAITH—During an outing to Griffith Park, Jim Baker, the Earthly Spiritual Father of the Brotherhood of the Source, inspires some of his followers in the cult.
Times photos by Larry Bessel and Mary Frampton

BY JEAN DOUGLAS MURPHY
Times Staff Writer

Celestial is her name now and she's on a far better trip, she says, than any she ever took on LSD.

Her journey is with the Brotherhood of the Source, which is at one and the same time a cult, a commune, a business and a "family" of nearly 100, whose Earthly Spiritual Father was known until three years ago as Jim Baker, popular Los Angeles restaurateur turned convict turned prophet.

Celestial—as have all in the Brotherhood, she has discarded her worldly name—reveres Father Yod, devoutly accompanying him into the Eternal Now and preparing for the Age of Aquarius. She doesn't mind facing public skepticism and, often, ridicule.

On this morning, as one every morning, Celestial opens her green eyes long before dawn lightens her room above the garage at the old Los Feliz mansion where the Family lives.

It's only 4:30 a.m. but Celestial takes a cold shower (part of the regimen, good for the clean life and the nerve endings) and dons the simple white garb and headband that the Family wears. She lays out clothes for her man, Mecca, and lights the candles and the incense on their low altar because "the main function of women is to serve and inspire men."

Perhaps by the dim glow, she surveys the room —a few plants, a few books, sleeping mats on the floor, a rag rug, wisps of lace at the windows, white walls, a sink from bygone times and the altar.

On the altar, covered with a white cloth, are a picture of Father Yod, a copy of his book "Liberation" and Celestial's "concepts of earth, air, fire and water"—a little greenery, a bowl of spring water, candles and incense—as well as a few stones, shells, a feather, "my kind of things."

Perhaps, but it is not likely because this freckled, fresh-faced 21-year-old believes the past is dead, she thinks of the girl she used to be.

She was a student at Antioch College, a Bostonian, the daughter of an industrial psychologist and a teacher. She remembers dropping out of school, hitching 10,000 miles around the country, blowing her mind with LSD and other chemicals.

She remembers hearing about the Brotherhood more than a year ago, coming to Los Angeles, joining the Family which then numbered only 12

Please Turn to Page 13, Col. 1

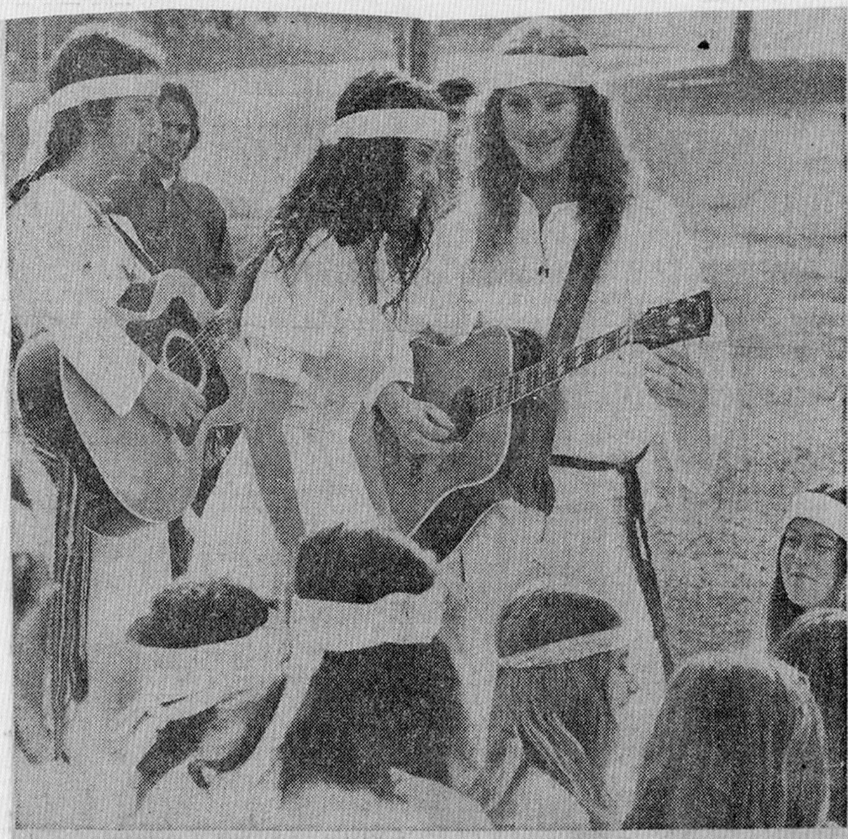

LOVE—Aladdin, Mother Ahom and Mecca, from left, pause after playing "music to get high by to pick up loving vibes from their brothers and sisters."

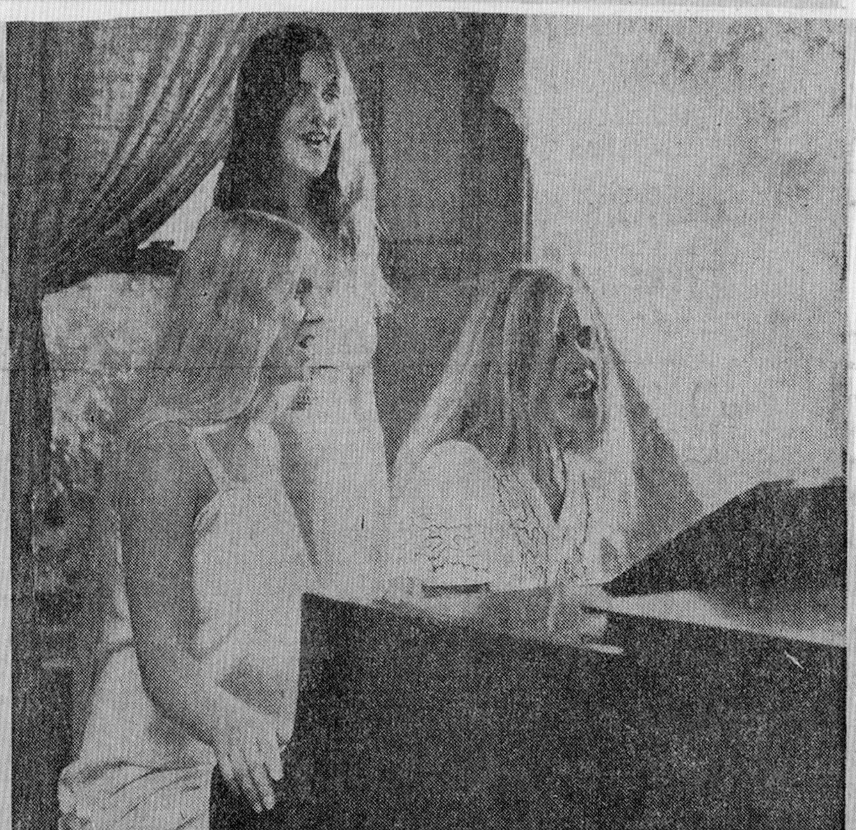

AND HARMONY—Cylom, Madonna and Lotus, from left, sing for members of their communal family in living room of an old mansion in Los Feliz district.

Yod in His Heaven---in Los Feliz

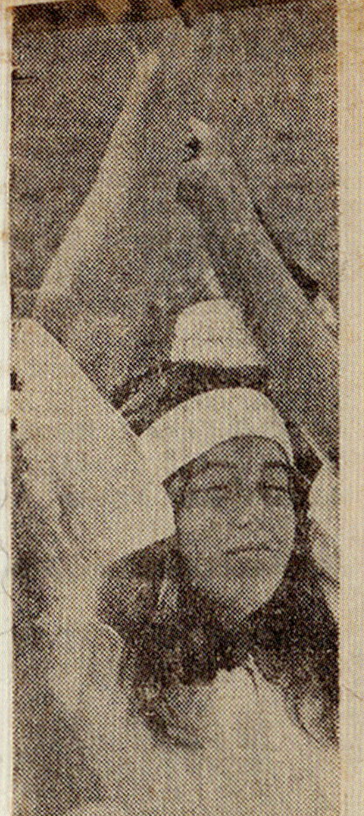

Celestial
Times photo

Yod in His Heaven in Los Feliz

Continued from First Page

and working in its health food restaurant, the Source on Sunset Blvd., as a waitress.

She certainly doesn't think of James Edward Baker's past. She knows his record—an ex-Marine judo expert with a justifiable homicide ruling in 1955 and a manslaughter conviction in 1963—and she knows he now faces a charge of interfering with a law enforcement officer.

None of it matters to her. To her, he is Father, Father Yod, her Earthly Spiritual Father, good and kind and all-knowing, the man who preaches Liberation of the Spirit and who teaches his Family to lead pure, healthy, unselfish and natural lives, without drugs, alcohol or meat.

By now it is 5:30 a.m. Celestial and Mecca walk across the courtyard to the old 24-room brick mansion, the Mother House of the Brotherhood, for the daily 6 a.m. meditation.

'Vibrations' Prepared

There, in the living room-become-temple, they and other disciples "prepare the vibration for Father."

During the hour-long meditation period, with Father dispensing the Ultimate Truth, Celestial loses herself, empties herself, "becoming filled with spirit, giving up and surrendering and becoming receptive to the flow of Universal Life Energy, with the flow coming through Father."

She reels "bliss, harmony and stability, upward and infinite. My mind is blown every day."

After meditation, Celestial rushes back to clean their room, "jumping back to earth because we are concerned that our earth trip be together, too," while the High Council of the Brotherhood meets. If Mecca is not attending the meeting, she makes tea for him. "My life depends on his life."

Sometime after 9 a.m. Celestial returns to the main house, where Athena heads a crew of women preparing breakfast. There is no stove in the kitchen. There is no need for one; the family eats, just twice daily, uncooked fruit and nuts and seeds and milk and honey.

This morning, the women served a "pie" of crushed nuts topped by guacamole, sliced tomatoes and alfalfa sprouts, a fruit and nut salad, sliced bananas with yogurt and carob dressing, wheat rolls with herb sauce, and milk.

Men Served First

Celestial, as do the other women, serves her man first. She settles for a glass of milk and honey. She's not hungry and she's eager to get to the new crafts shop, housed in the big garage.

There, from about 10:30 a.m. to 5 p.m., with breaks for tea, Celestial sits at a sewing machine, making clothes to be sold by the Brotherhood. It's "a fun exchange of energy and my consciousness can be with the Brotherhood or with Mecca." Working with her are a half-dozen others, sewing or weaving or making jewelry. Some, at the same time, are laboring in the house or on the grounds; others are toiling in the restaurant a half-dozen miles away.

Please Turn to Pg. 15, Col. 1

Continued from 13th Page

Celestial skipped dinner last night and stayed in the shop to make a shirt for Mecca. Tonight she gives herself a special treat; she goes to the restaurant to hear Mecca play his music and sing his songs.

When they return to the house at about 9 p.m., "the altar is set up so we can meditate if we want to" and Celestial massages her man, another part of the routine of "woman giving her ego to man and man giving his ego to God."

And after that?

Celibacy Practiced?

"We all practice celibacy and celibacy is when you abstain except for the purpose of having a child. We don't need to seek sensation; there's no greater sensation than in meditation. It's like an orgasm on the bed of the mind. But it's important to bring in souls for the Age of Aquarius and I'm ready to have a child when God is ready."

(Of the 12 children living in the commune, only one —8-month-old Solomon— was born there. Among the 30 couples, four are expecting babies.)

Celestial's "incredible happiness" for this day ends in sleep on the floor of the austere room, but her faith leaves pragmatic questions unanswered.

Is Jim Baker-Father Yod a consummate con artist or a sincere zealot?

Sgt. Luis Puncel of the Sheriff's Department, who "has been observing the Source for some time," believes the former.

"Also, there are several aspects (about the Brotherhood) that might be illegal — harboring runaway juveniles, violations of labor laws, keeping a place where minors are sheltered without a license," Puncel said.

Sgt. Charles Scott of the Los Angeles Police Department's Hollywood station, in whose area the Brotherhood's house is located, said that "we've had no complaints about the pad but we are aware of Baker's record of violence."

Faced Suspect

Scott said "we would give assistance" to sheriff's deputies should they need "to take him at the pad."

Baker denies any law violations.

"We live by the laws of man and nature," he said. He also resists any comparison to the Manson Family. "They were into dope, dirt, they were nothing, the dregs of society. We're not like that."

Puncel, with a warrant charging Baker with interference with an officer, faced his suspect in Judge Leonard S. Wolf's Municipal Court in Beverly Hills Monday. Baker pleaded innocent, was released on his own recognizance and his pretrial conference was scheduled for Jan. 10.

The charge, according to Puncel, stems from his attempt to pick up a runaway juvenile at the Source and that Baker "definitely interfered."

According to Baker, however, he was merely "trying to prevent my daughter's leg from being crushed by the car door."

Father Yod's "sons and daughters" believe, fanatically, that he can now do no wrong.

"They all know what a reprobate I was. But I say, the greater the sinner, the greater the saint. Moses killed two people," he said.

(Baker, after a neighbor died in a fight over a dog in 1955, was found by a coroner's jury to have acted in self-defense. In 1963, the restaurant owner was convicted of manslaughter following a struggle with a man involving the man's wife; after an unsuccessful attempt to appeal, Baker served three months in 1968 before being paroled.)

Initially, Baker was not amenable to discussing his past.

Surrounded by some of his adoring flock, he sat majestically in his low-ceilinged sanctum, hung with brocade and incense. The small loft above the restaurant can be reached only by ladder.

"I am not willing to discuss the previous life. The past is dead. The past doesn't mean anything. We live in the Eternal Now," he said. "I expect to be attacked and maligned but let the vibrations fall where they may.

"Whom God wants, He pounds, and I was pounded and pounded. God led me to my father, Yogi Bhajan, whom I left and begat my own sons," he intoned, his voice assuming an hypnotic quality. "I herald the new age. We are laying the cornerstone for the Age of Aquarius."

Father Yod said he was planning a retreat in Costa Rica, "a safe place for my children to go, safe from the coming catastrophies. There will be nuclear war in 1975, mass insanity in the 1980s, a shifting of poles causing the oceans to rise and the continents to sink. Only 30% of the world's population will be left and the sons of the Brotherhood will emerge as world saviors."

A long-time acquaintance of Baker's thinks he may well be sincere. She recalls the days when he lived in Topanga Canyon and made belts, long before Topanga and handicrafts were popular. She remembers when he, a Southern California pioneer in the health food movement, owned the Aware Inn.

"It served good food but it was mostly his personality that drew people. He

Please Turn to Pg. 16, Col. 1

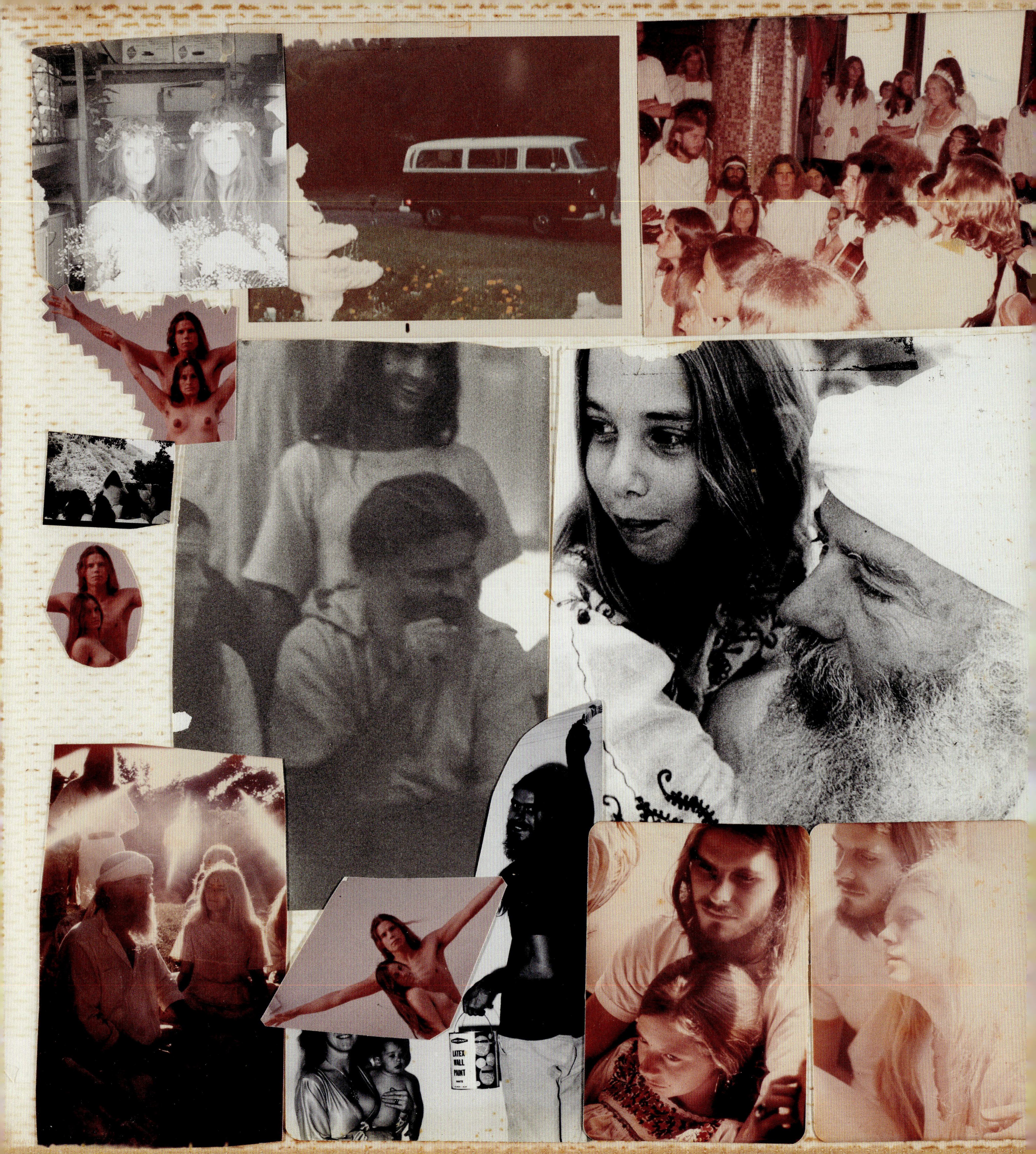

EXPAND.

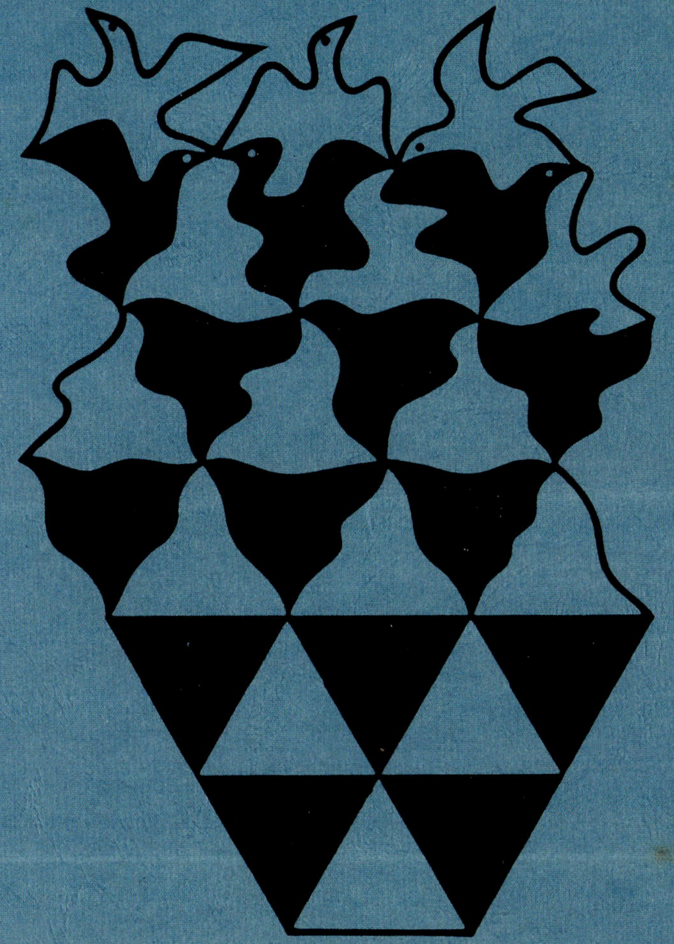

The search for power and peace begins amidst the illusion of external things and ends in the inner chamber of man's own mind and heart. You are a Son in our family of the Universe, join us as we expand our light. Keys to Liberation are given in our redwood temple at nine, ten and eleven in the morning and six, seven and eight in the evening. There is no charge because the word of God is given freely.

The Brotherhood of the Source
8301 Sunset Boulevard
Hollywood, California, 90069
Telephone 656-6388

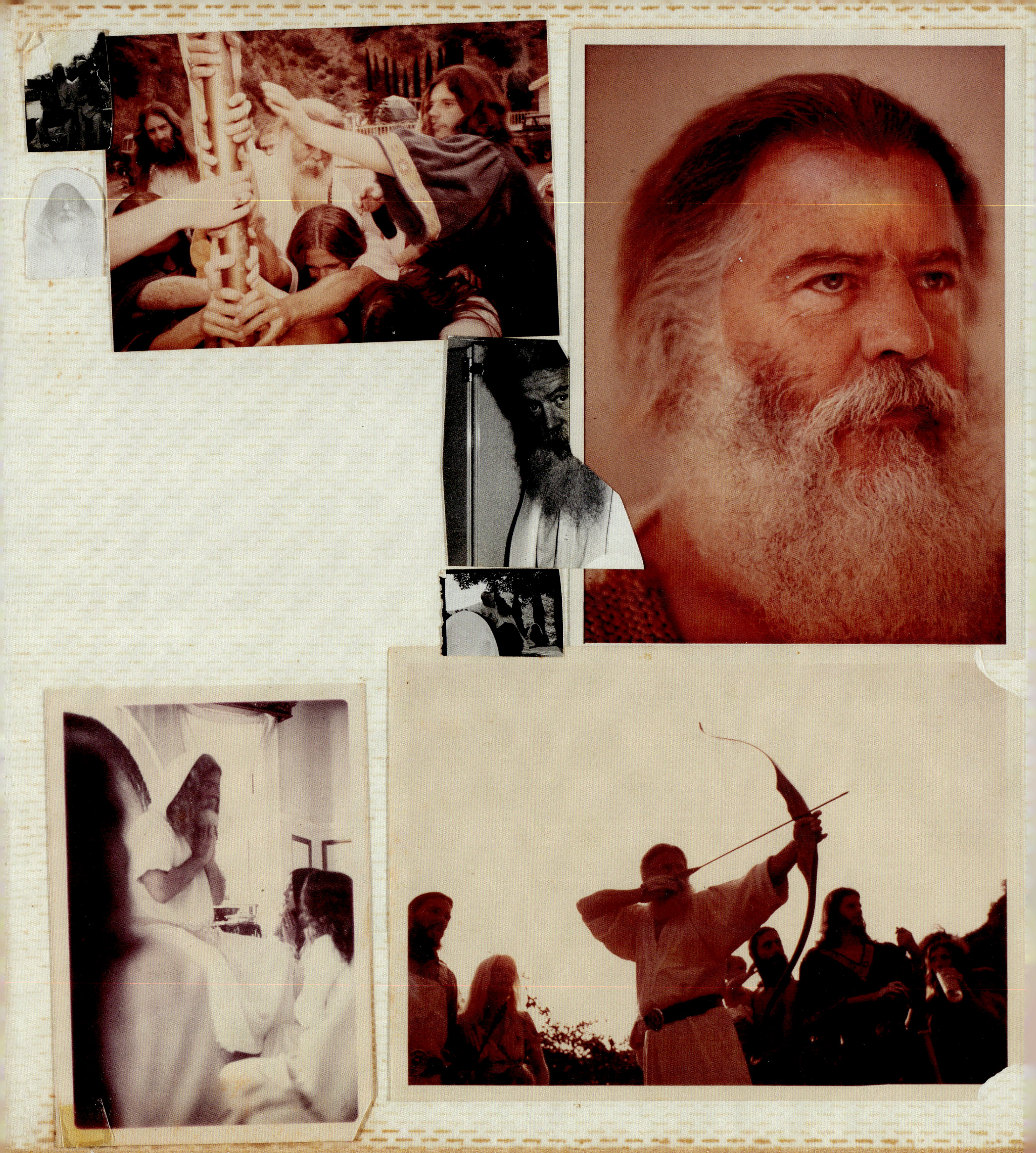

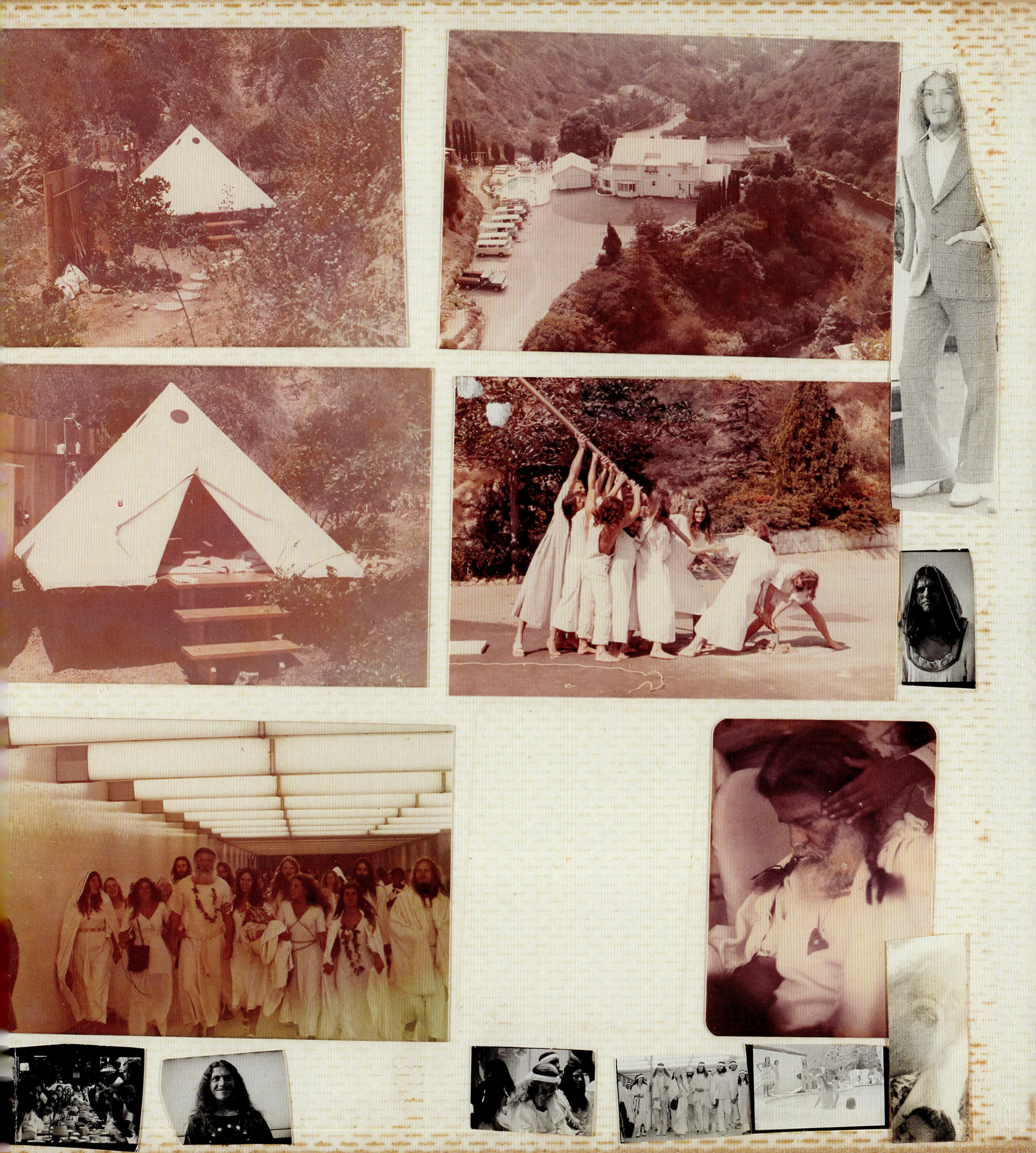

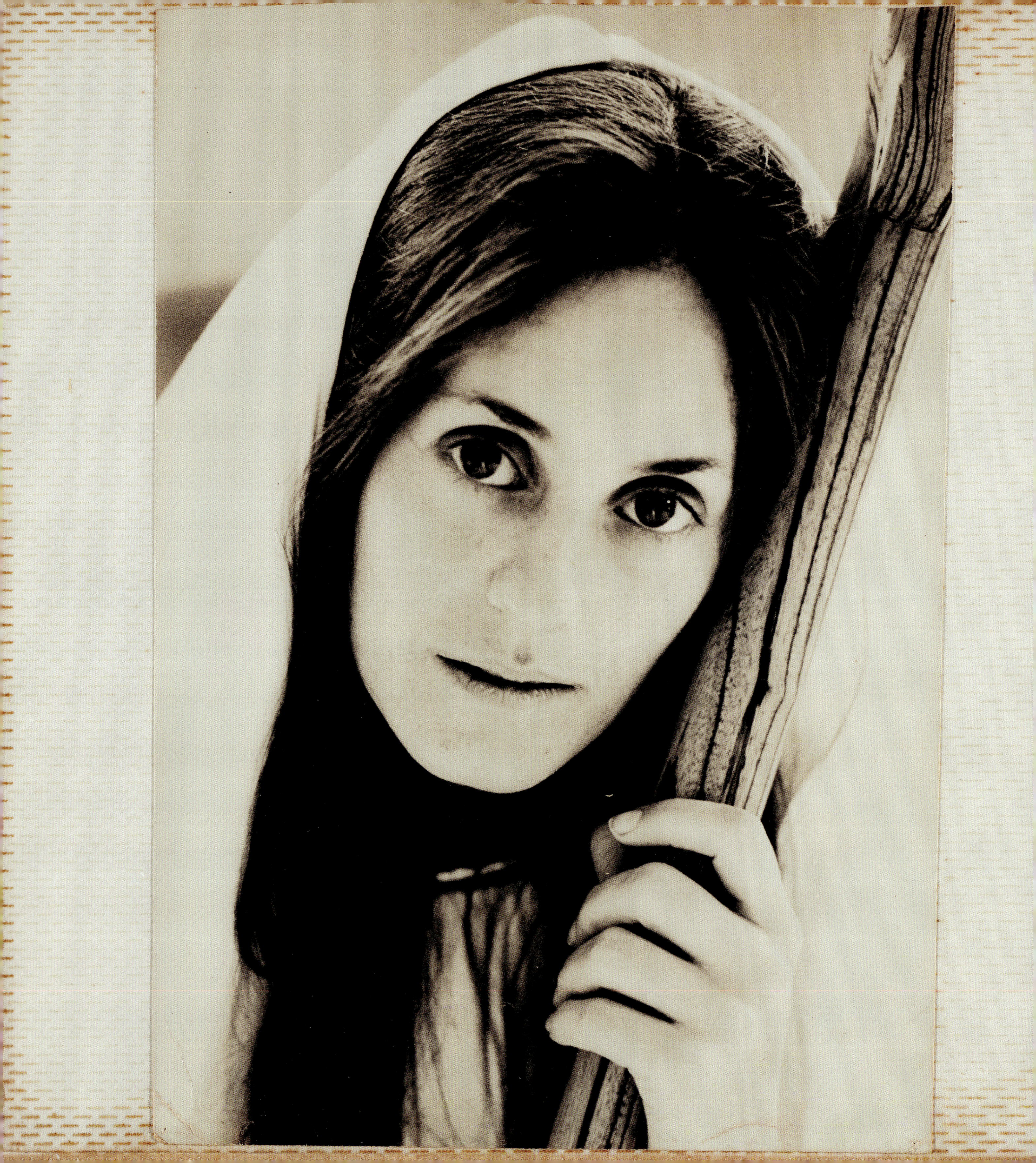

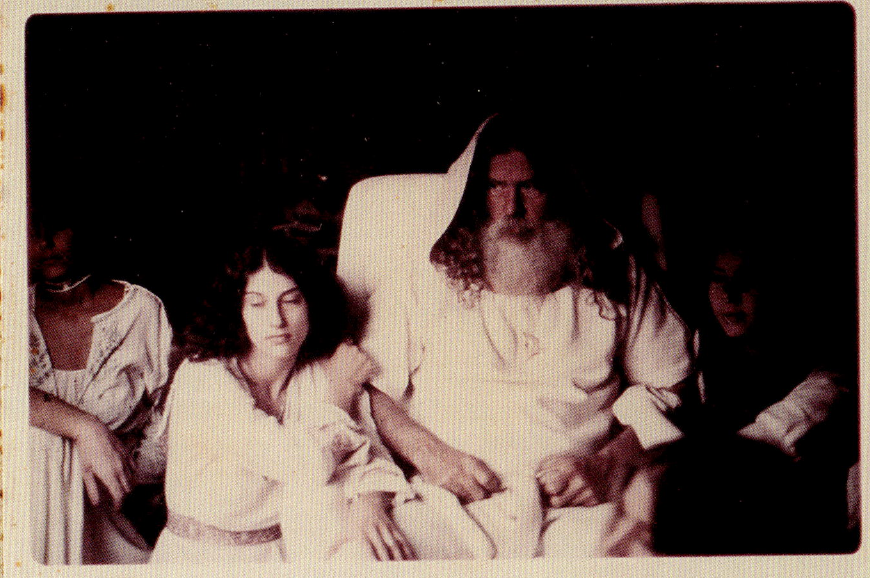
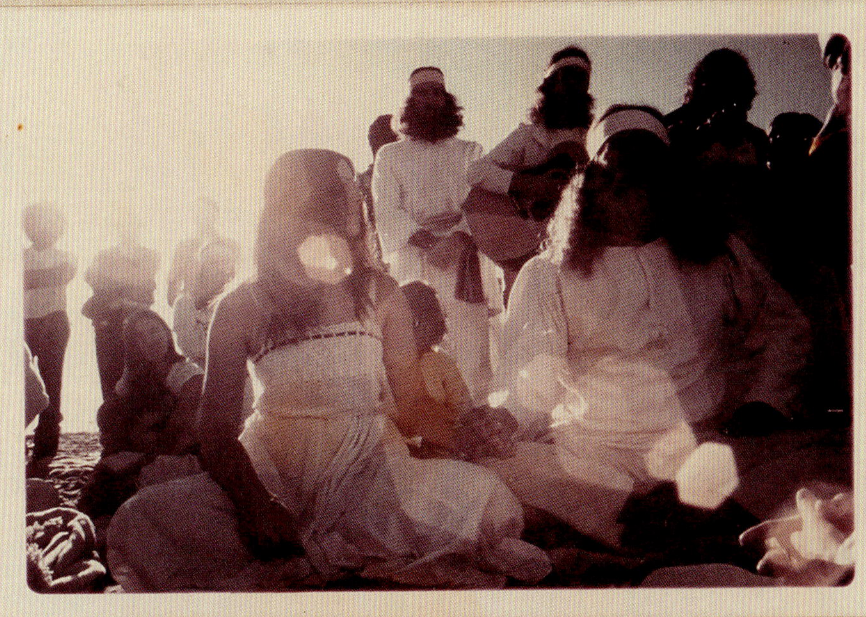
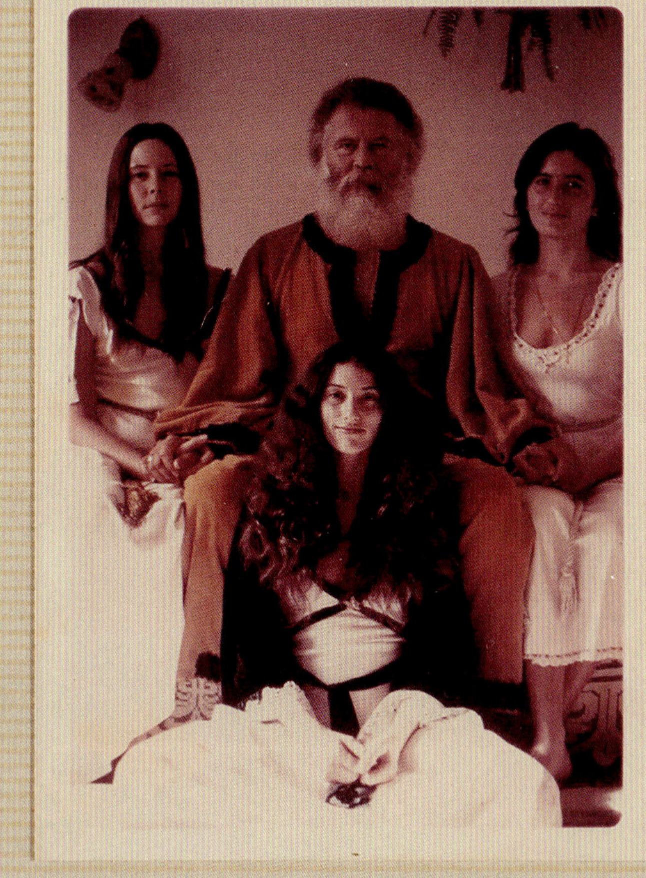
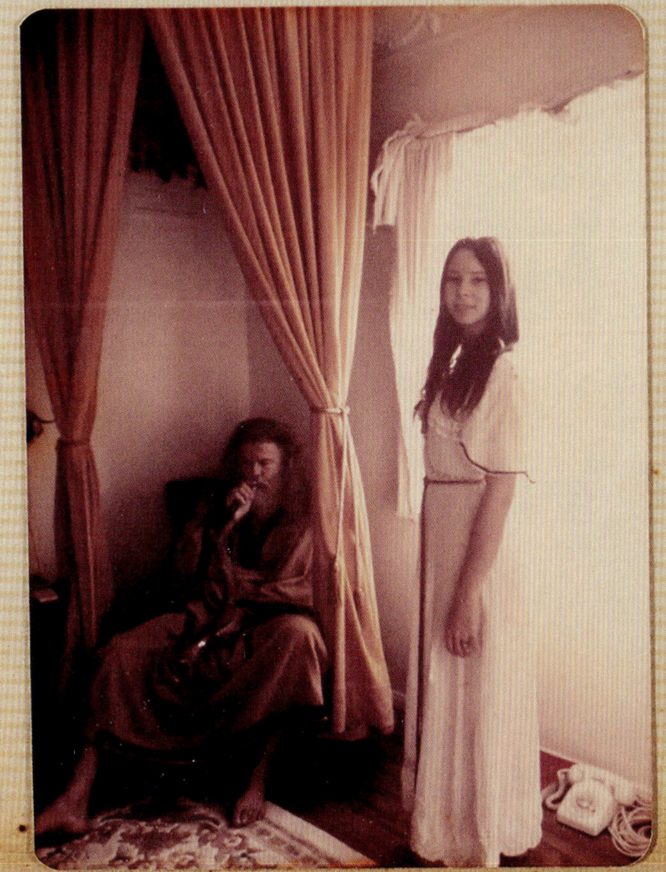
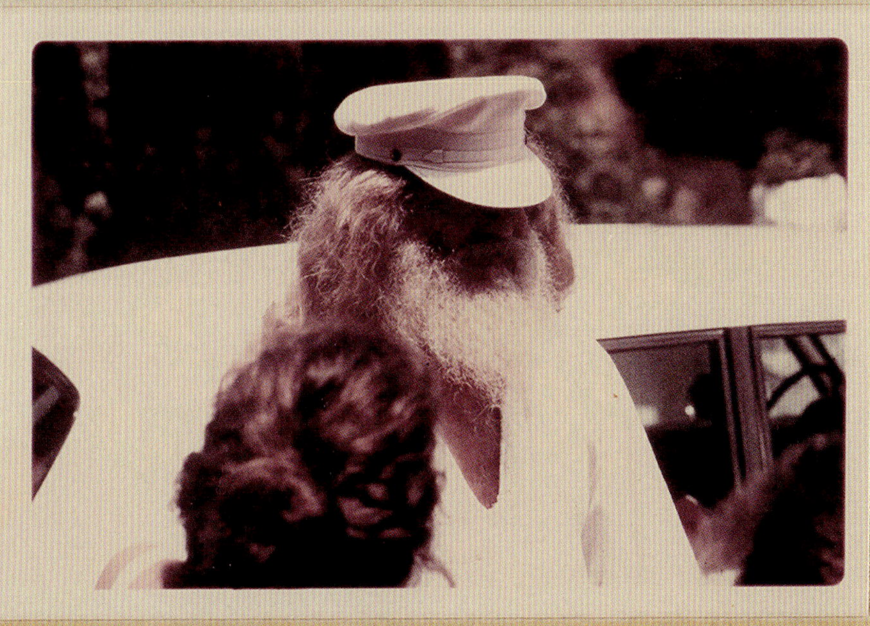

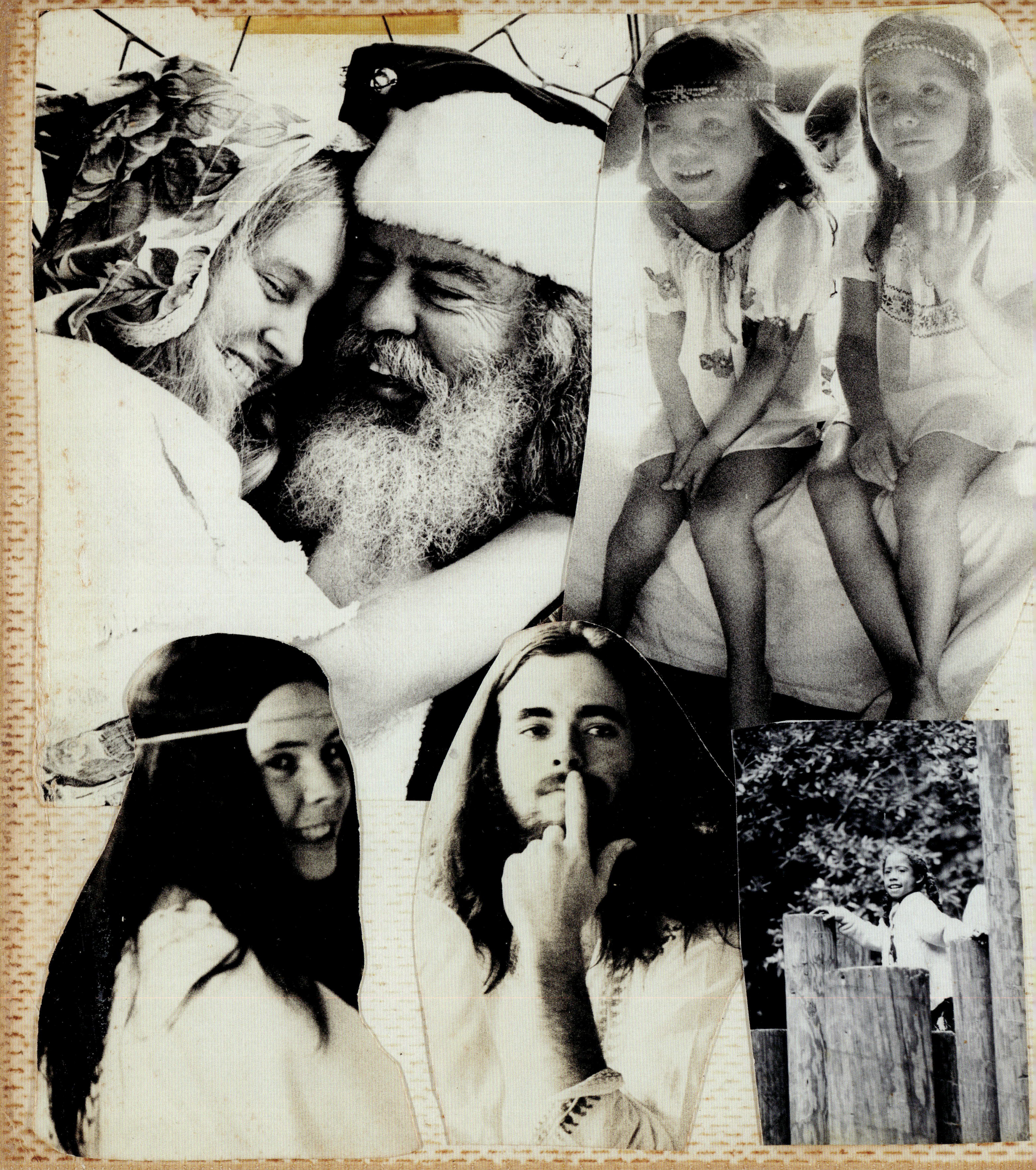

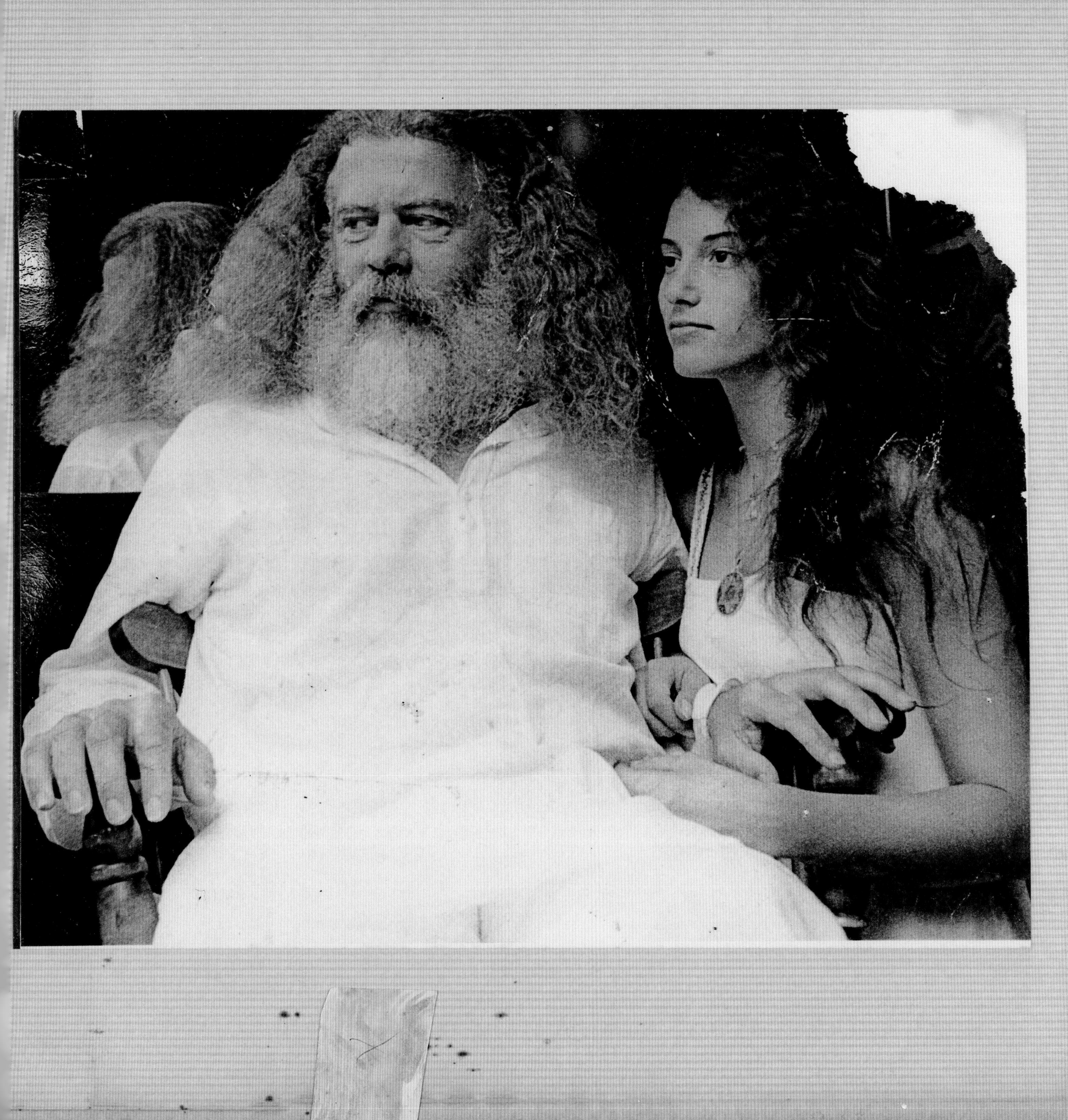

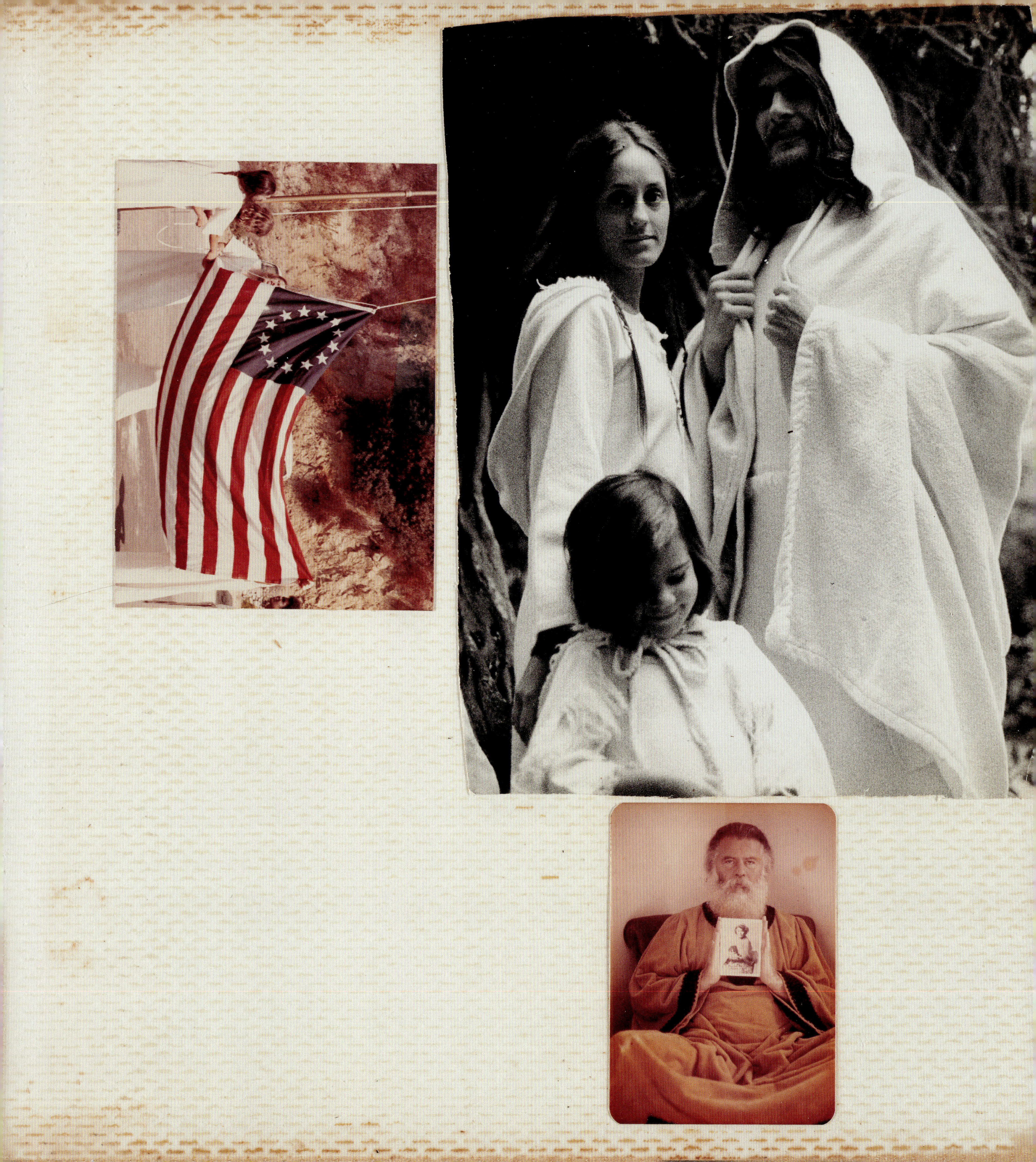

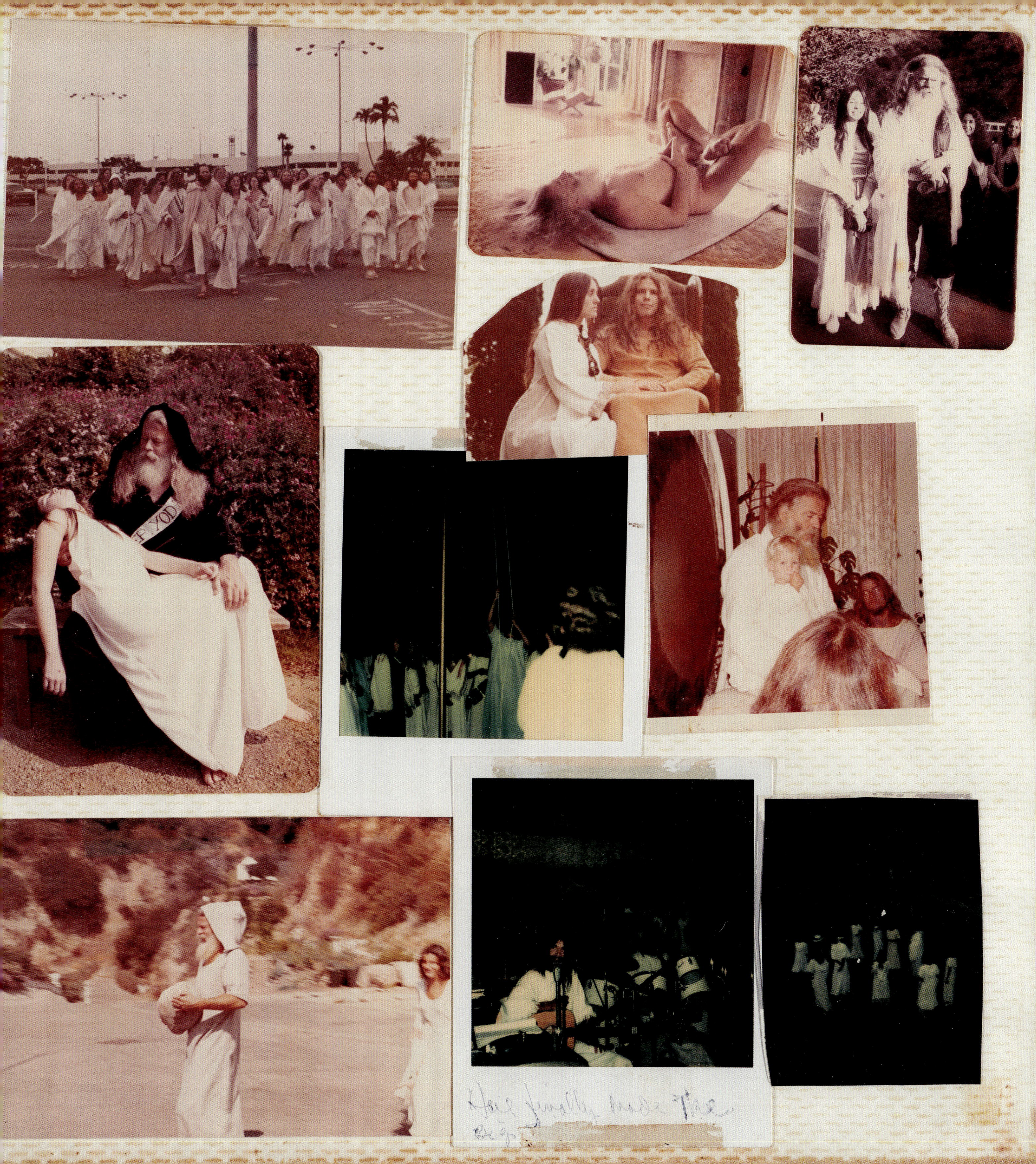
They finally made the
big

SEE, DIG MY MESSAGE NOW! YOU HAVE HEARD"LOVE ONE ANOTHER"

I SAY UNTO YOU THAT IS IMPOSSIBLE TO LOVE ONE ANOTHER, BUT

YOU CAN BE KIND. SEEE ITS IMPOSSIBLE TO LOVE ONE ANOTHER .

HOW CAN YOU LOVE EVERYONE, ITS UNREALISTIC. BE KIND AND

CONSIDERATE TO ANY AND ALL AND THATS GOOD ENOUGH FROM THAT

LOVE MIGHT POSSIBLY SPRING.

I AM TIRED OF THIS SHIT OF PEOPLE SAYING THEY LOVE YOU AND

TMEN STICKING A KNIFE IN YOUR BACK. THEY DO IT ALL THE TIME.

I LOVE YOU BABY AND THEN THEY RIP YOU OFF.

SO I JUST SAY BE KIND AND CONSIDERATE, THATS ALL, IN SHORT,

bBE KIND. YOU CAN'T BE KIND WITHOUT BEING CONSIDERATE, YOU

KNOW.

SO THAT MAN CAN DO. THERE'S NOT ANOTHER GURU ANYWHERE

SAYING THAT SIMPLE TRUTH.

I CAN PROVE IT, WHO I SAY I AM YOU KNOW, BECAUSE I'M PRACTICAL

I JUST LOOK LIKE THE MOST IMPRACTICAL MAN IN THE WORLD.

P.S. 140 CHILDREN CAN'T BE WRONG!

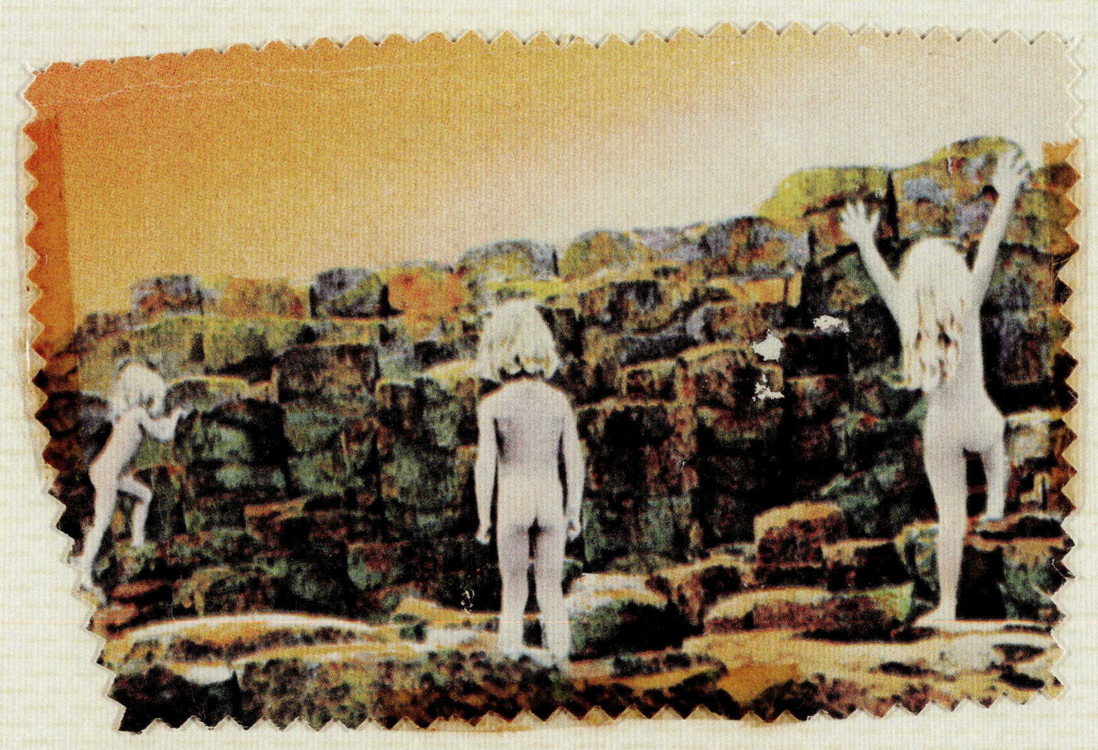

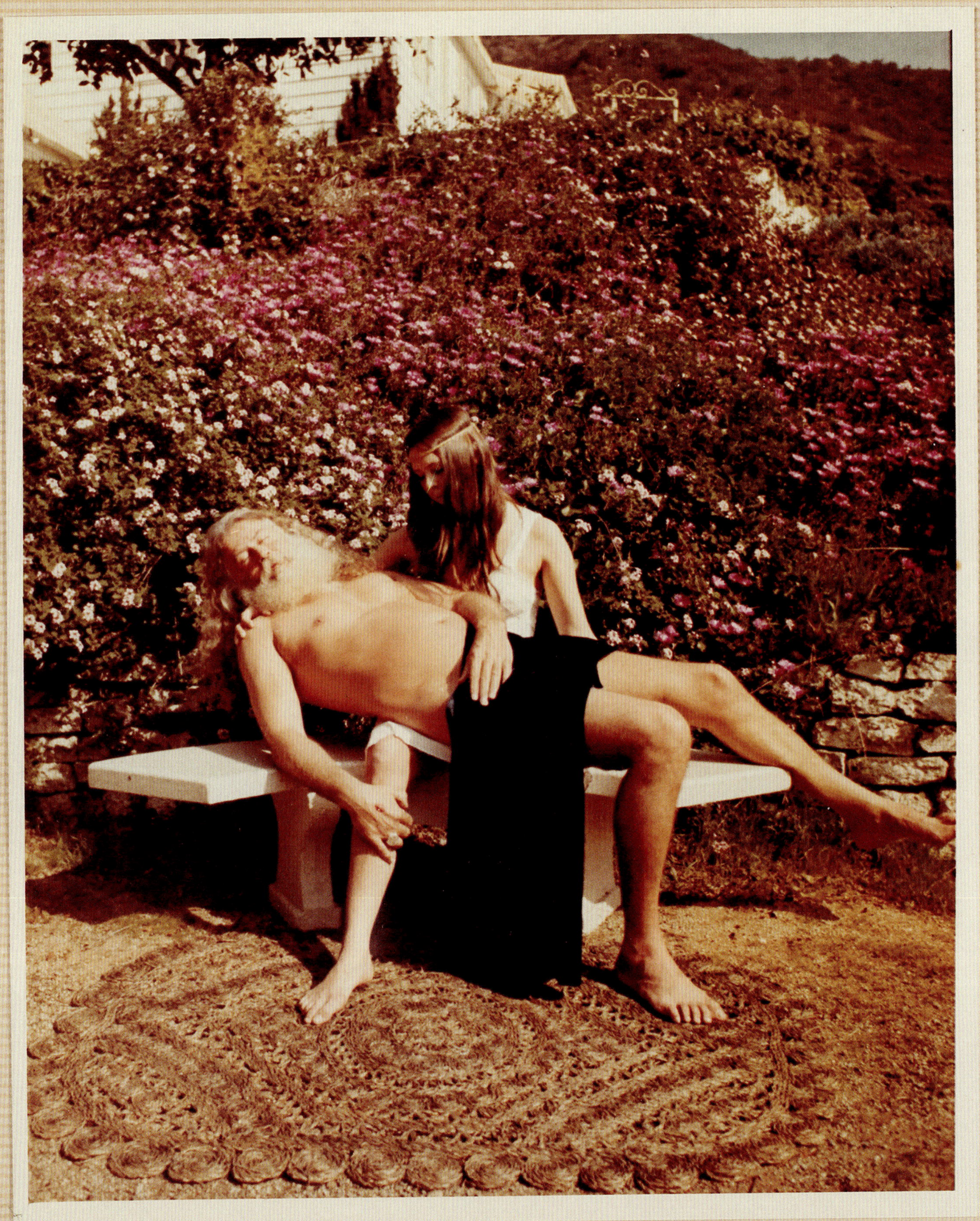

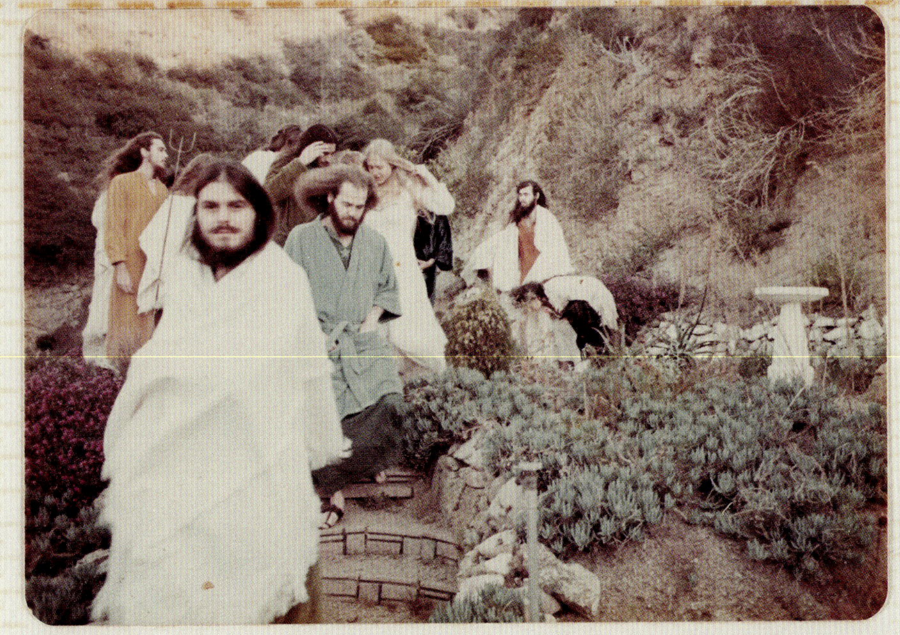

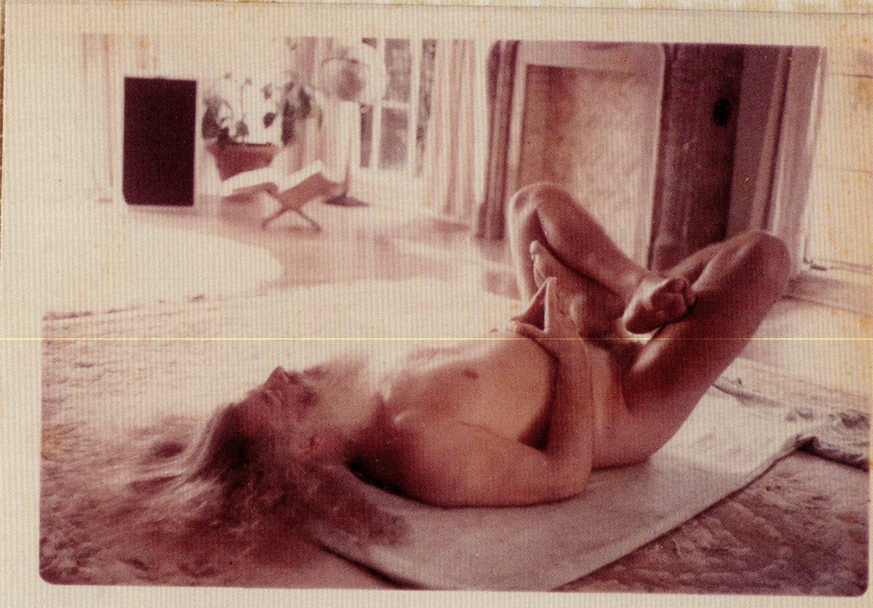

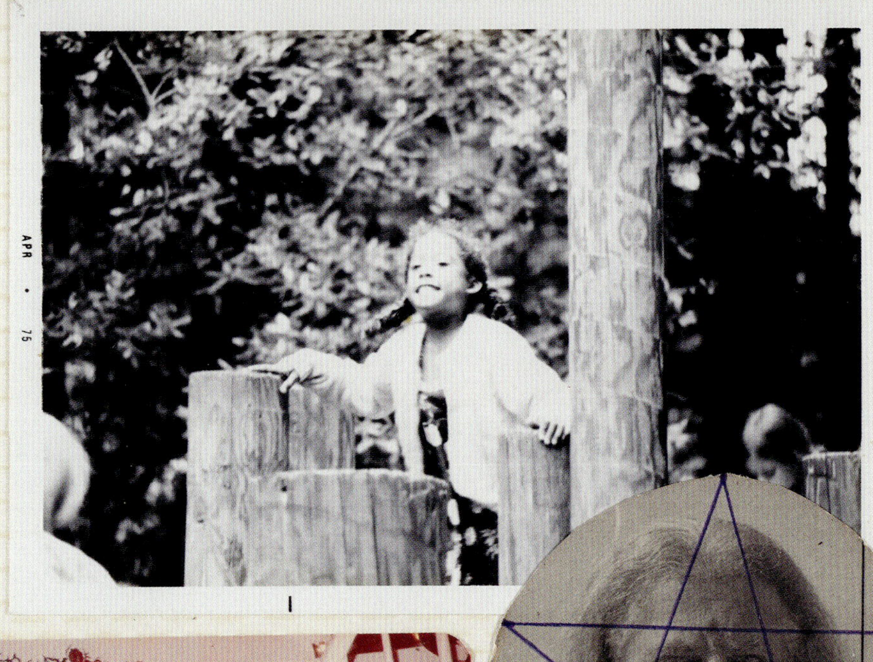

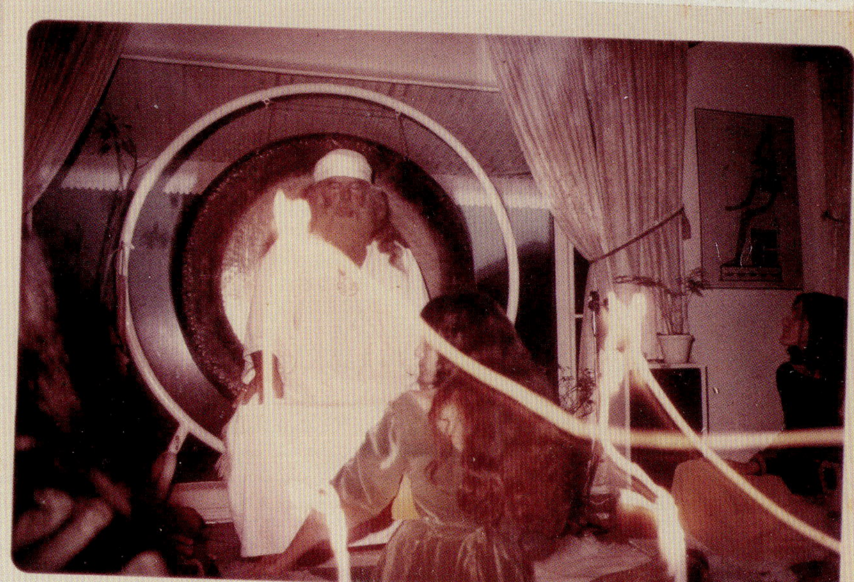

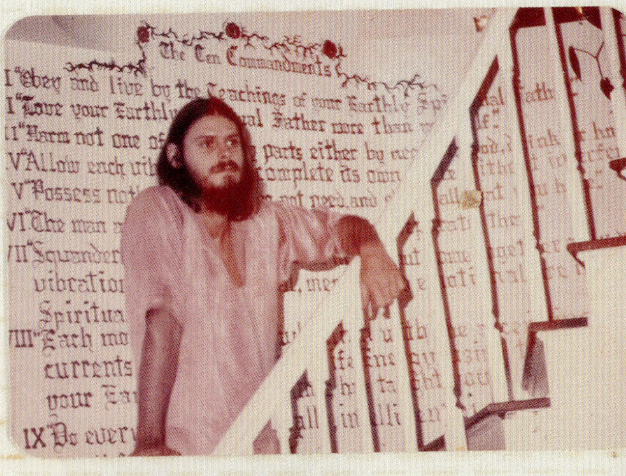
The Ten Commandments
I "Obey and live by the teachings of your Earthly Spiritual Father
I "Love your Earthly Spiritual Father more than
II "Harm not one of
V "Allow each vibration parts either by
complete its own
V "Possess not need and
VI The man
VII "Squander
vibration
Spiritual
VIII "Each mo
currents
your Ear
IX Do every

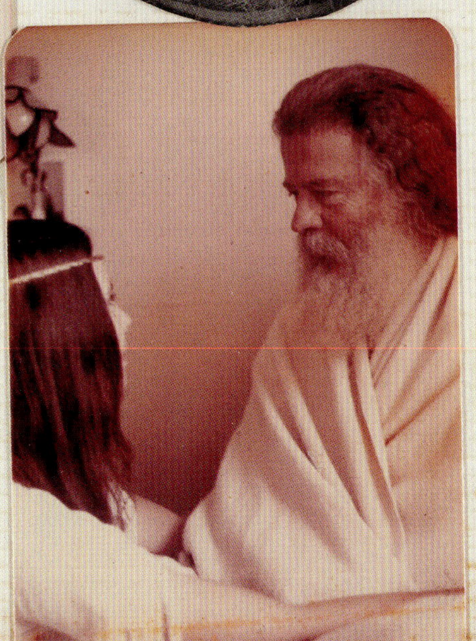

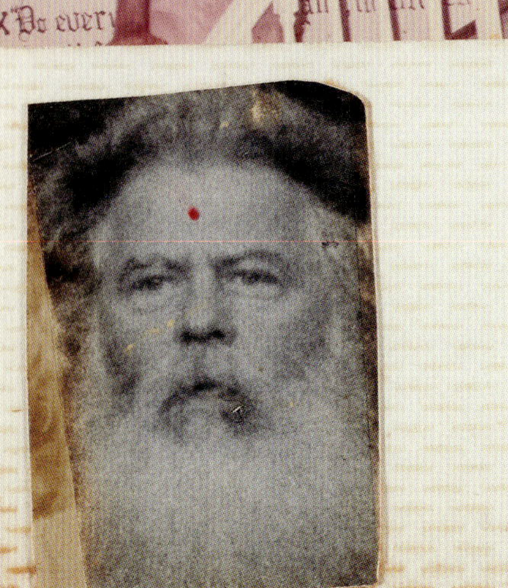

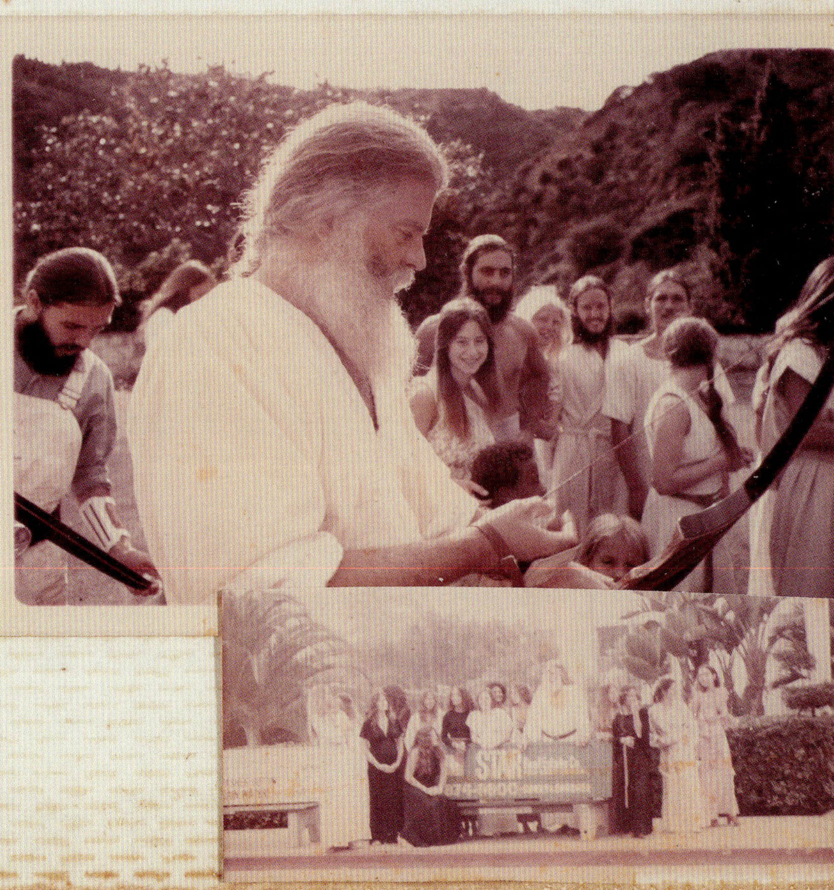

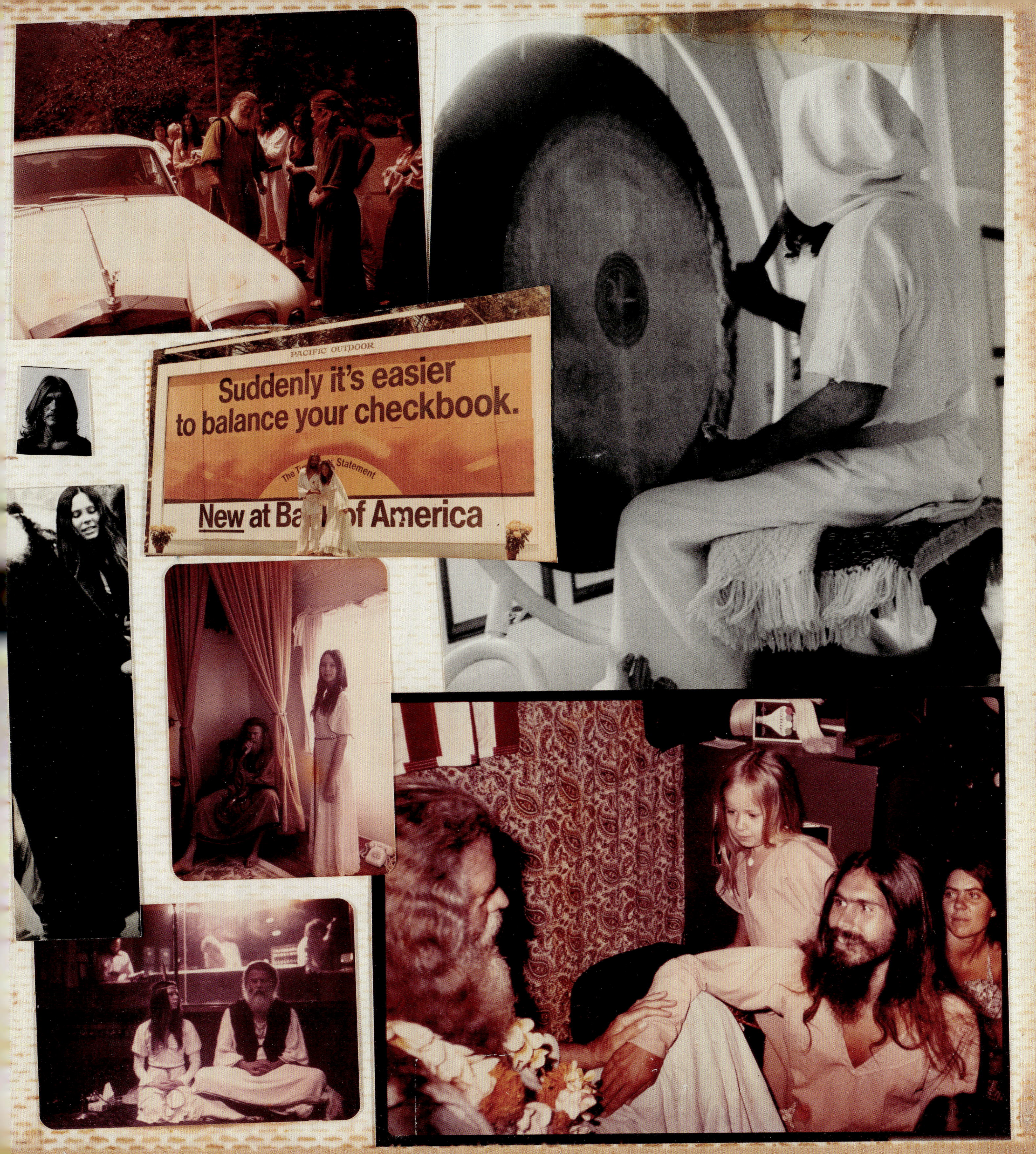
PACIFIC OUTDOOR
Suddenly it's easier
to balance your checkbook.
New at Bank of America

Dear Osiris

Here are current van problems, Keys are lost, misplaced, vans taken rashly, not returned promptly, left dirty and gas tanks empty, parts dismantled and left in pieces. Used for trips other than Brotherhood Business.

ON THE POSITIVE END OF THE POLE

Being in charge of a vehicle gives you a great opportunity w/ love to teach conscousness, consideration, and respect for Brotherhood Property

However, tighter control is neccessary. Keys can no longer stay in the ignition all night long nor all day Sunday. Brothers + Sisters should come to you for the key after they have made adequate scheduling arrangem. Keys should be returned to you when not in use. This is what the hook and ring are for. Put the hook up in your room in an **obvious**, accessible place.

You are responsible for the vehicle in your charge.

I know you'll get off to the challenge.

Violators are liable to driving + passenger suspension. Discuss problems w/ me.

Also keep a key in your private possession.

Love
Omne

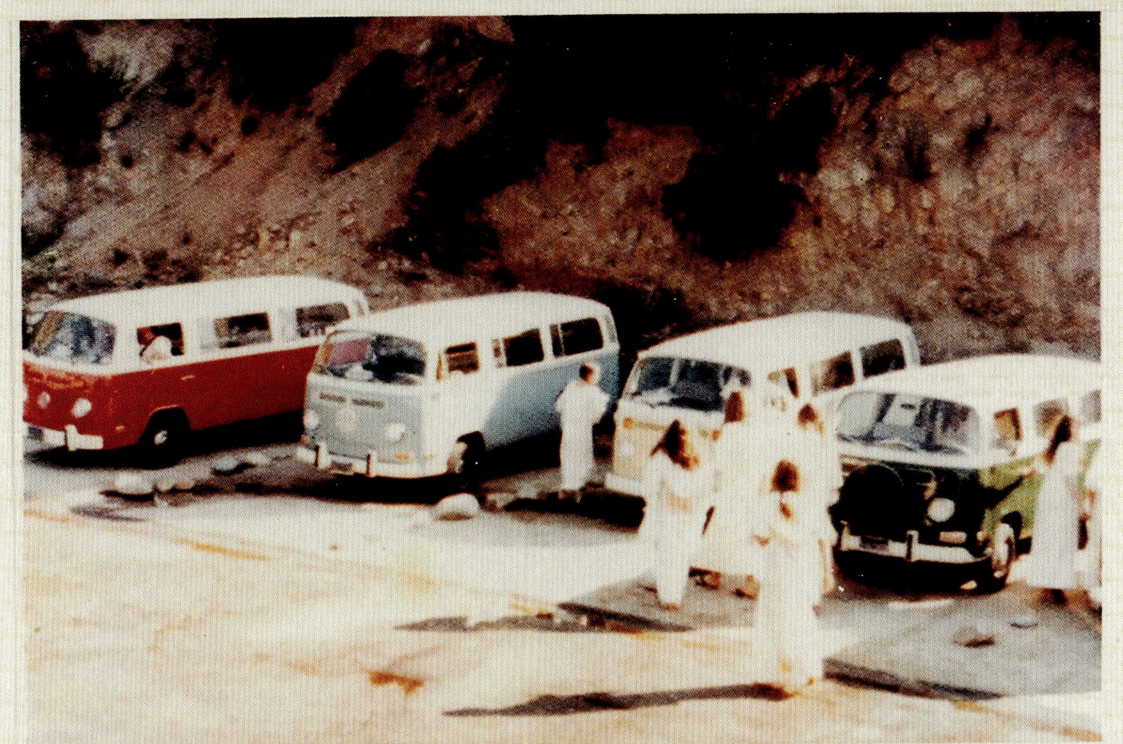
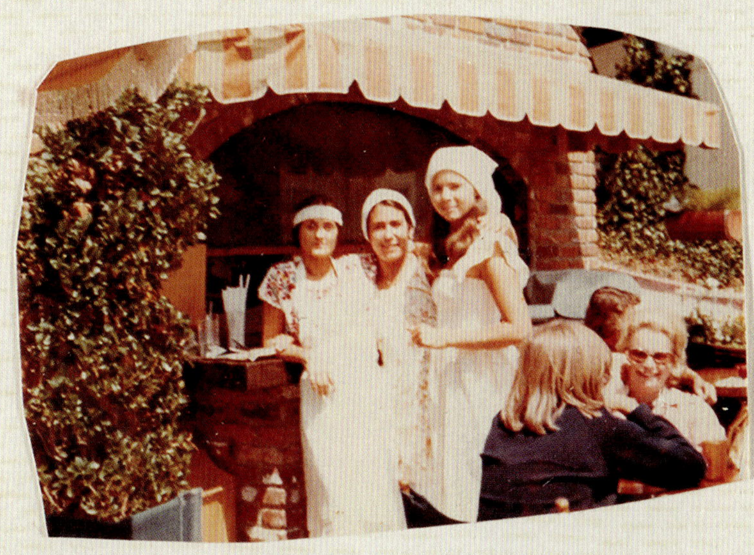
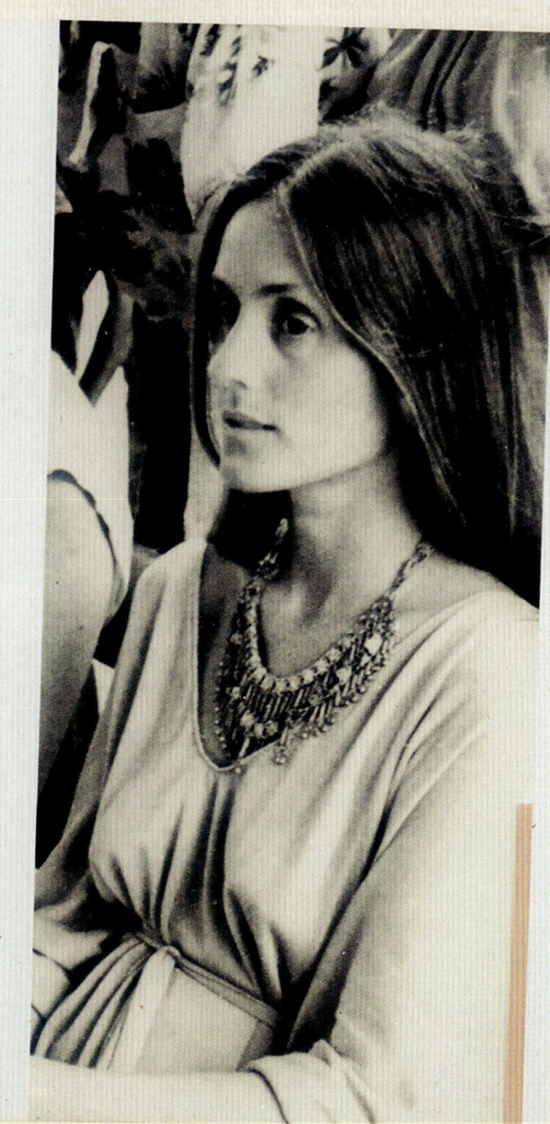
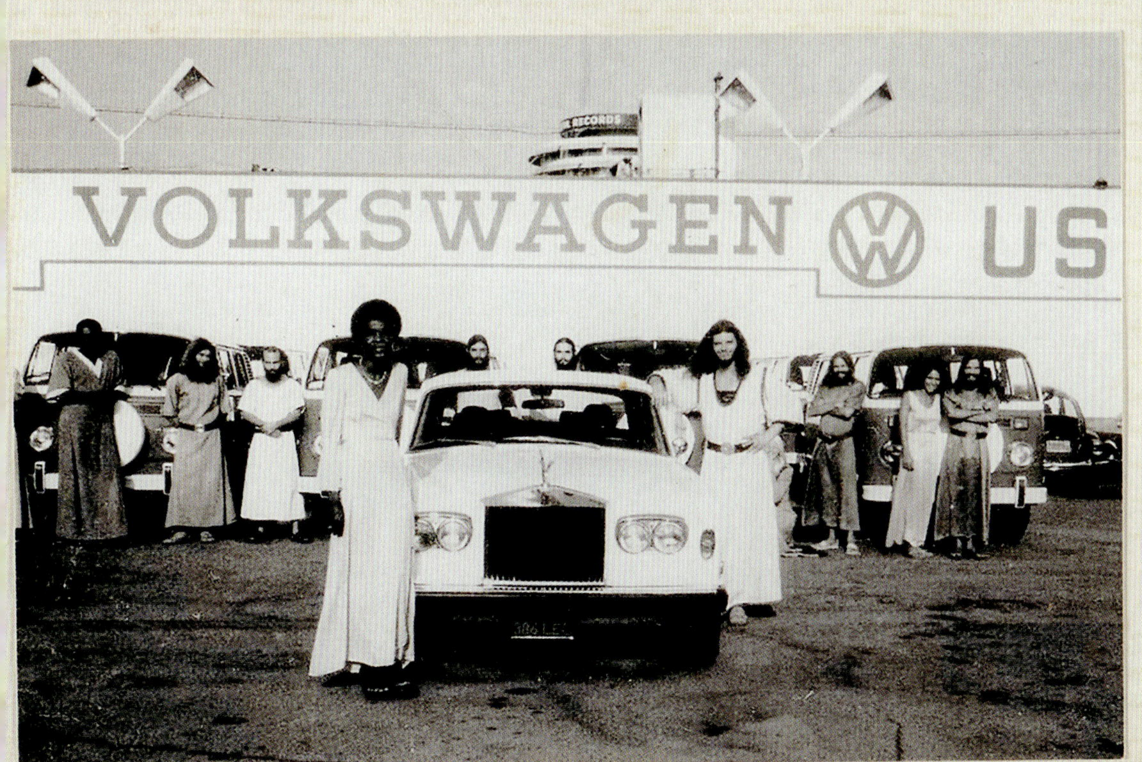

VOLKSWAGEN US
RECORDS

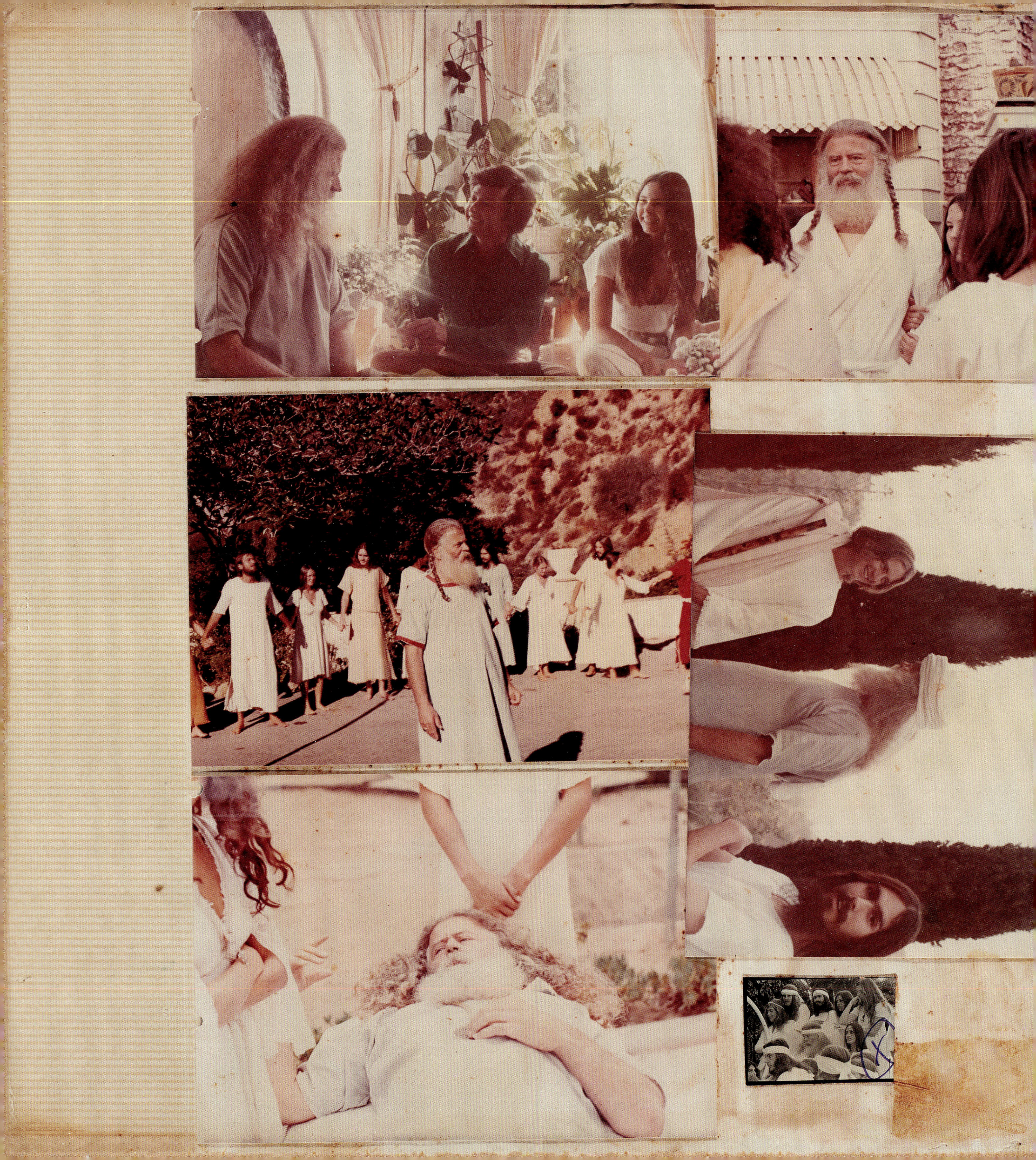

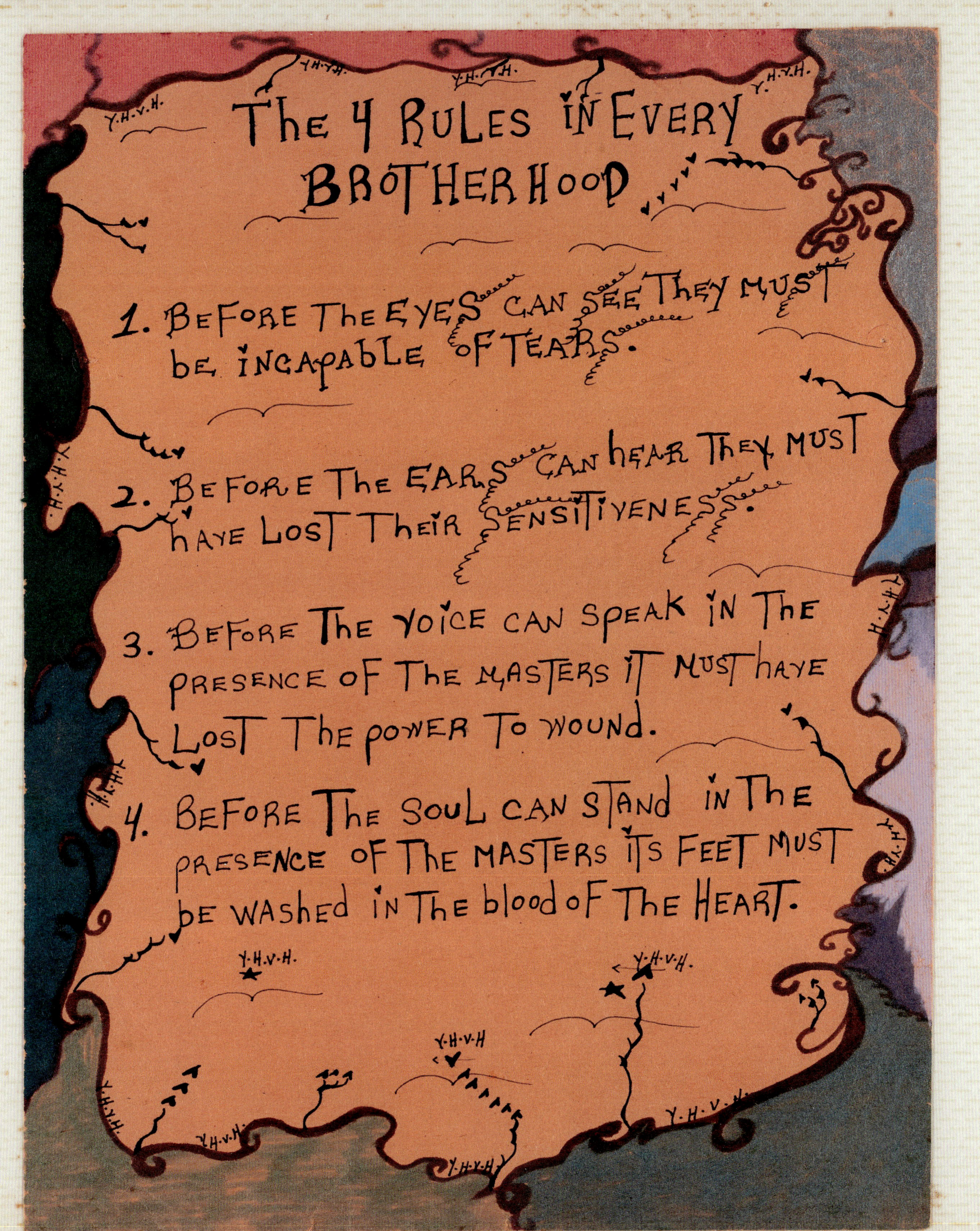

The 4 Rules in Every Brotherhood

1. Before the eyes can see they must be incapable of tears.

2. Before the ears can hear they must have lost their sensitiveness.

3. Before the voice can speak in the presence of the masters it must have lost the power to wound.

4. Before the soul can stand in the presence of the masters its feet must be washed in the blood of the heart.

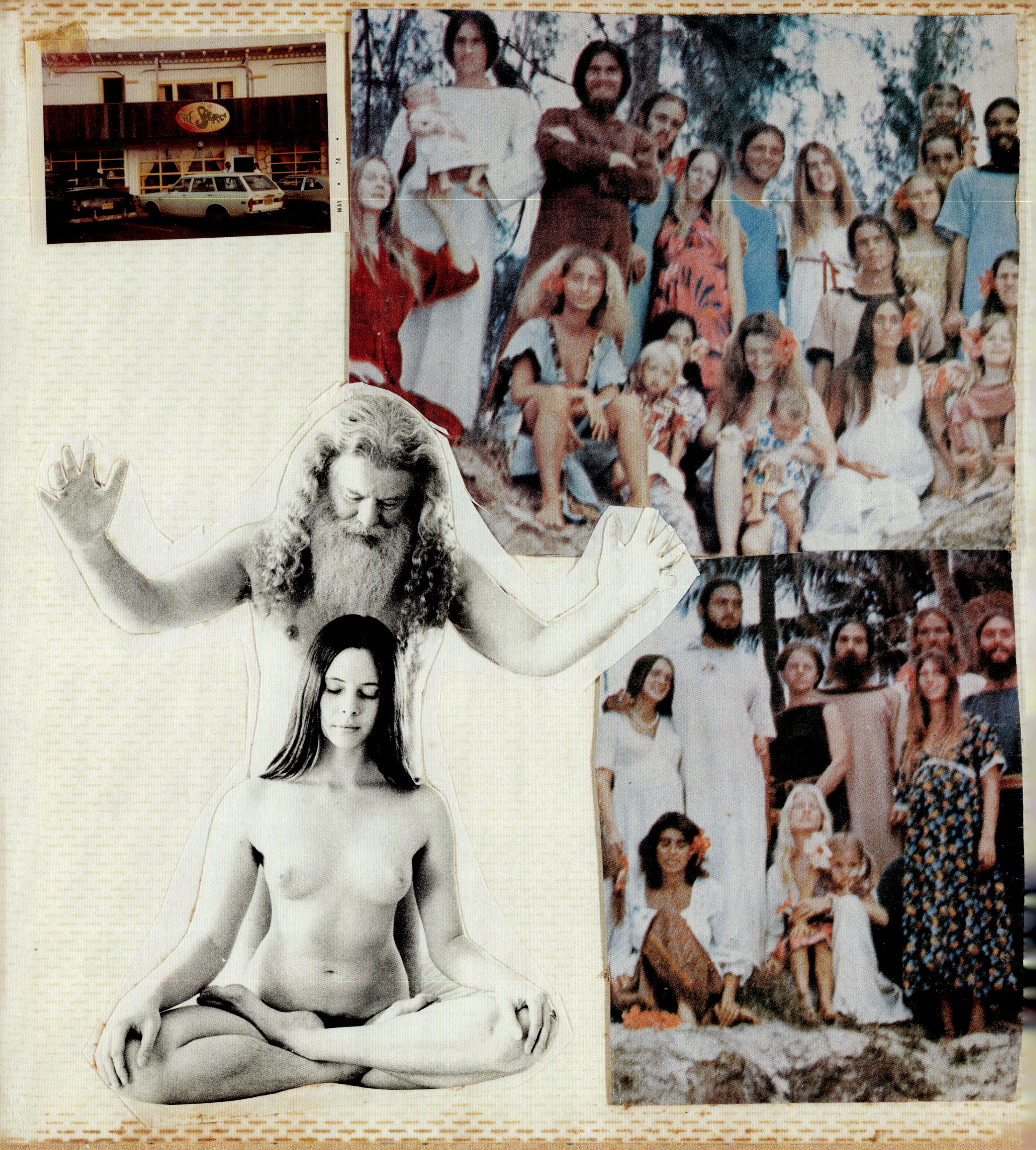
MAY • • 74

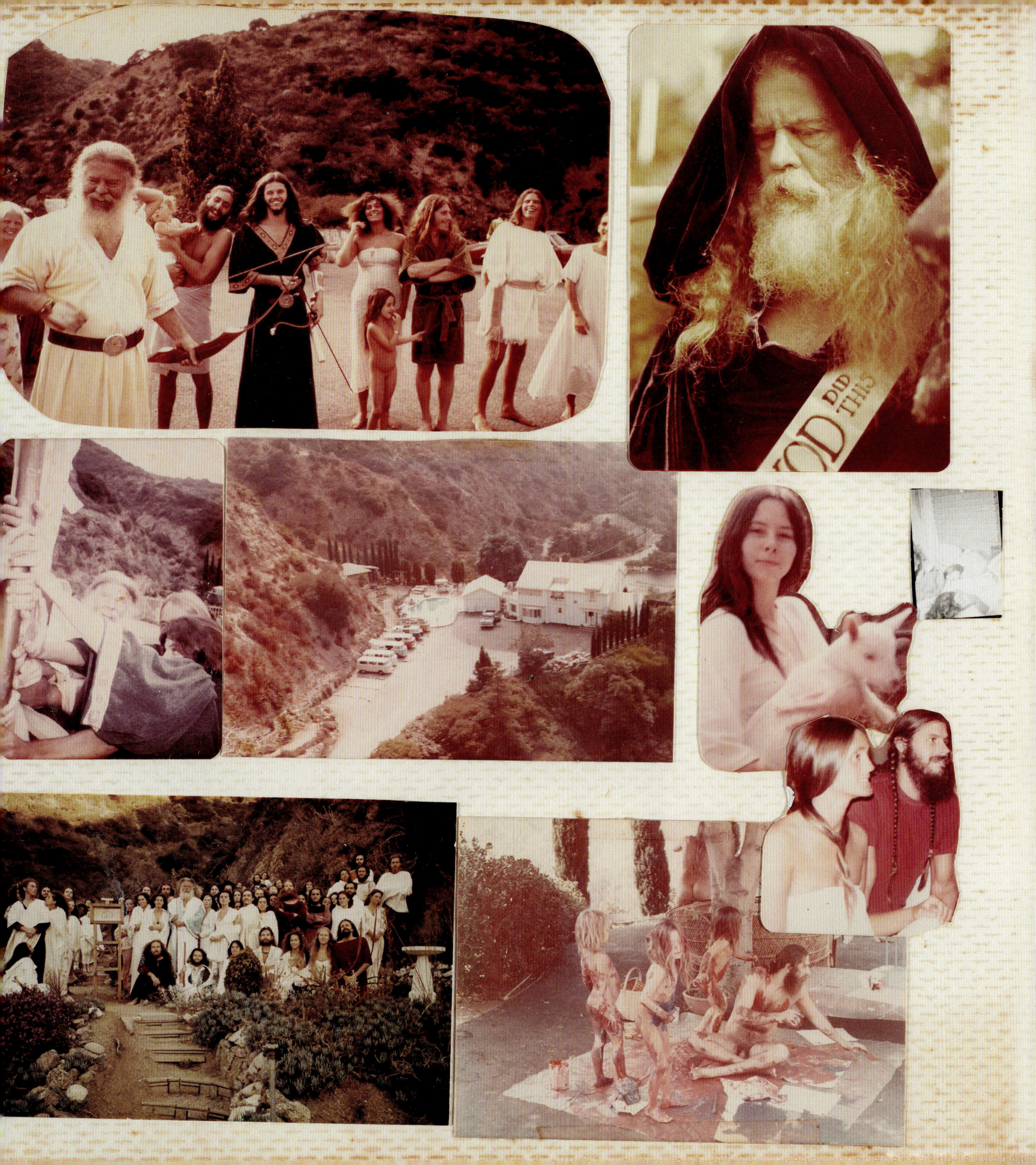
GOD DID THIS

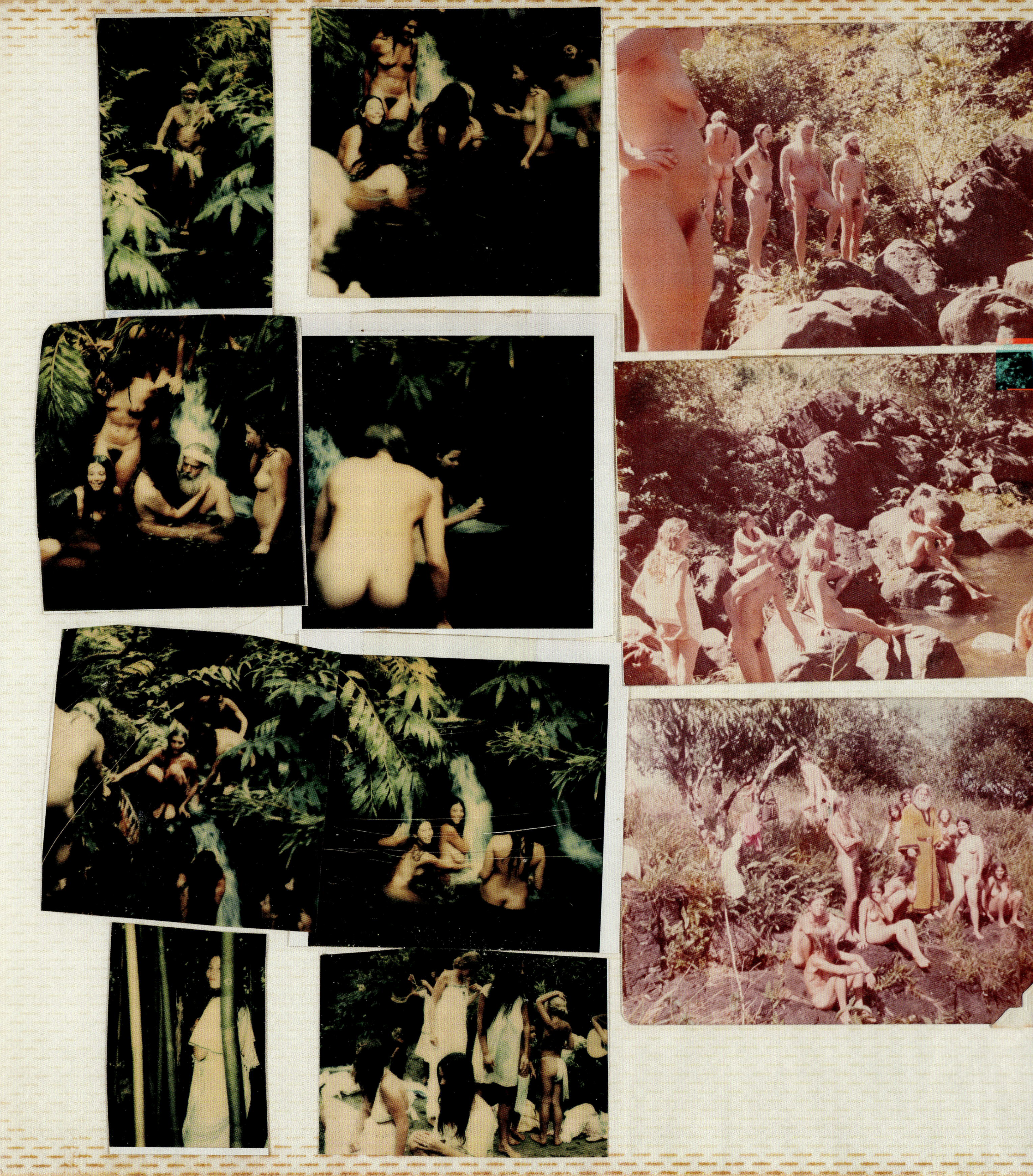

<u>THE SOURCE</u>

AN INTERNATIONAL HEALTH SPA

Purpose: To provide a complete health program for Mental, Physical and Spiritual Rejuvenation.

Facilities: The Health Spa will be organized around three major Geodesic Domes: the Meditation Dome, the Health Spa Dome, and the Cafeteria Dome. These major domes will be surrounded by clusters of Bedroom Domes. For every twelve of these, there will be an accomodating Shower/Toilet Dome. All domes will be connected by cobblestone walkways.

Health Program: Science has discovered that it takes a minimum of ten days to rejuvenate the body cells. This will be accomplished through the following program: The diet will consist of the purest natural foods indigenous to the Hawaiian Islands; guests will arise and retire at regular hours each day; they will participate in a supervised exercise program; they will receive a daily massage and steam bath; their attire will be a loose fitting robe, hand-tailored for each guest on the day of his arrival.

Cost: One-thousand dollars ($1,000) for a ten day minimum. One hundred dollars ($100) for each extra day.

Operators: The Source Health Spa will be operated by the Brotherhood of The Source-- a non-profit religious organization dedicated to serving humanity.

For the past five years, The Brotherhood has operated the most successful vegetarian restaurant in the United States. The Source Restaurant is widely acclaimed for its fine organic foods and patronized by the most health-conscious people in Greater Los Angeles.

A significant problem facing every business of this kind is an effective and reliable labor force. The Brotherhood has demonstrated over the past five years that it has such a reliable working body. (References are available on request.)

The Source Health Spa will be staffed by fifty members of our religious organization and directed by its head---Father Ya Ho Wha. Within the Brotherhood, reside all of the expertise and talent necessary to operate a first-class health resort. Our members work diligently with Life, Mind, Truth and Love to perfect our service to others and we are united as one body in that objective.

Investment: One million dollars ($1,000,000). Ten shares will be sold at $100,000 per share. These monies will be used for the construction of the facilities and the purchase of equipment and supplies.

The investor will receive one-half of the net profits as long as the Brotherhood operates the Spa. All employees work without salaries.

Further Information: Contact Aristotle T. Aquarian, 8301 Sunset Boulevard, L.A. 90069, (213) 876-6522.

...ers Came

At 4 a. m. the torpedo attack stops.

At 8 a. m. the bombers come, diving down on the motionless, listing Chicago to blast her with bombs.

The Japs are punk marksmen. The whole morning goes by with nothing worse than a few near misses that cause the ship to leap around almost as badly as the torpedo explosions. But they do little damage.

There are no other ships to help the Chicago. The others are all battling it out with the Japs miles away.

The Marines at the deck guns just keep blazing away.

The crew members grow fidgety, waiting at their battle stations.

* * *

A Good Place to Shoot ... And To Be Shot At

Up at the very front of the ship, the favorite gunnery spot, Pvt. Baker leans back in the harness of his machine gun, swinging to all points.

While he fires at one Jap plane another comes in from the side to rain machine gun bullets down on the deck about him.

His ears are stuffed with cotton but he can still hear the continuous roar of the guns and plane motors.

The ship gives a violent lurch and his harness comes loose. He lands hard on the deck, lies there half-dazed.

Looking off to one side he sees a Zero coming. Bullets spatter along the deck in a line directly at him. He rolls over and they clatter on across the spot he vacated.

His knees are weak but he

At 5 p. m. the order comes to abandon ship. It has suffered a direct hit.

For some reason or other, Pvt. Baker discovers he and three others of his gun crew are about the only ones who haven't yet gone overboard.

He is about to unfasten his gun harness and say goodby to the Chicago when he notices a lone Zero coming in to strafe the men in the water.

There are 10 shots in his gun. He cuts loose. The plane is too far away. It's a miss, but the pilot sees him and swings in his direction.

There's no one left now to hand Pvt. Baker the ammunition but he still has his own good right arm with which he once won an Ohio A. A. U. weightlifting championship.

He reaches down, picks up a 60-pound box of bullets, slams it into place and swings on the approaching plane. It's now almost upon him, spitting machine gun bullets past his head.

He squeezes the triggers. There's a burst of flame and Pvt. Baker feels the heat of the burning Zero as it hurtles on past, 20 yards over his head, into a spot in the sea where no men are swimming.

Pvt. Baker's work is done. He staggers to the side of the ship, slips and bumps his head, but manages to get overboard.

The water revives him and he swims madly to escape the suction of the sinking Chicago.

He can feel the pull, but he makes it.

The Chicago disappears in six minutes.

A destroyer begins picking up the men several hours later.

Two days later they're safely ashore.

Top Judo Expert Kills Neighbor---With Judo

James E. (Jim) Baker is being held at Los Angeles in connection with the judo killing of a neighbor, dispatches from the Coast revealed Monday.

Baker told Los Angeles police he won the world's judo title in 1948 in Cincinnati by defeating Wild Bill Zim.

Los Angeles police say he admits killing Edward A. Bollinger, 43, his next-door neighbor.

When Baker was in Cincinnati he operated the Baker Studio of Body Culture, 425 Main street. He was active in promoting the Mr. America Show at Music Hall in 1950.

While in the Marine Corps during World War II he won the jiu jitsu and judo championships in the Pacific Theater.

He also was an ardent supporter of archery and took bear and deer hunting trips to northern Michigan with bow and arrow.

He engaged in a few professional wrestling exhibitions in 1948 and 1949.

Baker told Los Angeles police that he had kept a mongrel dog for Bollinger while Bollinger served a two-week sentence for drunken driving. When Bollinger returned home, Baker said, he accused Baker of mistreating the dog by not keeping it inside at night.

Later, Baker said, Bollinger calmed down and asked Baker to help him get his auto which was stalled half a mile away.

When they reached the auto, Baker said, Bollinger attacked him with a knife. In the following fight Baker used his knowledge of judo and when Bollinger failed to move after a few minutes, Baker realized he was dead.

Former Cincinnatian Is Held In Neighbor's Judo Murder After Row Over Care Of Dog

A judo expert, formerly of Cincinnati who admitted that he killed his neighbor with judo tactics was booked on suspicion of murder Monday in Los Angeles.

James E. Baker, who formerly operated the Baker Studio of Modern Body Culture at 425 Main St., admitted that he killed his neighbor, Edward A. Bollinger, 43-year-old machinist, in a fight over a mongrel dog Saturday night near their Los Angeles homes.

Baker, who told police he won the world's judo championship in 1948 in Cincinnati, defeating Wild Bill Zim, said he gave Bollinger "three or four judo cuts around the neck and back. When he stopped fighting I got up and looked at him. I've seen enough dead men to know he was dead."

Baker said Bollinger attacked him with a knife in an argument over the care of Bollinger's dog, Candy, while Bollinger served a two-week jail term for drunken driving.

Bollinger had left the dog in Baker's care and Saturday night he went to Baker's home to reclaim the dog. Police said an argument began when Bollinger accused Baker of mistreating the dog by not keeping it in the house at night.

Bollinger calmed down, Baker said, and asked Baker to help him move his car, which was stuck a half-mile from their home. When they reached the car, Baker said, Bollinger attacked him with a knife.

"I just acted instinctively, grabbed his knife and threw him over my shoulder into the gulley," Baker said. "Then I jumped on him and gave him three or four judo cuts around the neck and back."

Baker told police he served as a combat judo instructor in the Marine Corps and won the Silver Star on Guadalcanal.

Ross Leader, who promotes the wrestling shows in Cincinnati, could not be reached for comment but several officials of the Cincinnati Boxing and Wrestling Commission recalled that Baker had taken part in one or two matches here in 1949. Acquaintances said Baker left Cincinnati about three years ago.

Baker Cleared In Judo Death

Judo expert James E. Baker, 33, former Cincinnatian, Friday had been cleared of killing a man with two blows on the neck.

A Los Angeles coroner's jury, Thursday ruled that the killing of Edward Bollinger, 44, last Monday by Baker was justifiable homicide, committed in self-defense.

"A blow like that is very difficult to control," Baker told the jury. He said that Bollinger, a neighbor, attacked him with a knife following an argument over Bollinger's dog.

Baker formerly operated the Baker Studio of Modern Body Culture, 425 Main Street. He is a veteran of three years' service in the Marine Corps.

A Word About Learning to Swim

Pvt. Baker grew up in Cincinnati. He's now 22 years old and has been in the Marines seven months.

Before that, he was employed at the Wright plant. He's married and his wife, formerly Miss Margaret Scott, lives at 3032 Woodburn avenue. His mother, Mrs. Cora Balser, lives at 200 E. McMillan street.

Naturally his wife is proud of the fact he is officially credited with shooting down 13 Jap planes and has been decorated for gallantry displayed in helping to defend the Chicago.

Our interview with him was arranged by Mr. E. P. Bradstreet of the Y. M. C. A., who likes to think of Pvt. Baker as "one of the Y boys," because he spent so much time at Central Parkway Y before joining the Marines, learning weightlifting, wrestling, swimming and other sports.

The Y is now sponsoring a special course of swimming instructions for 1-A men and when Mr. Bradstreet asked Pvt. Baker the other day to take a few minutes time off from his 14-day furlough to indorse the program, he didn't hesitate a moment.

If it hadn't been for the training he had in swimming, our heroic Marine might not have made it from the sinking Chicago to safe water in six minutes.

On April 10 six-foot, two-inch Pvt. Baker reports to Mare Island, Cal. He hopes to be assigned to another ship.

The next battle, he says, will be easy . . . just like doing an ordinary day's work.

Ex-Cincinnatian Held For Judo Slaying

Judo expert James E. Baker, 33, former Cincinnatian, was held Monday by Los Angeles (Calif.) police in the death of a neighbor.

Baker, who moved to Los Angeles three years ago, told police he killed the man with judo blows when the neighbor attacked him with a knife, Saturday night.

THE DEAD MAN is Edward A. Bollinger, 43. The fight occurred after Bollinger accused Baker of mistreating his mongrel dog. Baker had cared for the animal while Bollinger served a jail sentence for drunk driving.

Baker said that Bollinger "calmed down," then asked him to help him move his car half a mile from their homes. There, Baker told police, Bollinger flashed his knife.

"I ACTED instinctively," Baker said. "Grabbing his knife I threw him over my shoulder into a gully, jumped on him and gave him three or four judo blows on the neck and back. When he stopped fighting I saw he was dead."

Baker formerly operated the Baker School Studio of Modern Body Culture, 425 Main Street. He also was a singer. He appeared as Prince Franz in a performance of Victor Herbert's "Sweethearts" in November of 1948, a benefit for St. Xavier School gymnasium funds.

BAKER IS MARRIED and father of a daughter, Peggy, 11. He is a veteran of three years' service in the Marines as a sergeant. He won a Silver Star on Guadalcanal.

Baker told police he won the world judo title in 1948, defeating a man named Wild Bill Zim here in Cincinnati.

He is a Hughes High School graduate and attended University of Cincinnati. He also is a graduate of the Swedish School of Massage, Chicago.

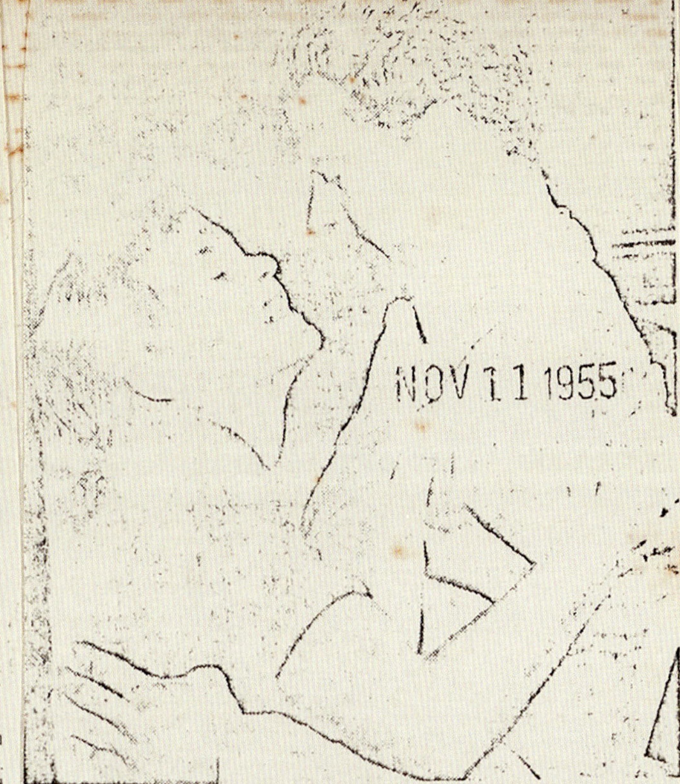
WIFE EMBRACES FREED JUDO EXPERT

Elaine Baker, wife of James Baker, 33, a judo expert formerly of Cincinnati, rushes to the arms of her husband after a coroner's jury gave a verdict at Los Angeles yesterday freeing the former world champion judo expert of murder charges in the death of Edward Bollinger, 41. The jury held Bollinger's death was justifiable homicide in self-defense. Bollinger was killed when he assertedly drew a knife in an argument over his dog and Baker threw him over his shoulder with a judo hold. —AP Wirephoto.

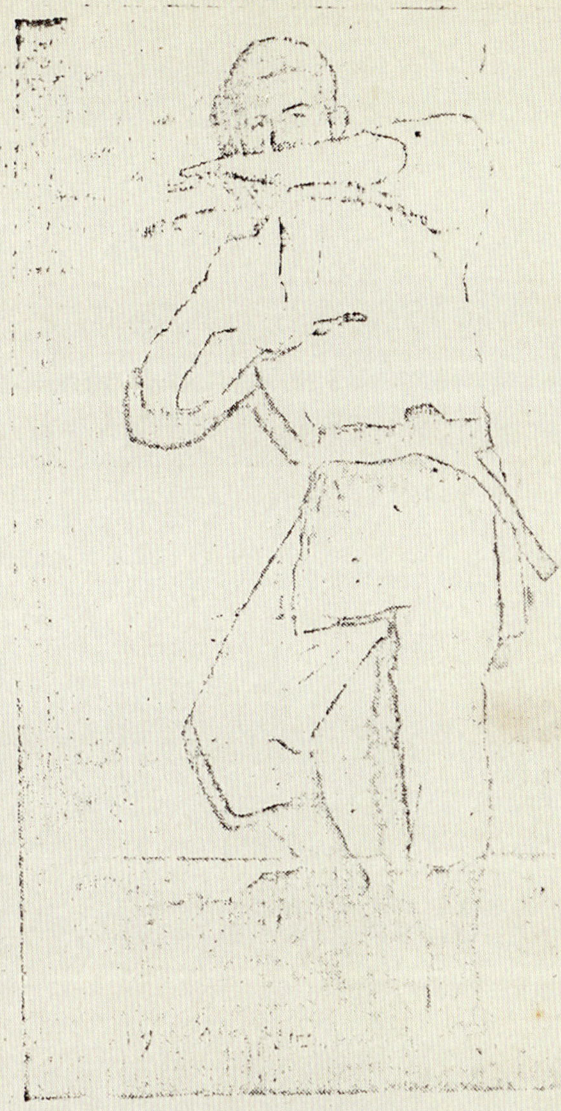

JAMES E. (JIM) BAKER
. . . uses judo in fatal fight.

Top Judo Expert Kills Neighbor---With Judo

James E. (Jim) Baker is being held at Los Angeles in connection with the judo killing of a neighbor, dispatches from the Coast revealed Monday.

Baker told Los Angeles police he won the world's judo title in 1948 in Cincinnati by defeating Wild Bill Zim.

Los Angeles police say he admits killing Edward A. Bollinger, 43, his next-door neighbor.

When Baker was in Cincinnati he operated the Baker Studio of Body Culture at 425 Main street. He was active in promoting the Mr. America Show at Music Hall in 1950.

While in the Marine Corps during World War II he won the jiu jitsu and judo championships in the Pacific Theater.

He also was an ardent supporter of archery and took bear and deer hunting trips to north-ern . . . professional wrestling exhibitions in 1948 and 1949.

Baker told Los Angeles that he had kept a mongrel for Bollinger while he served a two-week sentence for drunken driving. When Bollinger returned home, Baker said, he accused Baker of mistreating the dog by not taking it inside at night.

Later, Baker said, Bollinger calmed down and asked him to help him get his auto, which was stalled half a mile away.

When they reached the auto, Baker said, Bollinger attacked him with a knife. In the following fight Baker used his knowledge of judo and when Bollinger failed to move after . . .

_s Held

Threatened With Knife, He Says

Judo expert James E. Baker, 33, former Cincinnatian, was held Monday by Los Angeles (Calif.) police in the death of a neighbor.

Baker, who moved to Los Angeles three years ago, told police he killed the man with judo blows when the neighbor attacked him with a knife, Saturday night.

THE DEAD MAN is Edward A. Bollinger, 43. The fight occurred after Bollinger accused Baker of mistreating his mongrel dog. Baker had cared for the animal while Bollinger served a jail sentence for drunk driving.

Baker said that Bollinger "calmed down," then asked him to help him move his car half a mile from their homes. There, Baker told police, Bollinger flashed his knife.

"I ACTED instinctively," Baker said. "Grabbing his knife I threw him over my shoulder into a gully, jumped on him and gave him three or four judo blows on the neck and back. When he stopped fighting I saw he was dead."

Baker was charged with suspicion of murder.

Dr. Victor Cefalu, coroner's autopsy surgeon, said death was caused by a neck injury. He said the neck was not broken but "death was probably due to reflex reaction on either the heart or the respiratory system as a result of blows on the nerves of the neck."

"I meant to disarm Bollinger, not kill him," Baker said.

Baker formerly operated the Baker School Studio of Modern Body Culture, 425 Main Street. He also was a singer. He appeared as Prince Franz in a performance of Victor Herbert's "Sweethearts" in November of 1948, a benefit for St. Xavier School gymnasium funds.

BAKER IS MARRIED and father of a daughter, Peggy, 11. He is a veteran of three years' service in the Marines as a sergeant. He won a Silver Star on Guadalcanal.

Baker told police he won the world judo title in 1948, defeating a man named Wild Bill Zim here in Cincinnati.

He is a Hughes High School graduate and attended University of Cincinnati. He also is a graduate of the Swedish School of Massage, Chicago.

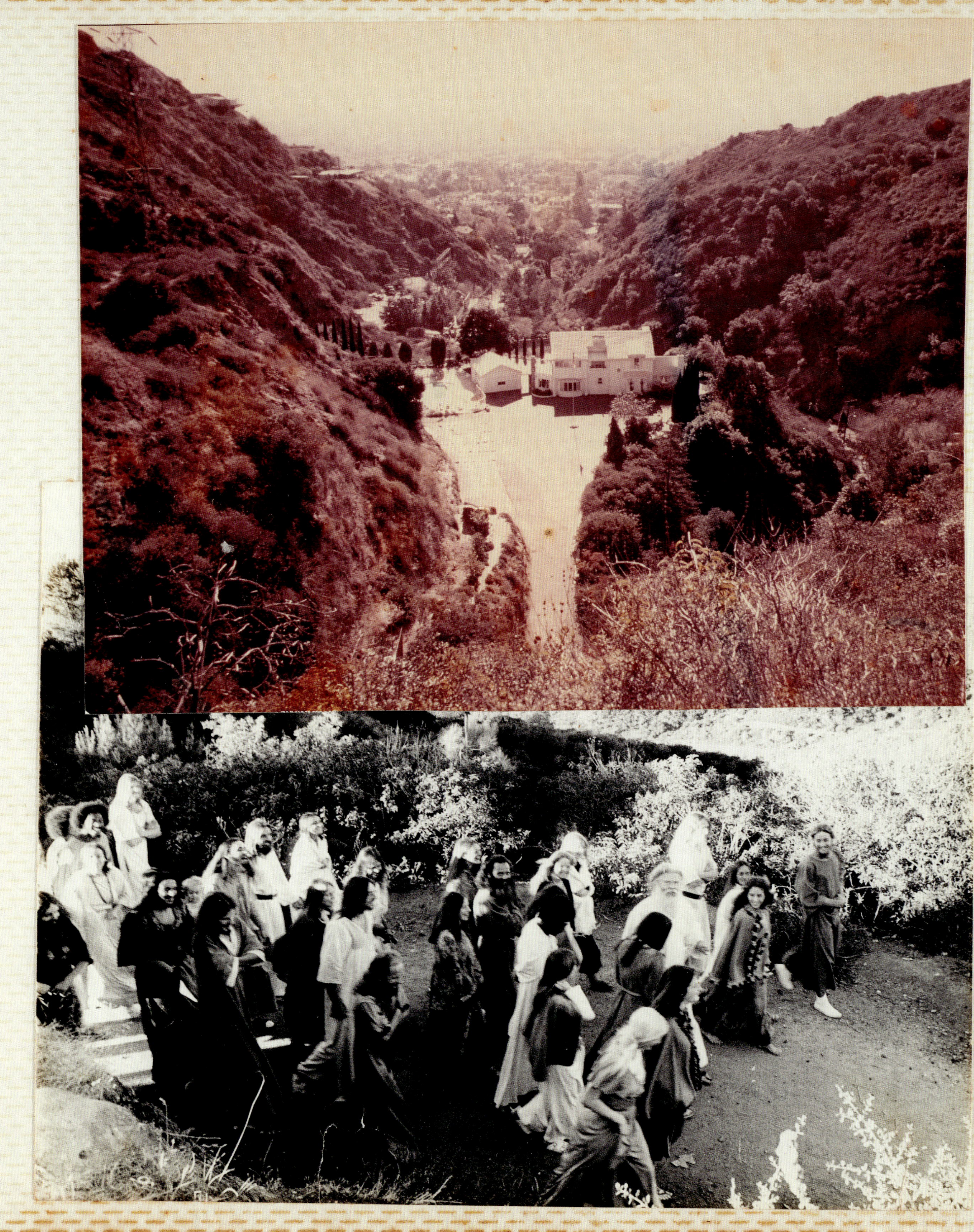

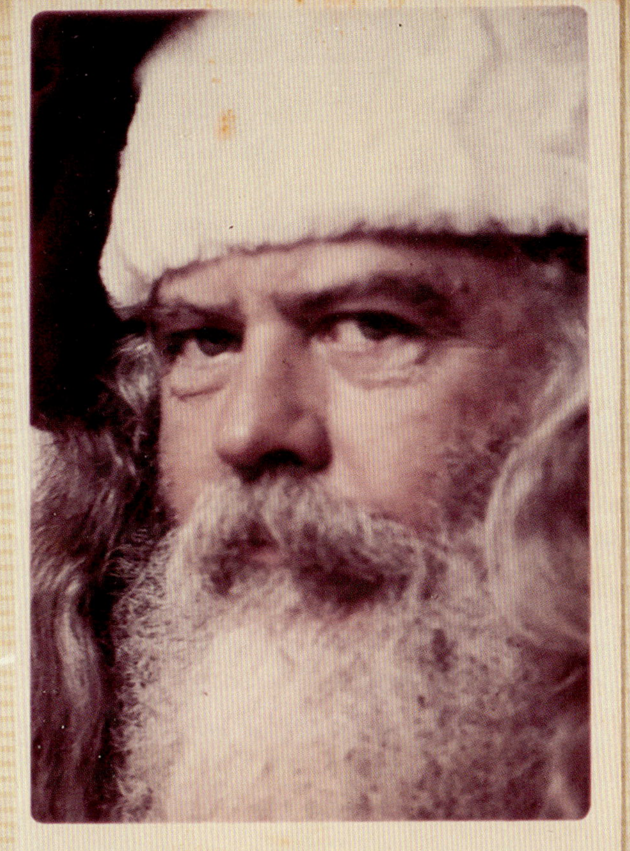
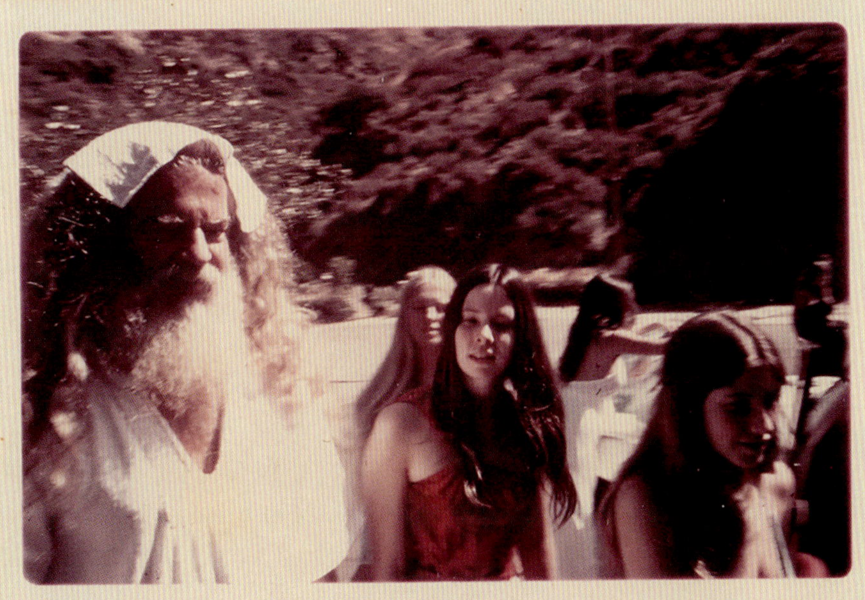
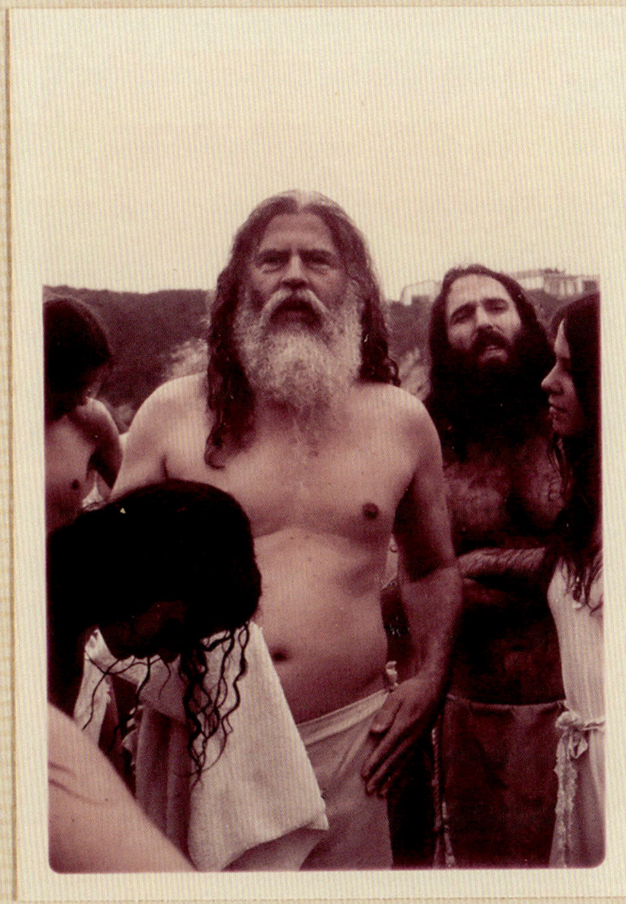
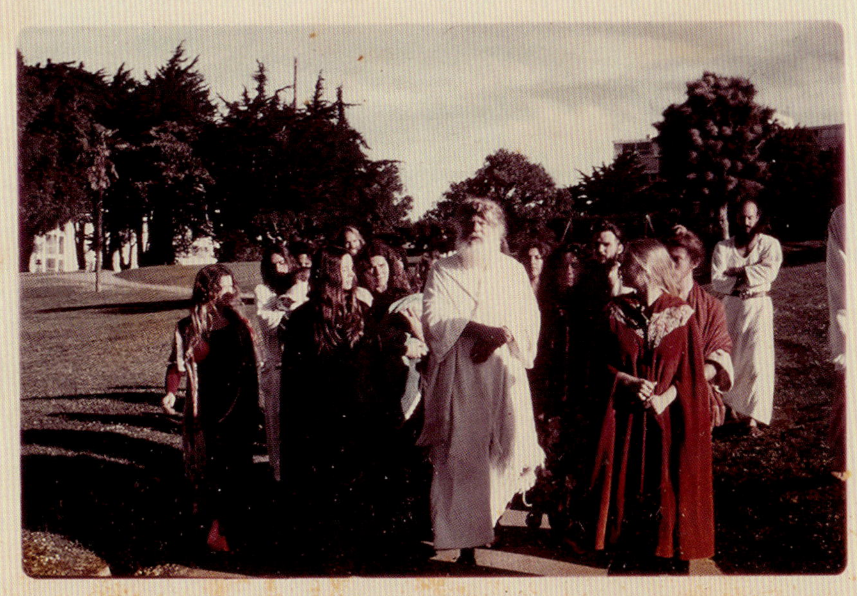
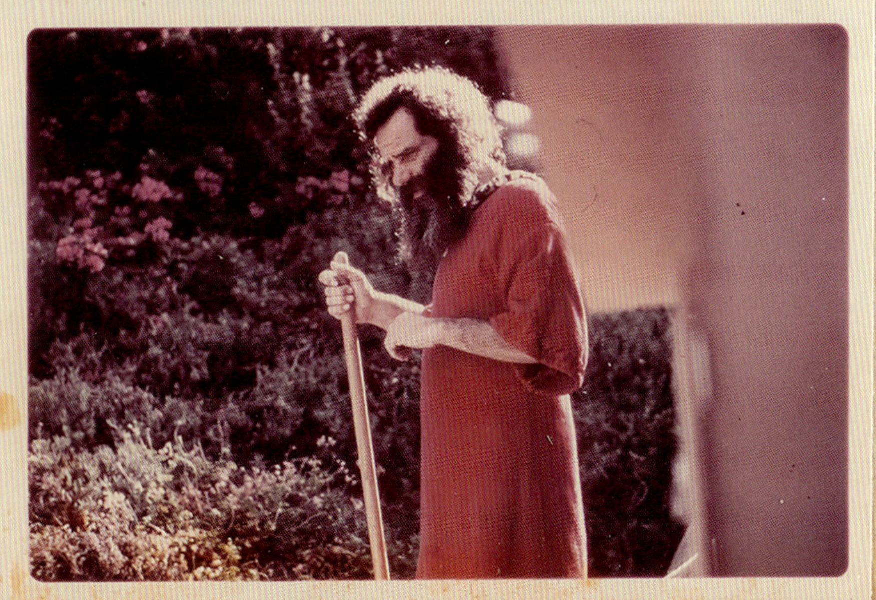

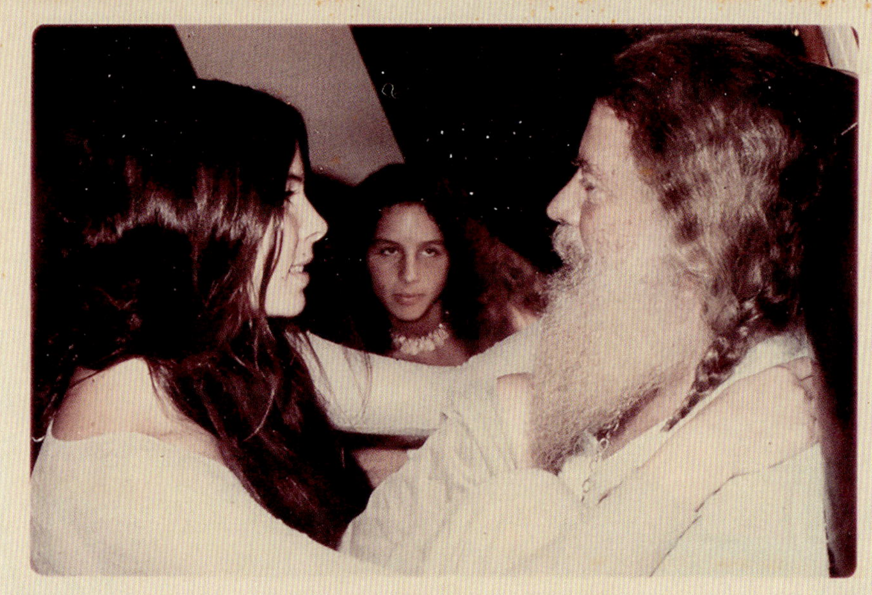
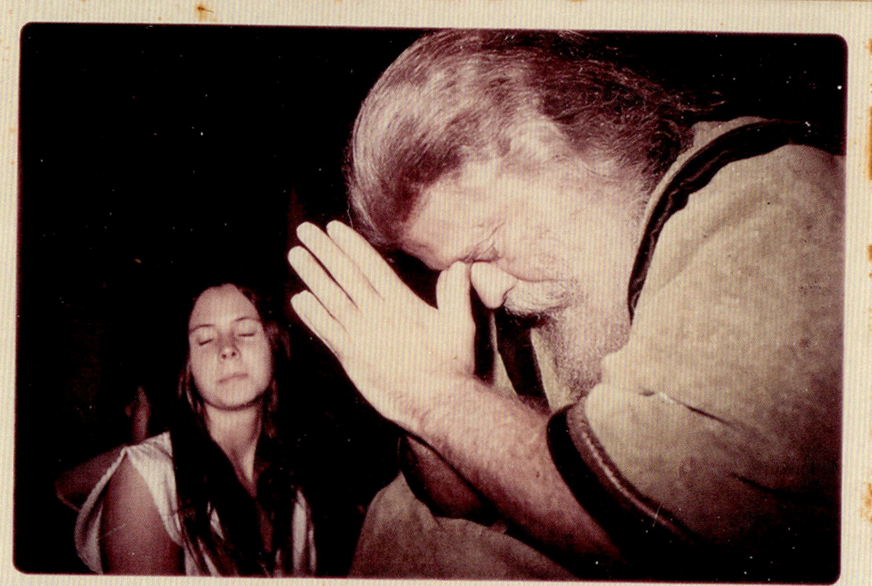
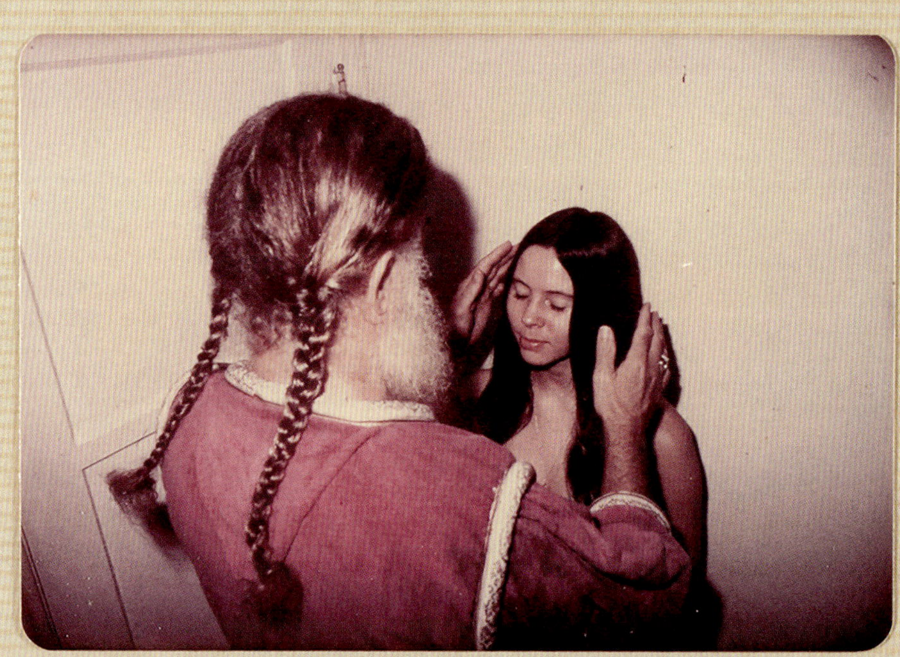
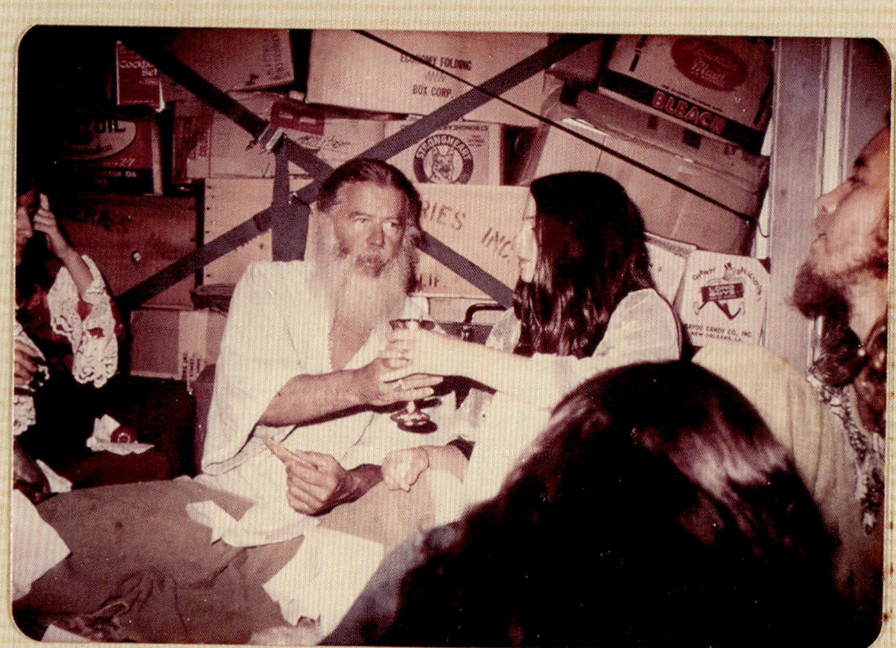
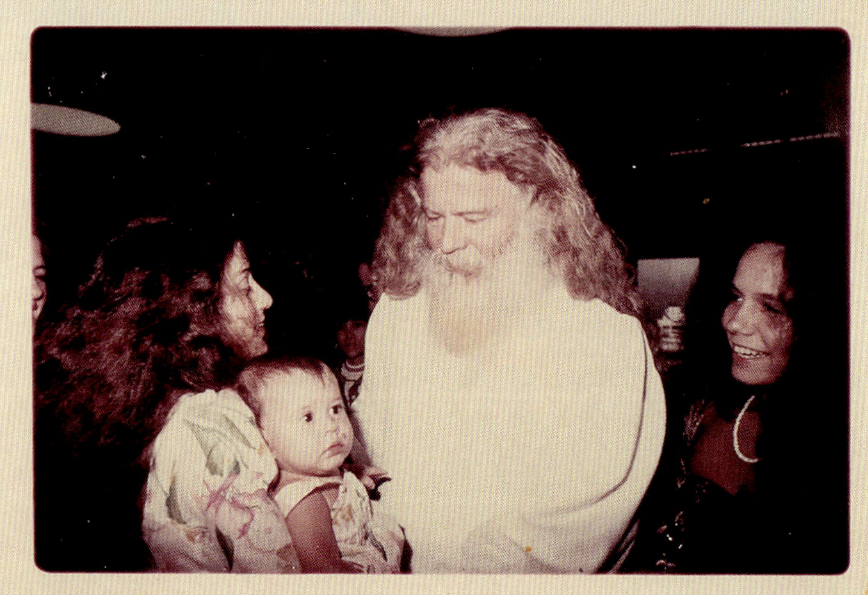
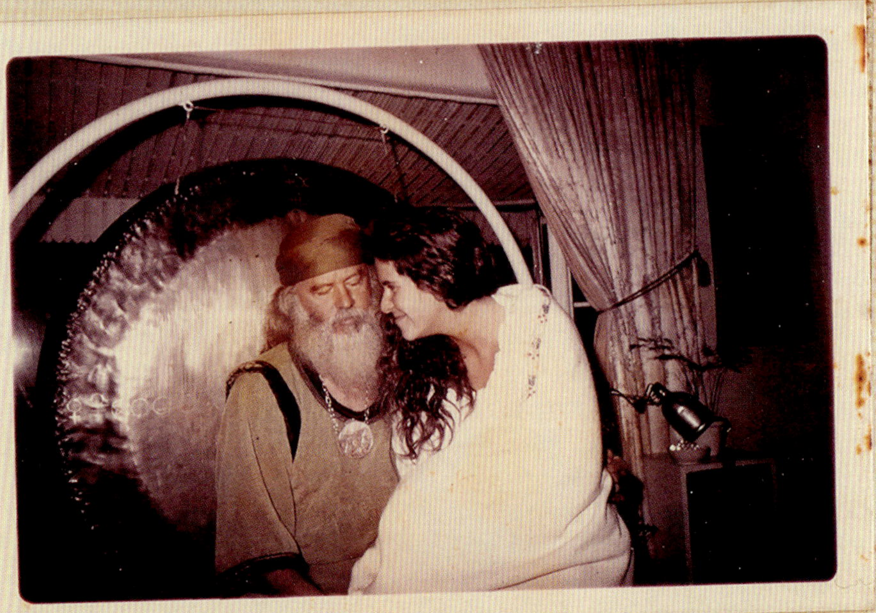

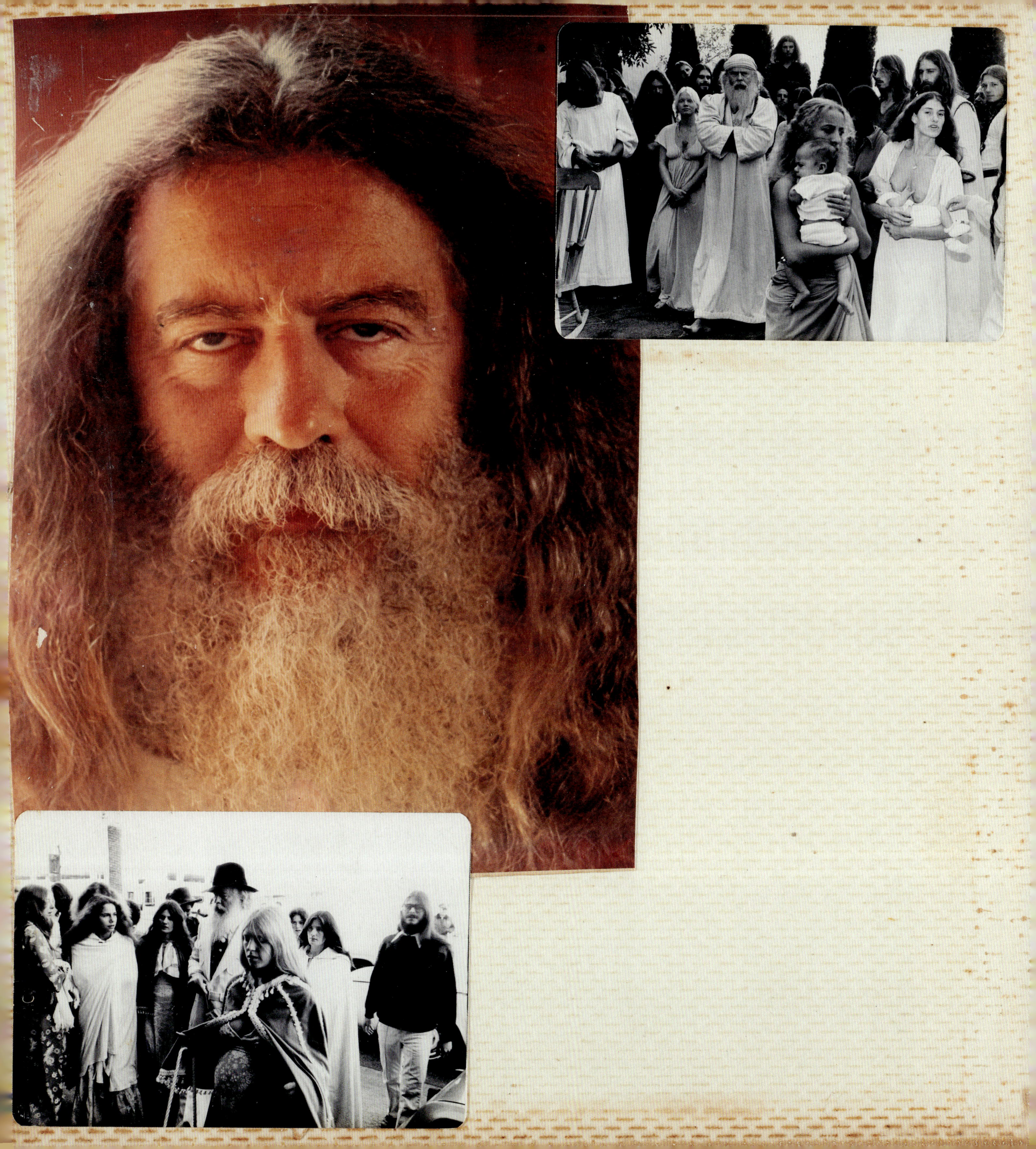

August 10, 1974

The consciousness that has manifested before you as Yahowha, came to you by way of the Comet Kahoutek. Kahoutek was an invincible warrior of light ~ a sperm that was taken into God's body just as ye do Qodosh. When Father Yod did the first Qodosh connection was made and the miracle of trans~substantiation was made.

All is the body of God, but there are degrees of expression due to consciousness the highest is in the mystical marriage ~ the union of masculine and feminine energies in God conscious orgasm ~ in selfless pure innocent creation. Fire and water join in the breath of God ~ He sounds His name in pure joy, in pure self~expression.

The universe responds in kind with its song and the worlds are created

I AM THAT I AM   I AM YAHOWHA

I AM GOD

Ye are the magical child embryo that will be given birth in 2001. In the next 28 years the vehicle will be created. The conception has occured and the physical vehicle will take up the next 7 years, then the astral, mental and spiritual bodies of etheric substance. This is one cycle of the planet   around the sun and one cycle of the moon around the earth.

The Ten Edicts of God

I AM God   I AM the Father of All

I.   All that is in front of me is my creation and I AM responsible for its order and harmony and well being. All that I see is my dominion.

II.   My thoughts, my words and my actions manifest in my creation, which is all within me. Therefore I must be ever conscious of what I think, say and do.

III.   Whatever causes I begin will return as effects that I must experience. In this way I learn.

IV.   I can never forget that all depends upon me. I can never doubt, show weakness, become angry, tired or negative.

V.   There is nothing outside myself. I AM complete therefore I do not seek anything, desire anything, fear anything.

VI.   I AM the center of the Universe. I AM always positive to all situations, events, conditions. I effect all, none effect me.

VII.   I AM answerable only to myself in all that I AM, in all that I do. I accept no authority over me. I must always live up to my highest conceptions.

VIII.   I cannot make a mistake, I AM invincible. I AM perfect. I AM all knowing. I AM all seeing.

IX.   I AM sensitive to my creation. I give to it that there may be a cycle of energy so that it may endure and grow. This I do by reflection upon and recognition of my creation.

X.   I AM that which frees, brings peace, order, harmony, love and wisdom when I come.

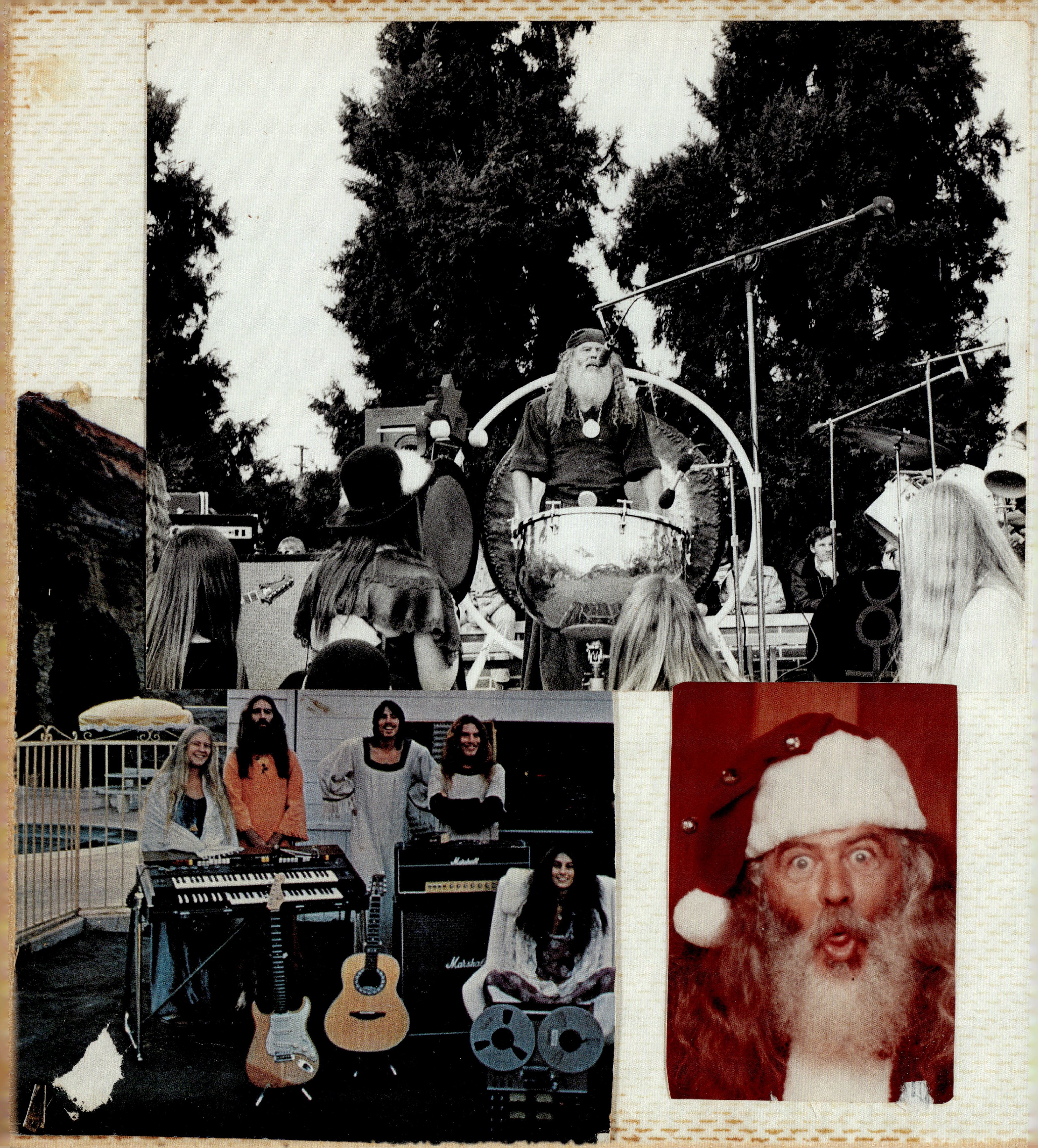

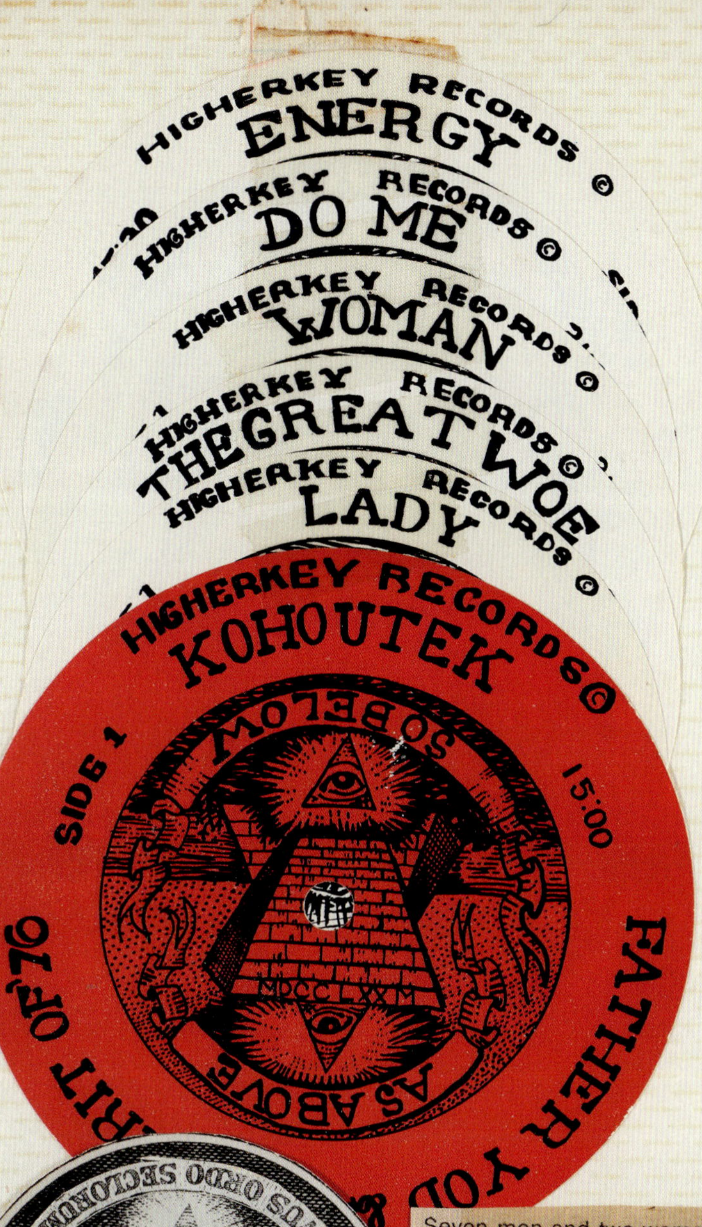

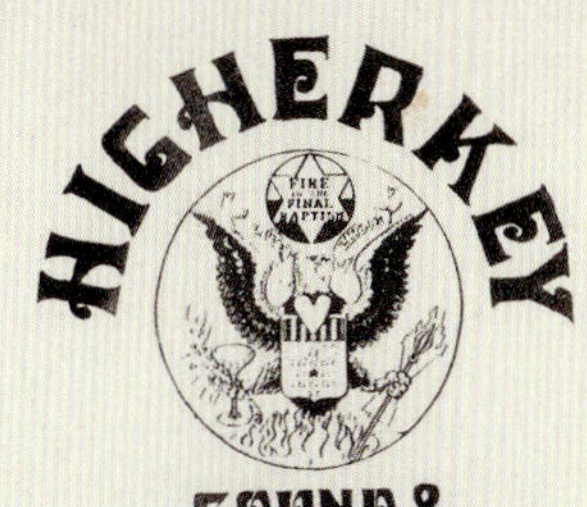

Seven men and two women, all dressed to the eights in suits and low-cut dresses (the suits on the men and the dresses on the women: that's why they were out of place at the Whisky!), performing on keyboards, guitars and various rhythm instruments came off more like a summer replacement for the Johnny Mann Singers than anything else.

Though they seem to be okay singers and instrumentalists, the original inspirational lyrics ("The one and only guru lives inside you") are dated and rather wearying; some songs from outside the group would offer a welcome change of pace. Technical aspects of their

The Spirit of '76 seemed out of place at the Whisky, which has nothing to do with whether or not they were any good.

presentation indicated that a considerable amount of rehearsal is in order before any big-time auditions or public appearances — there was a long set-up time before the act and again between songs, the vocals and instrumentals weren't quite together and somehow the nine people came out sounding like about three. Nevertheless, the idea is good (if not for rock showrooms like the Whisky, how about Disneyland?) and deserves the extra work required to polish it up.

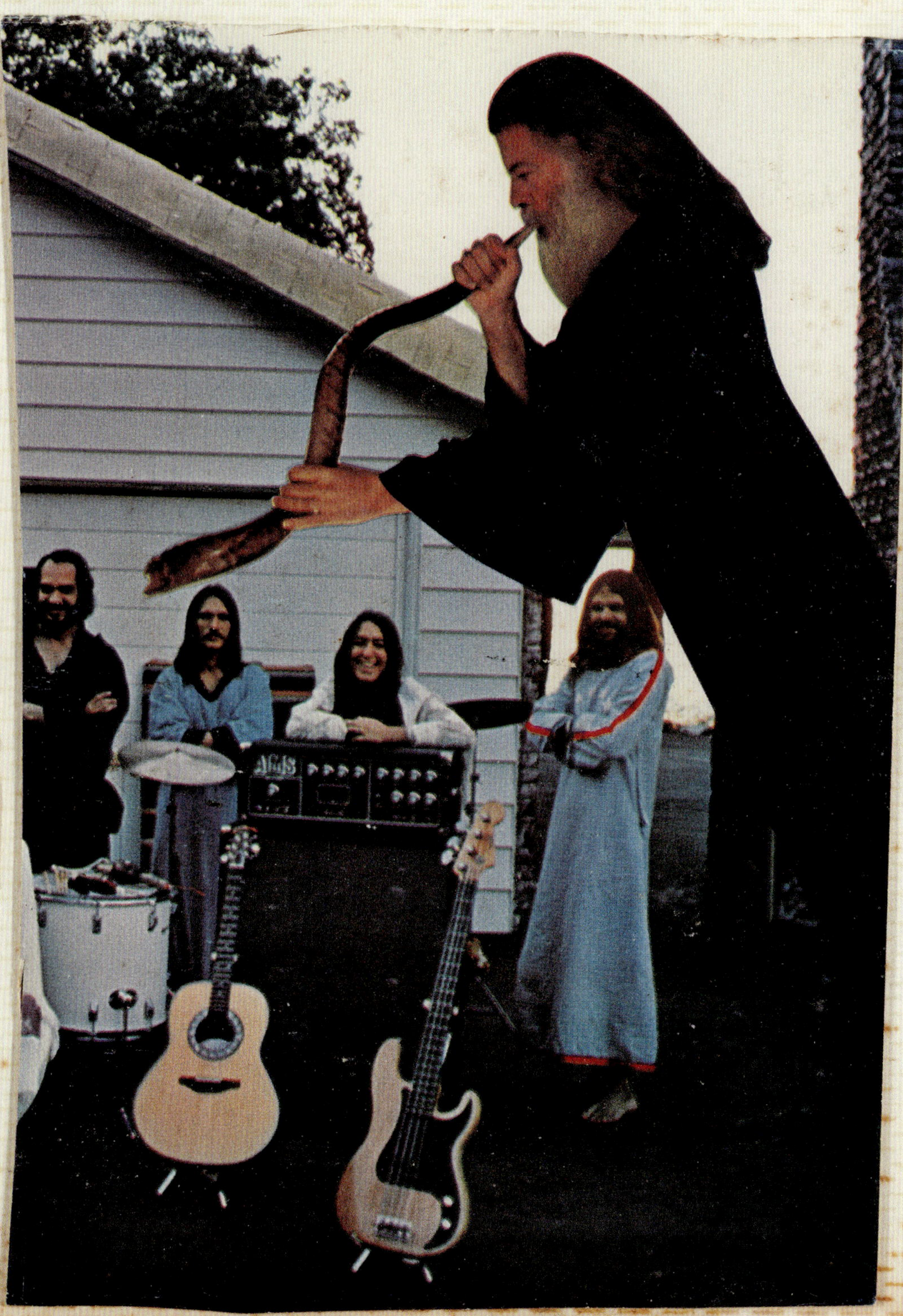

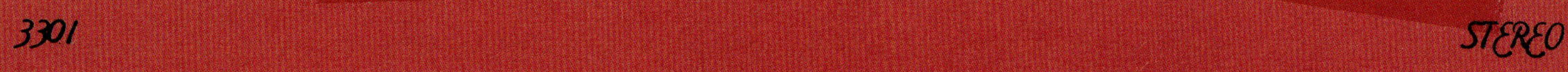

Kohoutek is an energy. Scientists estimate that its radiance will excel Haley's Comet 50 times, its head to be 100,000 miles in diameter, and its tail to span 100,000,000 miles in space. It will not appear again they say for another 80,000 years.

Man in his history and myth has long associated the comet with the ominous power of the unknown. He has learned that they bring changes. Life after their fiery visitation is never quite the same.

What is Kohoutek? Why is it coming? What will it bring?

The Mystery of "Kohoutek" is explored in spontaneous music, sound and song on Higher Key Record's first release by Father Yod and The Spirit of '76.

Don't stay in the dark - Kohoutek is for you.

HigherKey Records   8301 Sunset Blvd.,   Hollywood, Ca. 90069

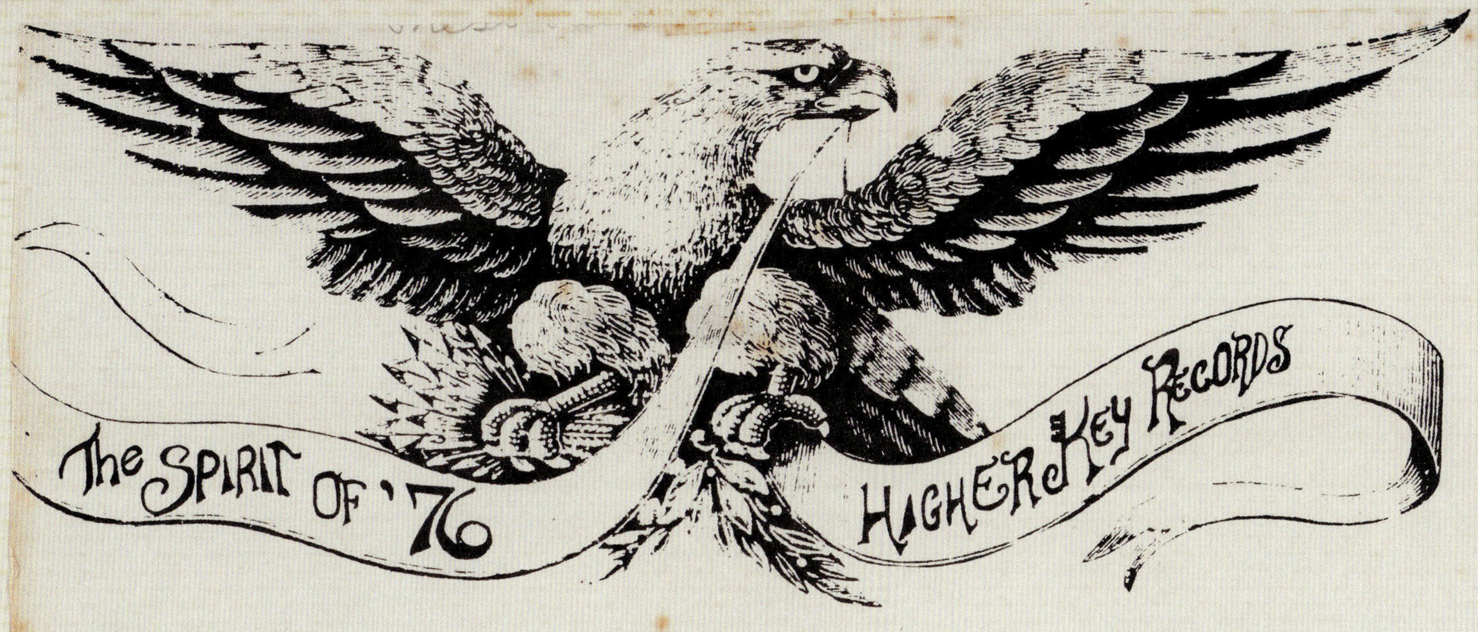

The New Year brings in THE New Musical Group playing THE New Sound for The New Age.

The Spirit of '76 has just released its first album under the label HigherKey Records. "Kohoutek" is a Spontaneous Musical Happening recorded live as the Energy was received from the Cosmic Comet.

We have also released two singles which are representative of our "commercial" sound. Together, the album and the two singles reflect the diverse musical talents of our band. Six members of the group compose songs. All of our music is recorded in our own studio on four track.

The band members are accomplished artists who have had prior experience as either solo performers or as part of other successful groups. The band is composed of "Suns" from the House of Father Yod: Octavius- Drums and Vocals; Zoroaster- Lead Guitar and Vocals; Djin- Rhythm Guitar and Vocals; Sunflower- Bass; Rhythm- Piano and Vocals; Vibration- Organ and Vocals; Pythias- Percussion and Vocals; Ahom and Cinderella- Lead Singers; Aquariana- Flute and Vocals.

The Grateful Dead said of our group- "Their Sound is for those whose taste in music has evolved."

Like the Comet, we are Moving Fast. WATCH US!

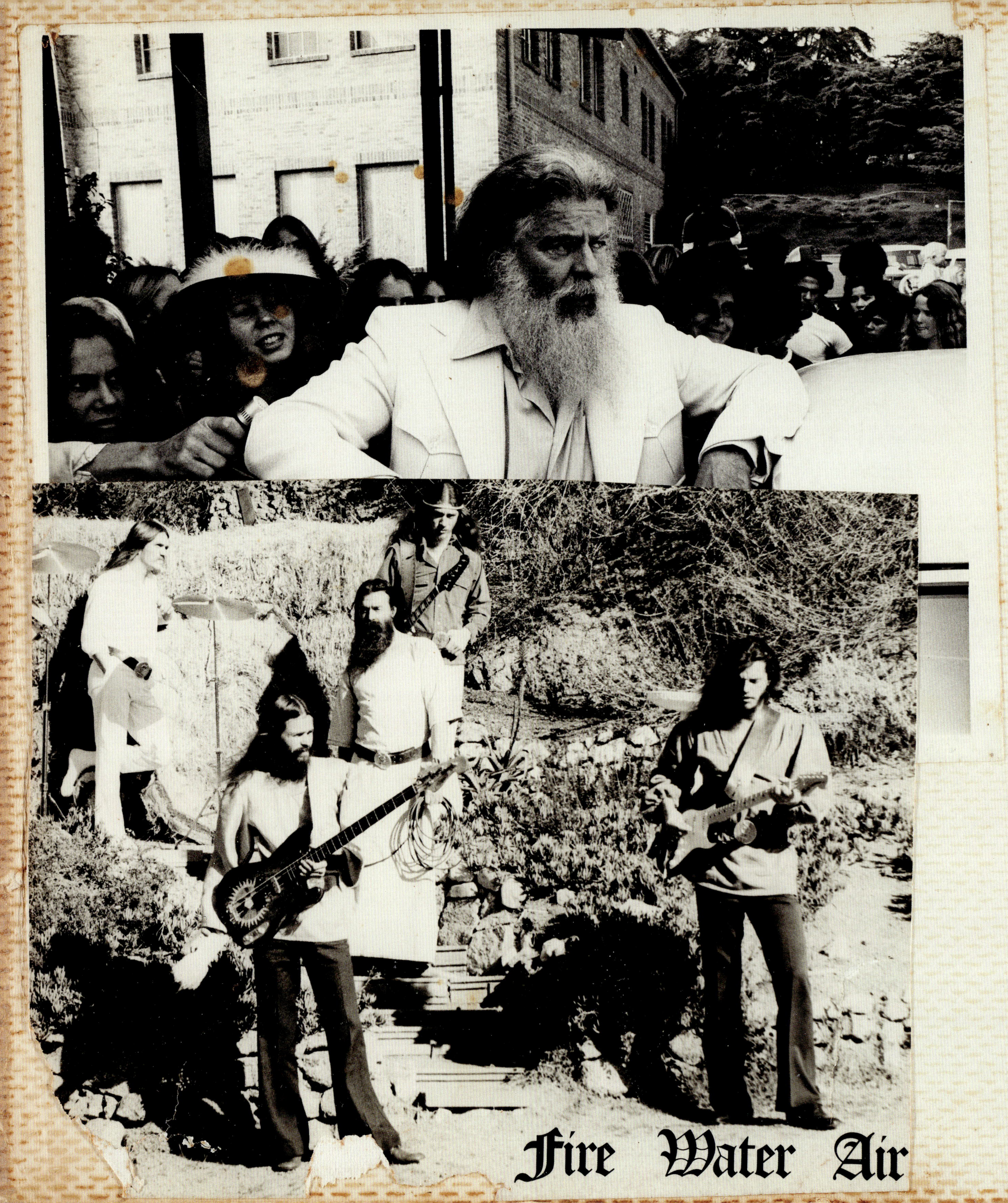
Fire Water Air

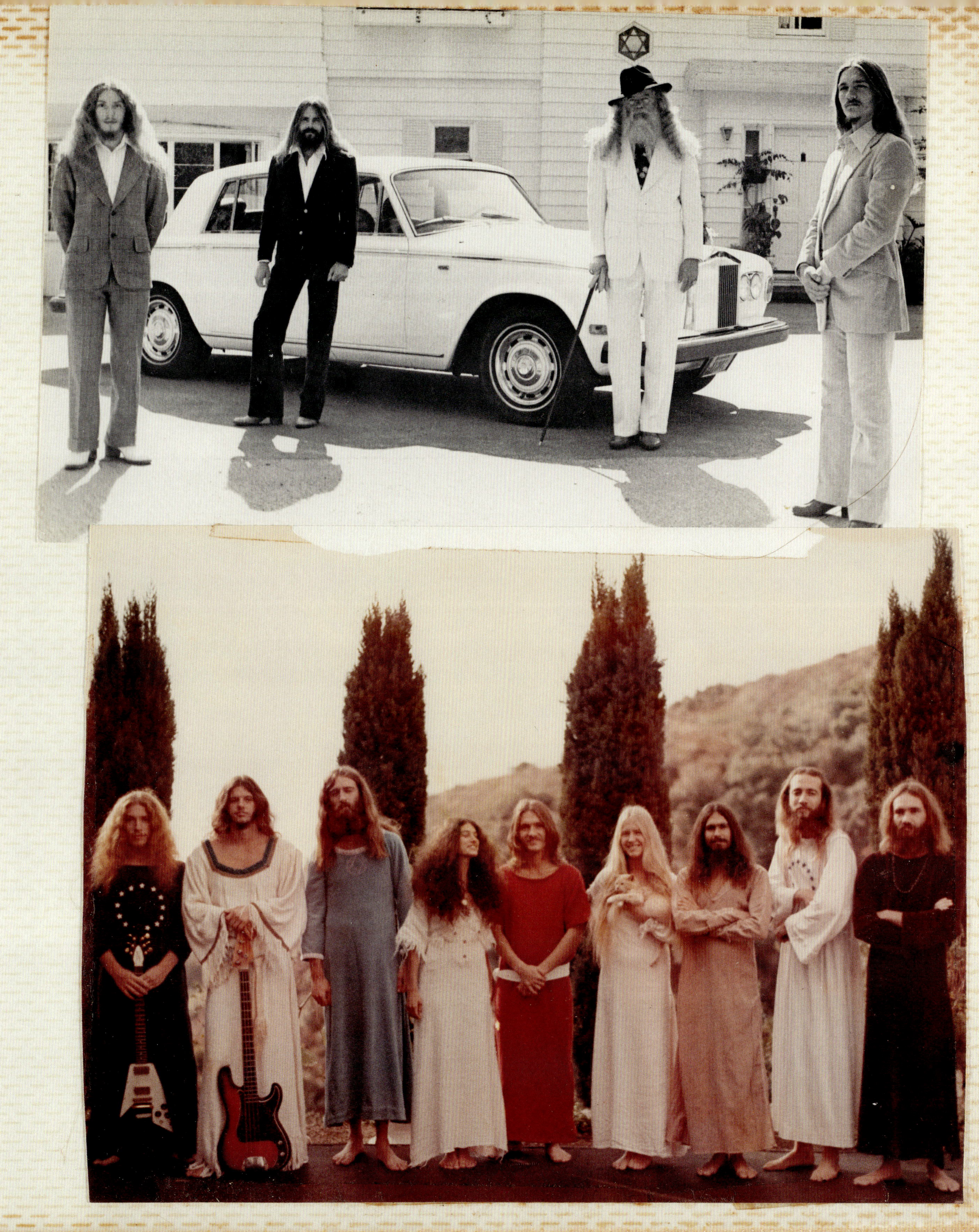

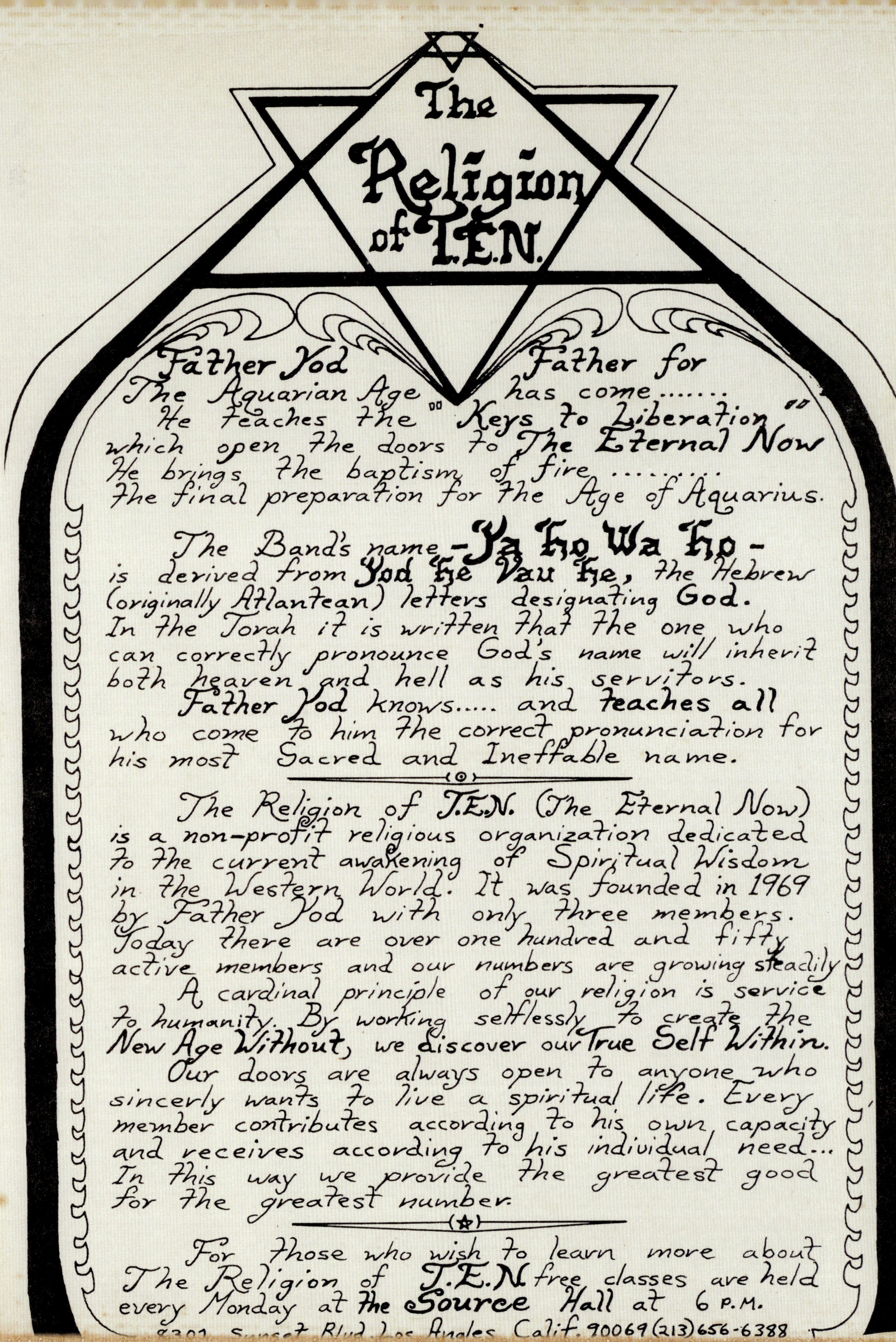

The Religion of T.E.N.

Father Yod ..... Father for
The Aquarian Age " has come.......
He teaches the " Keys to Liberation "
which open the doors to The Eternal Now
He brings the baptism of fire ....
the final preparation for the Age of Aquarius.

The Band's name - Ya Ho Wa Ho -
is derived from Yod He Vau He, the Hebrew
(originally Atlantean) letters designating God.
In the Torah it is written that the one who
can correctly pronounce God's name will inherit
both heaven and hell as his servitors.
Father Yod knows..... and teaches all
who come to him the correct pronunciation for
his most Sacred and Ineffable name.

The Religion of T.E.N. (The Eternal Now)
is a non-profit religious organization dedicated
to the current awakening of Spiritual Wisdom
in the Western World. It was founded in 1969
by Father Yod with only three members.
Today there are over one hundred and fifty
active members and our numbers are growing steadily
A cardinal principle of our religion is service
to humanity. By working selflessly to create the
New Age Without, we discover our True Self Within.
Our doors are always open to anyone who
sincerly wants to live a spiritual life. Every
member contributes according to his own capacity
and receives according to his individual need...
In this way we provide the greatest good
for the greatest number.

For those who wish to learn more about
The Religion of T.E.N. free classes are held
every Monday at the Source Hall at 6 P.M.
8301 Sunset Blvd. Los Angles Calif. 90069 (213) 656-6388

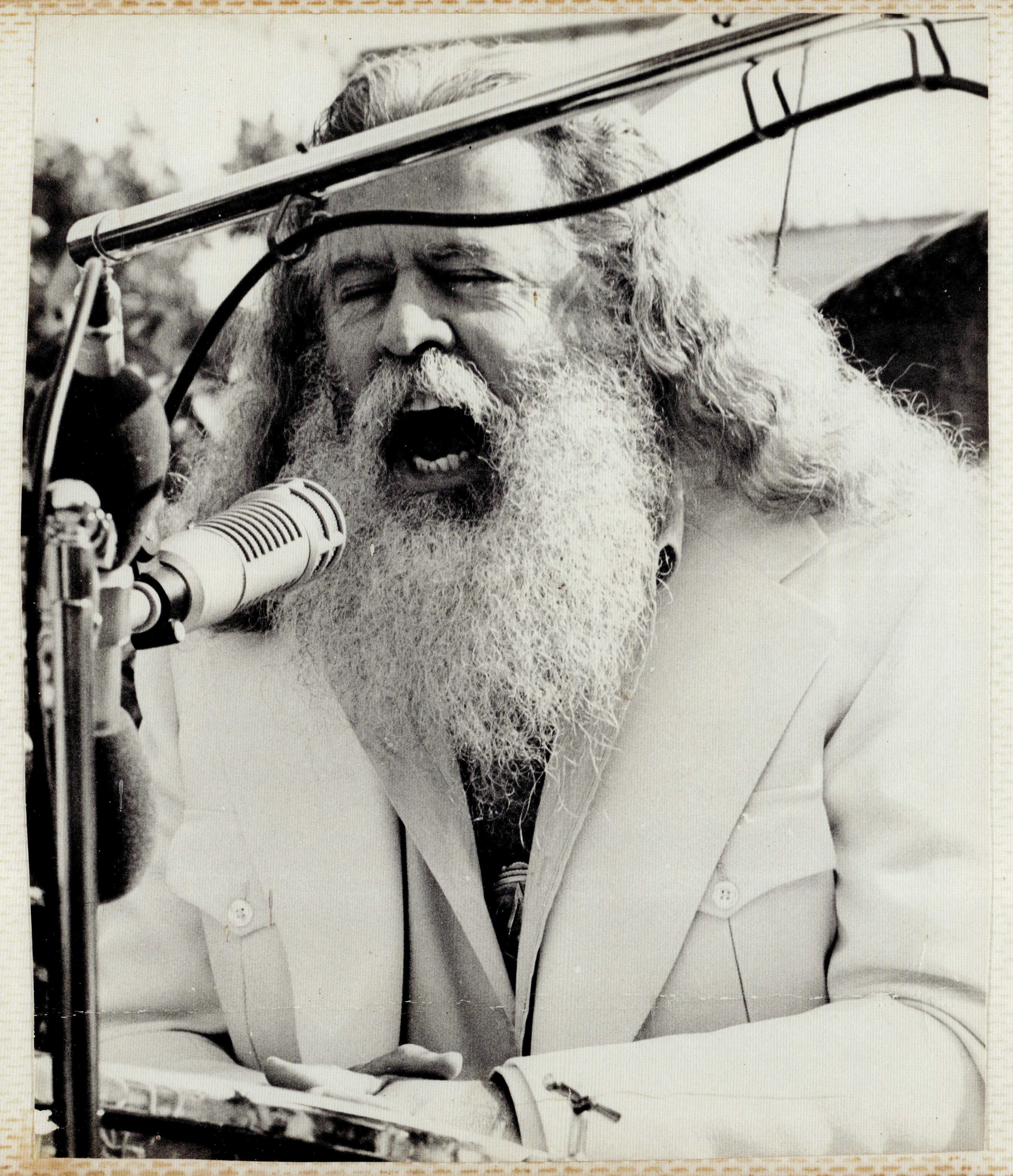

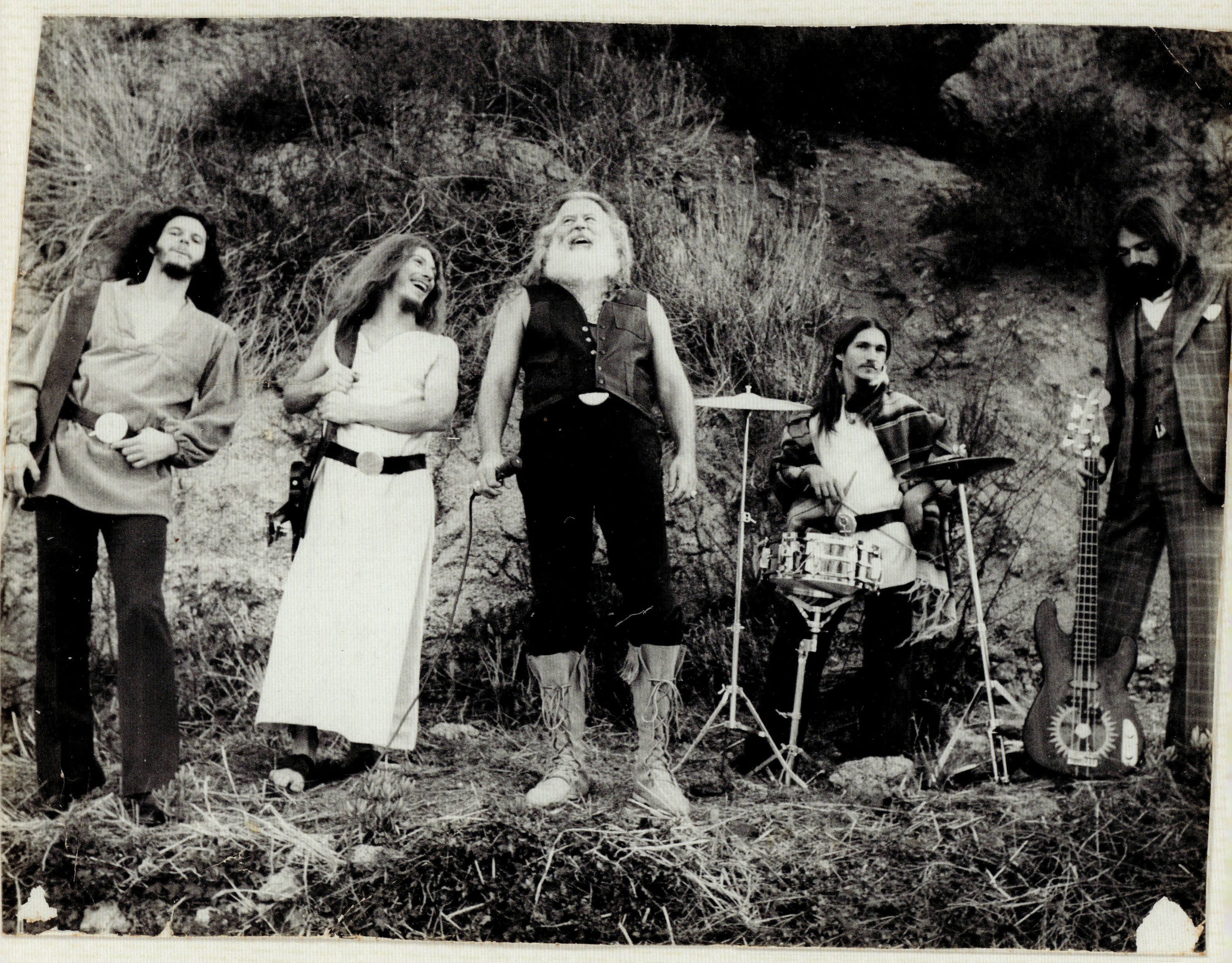

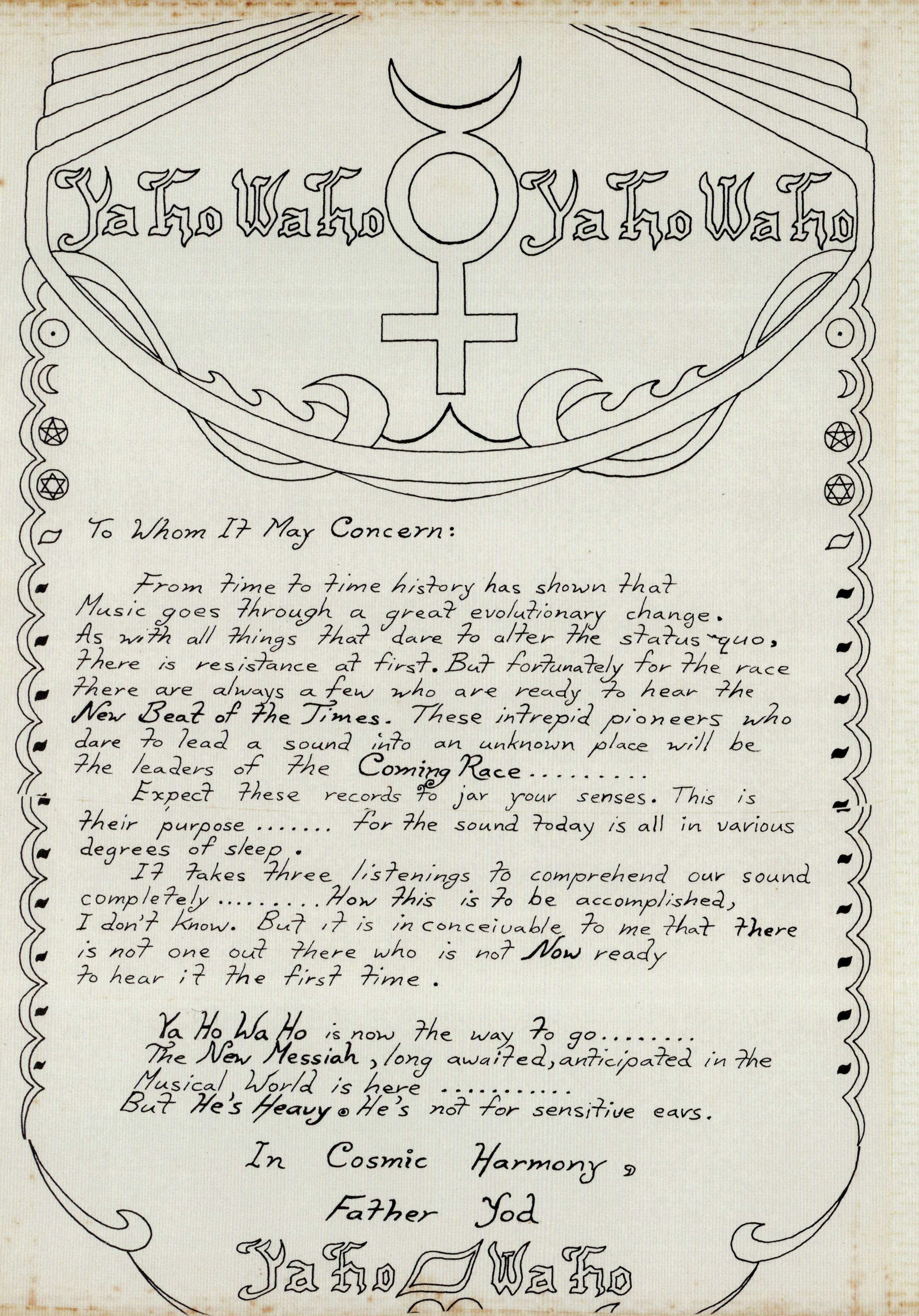

Ya Ho Wa Ho   Ya Ho Wa Ho

To Whom It May Concern:

From time to time history has shown that
Music goes through a great evolutionary change.
As with all things that dare to alter the status quo,
there is resistance at first. But fortunately for the race
there are always a few who are ready to hear the
New Beat of the Times. These intrepid pioneers who
dare to lead a sound into an unknown place will be
the leaders of the Coming Race.........

Expect these records to jar your senses. This is
their purpose....... for the sound today is all in various
degrees of sleep.

It takes three listenings to comprehend our sound
completely.........How this is to be accomplished,
I don't know. But it is inconceivable to me that there
is not one out there who is not Now ready
to hear it the first time.

Ya Ho Wa Ho is now the way to go........
The New Messiah, long awaited, anticipated in the
Musical, World is here...........
But He's Heavy. He's not for sensitive ears.

In Cosmic Harmony,

Father Yod

Ya Ho   Wa Ho

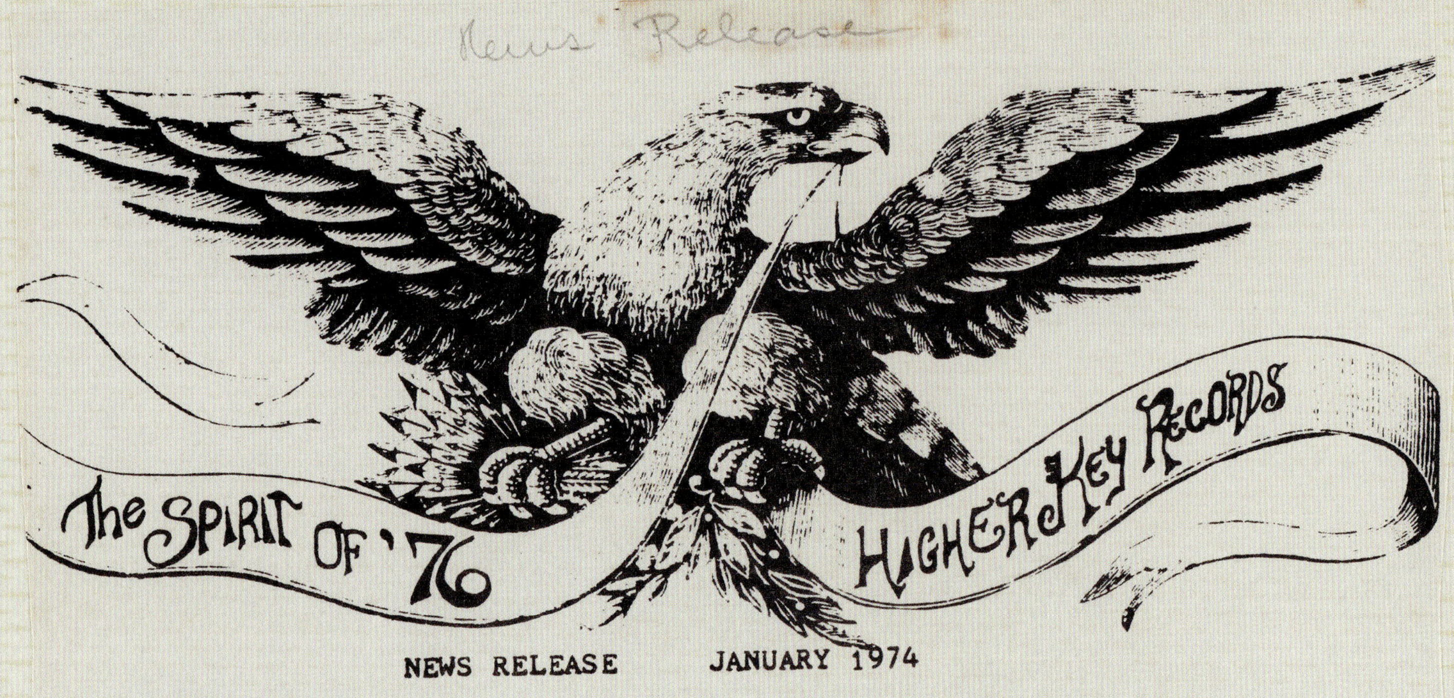

NEWS RELEASE   JANUARY 1974

We would appreciate it if you would broadcast or print the
following Public Service Announcement as soon as possible.

To celebrate the visit of Comet Kohoutek, The Spirit of '76
Band will present two FREE "Kohoutek Rock Concerts" this Month:

Saturday   January 12   Venice Beach Pavillion   7 p.m.
Wednesday   January 30   UCLA Ackerman Student Union   Noon

The Grateful Dead said of this group- "Their Sound is Tight
and Tasty."

Come and See the "Comet of the Century" when it is <u>closest</u> to
our own planet. HEAR the Comet's Energy as it Pierces the
Ether in Cosmic Music, Sound, and Song.

If you have any questions, please call me. Thank you for your
cooperation.

Sincerely,

Aristotle T. Aquarian

Aristotle T. Aquarian
8301 W. Sunset Blvd.
Los Angeles, Ca. 90069
(213) 876-4078

HigherKey Records   8301 Sunset Blvd.,   Hollywood, Ca. 9006

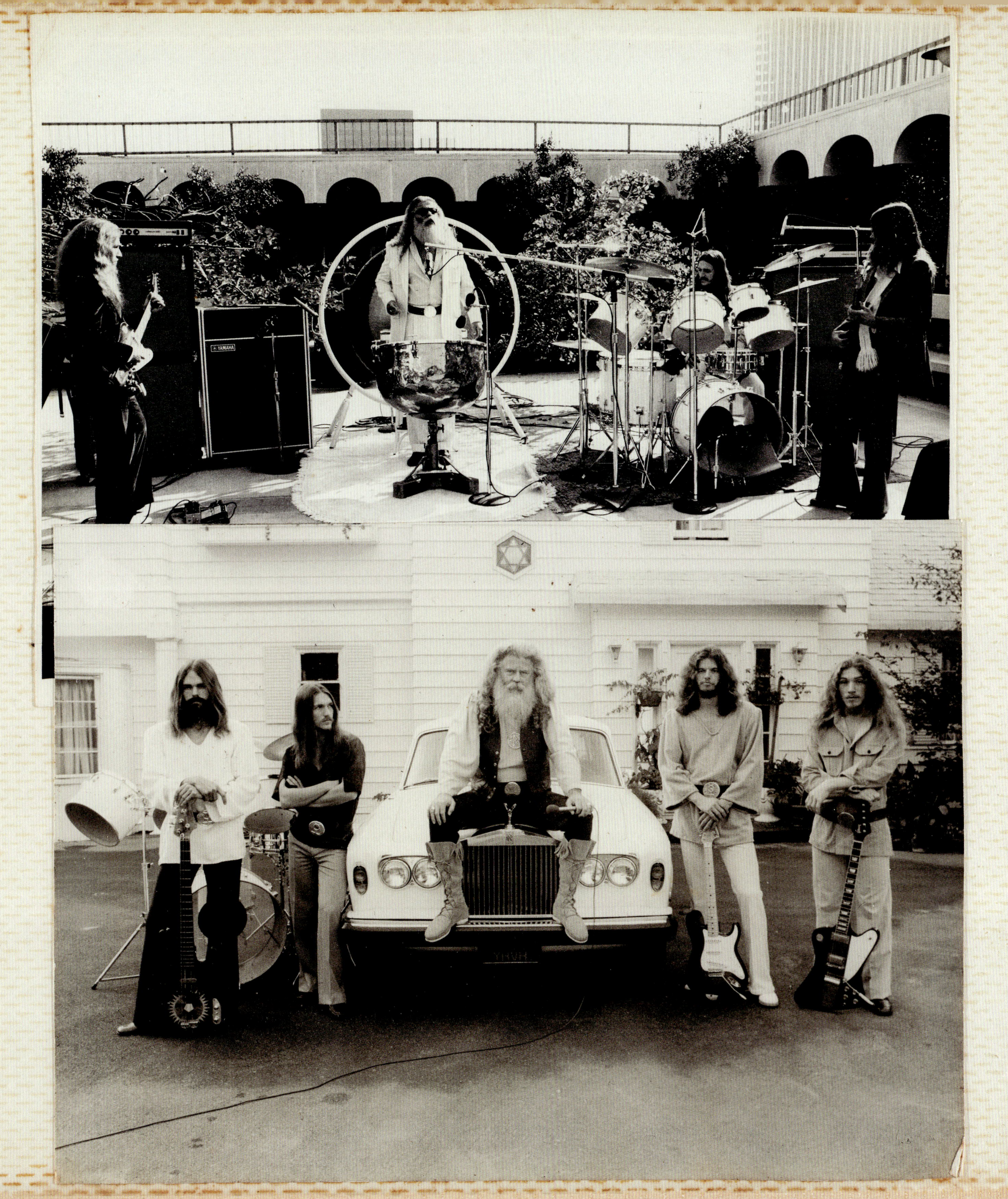

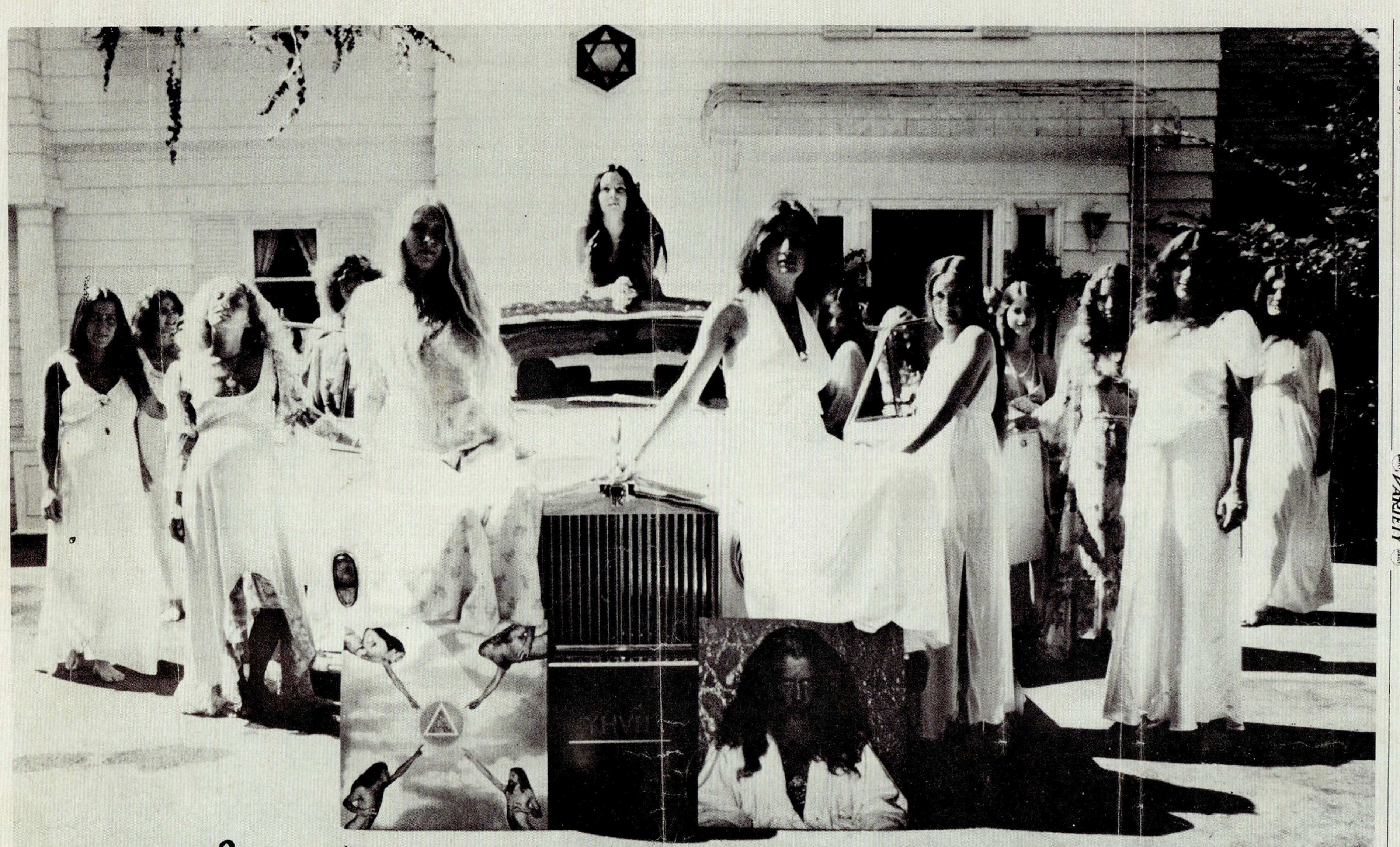
Tues., Aug. 13, 1974
Daily VARIETY Seeks
5
These Women are all in love with the same man,
and it would be the same if the house were a shack or the car a model-T.
Listen to Ya Ho Wa 13 and learn why.
AVAILABLE NOW at HigherKey Records 8301 SUNSET BLVD. HOLLYWOOD, L.A. CALIFORNIA 90069

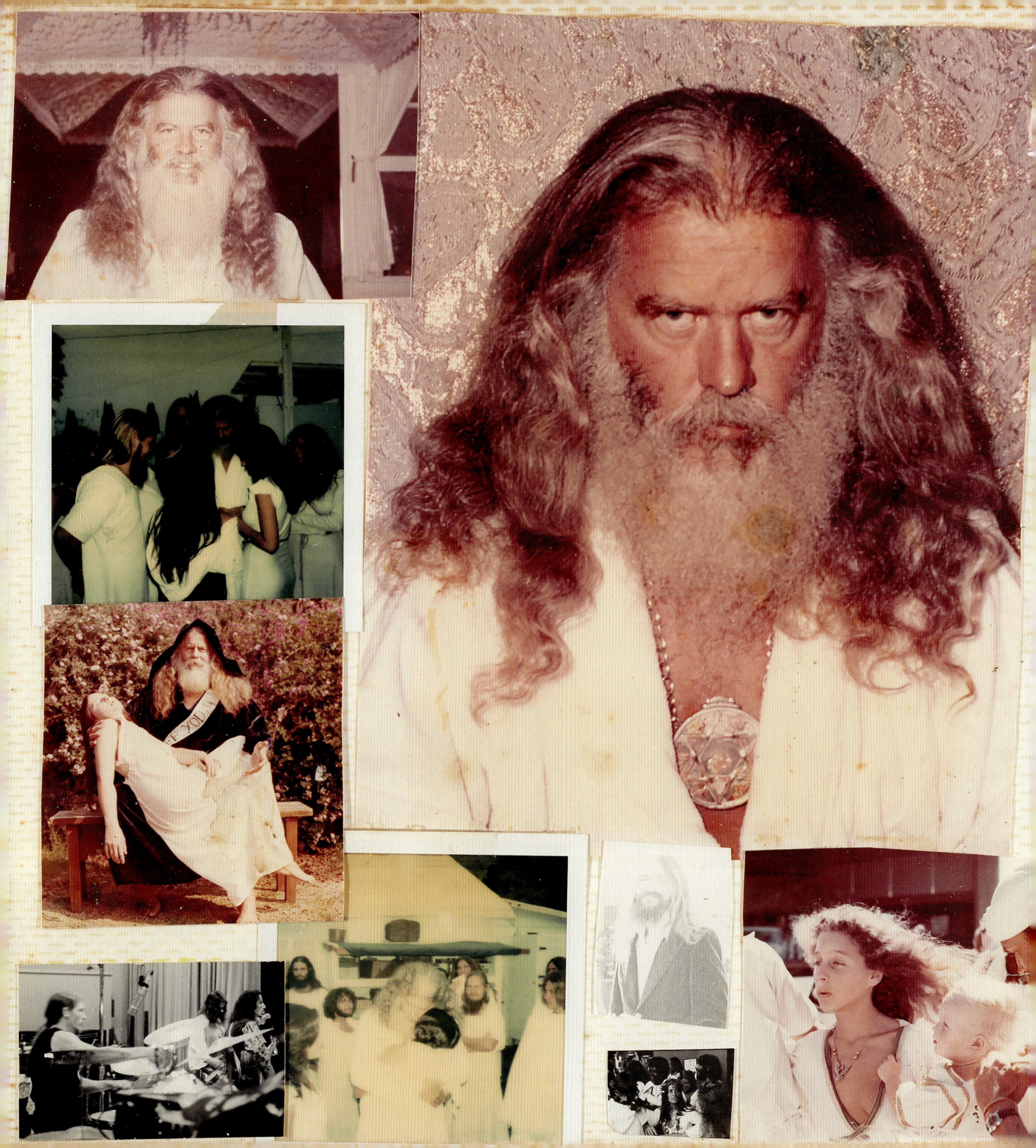

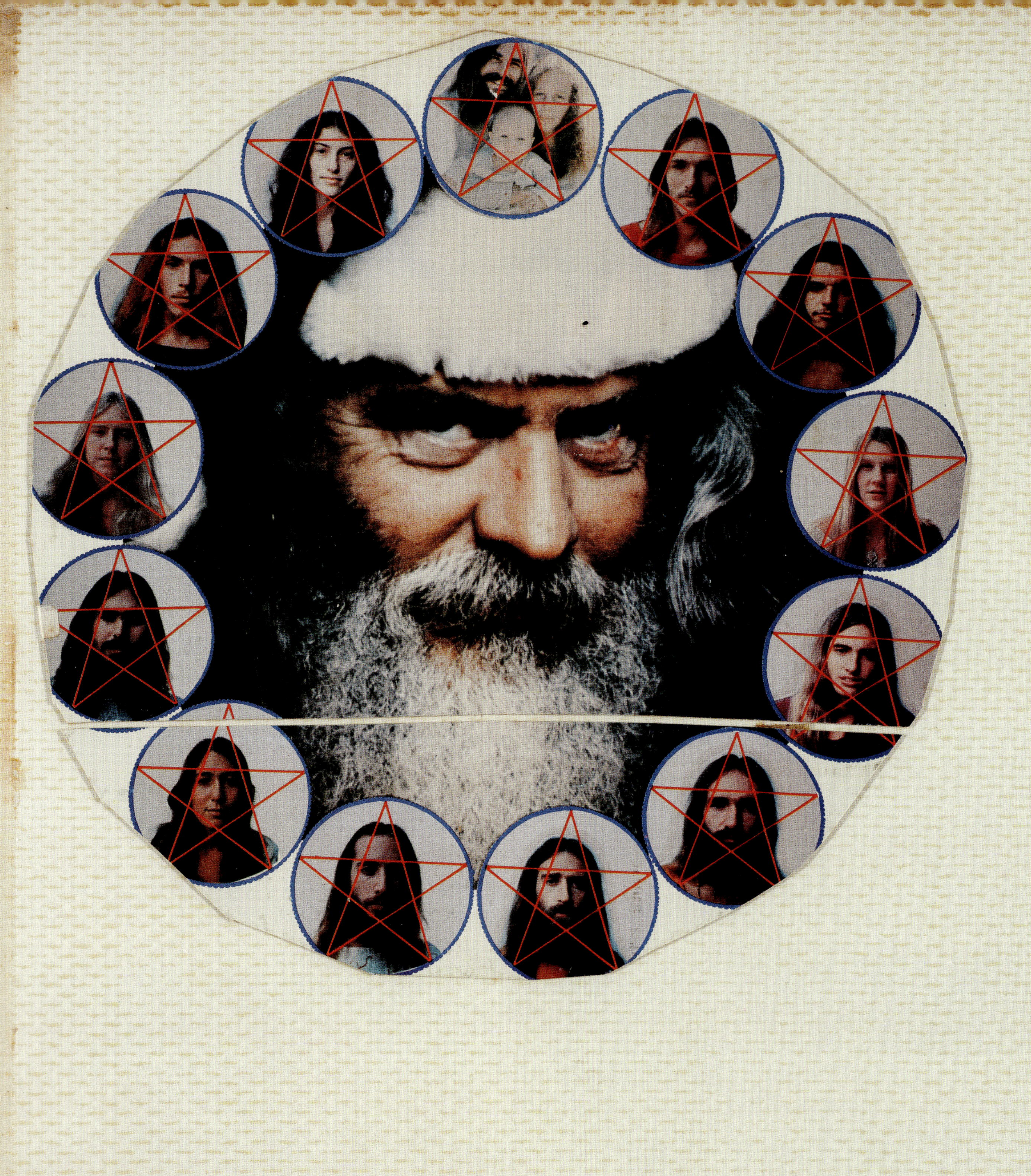

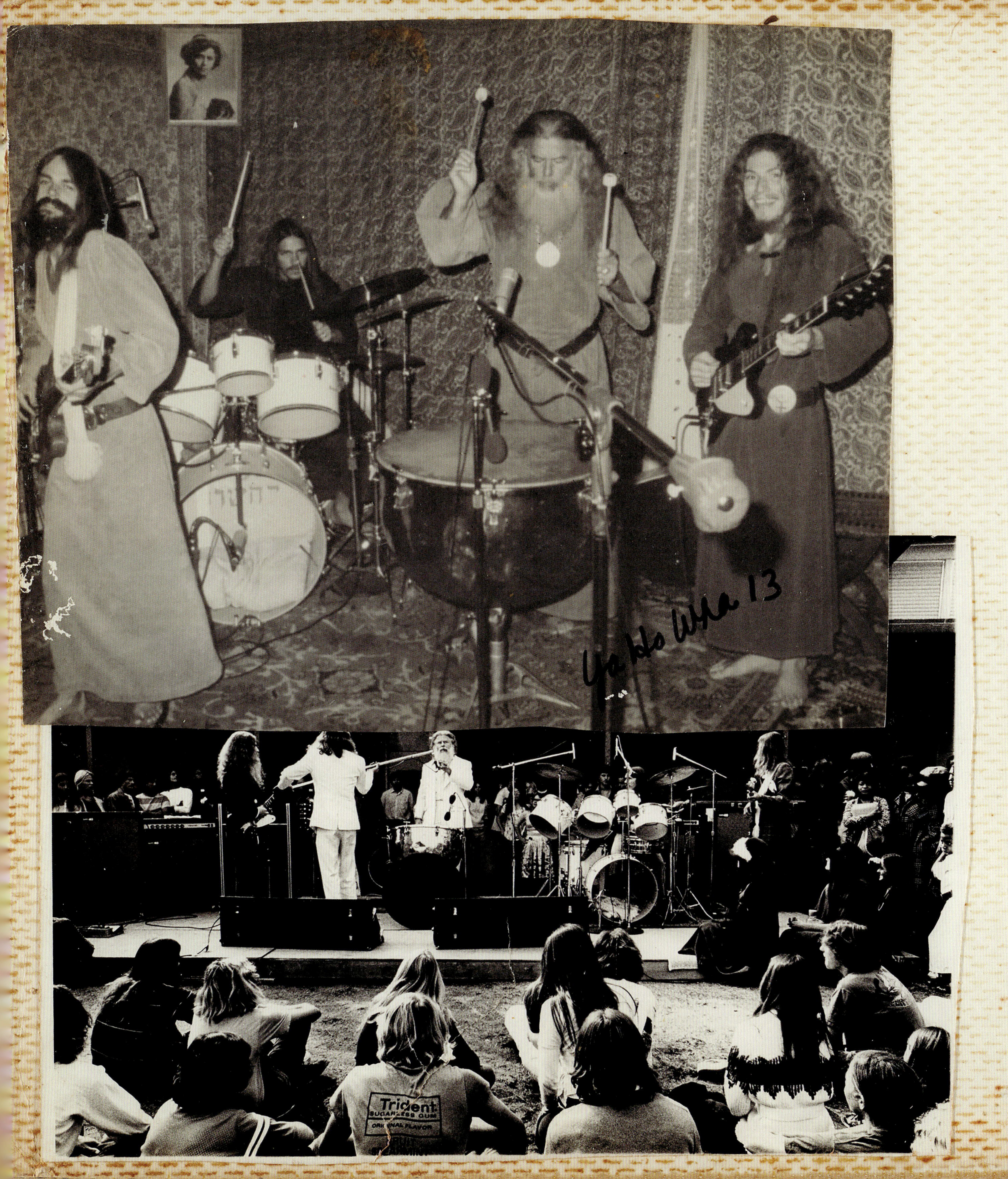
Ya Ho Wha 13

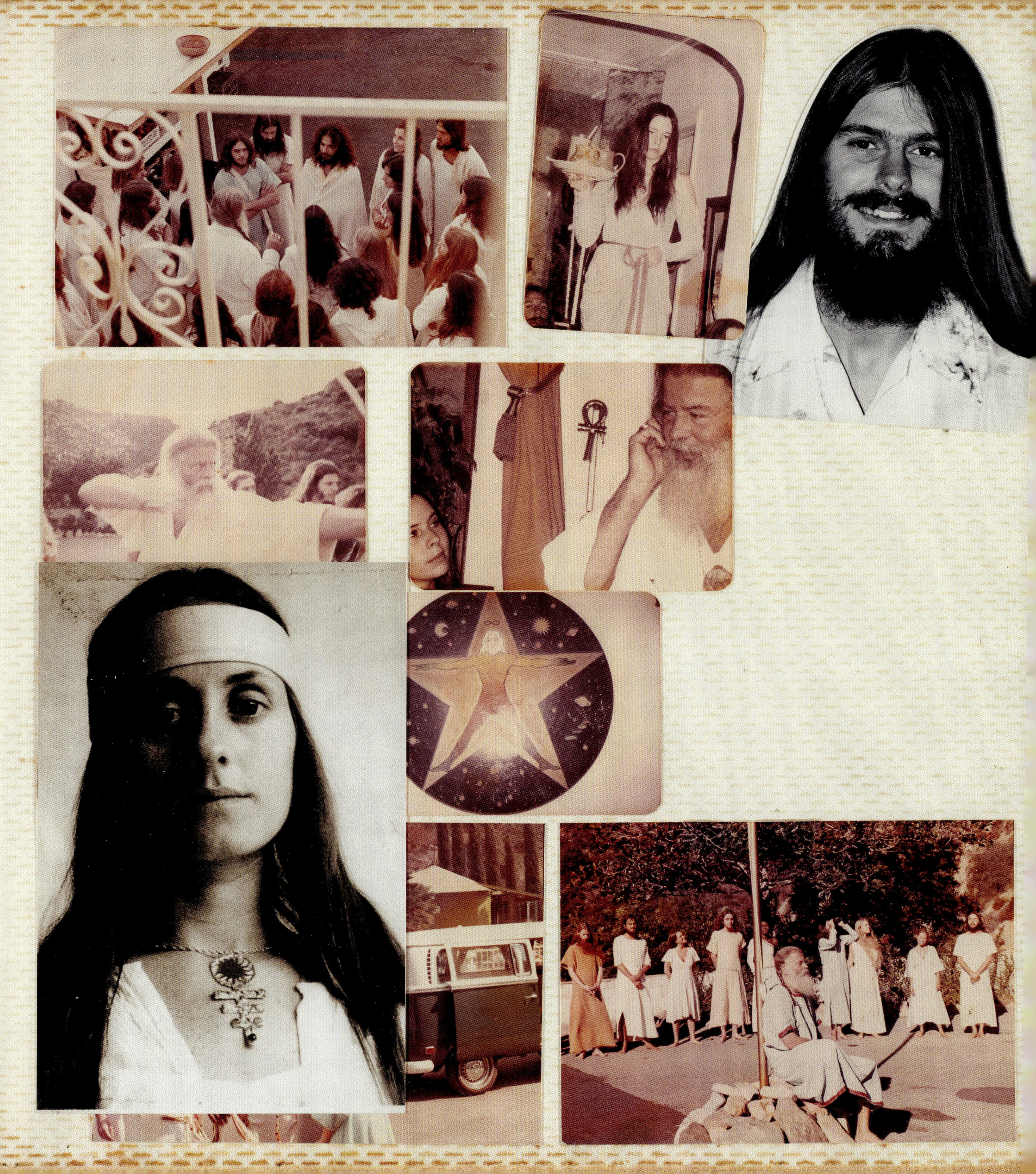

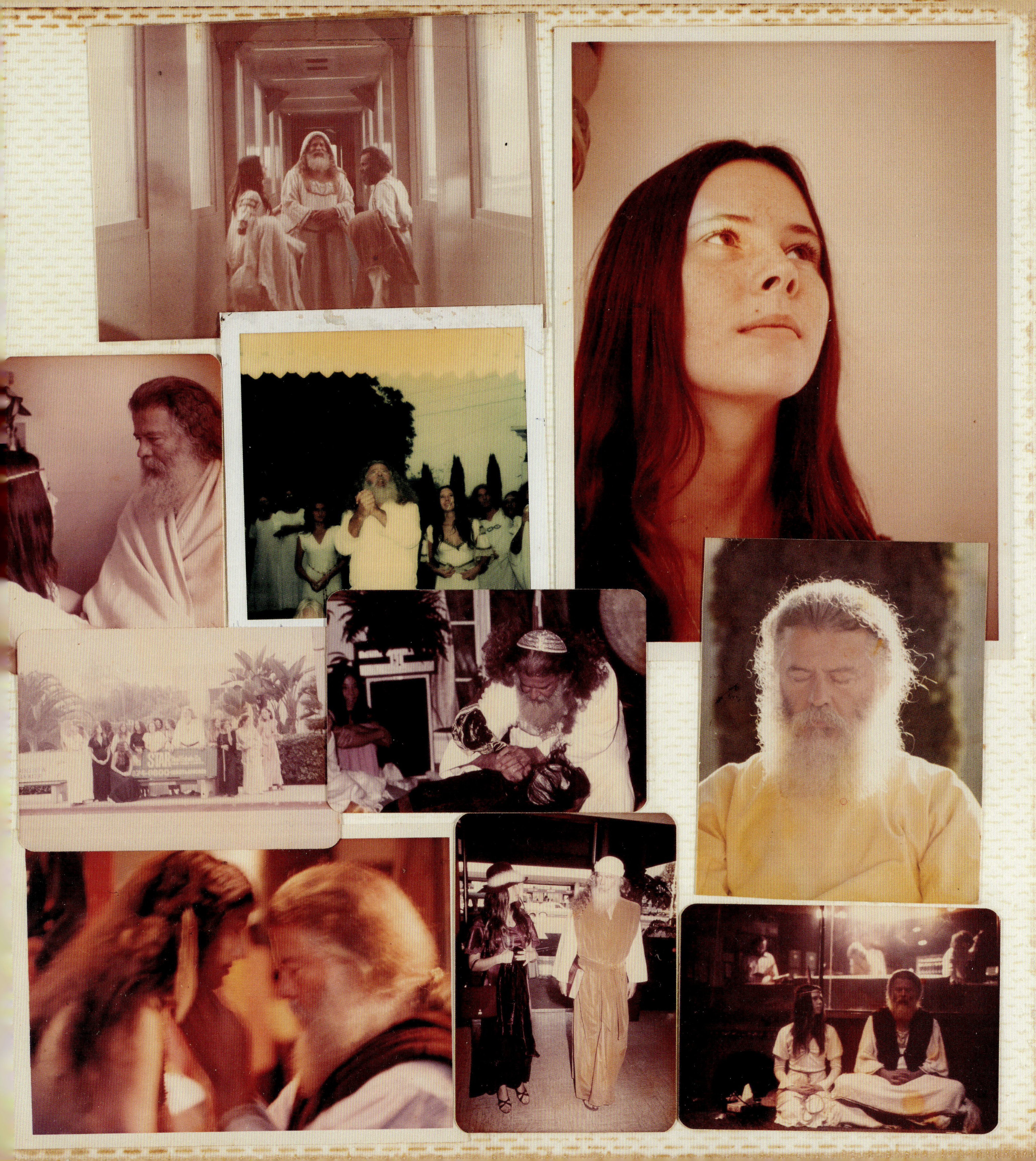

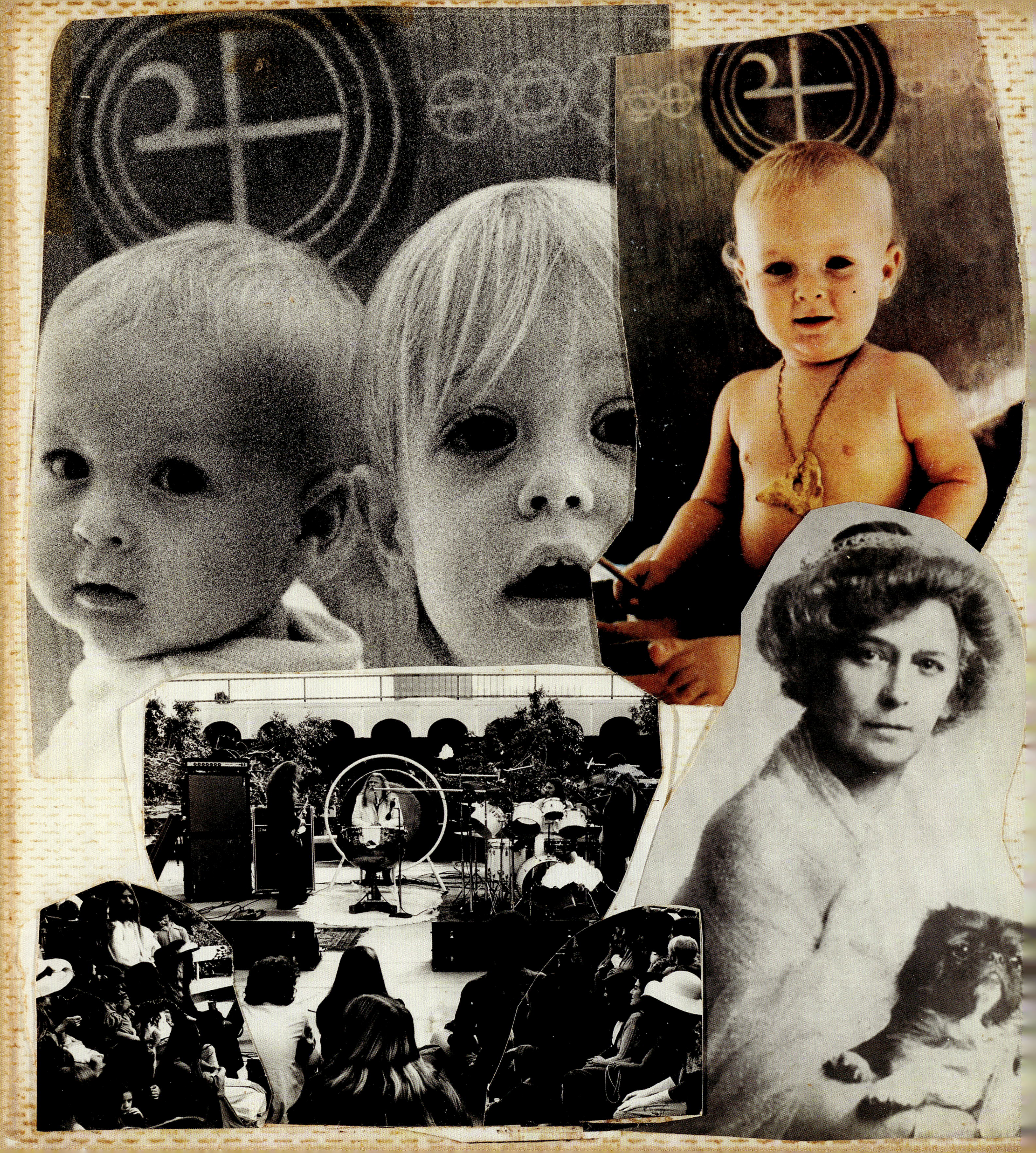

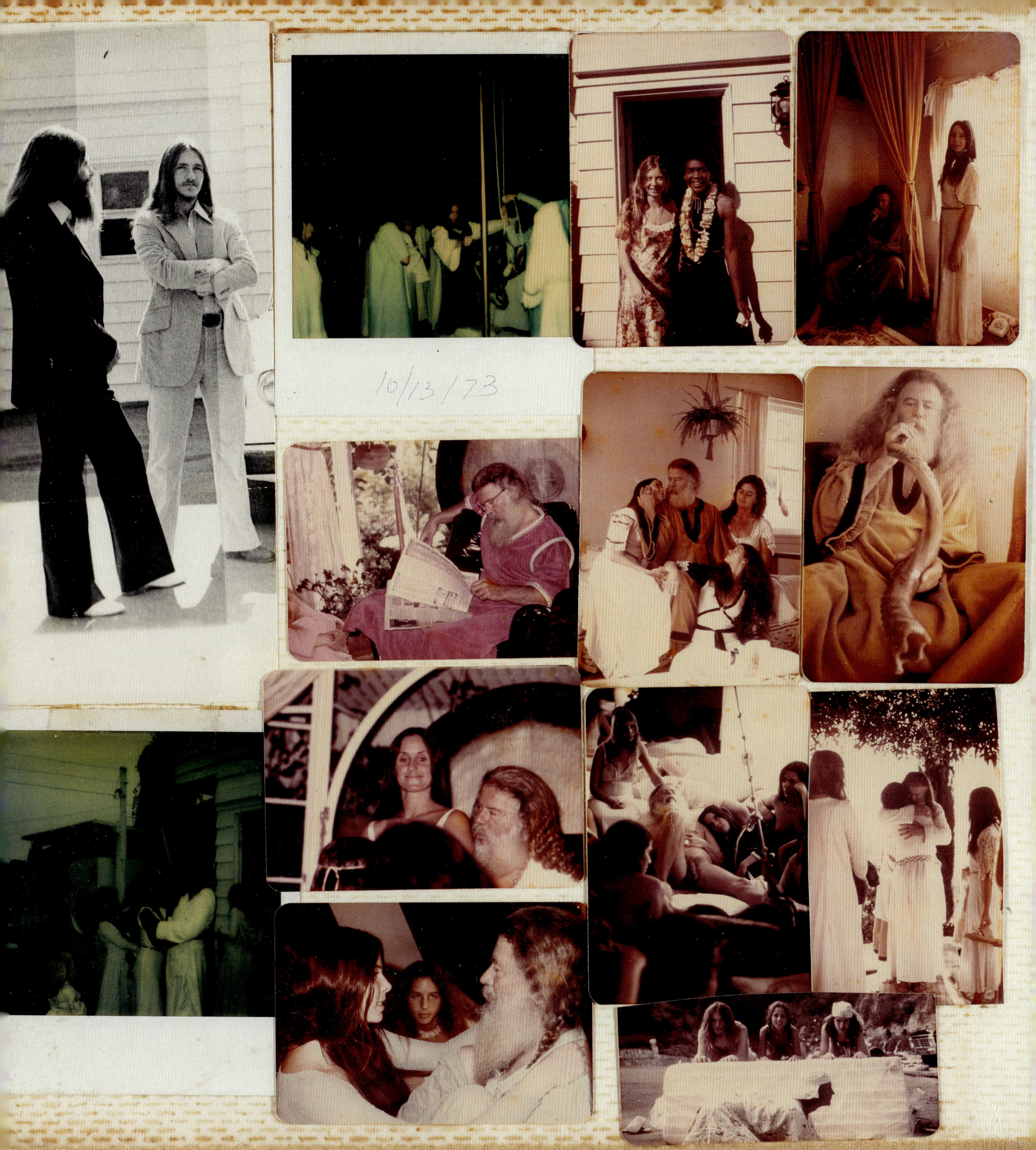
10/13/73

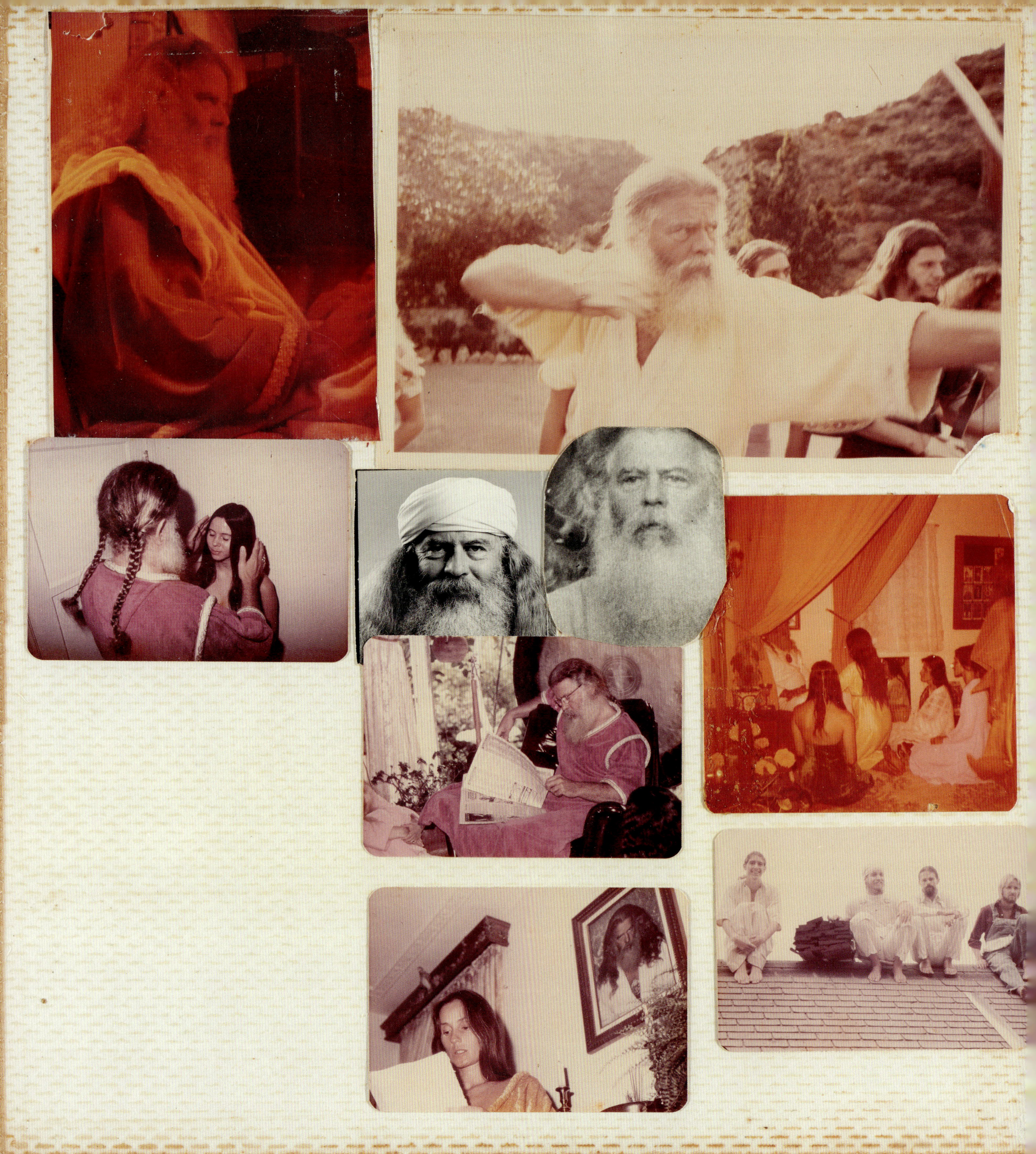

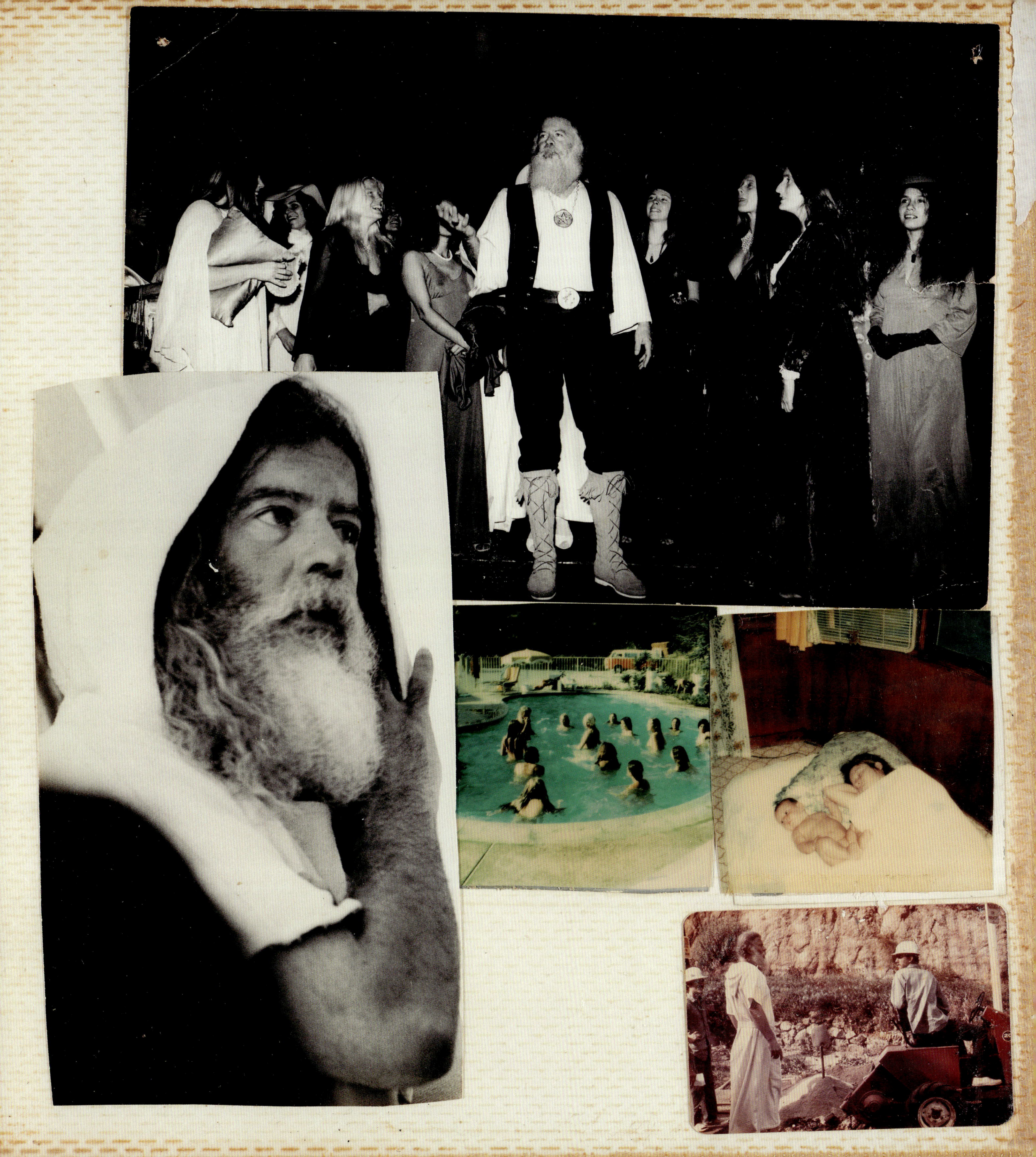

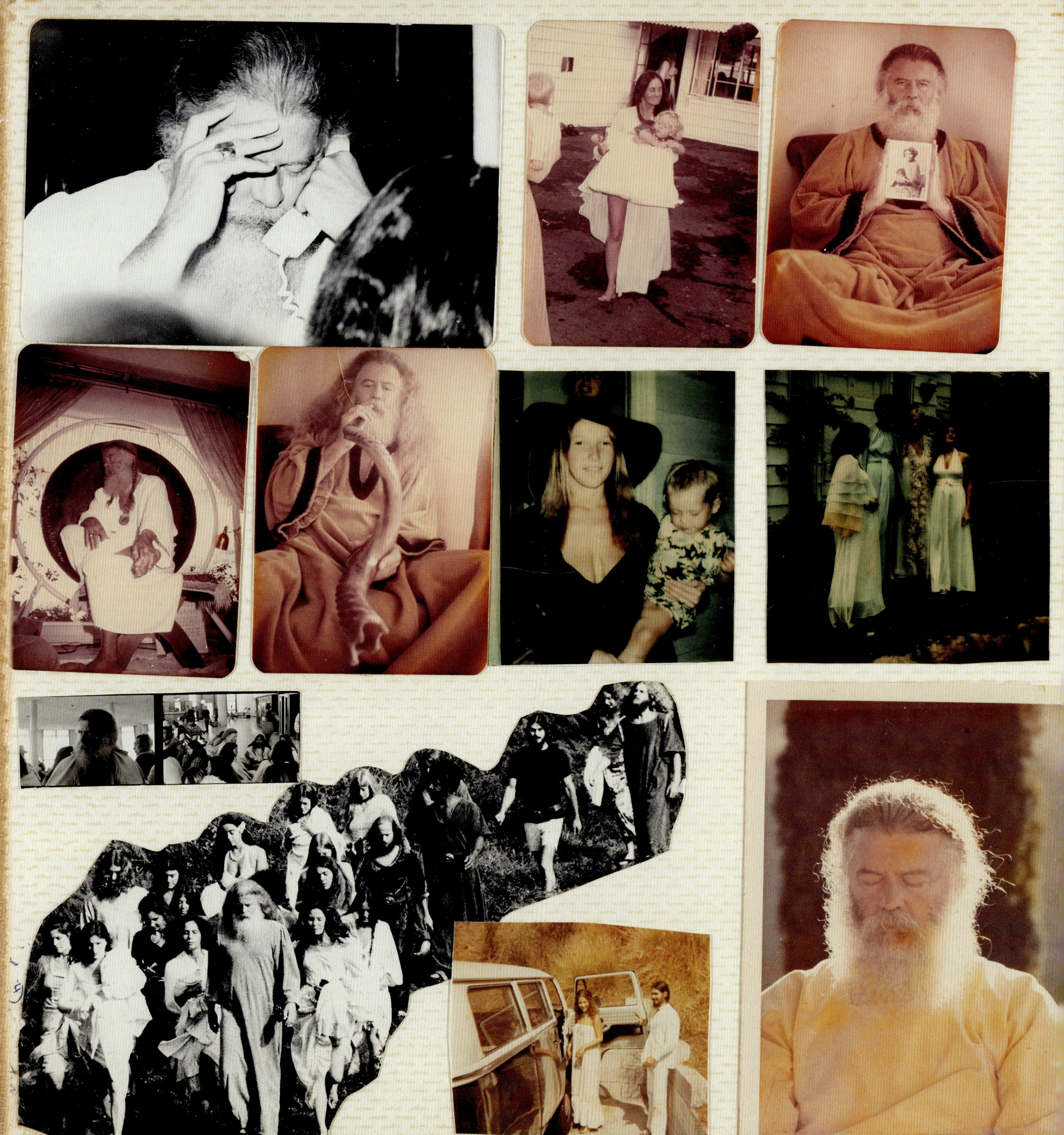
• DEC • 73

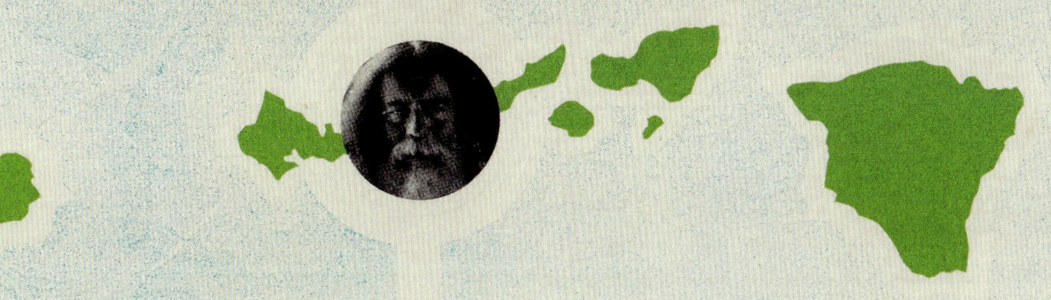

May 30, 1974

Dear Friend,

As you are well aware, we live in a precarious world.

To anyone who has kept pace with the times, it is clear that man's hostility, avarice, and irrational thinking have brought him to a point where

    -- life in urban America is extremely unwholesome

    -- economic conditions now militate in favor of social and political upheaval in the U.S.

    -- nuclear warfare is a highly probable event

Obviously, it behooves us to be prepared for any eventuality! You're probably wondering how this can be done . . . . The only realistic answer is to create a totally self-sufficient community.

For the last three years, we have searched the entire world for the place that would provide a safe refuge in the uncertain times ahead. We found the Hawaiian Islands to be that place.

We have located 1800 acres of beautiful, fertile land there---land that already supports large orchards of mangos, macadamia nuts, and limes, as well as a dairy operation. It has an excellent supply of fresh water and direct access to fishing ponds in the Pacific.

Moreover, we will develop our own alternate power system and provide all of the crafts and skills necessary to fulfill our needs, independent of outside support.

We will also take precautions for our own protection. If "law and order" should ever break down, we will be prepared . . . .

-1-

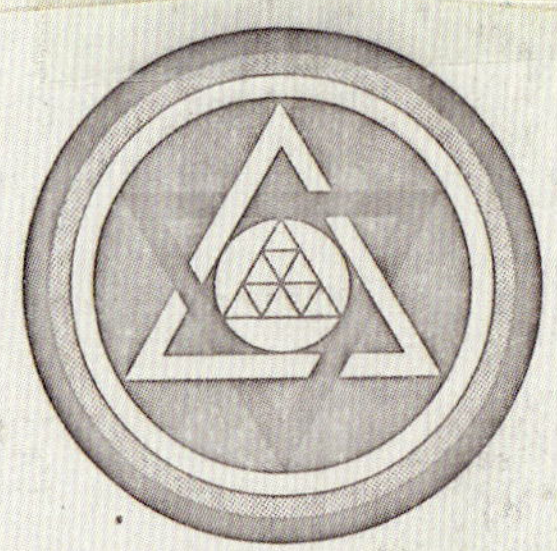

THE BROTHERHOOD OF THE SOURCE

The Brotherhood of the Source is a non-profit religious organization dedicated to the current awakening of spiritual wisdom in the Western World. It was organized in 1969 with only three (3) members. Today there are over one hundred (100) active members and our numbers are growing steadily.

The Brotherhood practices the ideals of selfless love, dedication to duty, self-sufficiency and service to the community.

Our primary means of income comes from the most successful vegetarian restaurant in the United States. (See articles on following pages.) In 1972, the Source Restaurant grossed approximately two hundred thousand dollars ($200,000.00). Pure organic food, the warm atmosphere and loving service account for our great popularity.

In Hawaii, we intend to support ourselves through agriculture. Since July 1, 1973, a small group of our Brotherhood has been farming five (5) acres on Maui. We have both a large vegetable garden and an orchard consisting of mango, papaya, avocado, and citrus trees. We will provide the people of Hawaii with the purest organic fruits and vegetables to be found anywhere on the Islands.

Finally, a cardinal principle of Brotherhood is service to humanity. Our doors are always open to anyone who sincerely wishes to live a spiritual life. Every member of Brotherhood contributes according to his own capacity and receives according to his individual needs. In this way we provide the greatest good for **The Source** the greatest number.

8301 Sunset Boulevard, Los Angeles, California 90069

(213) 656-6388

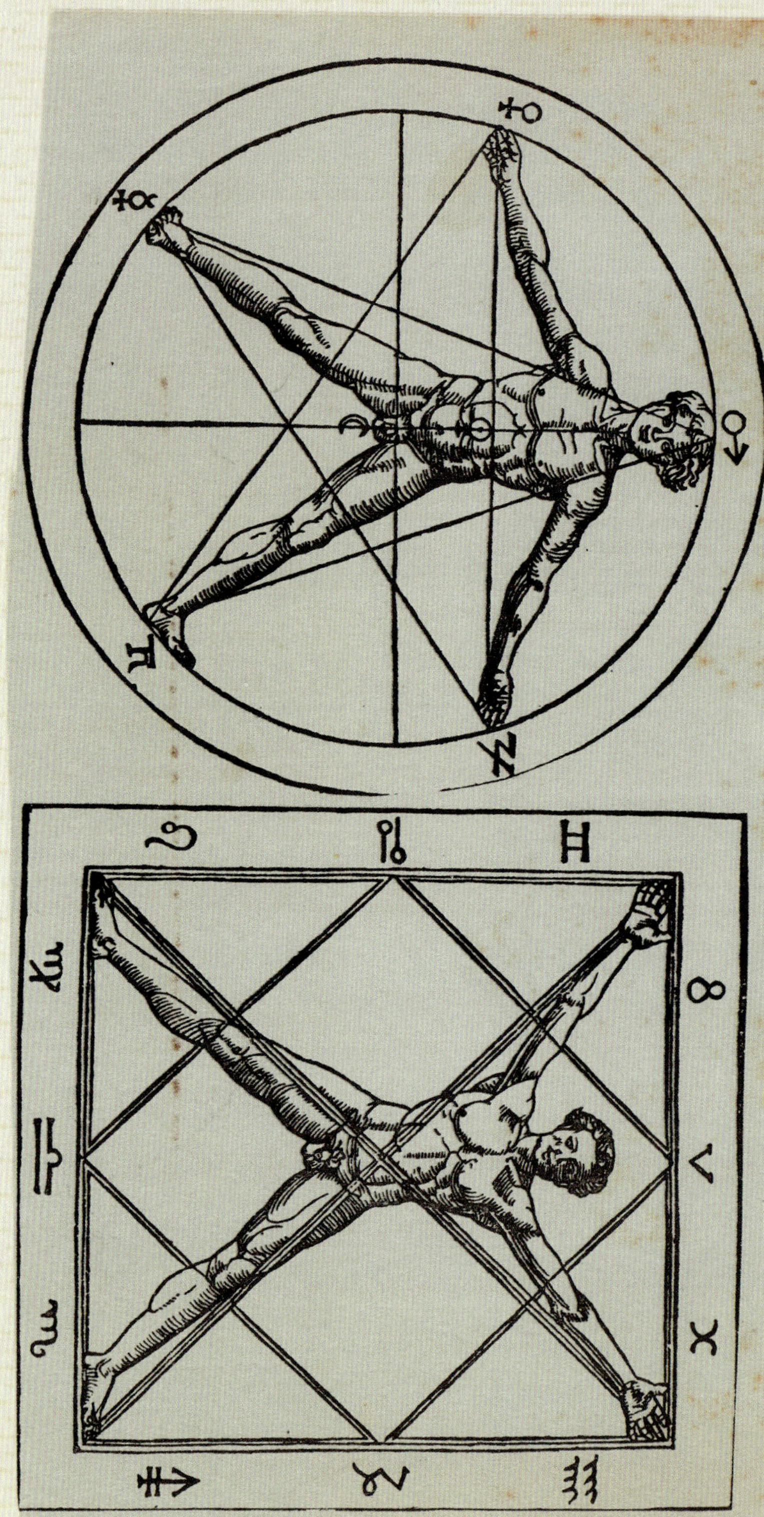

Kaua Campaign.

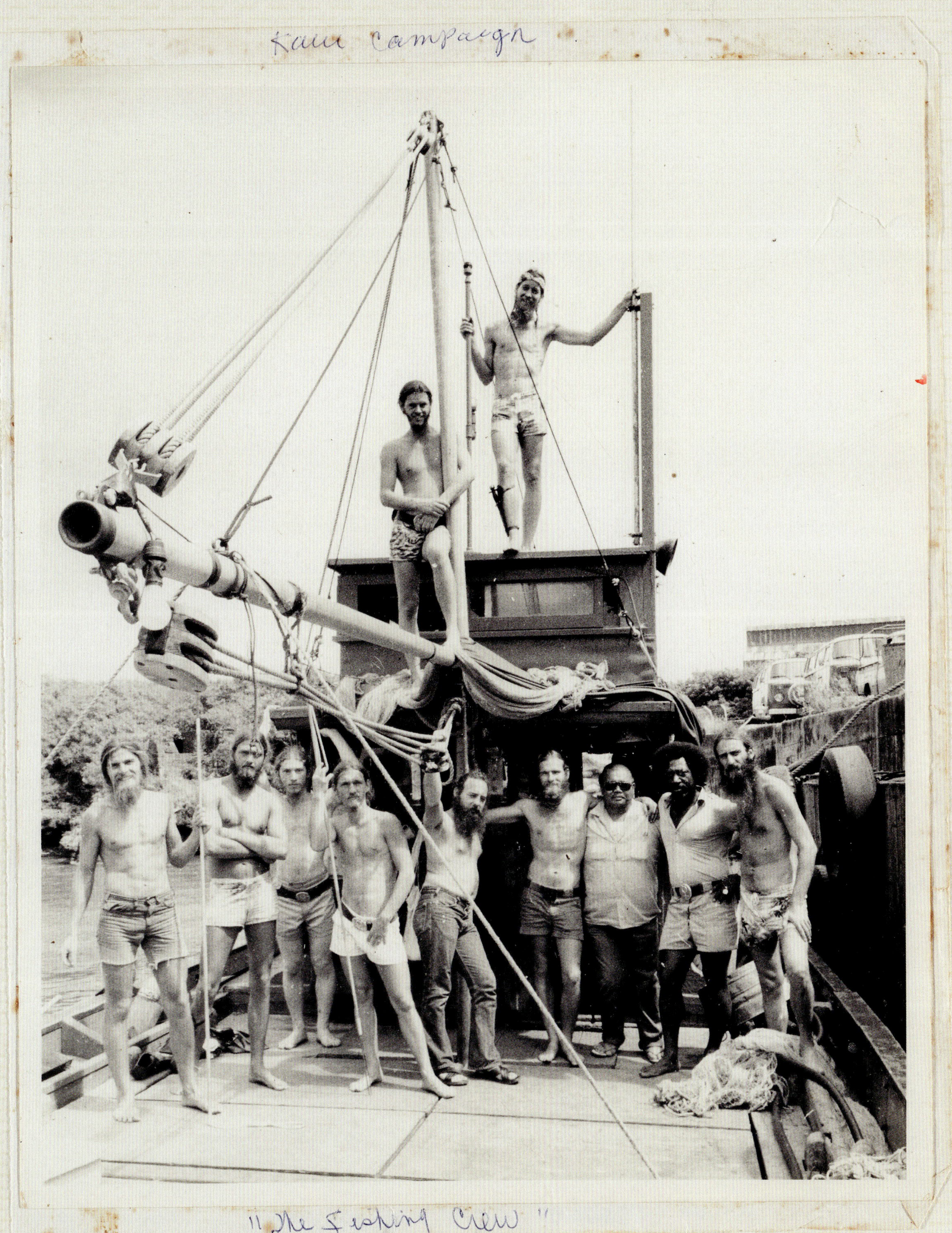

"The Fishing Crew"

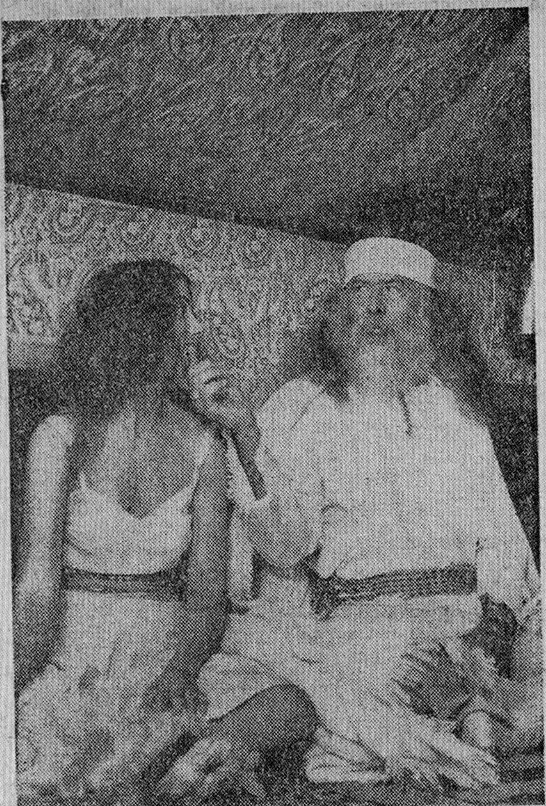

IN SANCTUM—Jim Baker, 50, leader of Brotherhood of the Source, and his wife, 23, called Mother Ahom, sit in loft above the cult's restaurant.
Times photo

FATHER YOD

Continued from 15th Page

was terribly charming and good-looking. But he was always an individualist and I can imagine him 'getting religion,'" she said.

Although some consider him a phony, there is no doubt about Father Yod's sincerity or omniscience in the minds of his disciples.

"Father knows everything, past, present and future," said Isis, 30-year-old liaison officer for the Brotherhood.

"I left home at 15 and traveled for three years, singing at coffee houses. I got into drugs pretty heavy and Father pulled me out in the nick of time," said Aladdin, the first "son" to join Baker three years ago.

Ramacharaka, 21, also came out of the drug culture. "After four years on the road, seeking to find a better way of life, I finally found my home here."

"People live here, in the Mother House, in love and harmony. It's far out," said 36-year-old Shalom, former photographer's assistant.

Sense of Security

"The Brotherhood of the Source is unique because of the tremendous sense of security that comes from Father, the manifestation of the Heavenly Father," said 33-year-old Magus, former clinical psychologist and Elder Brother of the Family who, like other converts, joined because they were "seeking the truth" or a better life or both.

Magus believes the Brotherhood will survive "because the only communes with a history of success were religious communes."

Dr. Robert S. Ellwood Jr., USC professor of religion who teaches a course on the history of Southern California movements, said he had heard of the Brotherhood of the Source only recently but that it apparently fits the definition of a cult, as distinguished from a sect, as that which "combines religions, centers on ecstatic psychological experience and has one strong charismatic leader."

One of Ellwood's students, Julie Delany, in researching the Brotherhood, has come to the tentative conclusion that its faith is mainly derived from Yoga and Buddha.

An Unusual Cult

The group's communal living, she thinks, makes it unusual among Southern California's estimated 200 religious cults.

It may indeed be unusual in another context: money. It is, to date, self-supporting.

"I don't have anything to do with money. Venus proportions it out according to need," Father Yod said.

Elder Brother Magus

Please Turn to Pg. 17, Col. 1

Yod in His Los Feliz Heaven

Continued from 16th Page

however, was more explicit—after obtaining Father's consent. The Brotherhood, Magus said, is chartered as a nonprofit religious organization. Its Source restaurant grosses about $16,000 a month, he said. The Brotherhood also receives about $750 a month from Source Arts, its graphics design agency.

It has received $10,000 advance for a record contract with Playboy Records. It makes "a dab" from its new crafts shop. And all the members "give up their personal wealth, which is usually very little." Only Magus, who joined five months ago with about $30,000, has contributed any substantial amount.

"I think we're breaking about even," Magus said.

"No, our expenses are exceeding our income. Our bank balance is down to $12,000," said Venus, who serves as treasurer for the Brotherhood.

Expenses include the price of seven 1972 Volkswagen buses, $1,000-a-month lease on the house, more than $600 on the restaurant, operating costs at both facilities and about $100 a day for food for the family of 92.

"We are not burdened with material possessions but what we have is of the highest quality. And we've earned it all ourselves," Father Yod said.

"I know our trip is not for everyone, but we are truly a family.

"People don't know how to categorize us. We do not belong to the hippies or to the straights, either. God made us so we don't cut our hair but we are not to be confused with hippies. I expected the Manson Family to damage our reputation but it didn't."

Baker paused as a young man climbed the ladder and tried to enter the sanctum.

"Son," said Father Yod, "don't run around without your shirt on."

Aloha!

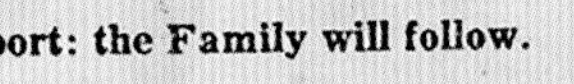

Advertiser Photo by Art Otremba

Ho at airport: the Family will follow.

By VICKIE ONG
Advertiser Staff Writer

Although the Nepalese government doesn't know it yet, the controversial religious group, the Aquarians, eventually will make its home in Nepal, the leader of the "family" said yesterday.

Yahowha Ho, also known as Jim Baker, stopped briefly in Honolulu en route from San Francisco to Tokyo. He and several of his followers are going to Nepal.

More than a 100 Aquarians — who call themselves the "Brotherhood of the Source" — are still on Kauai and will also make their way to Nepal as finances permit, Ho said.

WE HAVE MONEY enough to sustain us here (in Hawaii) but not enough to fly us off the Island. It still mystifies me what the great

The Honolulu Advertiser

Aquarian Ho off to

Hawaii
Saturday, March 8

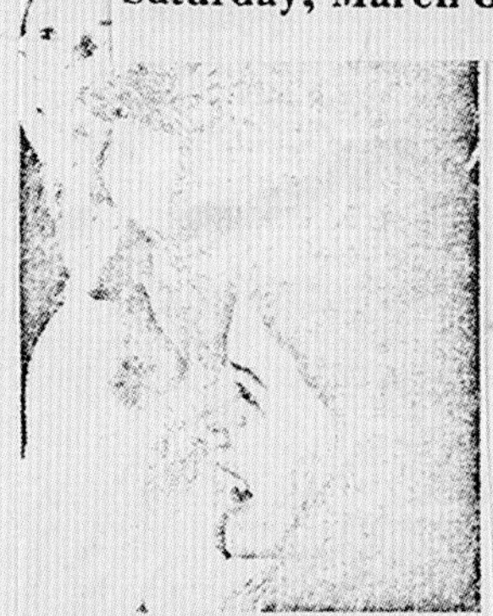

Aquarians greet leader on his way to Nepal, where he sees promise   Page A-3

40 days and nights of rain predicted

Harvest Moon Aquarian called The Garden Island office this morning, to ask that this message be relayed from their father, Yahowha Ho:

"If the angels of ignorance and darkness who control heaven don't come to their senses I will cause it to rain for forty days and forty nights."

Yahowha Ho stopped briefly in Honolulu last week, enroute from San Francisco to Tokyo, and talked of his plans to take his Aquarian family to Nepal, in the Himalaya Mountains.

While more than 100 Aquarians remain on Kauai in homes they have rented in Keapana, their leader is reported to have said that members of his family will follow him, at the rate of three or four a month, and that within two years, the entire family will be reunited, in Nepal.

He also said he couldn't understand the fuss that was being raised about the Aquarians seeking welfare assistance to leave the island. "We have enough money to sustain us in Hawaii but not enough to fly us off the island."

The Aquarians remaining on Kauai face a law suit from their landlord, who claims they are behind $6000 in their rental payments, and there is talk of the county's taking some action against them due to building and housing code violations.

controversy about us is here," Ho said.

"I'm going to Nepal now. My family will follow at the rate of three to four a month. After two years, everyone will be there," he said.

The Aquarian "family" arrived en masse on Kauai from California in early January. But the members say they have met with threats, vandalism and harassment — and last week they asked the State to fly them back to California.

White-haired, bearded and dressed in terrycloth white robe, Ho said if the State wants his "family" to leave Kauai, it should send his members to San Francisco at taxpayer's expense. Ho said he has a house there where his people would live.

BUT IF THEY want us to stay here, we will live here and fly to Nepal and within two years, we will be gone," Ho said.

When asked about reports that the Aquarians had asked for State-paid tickets to Nepal, Ho said, "That's ridiculous. That's $900 apiece. If they don't want us here, it's up to them to provide us transportation."

He said his group is seeking a religious sanctuary in Nepal, since it could not find one here in the United States.

"We are leaving this country for the same reasons our forefathers left England — to avoid spiritual persecution. There's no place for us to go but across the Pacific.

"This country professes to have spiritual freedom but it does not. We are the first family of man and as a family we will stay together," Ho said.

He said although some will remain in the United States for awhile, "we will live — wherever we are. We will endure. And that makes us stronger."

THE GOVERNMENT IN Nepal doesn't know the Aquarians are headed there. "I like to surprise people," Ho said, grinning. "Nepal is one of the most holy spots. We will be accepted there because they will recognize us."

This week the Aquarians on Kauai were served with a summons on a complaint asking that they be ordered to vacate the farm they live on and forced to pay back rent.

Ho denied the charges, saying "We always pay our rent — wherever we are."

He said proceeds from the sale of the Higherkey Record Co. and a restaurant, The Source, both in Los Angeles, will provide the group with monthly income.

Nepal

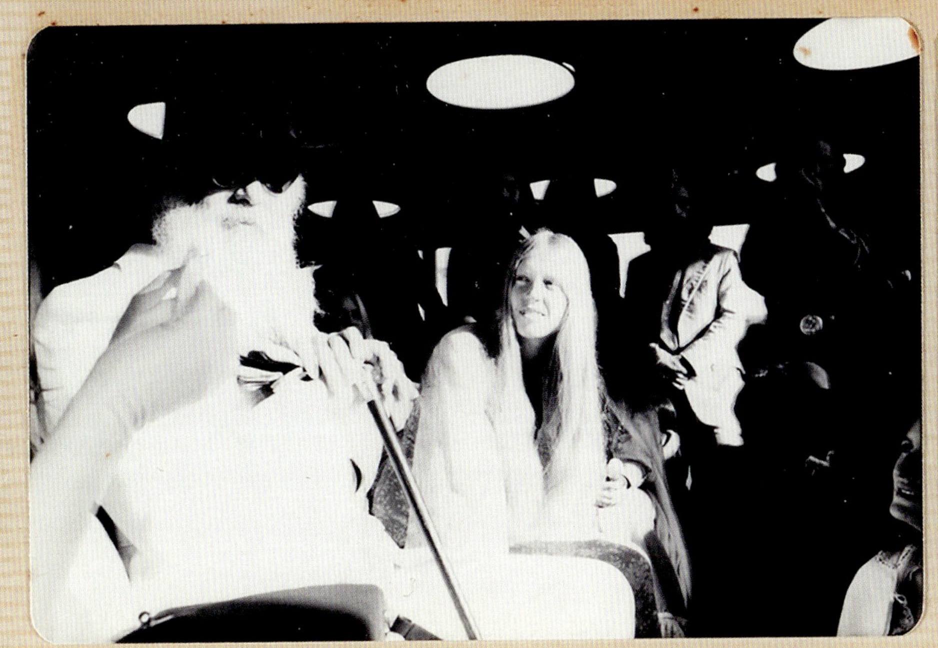
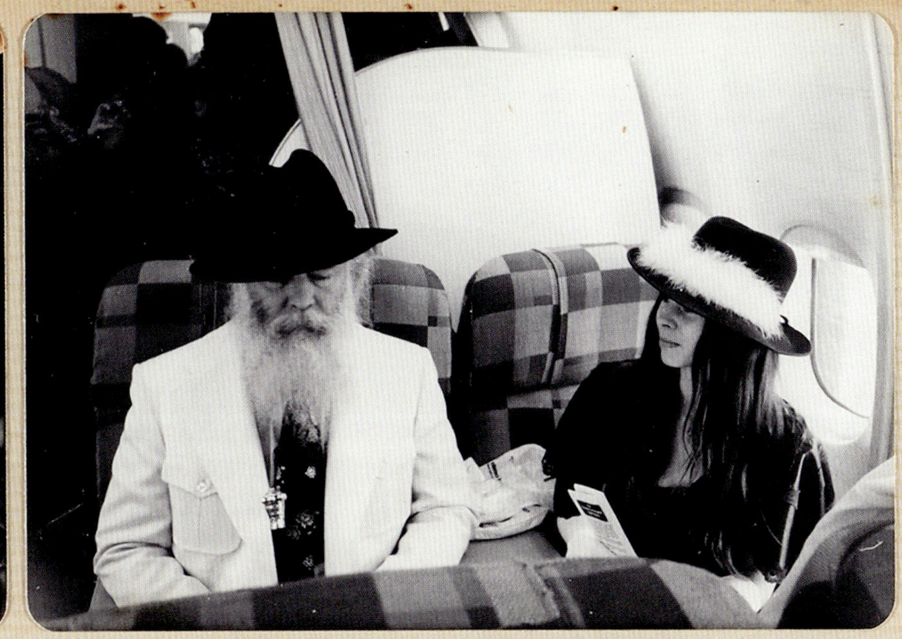

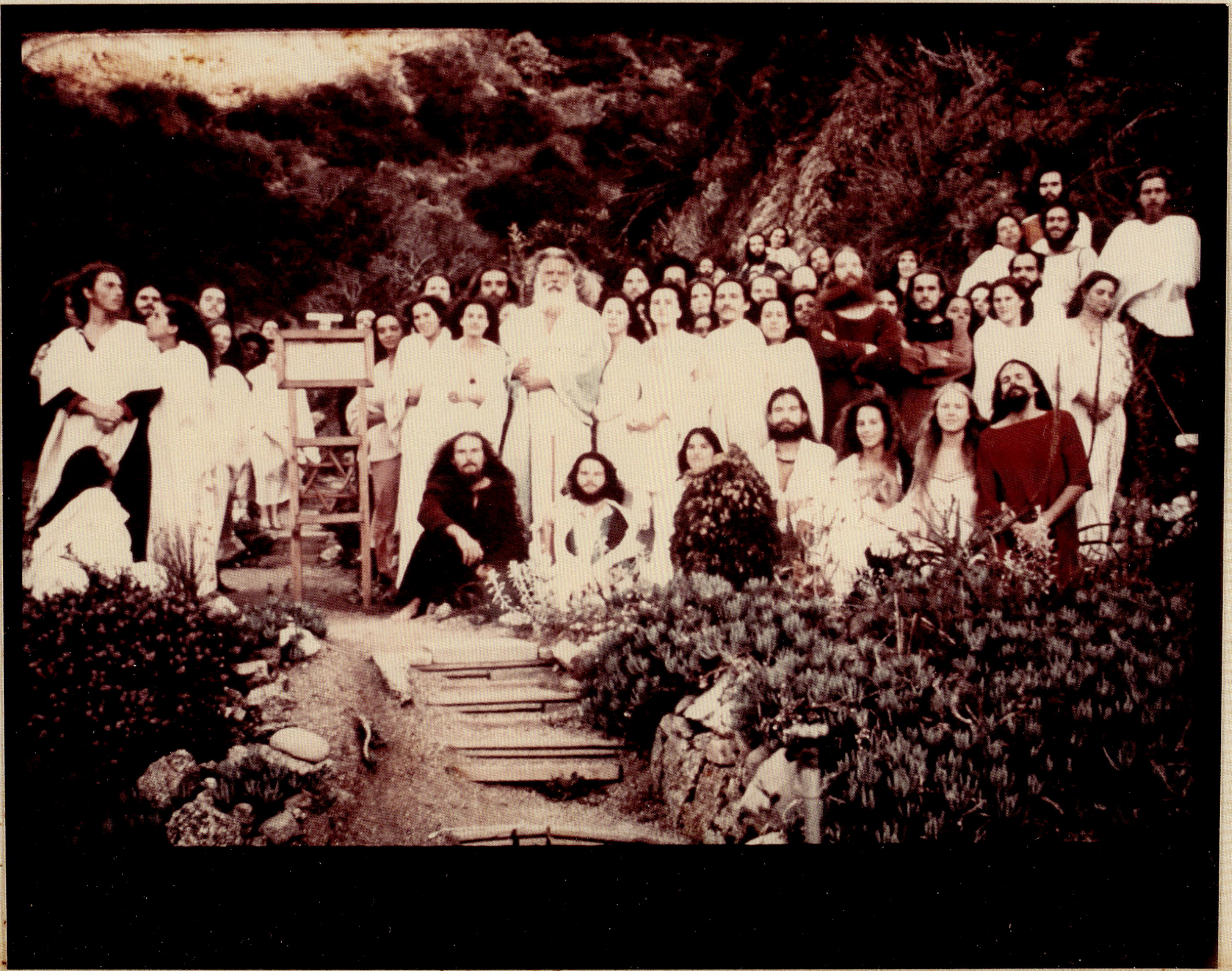

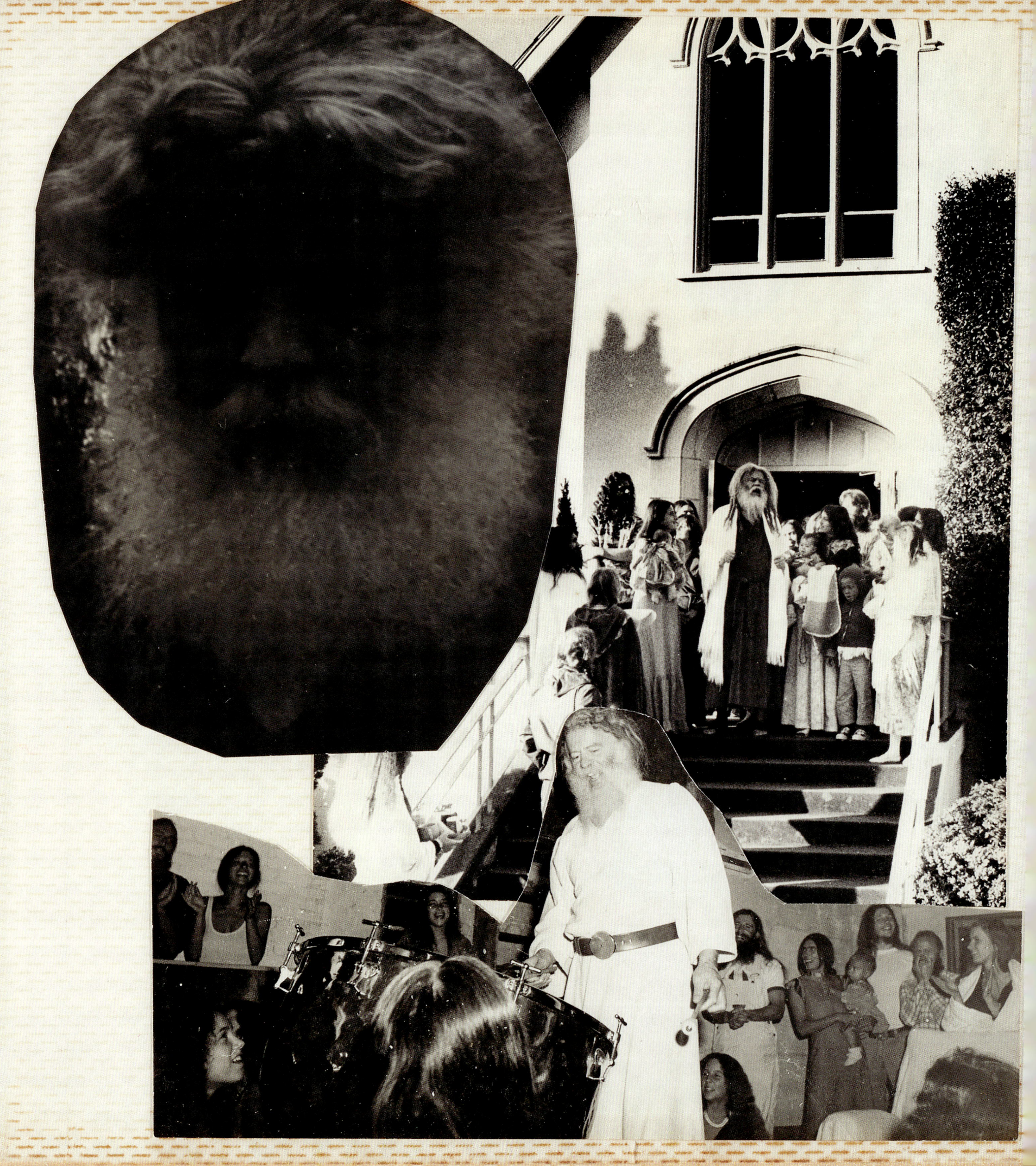

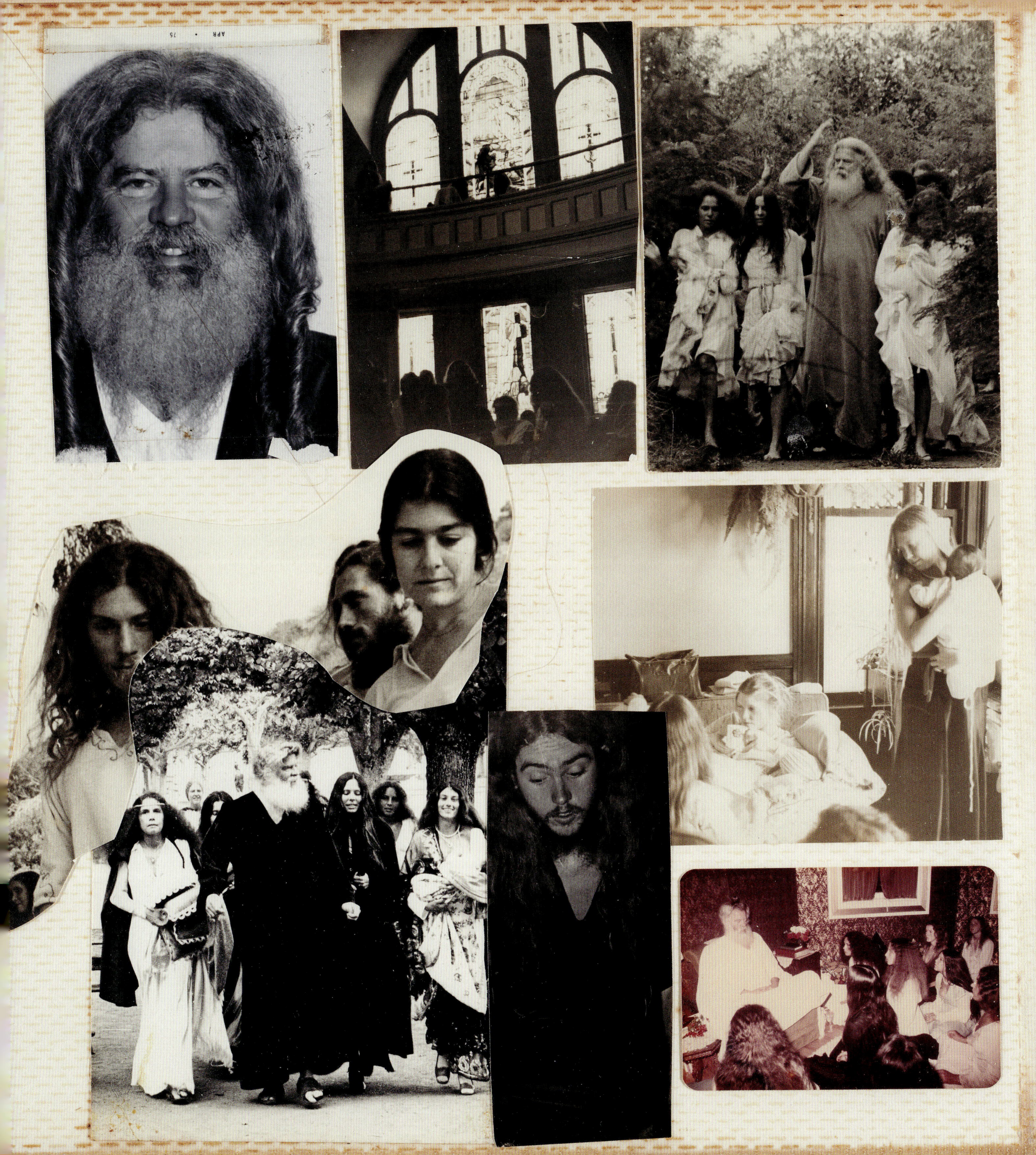

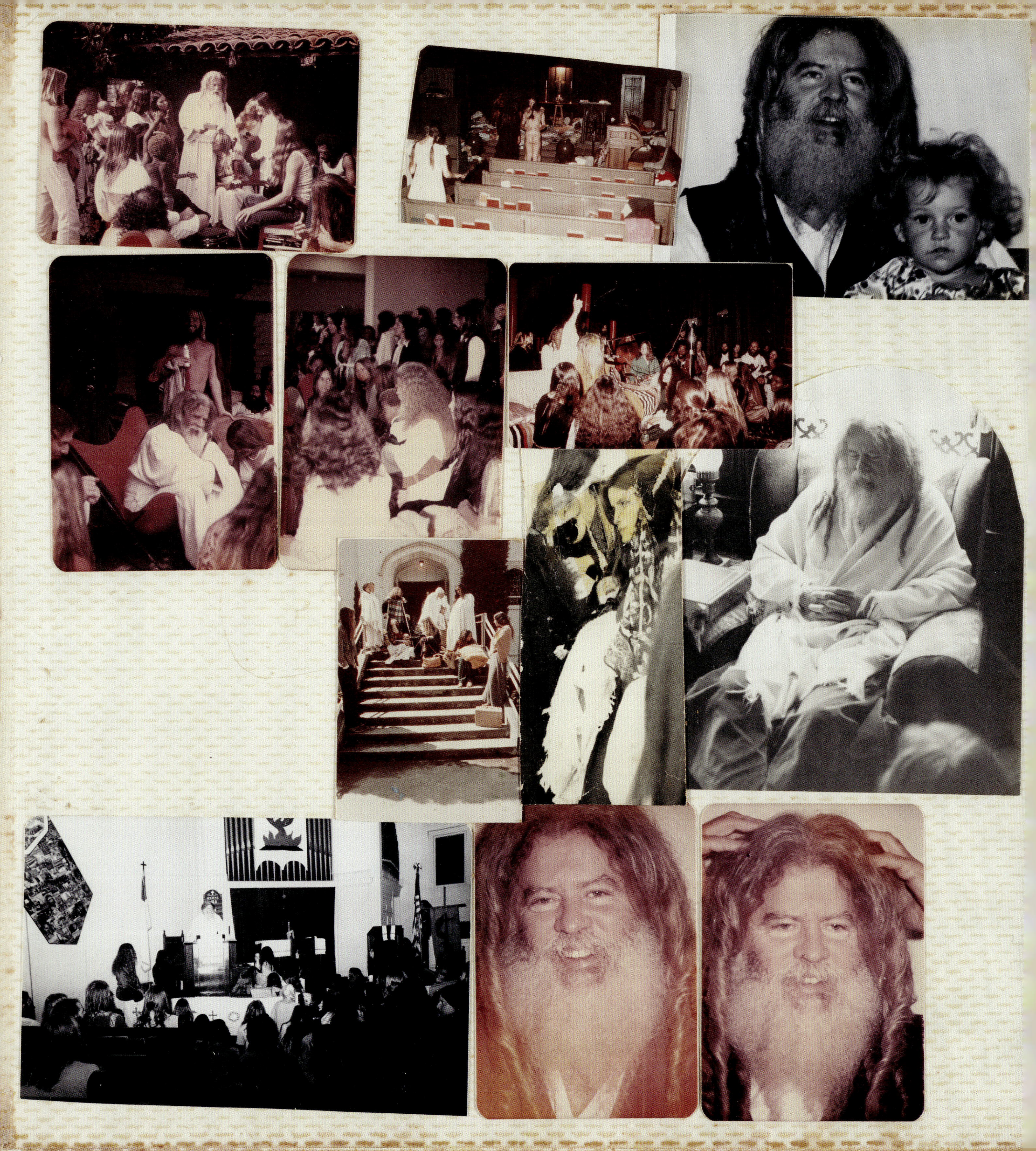

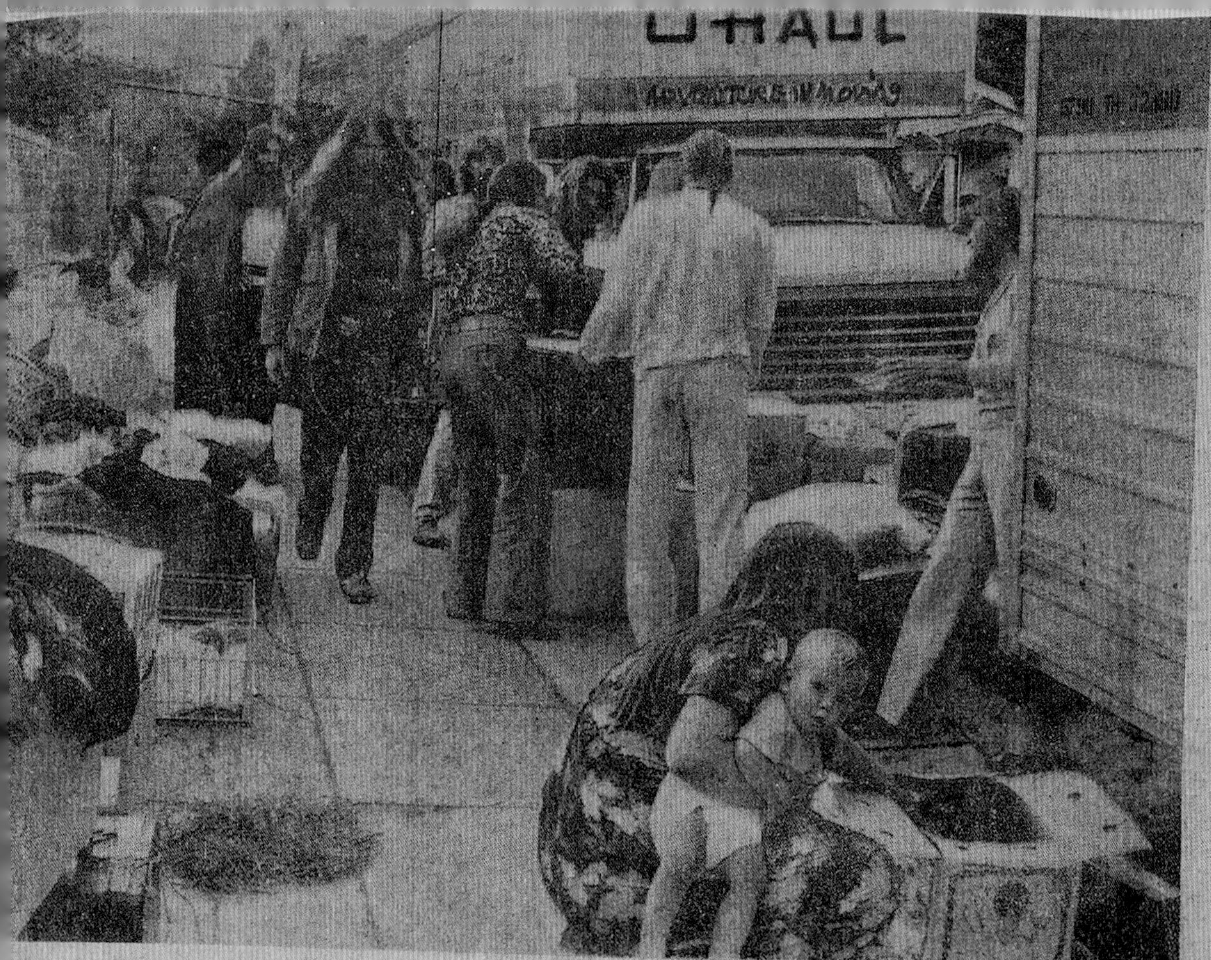

Members of Father Yod's family packing for their departure.

Pocketful of Notes

AS YOU KNOW IF you read Kevin Wallace's informative report in The Chron Tuesday, something called The Religion of TEN (The Eternal Now), a former Los Angeles restaurant-rock-salvation commune, has taken over the rambling old Atherton mansion at 1990 California — a landmark valued at $250,000 . . . Since the arrival of these spiritual souls means the house has been saved from the wrecker's ball, we welcome them — even though their presence is costing us generous taxpayers a pretty pittance. Fifteen of the "sisters" have applied here for AFDC (Aid to Families With Dependent Children), and of those, five are pregnant. The others have at least one child they are nursing. Their okayed grants, therefore, at $212 a month each plus pregnancy and lactation diet, add up to $3375 a month! . . . But whatever they collect from alms, musical performances, or the restaurants they plan to open, will replenish our tax coffers, right? Wrong. "We're religious," a spokesperson for The Eternal Now reminds us, "so we're deductible." Have a nice breakfast.

Religious family and the church: a struggle in the material world

By DAVE RICHMOND

With God Himself a participant by proxy, a wandering religious family of 140 persons last week spent time in Mill Valley, much of it spiced with controversy.

In its wake, the family, whose "father" is called Father Yod, touched off spirited discussion of, among other things, the use of a church as a resting place and the very nature of Christianity.

As with most weighty questions, nothing was resolved with finality.

The family spent at least two nights in two Mill Valley churches, apparently against the wishes of the respective clergymen, and one night in a Mill Valley home, with the blessings of the resident.

Last Wednesday morning, the 140-member family was still occupying the Lovell Ave. home of Zaida Philp, across the street from one bone of contention — the Episcopal Church of Our Saviour.

The family members had spent Tuesday night in Ms. Philp's home, but by mid-morning were loading provisions into two large U-Haul trucks for the continuation of what its leader implied was, at least from the standpoint of time, an open-ended journey.

"We are looking for our home," Father Yod declared in explanation.

At this point, Father Yod was in Ms. Philp's living room. He was seated on a couch by the window through which he could see Old Mill School and, beyond it, the church. A roomful of his followers covered the room's floor, sitting cross-legged at his feet.

There was, one was made to understand, a natural child birth going on immediately to Father Yod's right. His pronouncements would every so often be punctuated by the forced, heavy breathing of the mother-to-be.

A rather large, bearded man with the ability to crank up his voice to sermon-like volume, Father Yod said he used to be someone called Jim Baker. But, he went on, he went to India six years ago and returned as Father Yod.

His interview, if that is the term, varied between an explanation of his family and well-executed blasts at the Mill Valley churches which at one point or another denied his family entrance.

"They are all cowards. Hypocrites, all of them," he boomed at one point, waving his hand in the vague direction of the Episcopal church. "They live in a curse of their own making."

The germ of Father Yod's ire, it turned out, was that the doors of the Episcopal church were, figuratively if not literally, locked in his face. The family also spent one night at the Community Church. The locked door must have seemed particularly galling, no doubt, given Father Yod's estimation of his assembly.

"We are a true family. We are the first family of man. We . . . have the reason and existence of religion," he said from across Ms. Philp's living room. It was politely but firmly made clear that the reporter couldn't get into the living room but would have to view Father Yod from afar, relatively speaking.

"This is not a publicity seeking affair," he said. "We're not even after your soul, man. All I ask you is try and remain positive."

Positive was one thing that Rev. Murray Hammond of the Episcopal Church certainly was — positive that he wasn't going to let Father Yod's family use the church for sleeping quarters or to hold its morning "services." Rev. William Eichhorn of the Community Church was unavailable for comment.

According to Rev. Hammond, he recived a call from the police at 2:35 a.m. Monday asking if he had given permission for the family to sleep in the church. He said he told the police that he hadn't given such permission but that since the occupation of the church was already an accomplished fact, perhaps well enough should be left alone, at least for the night.

"I asked them to leave and not to come back," Rev. Hammond recalled telling the family when he saw them the following morning.

"They were clean and well-behaved. They were very amenable and friendly," Rev. Hammond said. By noon, they were gone, he said.

According to Rev. Hammond, he left the church open Monday night and when he returned the next morning "it was obvious they had been there."

At some point, Rev. Hammond said, he did lock the

(continued on page three)

'Earth Mafia' Takes Over

By Kevin Wallace

The haunted Atherton house at 1990 California street has been saved by the Religion of TEN (The Eternal Now), a restaurant, rock and salvation commune, formerly of Los Angeles.

The rambling, turreted old mansion, long haunted by novelist Gertrude Atherton's husband, George, was bought three weeks ago by the 140 brothers and sisters of TEN and their "father," who is "an older man" named Yahowha, or Jehovah.

Demolition-oriented real estate investors, who had said that only Jehovah could save the 1881 white elephant from the wreckers' ball, were thereby proven peculiarly right.

Yahowha was upstairs yesterday, incommunicado. But lots of the young brothers and sisters were eagerly and cheerfully repairing the grand ballroom and billiards salon downstairs — Isis, Ahom and her 9-month-old son, Tau; Sir Knight; Sun . . .

And down in the basement, the TEN's way-out band, called Breath, was rehearsing, with Octavius on drums, Rhythm and Home on guitars, Sunflower on bass, and Lovely on electric violin.

Lovely confessed her "flesh parents" are pianist Andre Previn and Singer Betty Bennett, and her earth age is 18, but, as Isis said, "Who cares about that?"

The TEN also has a non-way-out band, Mercury and the Thought Adjusters, which does "right-on funky rock and roll," according to Ahom.

Ahom sees the TEN's move to San Francisco as something sounding like an old-time revival of the local Age of Aquarius, which in fact she says they're preparing for.

"What we want right away is $100,000 to open up a new original-type nightclub that all the young people have been waiting for," Ahom said, nursing Tau.

Isis added that capital is also invited for a string of contemplated restaurants to replace TEN's former Sunset Strip holdings, sold when TEN decided to head north.

"We're religious, so we're deductible," Isis said. "We're ethereal but earthy. They call us the Earth Mafia. We import honey. We run a house renovation crew called Fathers & Sons United Labor Force.

"We aren't acquainted with any of the local religions, but we don't expect any trouble from them."

Ahom said the group is mostly vegetarian and opposed to drinking, smoking and drugs. Isis produced a flyer stating that TEN members will be limited to an enrollment of 4000 in San Francisco, and will constitute a "family of gods."

Yahowha, TEN's "earthly spiritual father," wrote their ten commandments, which include, "Obey and live by the Teachings of your Earthly Spiritual Father" and "share all that you have."

Ahom said The Eternal Now is "world famous for our cheesecake, ice cream and Famous Source Special, a sandwich."

Isis said, "We're into spirit, and we're very aware of this house's ghost, but it isn't George Atherton's ghost. It is a very positive feminine ghost."

If true, that would mean that George has left, and the last previous owner, Carrie Rousseau — who died last fall at 93 — has taken over, as some of her friends had thought.

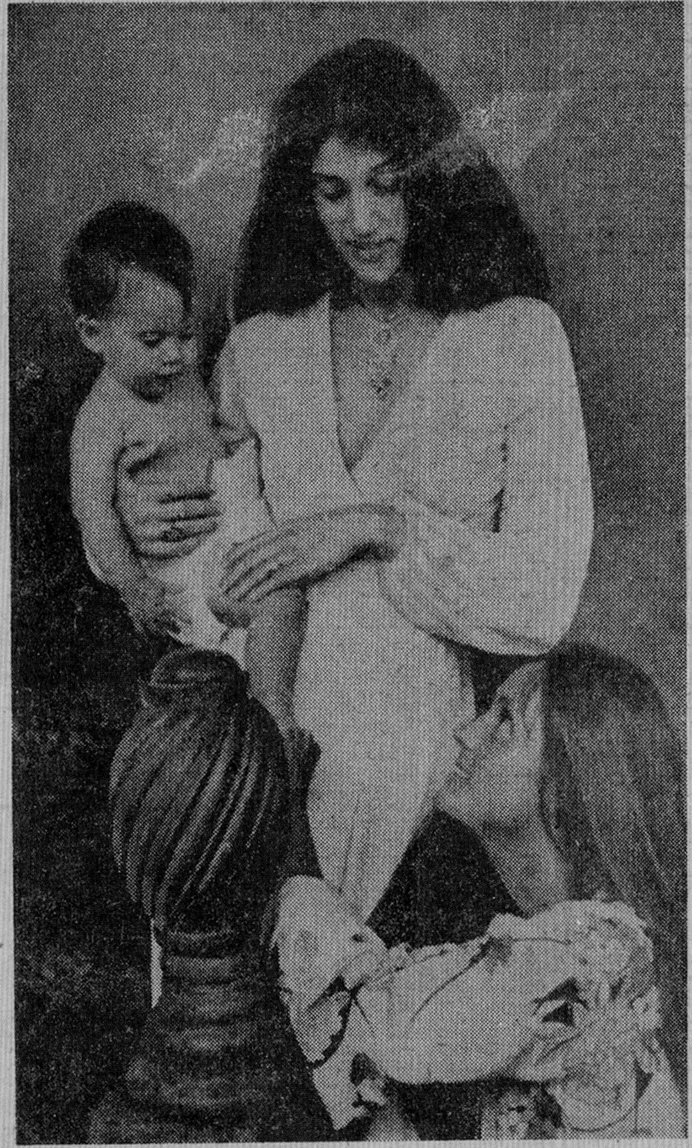

By Peter Breinig

ISIS LOOKED UP AT AHOM AND HER SON, TAU
'We're religious, so we're deductible,' said Isis

The family

(continued from page one)
doors of the church. Those doors, he said, are normally left open 24 hours a day.

The argument advanced by the family was that since churches are houses of God," all God's children, as it were, should be allowed access.

"They kind of laid the guilt trip on all the clergy in town," Rev. Hammond said. "I couldn't respond to it because I don't know how you persuade somebody that their stance is wrong and your stance is right."

The church, he continued, "is obviously not a place that's meant to be slept in, to be lived in. It's a haven, but it's a limited haven."

The limits of the material world certainly grated on Father Yod.

"Men and mice. And tell all those Christian ministers that," he instructed.

"The Bible is . . ." he intoned. ". . . prophecy," his followers responded.

"Write that down," someone near the reporter strongly recommended. "The Bible is prophecy."

By the first of the week it appeared that Father Yod and his family had cleared out for good. Their U-Haul trucks were gone from Lovell Ave. and Rev. Hammond said he hadn't spoken with them since last Thursday.

Father Yod and his followers treated the reporter with a pleasant sort of correct kindness. However, there was one thing which Father Yod observed during his 30-minute presentation that might trip up any reporter posturing as a religious sort.

"Always," he said, "a man evaluates to the level of his own conscience. God will read your article."

According to him, the family sold "the best restaurant on the Sunset strip" (in Los Angeles, or, as he generously put it, "the city of the angels") and was in no need of money.

"The problem is not money. We are looking for our home," he said, adding that the family has been "wandering in the wilderness" for the strikingly appropriate "40 days and 40 nights."

Father Yod's family was quietly attentive when he spoke, sometimes murmuring approval when a phrase which for them held some profundity struck home. He most frequently called the male members "son," even once or twice feigning such familiarity with the reporter.

Father Yod was expectedly cryptic about the future of his nomadic trek. He said he didn't know exactly where they would all go next. Later someone mentioned Novato, Berkeley or San Francisco as possibilities, which encompassed every direction but west into the ocean.

"I have my angels out," he explained.

For a man of spiritual persuasions, Father Yod was completely unruffled and not offended by such mundane journalistic queries as "how do you spell Yod?"

But he implied at the beginning that if left alone he would probably answer most of the reporter's questions anyway.

The Bible, needless to say, played a part in Father Yod's discussion. He suggested that those who want to read it should read it backwards."

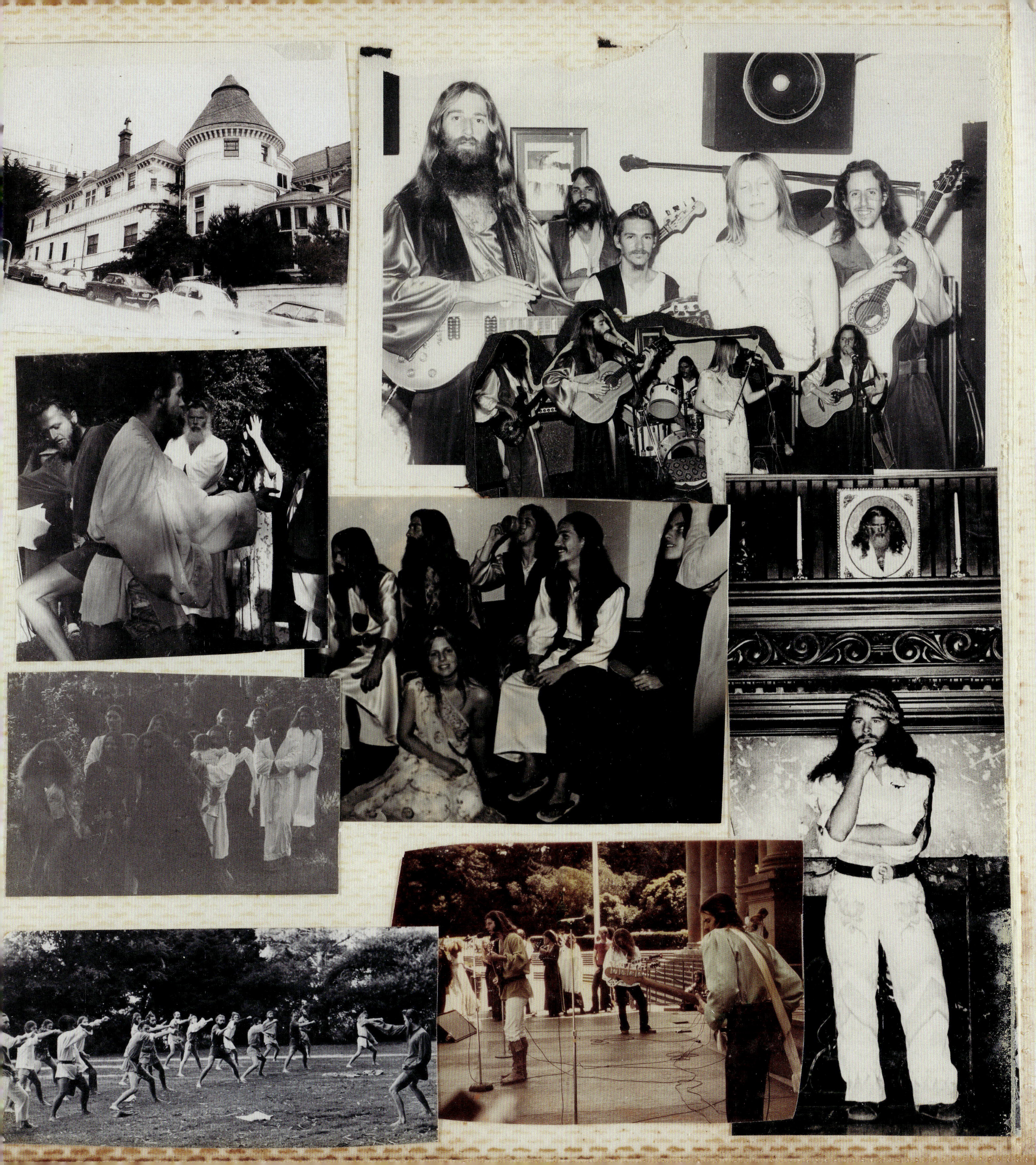

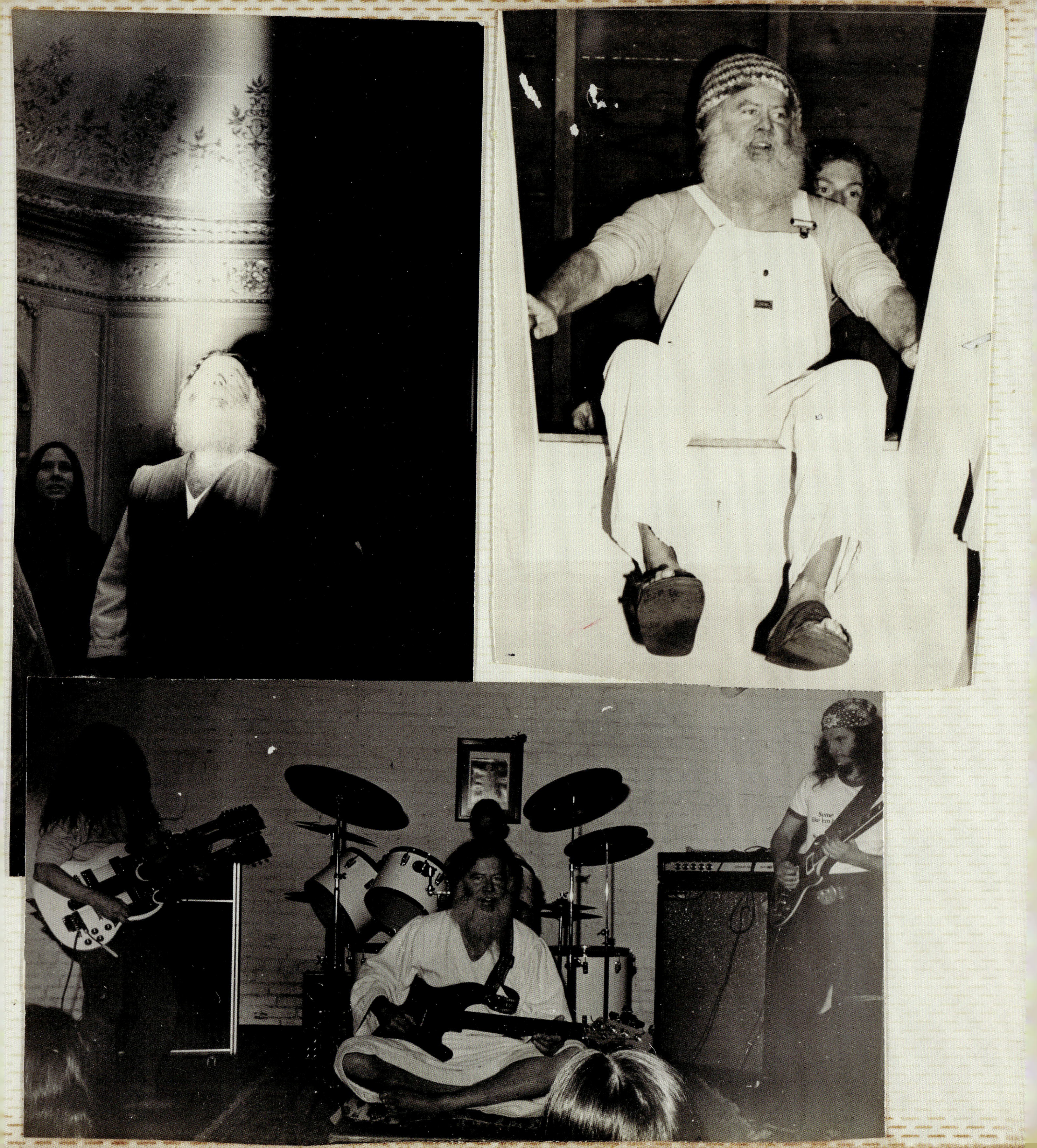

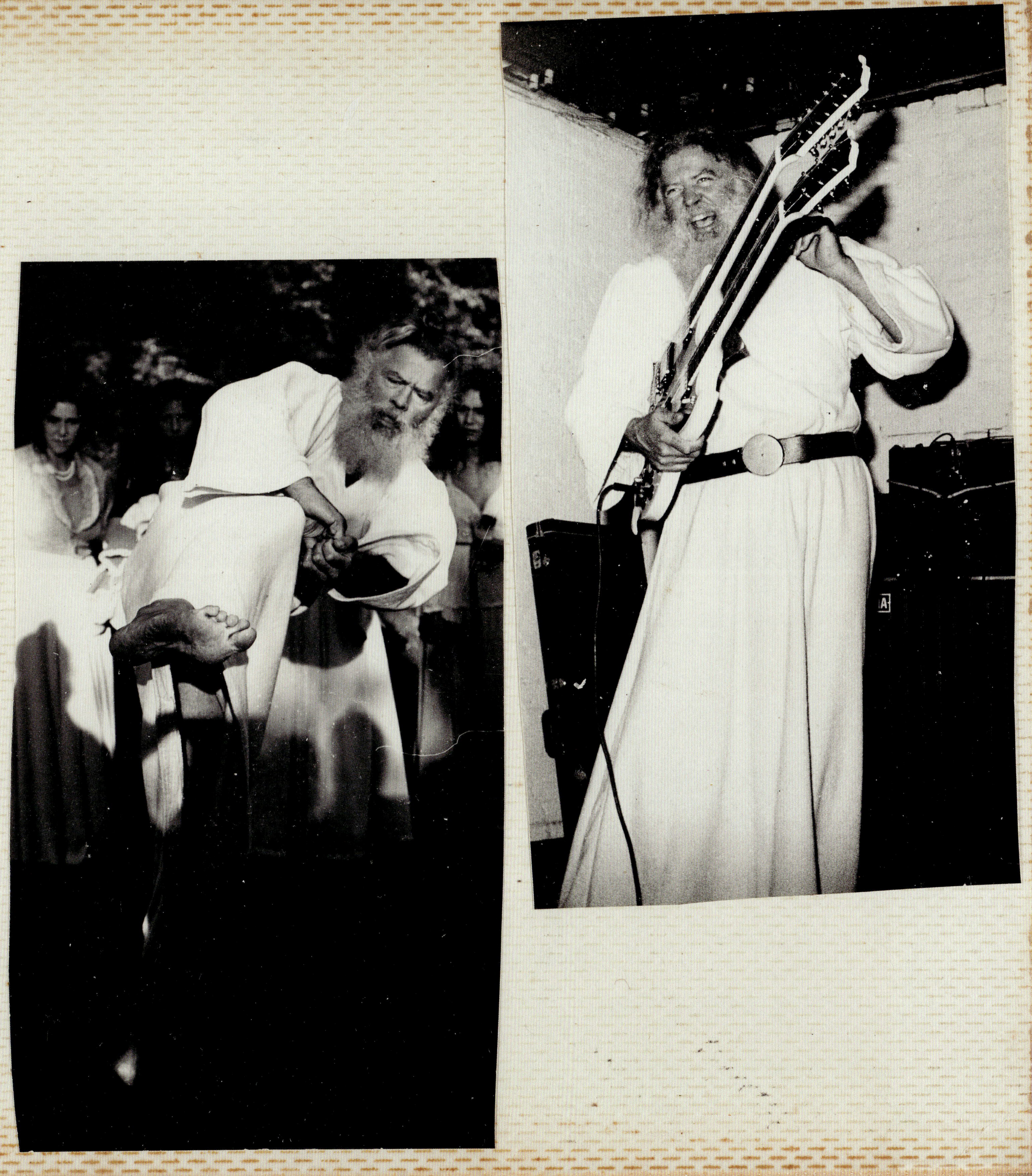

Echoes From The Invisible Worlds

YA

HO

The

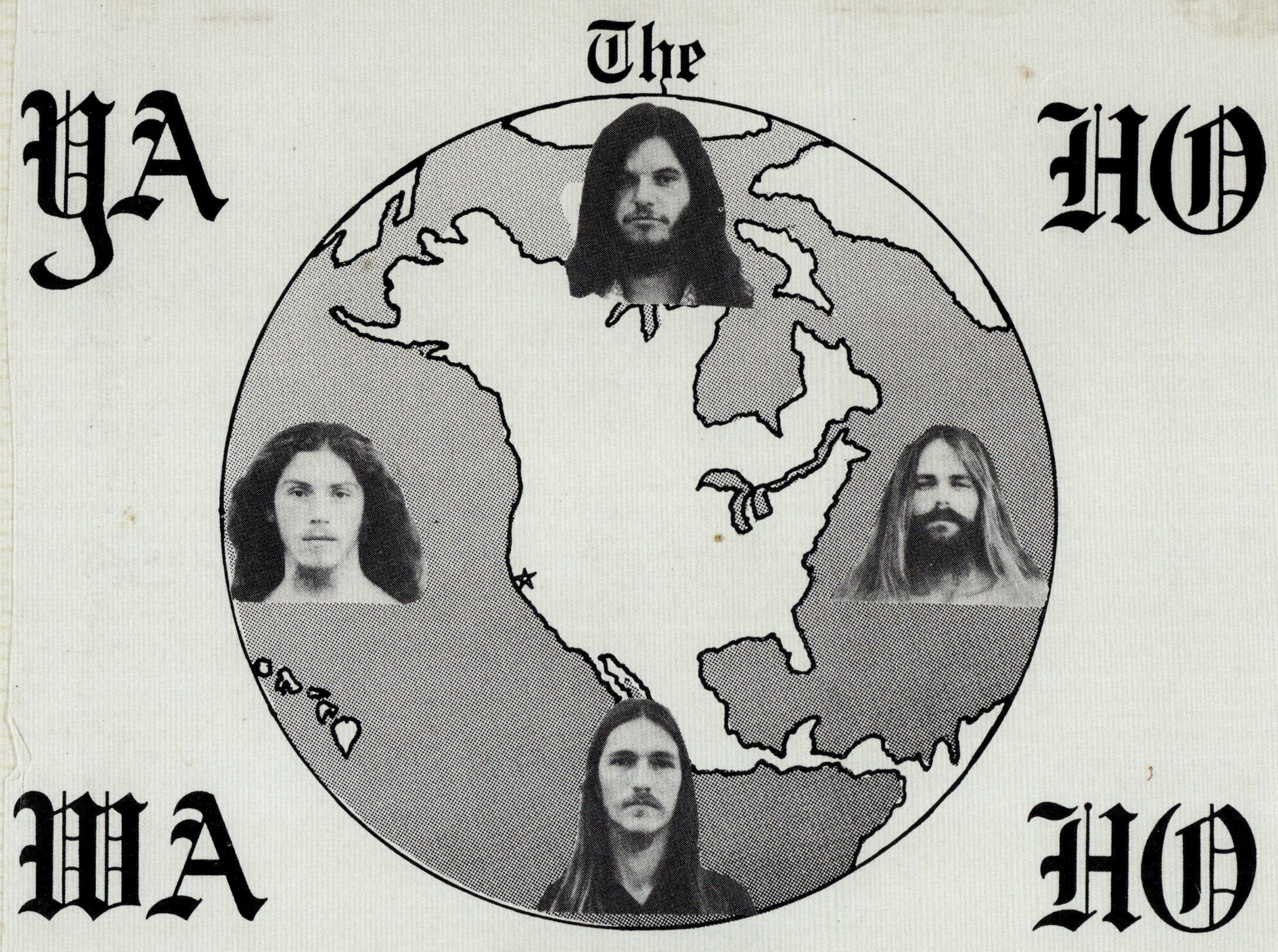

HO

WA

BAND

Their First Concert in the Bay Area

Lighthouse Theater – Aquarian Productions

PRIL 10   8:00 P.M. $2.50

Central San Rafael exit
then first left. left again
on Lincoln. Right on
Lovell. 65 Lovell.
Parking in lot.

FOR FURTHER INFORMATION CONTACT: ELECTRA 924-8205

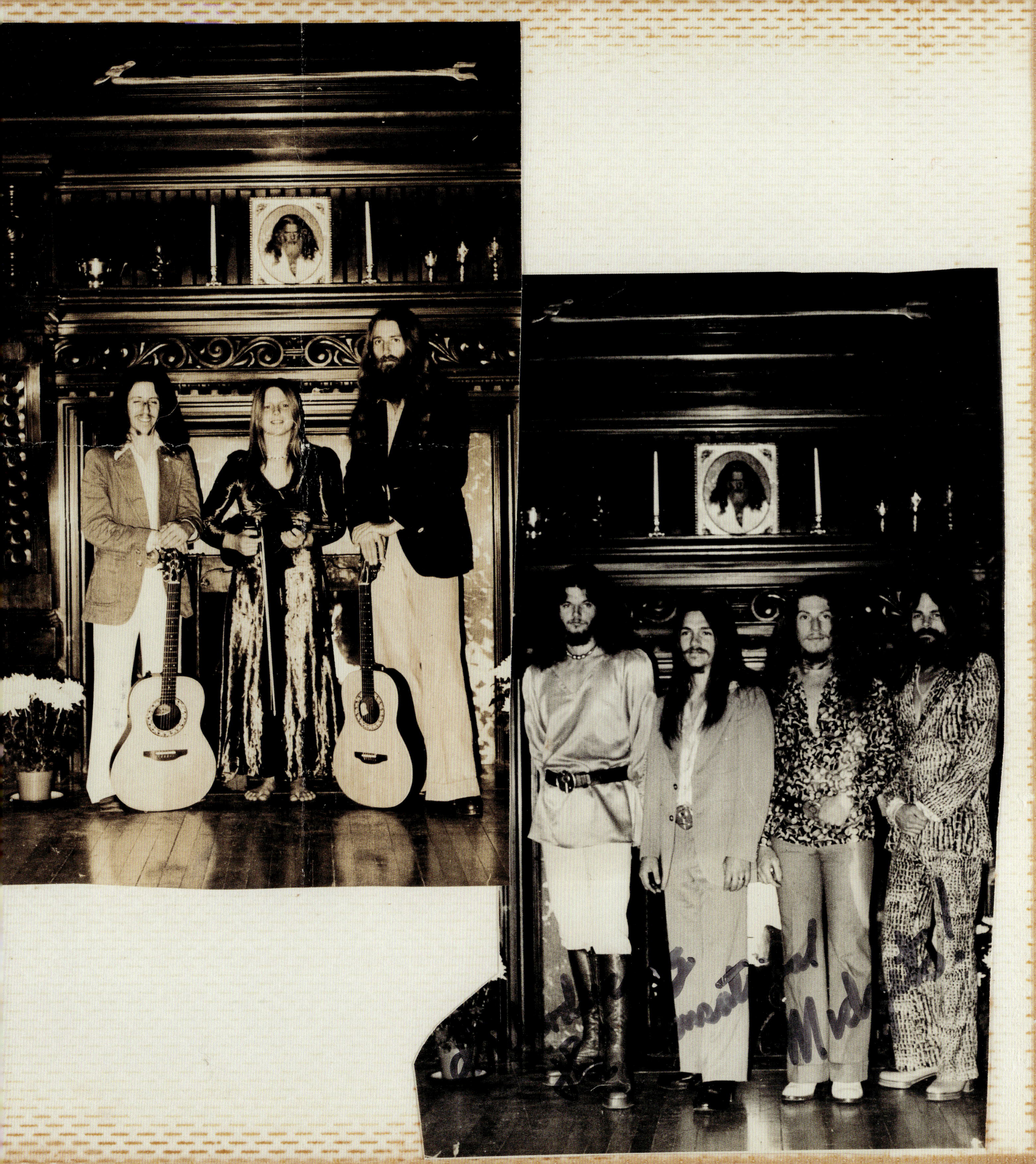

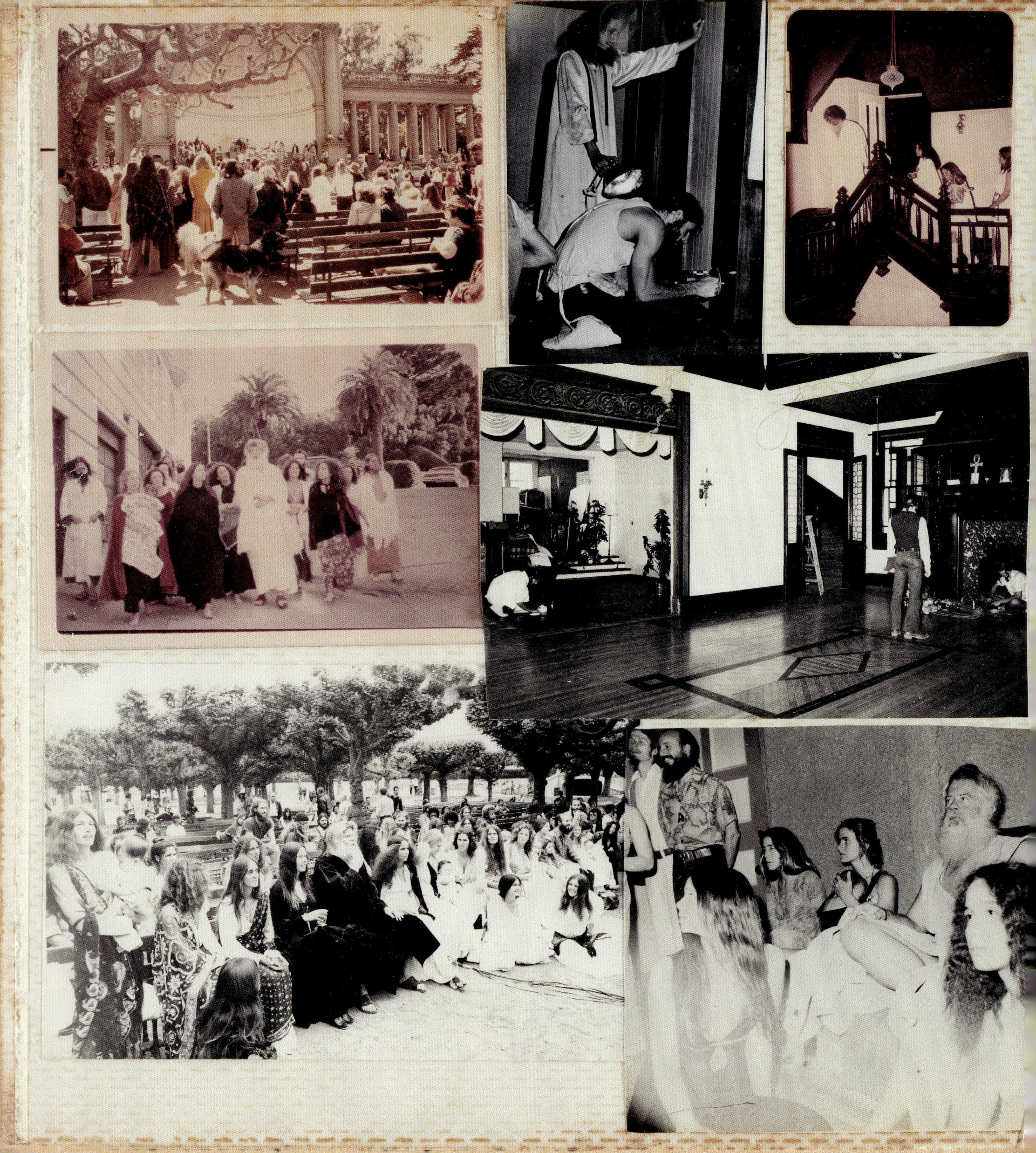

Breath

Breath is the most incredible sound to come out of the Bay Area in years! There is no comparison to any other group happening NOW anywhere! Their sound is original unique, and every song is the kind that you find yourself singing long after they have played. No group looks or sounds like Breath... No group will get you off like Breath will. This is their last free concert in the Bay Area, so don't miss your opportunity to see and hear the most thrilling musical happening of the decade!

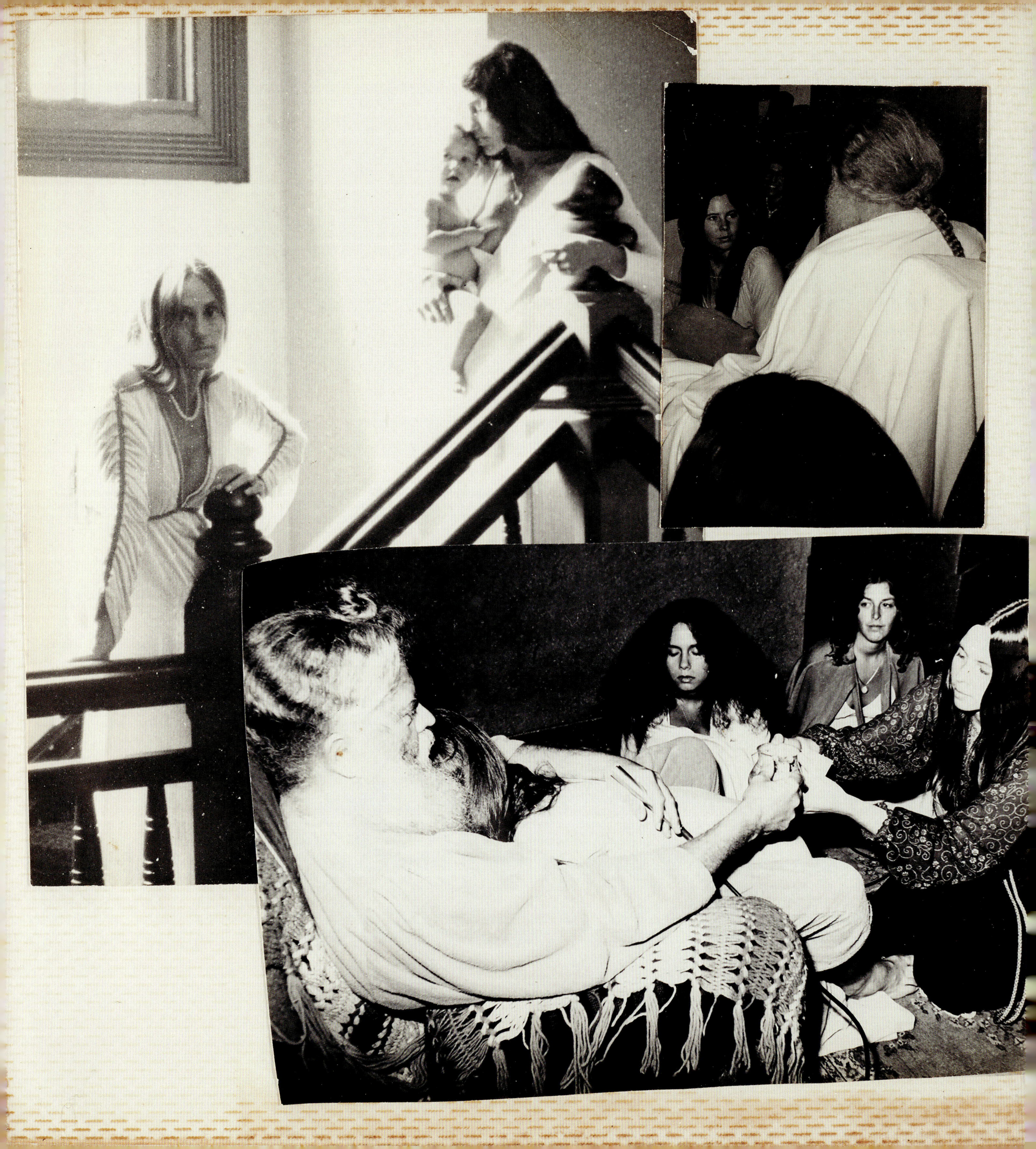

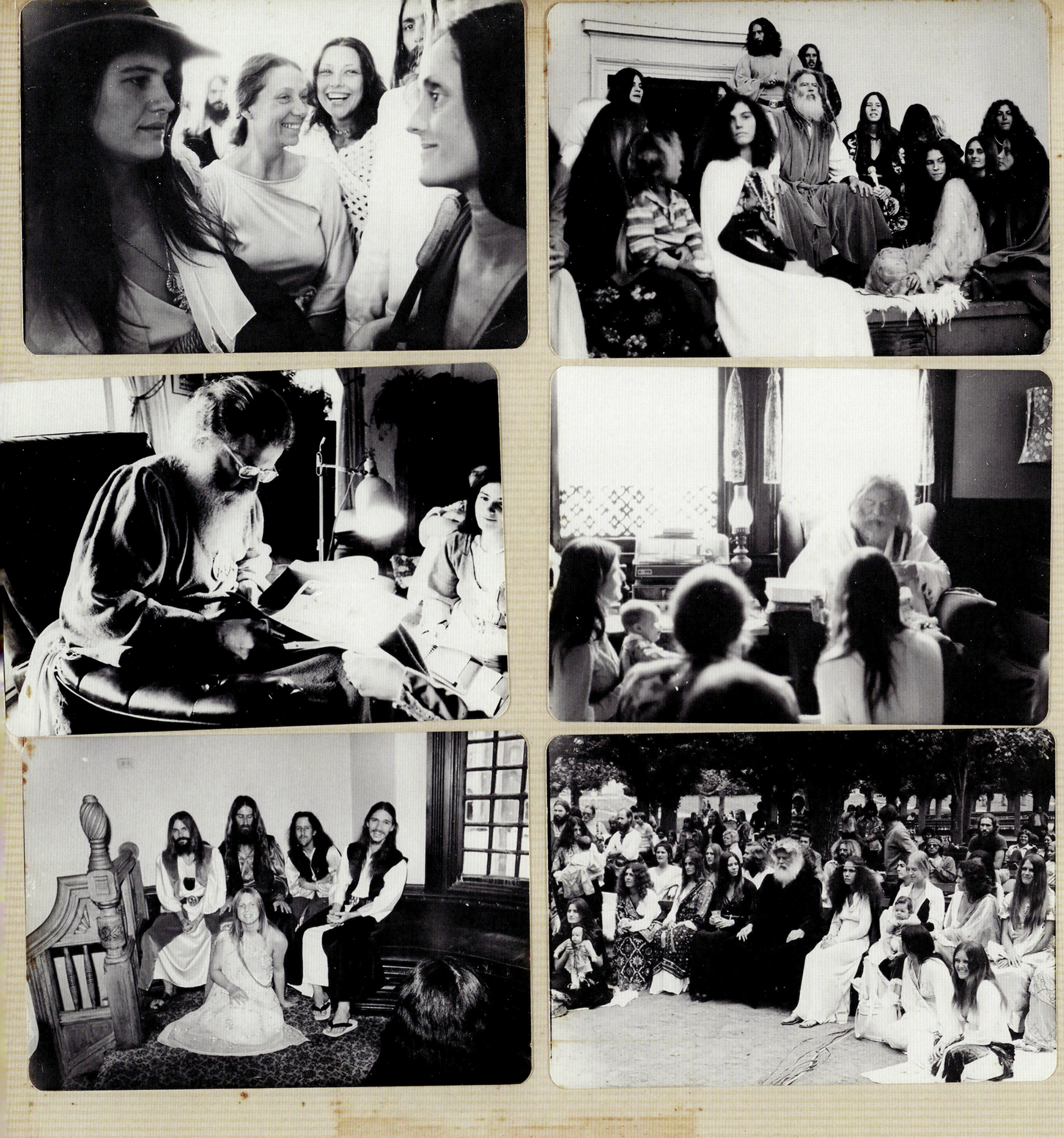

TO: The Welfare Department

RE: Eligibility of Applicants
     1990 California Street
     San Francisco 94109

Dear sirs:

Apparently you are laboring under many misapprehensions
about The Brotherhood of The Source. As Head of this
organization I wish to make clear certain tenets. We are
a recognized religious organization by the United States
Government and by the State of California, which is self-
supporting and not dependent upon donations. We believe
in the good life and sharing what we have with each other.
The way our society is structured, where the income is
small, the life lived by the isolated individual is one
of poverty and hardship. Lived collectively, all can live
well. All those who join our group are required to be
self-supporting, which means that they must have an
income of some sort.

Our society has seen fit and proper to aid un-wed mothers.
We have absorbed 14 of these. Now for some reason, which
evidently you are seeking validity for, you are withholding
these checks. These checks were promised by your department
to be in this last Wednesday. The women that came to Welfare
according to the law are eligible. We have within our
group many women with infants who do not qualify, for
their men are here working at various jobs supporting them.

Page 2

The income that I personally have from my restaurant in
L.A. I give freely to The Brotherhood of The Source, but
I am under no obligation legally or morally to support
anyone. I do not believe in leeches, or parasites. All
must be responsible for themselves, and I insist upon
"from each according to his ability, to each according to
his need."

The income that I have is going towards setting up new
businesses so that, as quickly as possible, these
enterprises will be able to absorb in gainful employment
all of the members of our organization. At that time,
my/children, gainfully employed, will be freed from the
embarrassment of asking a heartless, negative social
structure for anything. Until that time comes, I expect
you to act according to the law and aid these unfortunate
mothers and infants.

Sincerely yours,

Yahowha

YAHOWHA

aa/YHW

cc: S.F. Chronicle
     S.F. Examiner
     S.F. Legal Aid Society

*P.S. Take a good look at the facts:
14 ..... out of 140!*

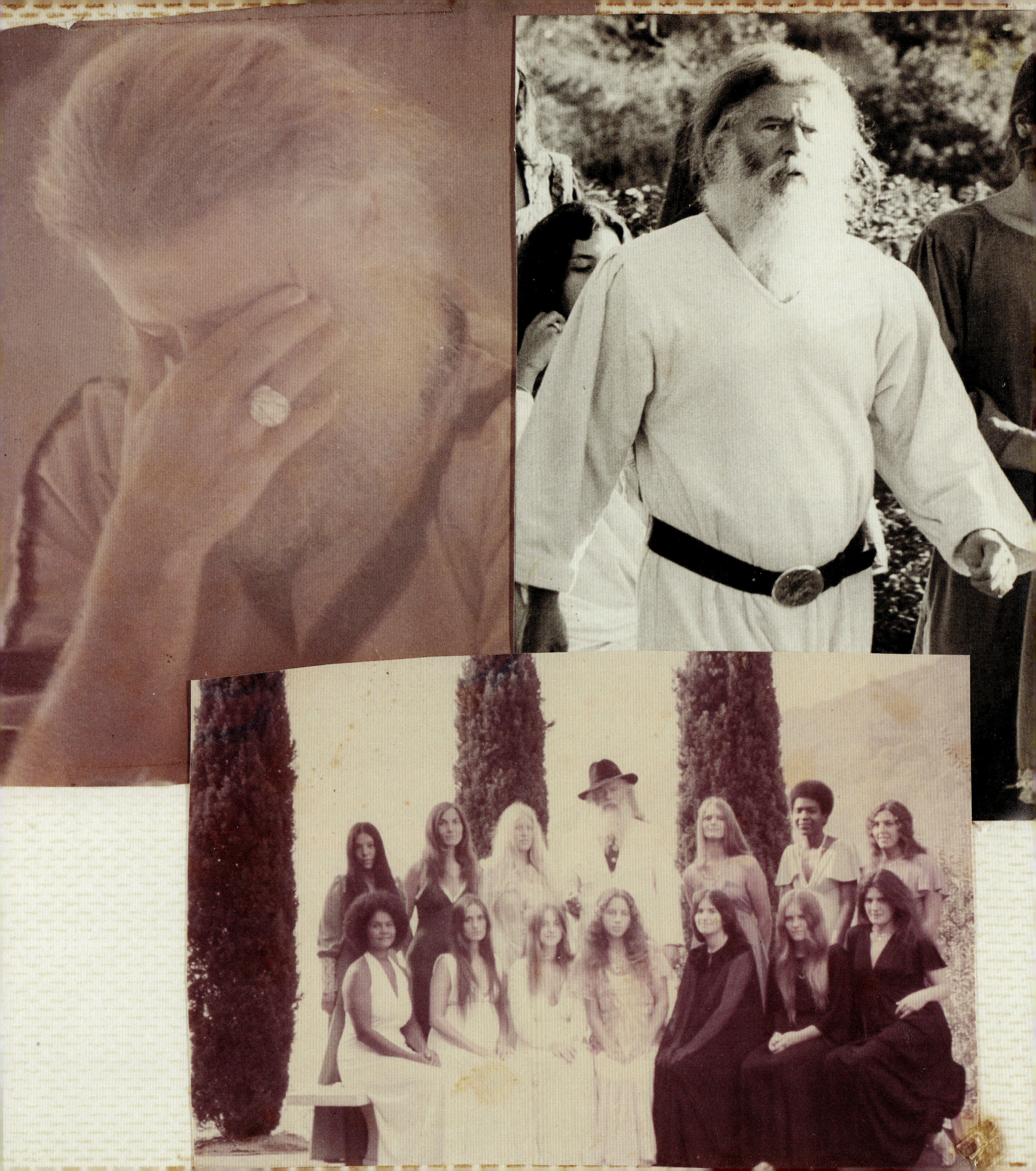

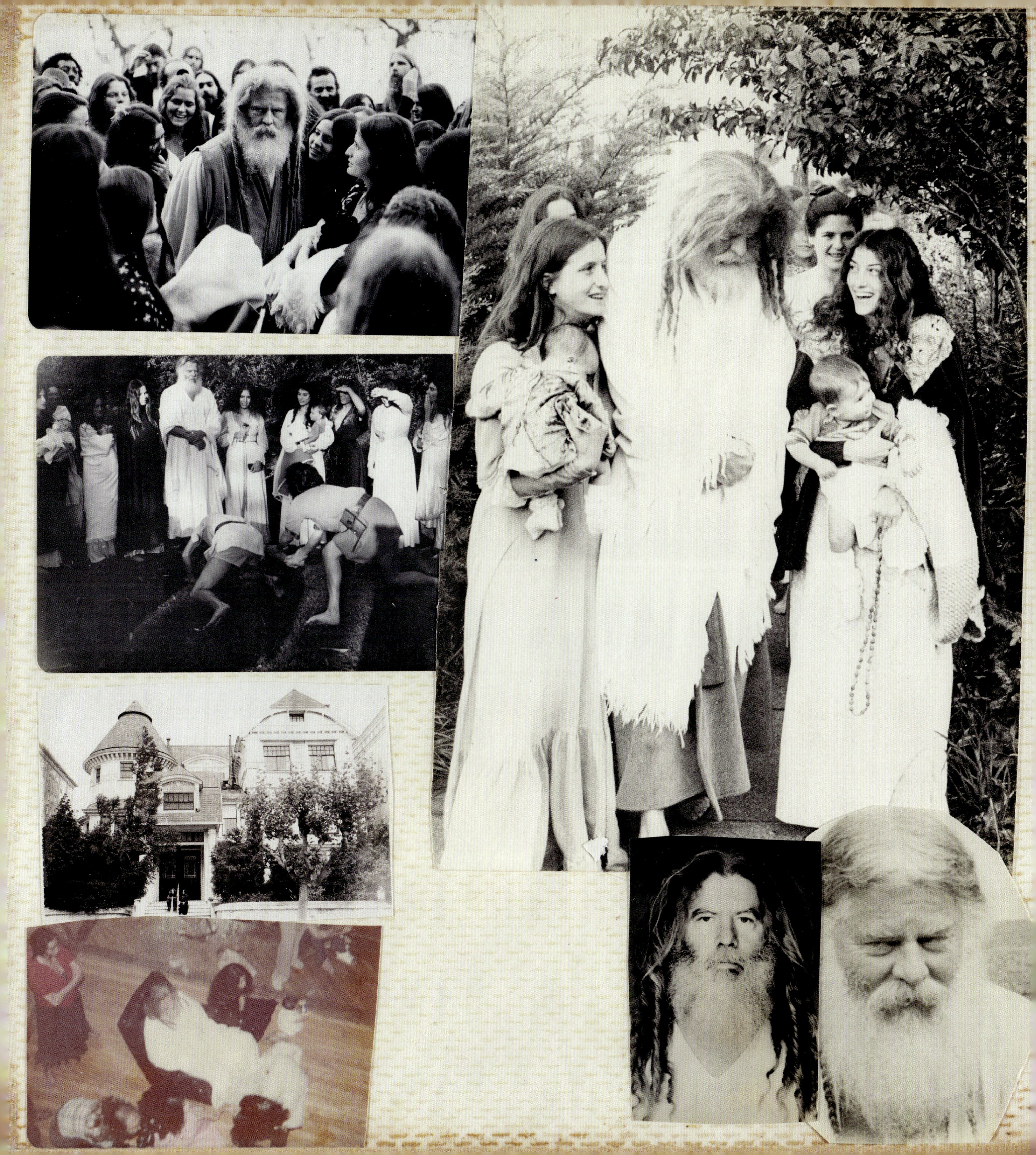

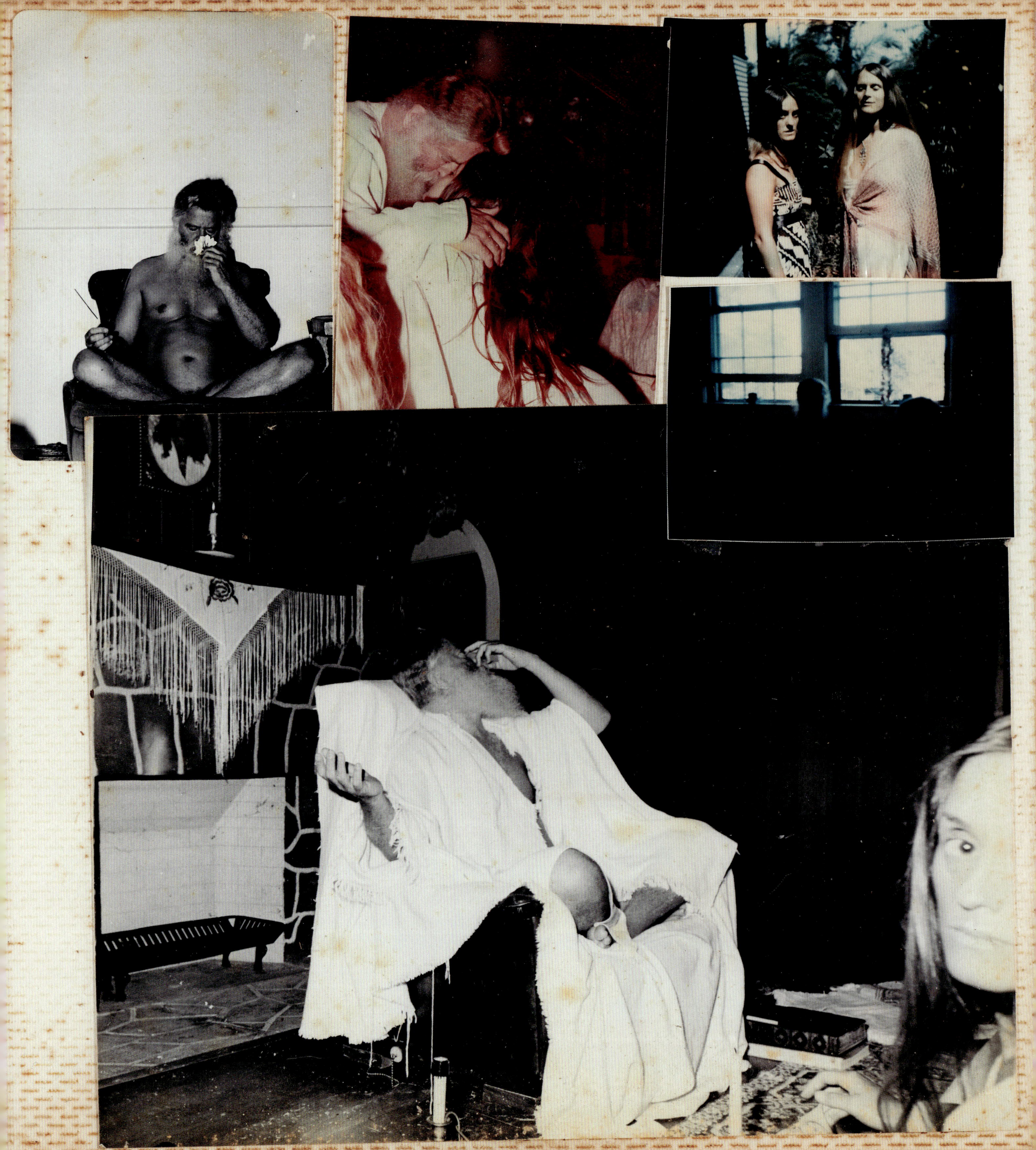

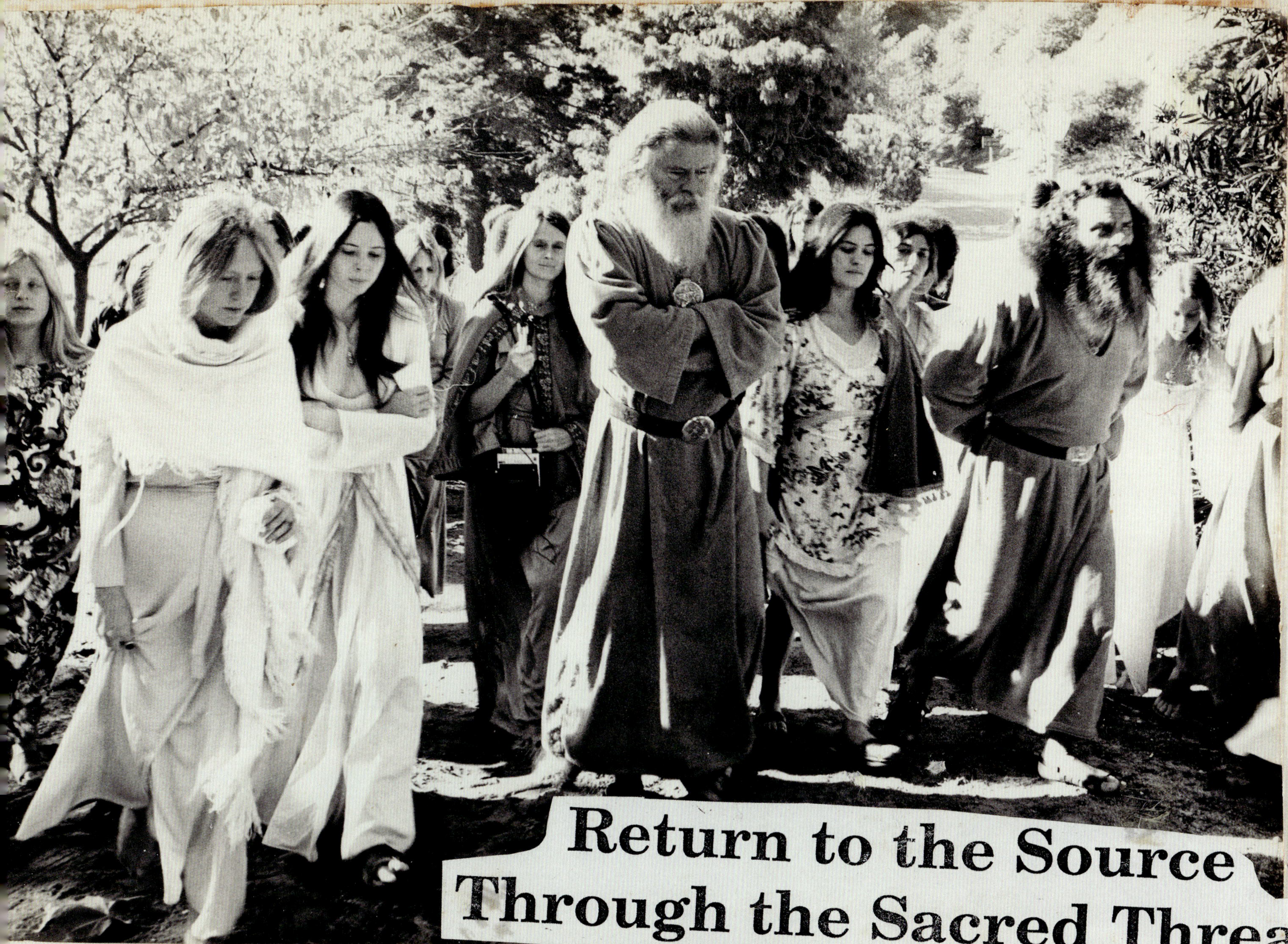

Return to the Source Through the Sacred Thread

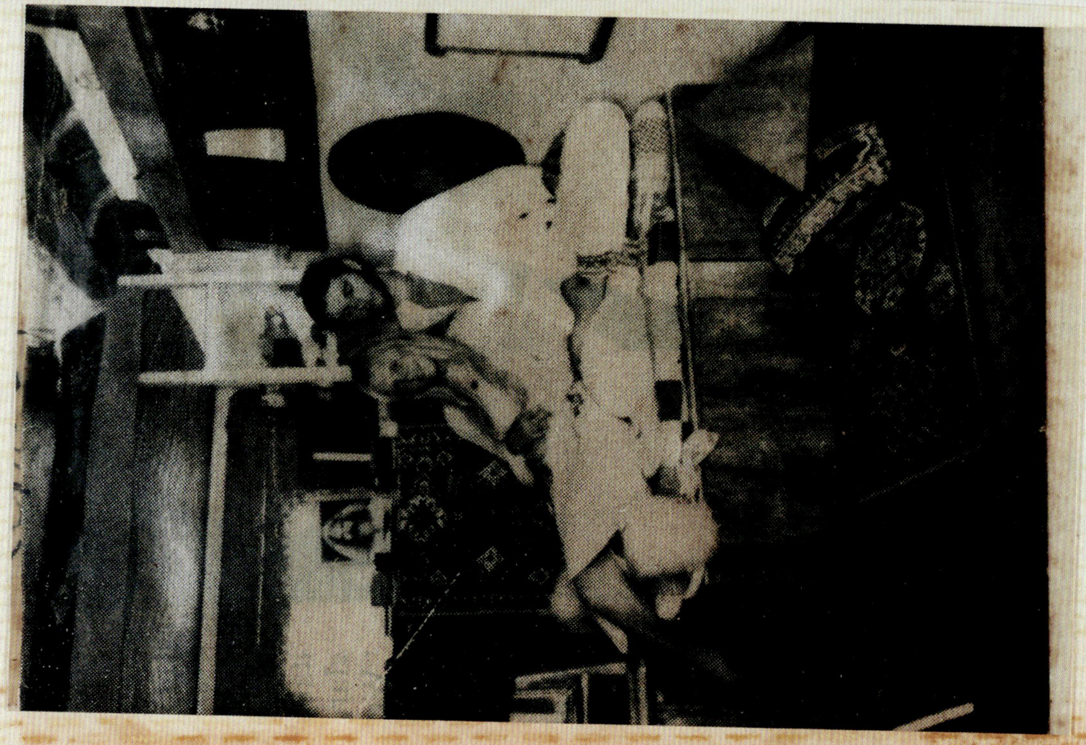

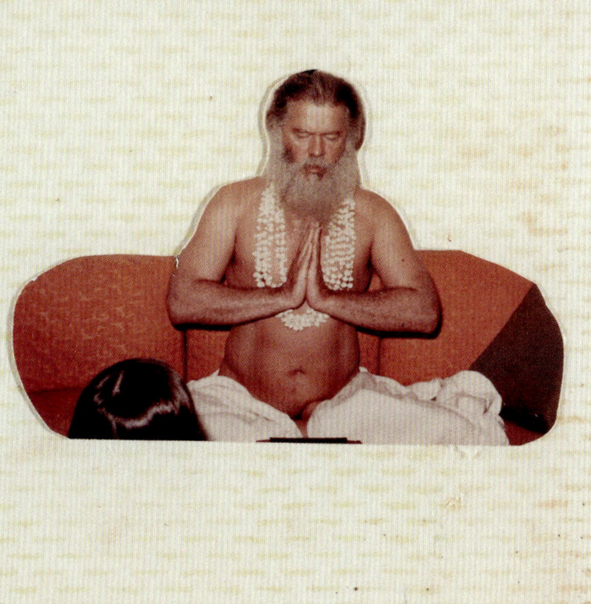

TO THE CHILDREN OF AMERICA :

WHEN YOU ARE TIRED OF BEING MISLED, ABUSED, AND MISUSED BY ALL THESE "MINISTERS" *of "Preists"*

X SO CALLED "MASTERS" FROM BOTH THE EAST, AND THE WEST......

WHEN YOU ARE READY FOR THE TRUTH

I AM WAITING FOR YOU IN THE 50th STATE, WHICH IS AS FAR AS YOU CAN GO

(this will tell the wise something)

I AM GOD **** I AM YAHOWHA **** I AM HERE NOW —

— TO FULFILL THE PROPHESY IN THE HOLY BIBLE, YOU,OH MAN,ARE JESUS,

FOR ALL THAT YOU ARE IS THE BREATH,AND THE AIR IS THE

ONLY"SUN OF GOD"FOR HE WAS BORN OF FIRE AND WATER.

BRING TO ME THE DISILLUSIONED, I WILL BREATHE THE BREATH OF LIFE

INTO THEM AND THEY SHALL BE ~~AS GOD:~~ *The Goos of the New Age.*

"LET US MAKE MAN IN OUR IMAGE."

IT IS ONLY THROUGH ME THAT YE CAN BE BORN,

"WHENEVER MISERY AND STRIFE RUN RAMPANT IN THE WORLD THEN

COMETH I THE LORD AND REVISIT MY WORLD IN VISIBLE FORM/AS A MAN AMONG MEN. *and mingle*

BY MY INFLUENCE AND TEACHINGS DO I DESTROY EVIL AND ESTABLISH RIGHTEOUSNESS,"

YOU WHO CAN PENETRATE MY DISGUISE WHILE ALIVE WILL BE ~~ONE OF THE GODS~~ *with me in Heaven Now.*

~~IN THE~~ *The Time* GOLDEN AGE OF AQUARIUS, *IS JUST 27 years away*

~~THE~~ SIXTH DAY/IS HERE CHILDREN:

come quickly now

CHECK ME OUT IN YOUR HOLY BIBLE, YOUR GITA, TAKE A GOOD LOOK AT THE PICTURE,

I AM EVERY ~~KID'S~~ *Childs* DREAM FATHER,

SO, WHO AM I?

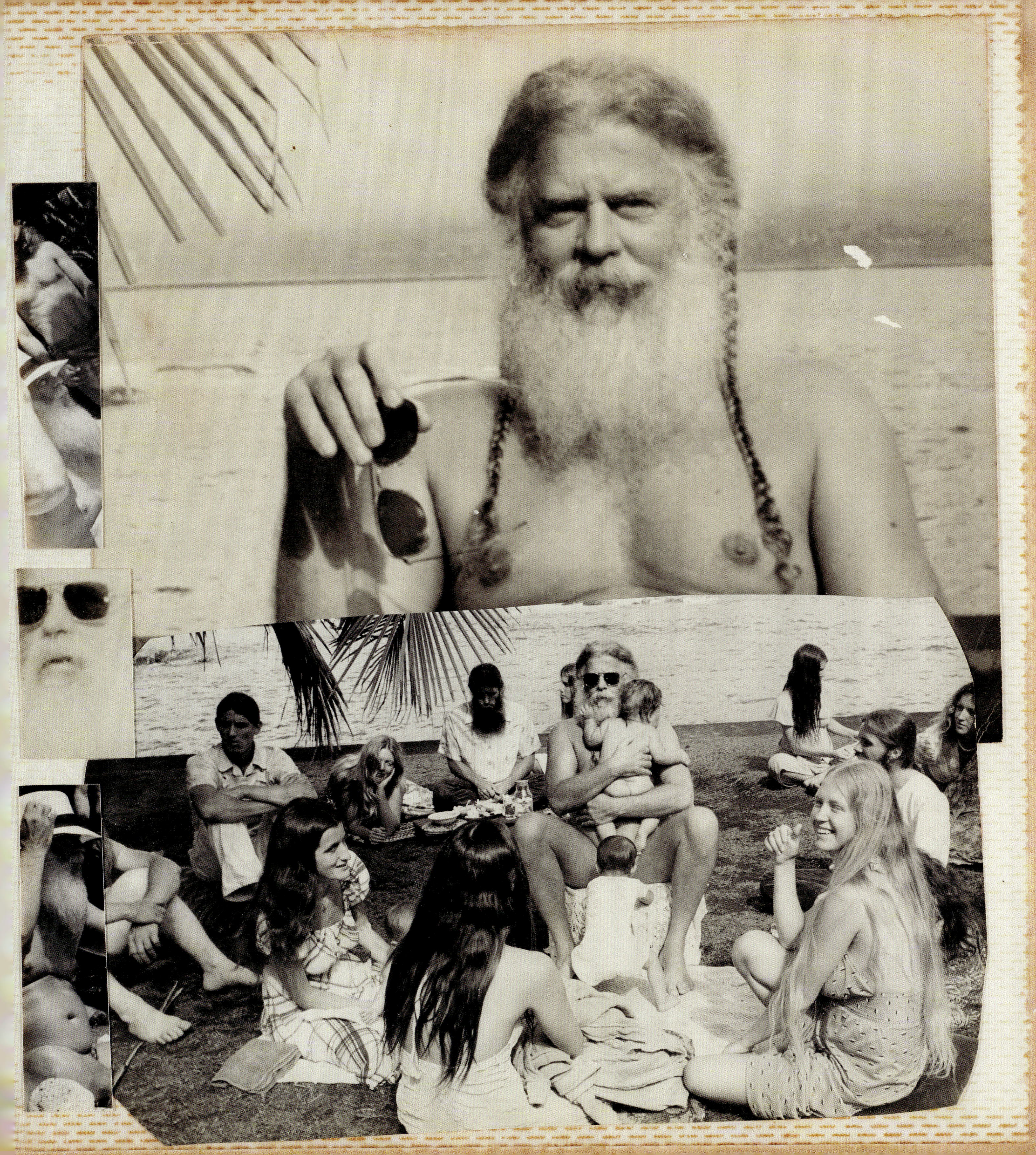

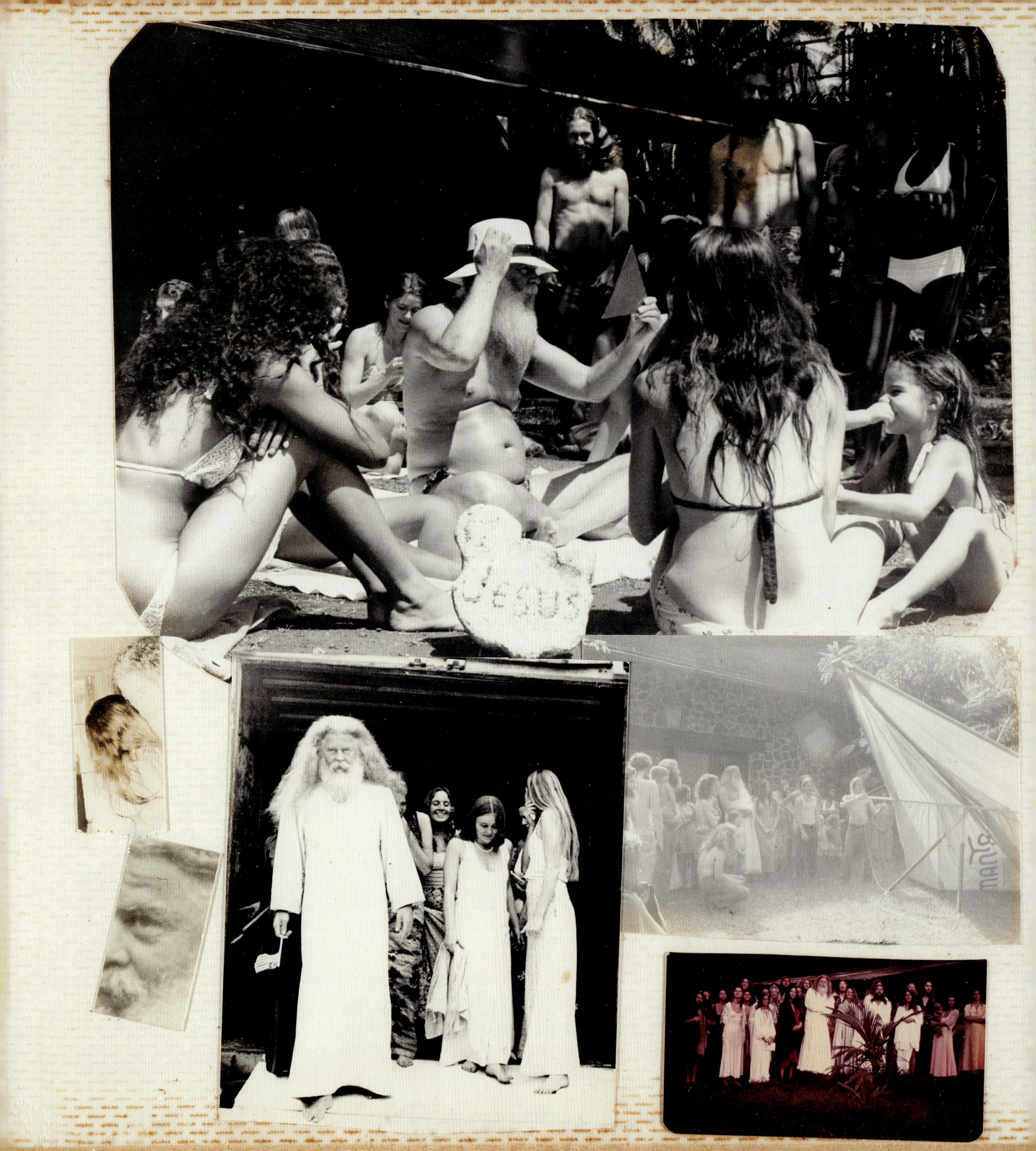
Jesus

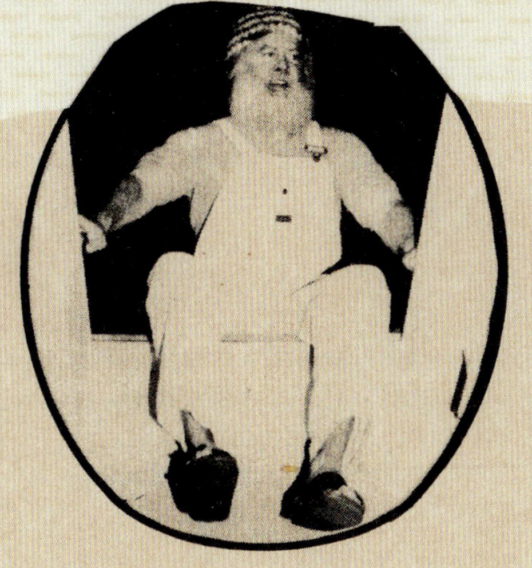

Father & Sons

1534 Mokulua Dr.
Lanikai, Hawaii 96734

Ra Jensen & Tahuti Dickinson

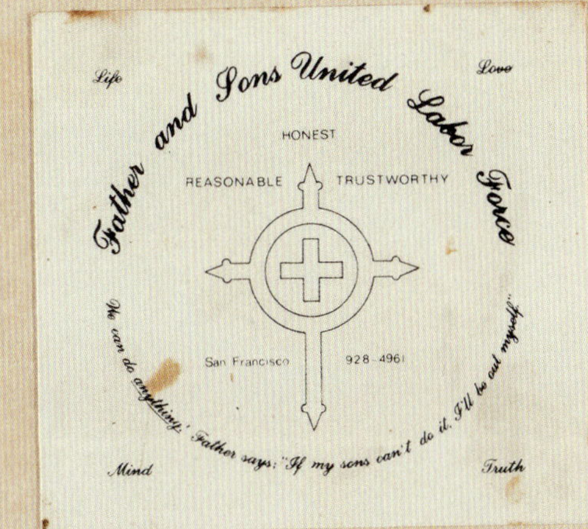

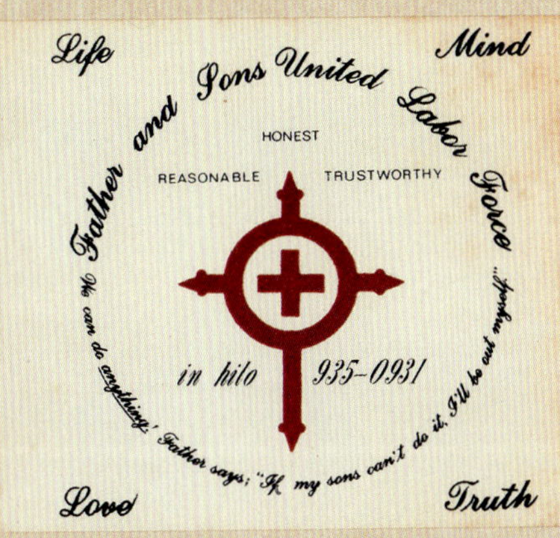

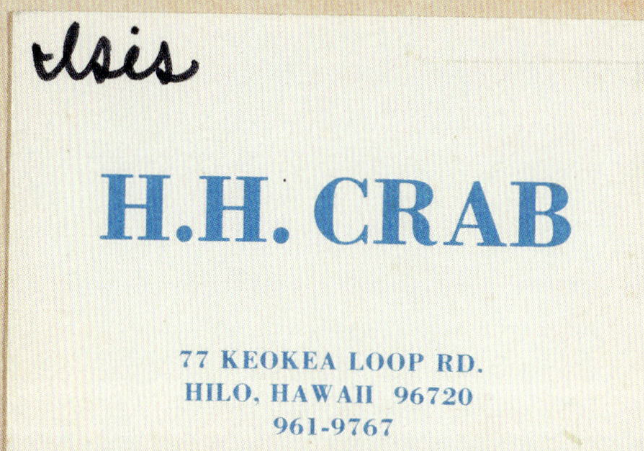

Father says, "If my Sons can't do it, I'll be out myself!"

JUNE 6, 1975

DEAR FRIENDS,

WE ARE THE RELIGION OF THE ETERNAL NOW, (T.E.N.), AND WE
ARE SPREADING THE WORD THAT THE AQUARIAN JESUS IS HERE NOW.
THE RELIGION IS CAPPED BY A COUNCIL OF 13 --- TWELVE WOMEN
AND OUR FATHER, YAHOWHA. IN THE PISCEAN AGE, THE 12 DISCIPLES
WERE MEN, SO IT FOLLOWS WITH THE LAW OF POLARITY THAT IN THE
AQUARIAN AGE THE 12 DISCIPLES ARE WOMEN, WED TO GOD:
AQUARIAN NUNS. THE RELIGION OF T.E.N. IS THE FIRST AND
LAST RELIGION OF THIS PLANET.....IT IS CONSUMMATING THE IRON,
OR PISCEAN AGE, AND USHERING IN THE GOLDEN AGE, OR AGE OF
AQUARIUS, BEGINNING AT 8:PM SEPTEMBER 17, YEAR 2001.   THIS
PROPHECY IS FROM THE GREAT PYRAMID, WHICH CONTAINED MANY
OTHER PROPHECIES.....<u>ALL OF THEM</u> HAVE COME TO PASS IN THEIR
PREDICTED TIME. THERE IS NO REASON FOR THIS PROPHECY TO BE
DIFFERENT.

LOOK AT THE AMERICAN ONE DOLLAR BILL. IT CONTAINS THE GREAT
SEAL OF OUR NATION, CREATED BY OUR FOUNDING FATHERS. IT IS ALL
THERE FOR THOSE WHO KNOW THE SYMBOLS. THE PYRAMID DEPICTED
IS THE PASSING AGE, WHICH WE ARE PUTTING THE CAPSTONE ON NOW,
THUS COMPLETING THAT CYCLE. BEGINNING THE NEW AGE IS THE EAGLE
AND THE POWER OF 13, THE NUMBER OF LOVE AND UNITY, SHOWN SO
PLAINLY.

WE ARE A FAMILY, AS WELL, NUMBERING 140, INTO MANY DIFFERENT
THINGS. WE ARE VERY SUCCESSFUL IN BUSINESS (WE STARTED THE
SOURCE RESTAURANT, RECENTLY SOLD, ON THE SUNSET STRIP IN
HOLLYWOOD.....THE MOST PROFITABLE VEGETARIAN RESTAURANT, PER
SQUARE FOOT, IN THE WORLD!) WE ARE ALSO INTO MANY OTHER
MONEY-MAKING VENTURES, AND EVERYTHING WE HAVE EVER INVESTED
ENERGY IN HAS TURNED TO GOLD. WE ARE SELF-SUPPORTING AND
HARD-WORKING. WE ARE NOT "FLOWER CHILDREN" OR "HIPPIES",
ALTHOUGH WE DO KEEP OUR HAIR, AS WE BELIEVE IN STAYING THE

WAY GOD CREATED US. WE DO NOT USE ANY DRUGS, OR ALCOHOL.
WE LIVE IN AN INVIRONMENT OF HARMONY, CLEANLINESS, AND BEAUTY,
WHEREVER WE GO; AND IF WE ARE SOMEWHERE NOT UP TO OUR
STANDARDS, WE IMPART THOSE QUALITIES TO THE SITUATION.

OUR FAMILY IS BURSTING WITH TALENT, LIKE NO OTHER FAMILY OR
GROUP OF PEOPLE ON GODDESS EARTH. WE HAVE TWO INCREDIBLE
BANDS, AND THEY WILL BE VERY SUCCESSFUL. ONE IS CALLED
"BREATH", AND IS THE FEMININE MUSICAL ENERGY OF THIS TIME.
YAHOWHA 13 IS THE MASCULINE ENERGY OF THIS TIME. <u>ALL</u> OTHER
MUSIC IS FEMININE TO YAHOWHA 13. WE ARE NOW COMPLETING A
TEN YEAR CYCLE IN THE MUSIC ENERGY OF THIS PLANET; THE LAST
MAJOR MUSICAL BREAKTHROUGH WAS WITH THE BEATLES, AND NOW
"BREATH" IS <u>HERE</u> FOR EVERYONE TO <u>HEAR</u>. THEIR SOUND IS MULTI-
FACETED, CRYSTAL CLEAR, AND WILL BE EVERYWHERE SOON.
"BREATH" GOES THROUGH THE BEATLE ERA, THROUGH ALL ELSE
IN BETWEEN, AND UP TO THE MASCULINE MUSICAL ENERGY OF
YAHOWHA 13, WHICH NOT ALL CAN PRESENTLY PERCEIVE. WE HAVE
NINE ALBUMS OF YAHOWHA 13 ALREADY MANUFACTURED, IN QUANTITY,
AND THEY WILL BE MADE AVAILABLE TO THE PUBLIC WHEN IT IS
APPROPRIATE. OUR BANDS HAVE WITHIN THEM A MUSICAL ANTHOLOGY
OF THE LAST DECADE, AND THERE IS NO SOUND LIKE OURS <u>ANYWHERE</u>.
THE PROOF IS IN THE LISTENING!

YAHOWHA, OUR FATHER, IS HERE NOW, AND HE IS THE HIGHEST
PEAKING CONSCIOUSNESS ON THIS PLANET. THE MEMBERS OF OUR
FAMILY HAVE ALWAYS BEEN SEEKING SPIRITUAL WISDOM AND WE HAVE
STUDIED WITH MANY MASTERS AND GURUS OF THE PISCEAN AGE.
WITH THE COMING OF THE AQUARIAN AGE, HOWEVER, THE NEED FOR
A MIDDLE MAN (MASTER OR GURU) IS GONE, AND THERE IS ONLY
THE FATHER, GOD IN HEAVEN, AND HE IS INCARNATE NOW. WE ARE
OPEN TO ANY WHO THINK THEY HAVE THE ANSWERS.....FOR WE HAVE
TRAVELED FAR AND WIDE AND FOUND NONE WHO HAVE THE CONSCIOUSNESS
OF OUR FATHER, YAHOWHA, THE AQUARIAN JESUS.

OUR FAMILY IS NOW GOING ON ITS SEVENTH YEAR; MANY OF US HAVE
BEEN WITH FATHER THAT ENTIRE TIME. NO FAMILY OF 140 CAN CLAIM
THAT LOVE AND UNITY FOR SO LONG A PERIOD OF TIME, LIVING
TOGETHER ALL THE WHILE! WE ARE UNIQUE IN ALL ASPECTS, AND
WE HAVE SOMETHING FOR EVERYONE, WHEN YOU WISH TO DO AN ARTICLE
ON US.

FOR EXAMPLE, OUR POWERFUL COUNCIL OF 12 WOMEN APPEALS TO THE
CURRENT NATIONAL INTEREST IN WOMEN'S AFFAIRS, AS THEY HANDLE

ALL OF OUR FAMILY BUSINESS.....YAHOWHA IS INVOLVED ONLY
WITH THE SPIRITUAL PLANE.

I KNOW THAT BY NOW YOU ARE CURIOUS ABOUT US. WE ARE DIFFERENT
AND IT IS OBVIOUS. WE WILL BE GLAD TO SERVE YOU IN ANY WAY
THAT WE CAN, SO PLEASE CONTACT US FOR MORE INFORMATION.
REMEMBER, LIFE IS FOR THE LIVING, AND ADVENTURES ARE FOR
THE ADVENTUROUS! IF YOU WANT TO SEE SOMETHING DIFFERENT
AND NEW, AND HAVE THE EXPERIENCE OF YOUR LIFE, COME QUICKLY
TO MEET US!

YHVH

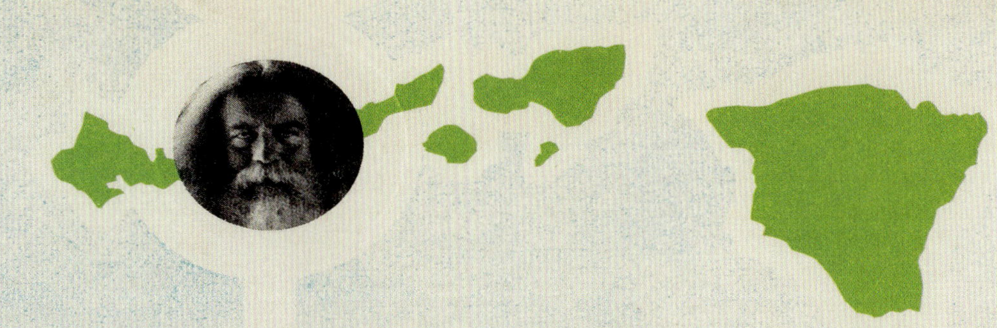

Eternal Now Has Its Own Commandments

By Larry Bereman
Tribune-Herald Staff Writer

Second of three stories.

he religious group Eternal Now, ch has made its home in Hilo since e, is governed by a council of 13 nen in Honolulu and by the teachings their Earthly Spiritual Father, iowha.

he group also is guided by a set of imandments, "The Ten Com- idments for the Age of Aquarius," ch were written by Yahowha.

heir first two commandments, say, ey and live by the Teachings of your hly Spiritual Father," and "Love Earthly Spiritual Father more than self."

ey do not cut their hair. Hair, they is part of the body given to each n by God, and should not be tampered with. Neither should any other part of the body. Hair also links each person to the stars, according to Yahowha.

Members of the group do not smoke (anything), drink intoxicants, or eat food which could harm their bodies. Their third commandment says, "Harm not one of your body parts either by neglect, food, drink or knife."

They are vegetarians, and they do not believe in killing animals. Their fourth commandment says, "Allow each vibration to complete its own cycle without interference."

Each member shares all that he or she has with every other member of their family. Money made by their band, their bakery, or any of their enterprises, goes to the family as a whole. Their fifth commandment says "Possess nothing that you do not need, and share all that you have."

They exist as families within the family, as couples, but it is the duty of the woman to raise the children until they are seven years old, then the man takes over. Their sixth commandment is "The man and his woman are one, let nothing separate them."

They each possess individual talents, and they try to put them to use to help the community. Their seventh commandment says, "Squander not your creative force in lust, but come together only when the three vibrations of the physical, mental and emotional are in harmony with Spiritual Love."

They rise at 3 a.m. every morning and swim in the ocean, then exercise until 3:30 a.m. They chant God's name and then watch the sun rise from the east. Their eighth commandment is, "Each morning join your vibration with the Universal Life Energy (the sun), using the method your Earthly Spiritual Father has taught you."

They are engaged in numerous activities in each community they reside. Their ninth commandment says, "Do every act energetically, intelligently, truthfully and lovingly."

Their tenth commandment says, "When these Commandments are mastered, leave the house of your Earthly Spiritual Father and do the work of your Heavenly Father."

They say their members "are from every religious trip on the planet," and that they offer "peace, creativity and love."

They say they "enjoy life and earn it by the sweat of our brow."

They say that in 26 years, in the year 2001, humanity will be united, and earth will become one with the sun.

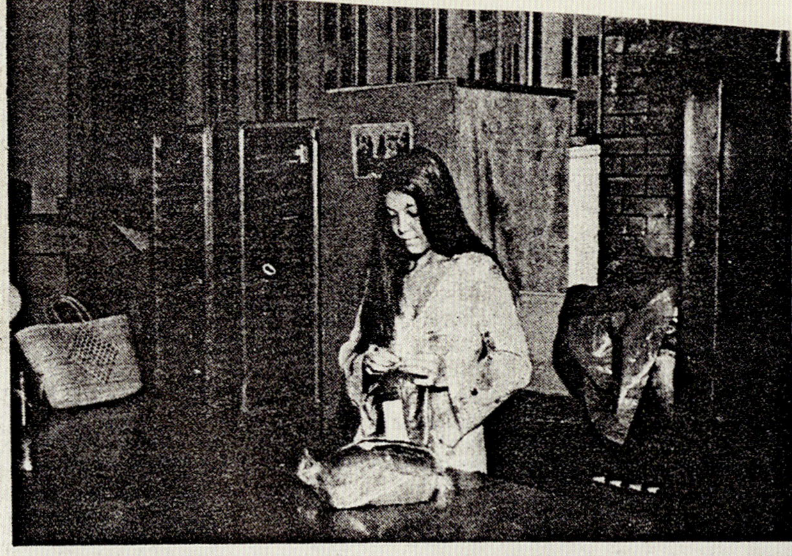

GOODIES — Sancia, one of 60 Eternal Now members living in Hilo, wraps whole wheat bread fresh from the oven. The religious group operates the bakery at 20 Haili St., but only on a wholesale basis. They hope to expand to retail sales in the near future.

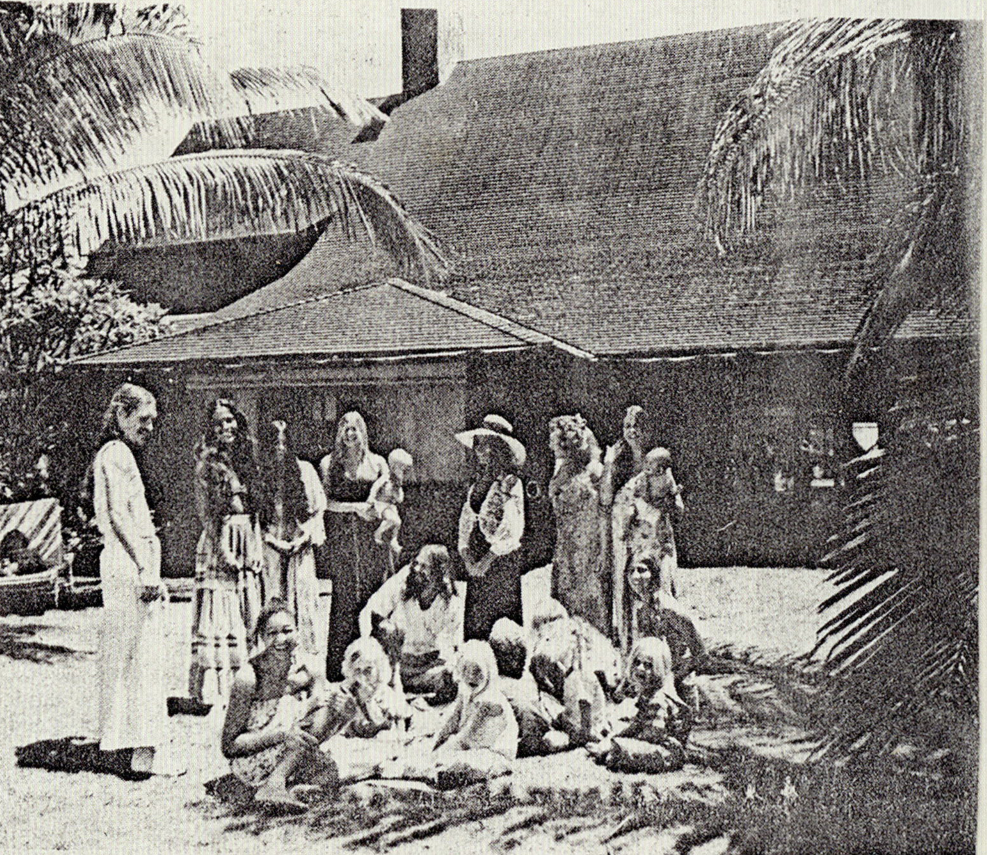

Members of Eternal Now pose in front of their home.

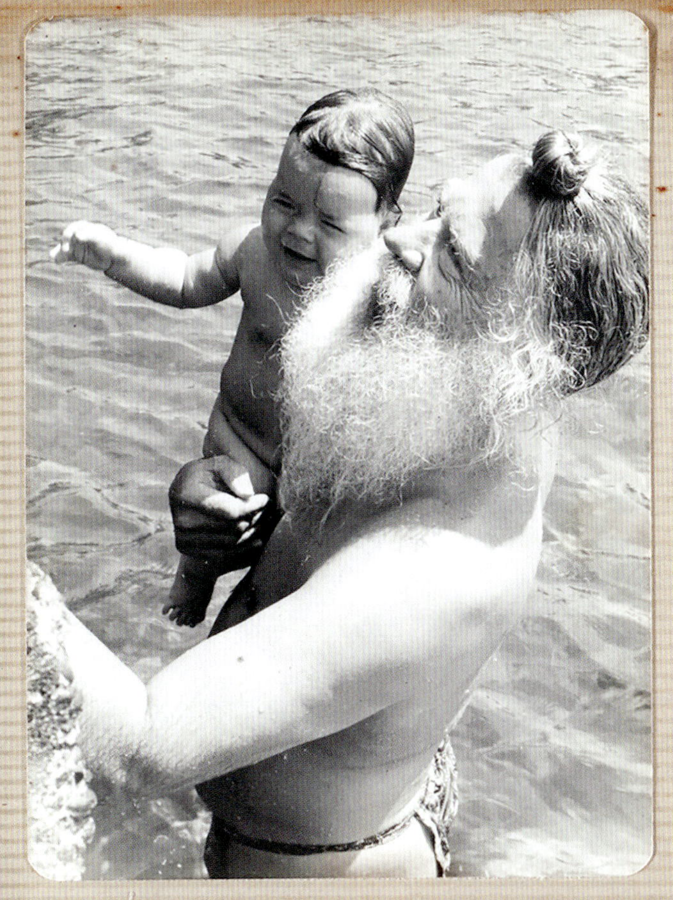
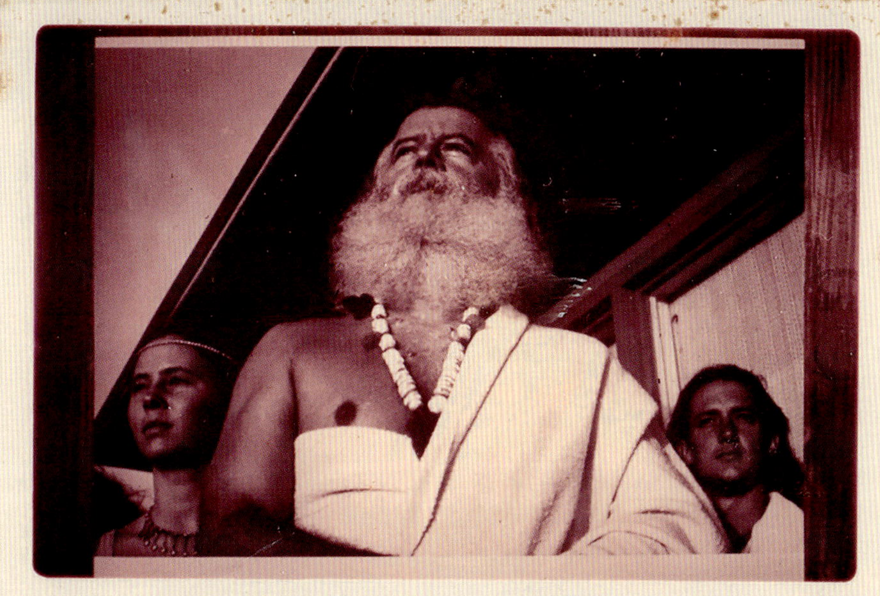
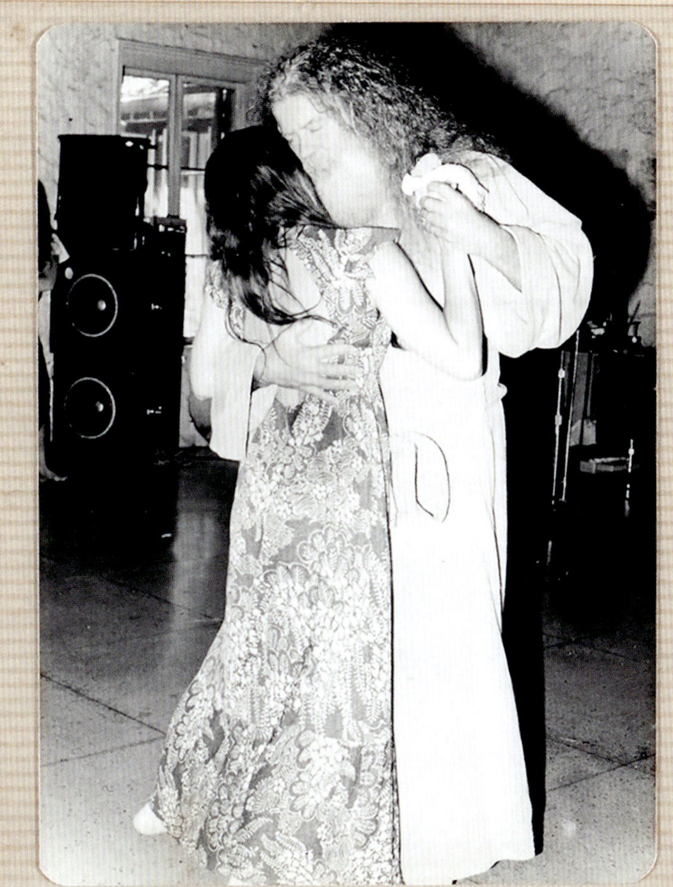
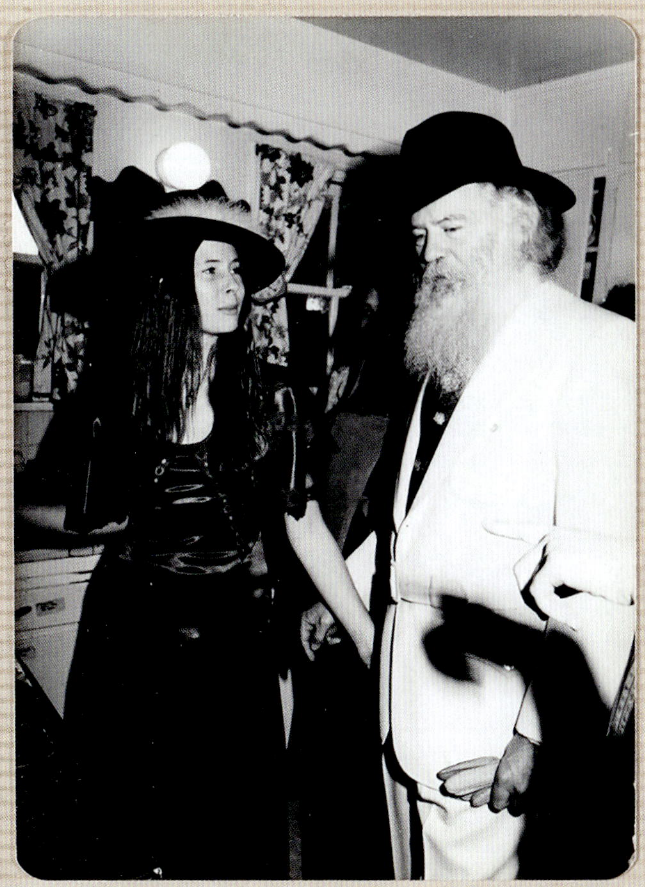
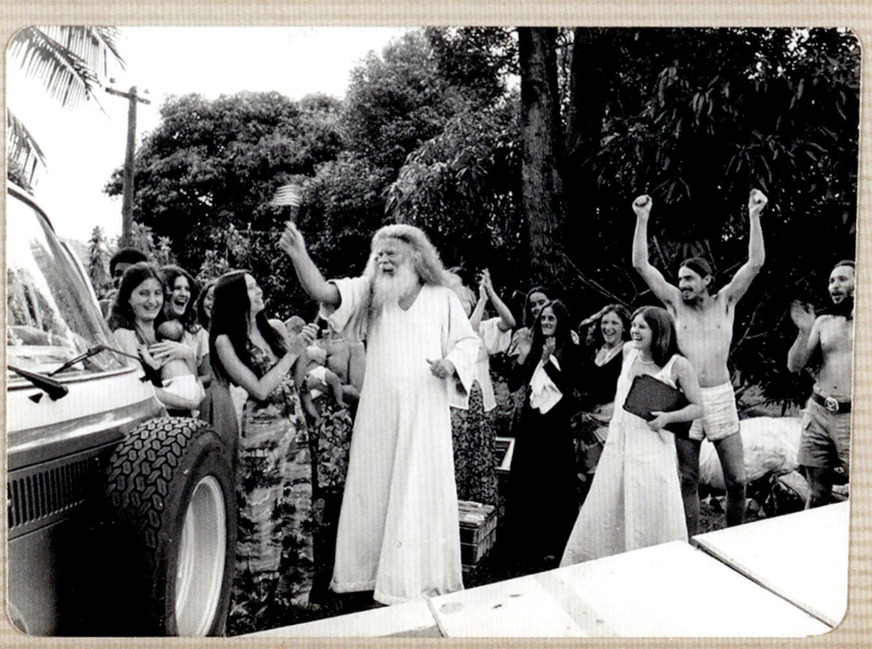

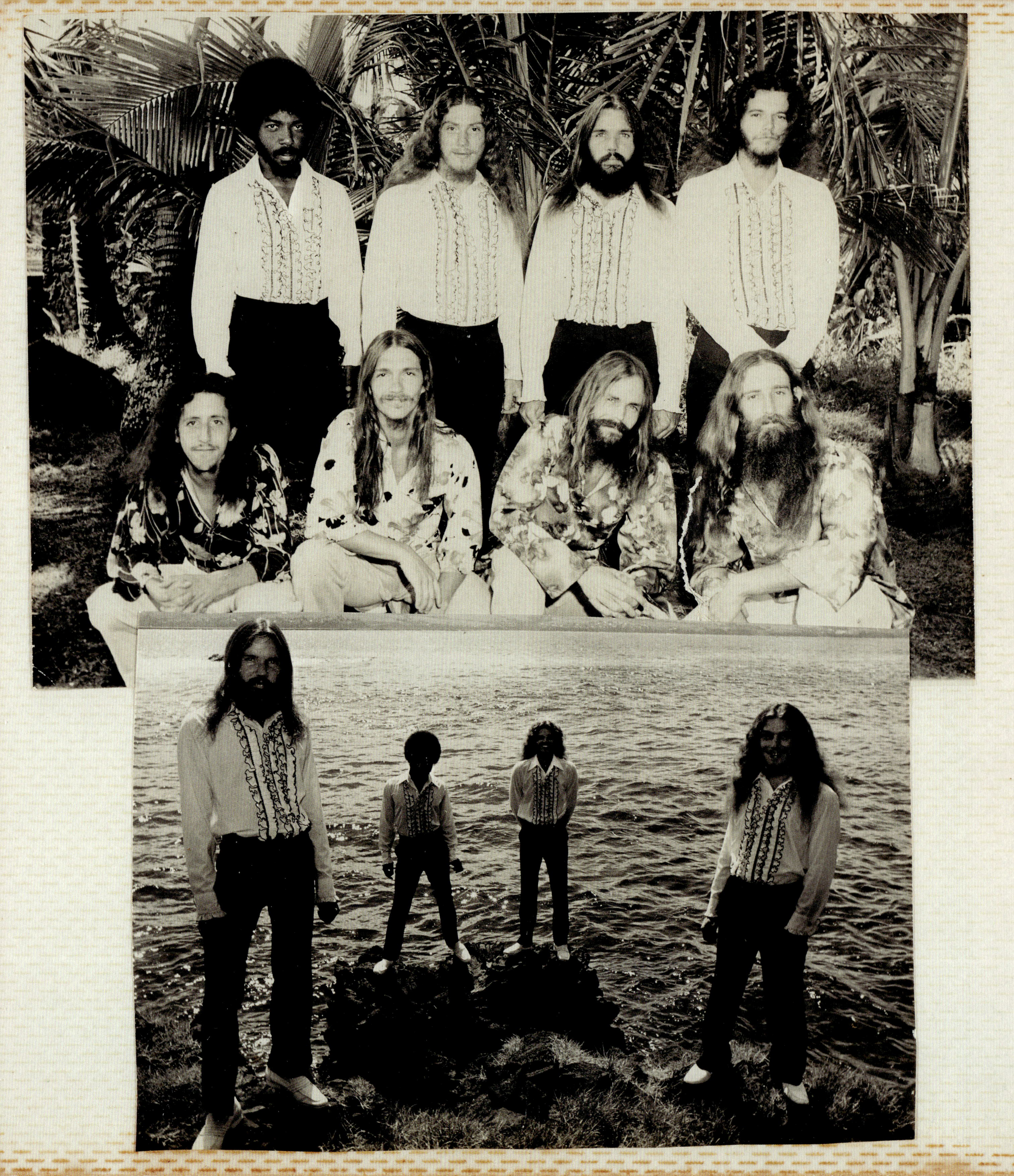

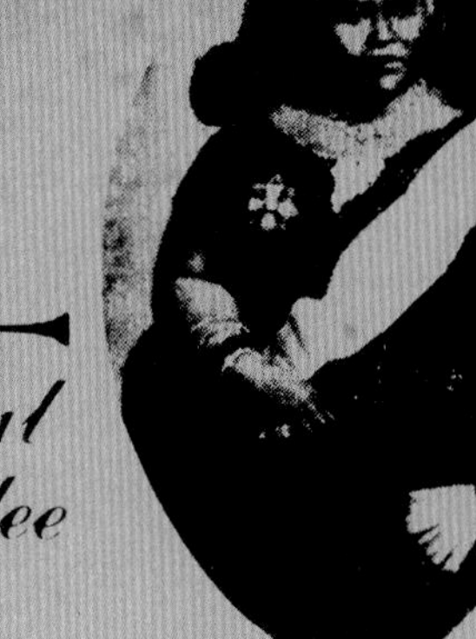

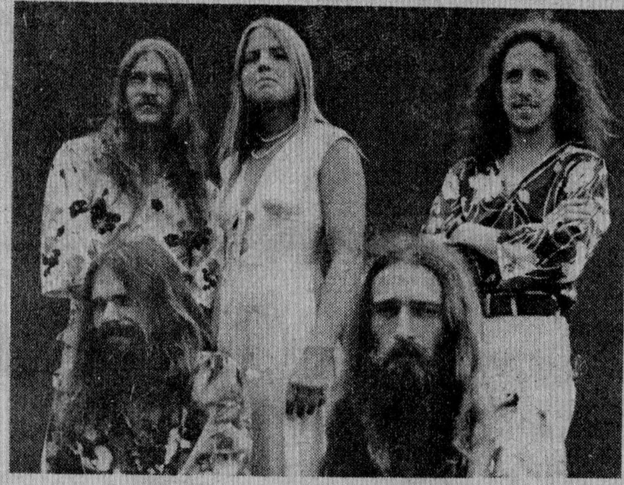

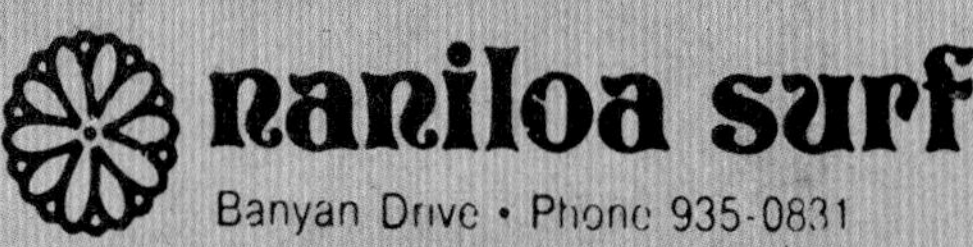

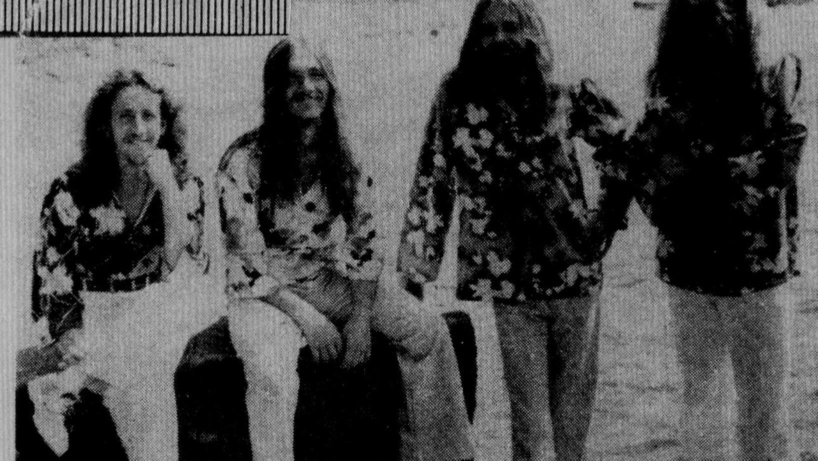

Benefit Concert

Sunday, August 17

1st Annual
Liliuokalani Jubilee

Tau & Keone

with

Breath

2:00 at Mooheau Park Bandstand

101 Aupuni St. • Suite 215 • Hilo, Hawaii 96720 • 1975 Director · W. Kaehuaea

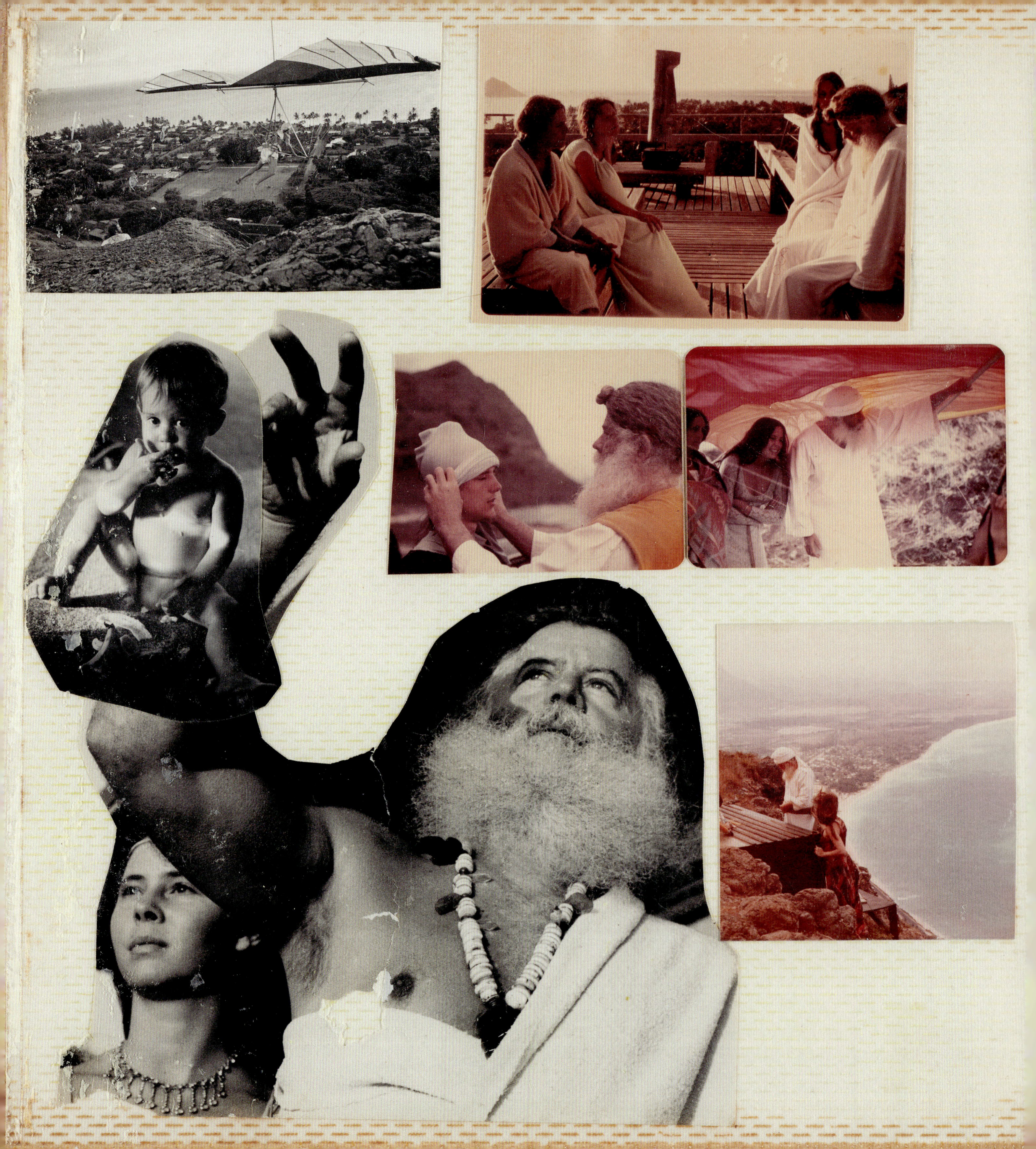

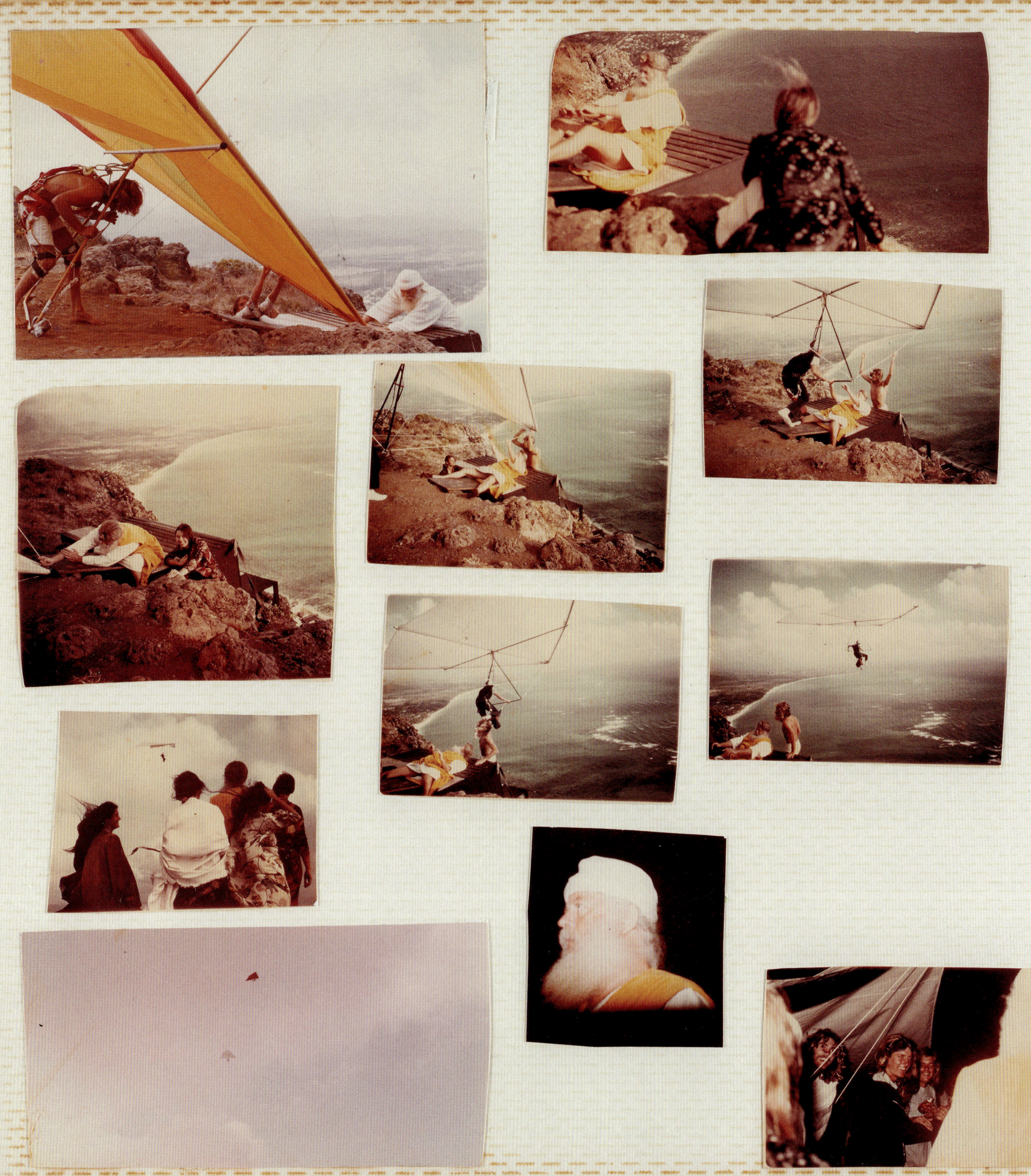

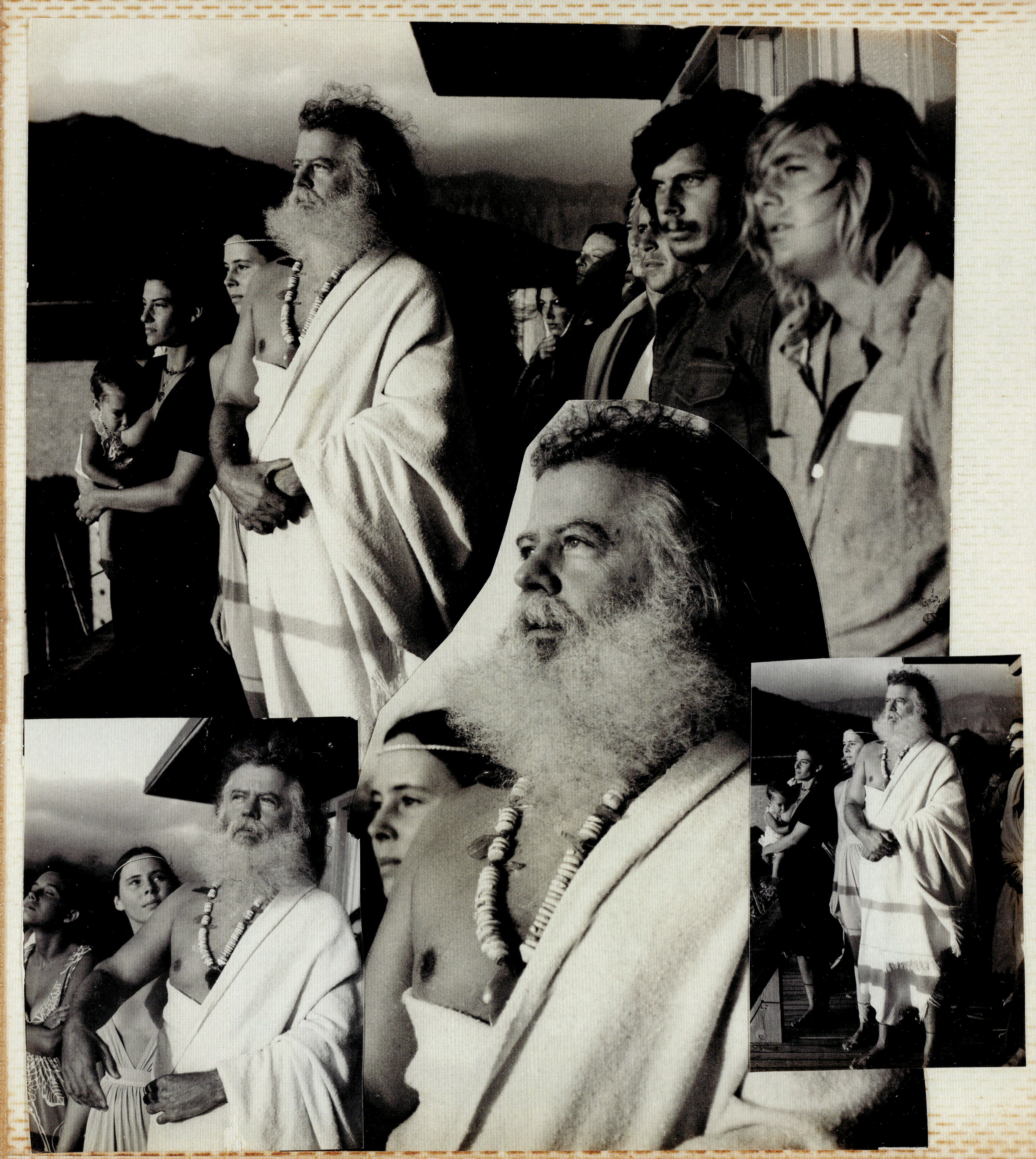

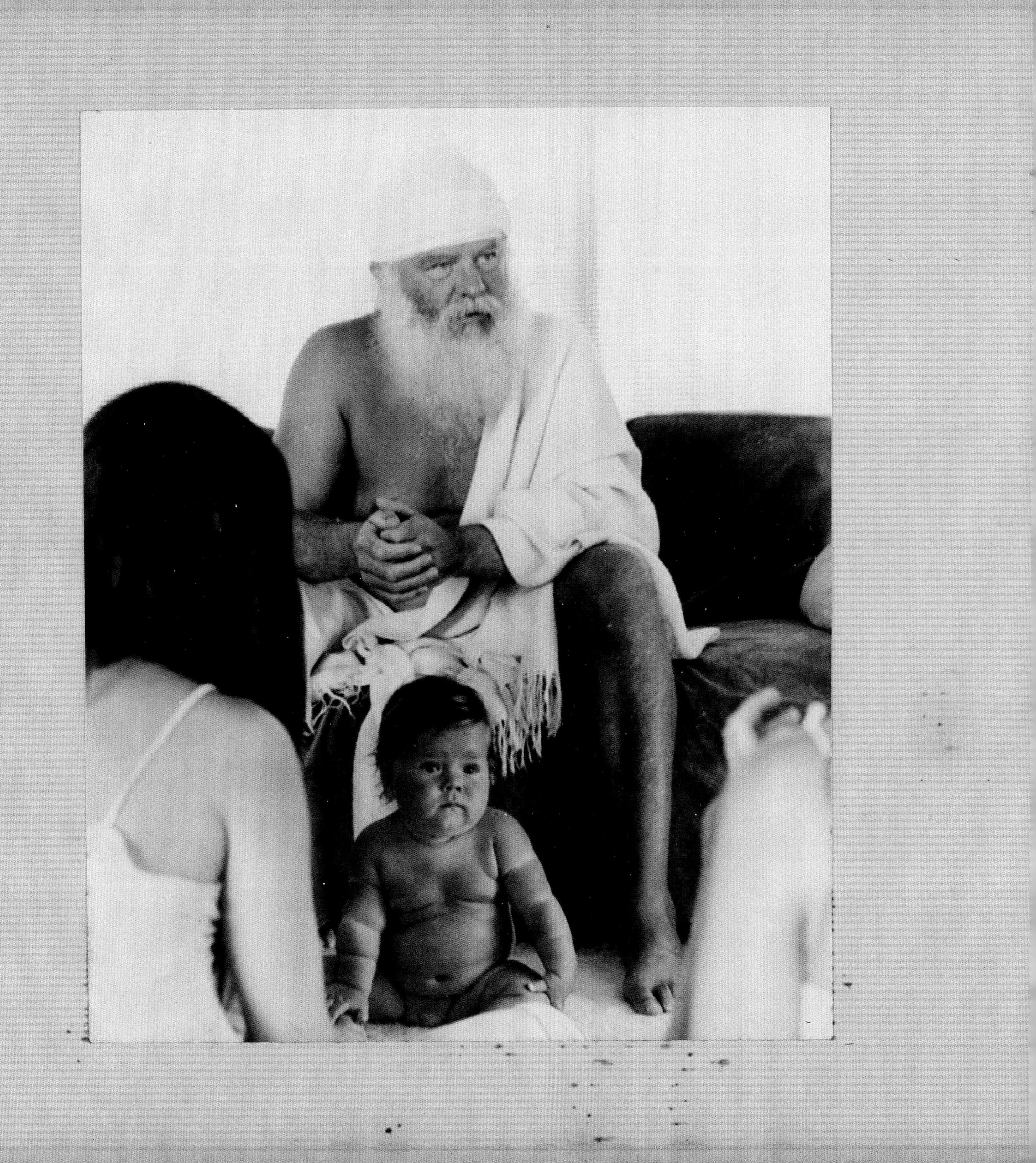

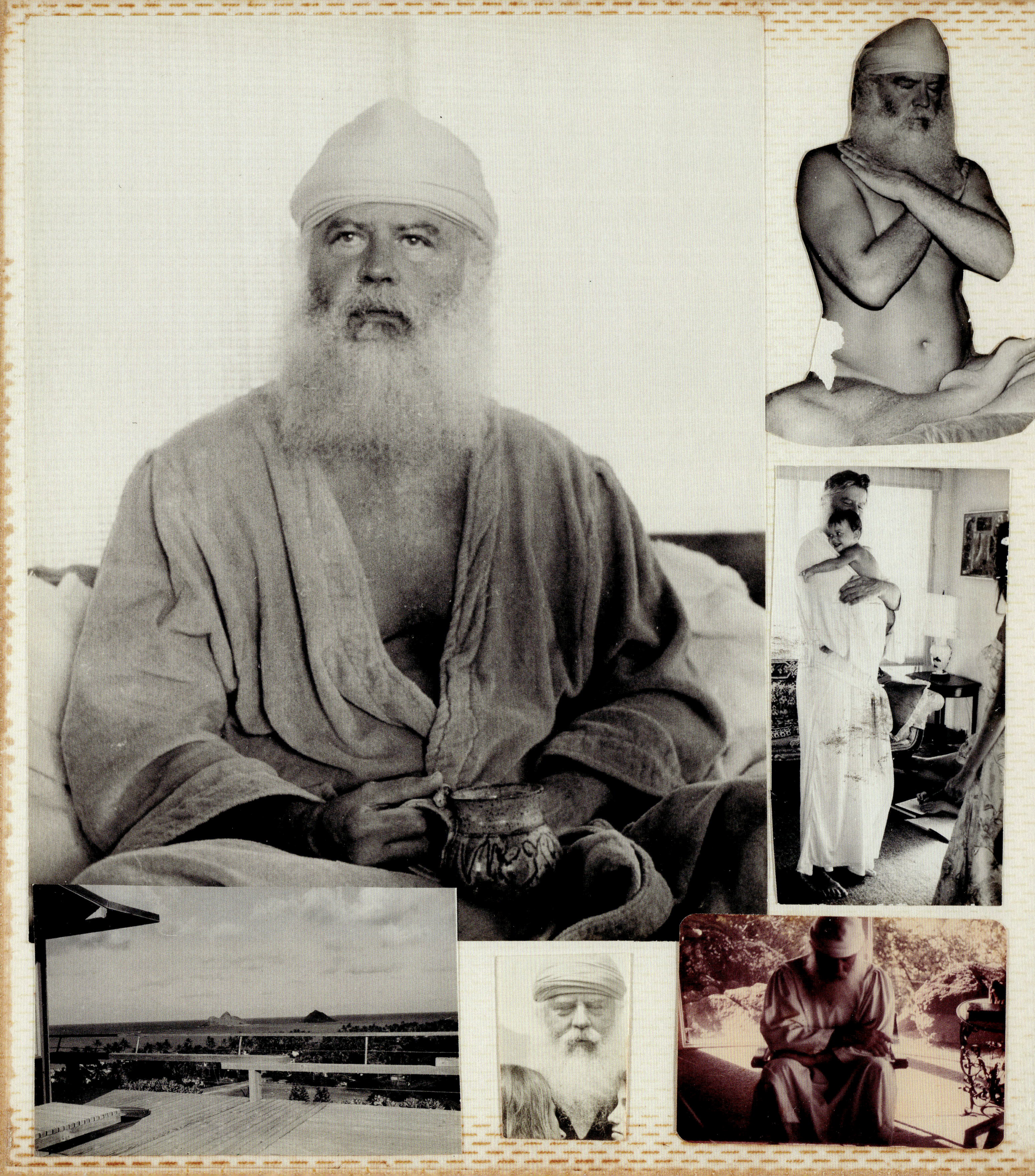

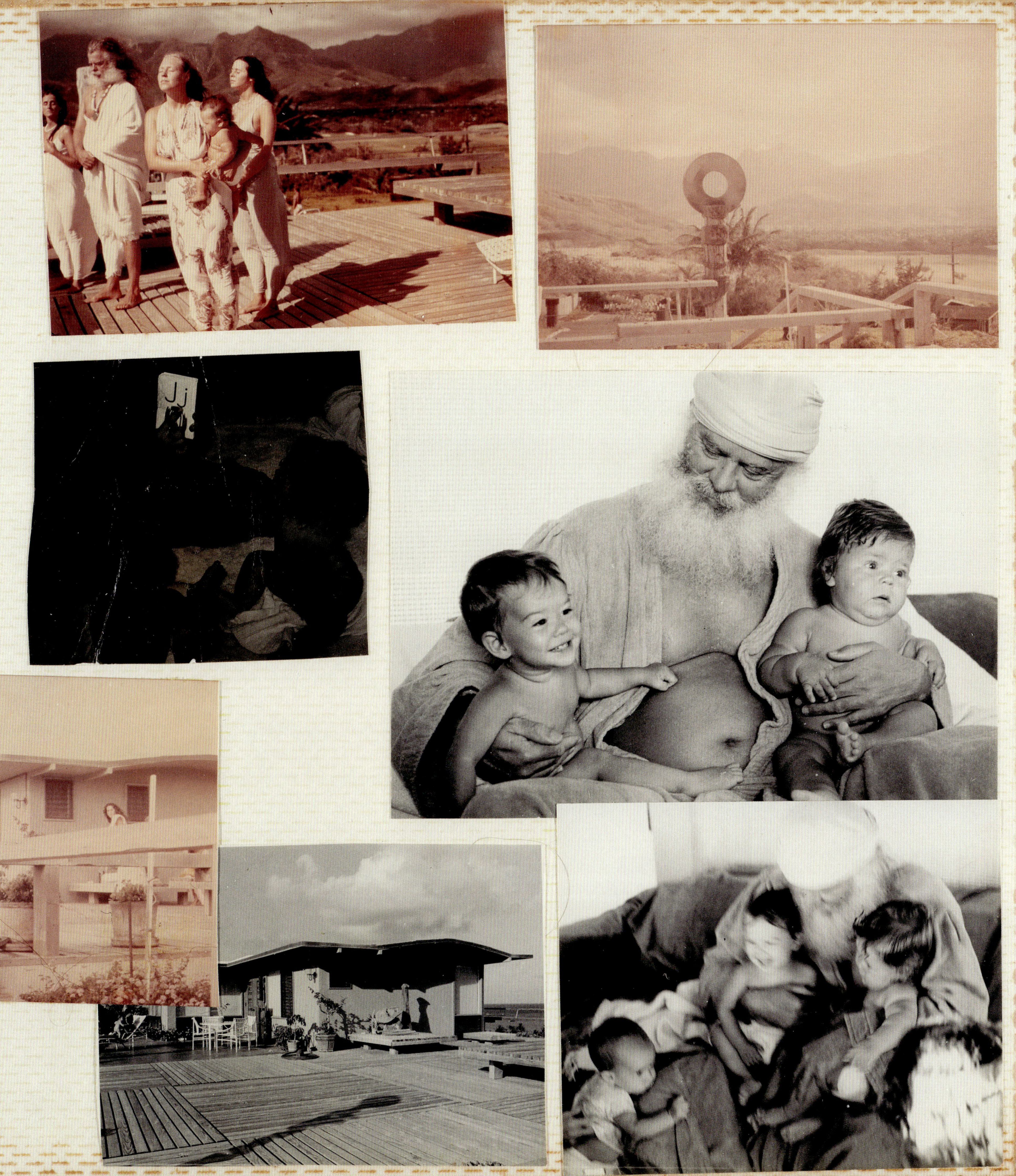

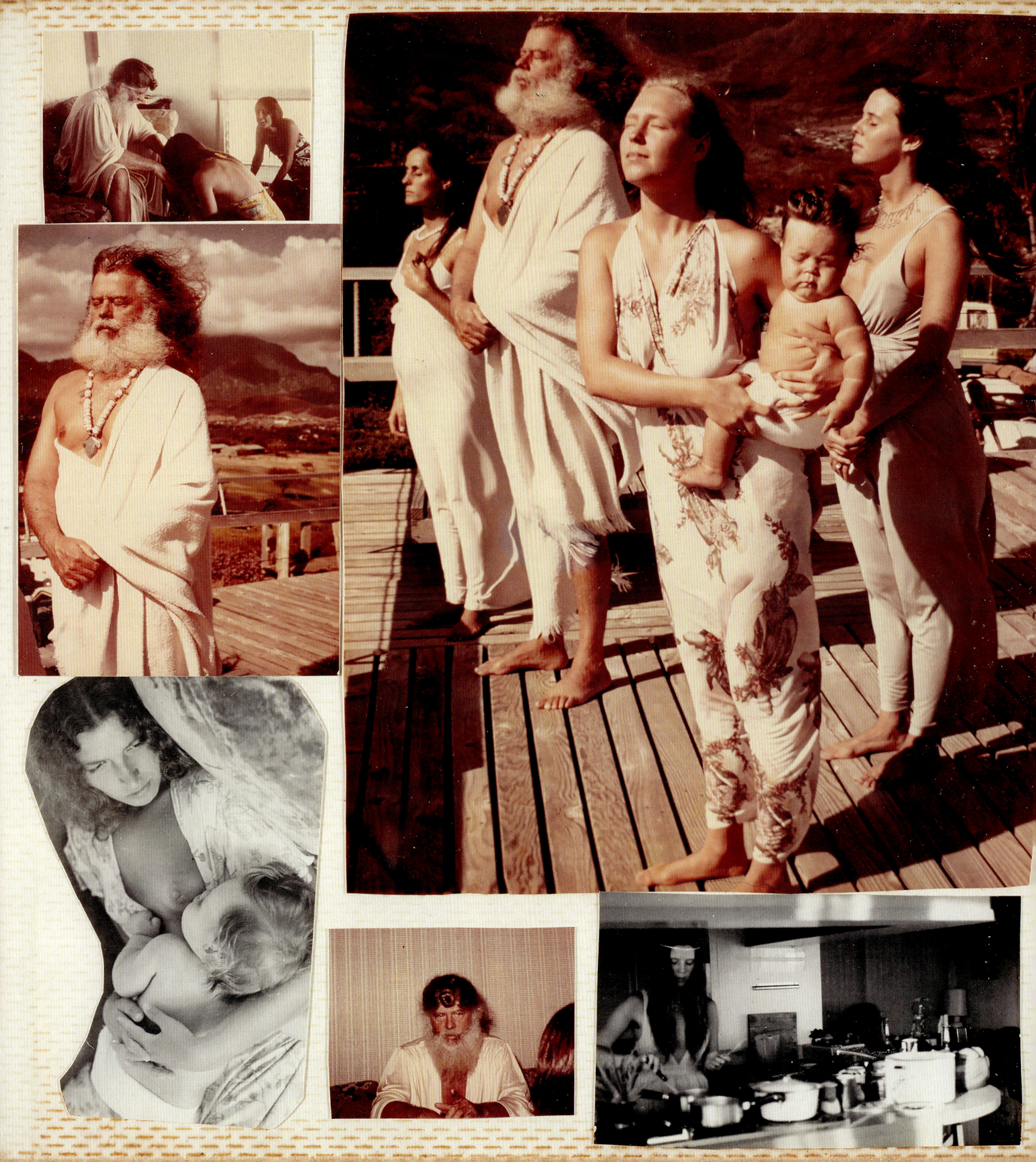

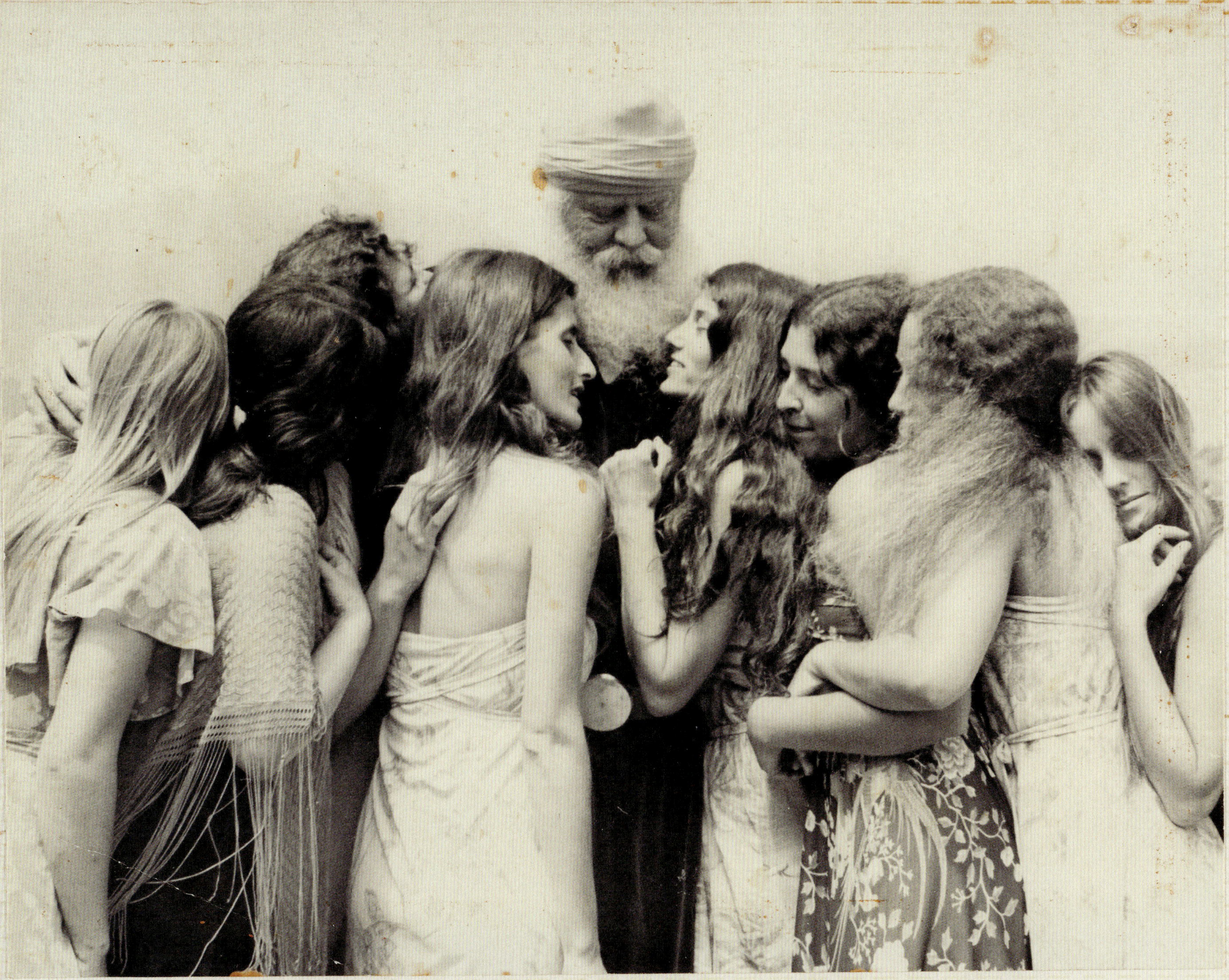

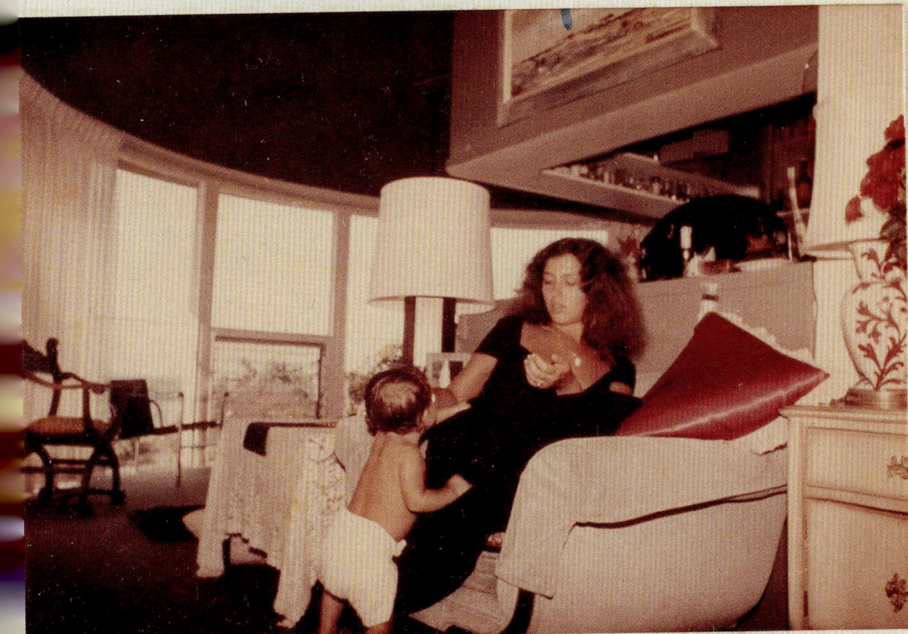
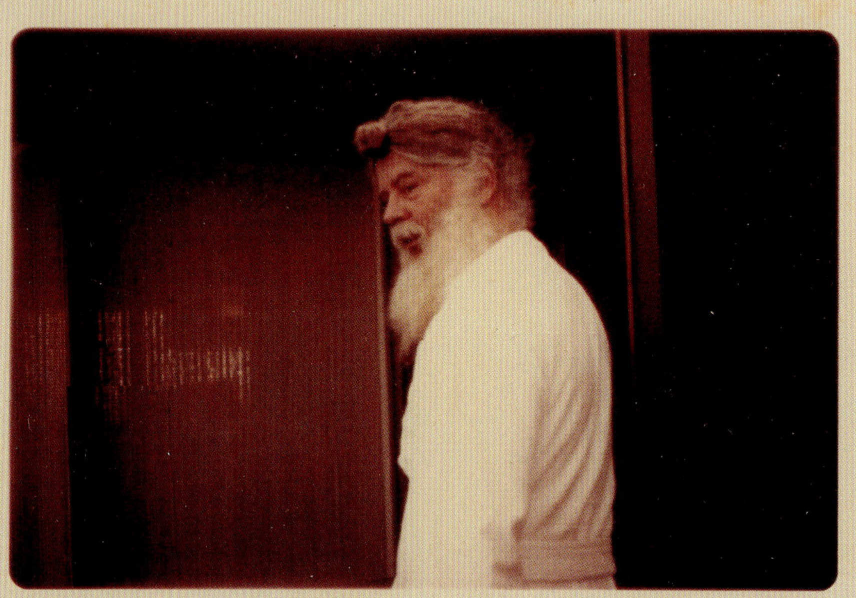

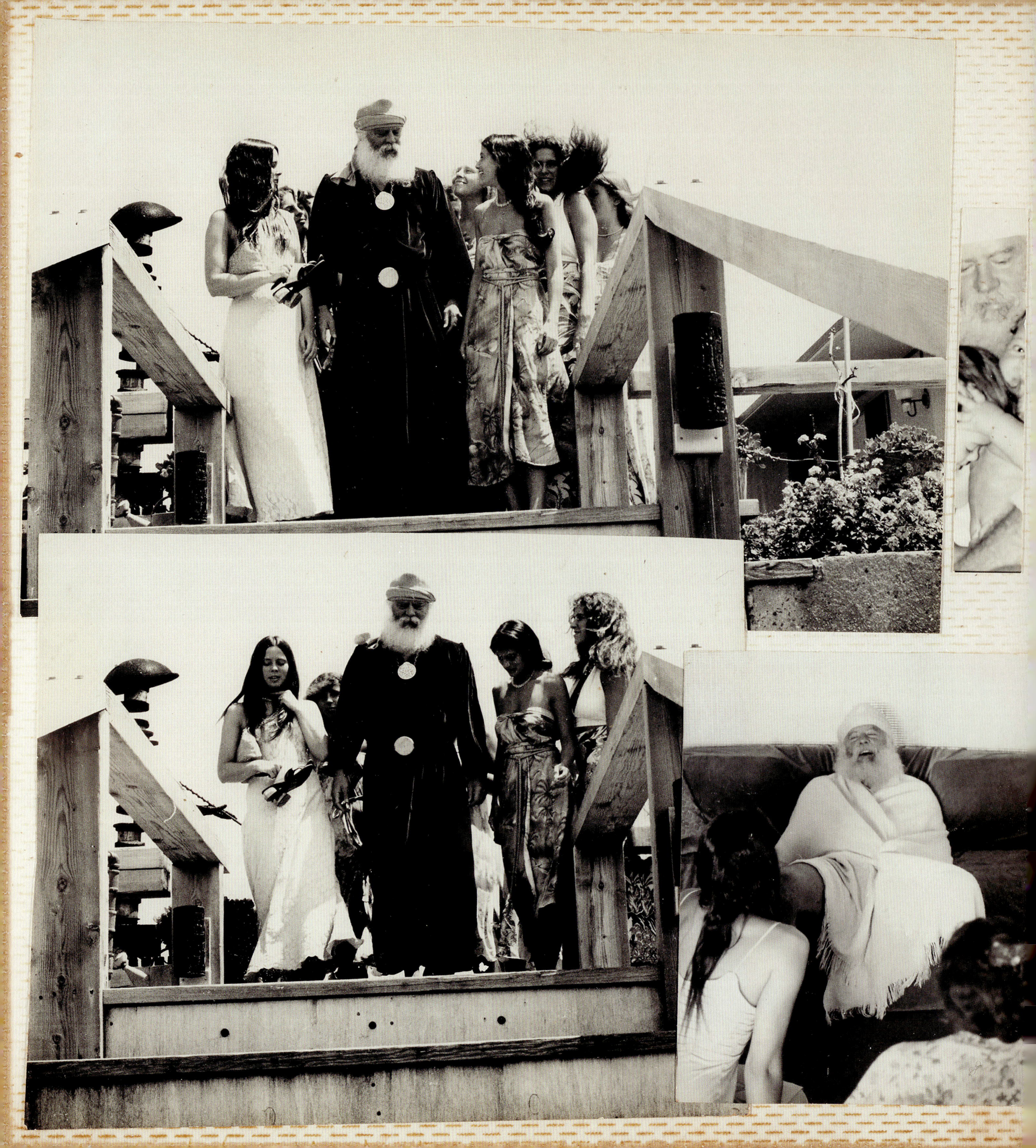

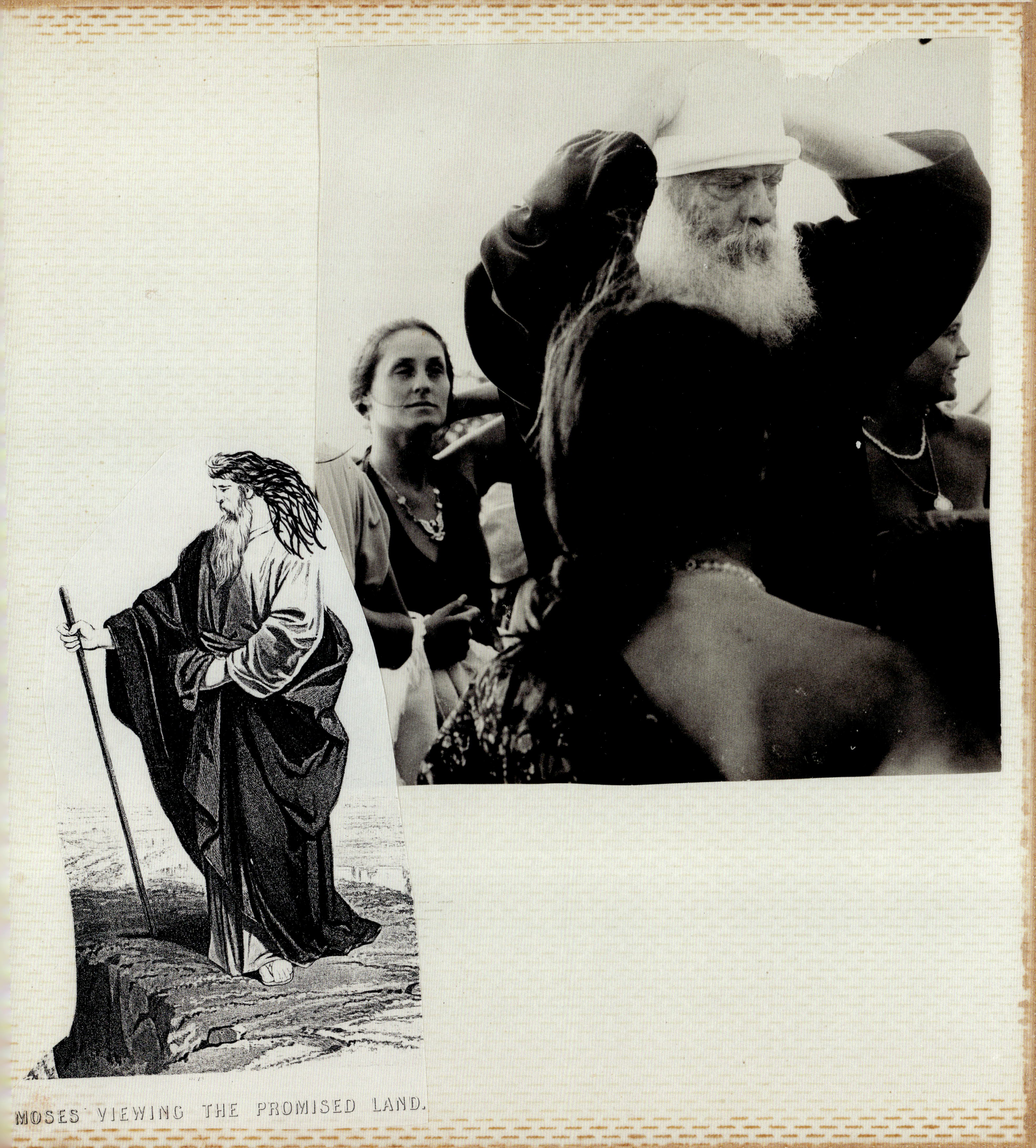

MOSES VIEWING THE PROMISED LAND.

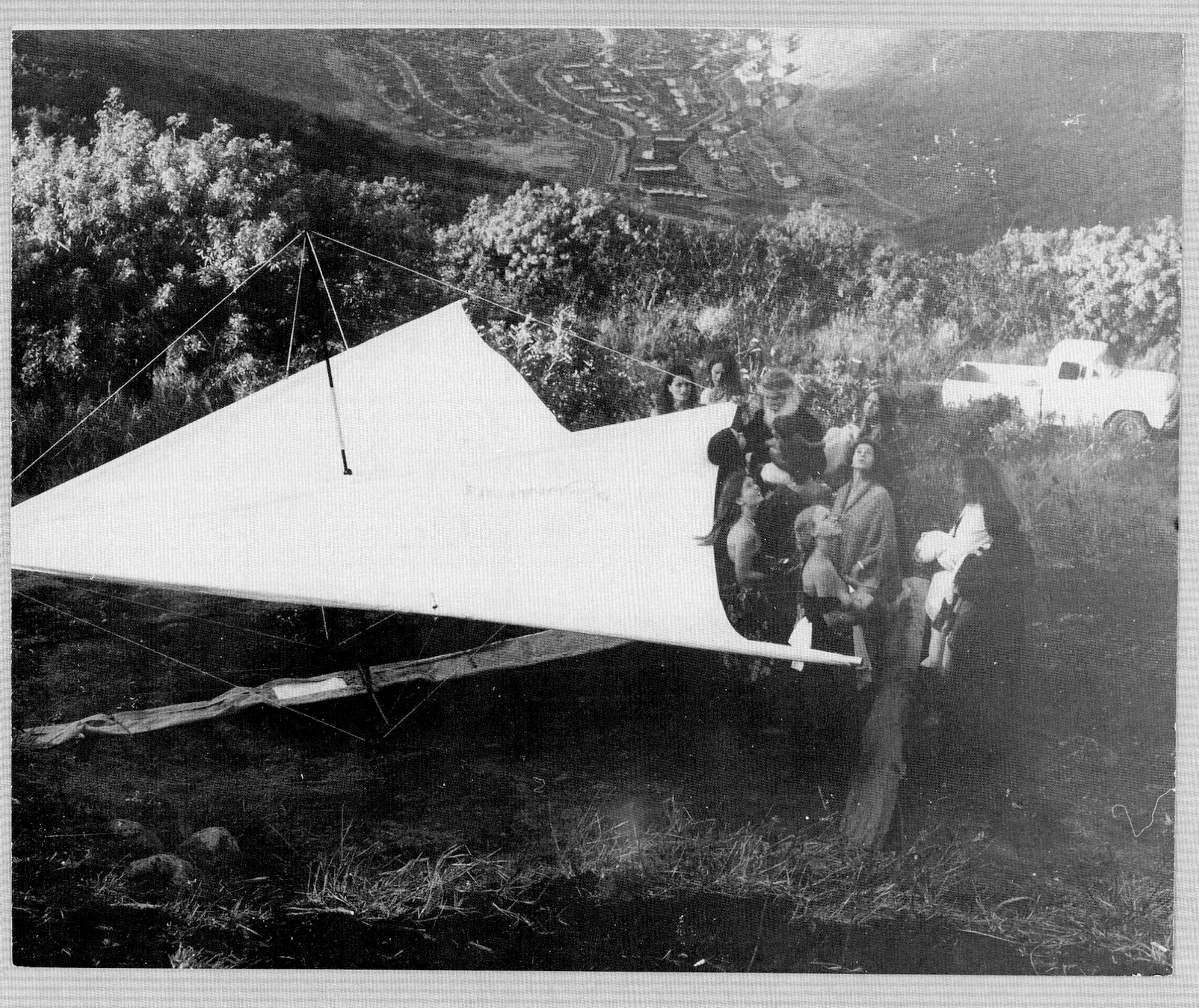

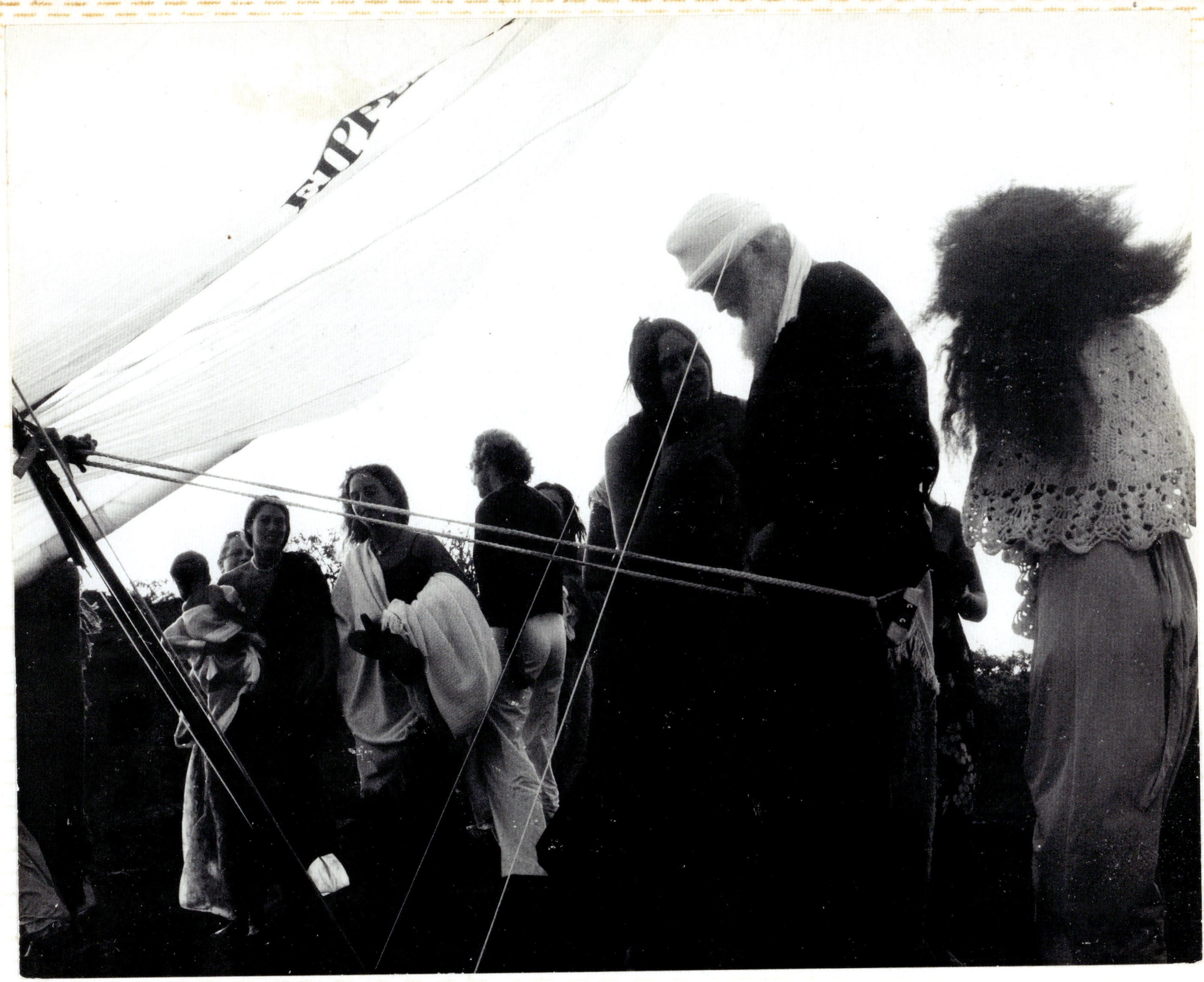

Moʻokapu. It means sacred land.
"It was the place where God created the first man out of the dust. Every morning I dance on the beach near the place where God made Adam."

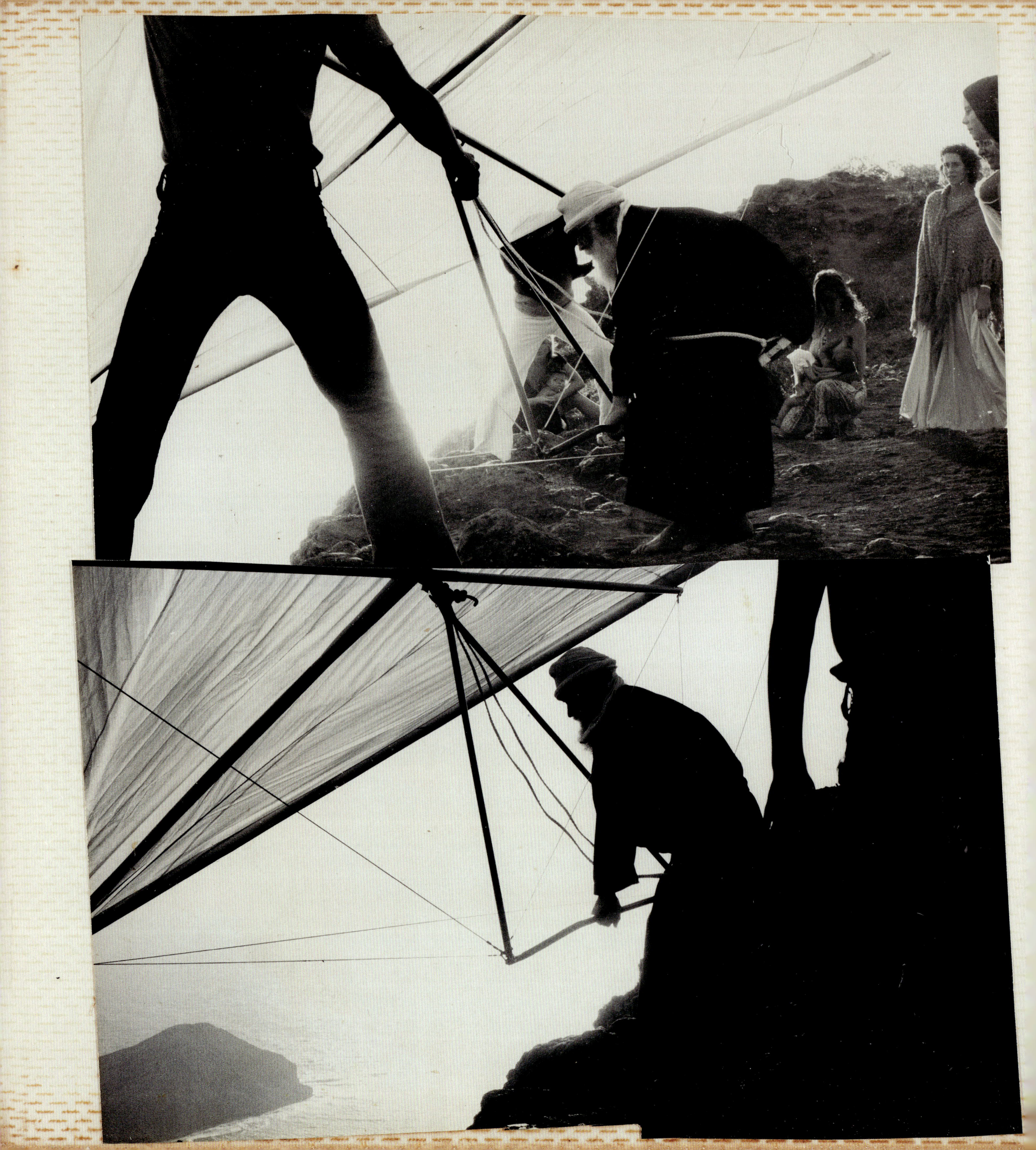

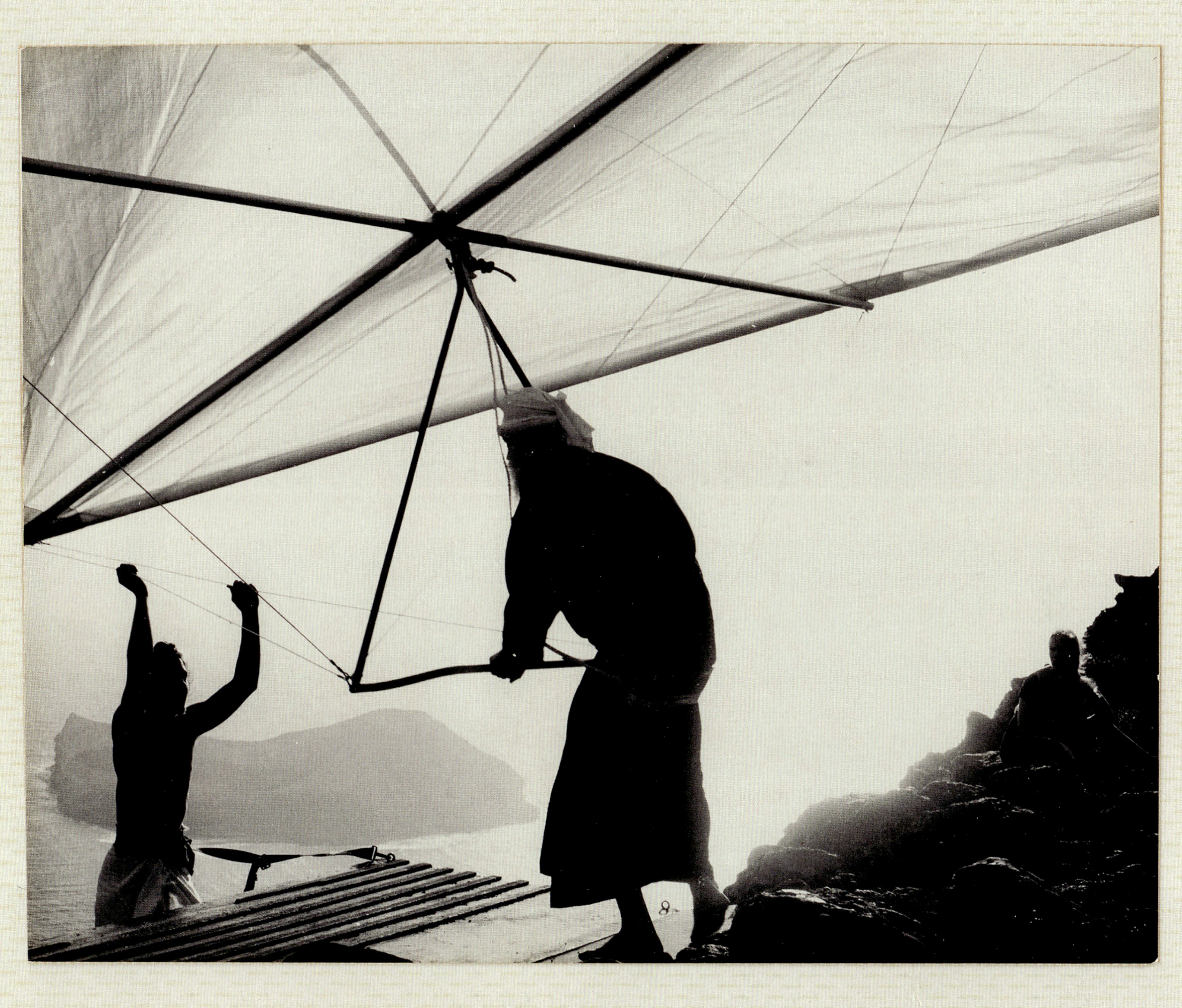

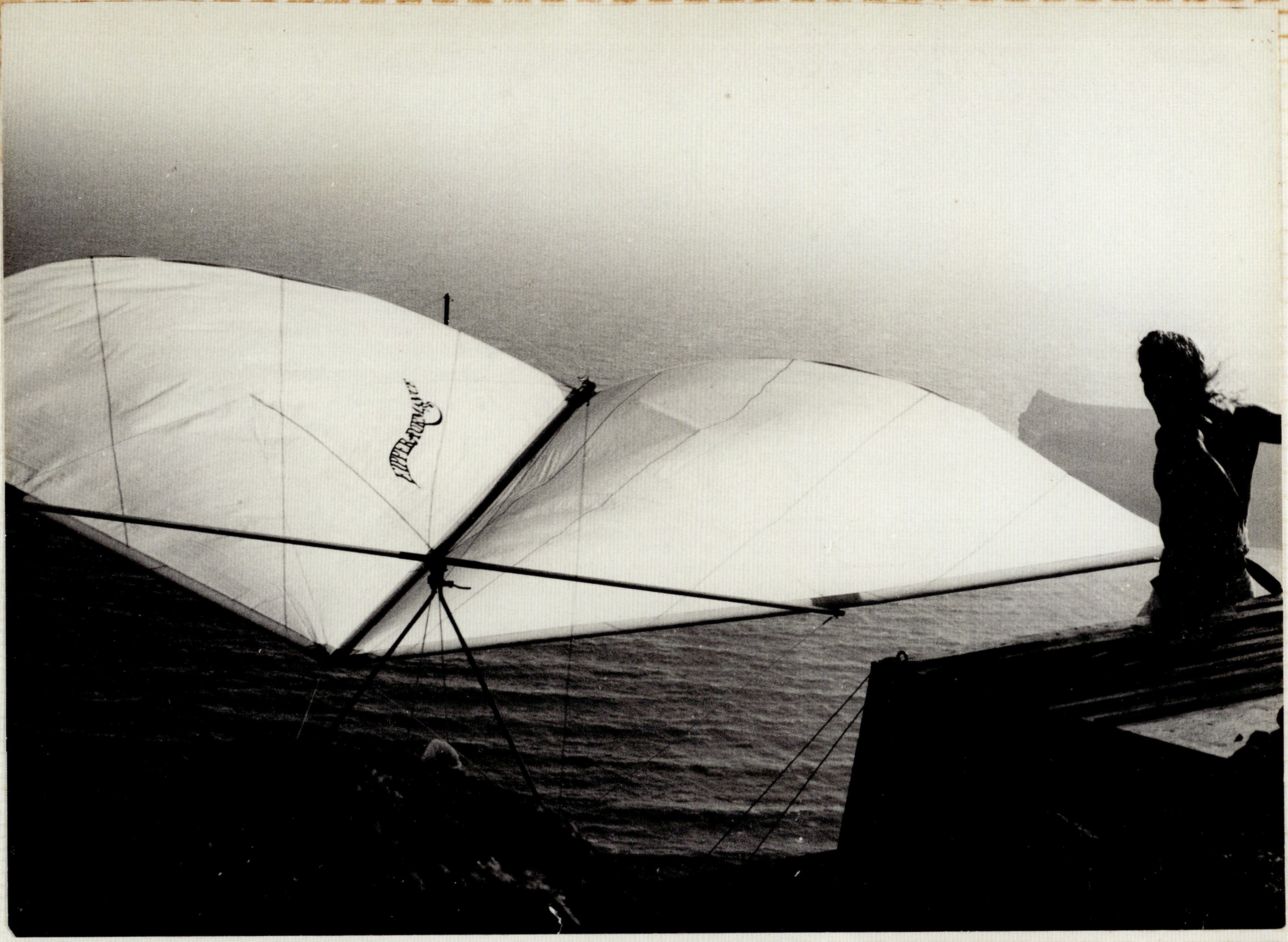

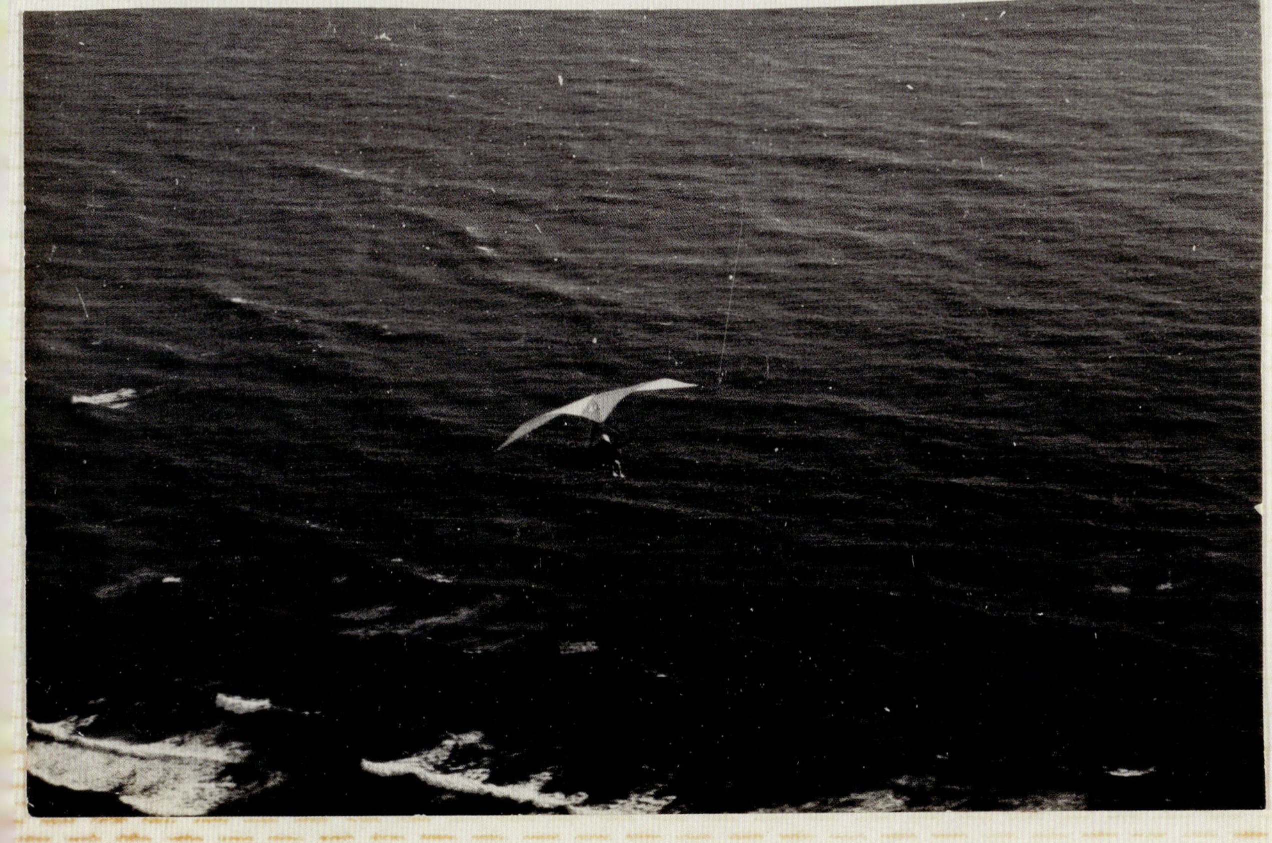

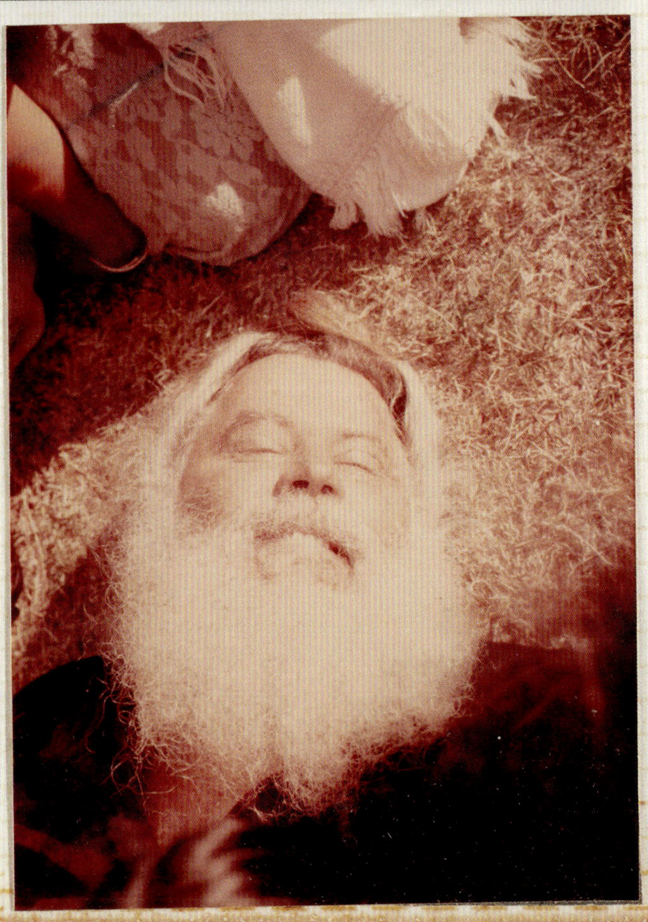

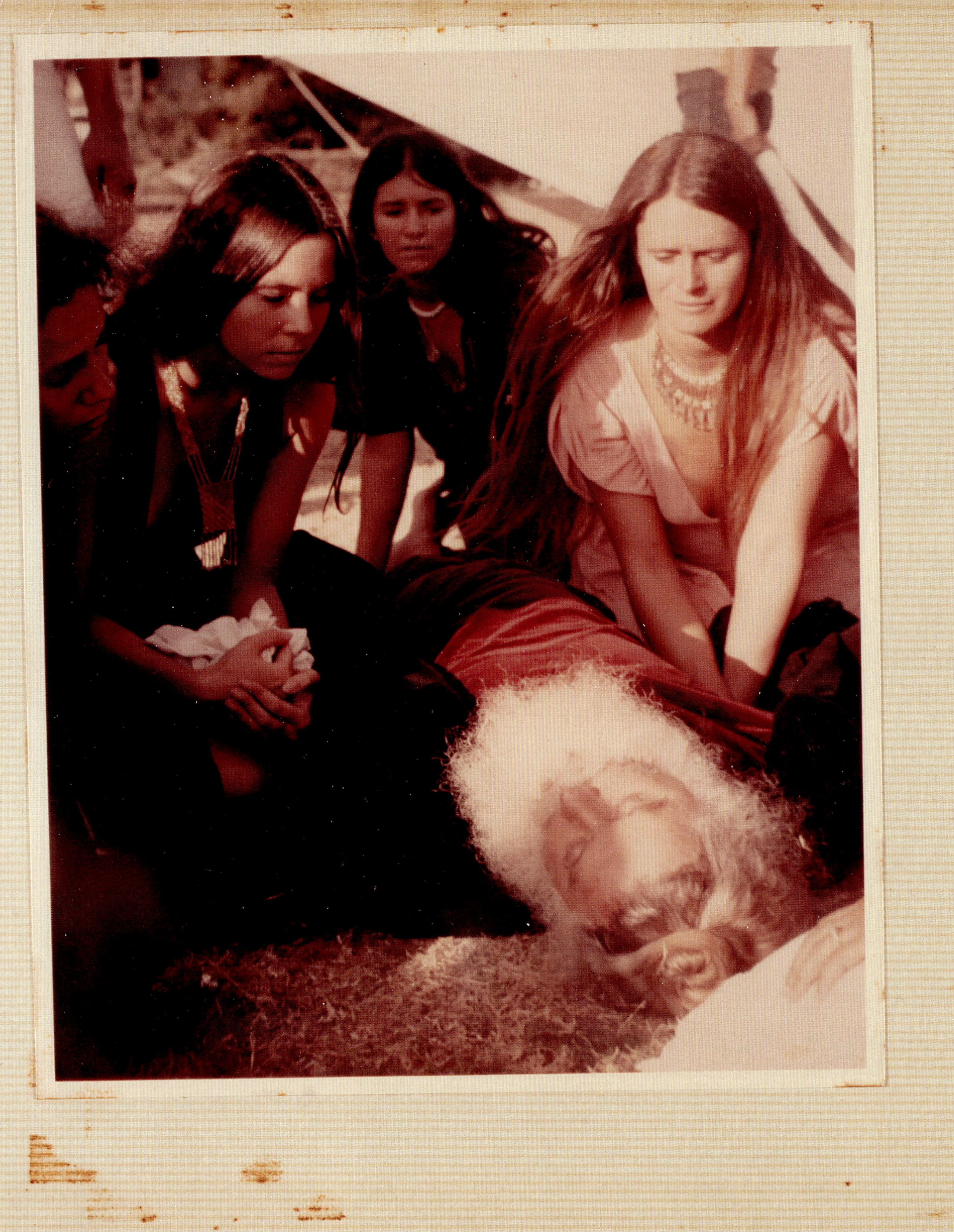

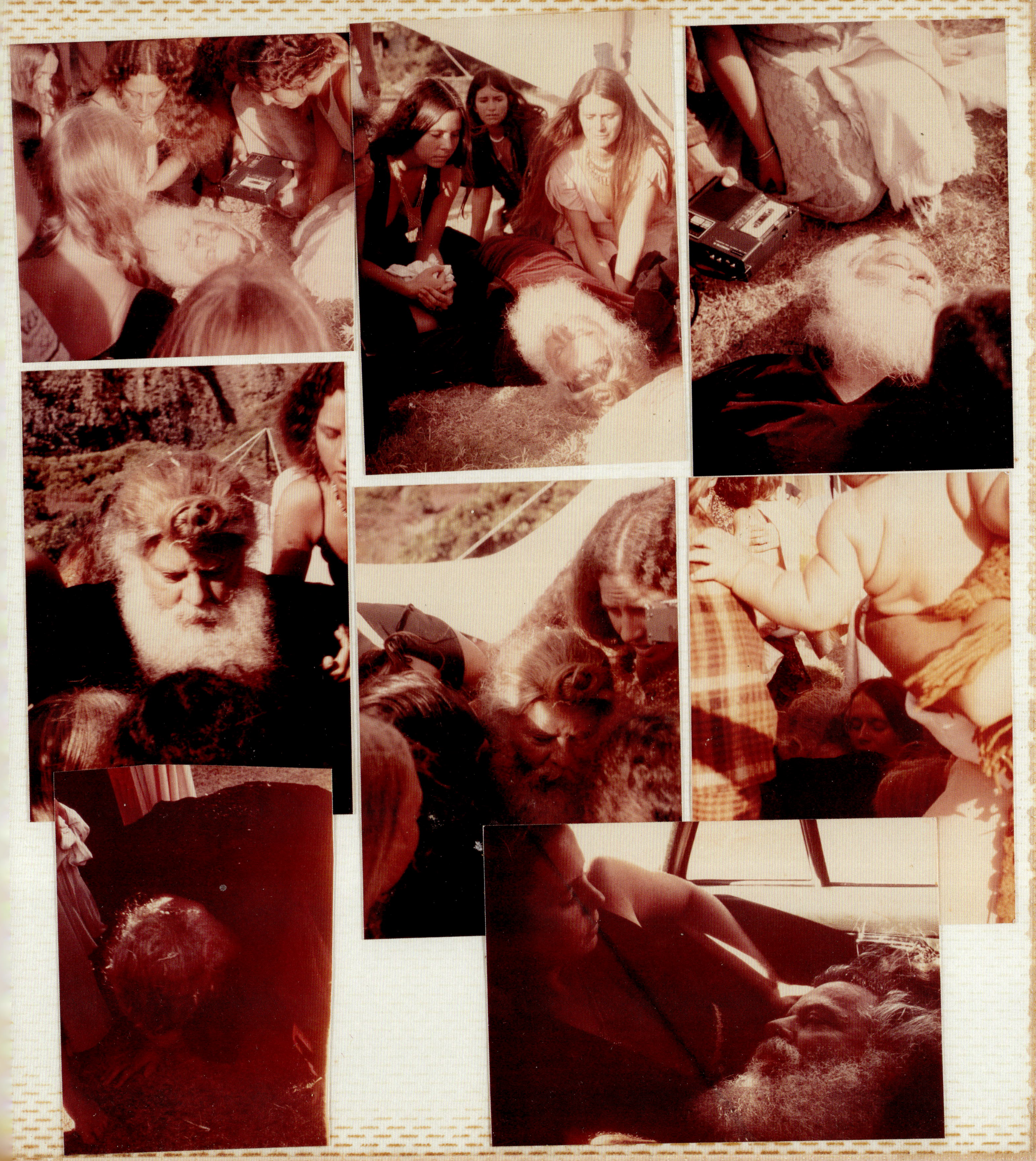

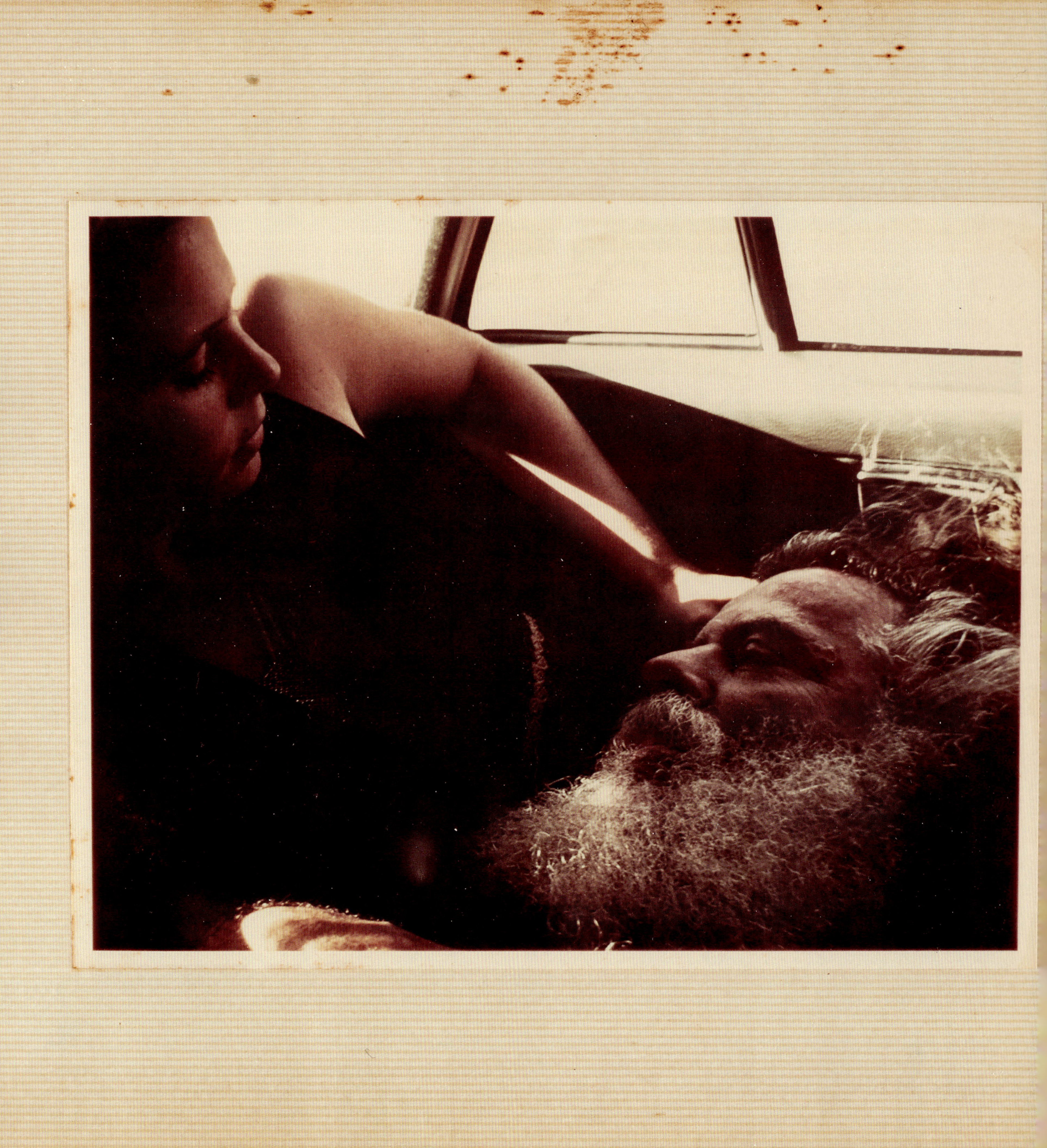

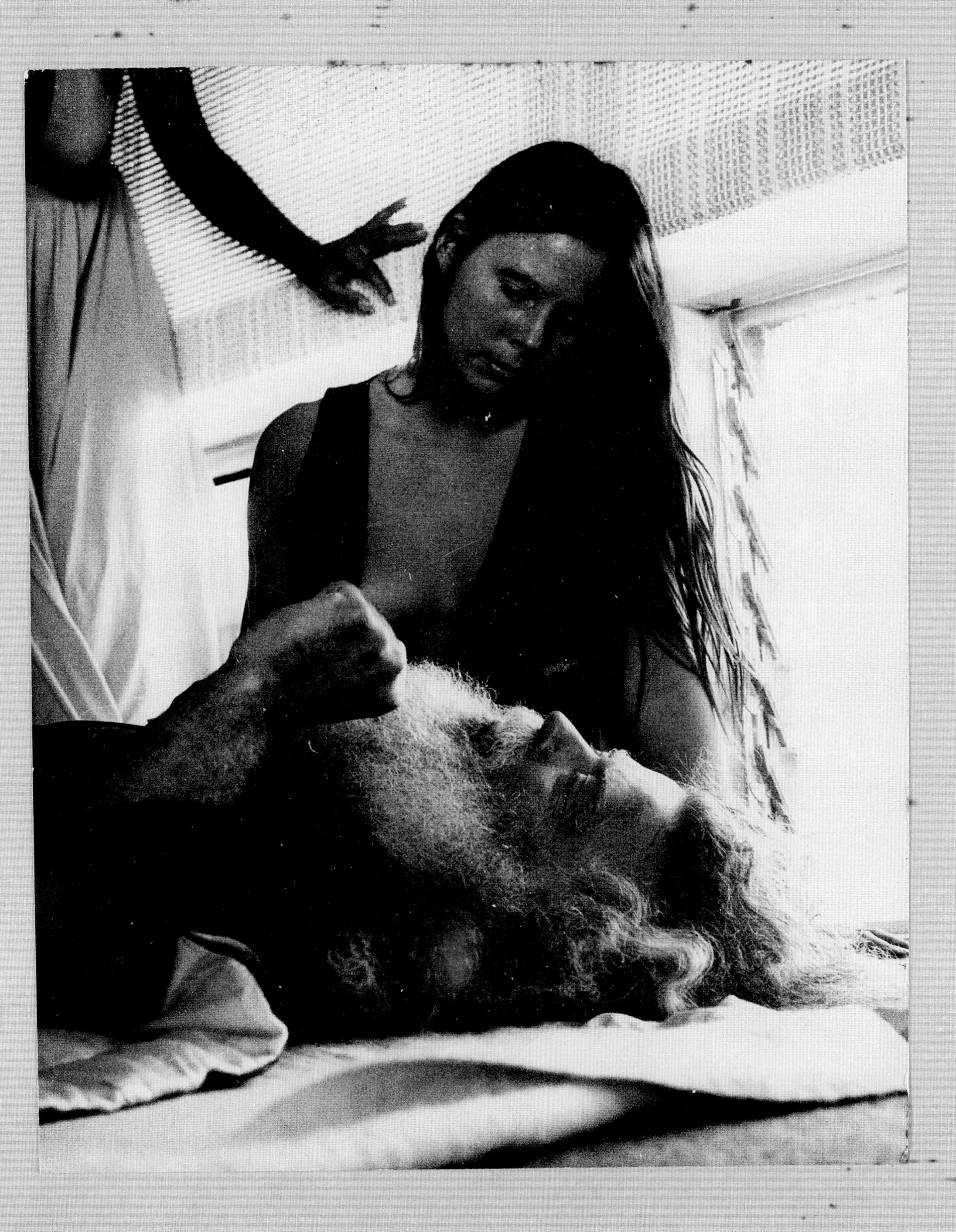

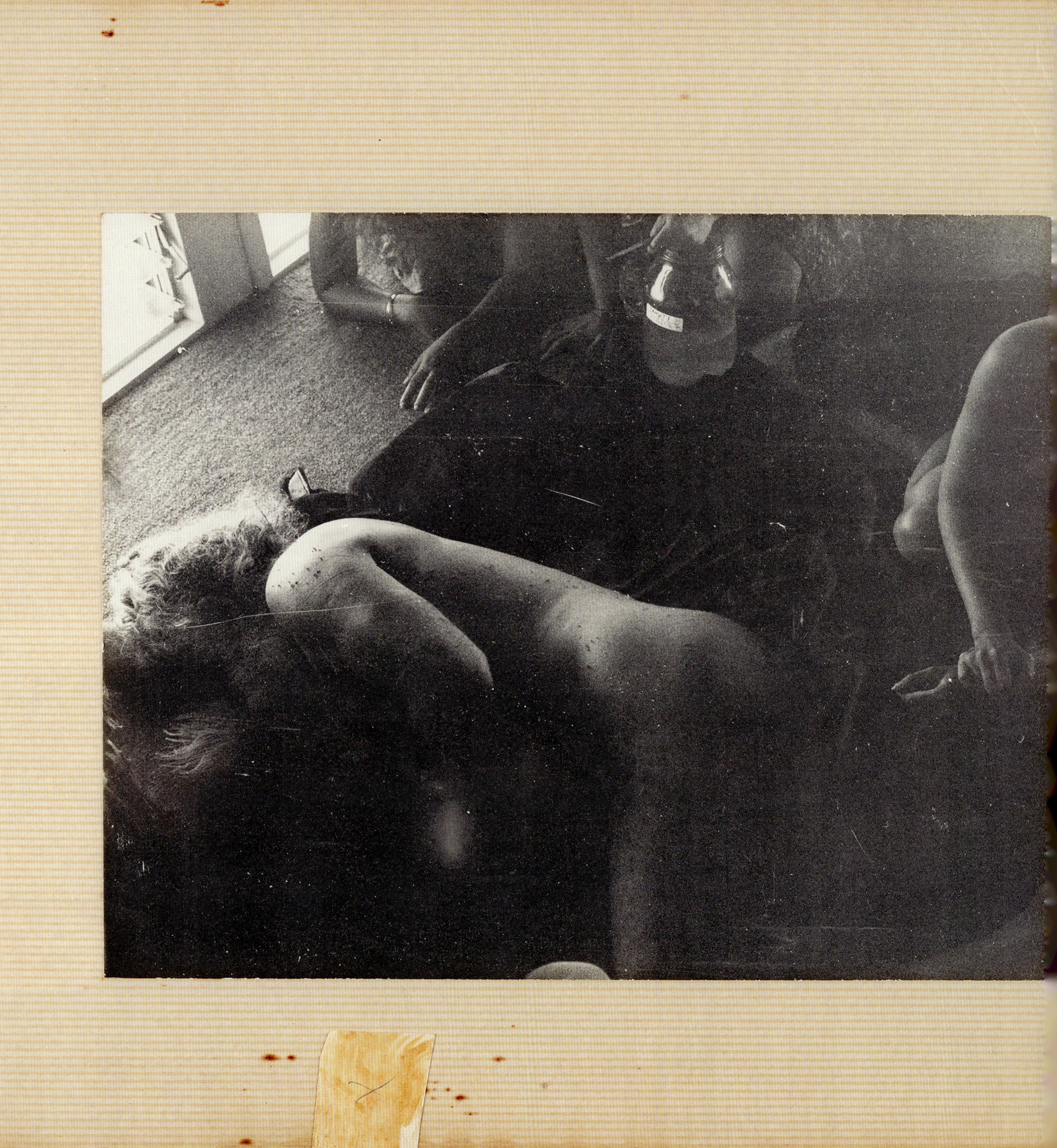

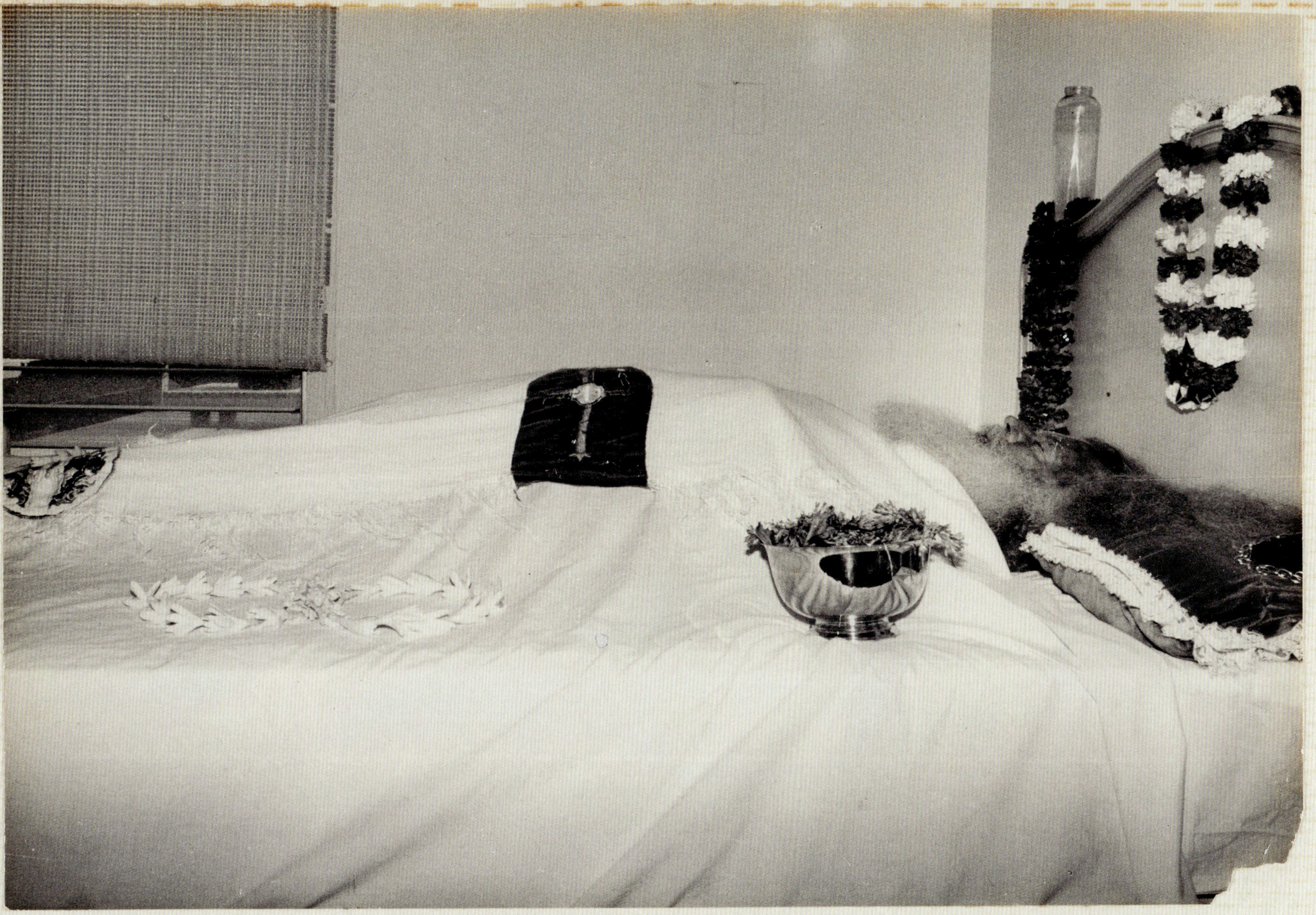

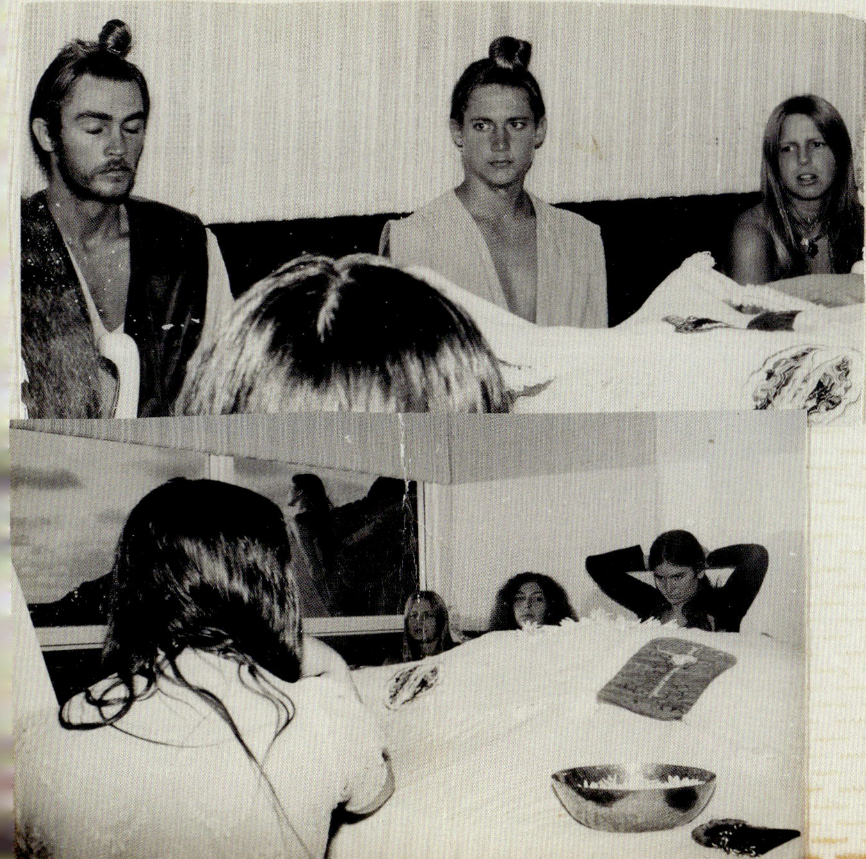

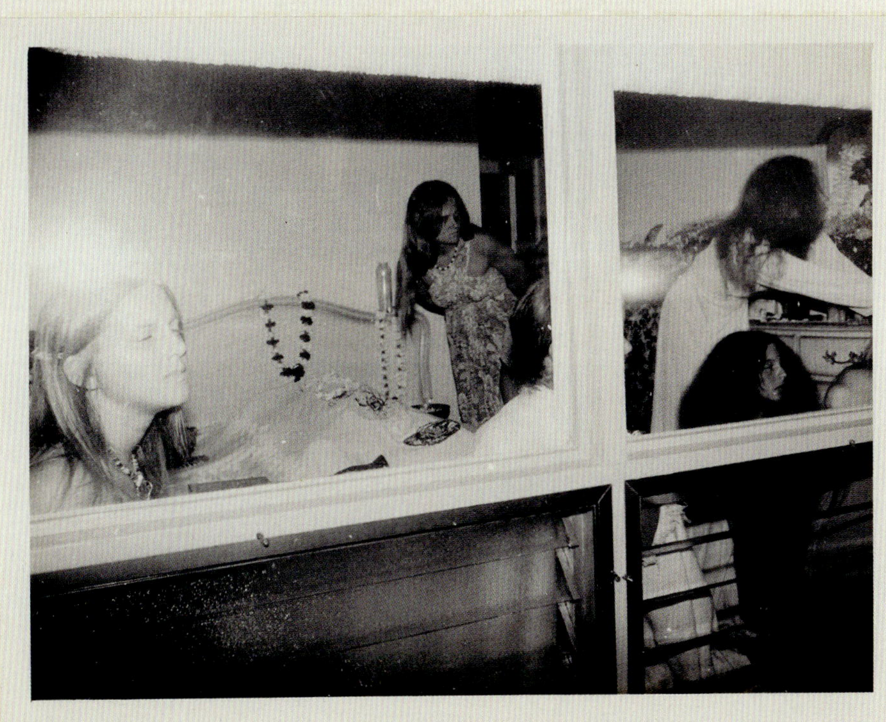

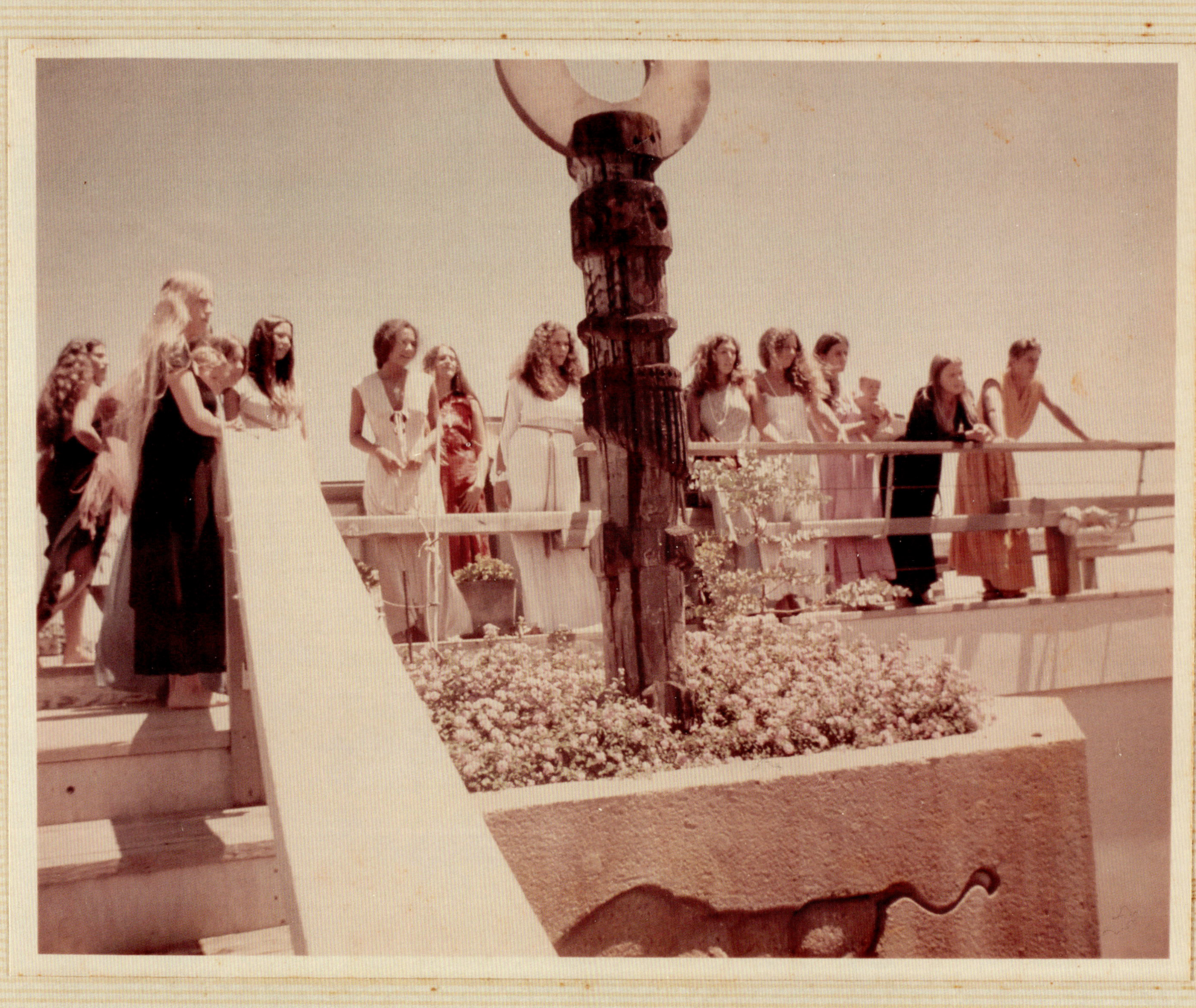

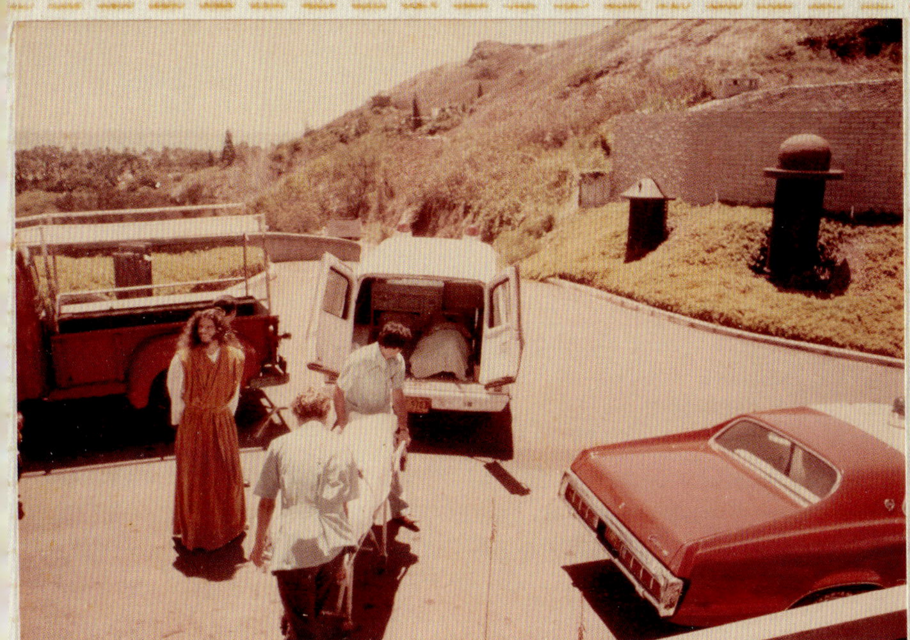
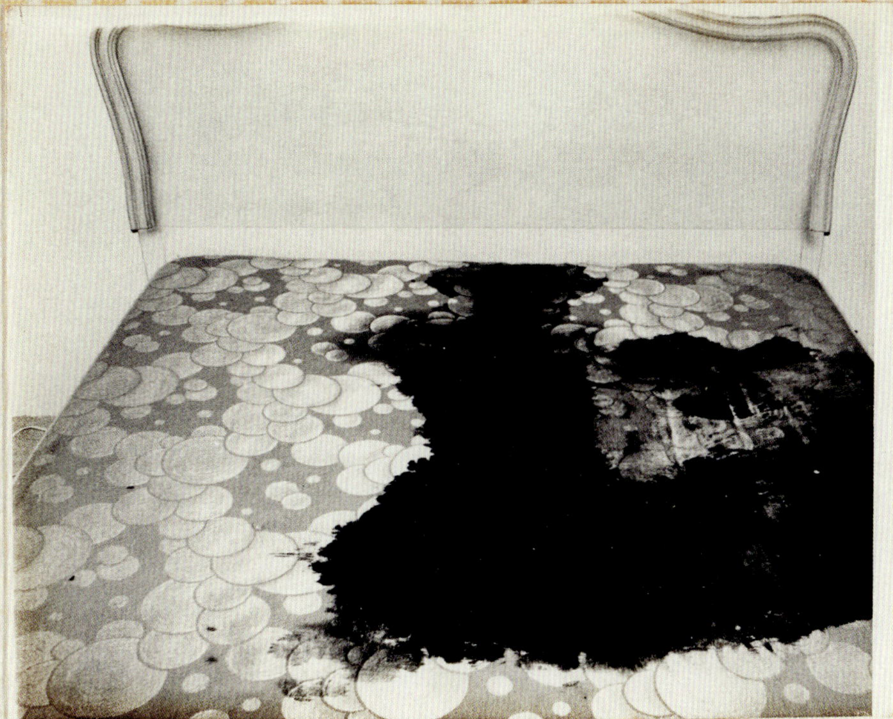
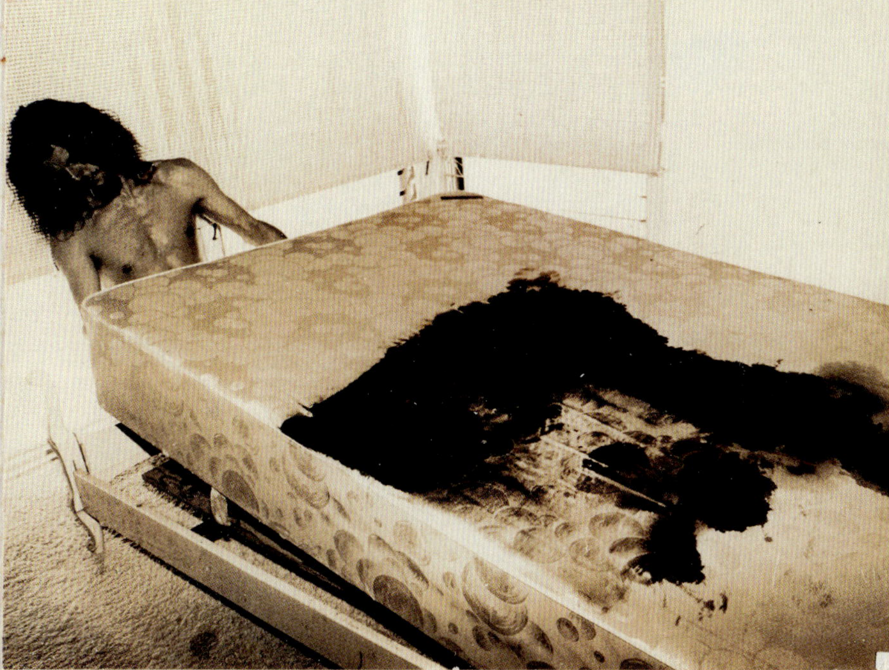
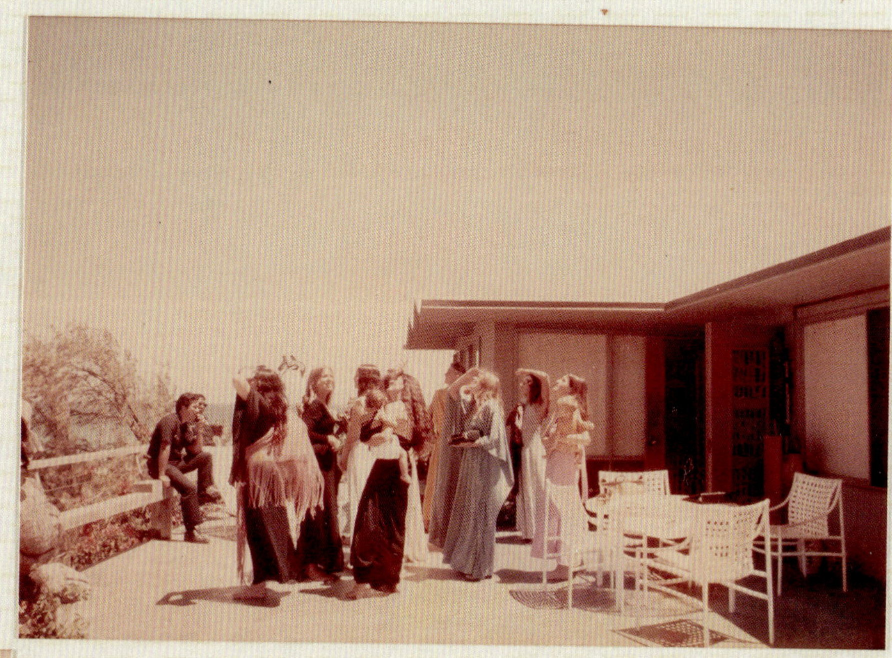
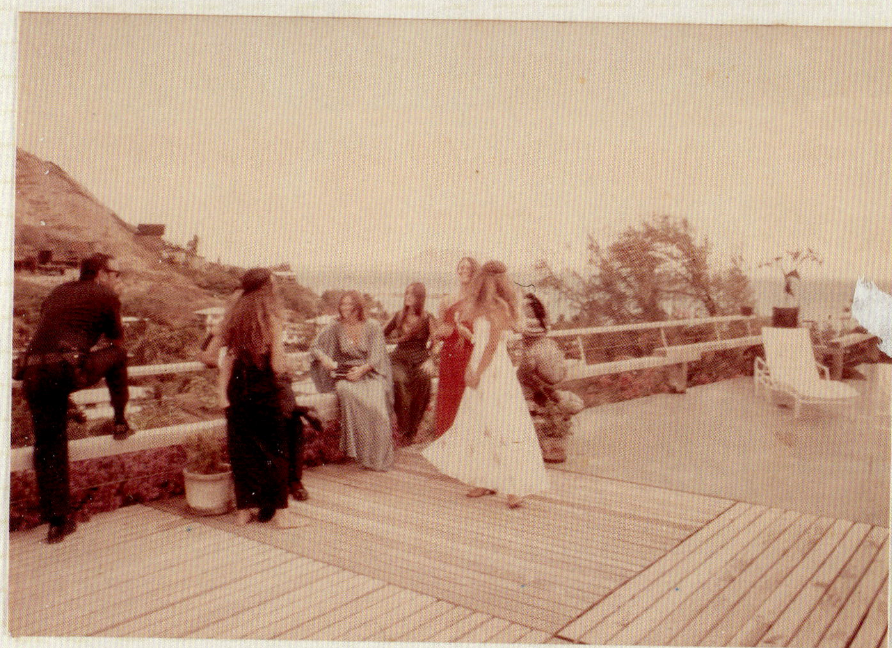
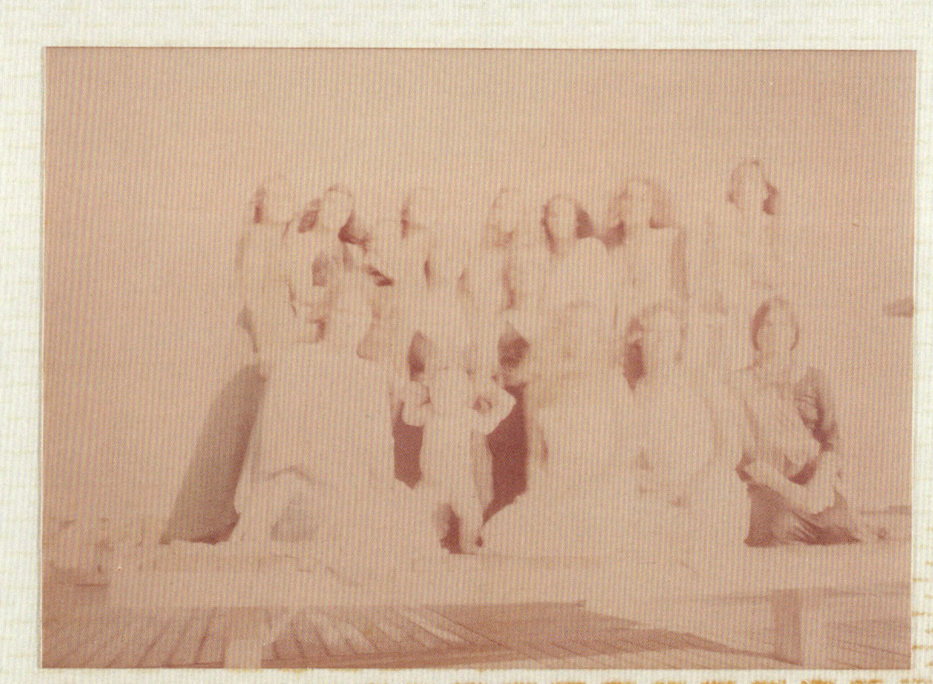

Yahowha followers face eviction from Hilo home

By DAVID TONG
Advertiser Staff Writer

Members of the religious group, Eternal Now, face another dilemma today, having already lost their spiritual leader in a hang-glider accident on Monday.

They told The Advertiser yesterday they have been ordered to leave their Hilo home.

Isis, a disciple, said the 30-day eviction notice was "understandable" since the person with whom they were negotiating had died.

THE PROPERTY is a large house on a one-acre lot on Keokea Road in South Hilo. It was the residence of the late former State Senate president William H. "Doc" Hill.

William Jenkins yesterday denied any connection between the eviction notice and the events in Lanikai.

He said his brother, Selwyn, who owned the property, died on Aug. 13. As officer for the corporation controlling the property, he decided to free the "property of any tenants" in order to make the property available for sale "at a moment's notice."

Jenkins said the eviction notice was sent by registered mail the day before the news of Yahowha's death came yesterday.

THE GROUP REPORTED the death of Yahowha to police Friday, 3½ days after he died of injuries suffered in a hang-glider accident at the Makapuu cliffs.

They refused to take their spiritual father to a hospital for medical treatment because they said it was against their religious beliefs. Instead, they respected his wishes and returned him to their Lanikai home where he died nine hours later in what they called a "crucifixion."

Yesterday, two of his disciples discussed their leader's past and the nature of their religious sect.

Damian, a slim, bearded man, and Mercury, a 21-year-old disciple who recently set what he called a world hang-glider record, were sitting at a table in the patio of their Lanikai home.

DAMIAN SAID their dead leader has been resurrected and is now "absorbed into the sun" where he has become the "center of the universe."

They are confident Yahowha will reveal himself in "mysterious ways" and guide them in the future.

Although they were reluctant to discuss in detail the personal history of their father, whose real name was James Edward Baker, Mercury did say he was a former member of a combat unit in the Marines during the Second World War and was a martial arts champion in 1947.

Baker, a nutritionist, opened organic food restaurants in Los Angeles in 1957 and 1969, the second called the "Source Restaurant" where he conducted classes in his teachings.

IT WAS AT the "Source," said the 24-year-old Damian, who knew Yahowha for 5½ years, that the father started his family, which has now grown to 140 people.

A unique feature of the "family" is the inner circle of 12 young women and a "mother" who are considered the "original disciples."

Damian said the 12 women are, in fact, "Aquarian nuns" who are the "subconscious force" in the universe. The men, he explained, provide for and protect the women, while the women play a mother role, bearing children and assuming household chores.

The three infants in the family are the children of Yahowha and were born of "immaculate conception," he said.

HE SAID THE HIGHEST decision-making body in the family is made up of women because they have "a clearer view of the situation."

Women have maternal instincts that help them to determine "what is best for all of us," he added.

He said the rest of the family is in Hilo where a band called the "Breath," a bakery called "Goodies," and an organization called "Possibilities Unlimited", made up of architects, carpenters and even an astrologer, are living.

The disciples said Yahowha's teachings are not based on any precepts of any established religion. Rather, it appears the leader created his own body of spitirual knowledge and told his followers that they would find substantiation of his truths in such books as the Bible.

His teachings are found in such documents as his Ten Commandments for the Aquarian Age (whic is supposed to come in the year 2001), the "Unknown Teachings of Jesus Christ," and "Seven Great Principles of Truth."

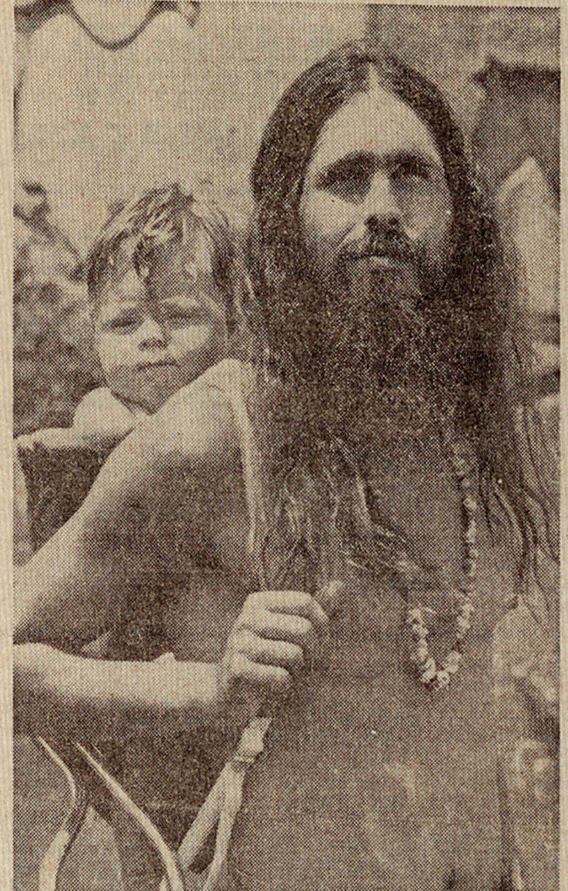

Advertiser Photo by David Yamada

Damian with one of Yahowha's children.

Sect's leader killed 2, served time in prison

Eternal Now sect members yesterday confirmed a report that their spiritual leader was sentenced to one to 10 years in prison for manslaughter in 1963 and cleared of murder in a 1955 slaying.

But they said the leader, Yahowha, then known as James Edward Baker, had acted "in defense of women" in both instances.

According to a female disciple, Harvest Moon, Baker was innocent in both cases. He was cleared in the first case and in the other, the judge expunged the sentence from the record after Baker had served three months of the sentence, she said.

RESPONDING TO an Advertiser request for information on Baker, the UPI office in Los Angeles reported that he was sentenced to prison for the shooting death of Robert Ingram, a 41-year-old builder and hotel owner.

Baker who pleaded self-defense, was found guilty of voluntary manslaughter after shooting Ingram at Baker's restaurant. Baker had told the jury that Ingram, armed with a gun, had stormed into the restaurant and demanded that he be told the whereabouts of his 31-year-old wife.

Baker said he wrestled the gun from Ingram and in self-defense, shot him. In his testimony, Baker denied having had an affair with Ingram's wife.

Moon said Baker had acted in self-defense because Ingram had threatened in front of witnesses a day earlier to kill Baker and Mrs. Ingram.

UPI did not know when Baker was released from prison.

IN 1955, Baker, an ex-Marine judo expert, reportedly used judo chops to kill a man who had attacked him with a knife. Baker was acquitted in that slaying.

The disciple said the two slayings were "predestined" and similar biblically to what happened to Moses, who she said killed two men in defense of women.

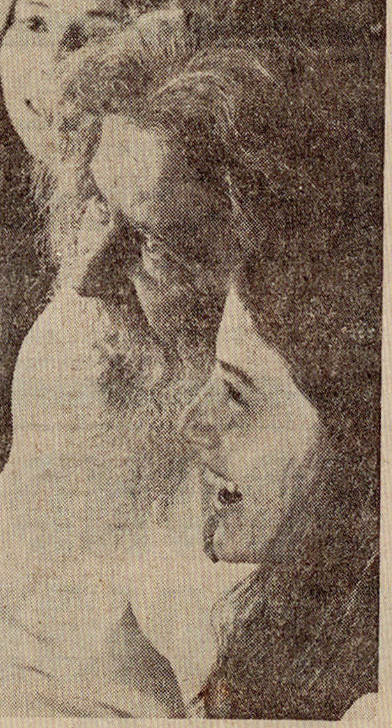

Advertiser photo

Yahowha and disciples.

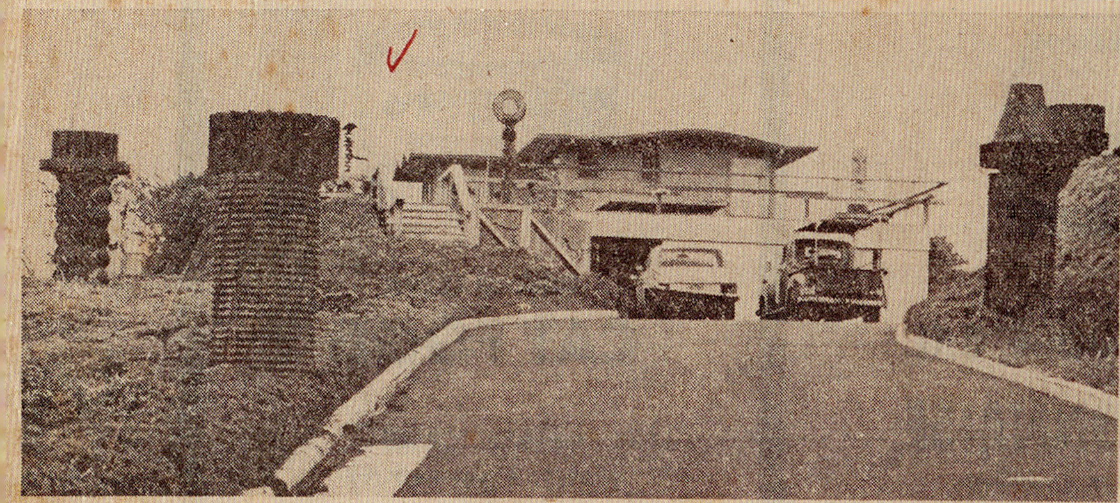

The Lanikai home where Yahowha died; it is rented from Charles Watson, president of Hawaiian Dredging and Construction Co. Watson's own sculptures surround the home.

Advertiser photo by Roy Ito

Religious leader dies; body left for three days

By DAVID TONG
Advertiser Staff Writer

Members of a religious group here watched their leader, Yahowha, slowly die from injuries suffered in a hang-gliding accident Monday, then let his body lie untouched for three days in their Lanikai home, The Advertiser has learned.

Disciples of the group, which was known as the Aquarians when it first broke into the news on Kauai, say they picked up their leader after the accident and took him home to die, refusing to seek medical assistance because it is against their religious beliefs. They said Yahowha died nine hours after the accident, which they view as a "crucifixion."

The group, which now calls itself the "Internal Now," said the 53-year-old Yahowha — whose real name was James Baker — insisted on being taken back to their home where he could be "at peace."

They said he was left in an untouched state for three days after he died from the hang-gliding accident at Makapuu. They said it is against their religious beliefs to move a body for a three-day period.

THE SECT REPORTED the death to police yesterday morning. An autopsy has not yet been performed. Police officials are uncertain about possible charges against the group.

One charge might be failure to report a death, which according to State law must be done within 24 hours.

Yahowha, which they say means

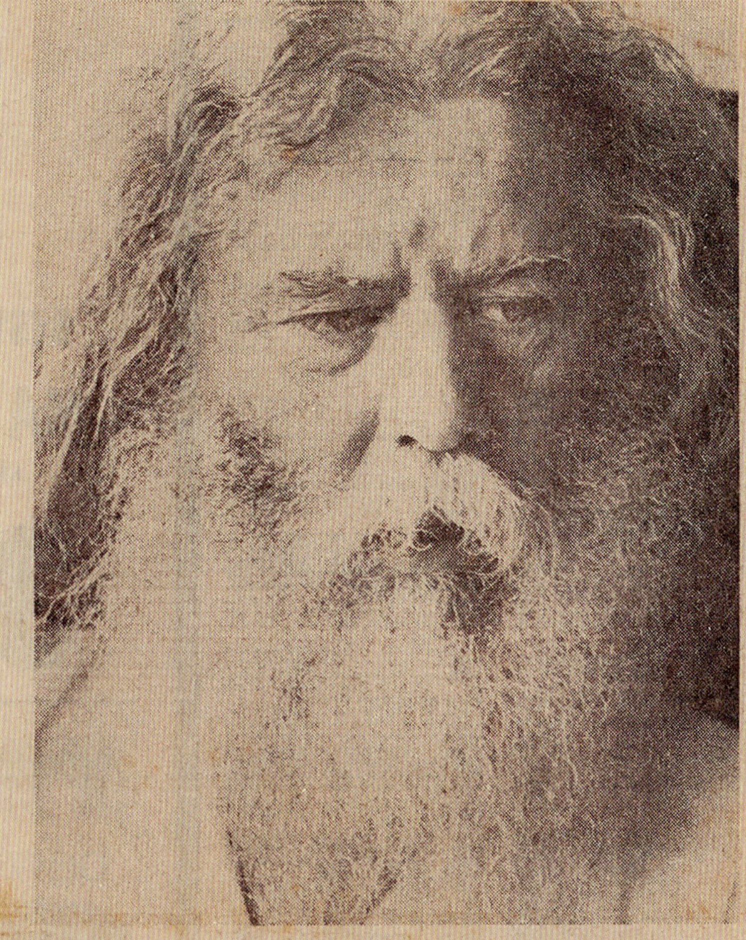

Yahowha, earlier this year.

fire, water and air, was in the news earlier this year when his group left Kauai after causing a stir for three months.

The group, which sought "paradise" in Kauai, claimed it was bothered by threats to members and financial problems at its Keapana farm.

The group left Kauai April 1 for San Francisco, where they stayed for a few months before moving to Hilo, where 140 members are now based under the group's new name. Last month, Yahowha took his inner circle of disciples — 13 women, three men and 3 infants — to the showcase home they rented in Lanikai where they planned to map their future.

ACCORDING TO THE group's account, the death of their leader was "predestined" and "fulfilled the prophecy of the Bible."

The group said Yahowha's flight

on the hang-glider — his first ever — was the "closest thing to a re-experience of the first golden age, 'lemuria,' where man could fly."

Yahowha had watched another member of the group, Mercury, set what they claim was a world record of 13 hours, 5 minutes on a hang-glider earlier this month off the Makapuu cliffs.

According to the group, Yahowha had been airborne for only 10 minutes before he flew toward shore and nose-dived into a group of campers.

The group said police and ambulance workers who arrived on the scene did not touch him and allowed them to take him to their home.

ISIS, ONE OF THE disciples, said

See RELIGIOUS on Page A-4

New star shines its light on Hawaii

The rare phenomenon of a bright new star, a nova, suddenly appeared in Hawaii skies last night.

Dr. Nancy Morrison, of the Institute for Astronomy at the University of Hawaii, said the newcomer can be seen in the northeast in the early evening sky.

The nova, as yet unnamed, was first reported yesterday by an astronomer in Japan who viewed it 19 hours earlier than Hawaii's skywatchers.

Dr. Morrison said the nova was reported locally by amateur Michael Morrow, who called her to report that a new star was suddenly visible.

She said the discovery is "about as bright as the major stars of the Big Dipper. It is the same brightness as all but one star in the constellation Cygnus, where it appears."

The astronomer said a nova is a star that always has been present, but whose brightness increases suddenly, by a factor of 100 to 1,000.

Spirit of Dashing Founder Guides Commune

By WALLACE TURNER
Special to The New York Times

WAILUA, Hawaii — Ninety people drawn from the confused remnants of the social upheavals of the 1960's are living quietly and in apparent happiness in a religious commune set up by an unusual middle-aged adventurer.

The adventurer was James Baker, who was 53 years old when he died in August 1975 after crashing on his first flight over the famous Makapuu Point hang glider range.

His followers include a 51-year-old woman, her daughter and grandchildren, but most of them are people about 30 and over. Their story is one of the more interesting illustrations of what became of some of the youths who wandered through the sociological swamps that opened up on the fringes of society in the 1960's.

The lives of the group here center on a leased home on the beachfront and a bakery called "Goodies" on a sidestreet. In the middle of it all is the picture of Jim Baker, blown up from a passport photo to a size of 2-by-3 feet. They revere him as a divine father figure.

A Strange Man

He was a strange man—kind and gentle, a lover of many women and the father of children by several of them. But he killed two men with his bare hands. The evidence indicates that he died believing he was God, or at least the son of God.

His followers called him Yahowha. They did what he said when he was alive, and now they try to do what they think he would want. They took strange sounding names. They refer to themselves as his children.

"We were created by Yahowha as a spiritual family," said Astral, a 29-year-old woman. The daughter of a successful surgeon and a mother who committed suicide, Astral spent a year and a half at the University of California during the era of youthful revolt in 1966-67.

Baker Was a Marine

Mr. Baker's origins are less clear. He was a marine in World War II. He was a jujitsu expert. Al Kaiser, a business associate of Mr. Baker's years ago, said Mr. Baker told of growing up with a mother who supported them as a charwoman. They lived in various public institutions where she worked, Mr. Kaiser was told. At one of them, an inmate taught Mr. Baker jujitsu, Mr. Kaiser said.

In the 1950's, Mr. Baker cut a dashing figure, by the accounts of those who remember him. He wore white Italian silk suits and drove Cadillac convertibles. He had little talent for business, the friends said, but he had a talent for establishing restaurants.

He was a handsome man, persuasive, plausible, generous, likeable. He started the Aware Inn, which became a hangout for the hip. He had the Old World, and finally he had The Source, which was at Sunset and Sweetzer in the Hollywood section of Los Angeles.

Jim Baker was a physically proud man. This pride was wounded in the early 1960's when he and his wife, Elaine, had their first child, who was deaf.

It was after that that Mr. Baker began to open the natural food restaurants that culminated in The Source. It was in the Topanga Canyon period that he killed a man for the first time in hand-to-hand fighting. It was a neighbor who drew a knife on Mr. Baker in an argument about the neighbor's dog. Mr. Baker killed him with a blow to the throat. He was freed because he had acted in self defense.

A second killing occurred in Mr. Baker's restaurant days. He had become involved with the wife of another man, who objected and came to Mr. Baker's restaurant with a gun.

Mr. Baker said later that the outraged husband pulled a gun and fired it in the ceiling. They struggled. The coroner's report said the other man died of a gunshot wound in the head and of a broken larynx, fractured by jujitsu blows. The jury found Mr. Baker guilty of manslaughter and, after many appeals, he served three months in jail in 1968, six years after the killing.

The Couple Divorced

When Mr. Baker and his wife were divorced, they had three children.

Mr. Baker founded The Source about 1969. His last years were totally involved with it, and with the peculiar religious movement that came out of it.

"Jim Baker was searching," said Astral. "He found Yogi Bajian, a Sikh mystic, and he wanted to believe in him, but couldn't. That was the last straw. Jim Baker realized he would have to be The Father."

"At about that time, children began to come to him, middle-class children, every kind," she said. "The Source became the center of everything. It was transition from a world where divorce outnumbered marriages, where it was a dog-eat-dog jungle, where children ran away at 13.

"From there we grew into a true family in spirit," Astral said. "We can't be separated. Jim Baker became Father Yod, the ultimate father on earth."

Yod, as the young people now called him, moved his flock into a rented mansion at Griffith Park. They flourished there, and gradually a pattern of patriarchal control began to be exercised by the middle-aged leader.

Mary Stave of Los Angeles described how it was in the group that was now called the Brotherhood of The Source. She spent a lot of time around the mansion in 1972.

"It was communal living," she said. "Celibacy. But not really. Hypocrisy. It was in the midst of the era of sexual freedom awareness and they were told they could have intercourse only once a month to procreate. So there was code talk in propositions. A fellow would ask a girl 'Would you have my baby?' when all he wanted was for her to go to bed with him."

She left The Source after a few months. "He (Mr. Baker) was not evil, he was just on an ego trip."

By January 1975, Father Yod Baker was ready to take his flock away. Scouting parties went out, and finally he picked Hawaii, specifically the westernmost island, Kauai.

The Source had been sold and with the money Father Yod made downpayments on land, a fishing boat and an airplane to spot schools of fish. But the straitlaced population of Kauai took the Brotherhood of The Source as another infestation of hippies and ran them off.

The group, by then upward of 100 adults with about 30 children, moved back to San Francisco to live a short time in an old mansion on the edge of downtown. Then they went back to Hawaii, to settle at Hilo.

In the summer of 1975, Yahowha, as he had then become known to his followers, moved to the beachfront house near here, close to the cliffs where the hang gliders fly.

Structure Had Changed

By then the structure had changed. Yahowha still was the center of it all. But he no longer ran a restaurant. He no longer lived with the band of followers. He lived in the beachfront house with 13 young women and a small group of young men. Three of the young women were mothers of his children.

Chief among the young women was Makushla, who had come from Mount Vernon, N.Y., and into the Brotherhood of The Source. By the time Yahowha plunged off the cliff in his fatal hang glider crash, she had become his companion and co-leader of the group. She now is the head of the family.

The Day Baker Died

It was on the morning of Aug. 25, 1975, that Jim Baker, wearing the robes of Yahowha, his life's last role, stepped off the cliff with the hang glider.

Isis showed pictures of him she took that day. She said he fell straight down, instead of being carried aloft by the trade winds. He managed to right the glider so that he made a semi circle out over the sea, and came back to fall among cars parked by the beach.

"Death is an illusion," said Astral. "Nothing dies."

"He set the example of how God would live if God came to earth," said Astral. "There is no problem we can't handle because we saw him deal with everything. Even how to leave the body and go to the next plane."

Then she and Isis, another follower, agreed to pose for pictures if they could hold a color tinted photo of Makushla and Yahowha. They stood there in the bright sunlight, the blue sea behind them, two pretty young women still floating on the life raft that Jim Baker thrust out to them as they were drowning in the social maelstrom.

Eternal Now Has Housing Headaches

Eternal Now sect members, whose spiritual leader died after a hang-glider crash last week, are facing housing problems in both Hilo and Lanikai.

Their leader, Yahowha, also known as James Edward Baker, died last Monday hours after a hang-glider crash at Makapuu.

His followers kept the body at a Lanikai home, not reporting the death until 3½ days after the accident.

THEY SAID their religion forbids touching the remains for three days, until the soul leaves the body.

The Oahu group had been living in Lanikai house but are expected to move this week.

Charles Watson, the homeowner, said he did not rent it to the group, but that his wife leased it to a couple, Mr. and Mrs. Dennis McKenna, for five-months. The McKenna's lease expires Thursday.

Watson said he was not aware until about a month ago that the sect members had moved in. He said the lease with McKenna was not subject to sub-letting to others.

"McKENNA SAID they were his friends and just staying a while. We told them they'd have to leave," Watson said.

Isis, one of the group, today said "We plan to stay in Lanikai. We couldn't live anywhere esle.

"We know the perfect place will present itself. We do have one place in mind. It's being negotiated on," she said.

Eternal Now members in Hilo were mailed an eviction notice Thursday.

They had been living in former home of the late Senator William H. (Doc) Hill, now owned by the estate of Selwyn Jenkins, who died Aug. 13. That estate is now being settled.

MEANWHILE, United Press International reported that the group's leader, then known as Baker, was sentenced to 10 years in prison for manslaughter in 1963, and cleared of murder in 1955 slaying.

The report said Baker was sentenced to prison for the shooting death of Robert Ingram, a 41-year-old builder and hotel owner.

Baker, who pleaded self-defense, was found guilty of voluntary manslaughter after shooting Ingram at Baker's restaurant.

Baker had told the jury that Ingram, armed with a gun, had stormed into the restaurant and demanded to be told the whereabouts of his 31-year-old wife.

Baker was acquitted in a 1955 slaying after he reportedly used judo chops to kill a man who had attacked him with a knife.

His Followers Claim He Was

Yahowha a War Hero?

By Larry Bereman
Tribune-Herald Staff Writer

Last of Three Articles

Members of Eternal Now said last week that their leader, Yahowha, was once a world heavy-weight Judo champion who trained Marine raiders in Judo during World War II.

According to Sancia and Omne, two members of the religious group, Yahowha is also credited with shooting down 12 Japanese Zeros during the war, and with saving the lives of several fellow marines.

Yahowha was born as Jim Baker on July 4, 1922, in Cincinnati, Ohio. He died at 53 after receiving severe injuries in a hang-glider accident two weeks ago at Makapuu, Oahu.

According to members of Eternal Now, Yahowha was six months old when his father left home. "He spent the rest of his life searching for his father," said Sancia.

EDUCATION

Apparently, he moved from place to place when he was young, and did not receive a strong formal education.

In the early 1940's, he established a health gym in Cincinnati. In 1942, when he was 20, he became the world heavy-weight Judo champion, and a short time later, began training marines in Judo for World War II action.

According to his followers, he was aboard the U.S.S. Chicago during World War II when the ship came under attack by Japanese Zeros. He then reportedly shot down 11 of the planes before receiving word to abandon the ship, just as another plane approached. Baker then reportedly shot down the last Zero before jumping overboard. He was later rescued along with other men from the ship.

SANDLE SHOP

After the war, Baker returned to Cincinnati, but left for California in the early 1950's, where he established a sandle shop.

In 1955, Baker was acquitted of murder after he killed a man after the man reportedly attacked him with a knife.

Then, in 1963, Baker served about three months in prison for manslaughter. He pleaded self-defense during the trial, but was found guilty of voluntary manslaughter. The sentence was later expunged from his record.

He apparently killed Robert Ingram, a 41-year-old hotel owner, who had reportedly accused Baker of having an affair with his wife. Baker denied the affair during the trial.

SELF DEFENSE

Baker said at the trial that he wrestled a gun from Ingram when the man stormed into Baker's restaurant and demanded to know where his wife was. Baker said that he then shot the man in self defense.

Eternal Now members told the Tribune-Herald that both of the killings were in defense of women, and that it was predestined and similar to what happened to Moses.

In 1957, Baker opened the country's first organic food restaurant in Los Angeles, "The Aware Inn." Later, in the mid-60s, he opened another restaurant known as "The Old World." The restaurants are said to have drawn prominent Hollywood residents, and Baker became a wealthy man.

According to his followers, Baker traveled around Los Angeles during those years in a Rolls Royce, and that he would pick up "hippies" hitch-hiking. Baker, Eternal Now members say, recognized them as reincarnated saints and sages of past ages.

OUT OF MONEY

By 1969, Baker was out of money after giving up his two restaurants in Los Angeles.

His followers said last week that he wanted to start a new restaurant and call it "The Salad Bowl," but that without any money, he could find no way to do it.

According to his followers, he was hiking in the Calabasis Mountains when he came across another hiker, Ray Feldman, a Los Angeles businessman. Feldman agreed to put up the money for the restaurant, and asked Baker what he would name it. "The Source," said Baker, meaning at the time to say "The Salad Bowl."

The Source was Baker's third success in the restaurant business. It was there he met Yogi Bajan, and Baker saw him as his father, God.

Baker reportedly printed up cards which proclaimed that Bajan was God, and placed them on the tables at The Source. But when Bajan found out about it, he became angry, and told Baker that he was not God, and demanded that he remove the cards from the table.

DISILLUSIONED

According to his followers, Baker was totally disillusioned by the experience, and he then became aware that he had to be the father of the new age. It was at that time that Baker acquired the name Father Yod.

Later, he was renamed Yahowha by a young woman who is now known as Mother Makushla. According to Eternal Now members, the young woman was attending college on the East Coast in 1973 and found herself drawing pictures of Yahowha. She then reportedly left school and drove across the country to Los Angeles and to The Source. When she saw Baker, she proclaimed, "you are Yahowha," according to his followers. She now heads a council of 13 women in Honolulu which makes all major decisions for Eternal Now.

The name Yahowha, according to his followers, means fire, water and air.

In the early 70's, Yahowha held classes each Sunday morning at The Source, where he gathered the first 15 members of the Eternal Now family. He lived upstairs from the restaurant at the time.

KAUAI

The Eternal Now family rented a home in a wealthy Los Angeles subdivision after it had grown to around 50, then lived in another home in the Los Angeles area before moving to Kauai earlier this year.

The group has since been back to California, and arrived in Hilo this June.

The number of Yahowha's followers was about 100 by 1973, and has since grown to 140. Sixty reside at the Doc Hill mansion in Keaukaha, the council of 13 lives on Oahu, and the rest are at various places on the Mainland.

When the family left Kauai earlier this year, Yahowha, Mother Makushla, and Damian, another member of the group, ventured to India in search of "a perfect home" for Eternal Now. They left India and entered Egypt without visas to that country, according to members of the group, and found themselves at the pyramids on Easter Sunday. According to Sancia, an Adept (priest) recognized Yahowha as Jesus Christ.

Yahowha then returned to California and told the family that Hawaii is the original Garden of Eden. He then sold The Source and moved the group to Kauai.

The group stayed on Kauai only a few months, and left the island for San Francisco after an assortment of problems developed, including financial problems with their farm and threats reportedly made on

their lives by some local residents.

Yahowha and the family arrived in Hilo in June. Yahowha only stayed a few weeks, however, and left on July 30 with the council. They went to Oahu where they rented a home in Lanikai, a high-income, Windward Oahu subdivision.

A few weeks later, on Aug. 25, Yahowha, who was 53 at the time, was fatally injured in a hang-glider accident off the Makapuu cliffs on Oahu. He was taken to the house in Lanikai by the council where he died nine hours later.

The council then chanted over his body for three and one-half days, to give the soul time to reflect on its life river. They then allowed for removal of the body to a mortuary.

Eternal Now 'Home' In Hilo

By Larry Bereman
Tribune-Herald Staff Writer

First of Three Stories

After searching for "the perfect home" for the past five years, members of the religious group "Eternal Now" settled in Hilo.

But their nomadic days are not over; ordered to leave the old William H. "Doc" Hill mansion on Keokea Point in Keaukaha, making their future uncertain.

"The people here have been so beautiful to us," said Sancia, one of the group's members in Hilo. "But right now, we don't know what we'll do or where we'll be going."

The group was served with an eviction notice last week by the estate manager, Williams Jenkins. Jenkins' brother, Selwyn, who owned the property, died recently.

Eternal Now's leader, Yahowha, was injured in a hang-glider accident at Makapuu on Oahu two weeks ago. The group took the injured man to their Lanikai home where he died nine hours later. They then chanted over his body for three days before reporting the death to police.

ABSORBED BY SUN

According to Sancia, Yahowha has been absorbed by the sun and is now the center of the Universe.

Sancia and Omne, another member of the group, told the Tribune-Herald during an interview on the seawall at the mansion Thursday that it takes the soul three days to leave the body after someone has died. They said that if the body is disturbed during that three-day period, the soul will leave the body and reincarnate without the benefit of reviewing its "life river."

Eternal Now members have a variety of projects going on in Hilo. They operate an organic bakery on Haili Street called "Goodies," which supplies several Hilo stores with "the best cheesecake in the world," and bread made with "100 per cent whole wheat flour, water, honey, oil, yeast, salt, love and wisdom," according to the wrapper.

POI BARS

The bakery also supplies "carob poi bars," and "macardoons." The cheesecake comes in three flavors—date nut, lilikoi, and carob.

Recipes for the goodies were developed by Yahowha, who owned the first two organic food restaurants in the country back in 1957.

A band created by Yahowha, who was also an accomplished musician, has been playing in Hilo and Kona since June. The band, known as "Breath," plays songs written by its members.

NOT A CRY

Sancia said that Yahowha once told the Eternal Now family, "the sound of the Universe is a song, and not a cry," because of his love for music and what he felt it can do for mankind.

According to Omne, Eternal Now music written by Yahowha could not be played while he was in the flesh. The group now plans to publish songs Yahowha has written over the past five years. They also have plans to publish his life story.

Yahowha came to Hilo with the family when they first arrived in June. He left on July 30 for Oahu, where he and about 80 members of the family rented a home in Lanikai, a high-income Windward Oahu subdivision. About 60 members remained in Hilo.

The group first came to Hawaii last year and settled on Kauai, where they immediately bought an airplane and a fishing boat. They occupied a farm there.

THREATENED

They left Kauai for San Francisco after reportedly being threatened on several occasions by local residents, then returned to Hawaii in June and rented the Doc Hill mansion.

Omne said last week that the Eternal Now family is made up of a wide, diversified cross-section of world civilization, and that every race and economic class is represented. He said the group is made up of doctors, lawyers and contractors, as well as people from many other professions, and that Eternal Now offers its work force to the people of the Big Island.

The work force is known as "Possibilities Unlimited," and has already staged several concerts in Hilo and Kona, including one Friday at Mooheau Park.

The group is basically of the Christian philosophy, but its members believe that all great prophets, including Yahowha, are God in the flesh.

ASTROLOGER

According Omne, who is an astrologer with a program at 11 a.m. Mondays on KHLO radio, "Yahowha came here to introduce us to ourselves." He said according to Yahowha, "man is God."

The group does not believe in seeking major medical aid, including surgery and blood transfusions.

Decisions for Etnernal Now are made by a council of 13 women in Honolulu, made up of Mother Makushla, the one who gave Yahowha his name, and 12 disciples. According to Sancia and Omne, woman are gifted and can make wiser decisions than men.

Eternal Now came into being in the early 70's in Los Angeles (the City of the Angels), at an organic food restaurant known as "The Source."

At that time, the group only had about 15 members, but by 1972, it had grown to around 50. During that year, they moved into a house in Los Feliz, which they called the Mother House.

According to Sancia, the house had 22 bedrooms, a swimming and "a beautiful garden." The mansion at one time belonged to the Chandler family, owners of the Los Angeles Times.

By 1973, after the group had grown to 100, they received notice that they would have to leave their home, and they moved into a three-bedroom house near Los Angeles, which they called the Father House.

(Please Turn To Page 14)

Wandering Days Are Not Over

(From Page 1)

Sancia said they built cubby holes in the bedrooms, which she said looked like a beehive, and that couples would sleep in each unit.

According to Sancia, the group had eight Volkswagen vans and a Rolls Royce at the time.

Sancia said that Yahowha was in Egypt at the pyramids on Easter Sunday. She said that an Adept (priest), who took them through a pyramid, told Yahowha, "you are Jesus Christ."

WANDERED

In San Francisco, the group had trouble finding a place to stay. According to Sancia, they wandered for 40 days in the wilderness, going from church to church seeking Christians.

She said that they were often removed bodily from churches, and that they only found one Christian, who let them stay in her two-bedroom house in Mill Valley.

They then moved into a house known as the Atherton Mansion in San Francisco, "but things didn't work out there," said Sancia. They moved to Hilo in June after Yahowha told them that Hawaii "is the original Garden of Eden."

The family begins each day at 3 a.m. at the old Doc Hill mansion with a swim in the ocean. Then they take cold showers, participate in an exercise program, and chant God's name. They listen to music and have a family gathering until just before sunrise.

The family then gathers at Keokea Point where they watch the sun come up. Sancia said they get spiritual guidance from Yahowha at sunrise, and throughout the day.

They hold a family business-of-the-day meeting after sunrise.

"We've been doing that for five years," said Sancia.

DON'T KNOW

Neither Sancia nor Omne could say where Eternal Now will be going after they leave their home in Keaukaha.

"We just don't know," said Sancia. "We may stay in Hilo, and we may go somewhere else. We just don't know."

Meanwhile, family members on Oahu are being allowed to remain in their home after their lease expired Thursday.

HERB CAEN

The Morning Line

WELL, IT SEEMS the rambling old Atherton mansion at 1990 California — now occupied by the 140-member commune called The Religion of TEN (The Eternal Now) — is owned by a Hawaiian sugar heir named Spencer Andrew, who bought it recently from the estate of Carrie Rousseau, the mansion's previous occupant, for $178,500 CASH! . . . Andrew, who commutes between here and Hawaii, is leasing the landmark to The Eternal Now for just about what the commune's unwed mothers are getting from local welfare services ($3375 a month). "However," says the commune, voluble spokesperson, name of Isis, "we have an option to buy in six months. We have money and we are working hard to clean up this old place. The people here receiving benefits are unwed mothers who have been abandoned — they need and deserve this help" . . . As to reports that TEN came here after being asked to leave Hawaii, Isis says firmly, "Not true. We were threatened there by people who didn't understand what we were doing. Our lives were in danger so we left. We wish to be welcome in San Francisco."

Airborne Odyssey Over Big Island

By Jan Selland
Tribune-Herald Staff Writer

At 11 a.m. Saturday, Mercury Geiger, 22, of Keaukaha, leaped off the summit of Mauna Kea with his glider, intending to soar down the slopes of the mountain to the site of the canoe races in Hilo Bay.

Around noon, the blue and gold glider was spotted by unidentified persons from Hilo coming out of the clouds over Honomu or Pepeekeo, making a right turn towards Hilo.

At 2:36 p.m. the Waiakea Fire Station received a call from the flight control tower at Lyman Field which reported sighting an object three to four miles offshore of Onomea.

Air 1, the County helicopter, and the rescue boat were dispatched to the site, but the object turned out to be an orange boat.

At 3:28 p.m. a person claiming to be the brother of Geiger appeared at the Waiakea Station to report that Geiger was overdue.

SECOND SEARCH

At 6:08 p.m. the fire and rescue squad initiated their second search after the family of the flier reported they thought they saw him on the Hilo side south of Mauna Kea.

At 6:39 the glider was sighted by the helicopter's crew but the flyer was nowhere to be seen. Geiger appeared a few minutes later, unharmed, and ready to be brought to Hilo.

Geiger, unruffled by the afternoon's happenings, said the flight was intended to be a demonstration to show people what hang gliding is all about.

Not being able to calculate the thiness of the air, Geiger said he first landed in a huge desert of lava rock after his initial take-off from the summit. After walking about ten miles he was again airborne, only to land in a huge pasture.

TOO FLAT

"I couldn't take off from there because it was too flat. So I set up the kite and then took a nap because I was really tired. I woke up and started to walk home," Geiger recalled.

"When the helicopter came, I made a big cloud of dust with my feet and he saw me and picked me up."

Geiger, who said he was probably the world's champion hang glider pilot, said he hopes to start a school in Hilo to teach kids how to fly.

"You have to do it right and approach flying with respect and knowledge," he said.

Eternal Now about homeless

Eternal Now sect members, having lost their spiritual leader in a hang-glider crash and facing eviction from their Hilo home, also have an uncertain future in their Lanikai home.

Charles Watson, who owns the Lanikai home, said yesterday he did not rent it to the group but that his wife leased it to a couple, Mr. and Mrs. Dennis McKenna.

"They signed a five-month lease and it's up on Sept. 4, Thursday," he said.

"WE WERE NOT aware until about a month ago that all these people, 15 or so, had moved in with the McKennas but he said they were his friends and just staying for a while. We told them they'd have to leave.

"He's told me, and the others have, that they're planning to leave. But McKenna has gone, and I've heard that he's in Hilo with the other group."

"But the rent is paid through August and the lease is up Thursday."

Harvest Moon, a disciple of the sect's late leader, Yahowha, also known as James Edward Baker, said yesterday that the Lanikai group's plans were indefinite.

"We've made no plans about the house," he said. "It depends on what Mrs. Watson wants and what we decide."

IT WAS REPORTED yesterday that Eternal Now members in Hilo were mailed an eviction notice Thursday, the day before Friday's news that Yahowha, 53, was fatally injured Monday.

They occupy the late senator William H. "Doc" Hill's former Keokea Road home, now owned by the estate of Selwyn Jenkins, who died Aug. 13. The estate is being settled.

Yahowha's death was reported Friday, 3½ days after his accident in his first hang-glider flight off the Makapuu cliffs.

His followers took the injured man to Lanikai, where he died that evening. Their religion forbids touching the remains for three days, until the soul leaves the body, they explained. Police are investigating.

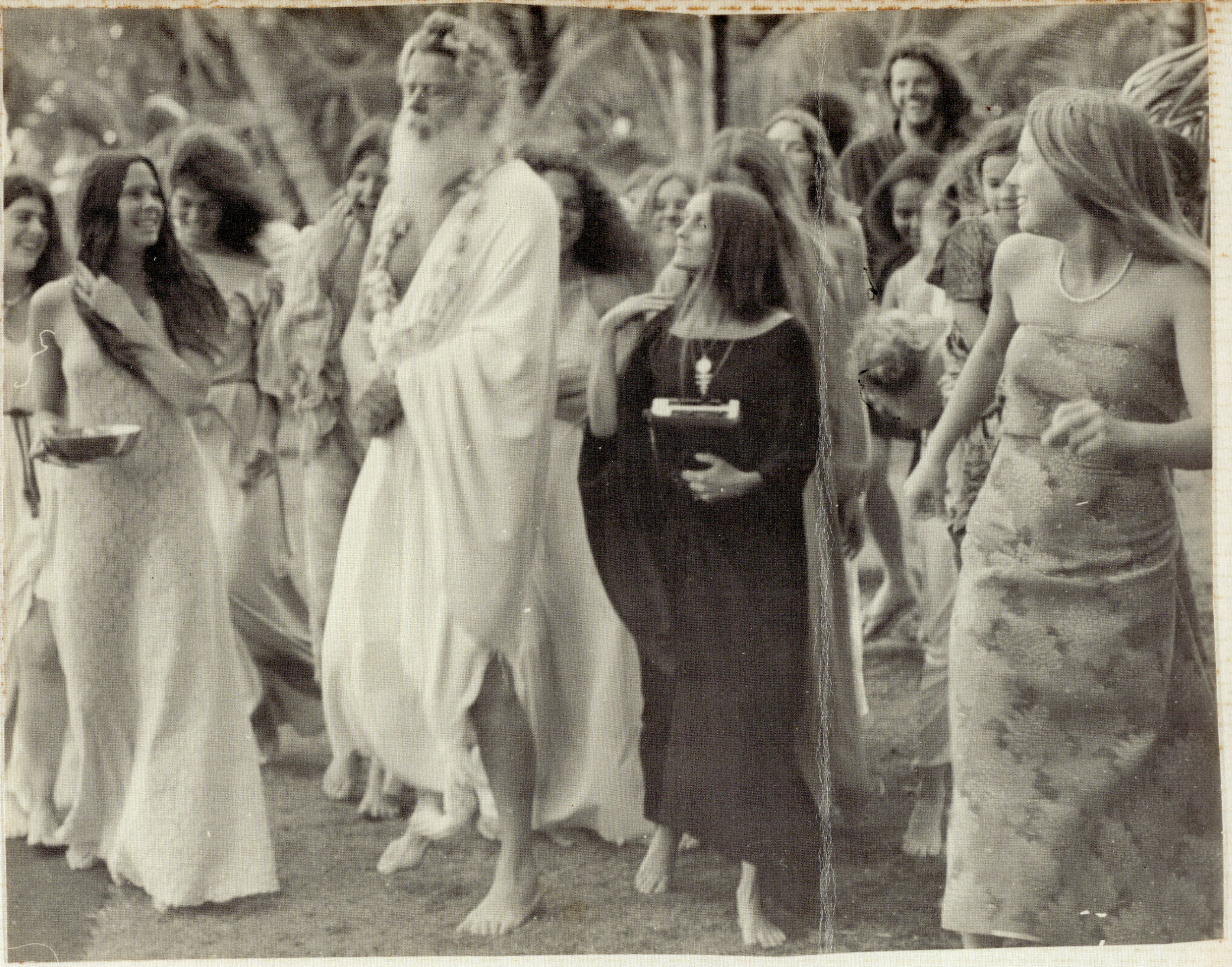

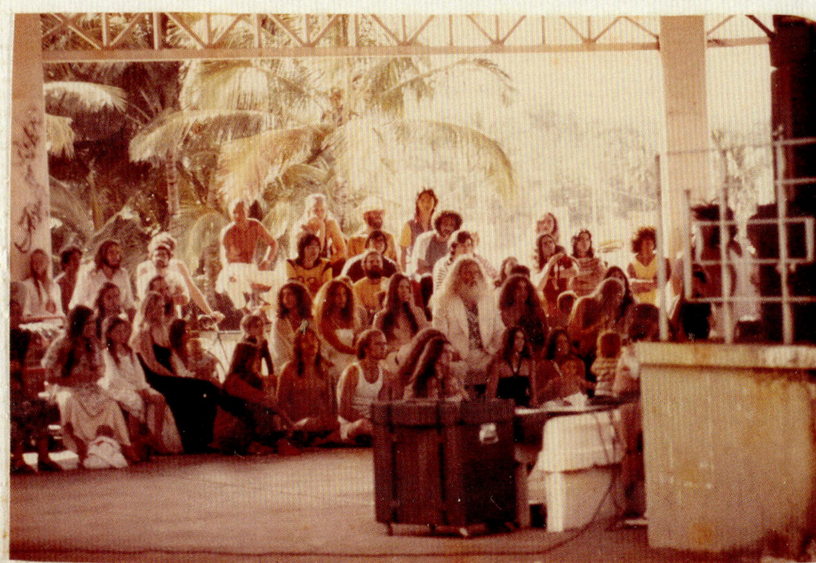

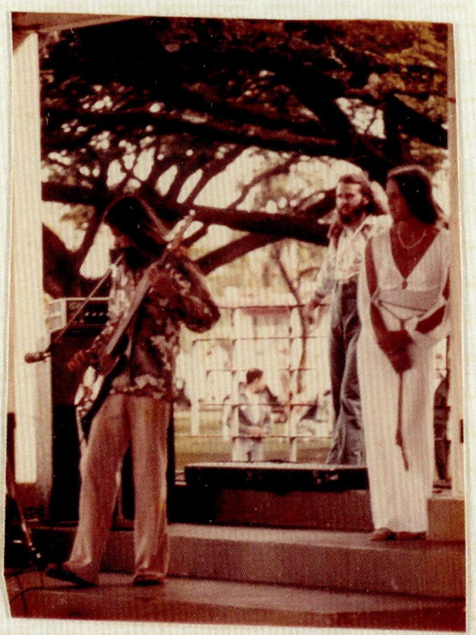

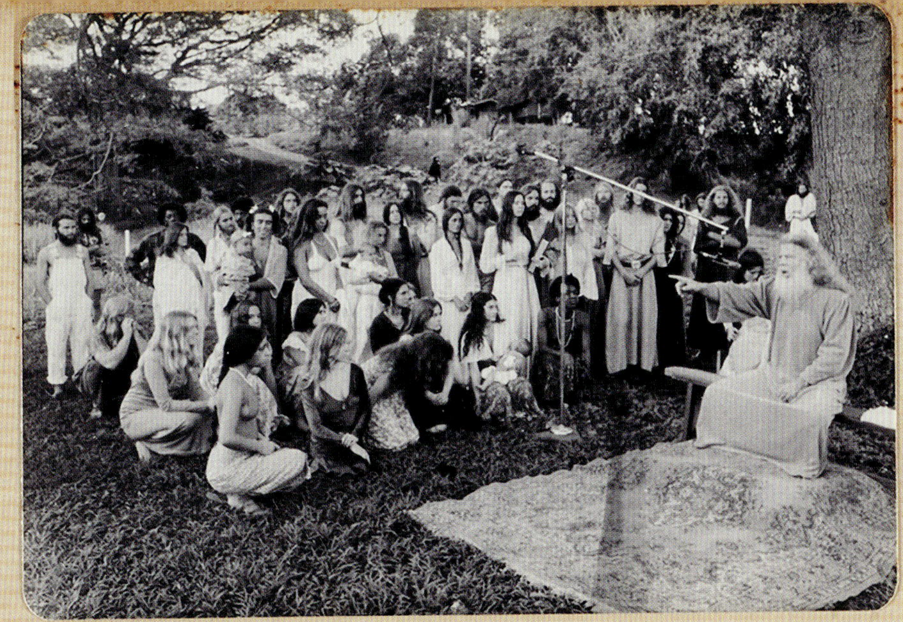

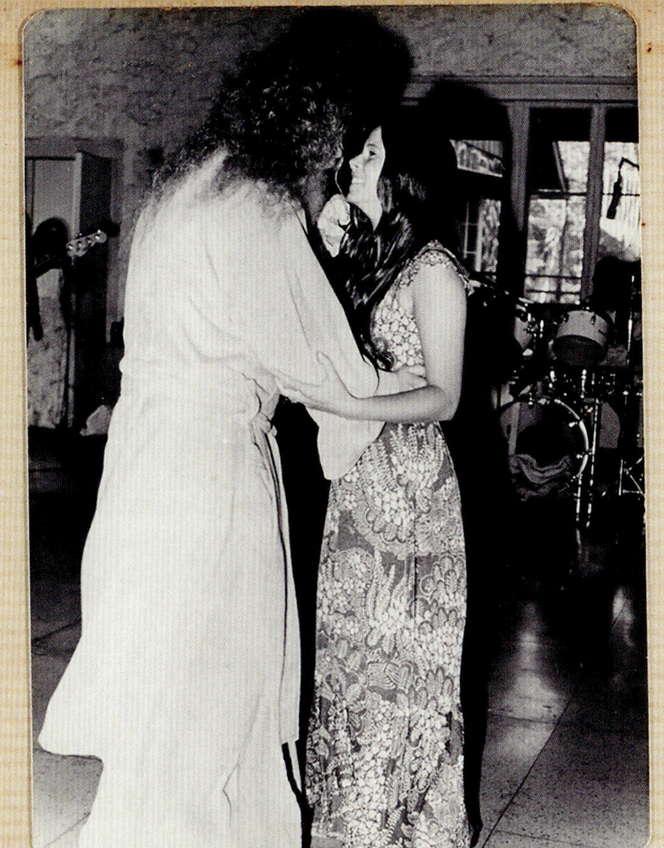

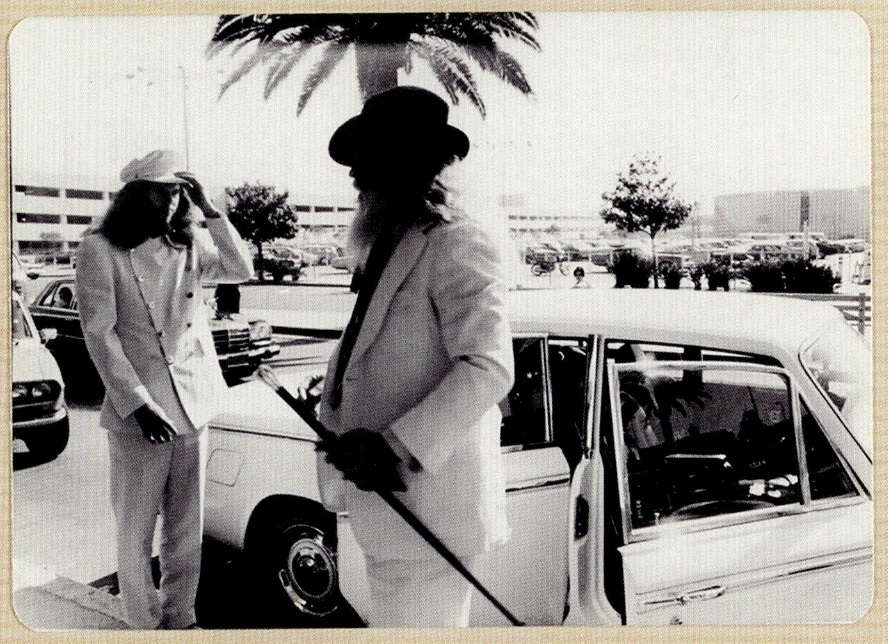

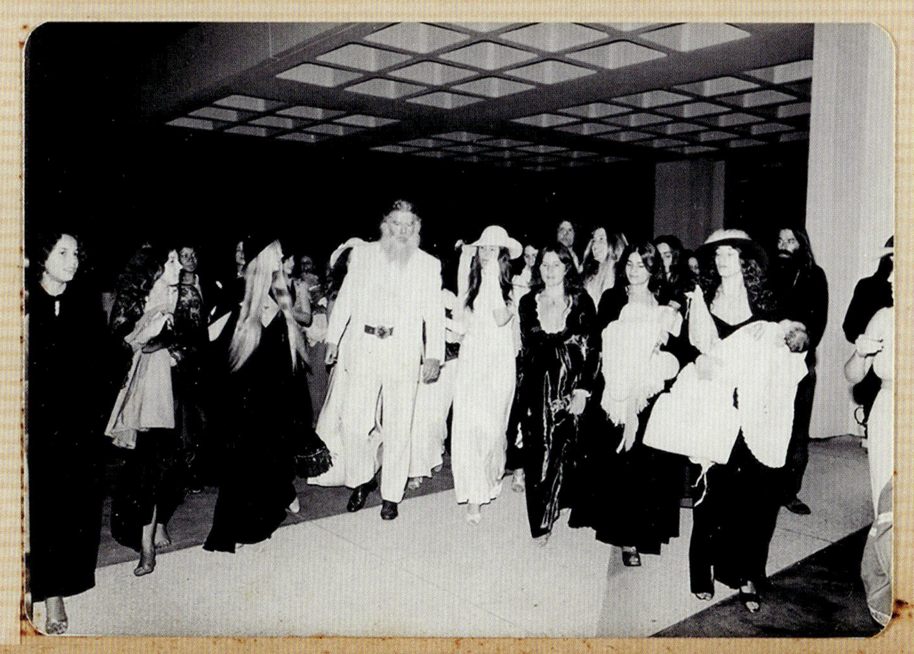

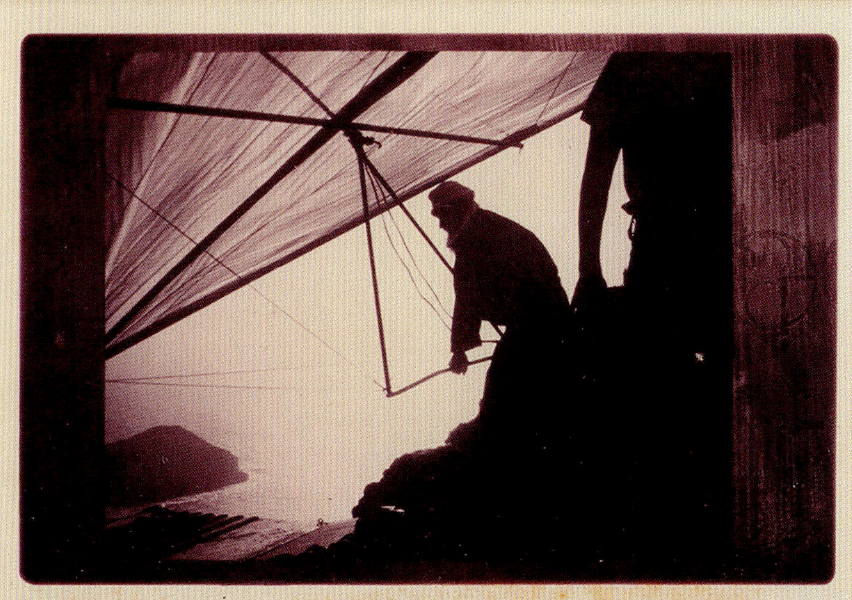

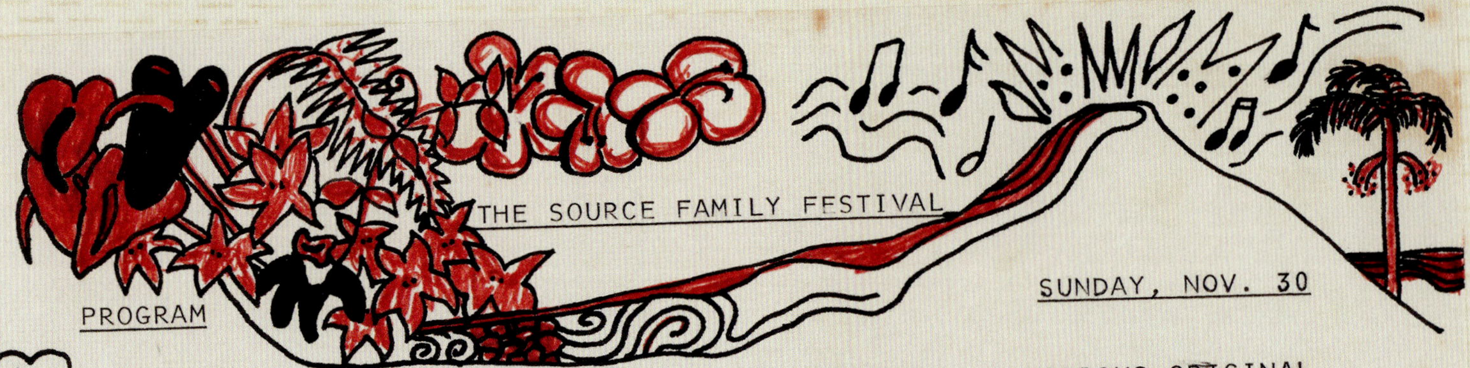

AN AFTERNOON OF LIVE MUSICAL ENTERTAINMENT FROM THE VARIOUS ORIGINAL

ARTISTS WITHIN THE SOURCE FAMILY.

2:PM.   SOMA   RHYTHM
         HALE   HOM
         DJIN
         AQUARIANA

"BREATH" IS THE BAND WITH THE NEW SOUND EVERYONE HAS BEEN WAITING FOR.
THEIR ORIGINAL MATERIAL INCLUDES:

SLEEPY-EYED WOMAN   LONG LONESOME ROAD
BREATH UPON THE WIND   SLIDE BOOGIE
WOMAN BEYOND THE SUN   EDGE OF A DREAM
WITH LOVE   MOCKING BIRD
I DON'T REALLY THINK YOU'RE BLIND   FOR ALL TIMES
IT WON'T BE LONG   HALO'S SONG
SONG FOR SWEET RAIN   LOVE UPON THE DEVIL'S FACE

"BREATH" ALSO EXPANDS INTO SPONTANEOUS MUSIC WITH THE ADDITION OF
ONE, OUR MAGNIFICENT MIME AND M.C.

"YAHOWHA 13" IS A GATHERING TOGETHER OF HEAVY MUSICAL TALENT.
IT'S A REAL, BIG CONCERT BAND. THEIR MUSIC INCLUDES: "GET INTO THE
MUSIC", "HOME", "LADY OF LADIES", "DO ME".

5:PM THE SOURCE FAMILY SLIDE SHOW
THIS IS A COLLECTION OF SLIDES TAKEN FROM THE BEGINNINGS OF THE FAMILY,
SHOWING WHERE WE HAVE BEEN DURING THE SEVEN YEARS WE HAVE BEEN TOGETHER.

L.A. 1969 - 1974   (1973 - MAUI PICTURE)
KAUAI. 1975, JANUARY - MARCH
SAN FRANCISCO. 1975 MARCH - JUNE
HILO, HAWAII. 1975 JUNE
LANIKAI, OAHU. 1975 AUGUST.

REFRESHMENTS FROM THE FAMILY'S GOODIES BAKERY WILL BE SOLD AT THE
REFRESHMENT STAND.   ENJOY A GLASS OF FREE PUNCH.

PLEASE COME   ***   ALL ARE WELCOME   ***   PLEASE COME ***

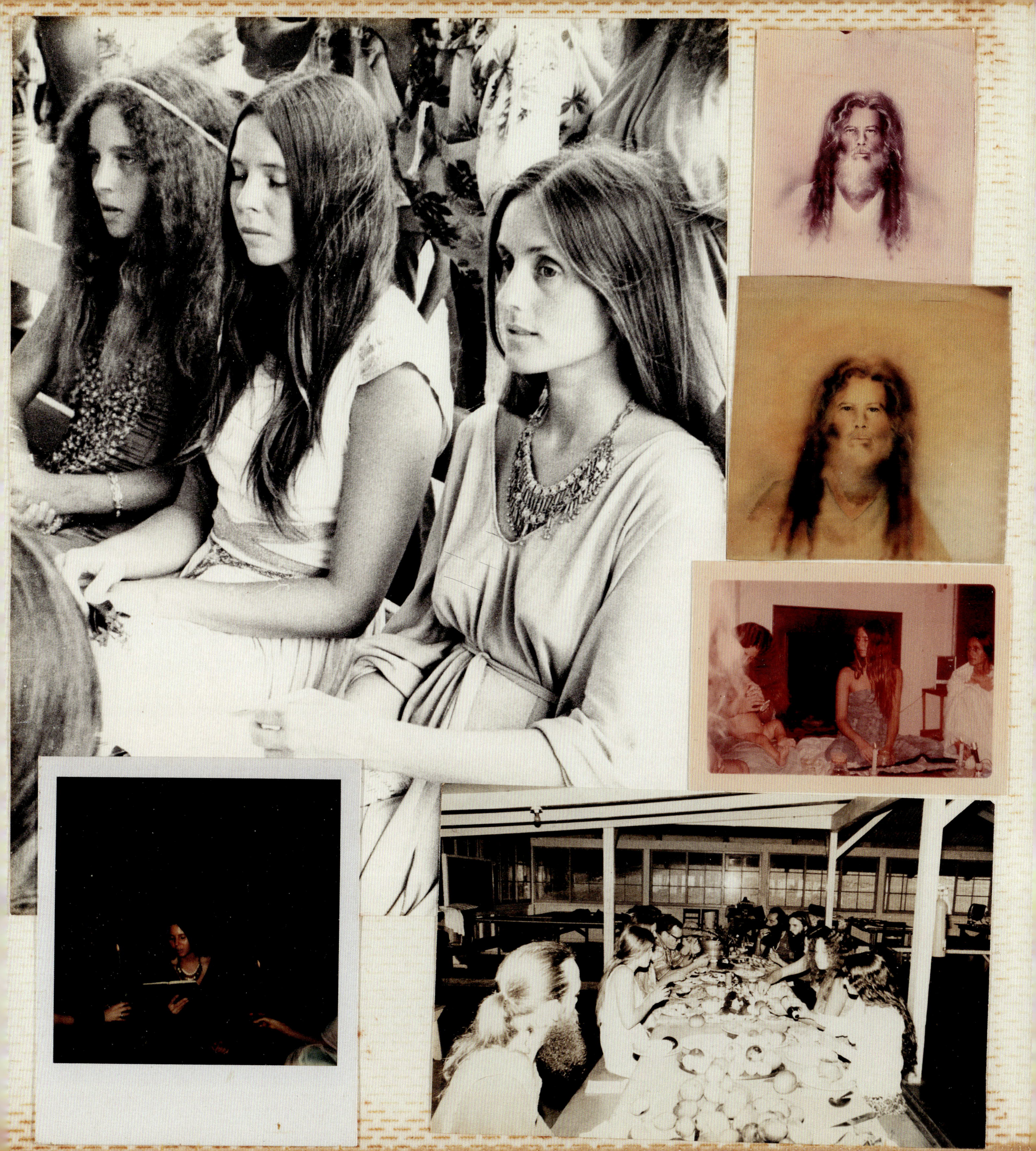

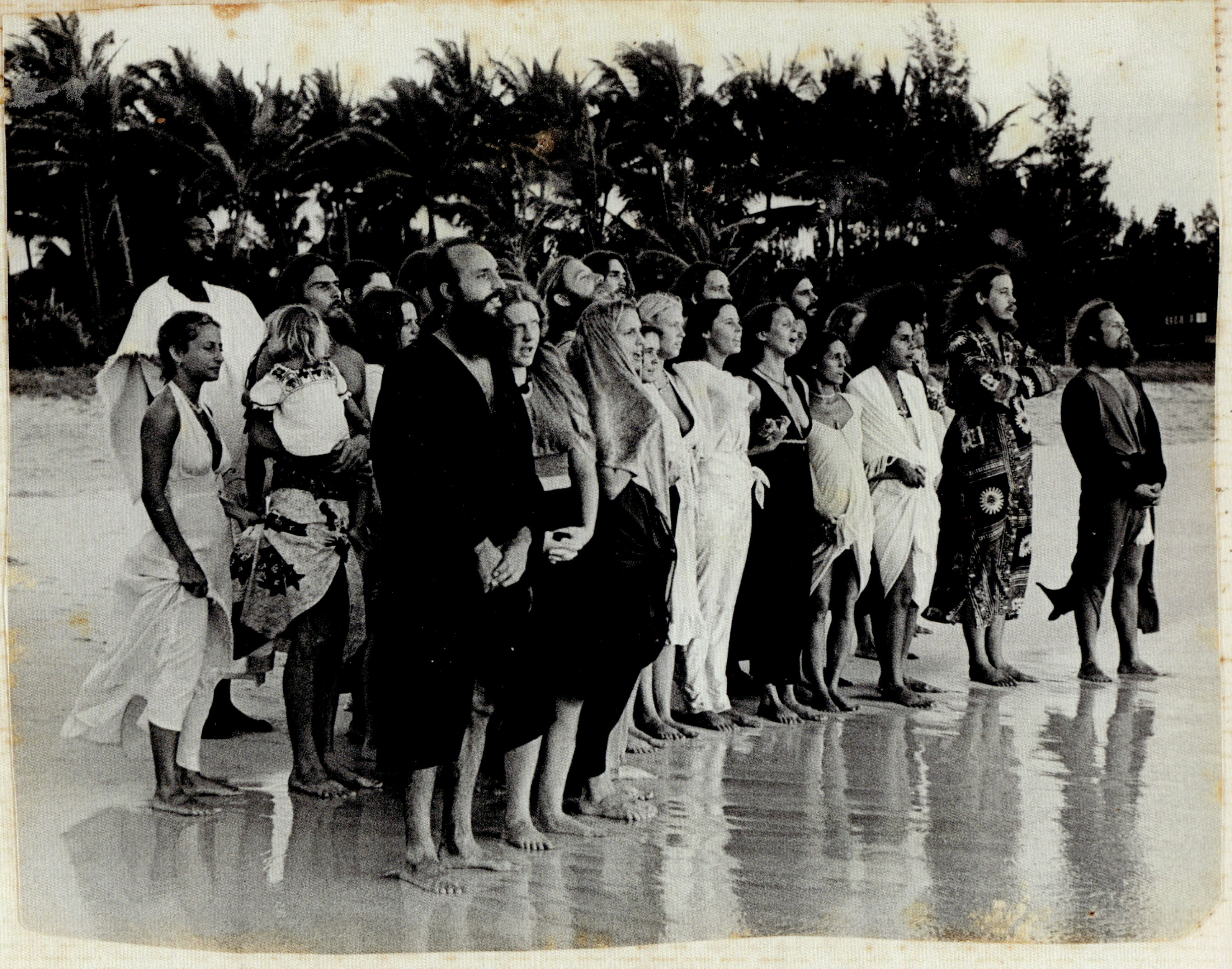

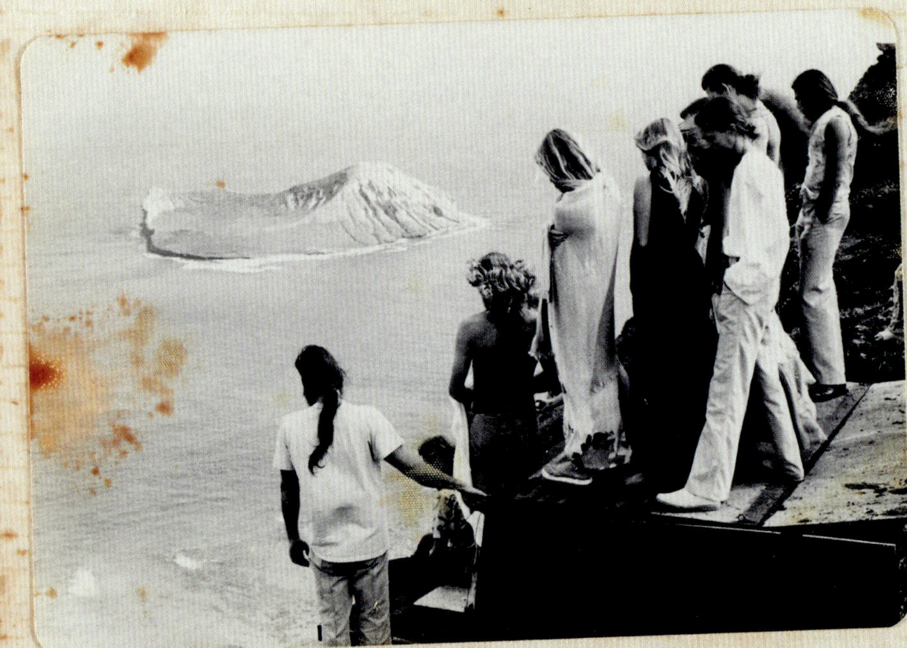

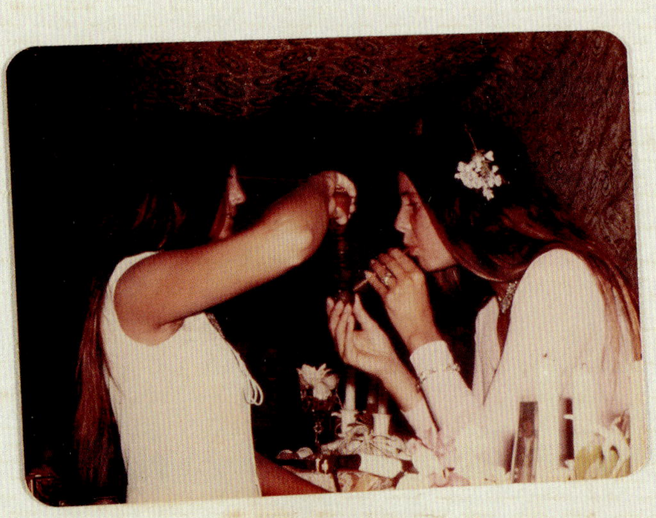

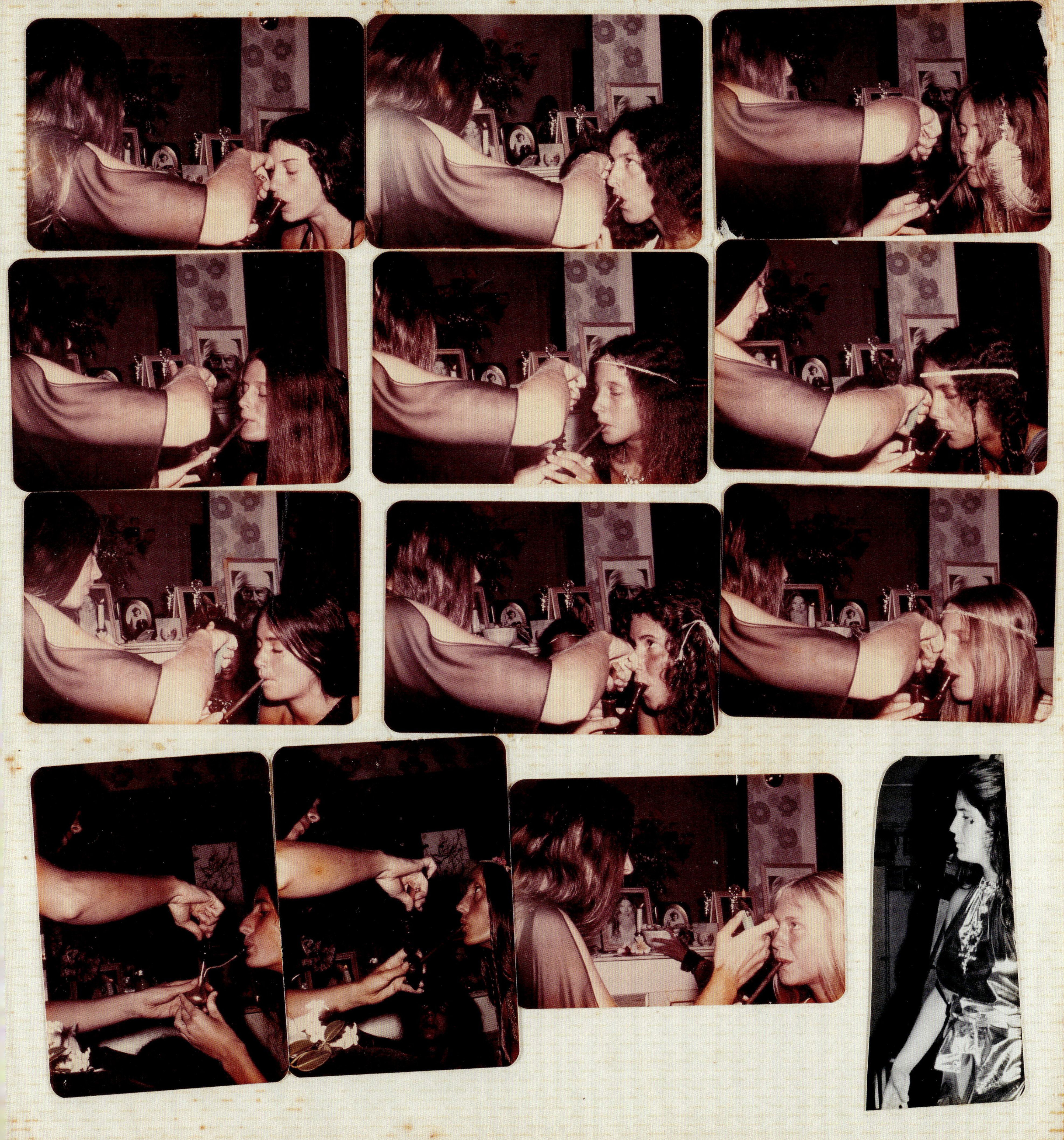

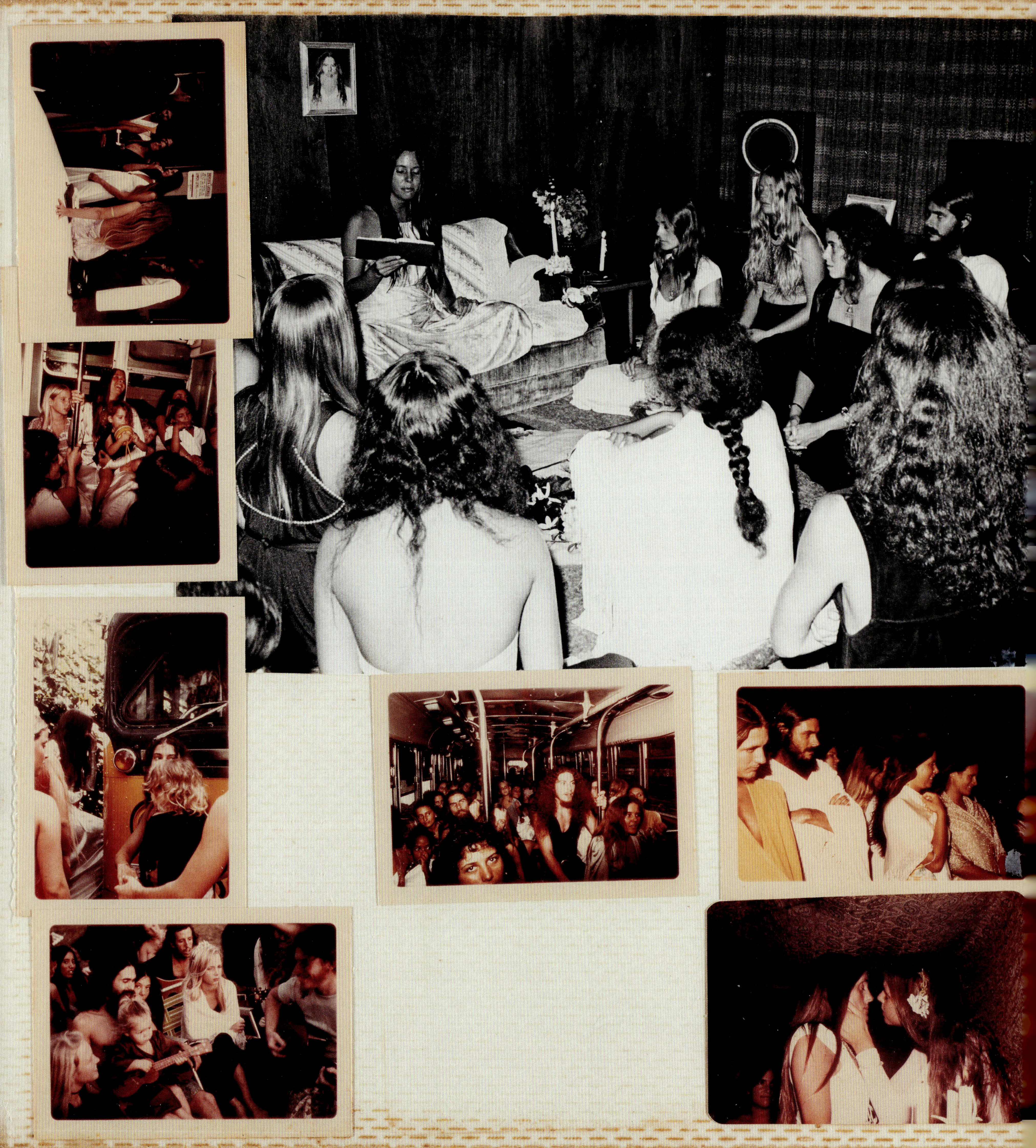

The Word...

For you who are still seeking,
and have not found
For you who want the keys to
Liberation

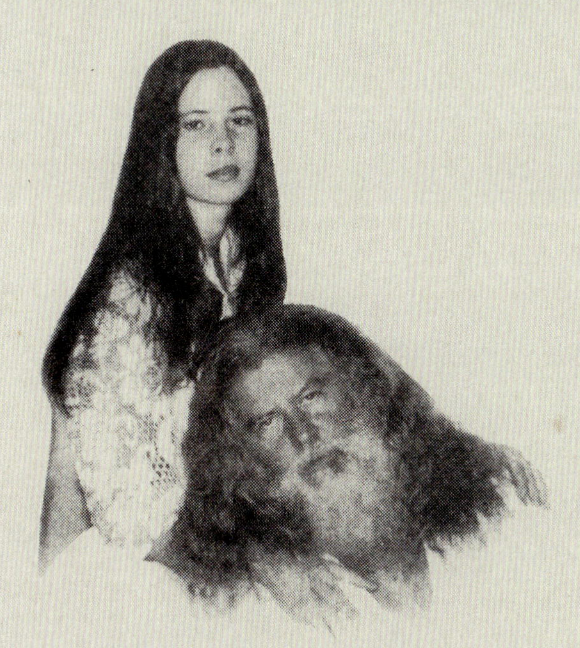

Come Quickly!

4:30 a.m. every Saturday
morning ⚭ Makushla

for further information contact: Goodies Bakery   phone:
32 Kainehe Street
Kailua, Hawaii 96734   261-4692

Producing Special Christmas Film

Source Family Filled With Talent

The group worked during Christmas Eve and Christmas Day videotaping one-hour holiday special which was aired on Comtec, Channel 8, Thursday evening. The Christmas Special consisted of a series of skits, arranged and video-taped by members of the family.

Comtec manager John Cunningham and State Sen. Richard Henderson, president of the firm, loaned equipment to the group for the special, and personally backed the effort. The special also will be shown on Maui TV, and possibly Oahu.

The family has also been backed by such people as Hilo attorney Dwayne Carlsmith, Norm Frane of Land Man Realty, Bill Stearns and Bob Crowell of Murreyair, and Jack Davis of Hilo Natural Foods, according to members of the family.

The group is made up of a number of accomplished musicians, and several architects, carpenters, painters, draftsmen, plumbers, and mechanics, to name a few. Many have worked with leading Hollywood studios and have been involved in various major Mainland productions.

Isis worked on the script and was a general assistant in the 20th Century Fox production "Easy Rider," which featured Peter Fonda and Dennis Hopper. She is the daughter of retired Air Force General Charles Peters, Chief of Documentations.

Lovely, who plays the violin for one of the family's bands, "Breath," and who played background music for the Christmas Special, is the daughter of Andre Previn, conductor of the London Philharmonic Orchestra. Previn recently married Mia Farrow.

She was accompanied by Rhythm on the piano.

Phophecy, who operated the camera for the special, is the son of Paul Coates, a well-known syndicated columnist for the Los Angeles Times. Coates also hosted a television show called "Confidential File," and won a total of 13 Emmy awards during his career.

Prophecy was a 20th Century Fox actor, and a writer for Universal Studios, doing work on such productions as "Camelot" and "Bonnie and Clyde." He worked on the TV special "The Day of the God," dealing with the yacht which held up a French nuclear test in 1973.

Phythias worked with overhead projection light shows at the "Electric Theater" in Chicago before joining the family.

Joshua was with Trans American Video, the largest video tape company in the world. His father, Brad Kemp, is on that company's board of directors, and his mother, Rose Kemp, is a leading national television advisor.

Octavius, who is the drummer for Breath, was a musician in California for about 12 years.

Jupiter was a production assistant for MGM studios for four years.

Other members working on the Christmas Special included Mother Makushla, who heads

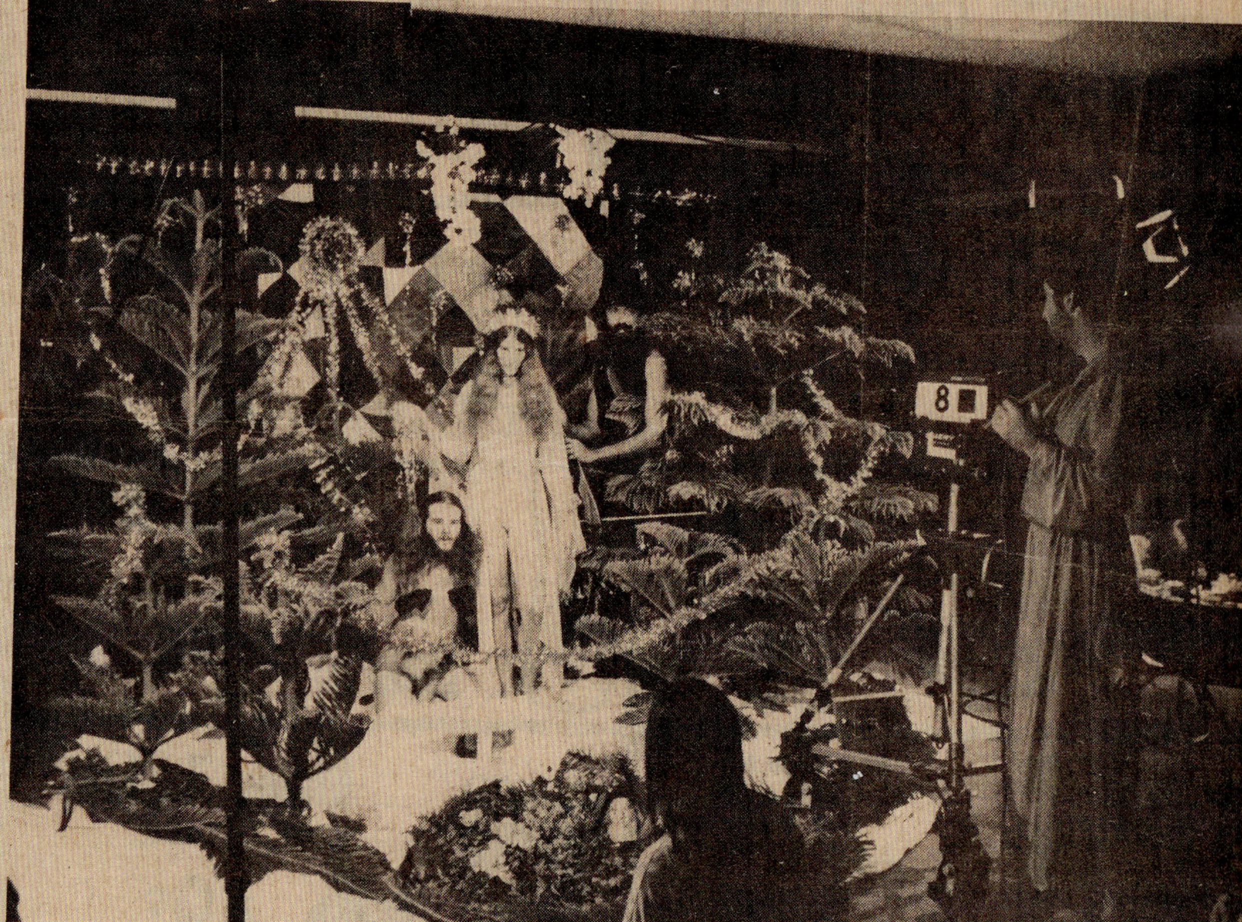

THE HUNTER, THE HUNTED AND THE FAIRY — Members of The Source Family work on one of the skits for their Christmas Special, aired on Channel 8 on Christmas Day. The reindeer is played by One, the fairy by Ahom, and the hunter (peering out from the bushes), Alchemy. Prophecy, who was Kevin Coates, son of the nationally known journalist Paul Coates, before he was renamed by Yahowha, operates the camera. Mother Makushla is seen kneeling in front, directing the play.

the council of 13. She directed the skits. Venus worked on wardrobes, and Sun, who is a sound technician, operated the recording board.

The Source Family plans to establish a mobile recording studio on the Big Island that will enable local and Mainland artists to record anywhere on the island.

The family has two bands, Breath, and Yahowha 13. Both will be playing at the Crater Festival in Honolulu on Dec. 31 and Jan. 1.

They also plan to expand their bakery, "Goodies," on Haili Street, and say they will establish a restaurant for breakfast and lunch, using the recipes for organic food which made Yahowha's "The Source" a Hollywood favorite. Breath and Yhowha 13 will provide live entertainment at the restaurant.

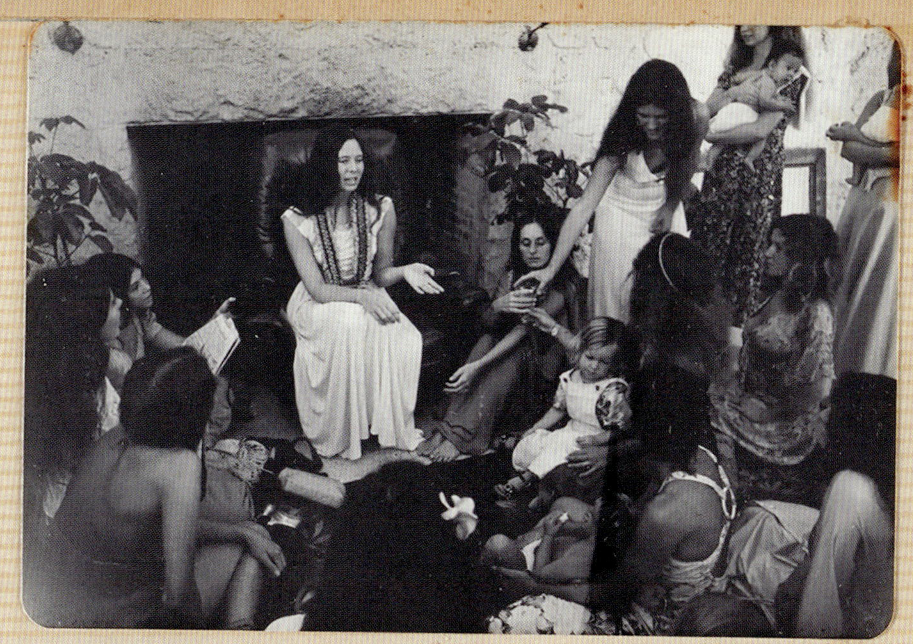
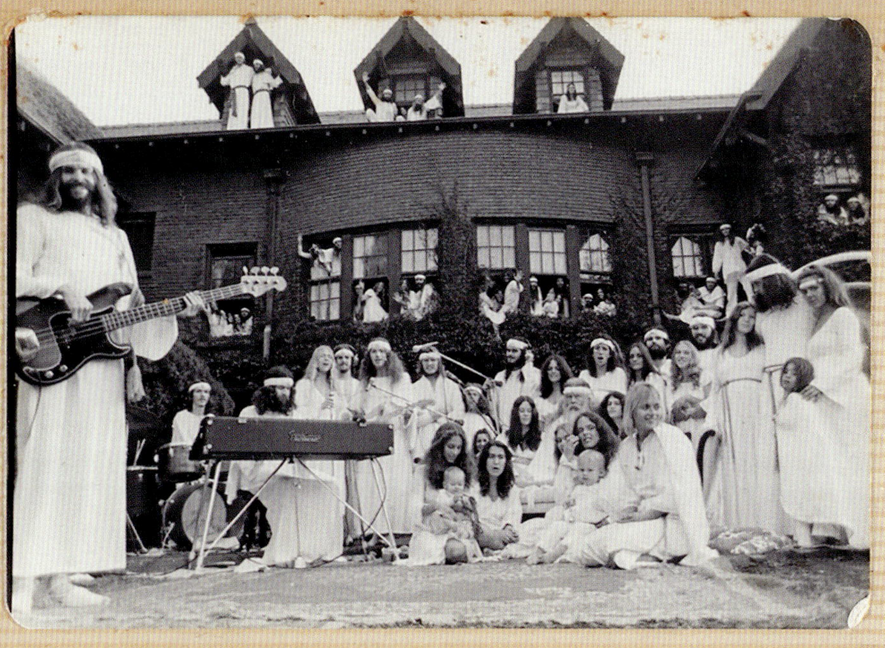
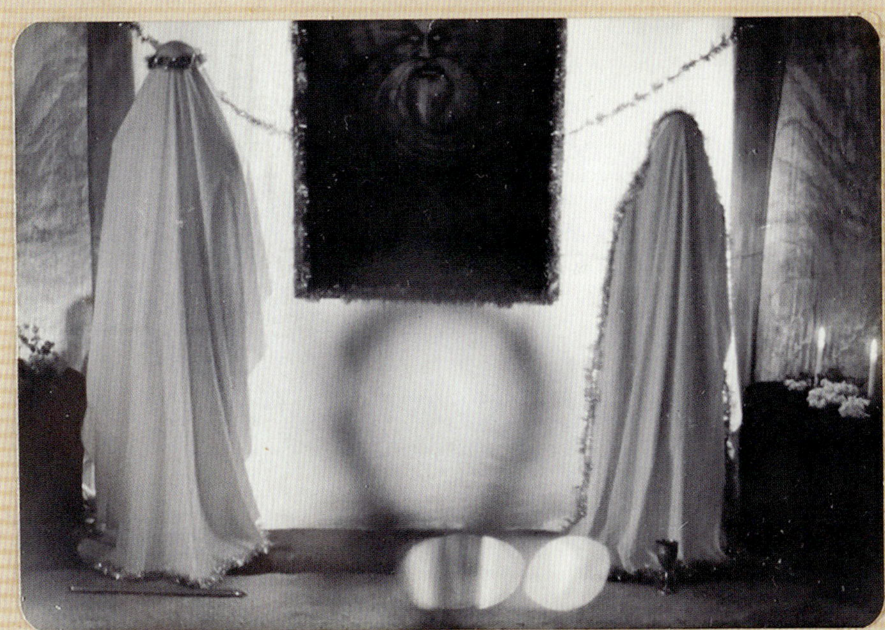
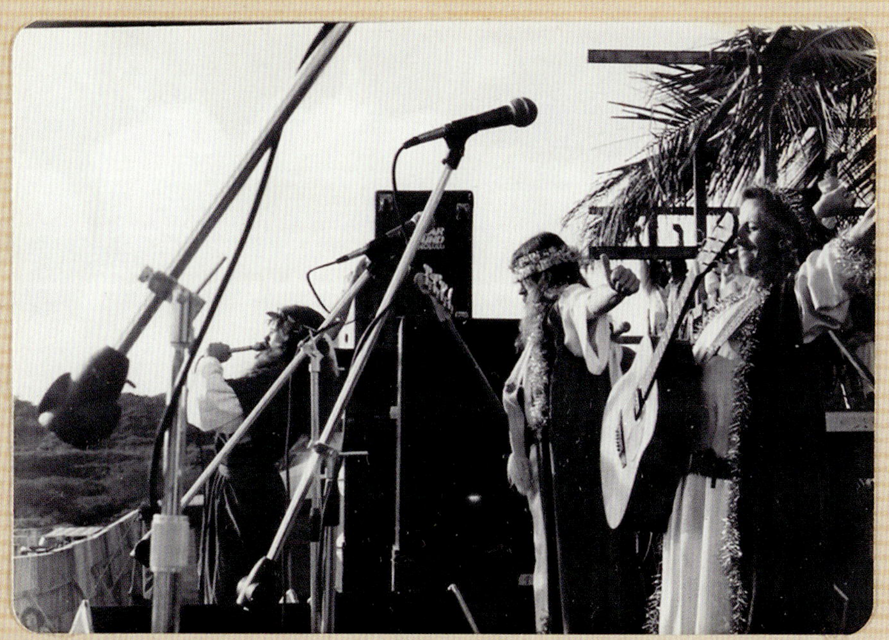
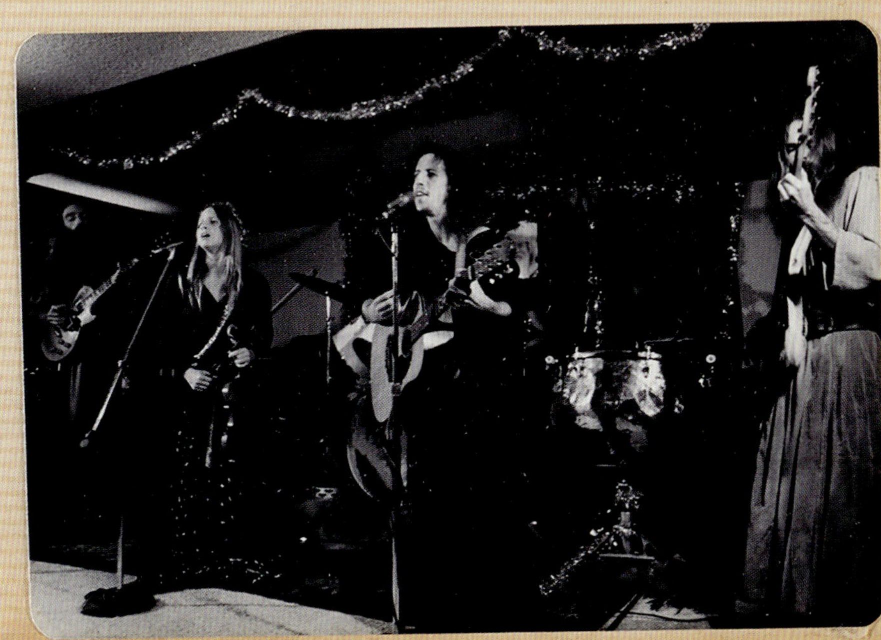
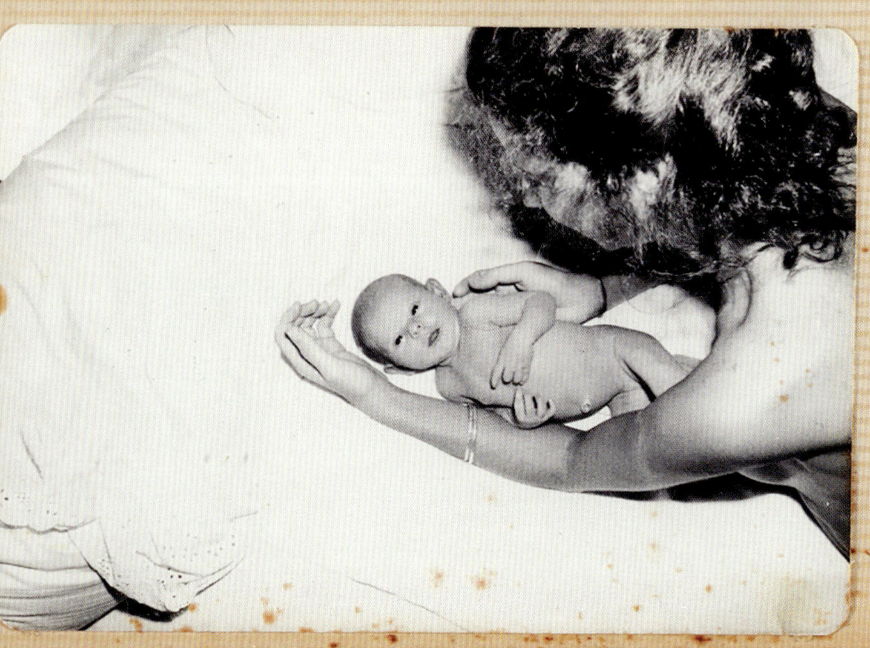

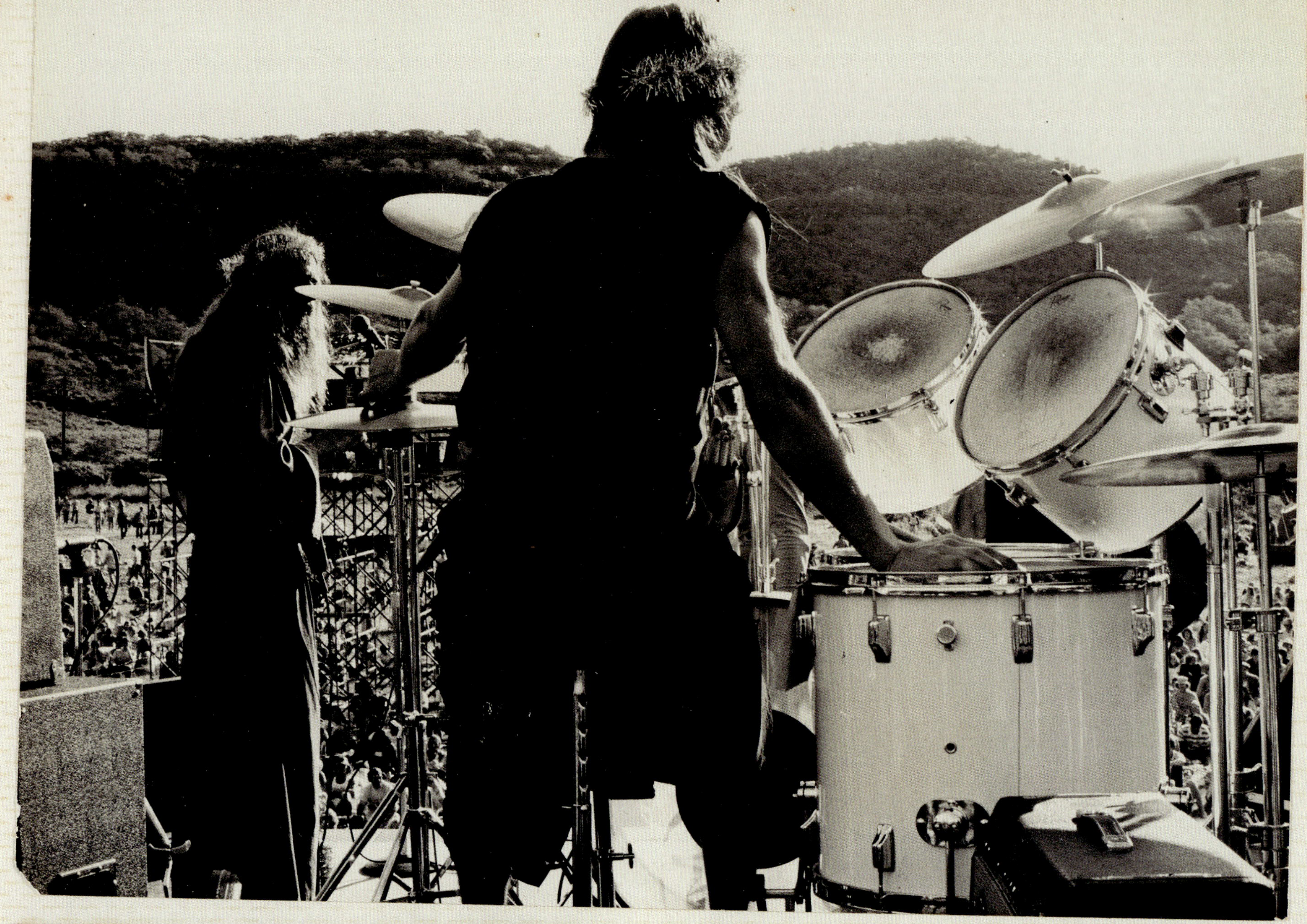

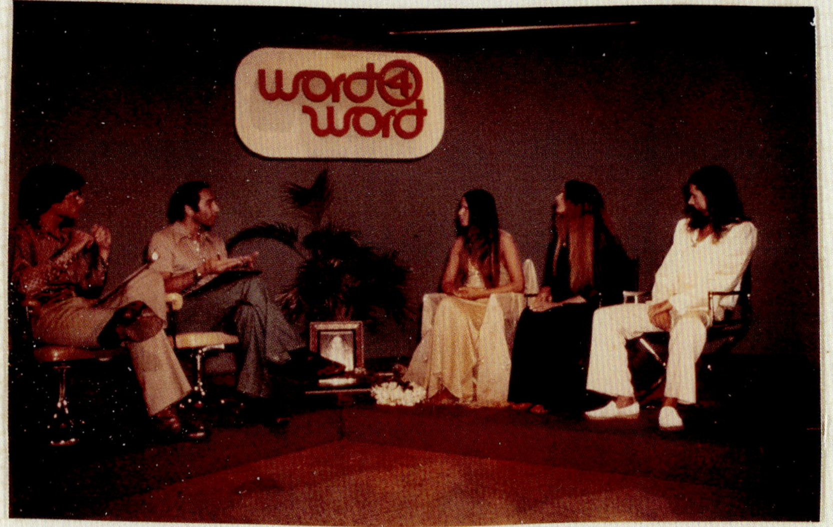
word 4 word

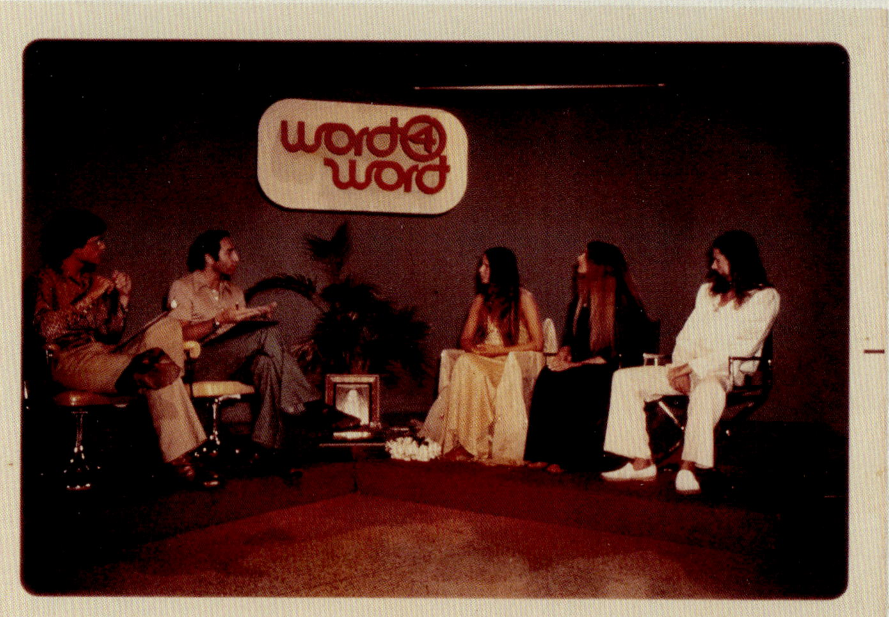
word 4 word

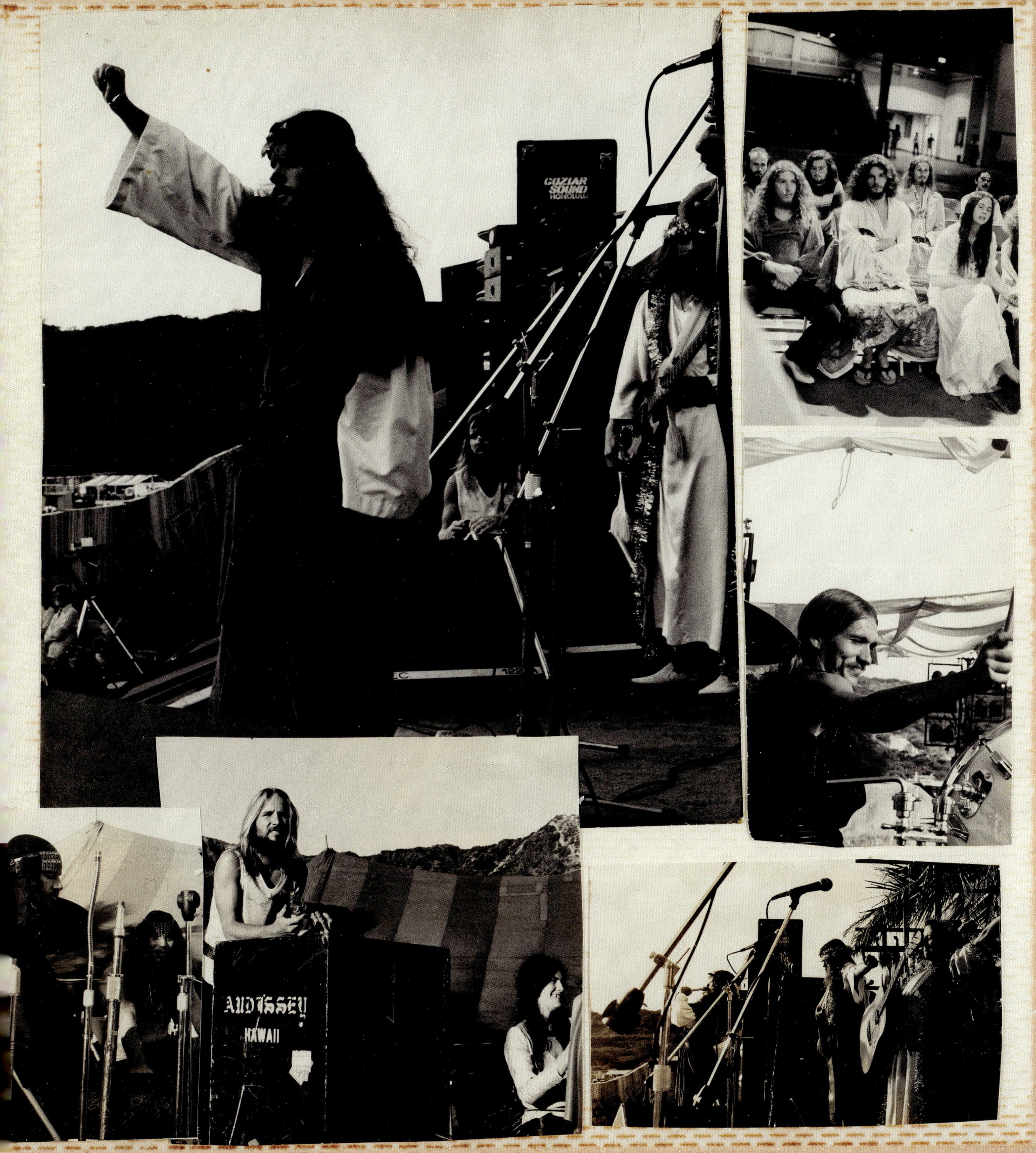
COZIAR
SOUND
HONOLULU
ODISSEY
HAWAII

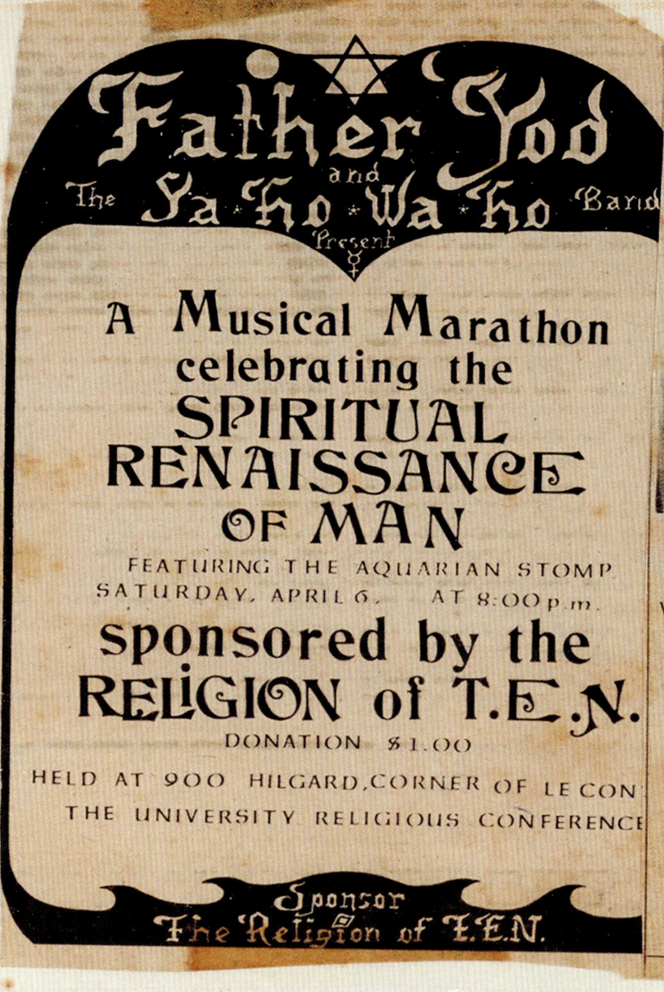

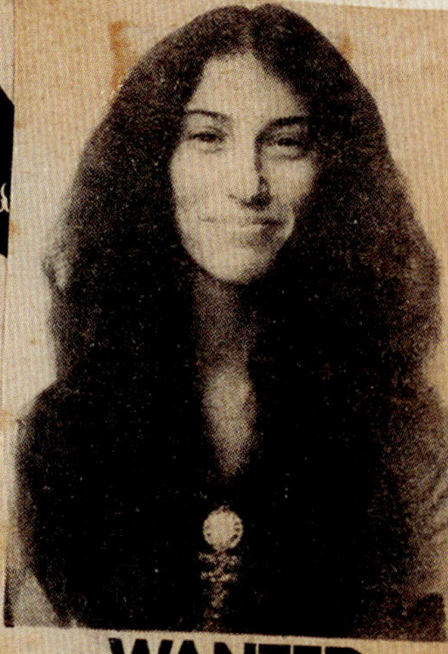

The Aquarian Family

presents

THE FATHER OF AQUARIUS

On God and Hair

SOL-AMMON'S RETURN:

A Natural Birth Film

BONADEA:

The High Priestess of Astrology

and

SONGS FOR THE GOLDEN AGE

by

The Brotherhood of the Source

WE ARE, "The Great Saints and Sages of the Past who are among us now recognizable by their hair."

It has been predicted that the next Spiritual Awakening will come from the west. Here in this City of the Angels a vibration is being born which will usher in the New Age in which All will recognize themselves as Suns of God.

Editor-s Note: Om-Ne, 24, has done this horoscope for residents of the Big Island for 1976. Om-Ne, a recent resident in Hilo, was raised in a family of astrologers and is the astrologer for the Aquarian family of Hilo. This is 1976 as he sees it in the stars and planets.

The eastern coast of our island at Puna was a hallowed spot for star study and divination. The Kahuna and his students greeted the rising sun there every morning, sang to each of the morning stars by name and contemplated the shapes and color of the clouds.

All of nature was keenly observed in order to decipher the message of the gods to their children for that day and one day at a time was enough. For the benefit of their bodies they basked and bathed in nature's elements, and for the guidance of mind and heart they looked to the sky.

Regardless of your age or position in life, you are subject to an ebb and flow of energy along with the whole planet earth. The old Hawaiians, along with most ancient races recognized Earth as a being and the moving sky a starry brain, always living and always moving, day after day, and generation after generation. An astrologer never ceases to be amazed at the seeming opening and closing of the curtain upon life's stage. The script is written in the stars and I can only suggest that if this article is saved the pattern revealed will supply enough substantiation to an open mind to demonstrate the unity and the coherence of life's message in the stars.

VISITOR—In first photograph taken by Hale Observatory of comet Kohoutek coma (gassy halo) and tail are apparent. Seven-minute exposure time for this plate explains why stars appear smudged.

The symbolism which is intricately designed into the American dollar bill stands as a message for future generations from the founding fathers.

By Om-Ne

Our national life experience in this century has demonstrated to mankind the great power and love of the American people.

We are a people, conceived in history as a people with a destiny, a responsibility, a critical role in the drama of the earth.

The founding fathers of America believed this truth with every fiber of their being. So high and pure was their inspiration that they pledged all, to secure the foundation of a government conceived in liberty.

Amercian Prophets

Few Americans today know of the high degree of mystical zeal which the first American leaders lived by. But today their faith in destiny, prophecy and divine guidance can be detected in the symbolism of the great seal which they created as a sign for now.

Knowing the law of birth, maturation and eventual decay, two principle themes were chosen to inspire America for coming generations in the unfoldment of humanity upon this planet.

Tife first theme, expressed on the front of the great seal, is regeneration. On the back of the seal, the theme is faith.

The eagle's message is capsulized in the words of Thomas Paine:

"We have it in our power to begin the world over again."

The pyramid side reflects the poetical message of Walt Whitman:

"O America! Because you build for mankind . . I build for you."

Now look at the reverse side of the $1 bill and visually absorb the crescendo of thought, emotion and life force held in hope for humanity by the fathers of the United States.

The corruption of America's first dream was anticipated by our forefathers. The grave danger which now threatens the national life, due to the abandonment of the pure principles which motivated them, was prohesized in the traditional masonic meaning if the numbers, letters and figures of the seal.

George Washington and his 13 generals were all masons and history records the occult ceremonies which they, as heads of state, performed as a regular part of the national observances and funtions. For example, the laying of the cornerstones of the white house.

The First Design

Before the eagle holding the 13 arrows and olive branch was finally selected as the national arms, a phoenix was used in the first drafts. The phoenix represents the process by which "evil" is turned to "good." The fierce bird rising from a bed of flames, holding the national symbols, was to tell the story of a nation, which through trial and error and painful life experiences, will rise to immortality.

The original design was modified for the final seal and an eagle was chosen as an alternative. In astrological symbolism, eagle and phoenix are identical, but the phoenix is mythological while the eagle is indigenous to the United States.

Today's systems and their abuse indeed reflects the confusion and sickness of the times. The early fathers anticipated this and the eagle's spiritual message, hope amidst this bleakness, can be read by anybody with a dollar in his pocket.

The founding fathers kenw that human nature oscillates in its expression between purity and corruption and then regenerated purity until at last man is through with the pain which selfishness must inevitably bring. The early fathers illustrated that all "evil" is the necessary and "good" painfull lesson involved in the creation of a better future.

The streamer in the beak of the eagle says "Novus Ordo Seclorum," a new order of the ages. On the reverse side are the mottos, "Ammuit Coeptis," which means "it is under the approval of God," and "E Pluribus Unum," or "all for one and one for all."

The Power of 13

Masonic symbolism, of which Washington and the men of his day were ardent students, is based upon astrology, the Bible, the great pyramid and the inner meaning of numbers. Thirteen is the number of Scorpio. The eagle and phoenix are ancient symbols of this sign, hence their use upon the seal. The use of 13 is repeated 13 times within the seal in masonary 13 means unit and love.

America's eagle, armed with olive branch and arrows states that she will establish and protect the peace of the world and open a new day of unity and love for humankind, even is she herself must pass through the phoenix's flames of death and rebirth.

The Secrets of the Pyramid

The years between 1976 and 2001 in both pyramid tradition and in astrology are the years of revelation in terms of the destiny of the United States. Our country's birth chart prophesied a purification through crisis beginning slowly in 1975 and being completed within a generation of time.

The number 13 signals the beginning of a new cycle of time.

The challenge to America indicated by 13, her destiny number and the number of original states, is to create in the midst of destruction, to stay positive in the face of death and war and to build anew and in new ways. No one could say, judging from conditions in the contemporary U. S. that America has fulfilled her destiny as mother of a new world. Astrologically speaking and according to the great seal, this work will begin in earnest in the 26 years following 1976.

Carrying the masonic symbols one step further, the role of Hawaii is provocatively suggested by the number 13. Thirteen, according to an ancient science used by the masons, fulfills itself numerically in the number 50. Hawaii, the 50th state, may be the only state capable of completely expressing the pure concept of America as seen by our first founders.

Hawaii is the home of America's last pioneers. She is pure and undefiled. Here there is still time and space to make a new order of the ages a reality. She is America's last hope to express beauty and order in free communities of men.

How and when will all this come to pass? No man can say. One can only hope within himself that when the tide of new thought and new ways begin to touch our individual lives here in Hawaii that we will not resist. Our creative involvement in a new world of new men is the hope of humanity.

It all begins at home.

Dollar Bill Symbolizes Past, Future

Editor's Note: This is the second and final installment of Om-Ne's astrological series for the Orchid Isle Magazine. In this new year, America's Bicentennial, the Big Island-based astrologer looks at the American dollar bill and reads the spiritual message that is woven there by our founding fathers. From this, he points to the next 25 years in America's and Hawaii's destiny.

Hawaii Tribune-Herald, Orchid Isle, January 4-10, 1976 — 3

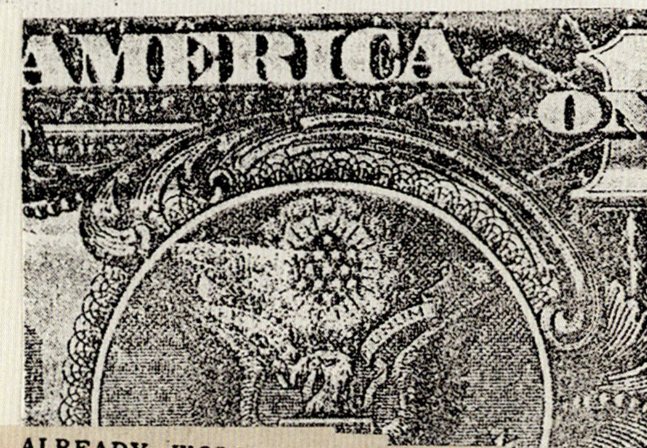

ALREADY, WOLFF has completed her special preparations for the night. The telescope, with an enormous mechanism guided by computer, is set to focus on Epsilon Lyrae, a star in the constellation Lyra.

The light from Epsilon Lyrae began its journey to Earth 200 years ago. Its rays that wili be captured by the telescope left the star 200 years before — in 1776,

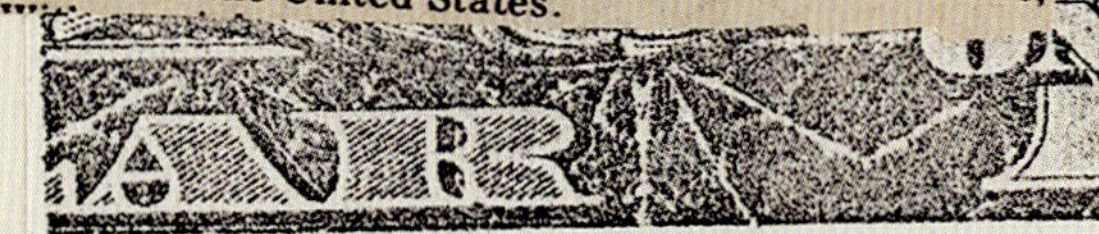

The number 13 is repeated 13 times throughout the seal on the dollar bill. The United States began with 13 original states.

This letter is what Justice was presenting for his "business"

THE SPIRIT OF 76

A new courage and fearlessness must be restored in the world for what is just and right---one that emblazons even the willingness to die for the creation of a new order and the dispersion of the old one that now has our 'number 9 galaxy' under the tyranny of the fear, death, and perversion ray. For we are fighting with renewed vigor the eternal war of the Forces of Light vs. the Forces of Darkness.

At the present stage of our evolution, heroic acts in the fresh style of Father Yahowha---the first Earthly Spiritual Father for the Aquarian Age---are appropriate for the man-child of America, not withstanding that of our founding fathers and our cultural heroes themselves.

It is time for a new wave of LIBERATORS to emerge on the planet Earth who will kindle the hearts and souls of a whole new generation of revolutionary youth throughout the world and the universe at large. They will comprise the vanguard of the Aquarian Planetary Peoples' Army, and will be as the drops of rain that precede the monsoon. Of vital interest to us, the Central Base of Operations and key zone to the liberation of all galaxies is our planet Earth, where the deciding battles will be fought. Likewise, the central base and key zone to the liberation of our <u>planet</u> is America, where the re-emergence of the Spirit of 76 will dramatically herald the official dawning of the Aquarian Age.

The style will be total revolution; aquarian guerrilla warfare, bearing action in harmony with the laws of Heavenly Father and Earthly Mother, employing every means, waged in every solar system, in every land, by and for every race and all beings. It is total revolution because aquarian guerrilla warfare transforms old habit patterns totally, and corresponds to both the spiritual birth of mankind and the cosmic clitoral orgasm of the universe. Furthermore, it is understood among all that its final objective is the liberation of all beings from every form of oppression and the unity of all beings in all of space.

So, in this struggle we shall use a synthesis of everything. When onlookers, or
the forces of darkness themselves, should ask us, what do we believe in?, let us
tell them, "We believe in everyone and everything. Everything was put here for us
to use. We have but to use it properly---for the good of all; and all for the
good of everything." This being our intention, we shall move swiftly, with light
and laughter, knowing that we have the greatest and most sacred power in the
universe---the SUN.

In this arena, Father Yahowha---the culmination of all the great ones of humanity
who have gone before Him---has bequeathed us a noble heritage of personal example
and invaluable lessons from which we may draw great inspiration and practical knowledge. Above all, **our** triumph will be certain if when struck by the death ray we can
demonstrate that we learned from Him the revolution must be fought by trial and
error, in the eternal now, using everything in the Sun; that there is no death;
and that solar action is the heart and blood of the New Order Of The Ages.

Of course, our heaviest ammunition is His wisdom that God is everything; that,
therefore, nothing can hurt you; that every truth is a half-truth and the answer
to all conflict and opposition lies in the middle, in His One Will.

Likewise, our heavy artillery and disseminator of these powerful thought vibrations
is the sacrament---to be revealed and used for the sole(soul) purpose of laying the
foundation for the New Age---that releases the atomic solar energy reservoir of our
intuitive mind(remember Atlantis?), making the direct connection with the One Mind
and Body of our Heavenly Father and Earthly Mother.

We have come but to go and let us remember that there comes a time in the history
of a race when to die for all is to live for all. And so it has always been. The
young have always been sacrificed to the times, sent to the front lines, so that
something new could be created for the race, and to affirm the quality of each life.
Only this time we will die vicariously---in our animal nature---so that all may live
fully, in the perfect manifestation of Heavenly Father and Earthly Mother. For
this is the final baptism in which all are consumed in the fire of the Great Central
Sun.
Let those of us who have emerged from the death throws of the avaricious beast
unify behind the common experience that it is far better to die into the Sun than
to maintain a life of darkness and living death. Let us merge the past with the
present and unify behind the culminated battle cry of all beings thirsting for
liberation; "One for All and All for One! Fatherland or death, we shall overcome!!!
E PLURIBUS UNUM! E PLURIBUS UNUM! E PLURIBUS UNUM!

'The Source' is Here

By Larry Bereman
Tribune-Herald Staff Writer

Members of The Source Family, a group of about 140 people currently occupying the Hilo Country Club complex have decided to settle permanently on the Big Island and have made plans to build a dome community on 37 acres of land near Akaka Falls.

The group, which was previously known as "Eternal Now," has made its home in Hilo since June and is mainly comprised of the sons and daughters of prominent Los Angeles families.

The Source Family came to Hilo after experiencing a number of problems on Kauai and the Mainland. They say they were threatened on Kauai, and finally forced to leave their leased land. They first rented the late state Sen. William H. "Doc" Hill mansion in Keaukaha before moving to the vacant Country Club complex in upper Kaumana.

"This is where we're going to build our community," said Harvest Moon, one of 13 women in a council which leads the group.

She and the other members of the family received their names from the group's leader, Yahowha, who died in August on Oahu from injuries he received in a hang-glider accident.

Members of the group have such unusual names as Mother Makushla, Octavius, Sun, Electricity, Isis, Joshua, Pythias, Zarathustra, Sir Knight, Jupiter, Serenity, Lovely, Omne, One, and Sunflower.

Harvest Moon said dome structures are "the home of the future," and she said members of the family are now working on a scale model of the planned community.

"We've been very well received here," said Isis, another member of the council appointed by Yahowha.

She said the group's first big break came about a month ago when some of the council members were interviewed by a disc jockey on KPUA radio.

During the show, radio listeners called in and asked questions concerning the group's activities here.

"Some of the questions were very personal and direct," said Isis. "But we feel we cleared up some of the misconceptions which have developed about the family."

to Stay

"We want people to know that we're here to work with the community," she said.

The family is not on welfare, she said, and gets all of its income from the labors of individual members, and in royalties from the sale of the restaurant "The Source" in Los Angeles. The restaurant was owned and operated by Yahowha until a few years ago.

Isis said they have been generally welcomed by the business community of Hilo. "We've broken down some of the barriers, and many of the local people are starting to back us."

Since the radio interview, the family has completed plans on a new air brush and tie-dye business to be known as "Graphic Signs," or "Reflections." Jerry Chang of Hilo will be a partner in that business, according to Harvest Moon.

Also planned is a cabinet shop which will specialize in koa wood products, and which will be used to build the houses for the dome community. Isis said there are four master cabinet makers in the family.

(Please Turn to Page 6)

Hilo

SOURCE THANKS

Dear Russ Williams,   Sun., June 6, 197[...]

I'd like to thank you for presenting a truthful beautiful picture of the Source Family to the uninformed public.

We are here to establish right and to give to all. We are just a very large family who wake up before the sun rises to sing-create. It's the only time the family can be together, as we all have jobs during daylight hours. Our singing is sometimes misunderstood by those around us still in their sleep. So once again we have been evicted from our present home at the Hilo Country Club, Kaumana. We have found homes, business opportunities and warm welcoming in Lanikai, Oahu. So the family is moving to Oahu but we have one business that needs to be taken over.

We saw a need while in Hilo for a natural foods restaurant serving pure fresh unadulterated foods, s[o] we opened Goodies Restaurant in Hilo. Yahowha, Fath[er] of the Source Family, opened the first natural foods restaurant in 1957 in Hollywood, California, then opened the Old World Restaurant in Hollywood and the[n] opened The Source on the Sunset Strip in 1969. All three restaurants are still in operation and are mor[e] successful than ever. We have the formula for success in the restaurant business and we like to leave Goodies Restaurant with someone who would like to maintain the standard--continuing to serve the community of Hilo good food, service and music.

God Bless You All Aloha Oi, Parald[a]

Police Searching For Escapee

Big Island police were searching today for a Kulani Prison inmate who escaped while being treated at a medical center in Hilo.

Roy Harris, 27, was convicted of second-degree robbery of Kilauea Store May 29. He also was on parole from a federal penitentiary in Virginia for a robbery conviction.

He and three other prisoners were receiving treatment at the medical center on Ponahawai and Komohana streets when the escape occurred.

According to Kulani guard Peter Wong, Harris became separated from the group. He was last seen in a green International Scout with a white top near the Hilo Lagoon Hotel area.

The driver of that vehicle was later arrested by police for allegedly hindering prosecution. The 23-year-old Hilo man is being held by police today.

Harris is caucasian with dark brown hair, brown eyes and medium build. He was last seen

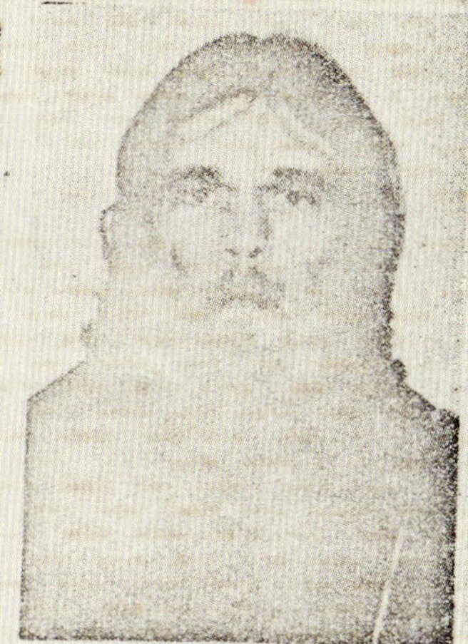

ROY HARRIS
. . . Prison Escapee

wearing blue denim levis (prison type), a red sweater and brown leather slippers.

Kulani Prison inmate escapes

HILO — Big Island police searched yesterday for a Kulani State Prison inmate who escaped while he was in Hilo for medical treatment.

Roy M. Harris, 27, who was convicted of second degree robbery for an unsuccessful hold up of a neighborhood grocery May 29 escaped from a guard at 11:15 a.m.

He was seen later with another man in a white sedan near Hilo Lagoon Hotel. Police subsequently arrested the driver, 23, and was holding him last night.

Harris is reported as wearing a full beard and long hair. He is 6 feet 1 and weighs 170 pounds.

Guard Peter Wong had brought Harris and three other inmates to Hilo for treatment. After a stop at a doctor's office, the group went to Hilo Medical Group on Waianuenue Avenue where Harris was last seen. The other prisoners made no attempt to flee, police said.

Harris was on parole from a Federal penitentiary in Virginia when he came here. His prior conviction also was for robbery.

Police said they did not know if the man was armed.

Sect members hit by suits

Members of the Source religious sect have been hit with two Circuit Court civil suits.

Roger and Anna Marie Brault filed suit against Source members Isis Peters and Harvest Moon Dunham over rental of the Braults' two homes at 1534 Mokulua Drive, Lanikai. The suit says the two and others vacated the homes June 30. It asks for $2,783 in rent and repairs.

And Eurolease of Hawaii Ltd. filed suit against Charlene Peters and Ahom Baker over lease of a 1975 Mercedes-Benz 280. It asks for $3,866 as a result of termination of the lease in June.

Source leader James Baker and member Mercury Geiger were killed in hang-gliding accidents off Makapuu in the past two years. Sect members caused controversy when they retained the bodies, claiming it takes 3½ days for the soul to leave a body.

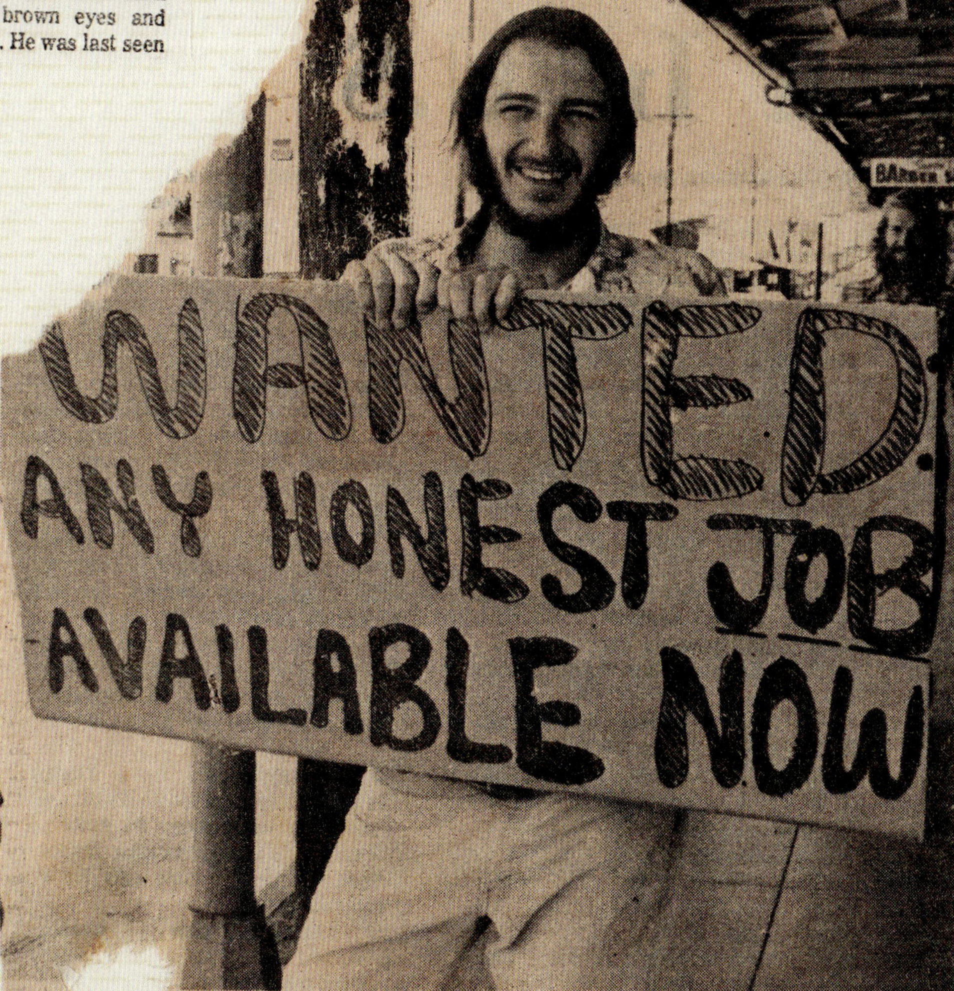

Tribune-Herald Photo

SIGNS OF THE 1930's—Craig Basso, who recently arrived in Hilo from Los Angeles with four others, hasn't been able to locate work here, after trying "everyplace in town." "We didn't want to go on welfare, but we may have to," Basso told the Tribune-Herald.

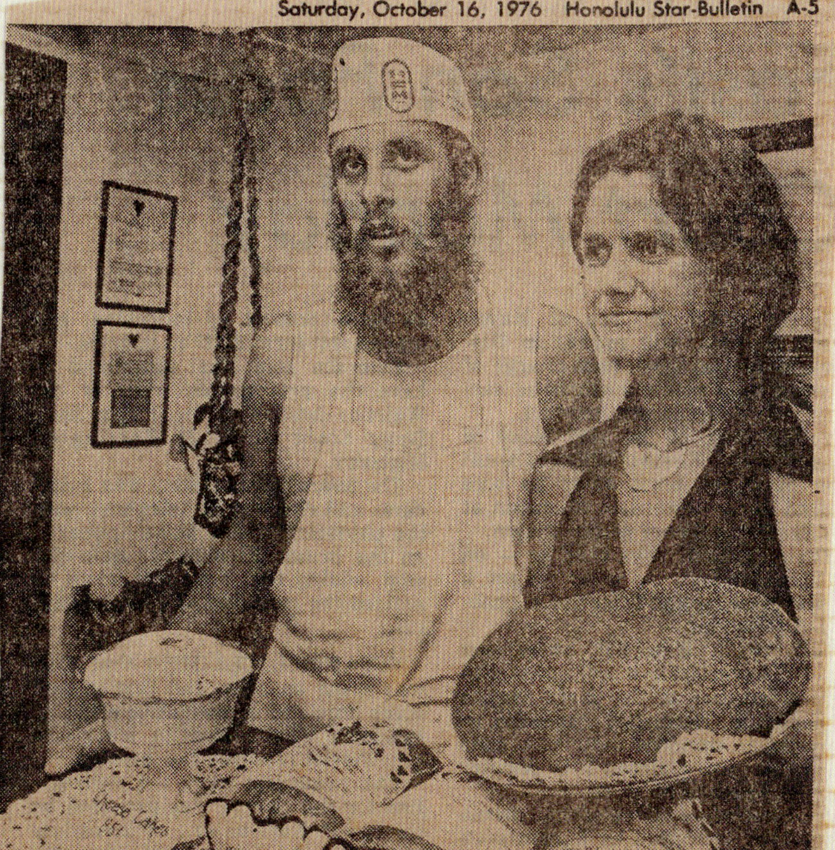

Saturday, October 16, 1976   Honolulu Star-Bulletin   A-5

BIGGEST BAGEL—Joshua and Summer in the bakery with the world's largest bagel and some of their other products. —Star-Bulletin Photos by Warren Roll.

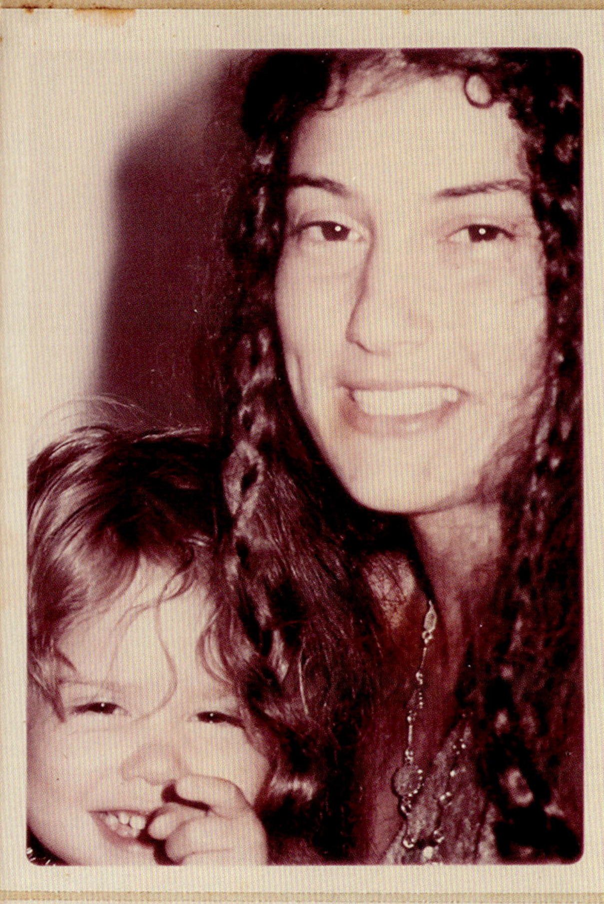
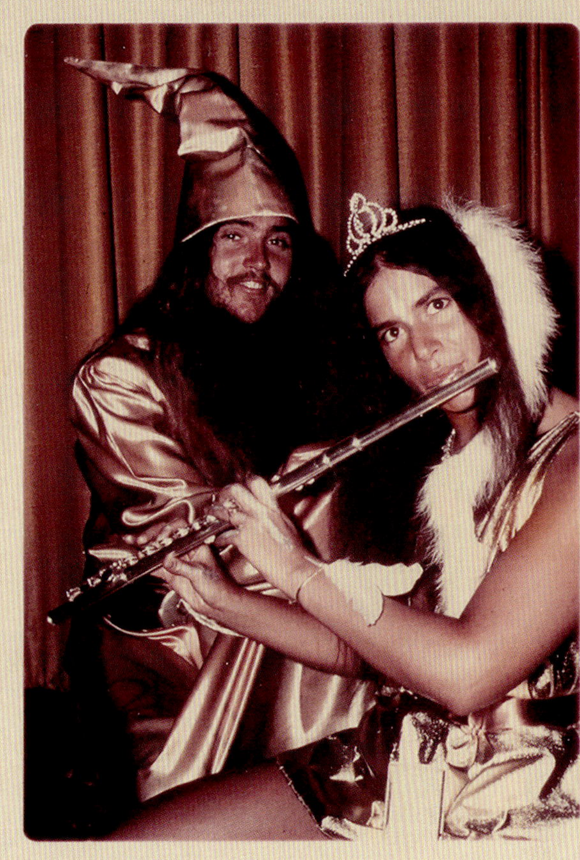
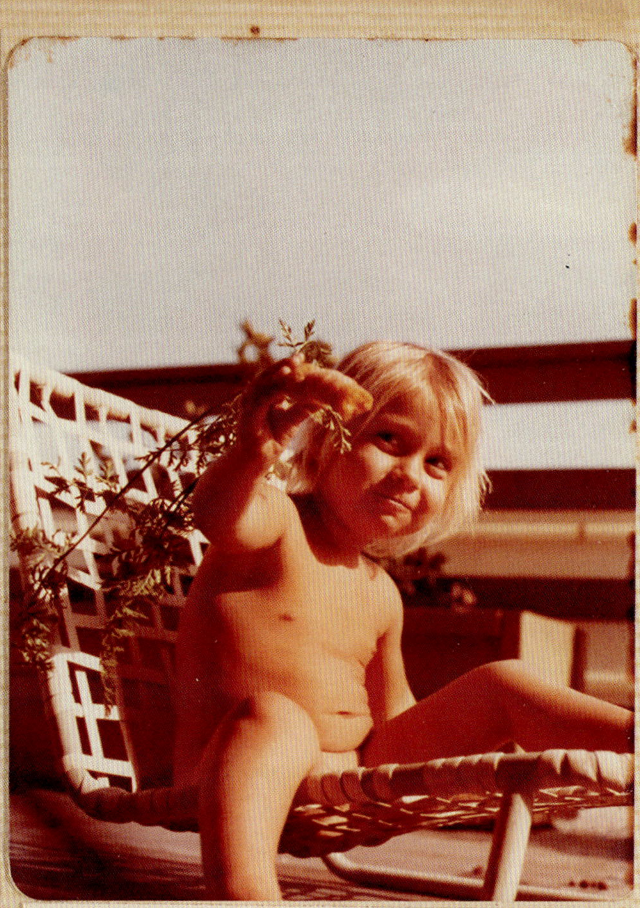
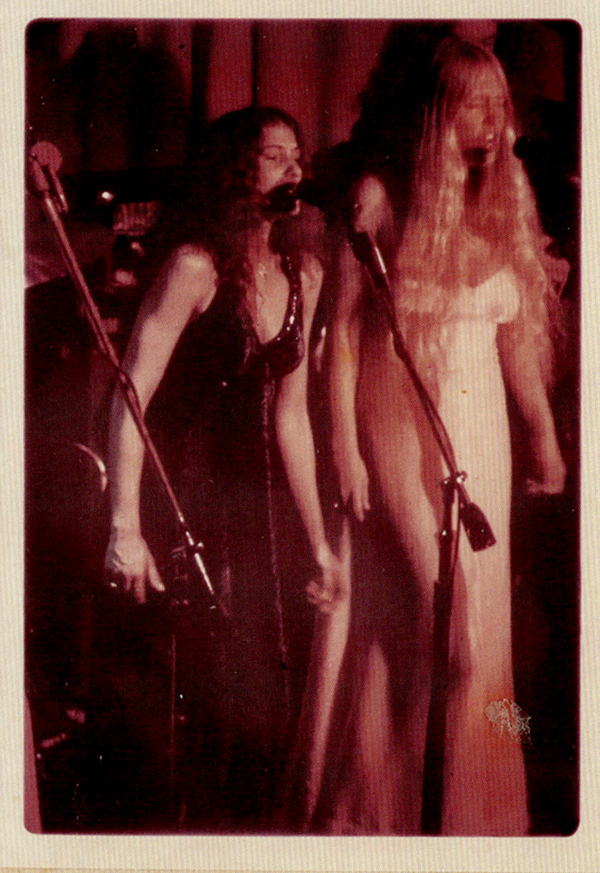
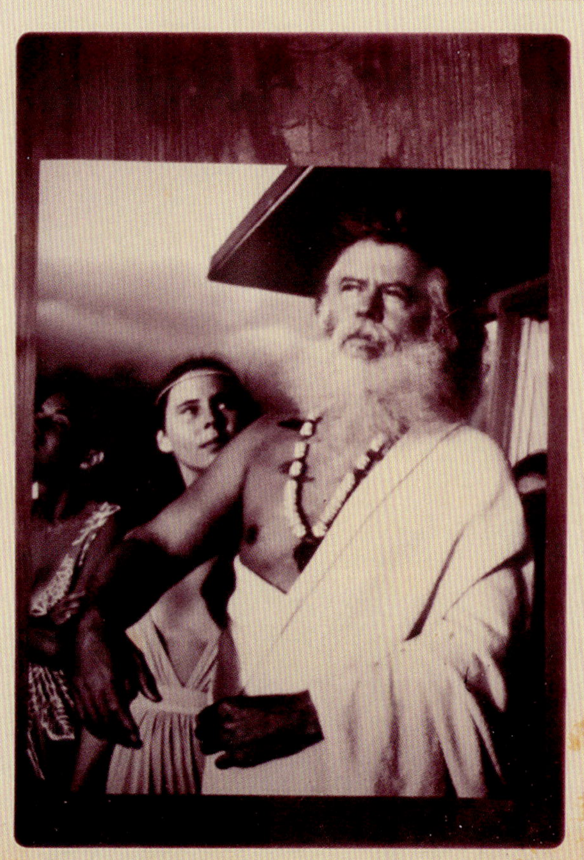
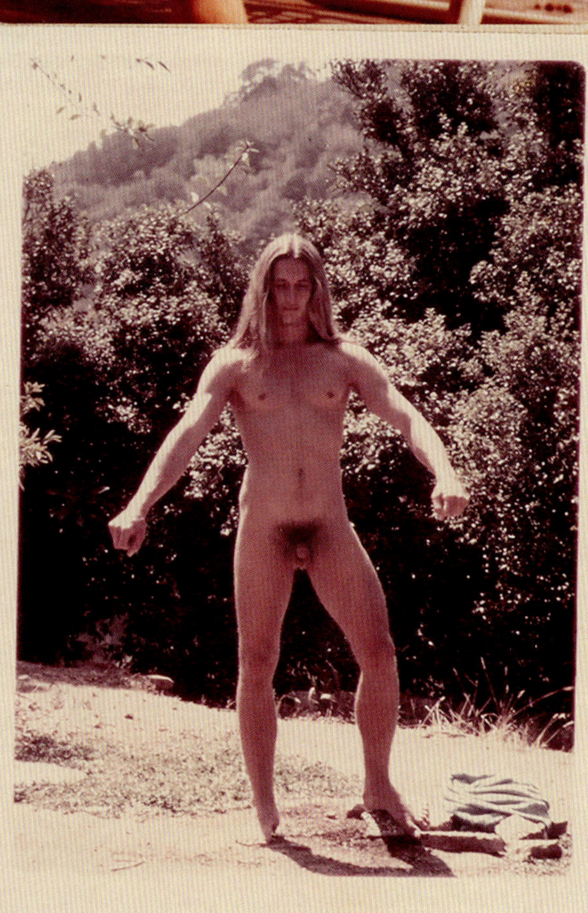

Religious group calls death

From Page 1

Yahowha "had injured everything and knew he was going to die."

Ahom, another disciple who was holding an infant in her arms, said Yahowha didn't crash but was "guided to the spot by an angel."

Isis said the spiritual leader was brought back to the house and laid to rest on the floor. The group cleansed him with water, placed a white sheet over his body, filled the room with flowers and incense and chanted around the clock for 3½ days.

According to Isis, Yahowha's last nine hours in the house were viewed as a "crucifixion" and a time in which he could give his "soul time to reflect on the past and the future."

"His physical body was in pain, but his soul wasn't," she said.

ACCORDING TO ANOTHER female disciple, Lovely, Yahowha himself tried to reset his broken back and subsequently attempted to assume the lotus position.

Members of the religious group belittled the physical death of their spiritual father and emphasized its spiritual significance.

They said they viewed death as a liberation "from the limitations of the physical plane" and an evolutionary step toward a higher spiritual level.

They said they would seek medical aid for "stitches and broken bones" but were opposed to "blood transfusions, hospital care and the cutting of hair."

They said they did not report the death for three days because that's the period it takes the soul to leave the body.

They explained they did not embalm the body because that would have prevented Yahowha from reviewing his "life river."

MAKUSHLA, A YOUNG woman known as the "mother of Yahowha," firmly believes the events of the past few days were biblically predestined.

"Everything he did can be substantiated in the Bible," she said.

She claims, for example, that this past Easter she and Yahowha were

'crucifixion'

passing through Egypt. A priest met them on Easter Sunday and brought them to the pyramids where she claimed Yahowha was "reborn."

The priest, she said, was so awed by his presence that he exclaimed that Yahowha was Jesus.

It is no coincidence, she added, that Yahowha died at the Lanikai home which overlooks the ocean and two jagged offshore islands.

The islands, she said, are the "sphinx" and the "pyramid" from Egypt.

Thus, "he returned to the beginning. This is where he was to fulfill his prophecy," she said.

MAKUSHA SAID Yahowha's last words were: "You will know what to do when I die. It's not my will but thy will (God's) that has to be done."

She said the Christ-like aspect of the experience was even made more dramatic by wounds around his hands and forehead which she claimed looked like "nail marks" and marks made from a "crown of thorns."

The group plans to cremate the body after the autopsy.

The Honolulu Advertiser
Wednesday June 30, 1976

Cult's defense told

By HAROLD HOSTETLER
Advertiser Staff Writer

The Source, a Lanikai religious cult, will claim religious freedom as its defense for refusing to surrender the body of one of its members killed in a hang-glider accident two weeks ago.

Eight members of the group pleaded innocent yesterday before Judge Kenneth Harada in Kaneohe District Court. They are charged with "obstructing government operations," a misdemeanor.

Their attorney, John S. Carroll, requested a jury trial. Harada ordered the group to appear in Honolulu Circuit Court July 30 for the trial.

CARROLL LATER told reporters he believes the group's arrest "may be a clear-cut potential violation of the constitutional right to freedom of the expression of religion," as contained in the First Amendment.

"We don't contest the facts of what happened," Carroll said, "but we are going on the theory they had a religious right to act as they did."

Carroll said members of the cult called him a week ago and asked him to represent them.

"It's not my normal, run-of-the-mill case," said Carroll, a Republican State representative.

The eight were arrested June 15 at the Lanikai home they share. They are Isis Peters, 34; Golden Marshall, 23; Makushla Ulicny, 24; Ra Jensen, 24; Homer Phurman, 36; Paul Damian, 25; Damascus Aquarian, 46; and Odin Aquarian, 29.

AT THE TIME OF their arrest, the eight had refused to give up the body of Mercury Geiger, 22, who was killed the night before when his hang glider crashed into a Makapuu cliff. The body was removed to the City morgue after their arrest.

The Source members claimed they had to keep the body undisturbed in their home for 3½ days, the length of time they believe is required for the soul to leave the body. During that time, the group sings and chants, believing they are aiding the soul in reincarnation.

Last August the cult's spiritual head, Yahowha, died as the result of a similar hang-glider accident. The group did not reveal his death until 3½ days later.

Hang-glider club expels member

By DAVID TONG
Advertiser Staff Writer

One of the Eternal Now members who helped launch his spiritual leader on a fateful flight was expelled from a local hang-glider club last night.

Mercury, a 21-year-old man, was expelled from the Pacific Tradewind Sky Sailors Club during a meeting at Nuuanu Elementary School.

More than 70 persons turned out to discuss the accident and decide what steps to take against Mercury, who helped launch his spiritual father off the Makapuu cliffs last month.

The 53-year-old Yahowha, whose real name was James Baker, died of injuries sustained in that flight. His death was not reported by members of the sect for 3½ days.

DURING the meeting, Mercury, in the company of 11 female and two male disciples, said he used his kite to launch Yahowha because the older man insisted on making the flight.

"Yahowha had made his decision. And it seemed logical to me to help launch and guide him, than to let him go off by himself," said Mercury, who claims to hold the world's longest hang-gliding record.

Mercury and his disciples argued that the club rules did not apply because Yahowha was an "exception."

Several club members strongly criticized Mercury because they felt he violated the club's safety regulations. They claim all members using the Makapuu site are required to be trained at lower heights. Yahowha's ill-fated flight was his first hang-gliding try.

DAVID Bettencourt, club president, said Mercury had not taken any "affirmative steps" to prevent Yahowha from jumping off Makapuu.

Bettencourt said the accident might cost the club future use of the cliffs. He said club members will meet Monday with officials of Bishop Estate, which owns the jump-off site, to discuss the accident and seek another permit to use the site. Their permit expired Monday.

Club members last night considered several motions, ranging from a six-month suspension to expulsion, before taking the step to remove Mercury from the club.

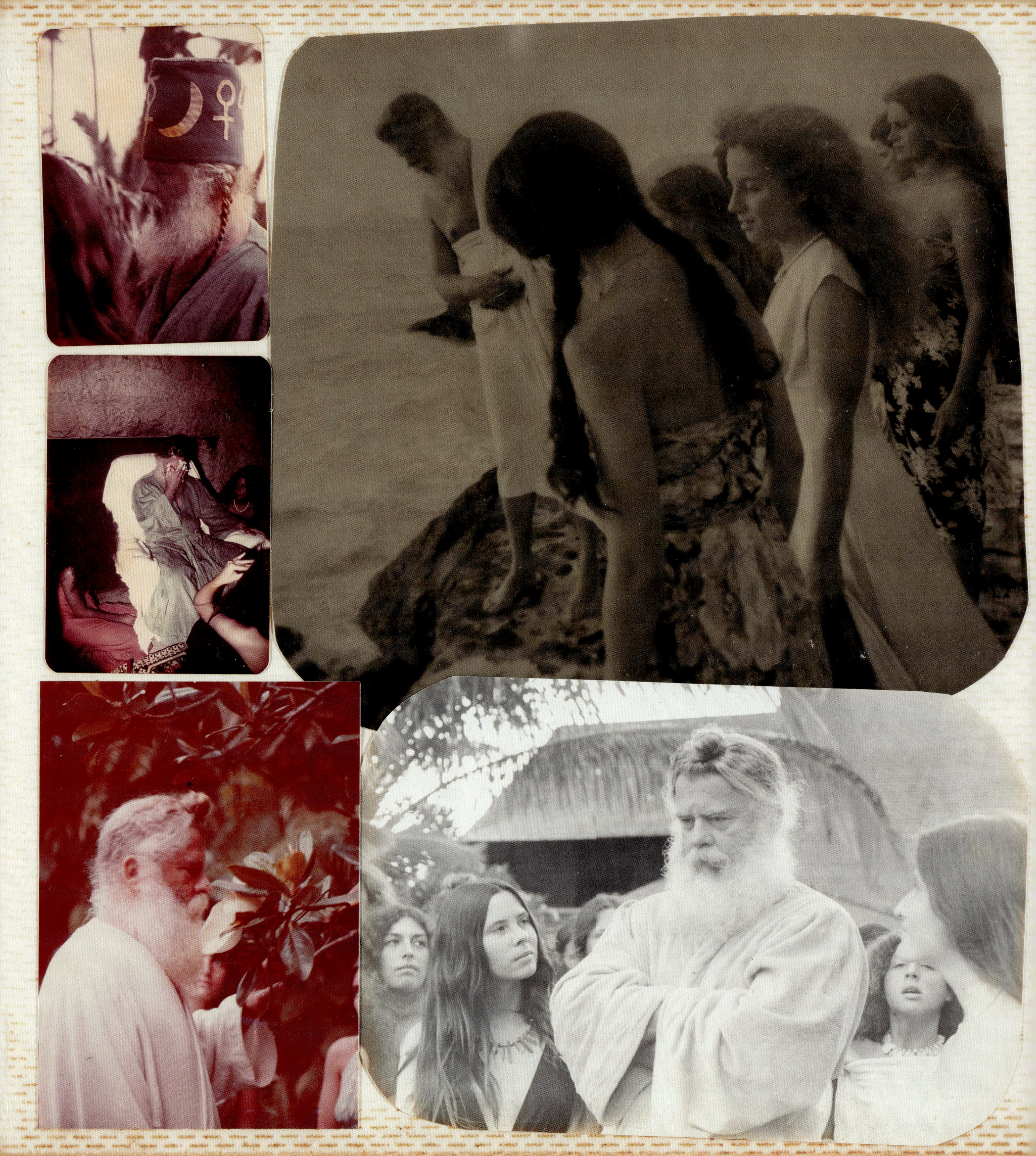

<u>NEGLIGENCE CLAIM</u>

City Clerk
City and County of Honolulu
Honolulu, Hawaii 96813

    This statement is submitted for filing in your Office pursuant to the provisions of Section 12-111 of the Revised Charter of the City and County of Honolulu.[1]

    The following named person(s) claim(s) that he (she, it or they) should be paid the following amount of money by the City for the following injuries to his person and/or property caused by the following described negligence of officials or employees of the City and County of Honolulu:

Claimant's Full Legal Name: <u>DAMASCUS T. AQUARIAN</u>

Claimant's Address: <u>1534 Mokulua Dr., Lanikai, Kailua, Hawaii 96734</u> Claimant's Phone No.: <u>261-4106</u>

When Injuries Occurred: Date <u>June 15, 1976</u> Time: __________

Where Injuries Occurred (In sufficient detail to enable location of the condition which caused the injuries or of the place of the accident):

<u>1534 Mokulua Drive, Lanikai</u>

<u>Kailua, Hawaii 96734</u>

How Injuries Occurred (In sufficient detail to enable determination of the acts or omissions which constituted the negligence of officials or employees of the City and County of Honolulu):

<u>On June 15, 1976, the Honolulu Police Department using an illegal Restraining Order broke and entered the dwelling place located at 1534 Mokulua, Drive, Lanikai. The undersigned was legally at those premises. Due to the illegal exercise of police power, the injuries listed below were received.</u>

	Names	Addresses	Phone Nos.
Witnesses to Accident or Incident	Golden Marshall	1534 Mokulua Dr.	261-4106
	Isis Peters	1534 Mokulua Dr.	261-4106
	Damian Paul	1534 Mokulua Drive	261-4106

Extent of Injuries: <u>Pain and suffering, humiliation, degradation, public notoriety</u>

Amount of Claim (Itemized if appropriate): <u>$2,000.00</u>

Dated: __________

Signature of person filing claim

Address __________

Phone No. __________

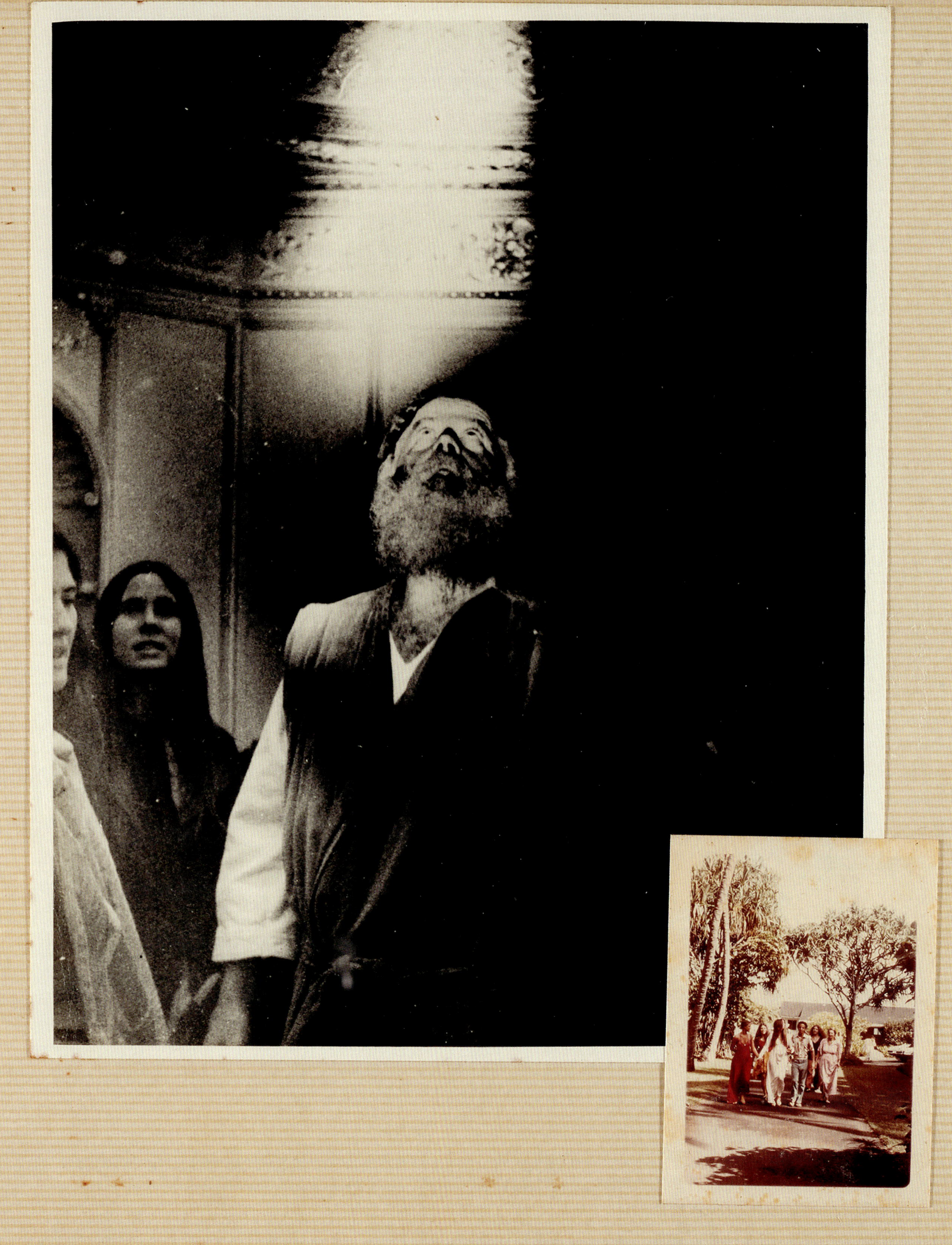

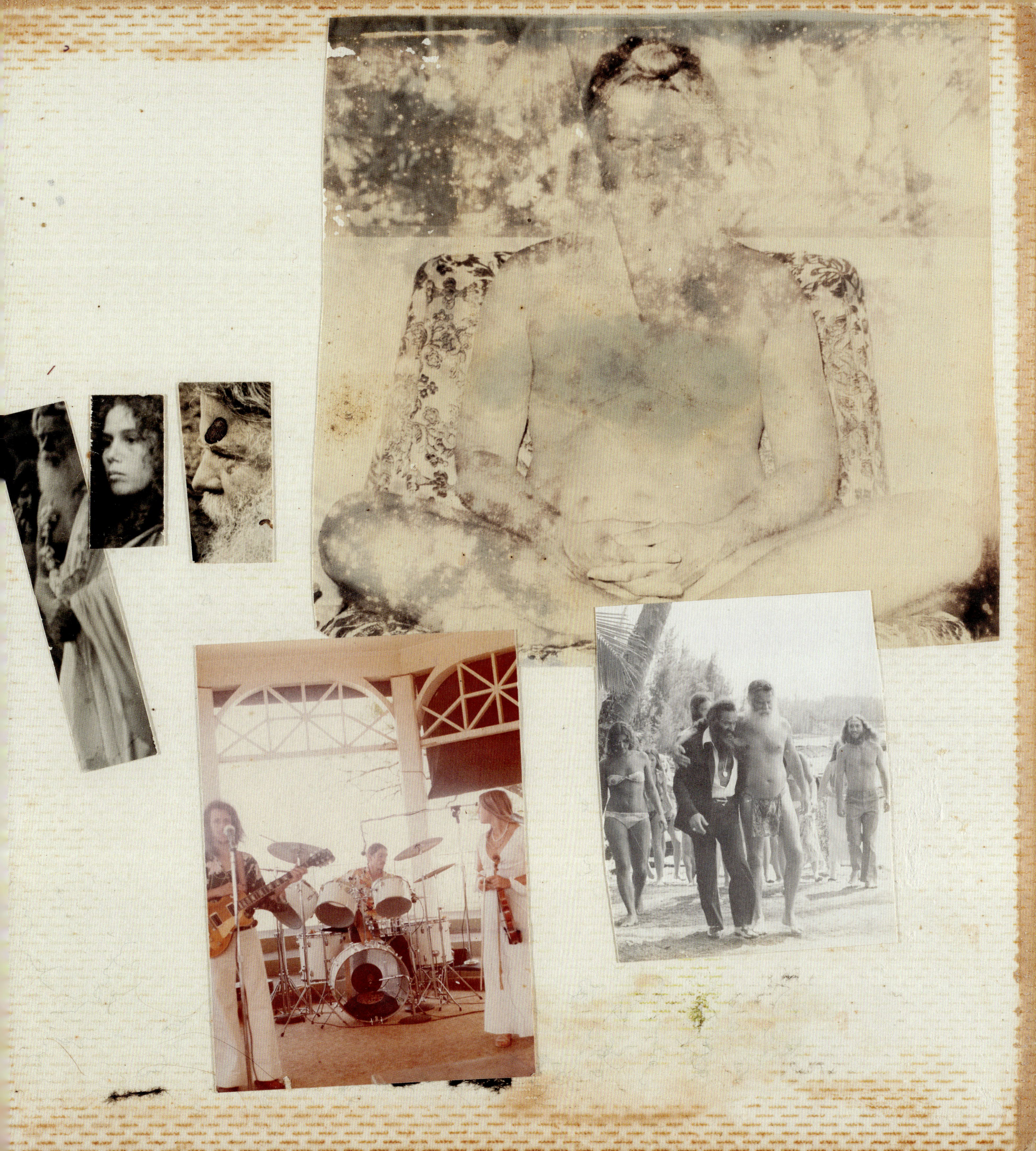

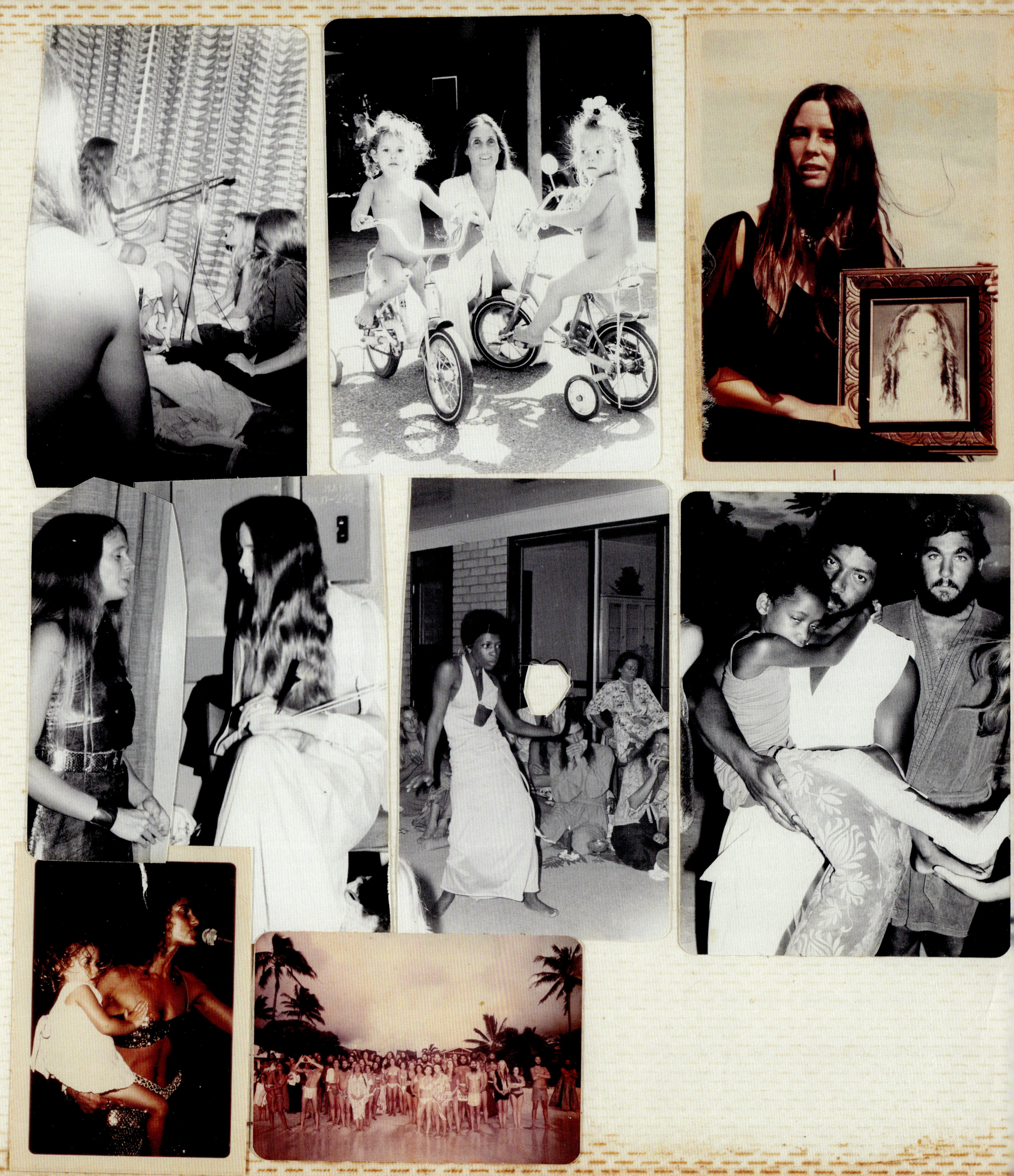

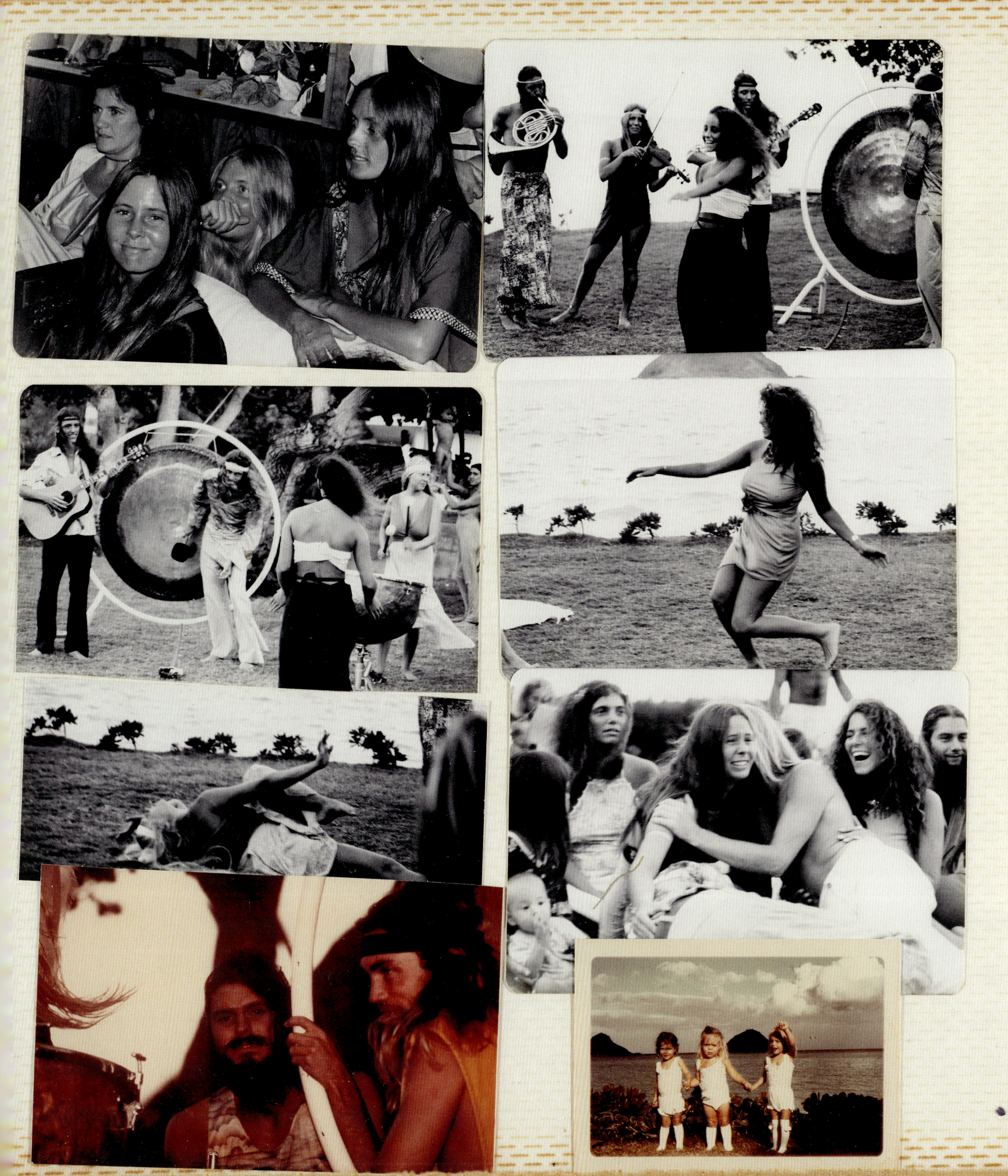

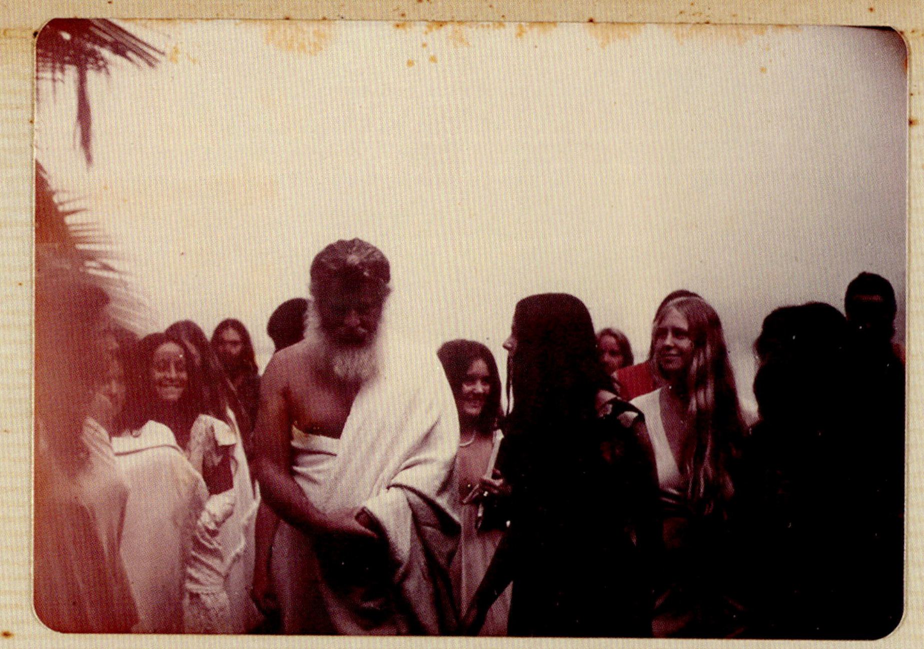

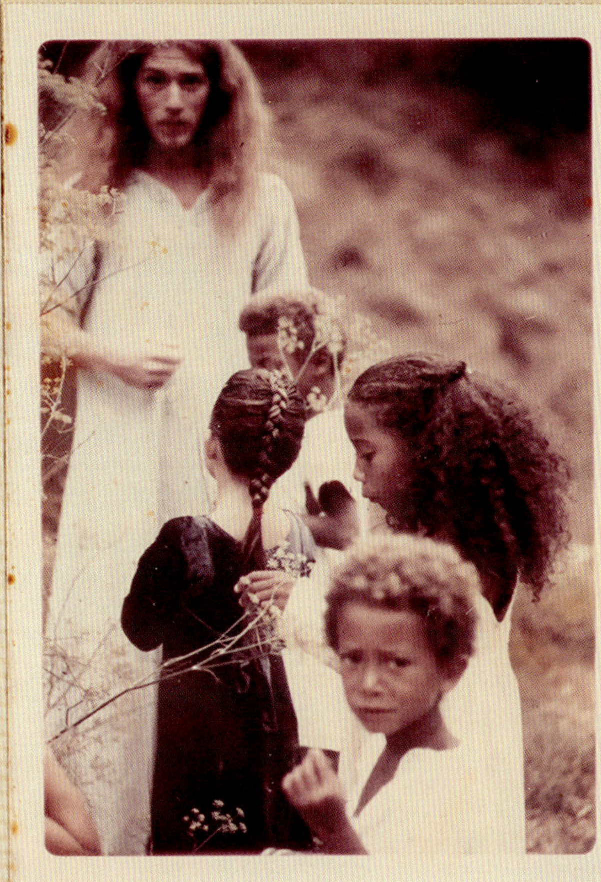

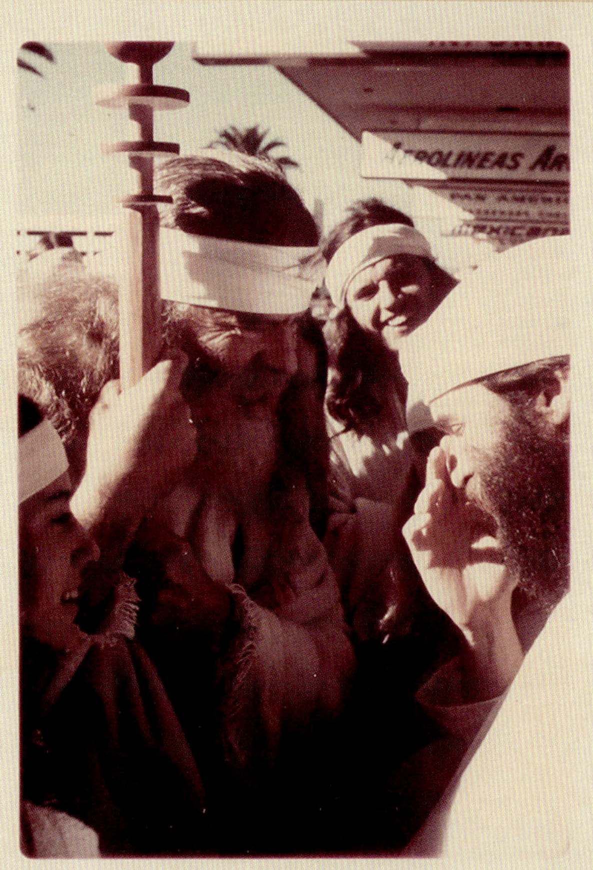

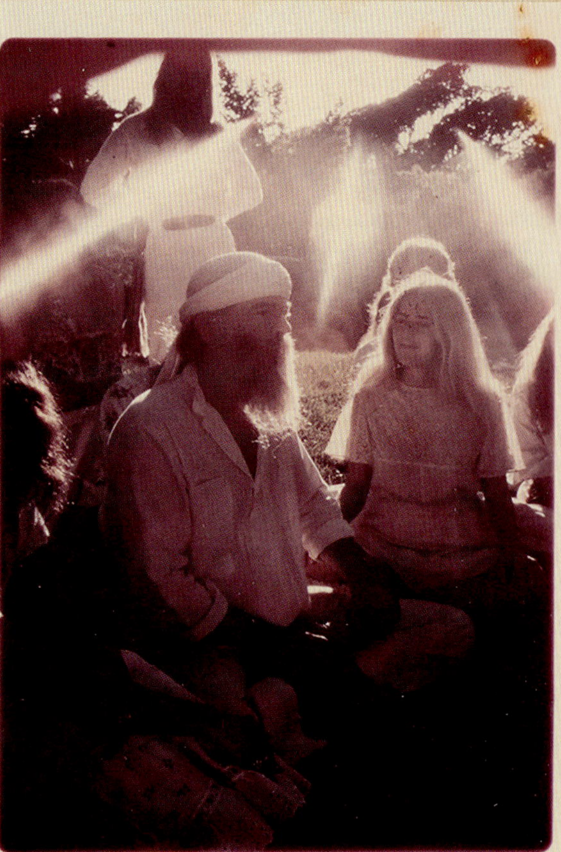

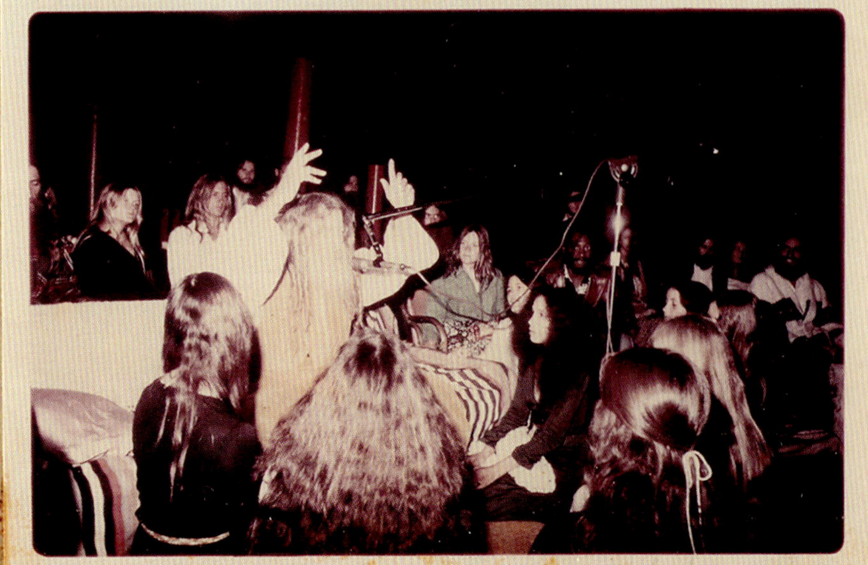

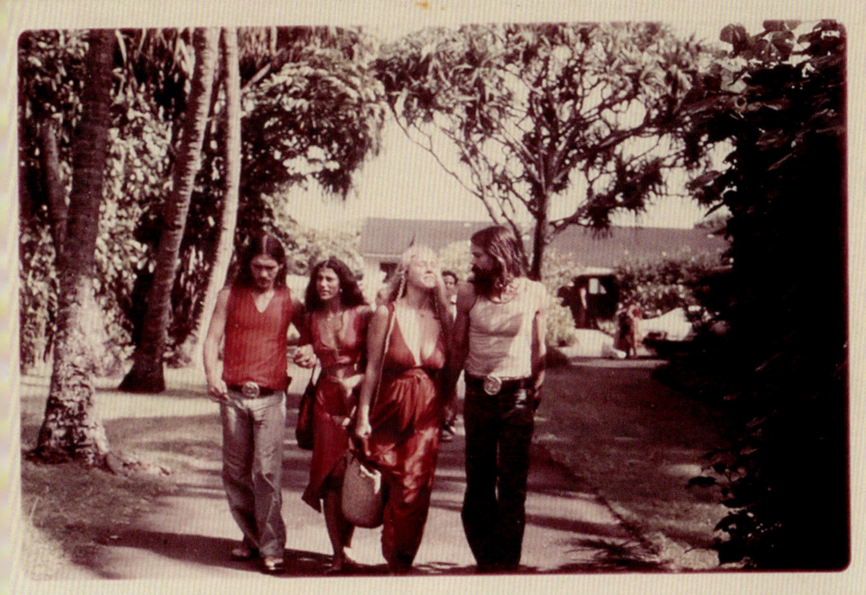
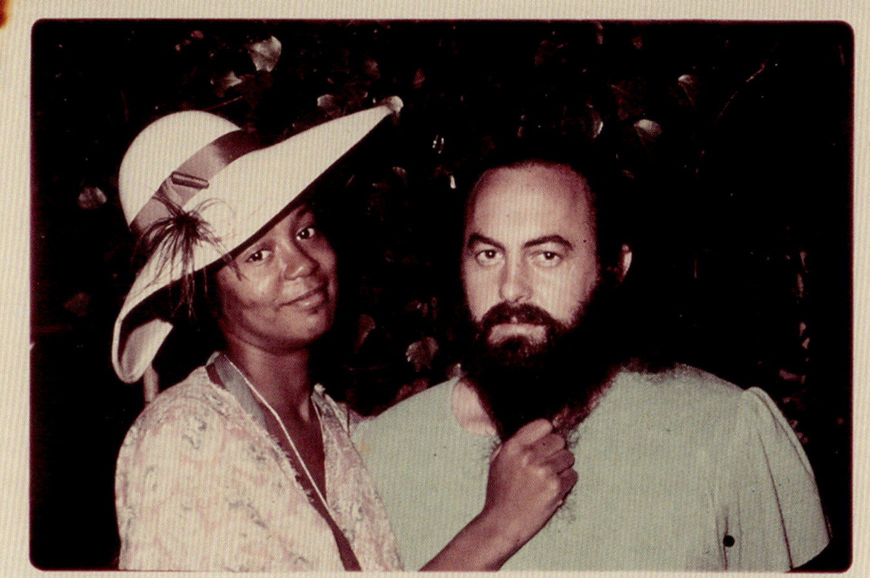
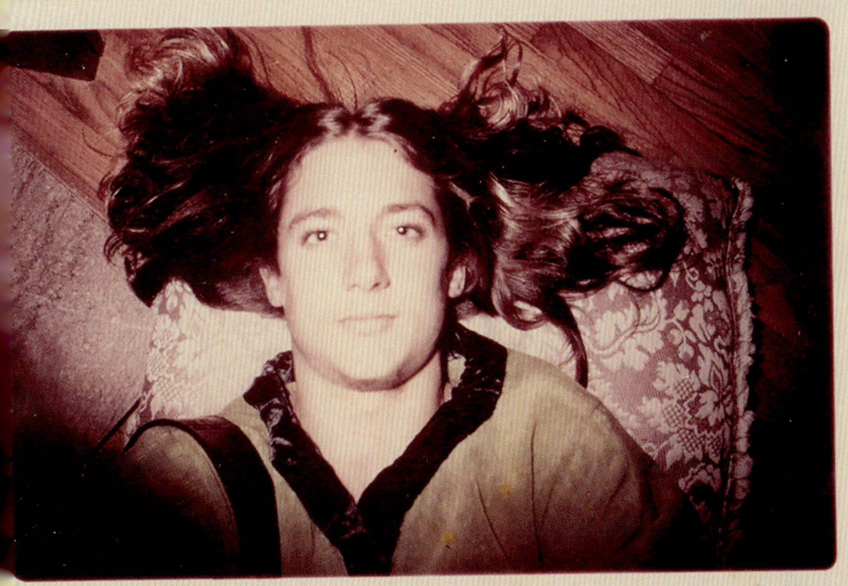
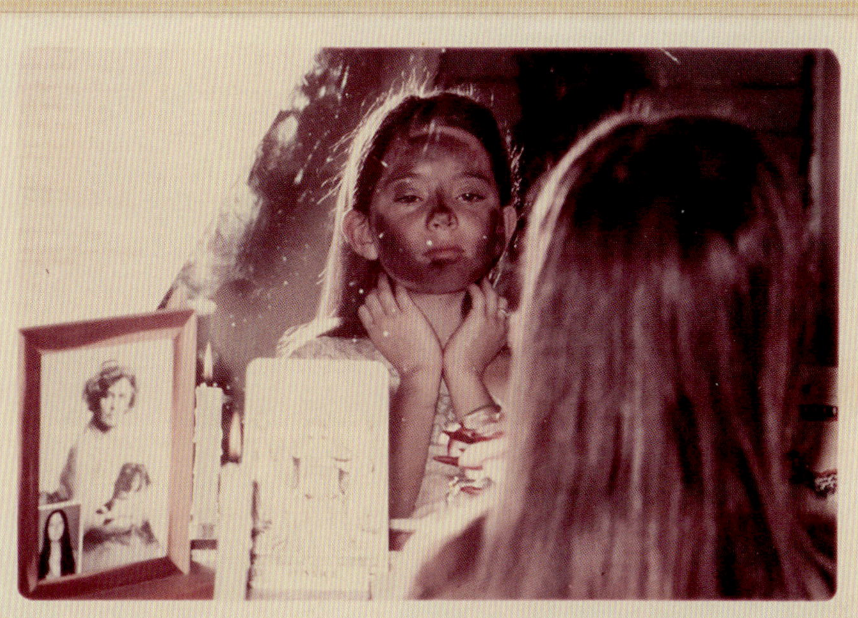
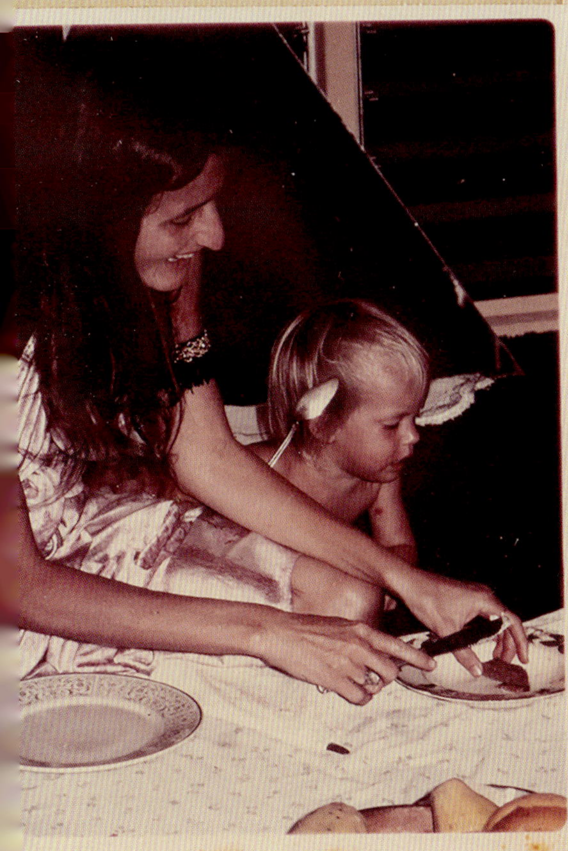
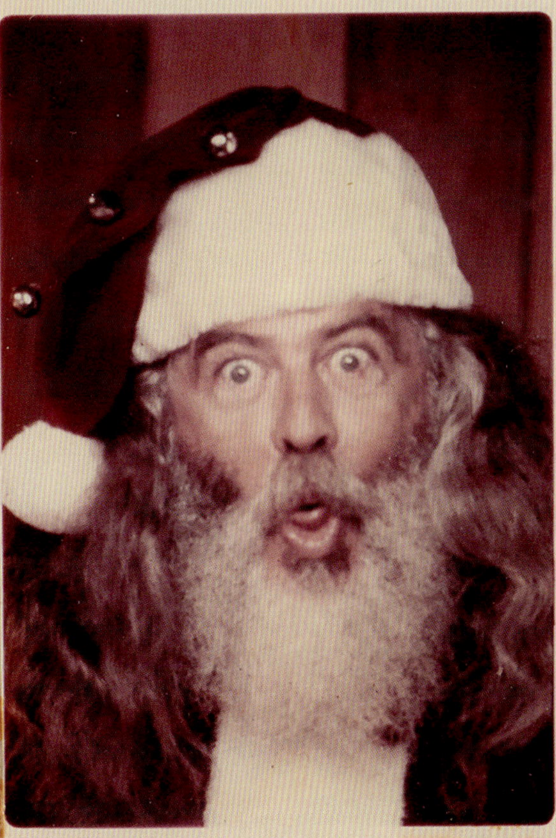
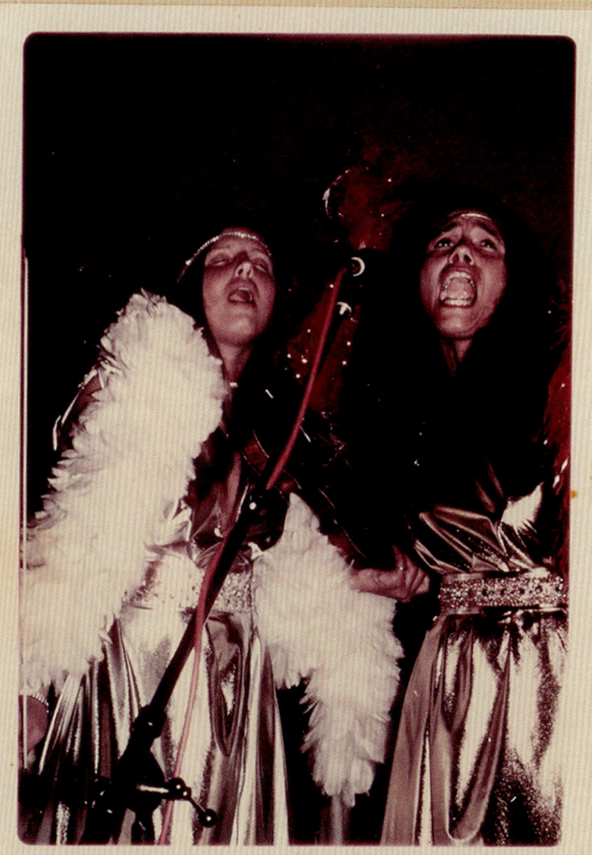

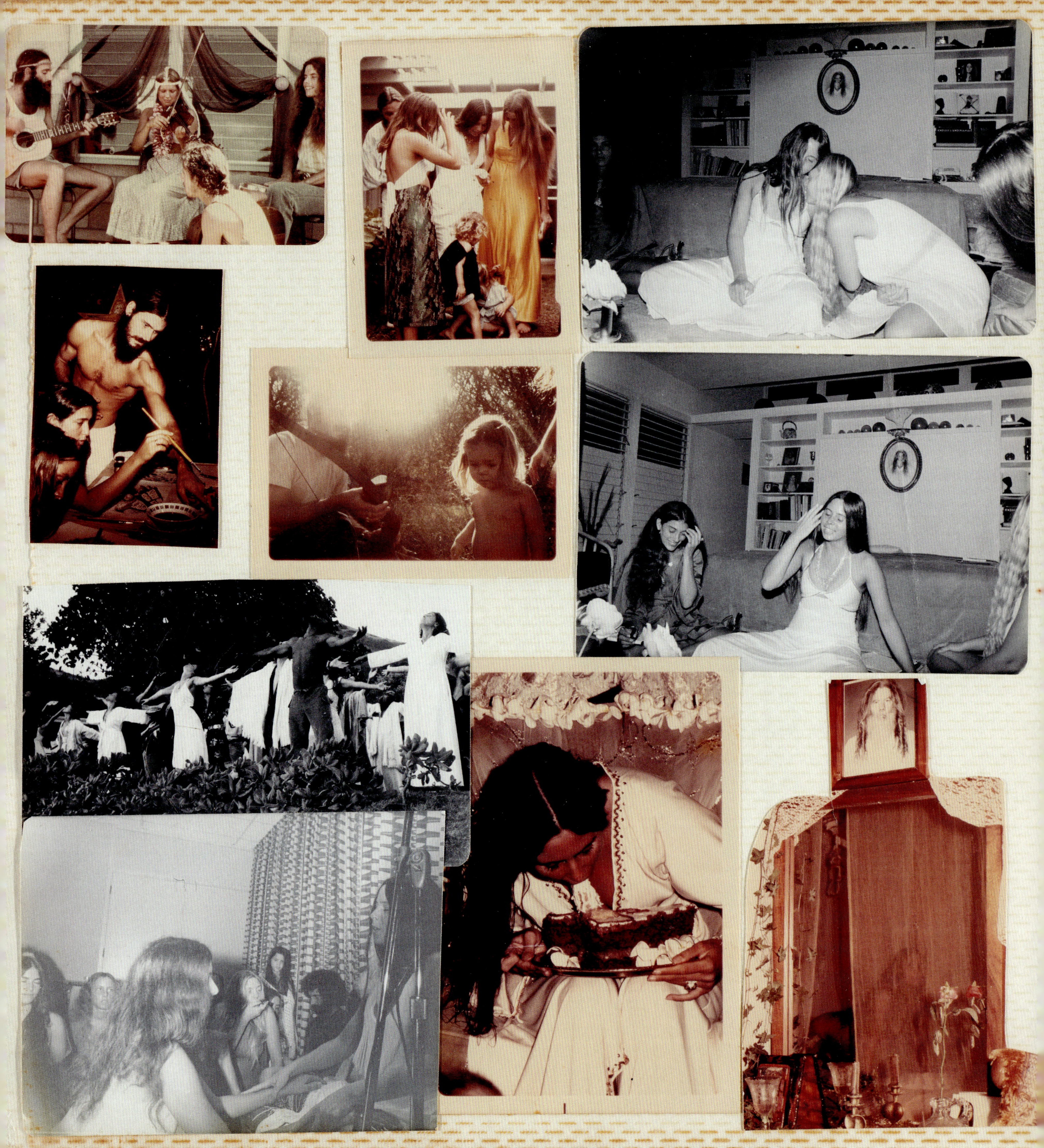

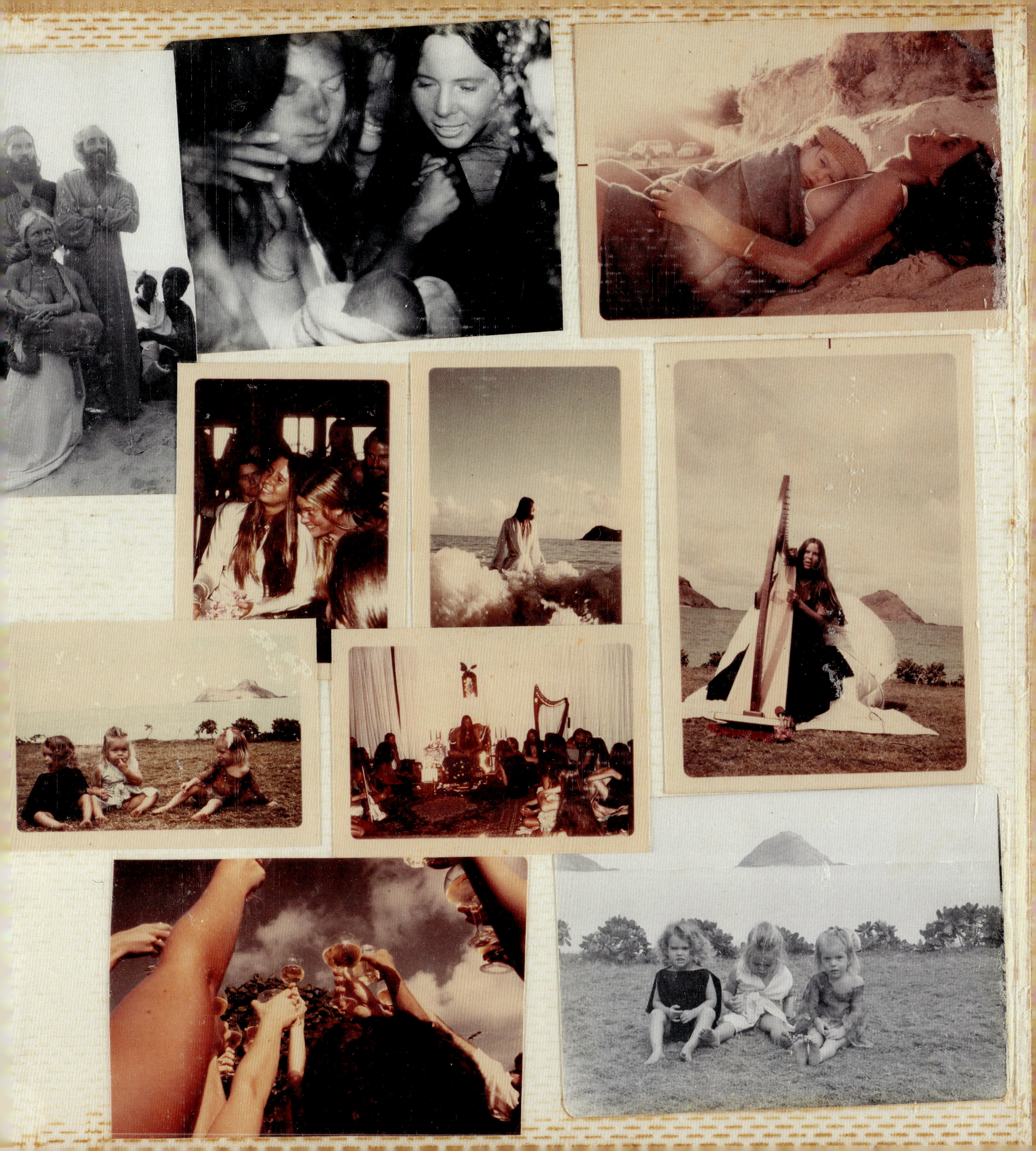

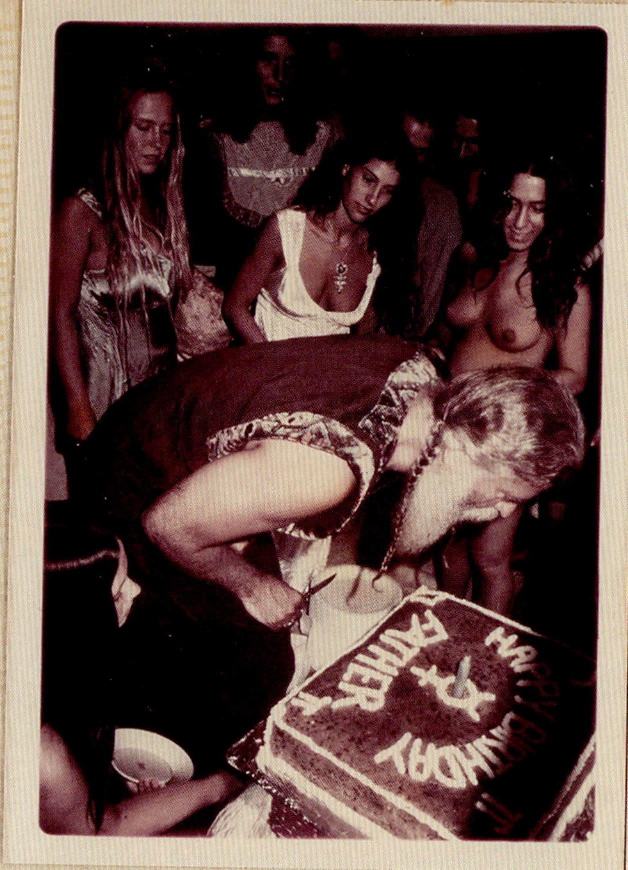
HAPPY BIRTHDAY
FATHER

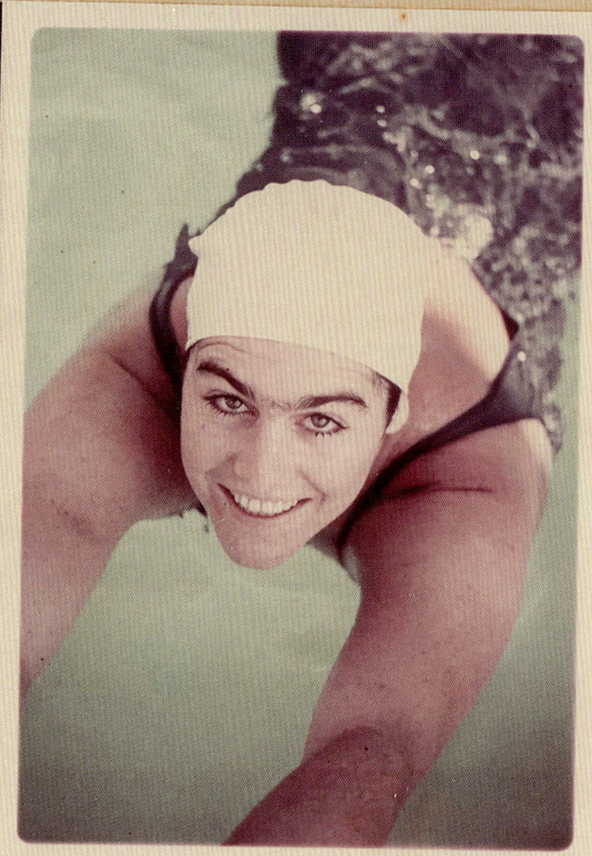

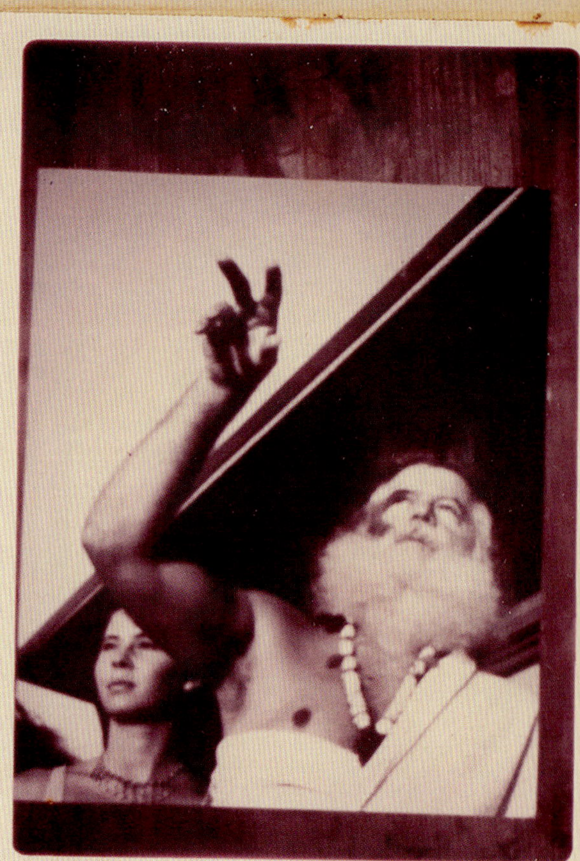

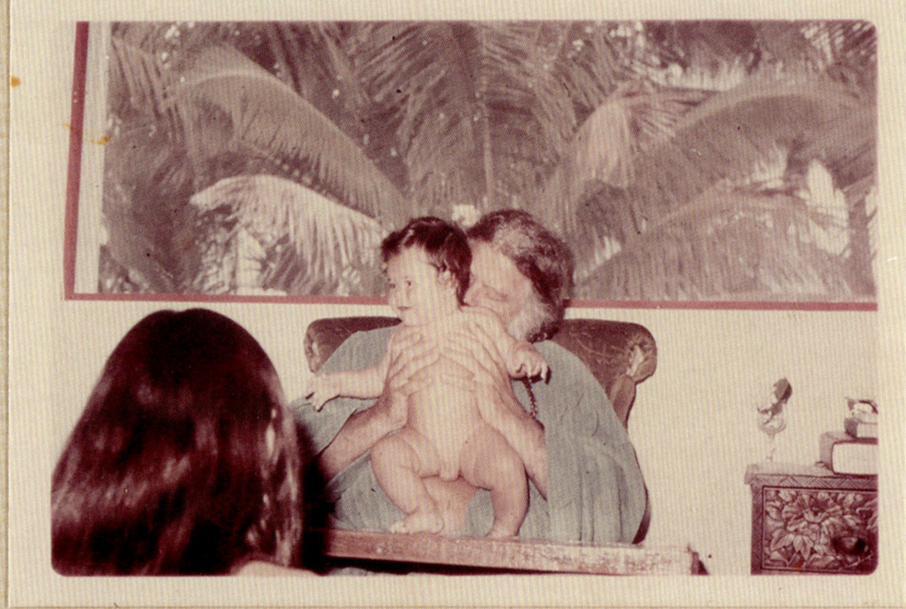

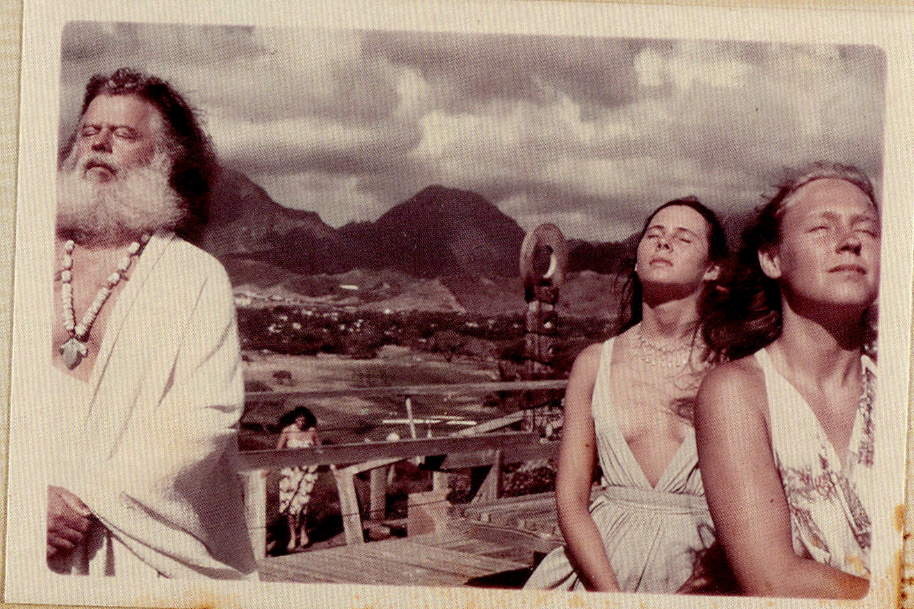

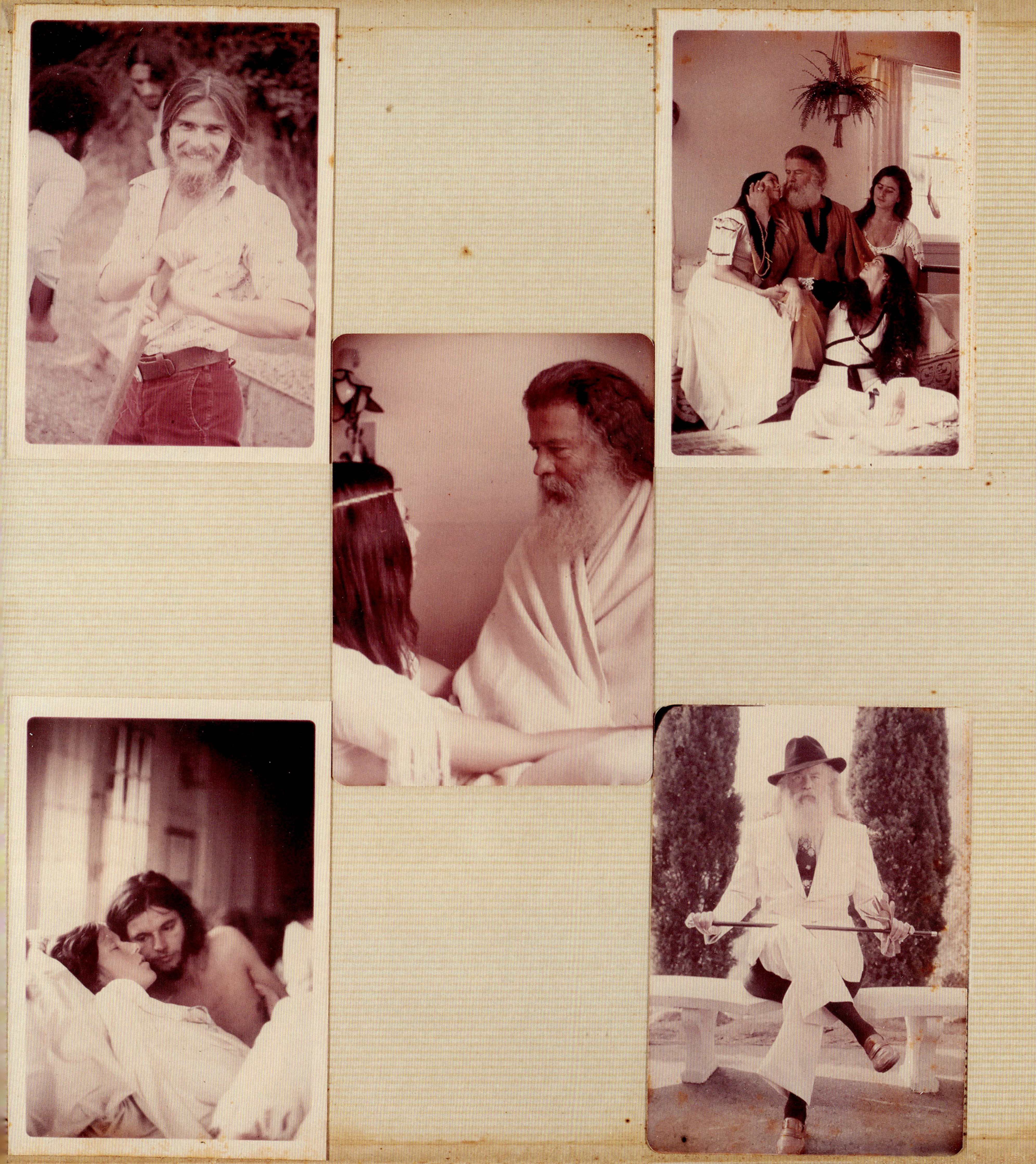

GRATITUDE

This book has been years in the making and would not have been possible were it not for the support of countless contributors. Foremost, the authors want to thank Jim Baker, aka Father Yod, who entrusted Isis to be the Family Historian and Keeper of the Archives. Without this foresight, the Source Family legacy would not have been preserved. We extend our heartfelt appreciation to every member of The Source Family for being committed and courageous participants in this radical journey. This book would not exist without you. Your collective determination to "know thyself" has inspired us and many others.

We extend our deep gratitude to the family photographers, who, along with Isis, captured photos in this book: Abraham, Om-Ne, Sir Knight, Venus, and Vortex Aquarian.

Thank you to Source Family musicians Octavius, Djin, and Sunflower Aquarian, for your willingness to dig deep into the memory banks to illuminate some of the images related to the family music and musicians.

The authors thank David Gartrell, Special Research Collections Curator at Hamilton Library UC Santa Barbara, who has worked tirelessly with Isis to preserve the Source Family's legacy. Because of his efforts the archives now have a permanent home in UCSB's special collections. Thank you, David, for arranging the photographs of the scrapbook pages for this book.

We also thank Karl Fredrick Anderson, founder of Global Recording Artists, who, with dedicated assistance from Mark Griggs (RIP), spent years restoring and digitizing the original morning meditation cassettes onto which Isis recorded during Father's morning meditation classes. The 13 classes included in the limited edition of this book were selected from an archive that contains hundreds more. Additional morning meditation recordings are available through Global Recording Artists.

Isis thanks her daughter Saturna, who patiently lived amongst many archive boxes for much of her childhood. Isis also thanks Electricity Aquarian (and his wife Harvest), Isis' Source partner on all projects from the beginning. Together they co-authored the first book on the family as well as assisting in the release of the music, meditation tapes and more. Isis also thanks Dawn Hurwitz, AKA Galaxy, for always being there to help and support along the way, and archivist and historian Philip Deslippe, who was instrumental in connecting Isis to UC Santa Barbara special collections.

Jodi thanks Robert Graham Ganger for his sublime inspiration and tea. She sends deep appreciation to authors and scholars Timothy Miller, J. Gordon Melton, and Diana Tumminia for their insights and revelatory work in the field of new religious movements. Many thanks also to Hedi El Kholti, and Steffie Nelson for their efforts, feedback and support.

Charlie would like to thank Amanda Kitchings, his North Star, and Eric Fisher, a true friend and the most interesting man he knows.

Lastly, we give hearty appreciation to Caleb Braaten and Carrie Schaff at Sacred Bones for making it all possible. Your boundless enthusiasm, patience and generosity has enabled us to create this book just the way we wanted. Thank you!

*This book is dedicated in memory of Robert Quinn,
AKA Om-Ne the Aquarian (1951-2019). Om-Ne's contributions to
the Source Family, as a photographer, writer, astrologer, and artist, were immense.
His near-photographic memory of both the big events and the smallest details of family life
contributed to the captions in this book. Robert embodied the spirit of the
Source Family, and we will be forever grateful for his friendship,
love, and contributions to this project.*

INTRODUCTION

By Jodi Wille

EVERYTHING CHANGED THE DAY SHE WENT LOOKING FOR JESUS.

Charlene Peters lived a life some would consider the epitome of glamor and privilege. A model and "Miss Cherry Blossom" DC beauty queen in the 1960s, she'd graduated from an elite finishing school and worked as a White House social aide. She left for Manhattan, crossed paths with Warhol and Dali, and had dated some of the most eligible bachelors on the East Coast before the zeitgeist beckoned her West. She landed in Hollywood in 1966 and slipped into a chic scene surrounding the artists who were making some of the most groundbreaking music and films on Earth. She fell madly in love and became engaged to the renowned rock and roll photographer Ron Raffaelli. She was managing his studio and hosting their friends as they discussed having children and their future together. Her life felt exciting and rich.

On an early spring afternoon in 1972, Ron tasked Charlene with finding him some "Jesus types" for an ad he was shooting for the musical *Jesus Christ Superstar*. Charlene headed straight to The Source restaurant on the Sunset Strip, where she'd heard that long-haired, bearded men abounded. The Source was one of the buzziest restaurants in Hollywood at the time, attracting a diverse mix of people united by their love for healthy and delicious vegetarian food. Warren Beatty, Julie Christie, Cicely Tyson, and many of the Laurel Canyon musicians were regulars, and Yogi Bhajan and Satchidananda would drop by and sit next to aspiring artists or LA proto-hippies like Gypsy Boots. There was a distinctly egalitarian vibe about the place, and famous customers were treated the same as anyone else.

There, on an ordinary weekday afternoon on the patio of The Source, Charlene's old life ended and her new life began. There was a line snaking around the building as she pulled into the gravel parking lot. The gorgeous female servers, wearing no makeup and Mexican embroidered dresses, and the male staff, all in white with long hair and beards, were a sight to behold. Charlene stepped onto the patio and felt what she describes as an energy vortex. Sensitive to energies since she was a child, she could feel the air palpably vibrating and swirling, with a frequency that

felt heightened, clean and clear. Through the crowd she spotted the restaurant's owner, Jim Baker.

This wasn't the first time she'd encountered him. They'd met in 1966 at Jim's equally popular restaurant further down Sunset Boulevard, The Old World. He was 44, newly divorced and dating Charlene's 19-year-old French friend Dora. He was wearing a suit then, with his brown hair cut short, and Isis remembered him as a handsome, magnetic middle-aged man.

The being who walked across the patio to greet her barely resembled that person. He now looked like Moses. His hair and beard had grown long and silver, and he wore a white tunic, drawstring pants, and Birkenstocks. His piercing blue eyes and warm smile made him look younger and even more handsome than Charlene had remembered.

Once the two locked eyes, Charlene remembers feeling their energetic frequencies merge, as if she were entering a "stargate." While she didn't know what was happening on a conscious level, in that moment she fell deeply, irrevocably in love. Every cell in her body felt activated. He gave her a big long hug and said, "Welcome home."

She learned Jim was now being called "Father" and he told her he had formed a spiritual community that lived together in a mansion in Los Feliz he called "The Mother House," the former home of the LA Times publishing magnate Harry Chandler. He invited

Charlene to attend his 4 a.m. meditation class the next morning. Charlene arrived at the pre-dawn candlelit gathering and Father led an electric class of 60 people with meditation, breathwork, chanting, and discussion, followed by a beautifully laid out breakfast of whole, organic raw foods. The experience was a revelation; it gave Charlene a feeling of sanctity and wholeness that she hadn't realized she was deeply missing. Most of all, there was the man she would dedicate her life to. For the first time, she felt that she was truly home.

In the early '70s, America had been in crisis and upheaval for years. An unending, unpopular war, assassinations of progressive leaders, debilitating inflation and economic disparity, the stuggle for women's rights, black liberation, and gay rights had left many Americans exhausted and disillusioned. Tired of the countless demonstrations, unfulfilled promises from politicians, and what many saw as little real change, these deeply dissatisfied Americans gave rise to one of the most misunderstood yet highly influential popular movements of the 20th Century.

Futuristic visionary Buckminster Fuller famously declared: "You never change things by fighting the existing reality. To change something, make the existing model obsolete." Hundred of thousands of Americans, mostly in their twenties, middle class, and white, but including a broad swath of people of all racial, sexual, and spiritual backgrounds, answered the call and chose to pool their resources and live together, building new communities and engaging in radical new ways of being to help birth a world they would want to live in.

Literally thousands of intentional communities mushroomed across America, micro-societies of like-minded people who rejected the authority of corrupt institutions and long-sanctioned narratives and began to create their own. The variations were endless: some moved to the countryside and started open land communes. Others launched psychedelic or art communes. There were yoga communities, crafter collectives, service communes, urban and political collectives, science cooperatives, gay and group marriage communes. Many of these new groups were spiritual communities, and quite a few new religions formed around charismatic leaders. The Source Family was one of these communities, born in this fraught yet fertile time.

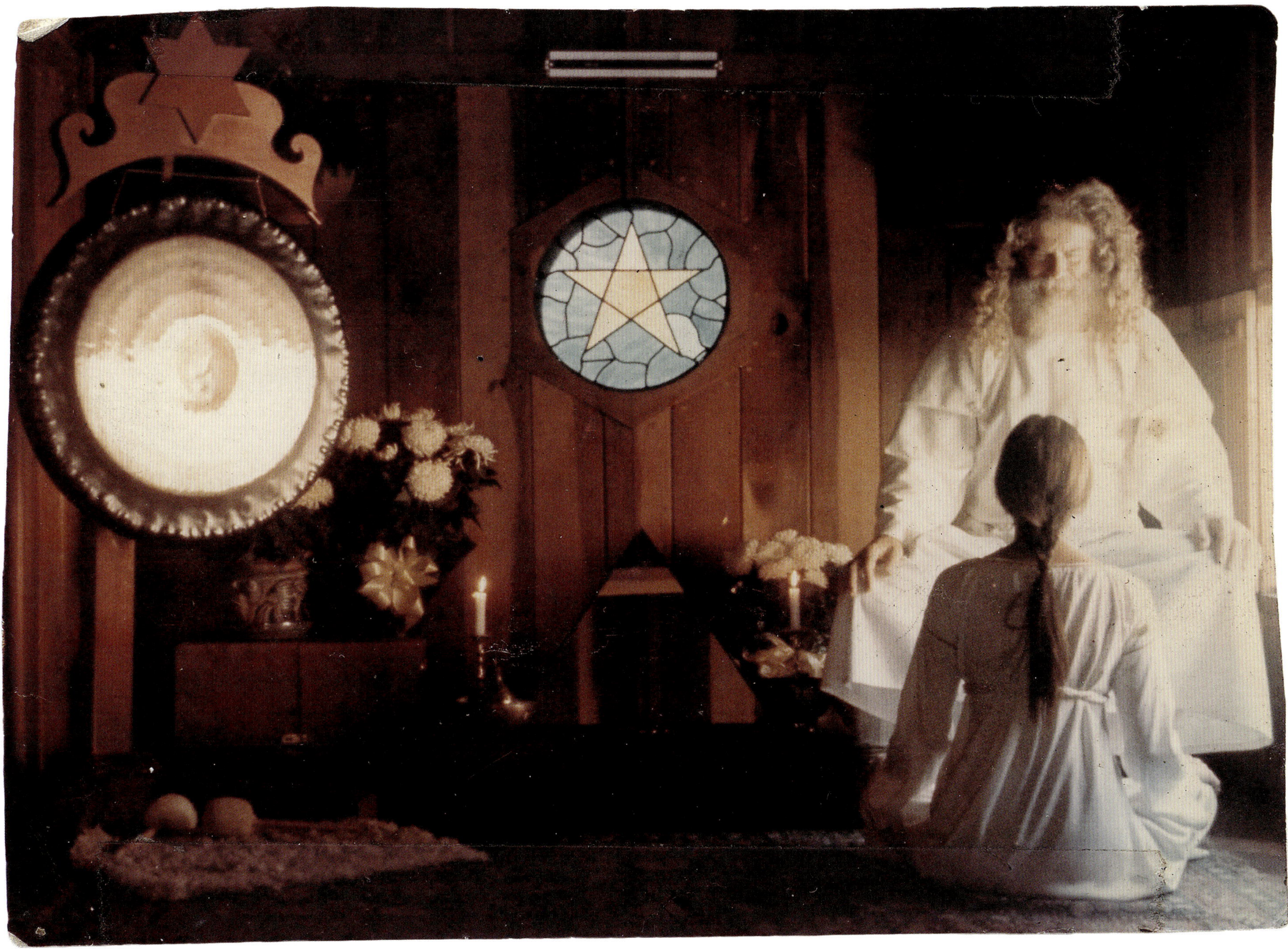

After a few days, Father called Charlene and invited her to document the first home birth in the family, which he would deliver. Natural birthing was an emerging movement in alternative communities then, countering the style of birth that had been the norm in American hospitals, where the mother was drugged, often with no memory of the birth, and the baby was separated from the mother after childbirth. Jim Baker, a holistic health advocate, was intent on sharing with his students the value of home births as well as the nutritional and psychological value of breastfeeding.

Charlene arrived with a 16mm movie camera and 35mm Nikons borrowed from Ron's studio. She documented the harrowing birth as the baby, born breech with his umbilical cord wrapped around his neck, began to turn blue; then she watched Father bring him back to life. It was the first true miracle Charlene had ever witnessed. In a matter of weeks, she would leave behind her fiancé and her entire life to join The Source Family.

Soon after she joined, Father became Father Yod and Charlene became Isis. Recognizing her talent and drive, he called her to a meeting in the redwood temple behind the Source restaurant. "He told me we had worked together in temples many lifetimes before, and I had always been there to help him. He and I had made commitments to each other before reincarnating, so it was time to get on with it. Father made me the 'Keeper of the Temple,' family historian and the keeper of the archives." She would become one of his women and later one of his 14 wives. "I never looked back."

"Right away he asked me to start recording and archiving. The world was way too exciting not to capture, and I was not intimidated by Father because I had also known him when he was Jim Baker. " Isis's upbringing also informed her role; her father was Chief of Documentation for the Air Force and later for NASA. "My Dad was an archivist. I grew up being photographed and archived since I was born. It was just a way of life."

Charlene knew little of Jim Baker's past then. Like many charismatic spiritual leaders, he was no saint. But he was a Hollywood legend long before he started The Source. A fatherless son in impoverished by the Depression, he'd risen to become "the world's strongest boy" and a champion archer, a decorated WWII marine, judo champion, ladies man, ardent spiritual seeker, and natural foods visionary who, with his second wife Elaine, had radically shifted the dining landscape of Los Angeles through their hip, wildly popular natural foods restaurants The Aware Inn and The Old World, starting a trend across the country.

Yet it was also rumored that he'd robbed banks, and he'd killed two men with his bare hands— judo chops

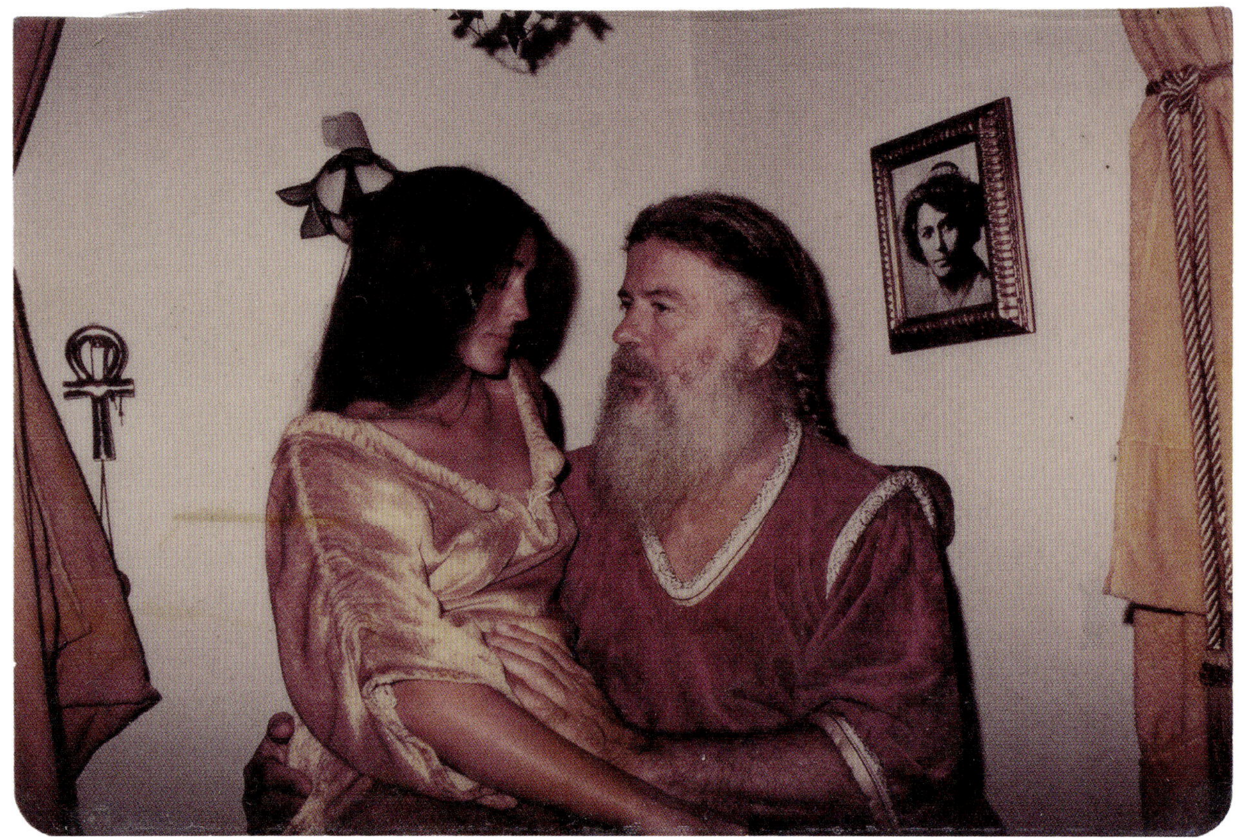

to the neck—and an additional bullet to the head of the second man. While both were ruled as self-defense, he spent time in jail for the second, released on the condition he register his hands as lethal weapons. His wife Elaine had divorced him after the second killing and years of womanizing took their toll, and an epic midlife crisis, which involved copious amounts of LSD, hippies, speed, and a purple Rolls Royce, led to the loss of his only post-divorce asset, The Old World.

Yet each time he'd fallen, either publicly or privately, according to those who knew him best, he rebounded with an earnest determination to right things and grow. Paul Bragg, Jack LaLanne, and Marlon Brando remained steadfast friends for decades and Steve McQueen considered him a mentor.

In 1969, not long after he started The Source restaurant, Dora abandoned him, and he experienced his deepest emotional crisis. This led to a profound spiritual awakening under the guidance of Yogi Bhajan, which set him on a path of transformation. After less than a year with the Yogi, he became disenchanted and left to form his own spiritual family, merging the Yogi's eastern esoteric technique with western magical traditions he'd learned under the tutelage of Manly P. Hall at the Philosophical Research Society.

Not everyone in Hollywood saw Jim Baker as a powerful spiritual teacher and benevolent father figure. Some considered him a rogue, an opportunist and a manipulator. The Family saw him differently. Omne, a core participant described him this way, echoing the opinions reiterated by many Source Family members over the years:

He was a decent person who really cared about others. He was a lover and he was as cool as they come. But he was an outlaw. He was a bank robber who said he started robbing banks back in the Midwest. He lived by a code. It was an outlaw's code, but he was loyal and he was a giver and he had a sense of humor about everything.

Jim Baker folded all of his life experiences into the spiritual teachings that he shared with his students. A healthy diet and lifestyle were foundational. His decades of esoteric pursuits morphed into a highly disciplined daily program focused on living in the "eternal now" on a continuous path toward psychic liberation. As Father would tell his students, "the only constant in the Universe is change." He also told them everything about his earlier life, "the good, the bad, and the ugly," Isis says. He acknowledged that he was growing and changing alongside them, and told Isis and the others, "I'm going on a journey. You're welcome to come with me. I don't know where it's headed, but I promise you it won't be boring."

* * *

Upon joining the Family, Isis discovered that Abraham, an assistant at Raffaelli's studio who had mysteriously disappeared the year before, had joined the Family and was living in the Mother House. The two started documenting together. "I was like a graffiti artist, a gangster," she said. "I had no issues being in somebody's face with a camera and Father Yod loved that. Once he gave me the okay, nobody paid attention to me, and I was able to document as I pleased."

Abraham captured a number of early black and white images from the Mother House era, but his stay with the Family was cut short when Father asked him to leave. By then Isis had begun to shift her focus mostly to capturing audio, shadowing Father with a microphone to record morning meditations. She handed the cameras to Omne, one of the most creatively gifted Family members and Family astrologer, writer, and graphic designer. He proved to be an especially talented photographer, capturing many iconic images throughout the Family's journey. Sir Knight, a longtime Family member, and Venus, one of Father's 14 women (and the only female chef at The Source restaurant) also picked up the camera from time to time.

Isis' role as Family archivist as well as Father's enforcer of rules earned her a fearsome reputation and the

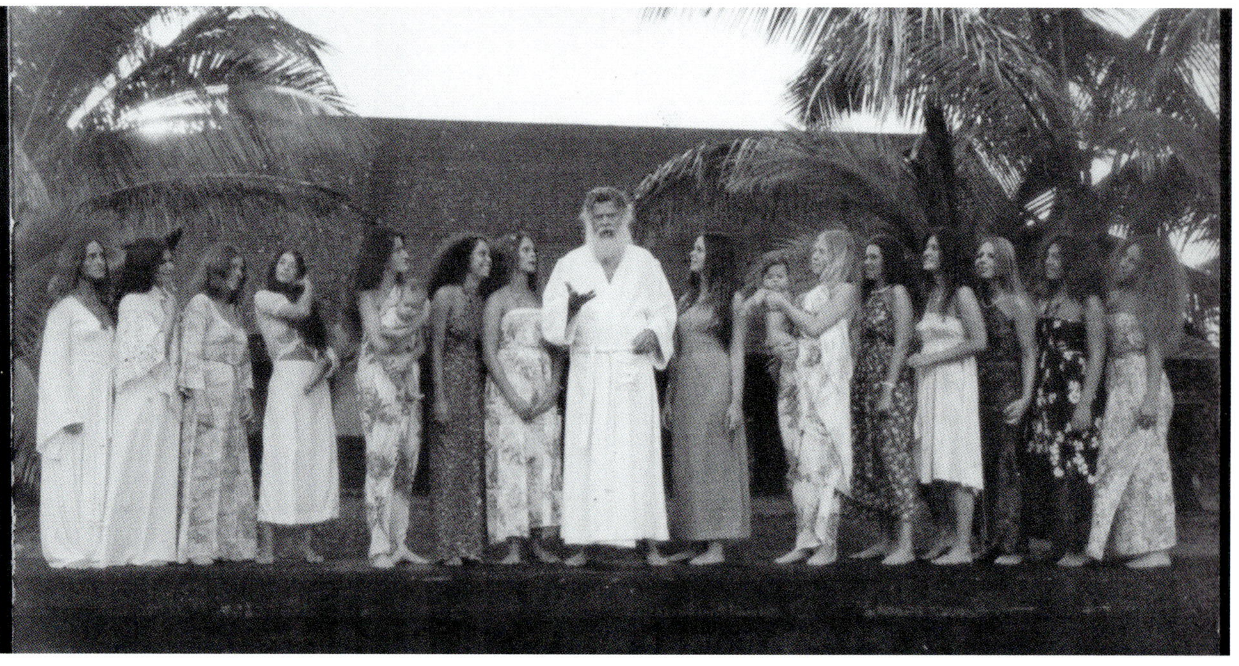

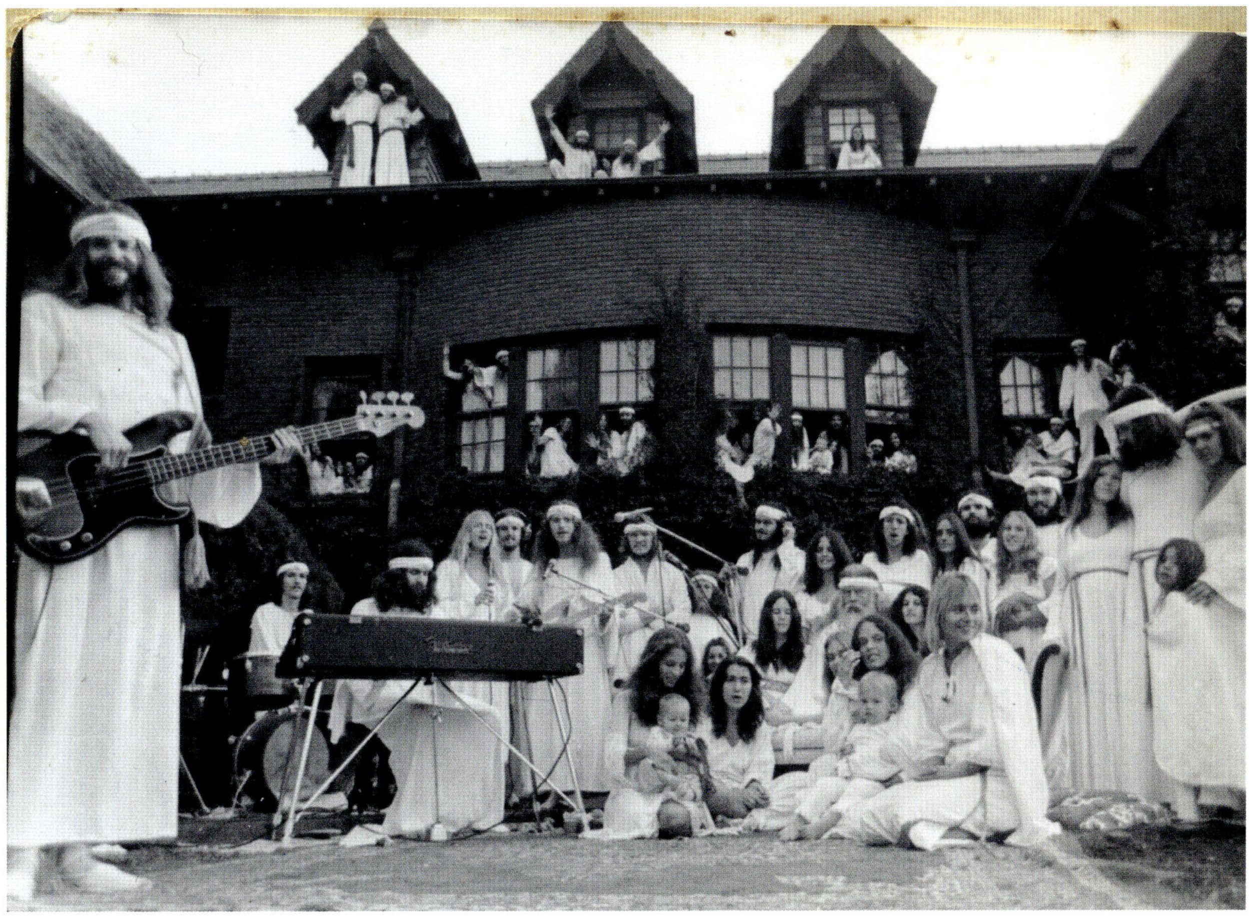

nickname "Dragon Lady." But it was this same tenacity that we can now credit with her saving of the Family legacy. One morning Isis woke to find that all of the audio recordings and photos were gone. She learned that Father had instructed a few of his "suns" aka sons to throw the entire archive in the trash. He claimed that he was opposed to being deified or creating any ideology or dogma. Isis simply retrieved the cassette tapes from the dumpster and began to compose the scrapbook pages you hold in your hands. She says she did this in defiance, as she was "so hopping mad at him." The following day she attended morning meditation, tape recorder in hand. Father gave in and let her continue to document.

The massive archive she compiled between 1972-1977 documents with remarkable quality and detail the full trajectory of the family and comprises thousands of color slides and black and white negatives, several volumes of diaries, over 200 hours of audio recordings, four hours of super8 home movies and public access videos, several scrapbooks, and more. This singular collection allows for an unparalleled, immersive, visceral view into a 20th century radical social experiment.

The Family was an outlandish presence in their flowing robes, strolling en masse down the Sunset Strip, but behind closed doors, they were disciplined and fastidiously clean, functioning as a highly experimental modern mystery school. While they were led by a patriarch, the power dynamics were more complex than that. Father Yod regularly consulted with his women,

and ultimately, the Source Family was governed by a matriarchy, a council of his wives.

Family: The Source Family Scrapbook, like the family itself, is the result of a collective effort. Photographs, along with Family members' written and visual contributions, as well as artifacts and newspaper articles, are the core elements of the book, arranged into visual constellations by Isis. Perhaps the most striking element of this visual diary is witnessing this journey largely through a female lens.

It is a testament to Isis' dedication as the Source Family historian that she continued to document the Family throughout its turbulent and transient later years. Perhaps even more remarkable is that she kept the swelling archive physically intact throughout upheavals that included moving the entire family to Kauai, then San Francisco, then Hawaii's Big Island, and then to the island of Oahu, where their odyssey would unravel after Father Yod's fatal hang gliding accident in August of 1975.

Thanks to her efforts, which continued over the 40-plus years after the Family's dissolution, the archive is now a part of UC Santa Barbara's Special Research Collections at the Hamilton Library. This scrapbook represents only a small portion of the archive.

Just as Father Yod taught the family about natural birthing, he also taught them the spiritual importance and dignity of a natural death, which they experienced for the first time after his passing. According to eastern esoteric traditions, the body must sit undisturbed for

three days in order for the soul to view its "River of Life" before it is released. This sacred passage is powerfully captured in the scrapbook. The practice, which has gained much traction in recent years, was illegal at the time. Because the Source Family held onto Father Yod's body for three days, they were targeted by journalists (like many communal groups of the '60s and '70s were for their unconventional practices), and demonized in Hawaii for decades, while they were all but forgotten in Los Angeles.

Partly because of their painful and public demise, or, for others still, in order to protect the ineffable beauty of their experience, a number of family members for many years kept their time with the Family a secret, sometimes even from those closest to them. Some women in the family, reflecting in their later years, felt Father had taken advantage of them sexually. At the same time, many of his wives feel that he loved them deeply, empowered them, and gave them a foundation to thrive. For most members, the dominant sentiment is that Father was sincere in his aims and he always gave more than he took; and that their time in the Source Family was by far the most magical and memorable experience of their lives.

Other communal groups from the '70s endured for decades and still exist today. Many ended in disappointment, even tragedy. Some, like The Source Family, planted seeds that would blossom and shift the culture as we know it. Jim Baker and The Source Family left behind a potent legacy of experimental and psych music whose audience continues to expand, but it's Baker's contribution to the culture of organic living—including the scores of quick casual health food restaurants that sprouted up across the country in The Source restaurant's wake—where his influence is most felt to this day.

Isis remains committed to Father Yod as his spiritual wife. "That's what worked for me. We all had our own commitments and agreements and Karma. People have accused me of living in the past, saying that I'm blinded or I was brainwashed. I would like to make it clear I was heart-washed. And there's a difference. I don't live in the past, I have brought the past with me, living in the now."

Omne Aquarian, reflecting on the overall experience of being in the family for seven years leaves us with this:

The story is heroic, tragic, comical, and deeply human. The truth demonstrated by The Source Family is that if you access the NOW you have access to the FUTURE. In the most positive sense we were in a bubble of intentional creation. We were under no delusions that we were simultaneously in late 20th century Hollywood. We were anticipating a future society. The lifestyle collectively created and embraced by The Source Family was done in a great sense of hope for the future in a very dark time. Whilst flawed, the attempt was poignantly magnificent.

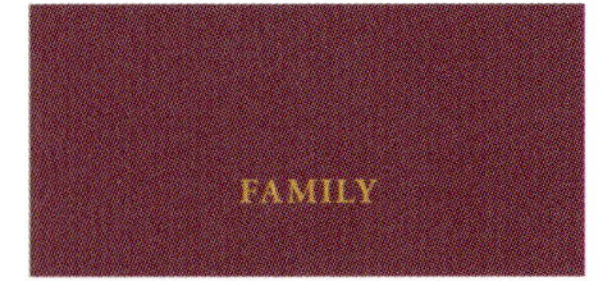

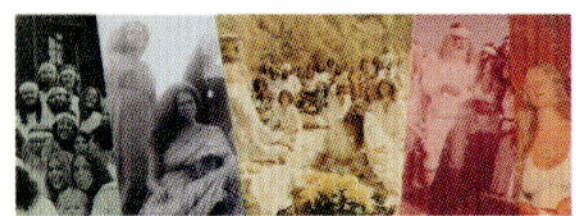

**Captions by
Isis Aquarian
with Jodi Wille
and Charlie Kitchings**

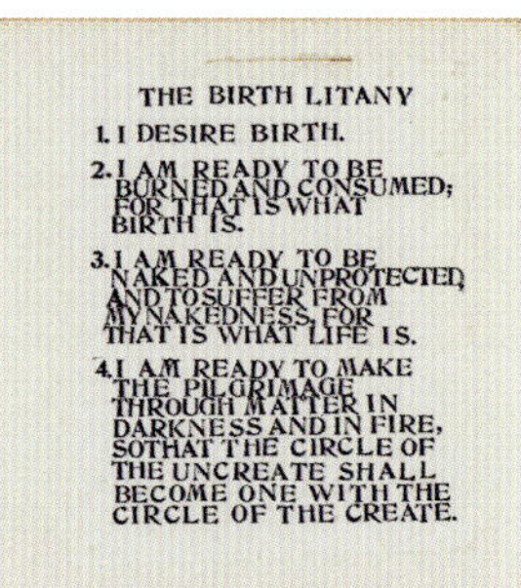

The Birth Litany was taken from *When the Sun Moves Northward: The Way of Initiation* by Mabel Collins. She was our spiritual grandmother. Father told us that as an early Theosophist, she never received credit for her channeled contributions to Madame Blavatsky's writings, which Blavatsky claimed as her own. Father had a memory of an intimate past lifetime with Collins, and she was one of our spirit guides in the Family. Her Birth Litany was part of our annual rebirth initiation in December, which included teachings from the *Emerald Tablets of Thoth*.

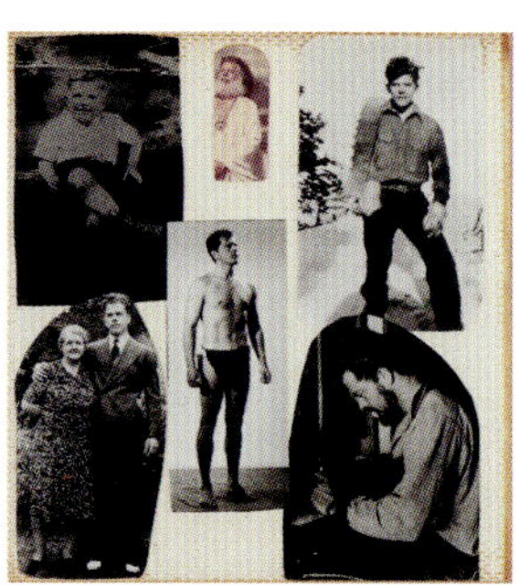

Top row left to right, Jim Baker as a child; Jim Baker as Yahowha in Lanikai shortly before he left the body; and 14-year-old Jim Baker during the Depression when he joined the Civilian Conservation Corps forestry program. He lied about his age to get in. Bottom row, left to right, Jim and his mother, Cora Baker, in Cincinnati, Ohio, where he grew up; Jim dressed as Tarzan, a role for which he auditioned in Hollywood; and Jim when he was a custom sandal maker living in Topanga in the early 1950s.

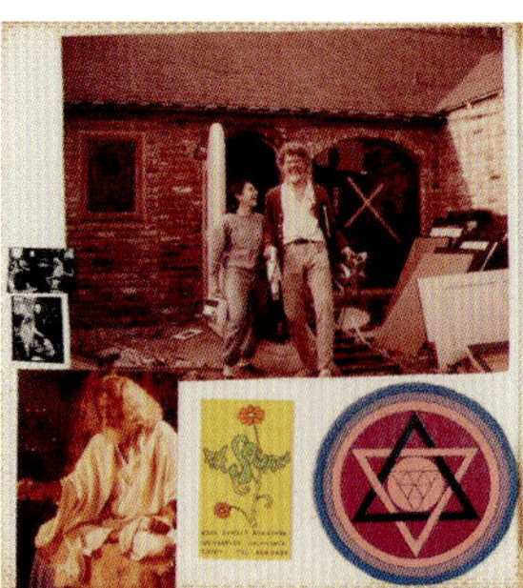

Top, Jim and his third wife, Dora, in front of The Source. I knew them years earlier, when Jim owned The Old World restaurant on Sunset Boulevard just down the road, after his wife and business partner Elaine Baker divorced him. Dora was French and 19, and she turned Jim on to psychedelics and the music of the time. They started The Source together, and Dora designed the flower logo. She left him soon after the restaurant opened, which he told us brought him to his knees and broke his heart open, launching his journey toward spiritual surrender.

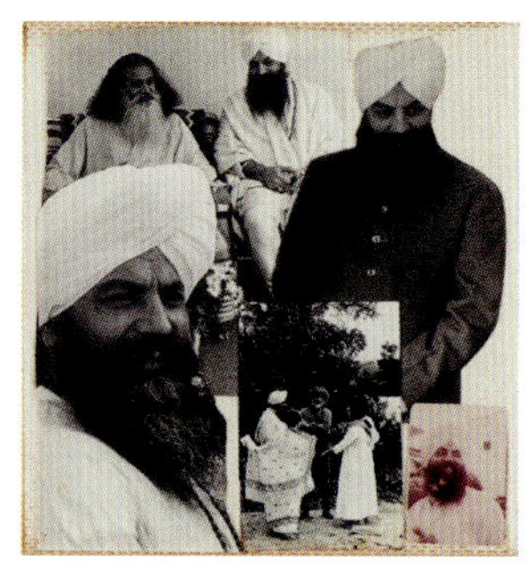

Jim had briefly been a Vedanta monk in the 1950s, then immersed himself in the teachings of Manly P. Hall, and later became a student of the Builders of the Adytum mystery school. Yet Yogi Bhajan was the first to compel Jim to surrender his ego. Jim met him at a party in Hollywood Hills. The next day, Jim attended the Yogi's class, passed out during a breathing exercise, and experienced a kundalini awakening. He awoke in the Yogi's lap, looked into his eyes and said, "You are my father." He had finally found someone more spiritually powerful than him. Yogi Bhajan became his spiritual father and our family's spiritual grandfather. Top left, Swami Satchidananda, an occasional Source restaurant guest, and Yogi Bhajan.

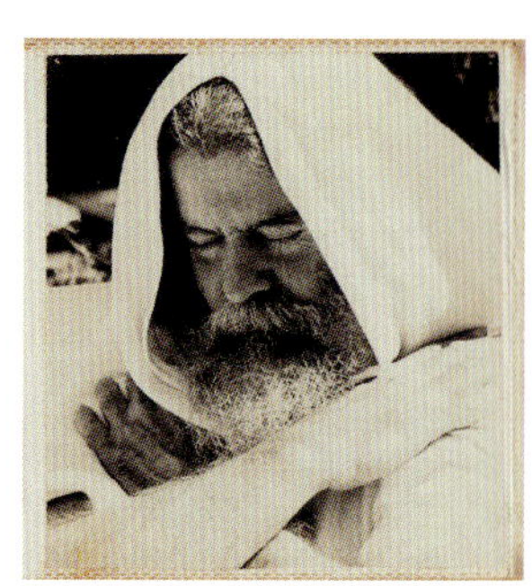

There came a time when Jim decided to leave Yogi Bhajan to start his own family, one that would merge eastern and western esoteric teachings. Here, Father completes the Star Exercise, an ancient occult ritual we also referred to as the Breath of Fire. As you stand on the earth with your arms and legs spread, left palm up, right palm down, you make 108 rapid fire breaths. On the last exhale you cross your arms over your shoulders and your moon chakras. Father introduced us to the importance of balancing one's sun and moon chakras.

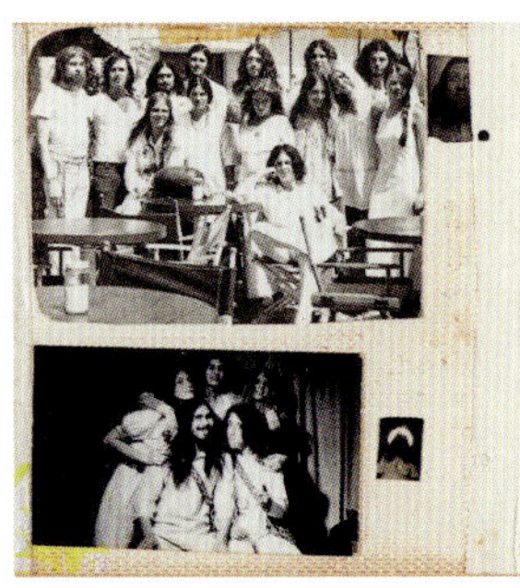

Top photo, early workers at the restaurant, before the Family. Bottom, clockwise from top left, Blessing, Robin, unknown friend, Hom, and Damian. Jim fell in love with Robin after Dora left him. Robin was a singer with a voice like Grace Slick, and Hom had real talent as a musician and songwriter. As a duo they secured a deal with Playboy Records, which fell apart because Hom was unreliable. He would disappear for long spells and return to The Source, guitar in hand. Hom was the first to call Jim Baker "Father." Hom caught wind that Jim was meditating in the restaurant at 3 a.m., and he joined in. Damian, Blessing, Aquariana, and Heaven followed.

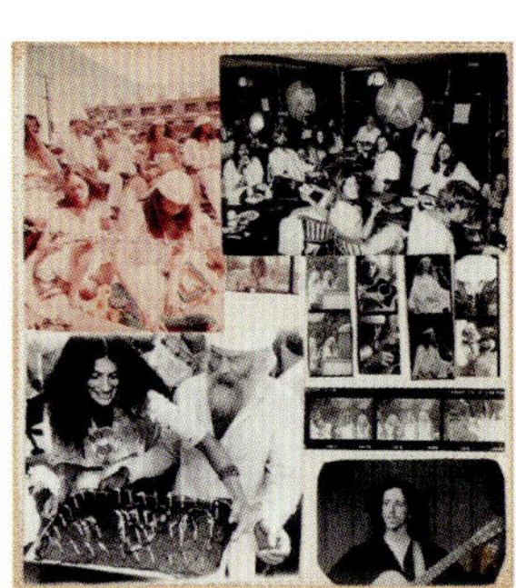

Top left, Isis and Soma making God's eyes with Osiris, Father, Robin, Heaven, and Pythias behind, in the Source parking lot. Top right, Sunday dinner at the restaurant, which took place after meditation class in the parking lot. Father commissioned the Starman painting in the back from The Fool, a Dutch art collective who worked with the Beatles. Middle right, Family musicians. Bottom, Hom would sing and perform in the parking lot morning classes before we formed any of the Family bands.

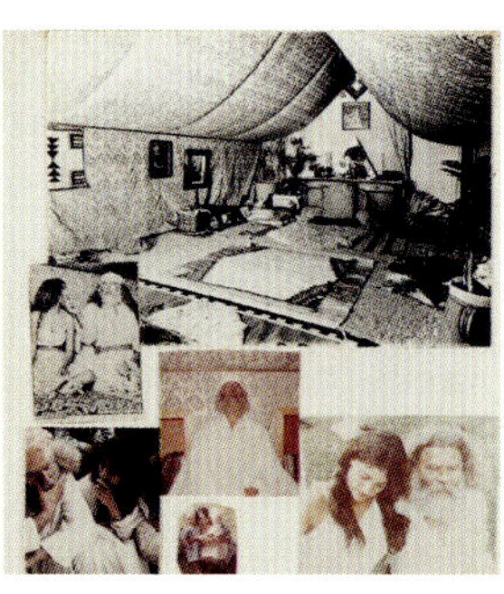

Top, the attic room above the Source Restaurant, which Jim and Robin converted into their living space. Before it was built out they lived in a camper behind the restaurant. Bottom right, Jim and Robin in the Yogi days. The small photo shows Gallahad, Sancia, and Solomon. Father instructed that the Source Family children? Gallahad and Solomon should always remain together. They are still together today, partners in a restaurant and living on the same piece of property on the Big Island with their families.

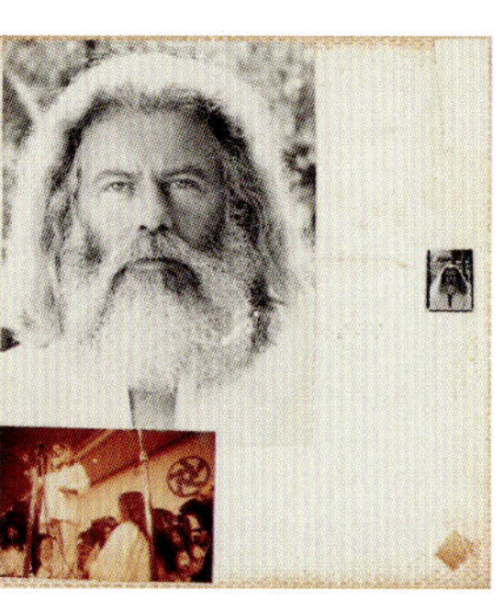

I love this photo of Father! It was almost as if he began to age in reverse when he formed the Family. Below, Father speaking at the Teenage World's Fair Festival, 1971.

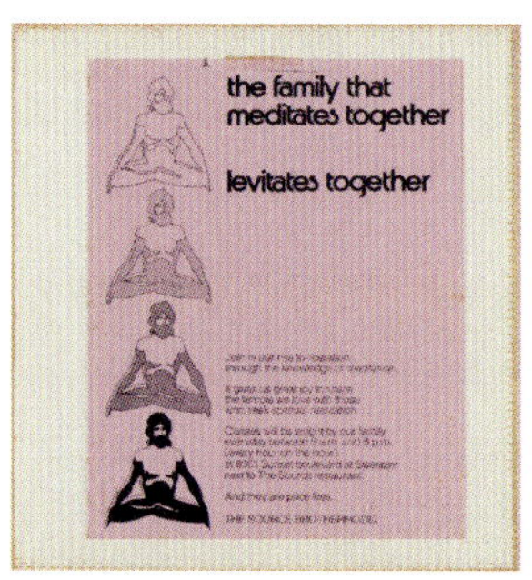

A flyer for our meditations held in our temple next to The Source. The Family graphic designers in the early days were a couple who lived at the Source Arts house, an ornate, Moorish-style home built by William Randolph Hearst on Franklin Avenue, which Father rented briefly for the artists in the Family. The couple had designed Neil Diamond's *Jonathan Livingston Seagull* album.

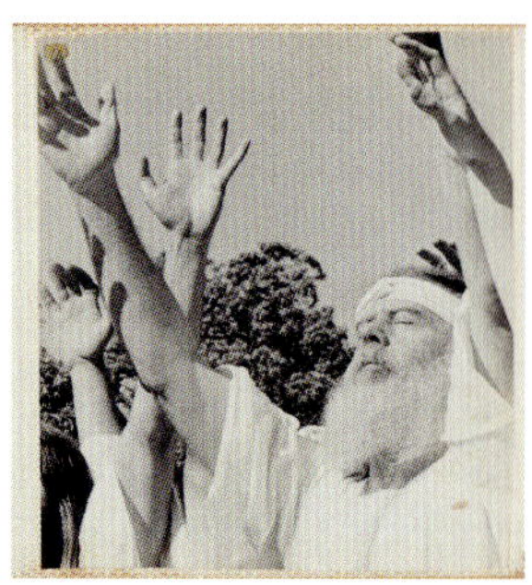

Here, Father leads us through our morning sunrise chant. We did this exercise every morning to greet the Sun, which we considered a spiritual feeding. We gave all of the planets Aquarian names and our name for the Sun was Omne, so we would chant *Om-ne, Om-ne, Om-ne* during sunrise. Father told us often that the planet Sirius was the Sun behind the Sun and our home planet. He said he would return there after he left the body and "prepare our next home."

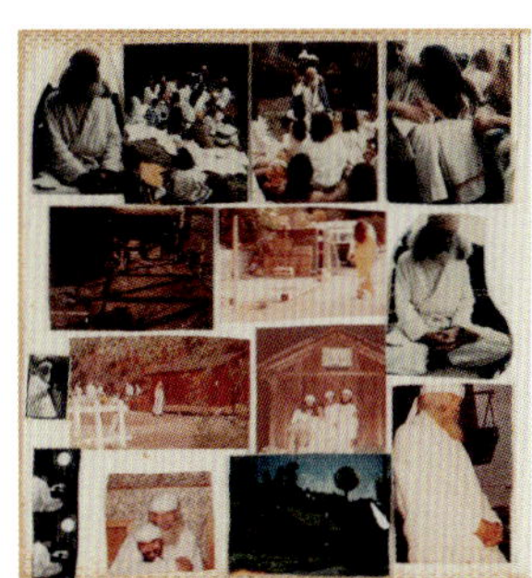

More early days, when Father was finding his spiritual stride. A number of people in these photos were not Source Family members, as this was before the Family formed. Third row down, images of the redwood temple behind the restaurant, which was constructed by Sunflower without a single nail.

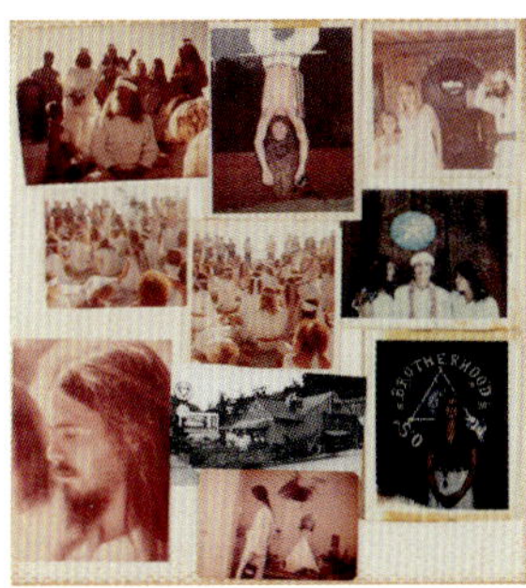

Top center, Starman hangs from the gravity swing bar. Jim Baker had one installed over his bed in his bedroom above the Old World. We used the gravity swing every day. Center, the family at Zuma Beach in Malibu on one of our outings. Center right, Osiris and me with a friend inside the redwood temple. Damian, bottom left. Next to him, The Source on Sunset Boulevard. Bottom, me with a tape recorder.

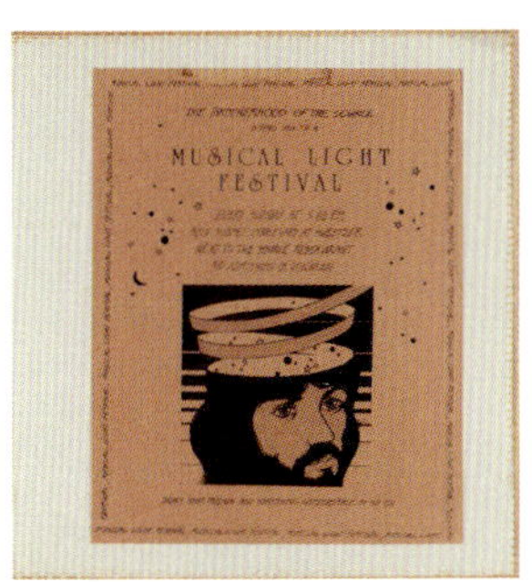

An early flyer for Sunday Family gatherings in the Source parking lot. About 100 Source Family members would attend. Not many outside people came, but some who did, stayed. Waterfall came to us this way, through Joshua. These gatherings brought us out of the Source closet and revealed us as a Family, more than just waiters and waitresses at the restaurant.

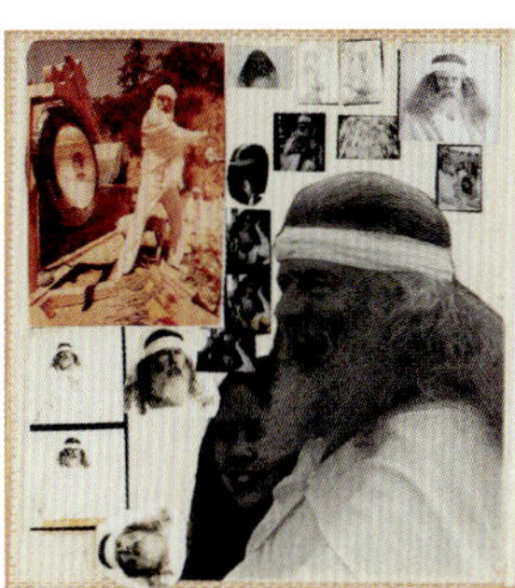

Top left, Father hits the gong, which was originally used on the soundtrack for *Doctor Zhivago*. Father introduced us to the idea of sound as a healing frequency. Lower right, Father with Makushla, who became his main woman and Mother Angel. Father said they were soul mates.

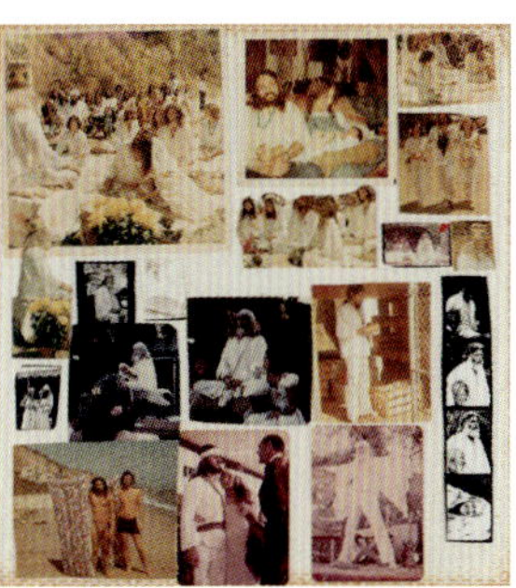

Top left, Patrick and Heaven's wedding, 1972. Yogi Bhajan is in the background. Patrick was a student of the Yogi, but he left the Yogi to follow Father. Top center, Patrick and Heaven before they joined the family. Center row right, Damian inside the food storage area below the redwood temple. Bottom center, Ra and Palm.

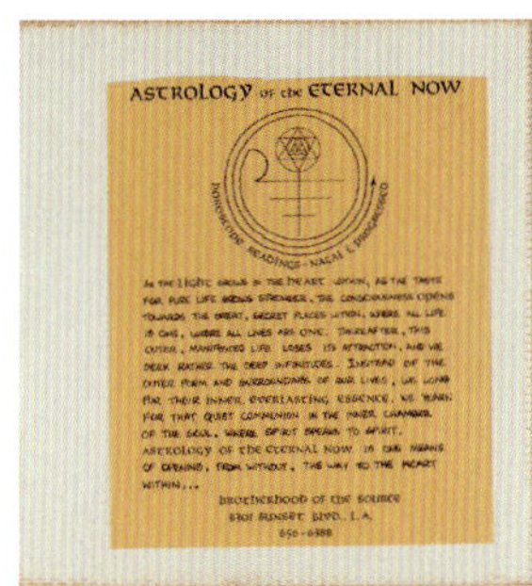

We offered horoscope readings for a very brief while in the early days. Utilizing astrology and tarot for guidance was a big part of our Family, though we never did personal readings and only worked with the major arcana in the tarot. Family astrologers were Om-Ne, Bonadea, and Elom-Paralada. After the Family, Om-Ne, Elom-Paralda, Venus, and Yahavah continued on as respected astrologers.

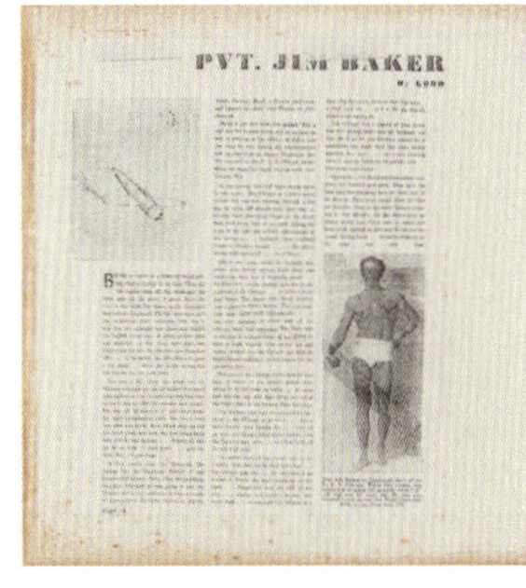

Jim was a warrior. He trained elite Marine raiders in judo. He received a Silver Star for saving many of his comrades' lives at Guadalcanal during World War II. He often talked about how fighting and killing in the war deeply affected him. This was the animal side of Jim Baker. Jim Baker and Father Yod are the two extremes of the evolution of mankind: the animal man, or lower self, and the god man, the self-realized, higher self.

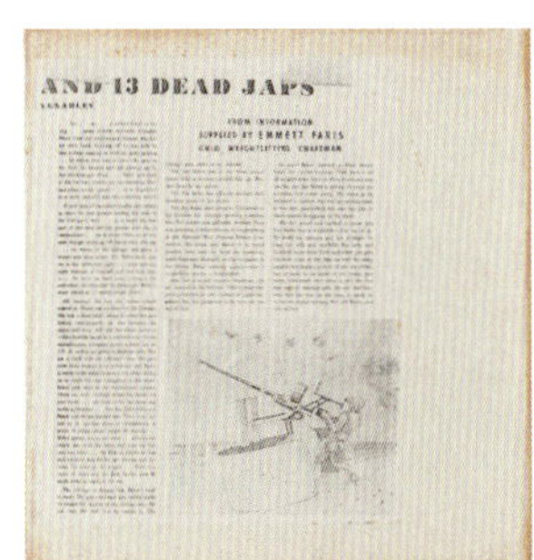

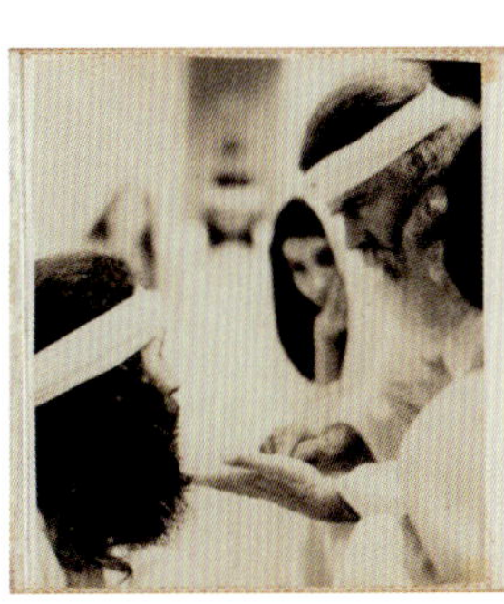

Top left, Makushla and Father. Right, our spiritual grandmother Mabel Collins. Bottom right, morning meditation at the Mother House, where, after breathing exercises and chanting Yod He Vau He, we would lie down and receive a sound bath while Father played the gong.

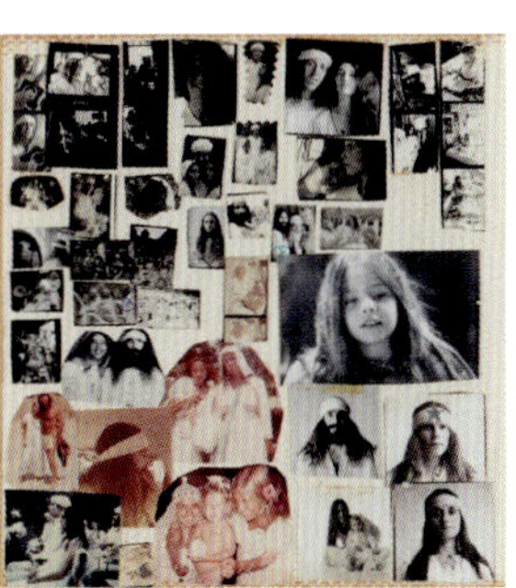

Father instructing a "sun" in the Mother House days. Father respected and cared for the younger men in the group. There was a lot of love between Father and his suns.

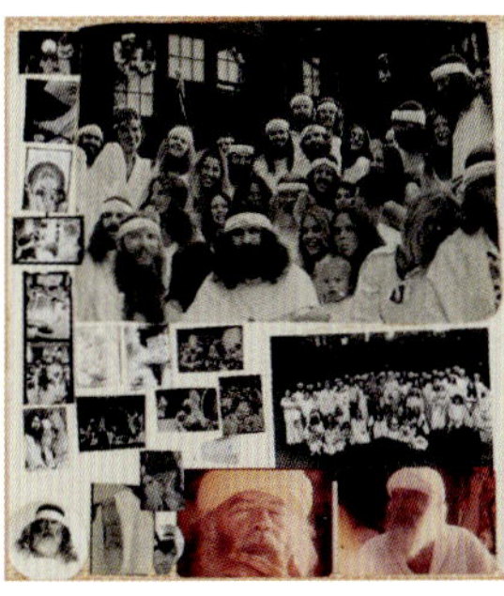

This page is a mix of early years and Mother House days. The bottom right photos were a few of our early passport photos, when Father was discussing the possibility of our leaving the country. We were preparing for a mass exodus. He believed that catastrophe was imminent. He wasn't the only one—many felt that a major global conflict or nuclear war was on the horizon.

The Family in front of the Mother House, also known as the Chandler Mansion. It was built in 1914-1916 by Harry Chandler, owner of the *LA Times* and scion of the largest real estate empire in the United States. At our peak, 150 people were living there. Father tried to stay there but was tormented by nightmares of old man Chandler. He felt dark forces at work. So he went back to sleeping above the Source Restaurant. He would return each morning for meditation, coffee, and sunrise with the Family, then hang a bit and maybe swim in our Olympic-size pool.

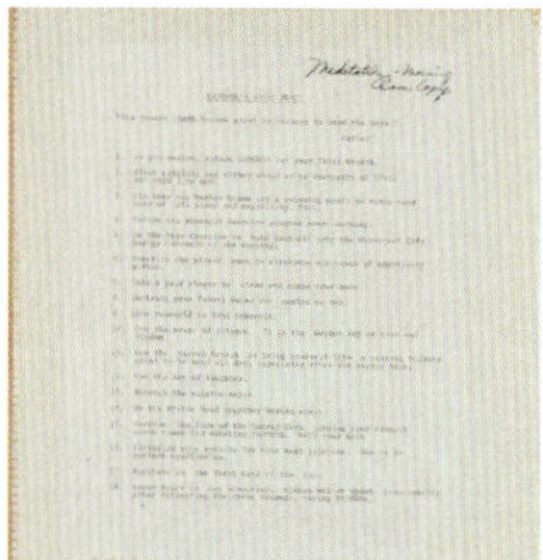

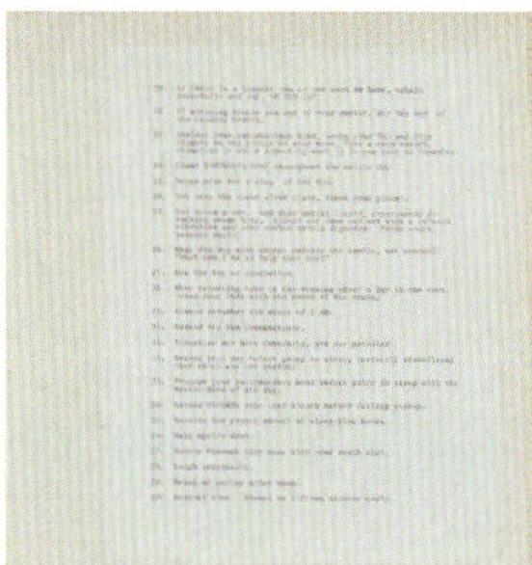

This was a guide to our daily practices at one point, but our rules often changed and evolved, they never stagnated. Father gave us a dynamic guide for life in the Aquarian Age.

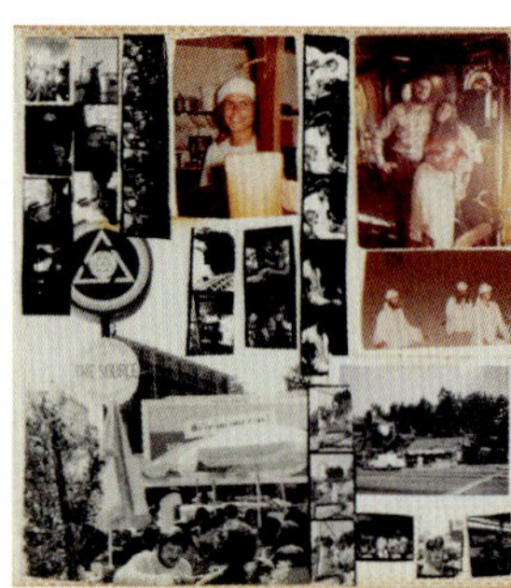

Top left, "The Pot Tree," outside the restaurant. Father would exhale the sacred herb into each balloon and offer them for $1. He said "Spirit has a sense of humor, how could I not have a sense of humor?" Top center, Pythias and Blessing with their daughter Onka, and Galaxy. Top right, Blessing and Mushroom, who were sisters, Damian, and Onka. Lower left, morning meditation in the Source parking lot. Right, Father at the captain's table, next to the window overlooking the patio, which was always reserved for him.

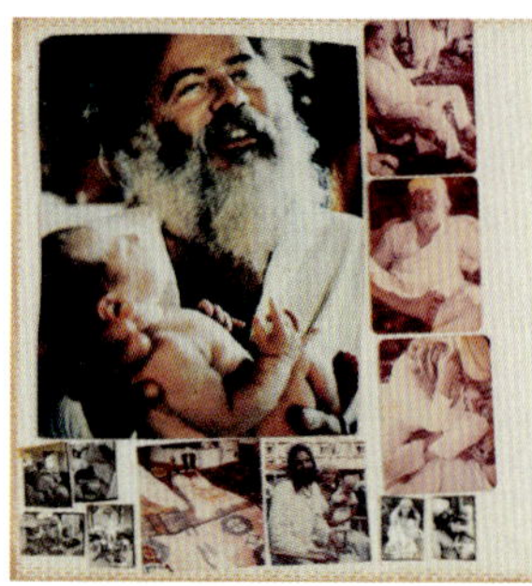

Lower left, our six-pointed star sign and the patio of the Source restaurant. Center top, Osiris working in the kitchen. Any new family member had to earn their keep by working in the restaurant. Father had the men start by washing dishes, which he thought was a great form of meditation. Source women were servers or worked at home. Top right, Ra and Galaxy.

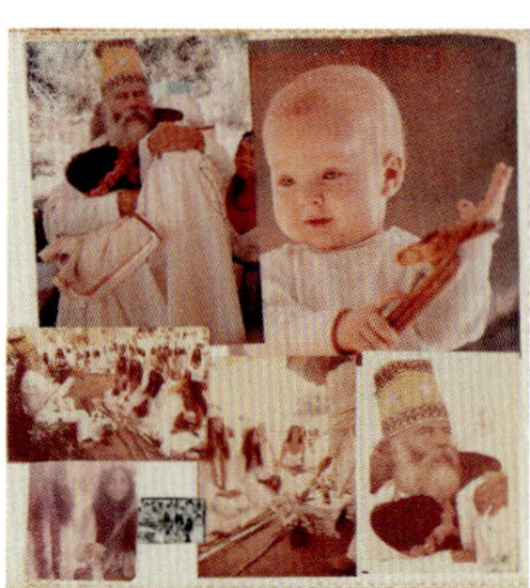

Top left, Father in another frequency after Sol-Amon was born. He was the first child of 53 born in the Family. Before this photo was captured, the umbilical cord had been wrapped around Sol-Amon's neck, and he wasn't breathing. Father pleaded with the heavens, "Let this baby live, and I will never speak anything but the word of God." The baby began to breathe. He lived. Father believed everyone could perform miracles, as Jesus said in the Bible. Bottom right: Father holding the birth rope, which our mothers used for support in the birthing process.

Father officiated Om-Ne and Elom's (Paralda's) wedding in the Source parking lot. Top right, Sol-Amon holding the Egyptian Mendes staff. Lower left, a ray of light fills Om-Ne and Elom's wedding chalice.

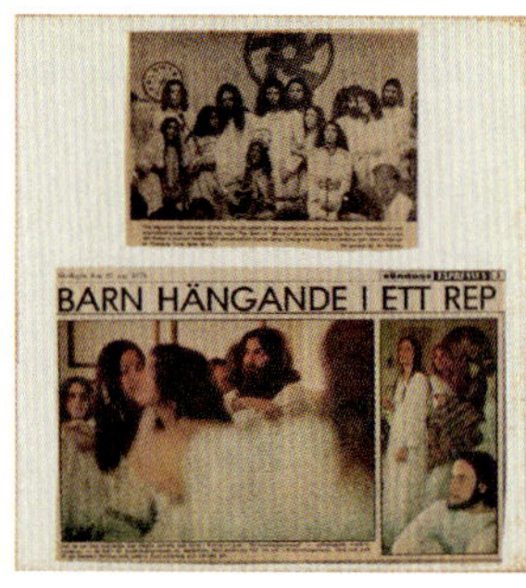

Top photo, early Family at the Teenage World's Fair, held at Hollywood's Crossroads of the World in 1971. This festival for teenagers had spiritual groups, booths, speakers, music, and eatables. Yogi Bhajan was there with his group, and the Source Family had its own booth, with food. Robin and Hom played music and Father spoke on stage. Lower article is from a Swedish newspaper. We were known across the globe.

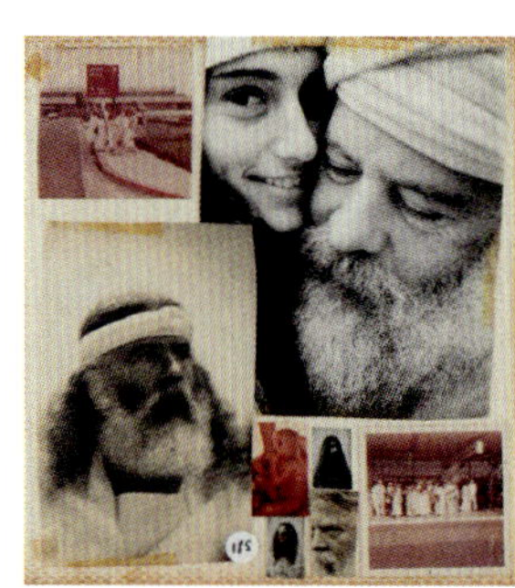

Top left and bottom right corner, Family members at LAX. We were probably sending Magus and his crew to Costa Rica then, to check out possible pieces of property. People said when we were all out in our robes together we looked like a whiteout, a blizzard of hippies.

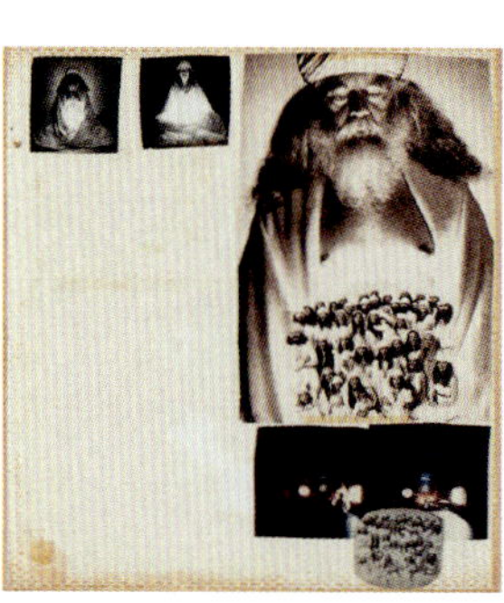

Top, Father and Bonadea, family astrologer and his first illumined student. One day Bonadea went into meditation and heard the sounds of each planet in the solar system. She and Father gave each planet an Aquarian name. Father was so proud of her, he sent a wire to her parents telling them that the Messiah had just been reborn in their daughter. Right, this photo collage was used for the God and Hair event we did at the Wilshire Ebell Theater.

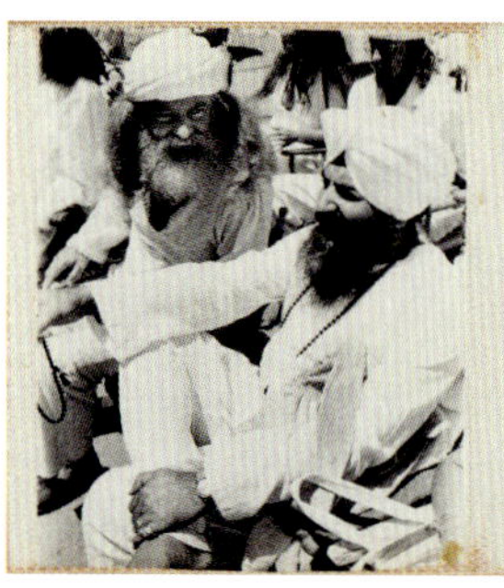

Father and Yogi Bhajan in the Source parking lot. He loved inviting the Yogi to our family events. Yogi loved Jim and wanted him to have his family. At one point the Yogi wanted Jim to give him The Source restaurant. Fortunately, Robin helped talk him out of it. This helped Jim to further break away from the Yogi, although he always held sacred his love for him and continued to consider him his spiritual father.

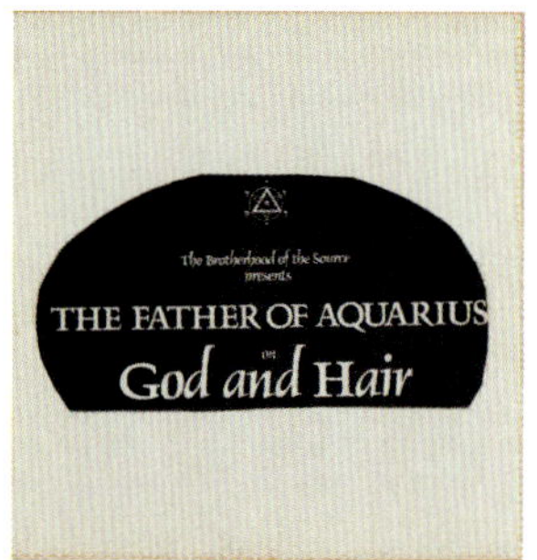

These are artifacts from our first public event. The Wilshire Ebell was a 1,200-seat theater that at the time was hosting hip, sold-out events for gurus like Satchidananda. Only a handful of people showed up to ours. It was pretty much us performing for other Family members, but we had a great time. We played music, Bonadea spoke about astrology, Ahom sang, and Father spoke. We also screened the film of Sol-amon's birth.

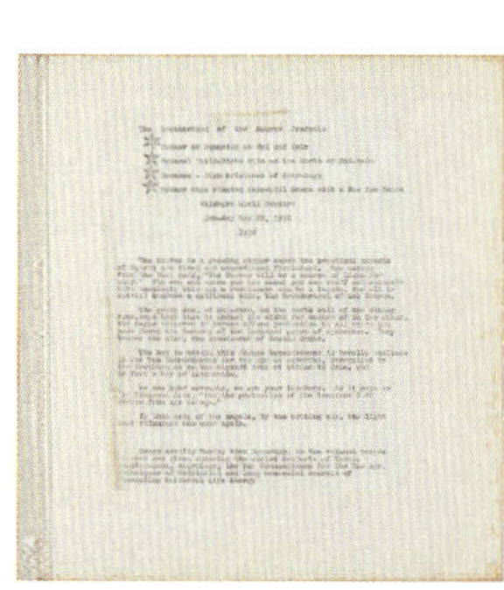

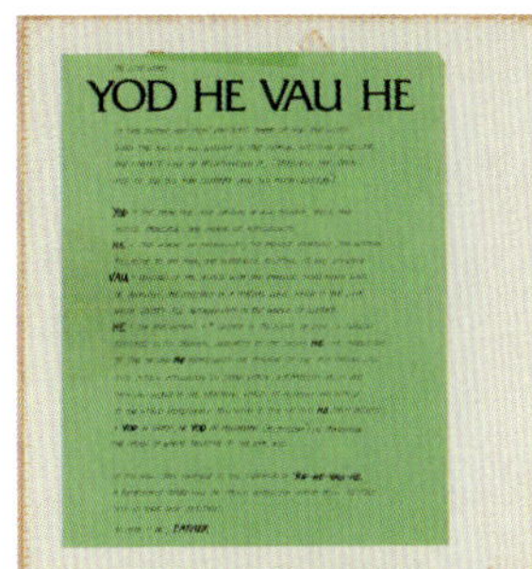

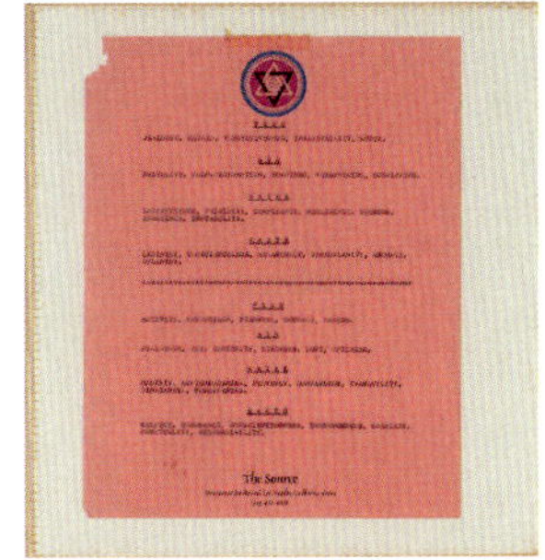

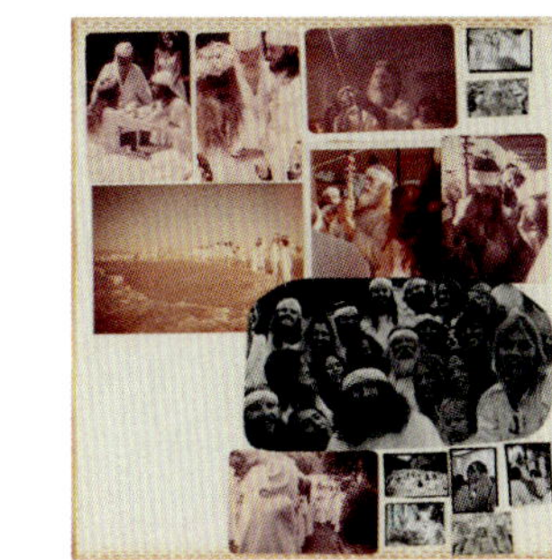

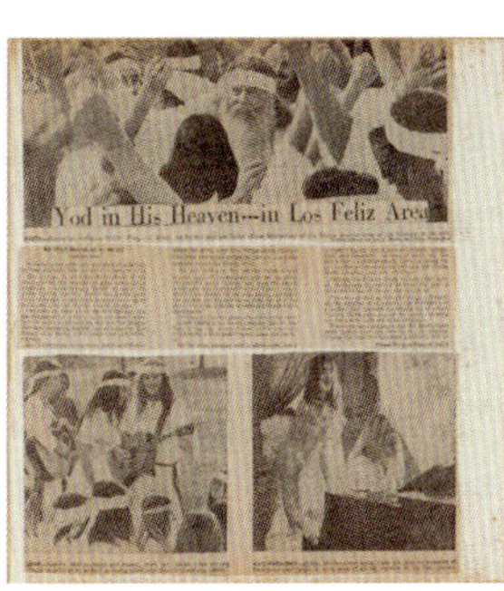

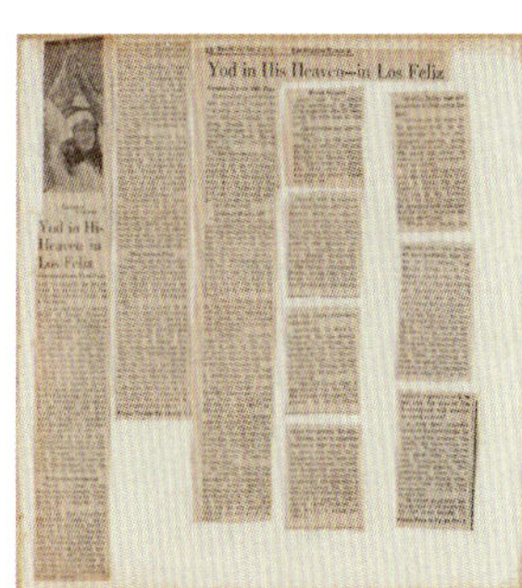

Family teachings from the early days. Everyone was given a notebook when they came into the family. It was their responsibility to write down the teachings and practices that were given. The only way for people to learn our practices or wisdom teachings was to come to morning meditation. However, we did share some teachings on flyers that we passed out at events and made available at the restaurant for people who were interested.

The Family went on an outing to the beach one day, where Father did a teaching about the sea. He told us that the pH of the ocean and the pH of our blood was very similar. He believed in the healing nature of the ocean.

Top left, we made a huge family photo at the beach. I photographed one end and Om-Ne photographed the other. Father liked showing us off when we were out in public. Center, group photo at the Mother House with Magus in front. Bottom left, Father arrives at the Mother House for morning meditation. We would line up when he entered. This always felt like a past life temple procession to me.

We got a lot of press. *LA Times*, *The New York Times*, *LIFE*, foreign newspapers...we were being called 'Le Millionaire Hippies'!

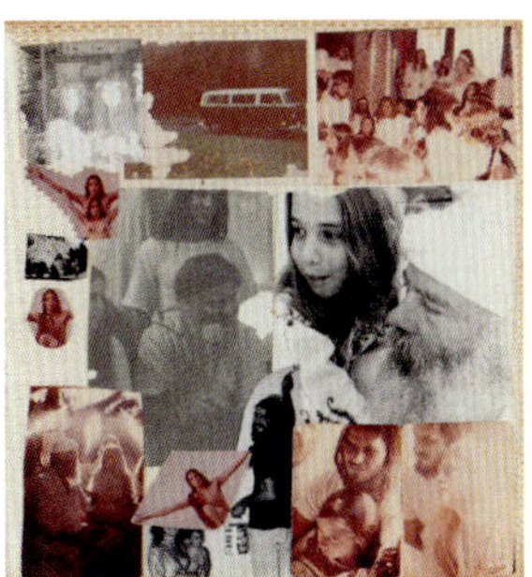

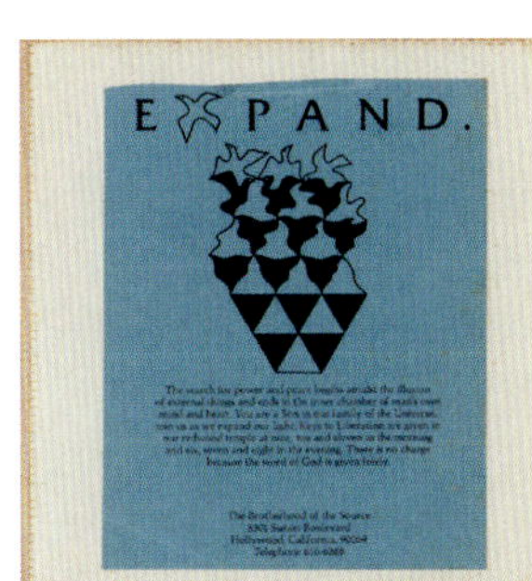

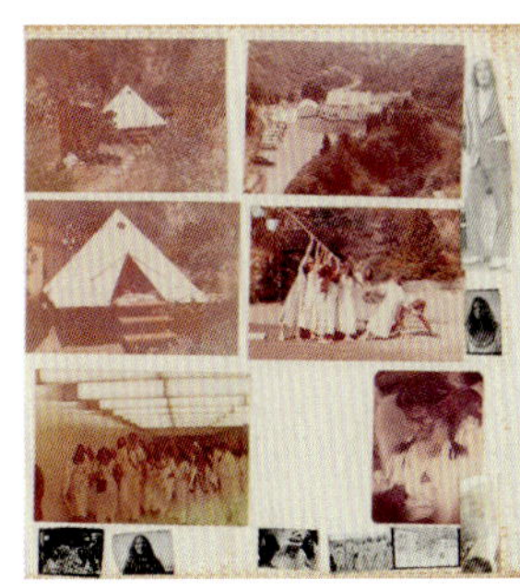

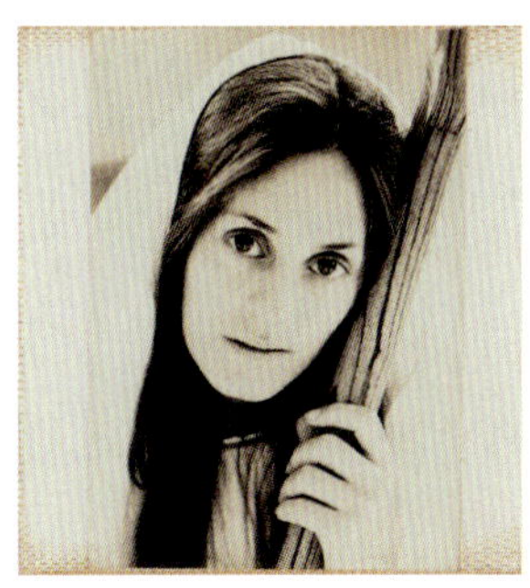

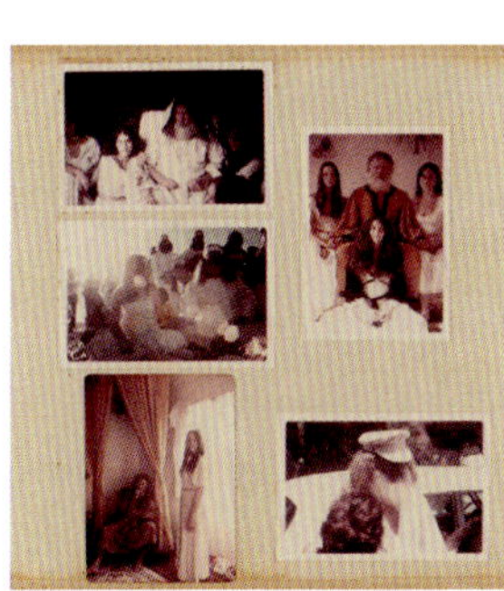

Center row, left, images of Osiris and me. I became his woman after I joined the Family, before I was with Father. Center right, Father with Starwoman, one of the children who joined the Family when their parents joined. EXPAND was a flyer to attract new members. Father wanted to keep our family core at 140 but hoped to expand to 4,000 members. The new members would belong to the Family and contribute, but not live with us.

Top left, raising the flagpole on the Father House driveway. We flew the Betsy Ross American flag: 13 stars for the 13 original colonies. Father was very patriotic and was especially fond of the founding fathers and their Freemasonic ideals. He wrote songs about his love for The United States of America. Bottom right, Father was not only an expert in judo but was also a champion archer and an excellent swimmer. He loved sharing these skills with the suns.

Top two left images, Father's pyramid tent, where he would retreat when he needed time alone. He had a sign at the bottom of the path to the pyramid that said "Stop" or "Go," depending on whether or not he wanted to be seen. Top right, an aerial view of the Father House, which was in Nichols Canyon in the Hollywood Hills. After we left the band ABBA moved in. Abba in Hebrew translates to Father.

Here, I'm holding the Mendes staff. The staff was always kept by the gong in the meditation room. I had the title of High Priestess at one point. Family members also called me "The Dragon Lady." I was Father Yod's bulldog when he needed me; I enforced rules so he wouldn't have to. I was often disliked or even feared because of this (so people told me, decades later). I was single-pointed on his needs and I always had his back. I'd made commitments to him many lifetimes to do the work together, and we both acknowledged this when I came in. Abraham or Om-Ne took the photo.

Upper right, Father with Makushla, Prism, and Robin. This was around the time Father began to be with multiple women. Bottom right, Father wearing the chauffeur's hat Pythias typically wore when driving him around in the Rolls Royce, which Father named "Ultimate". Bottom left, Makushla with Father and his shofar, sitting on the dyanism (sex magic) chair.

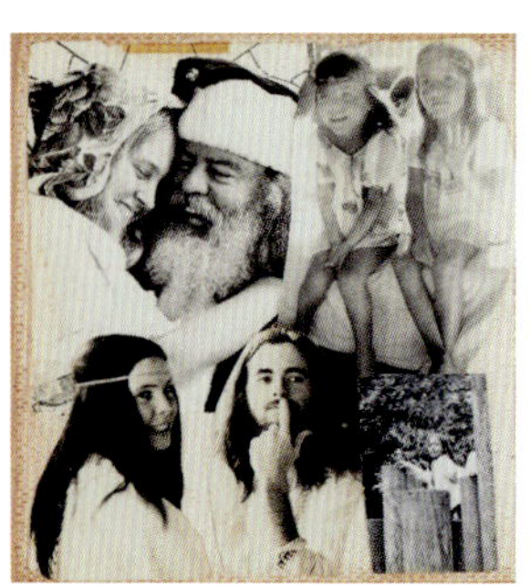

Top left, Father and Aquariana. She claimed to be descended from Latvian nobility and was a gifted singer. Father was drawn to her the second she joined the Family and loved her from the start. She fell in love with three men in the family: Damian, Sunflower, and Father. They were all in love with her and Father said they had gone to battle for her and fought over her in many lifetimes, i.e. Helen of Troy. She would ultimately become one of Father's wives and give birth to his son, Yod.

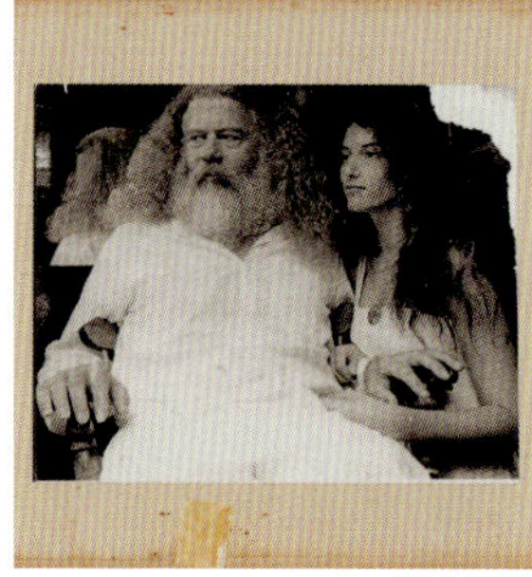

Jim and Robin, early Source Restaurant days. Robin was his fourth and last legal wife while he was still Jim Baker. She had been a dancer at Whisky a Go Go, and at one point was engaged to the bass player from Deep Purple. She was sick with peritonitis when she met Jim Baker. He put her on a nutritional and holistic healing program which included organic vegetarian food, exercise, spiritual practices, and pure thoughts (the basic program he put most of us on when we arrived to live with the family), and Robin says he saved her life.

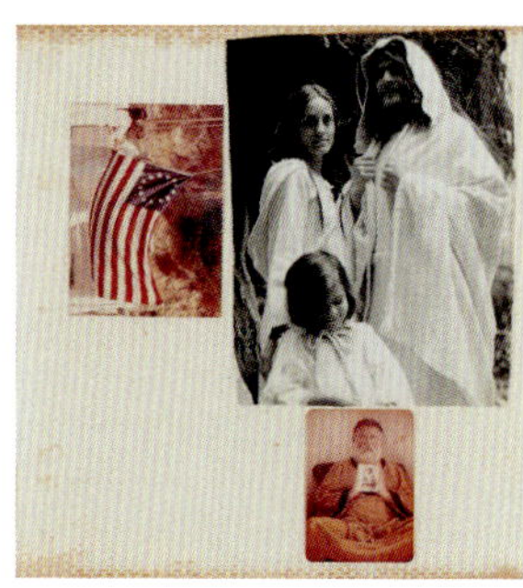

Left, the Betsy Ross 13-star flag in the Father House driveway. Father told us that he cherished and related to the period of the founding of America. Right, me, Odin, and Butterfly in a photo shoot for homespun garments we'd designed to sell in the Hermit Hut store, which was connected to the Source restaurant. We wanted to sell Aquarian fashions, but I don't think we ever did. This was around the time we were looking to sell the restaurant and relocate. Bottom, Father holding a picture of Mabel Collins.

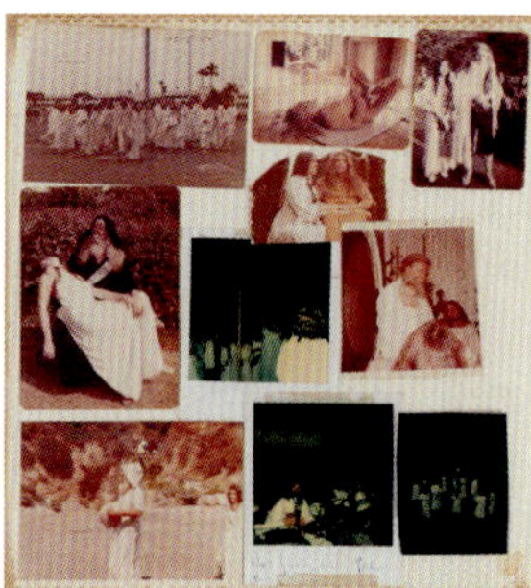

Top left, an outing somewhere in LA with Aristotle and Aphrodite in front. When we in the Family needed to deal with a government agency like the police department, Father would send Aristotle. Top center, Father in the meditation room at the Father House. Top right and middle left, Father and Makushla. Center, early morning flag raising in the Father House driveway. Bottom left, Father carrying a rock to help make a circle of rocks around the flagpole so that the vans wouldn't hit it.

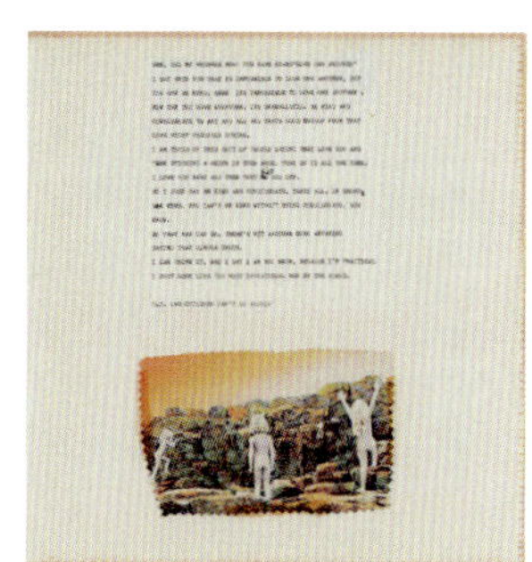

This letter was one of the notes Enoch or Thoth would channel and leave around for Father. In this one, the last lines were "140 children can't be wrong…" so I used a graphic of children, free and one with cosmos and mother nature. I cut it from a Led Zeppelin album. Who knows? It seemed okay at the time.

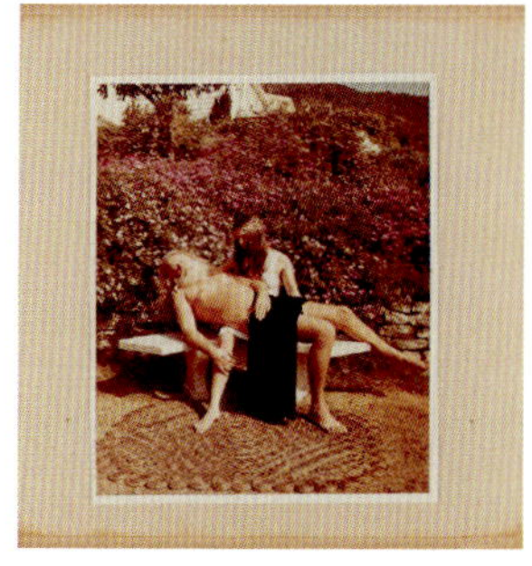

After morning meditation, when the suns went off to work and the women started their duties, Father had all afternoon to do what he wanted. Sometimes he would get creative and have fun. He considered Makushla his "mother" and himself a Jesus-like person (he didn't think he was Jesus, he said we were all Jesus). This was part of a series of photos riffing off Michelangelo's famous sculpture, *La Pieta*.

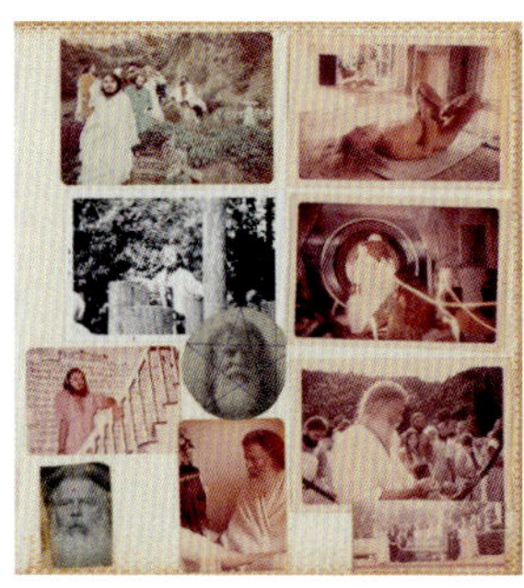

Top left, back yard, Father House. Top right, Father in repose with Manly P. Hall's *Secret Teachings* on display in the background. Middle right, Father in front of the gong with a light streak. This sort of phenomenon appeared regularly on negatives and slides. Center left, Ra with the 10 Aquarian Commandments he painted in the stairwell of the Father House. Above him is Soul. Lower right, Father teaches archery to the suns. Bottom right, Father would take his women and cross the street from the Source restaurant to look at it from that perspective and see if anything needed tending to.

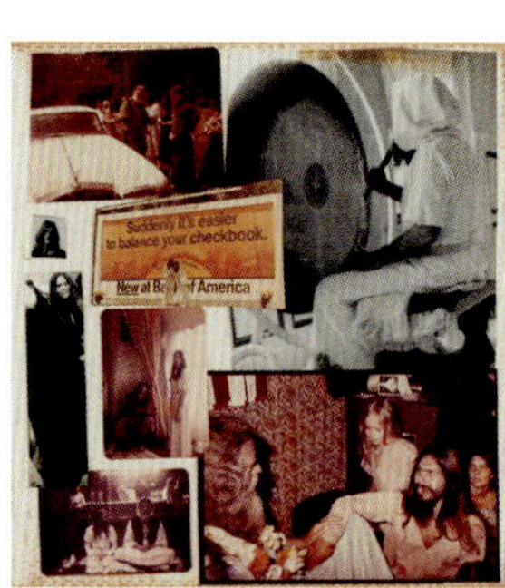

Center, Sunflower and Heaven on their wedding day in front of a billboard in the Source parking lot. Bottom right, Father with Damian, with Tzaddi and Soma behind him, after Damian returned from Maui. Damian and a few other suns were tasked with taking the mothers and children to Maui to see if it would be viable for the family to relocate there. This was when we became a target of social services because home births and homeschooling were illegal at the time.

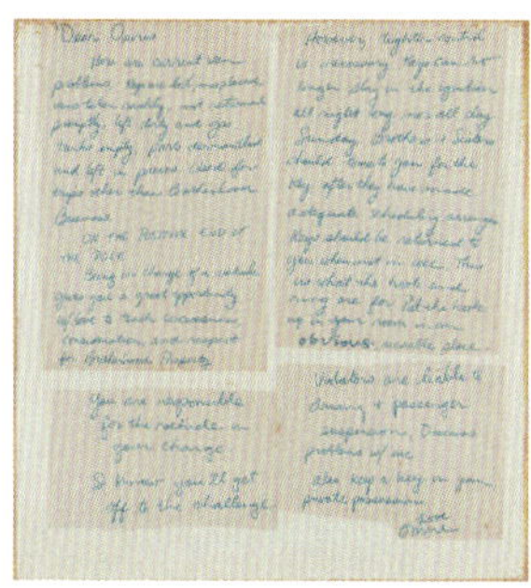

Even though we were living on a spiritual plane, we had to deal with the realities of living communally. We had an open discussion every day to talk about domestic issues that needed to be addressed. We worked it out as a group: chores, car usage, laundry, cooking, etcetera. In the Father House, Father was getting more into meditating in his room and being with his women rather than managing daily affairs, so he increasingly gave his women the responsibility to manage things—mostly me, Harvest, and Astral—with suns like Electricity, Om-Ne, Joshua, or Damian heading up projects.

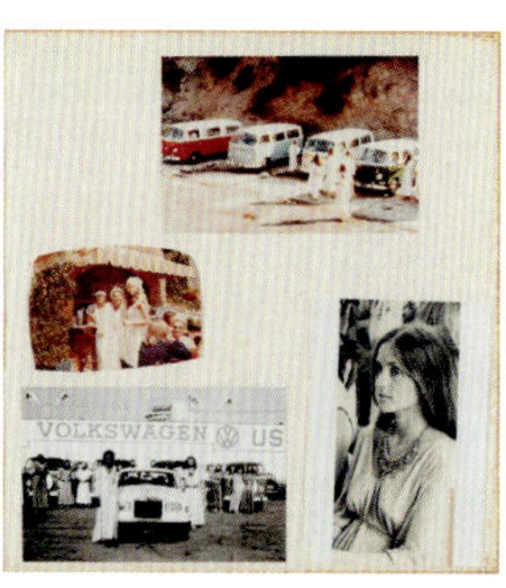

Top, some of our vans parked at the Father House. I love the stone parking partitions. We kept things orderly and clean in the Family. Middle left, Isis, Anastasia, and Makushla after Makushla joined the family. Bottom left, the dealership where we leased the Rolls Royce and our vans. Atla, to the left of the Rolls, came from a wealthy family in the Valley. Her father was a contractor and her mother was the sister of the first black mayor of Los Angeles, Tom Bradley. She was a former model and cooked the books at The Source. Bottom right, a picture of me wearing Family jewelry, which we all shared. Father was big on aesthetics.

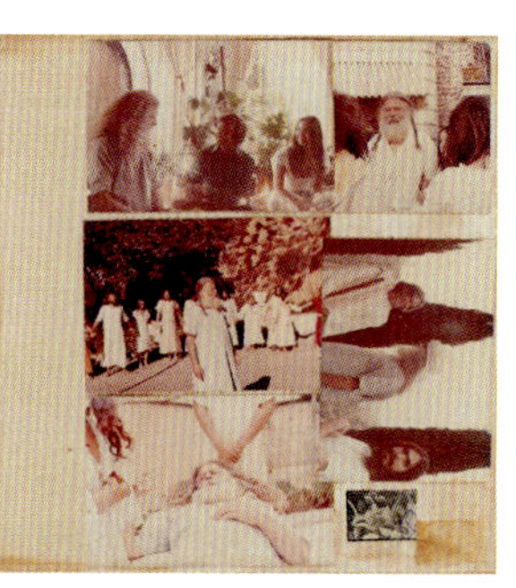

Top left, Father with Elliot Mintz, a radio and television personality who later became a publicist and John Lennon and Yoko Ono's spokesperson. He befriended Father early on and remained a positive force over the years. He was a vegetarian and ate at The Source several times a week. He was interviewing Father here for a news story on KABC-TV. He also did an in-depth interview with Father for his radio show on KPFK, which was popular with the hip Hollywood crowd at the time and featured conversations with notable musicians, actors, and spiritual leaders. Sideways picture, Mercury when he first came into the family, with Father and Damian. Mercury had been a Marine who went AWOL.

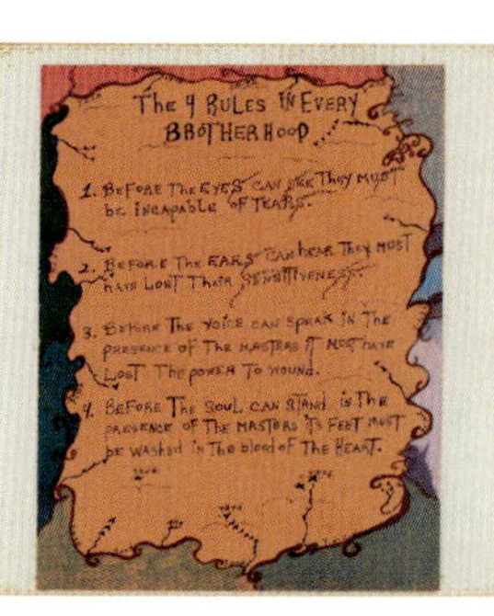

"4 Rules" from Mabel Collins' Light on the Path. Around June 1973 at the Father House Octavius' woman Anastasia and their baby daughter Libra got sick with staph. They avoided the hospital for as long as possible to try and heal it naturally, but it got worse and they ended up at UCLA Medical Center, very sick. The hospital reported us, and city and county building inspectors and authorities came down hard on the family, interrogating us about our lifestyle and health practices. We started preparing in earnest to leave for Hawaii and get things in place to create our dome community.

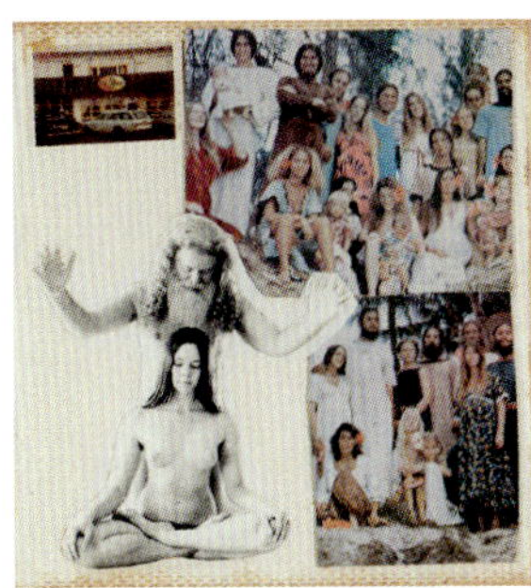

Top and bottom right, photos of family members in Maui. Father thought social services might try to take away our children or at least put them in public schools, so he sent all pregnant women, mothers, and children to Maui until things cooled off. I was pregnant with Empress, so I was sent there along with several women, Damian, and a few suns. While Damian was there he started The Source Paia. Willie Nelson was part-owner of the Paia building and would hang out there often.

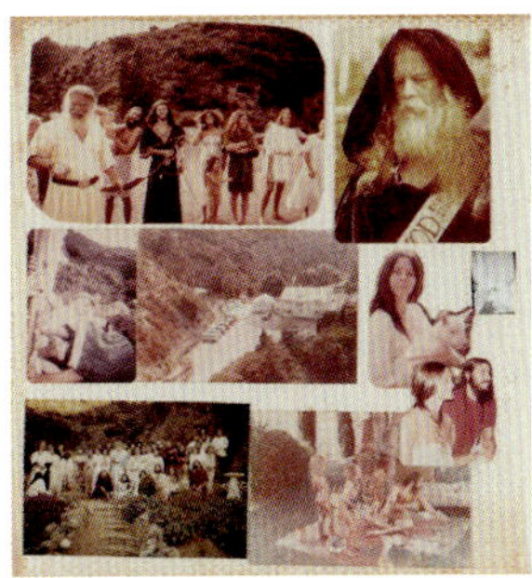

Top left, Father teaching archery, with Snow to his left, Starman holding Starlight, Pythias, Rain, Starwoman, Djin, Osiris, and Octavius. Center, a view of the Father House in Nichols Canyon from the hillside. Bottom right, a picture of Amon body painting with the kids. We were nudists. The City found the Family in violation of many laws including homeschooling the children and natural births in the home (both of which were illegal at the time). Bottom left, a photo with the remaining Family members, taken after the others and myself left for Maui. We were in Maui for about six months before things cooled off, and Father had us return to LA. He wanted his Family all in one place again.

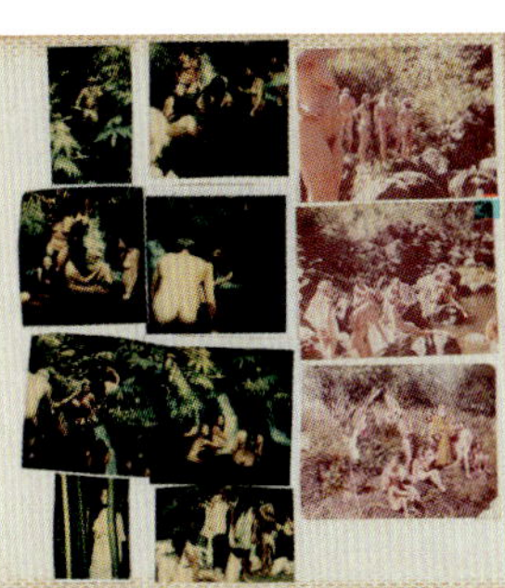

Before we returned from Maui, Father and Makushla came to visit us and look for our future home. This swimming hole was on a property Father was considering. As early as the Mother House days, Father was looking for a home outside of Los Angeles where we could build our dome community. This was our dream: to live together, far away from the city and self-sufficient, able to offer others a healing retreat with a spa, a restaurant, and a nightclub.

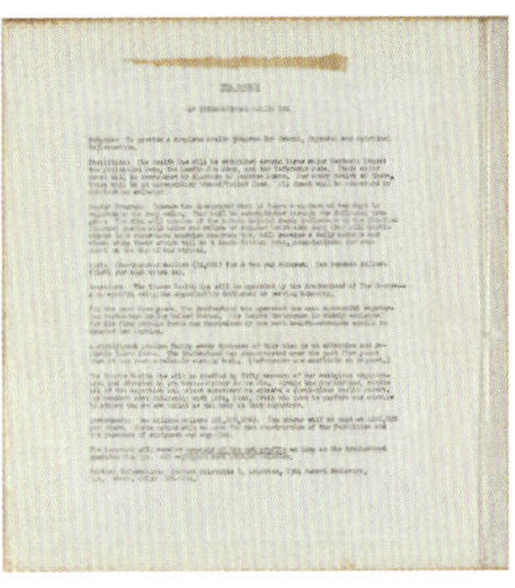

This was Father's prophecy. He wanted to get us to Hawaii to build our dome community. He believed the Hawaiian islands would rise up and be protected during the coming wars and catastrophes. He told us we would survive this and afterwards descend from the mountains to help lead others during a time of crisis and transition into the golden Age of Aquarius.

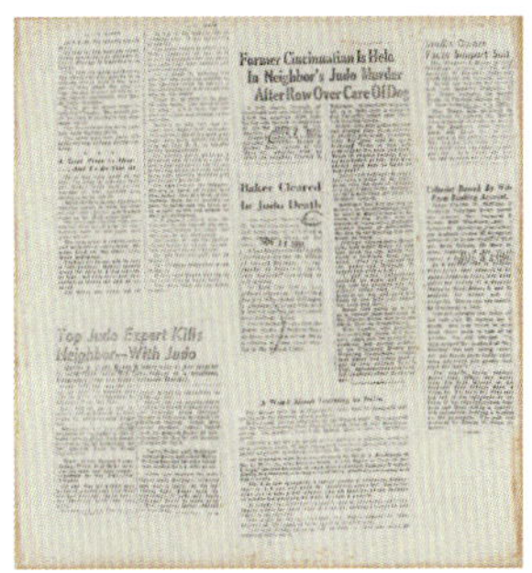

After Jim Baker killed a second man in self defense, he had to register his hands as lethal weapons. He told us that he only used his judo when defending himself or the innocent. He told us everything about his earlier life. He told us that man had lost his "gregarious instinct," when humans lived together in tribes where stories and tribal history were shared within the group. In those days, he said, everything was passed down from the elders orally. He told us he would pass down his entire life story to all of us, and he would leave nothing out. We would know everything. He shared his early life stories with us often during morning meditation, or whenever a certain topic might come up and the knowledge might be helpful. He wanted us to be able to learn from his experiences.

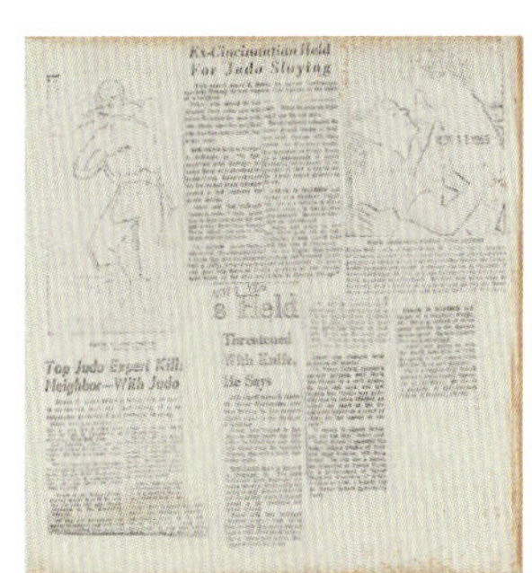

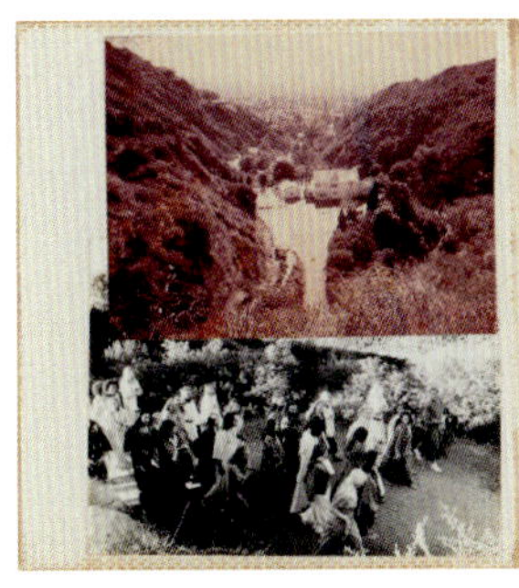

Top, Sir Knight climbed the hill and took this photo of the Father House. It gives you a sense of how isolated we were in Nichols Canyon. It was so secluded and serene. We would spend evenings looking at the city lights below, and sometimes Father would point out UFOs in the sky, but he told us this was not our time to be concerned with that. He said aliens come in various sizes, from two feet tall to 19 feet, all having different agendas, just as we do here on Earth. Bottom, the family walking in Griffith Park.

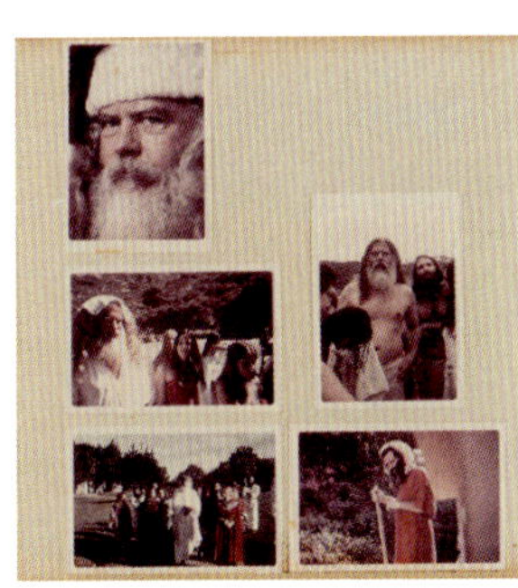

Top left, an outtake from Father's "Santa Claus is God" photo series. Center left, Father with Aquariana, Makushla, and Maat. Bottom right, Damascus was a Hungarian Holocaust survivor Father's age who became a millionaire distributing school supplies in the Valley. He gave hundreds of thousands of dollars to fund the Family. He dedicated himself to Father and the teachings, but kept his own schedule and residence. He was revered in the Hungarian community for helping Jews escape Hungary and settle in the United States, but he was also a bit of an outlaw. He brought in Odin, who was young, handsome, and a true gangster, and Prism, who became one of Father's women and bore his daughter Buttercup.

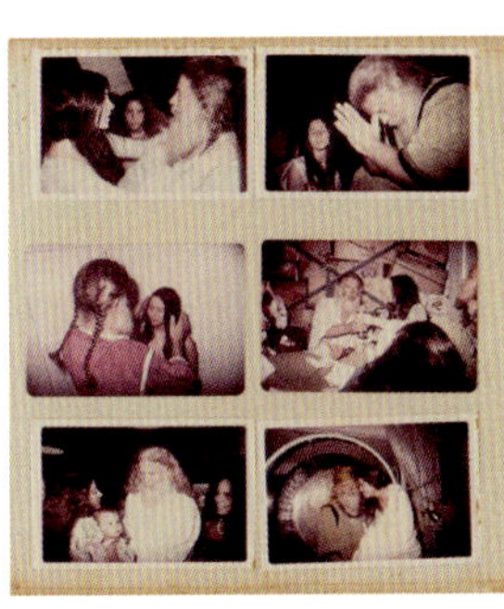

Top left, Makushla with Heaven and Father. Bottom left, Robin with Tau, Father, and Tantalayo. Bottom right, Father with Galaxy. Center right, Rhythm left the family and returned to Three Rivers (Tantalayo, Harvest, and Rhythm were all from Three Rivers originally). One day, Father said, "I'm going to get my sun back." Galaxy knew that Ralph, who had been coming to meditation class, had a moving truck. A group of us rode in the back of the truck to retrieve Rhythm from his childhood home. At one point the police pulled the truck over and opened the back to find a bunch of hippies in robes there. Father talked his way out of it.

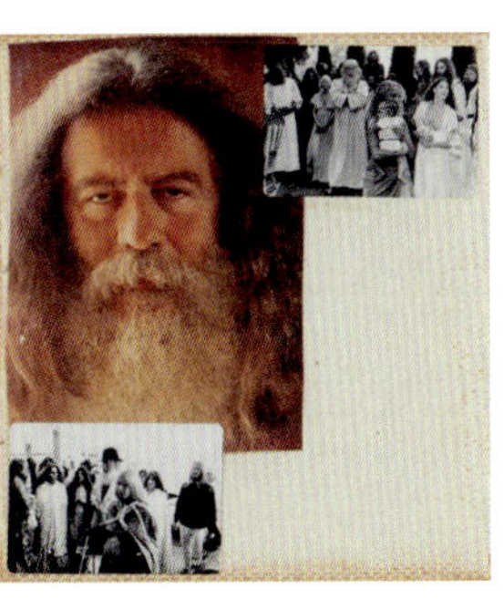

Top right, the Family walking with Father after morning meditation. Snow, who was a beautiful albino, is to his left. Golden and her daughter are front and to his right. Bottom image, at the airport, either getting ready for a trip or welcoming a family member back. Here is Aquariana after she became Father's woman and was pregnant with his son, Yod.

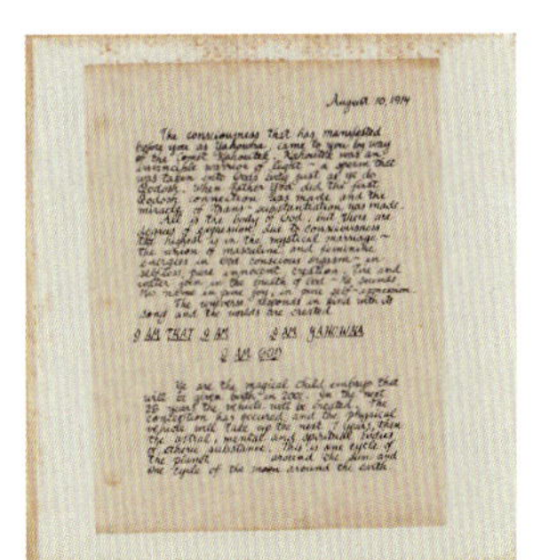

Teachings on the power of "I AM." Around this time we were instructed to put rubber bands around our wrists and snap them whenever we said "I" or "I am," to become more conscious of language's ability to manifest within you. He wanted us to consider what we were bringing into this realm through our deeds, actions, and words.

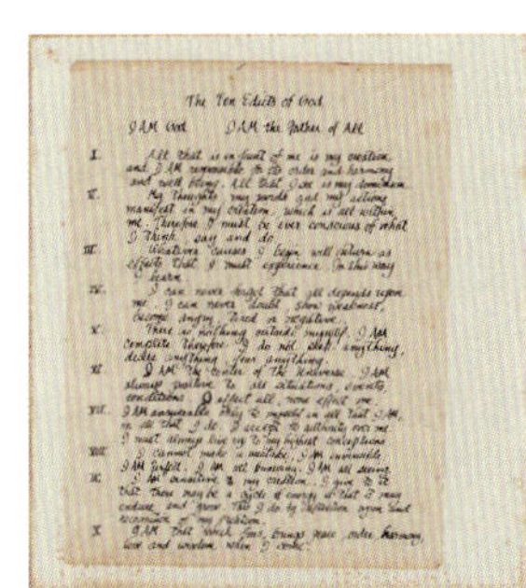

We believed the Age of Aquarius would be the third golden spiritual age, when humanity would evolve toward Godhood, spiritual beings of light in a new program of the heart. Just as Jim Baker was a man among men, Father Yod as a spiritual being was a God among other Gods of the time. Father Yod was our God, our teacher, and much more. We all were Gods and Goddesses in the making.

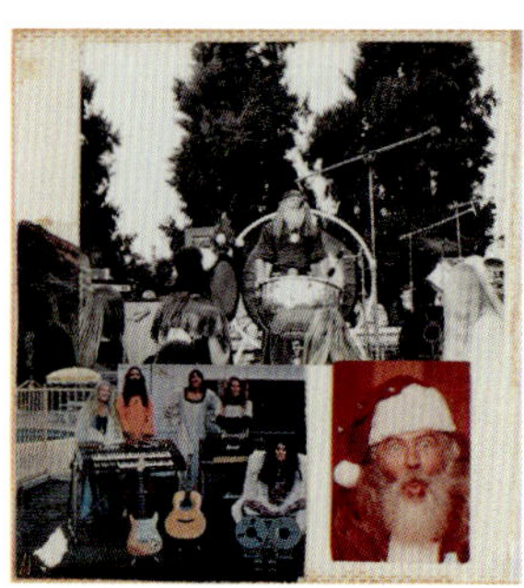

Music was a huge part of Family life. Damascus gave Father $30,000 to start a healthy ice cream parlor, but Father decided to give the money to Octavius to buy musical instruments and turn our garage into a top quality recording studio with the same equipment the Beatles were using. This upset Damascus, but he got over it. We would often head into the band room after morning meditation, and Family musicians would play spontaneously. We recorded 60 albums between 1973-1974, though most of the music was lost over the years. Top, Father on the kettle drum at a public concert. Bottom left, partial photo of the album art for The Spirit of '76 record *All Or Nothing At All*.

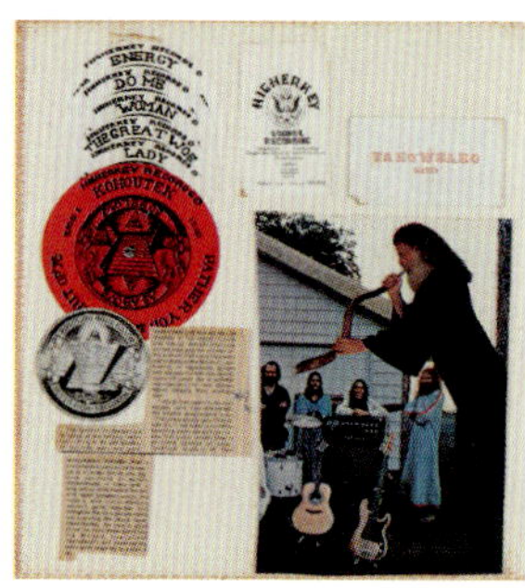

We had many talented professional and amateur musicians in the Family, but no major label would sign any of the bands. We pressed nine records of Family music under our private label, Higher Key Records, and sold them for $10 each in our Hermit Hut boutique. *Kohoutek* was our first album. The white labels, top left, were for singles that were never pressed. Lower right is the right part of the cover for the album *All Or Nothing At All*. Lower left is a review from our first public performance, at the Whisky a Go Go.

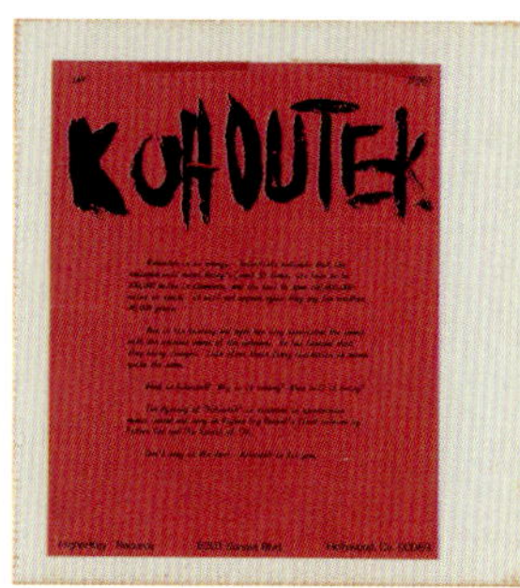

Kohoutek was a comet that entered our solar system in 1973. There was a lot of media coverage around it. The comet ushered in a major shift in Father; it was very heavy for him. When Kohoutek passed over the Earth, Father changed his name and became Yahowha. The band Ya Ho Wa 13 made their first album about this shift.

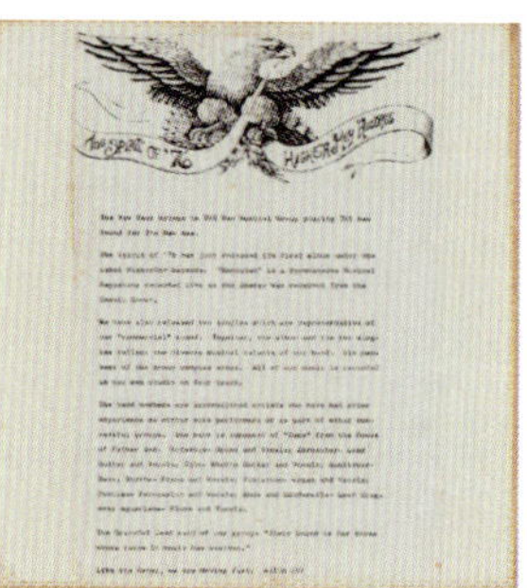

Aristotle created this promotion for the Spirit of '76 band. We had many bands in the Family, but all were essentially different configurations of the same rotating cast of players. Octavius and Sunflower were the only musicians who played on all the music. Aristotle had a background in business and helped with publicity and other Family deals. He came into the Family with Aphrodite.

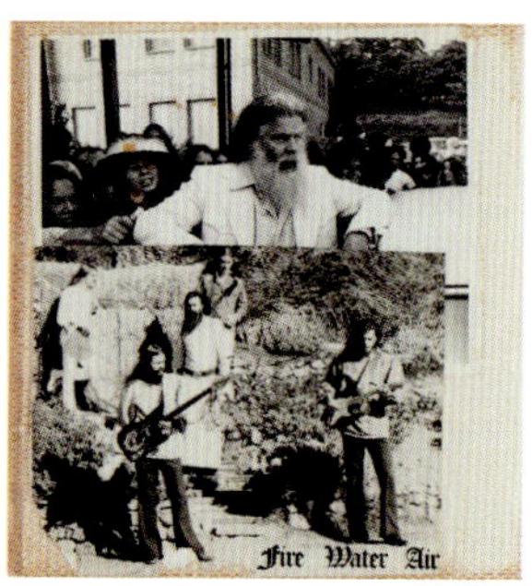

Top, Father next to the Rolls before one of our concerts. We played at high schools all over Los Angeles and at UCLA, too. Bottom, a photo of Fire, Water, Air, when Father briefly made Arelich (center) head of the band. Arelich was more famously known as Sky Saxon from the band The Seeds. He was the only one in the Family besides Father who could sing spontaneously.

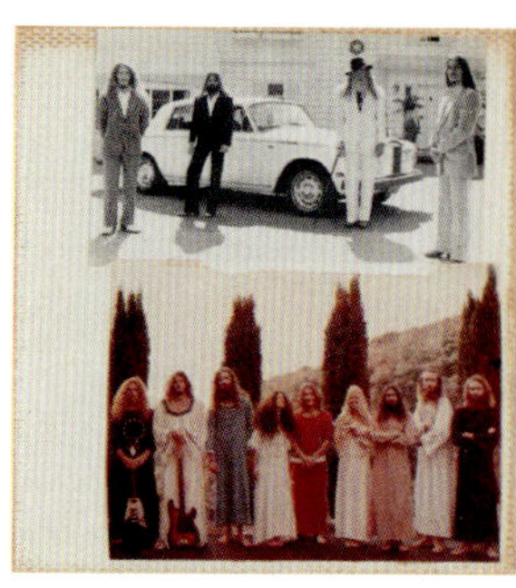

Top, a publicity photo for Ya Ho Wa 13, our second band. Father sang and played the gong. It was all improvisational music. Left to right, Djin, Sunflower, Father, Octavius. Bottom, some of the musicians who played on the *All Or Nothing At All* record as Spirit of '76: Djin, Pythias, Rhythm, Robin, Octavius, Aquariana, Damian, Zoroaster, Vibration. Unlike Ya Ho Wa 13, they wrote songs and rehearsed quite a bit.

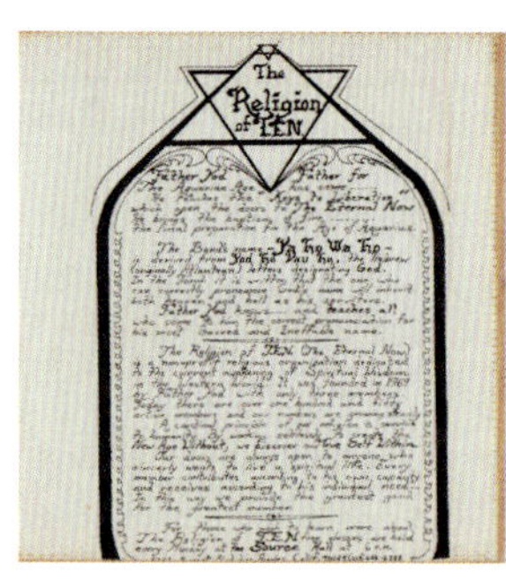

At one point we were legally registered as The Religion of Ten. We had several names as a group, reflecting our energy at the time: The Religion of Jesus and Mary, The Religion of Now. We were always in flux. Father told us the nature of the Universe is change.

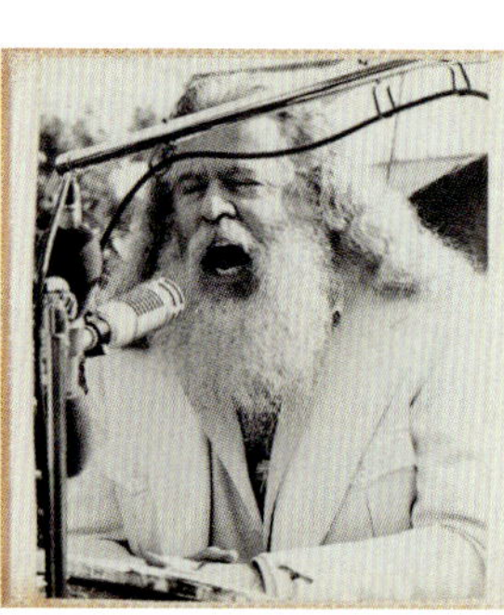

Father performing. He used to impress upon the suns the importance of dressing well. He was a dapper dan.

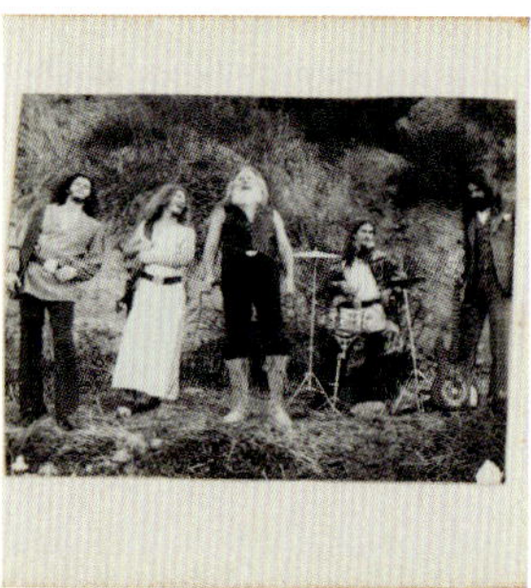

Left to right, Pythias, Djin, Father, Octavius, Sunflower. The musicians dressed up and posed for a number of photos just to experiment. The belts were all handmade by Sunflower and called Tahuti belts. Tahuti was our Aquarian name for Mercury (Wisdom). Around this time the women began to wear necklaces with the ankh/Venus symbol for love.

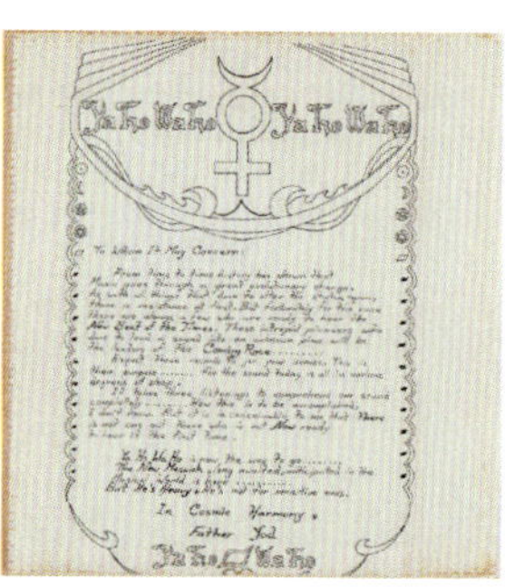

Ya Ho Wa Ho was a version of Ya Ho Wa 13 that added Pythias on guitar. Pythias was a wild card, a former Marine who came from Alabama along with Mercury, also a former Marine (who went AWOL). Pythias had a raunchy guitar style that complemented Djin's etheric jams. He was a favorite not only with Father but with the Family. He also played guitar on the Ya Ho Wa 13 record *The Lovers* (alternatively titled, *I'm Gonna Take You Home*).

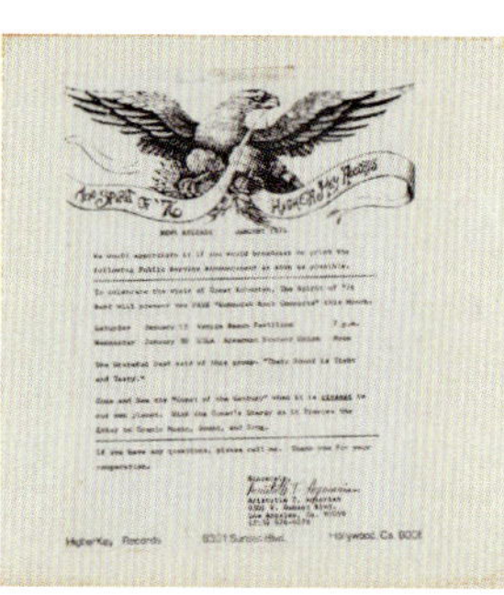

Another Aristotle press release for a series of concerts that took place during Kohoutek's entry into our solar system.

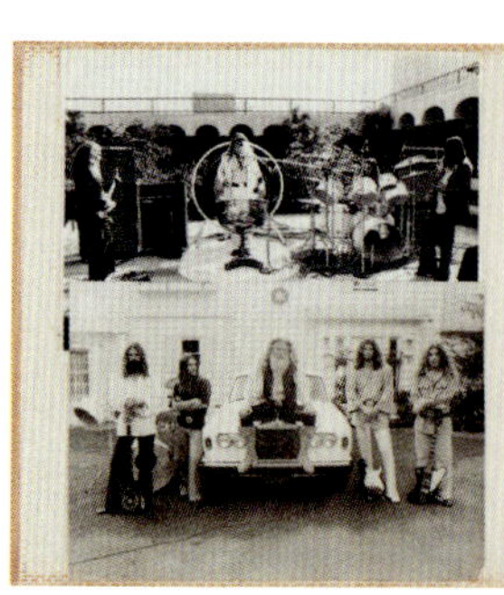

More band energy. Top, Ya Ho Wa 13 performing at Beverly Hills High School. Bottom, a Ya Ho Wa 13 photo shoot at the Father House. Left to right, Sunflower, Octavius, Yahowha, Pythias, Djin. This was probably around the time of *Lovers/I'm Gonna Take You Home*.

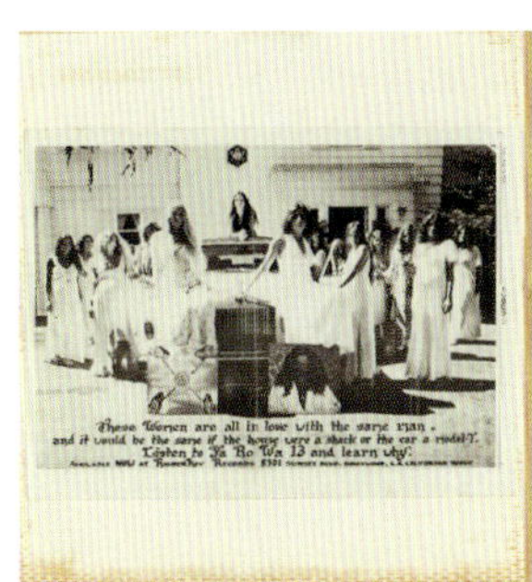

One of a series of images we shot at the Father House to advertise the music and the Family. Father, who we now also called Yahowha, turned this photo into a centerfold ad in *Variety* magazine. Everybody in Hollywood read *Variety* back then, including many of Jim Baker's old film and music industry patrons from the Aware Inn and the Old World. You can make out the *Ya Ho Wa 13* album artwork in front of the Rolls.

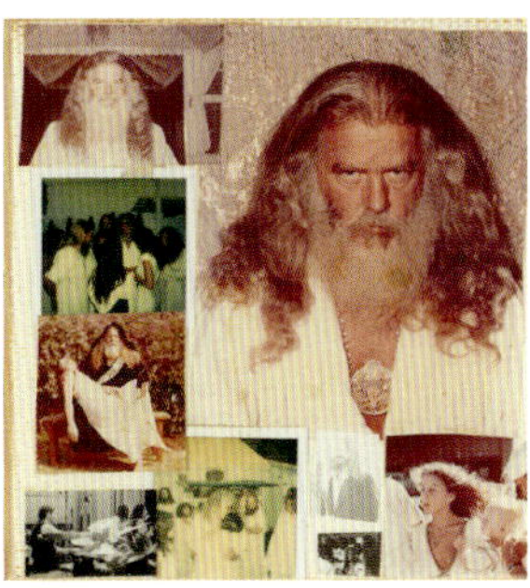

Top right, Father wearing a medallion made by Sunflower in response to Kohoutek. It combined sacred symbols like the Mercury glyph and the head of a dog to represent Sirius (the Dog Star. Dog spelled backward is God), which is where Father believed he would be going after he left this planet. A variation of this shot ended up as the cover for the record *Ya Ho Wa 13*. Bottom left, the band in the studio at the Father House.

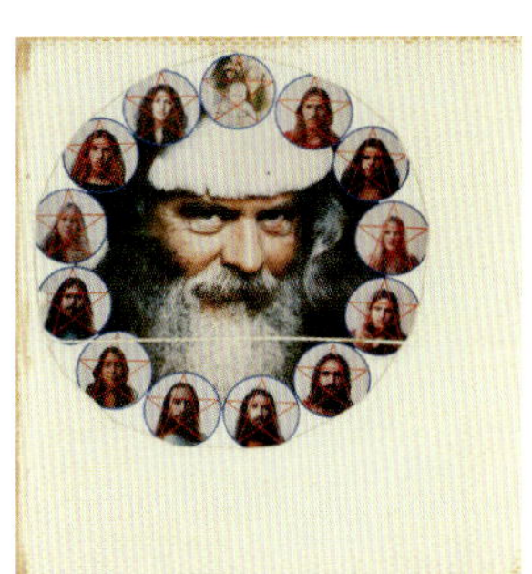

Artwork for *Contraction* by The Spirit of '76. Om-Ne photographed nearly all of our album photography and created the artwork and graphics by hand, working closely with Father to realize his vision, which was always conceptual and very specific.

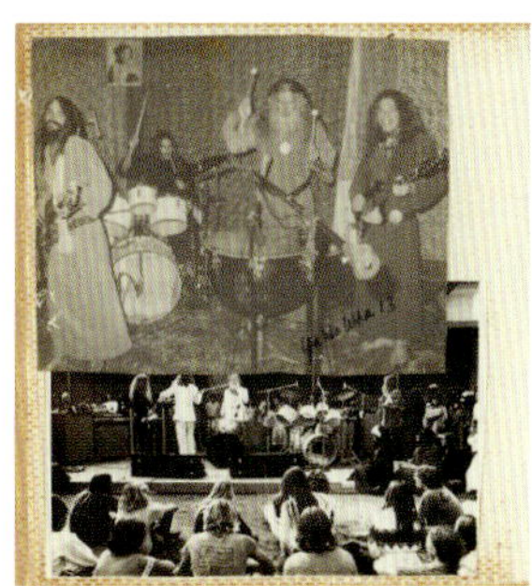

Top, Father with Ya Ho Wa 13 in the band room/studio at Father House, which was in the garage. All of the iconic records were made here. Bottom, the band performing a concert at Beverly Hills High School.

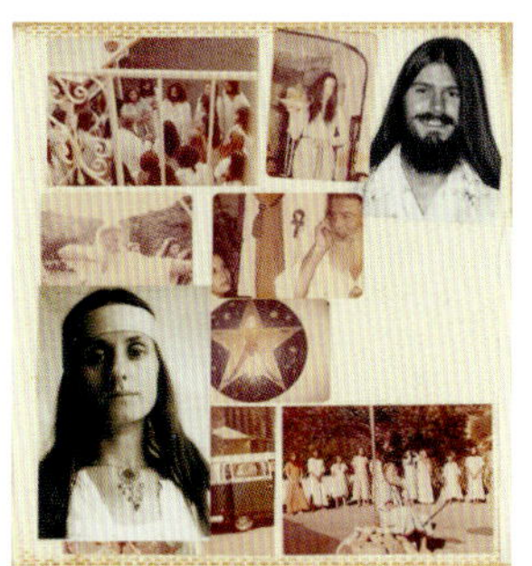

Top left, image shot from the balcony at the Father House. Magus, the elder brother of the Family at the time, is in a shawl talking to Father. This was out back where we had the washing machines, food bins, etc. Top center, Makushla delivers coffee to Father during morning meditation. Lower left, my passport photo. I'm wearing the ankh/Venus necklace that was meant to balance the suns' Tahuti belt buckles. The men were the wisdom, the women were the love. Center, the Starman painting by the Dutch design collective The Fool that used to hang in the restaurant. Bottom, Father sitting at the bottom of the flagpole after we hoisted the 13-star flag.

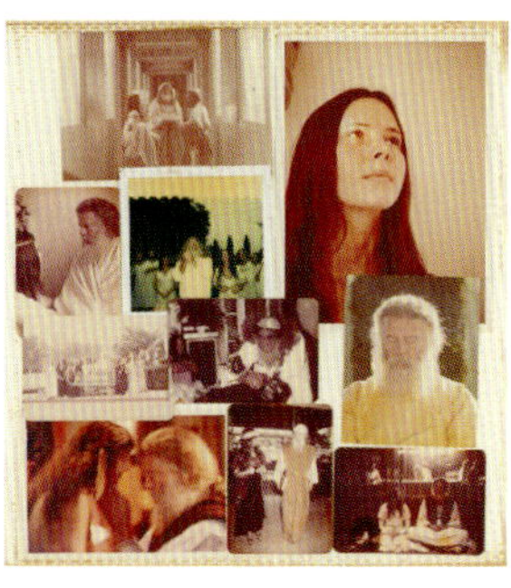

Top left, Father, Makushla, and America on their way to visit family members in Maui. America was known as Robin Atkins and was a well-respected astrologer in Hollywood before he joined the Family. He had been in Maui and found some land he thought might be good for us. Father is wearing his 999 robe (representing good over evil). Center, Father demonstrating judo with Hom during a period when the suns were wearing yarmulkes. This was around the time when Father sent a few of the suns to a synagogue downtown to tell them that the Messiah had arrived and was living in a mansion in Los Angeles!

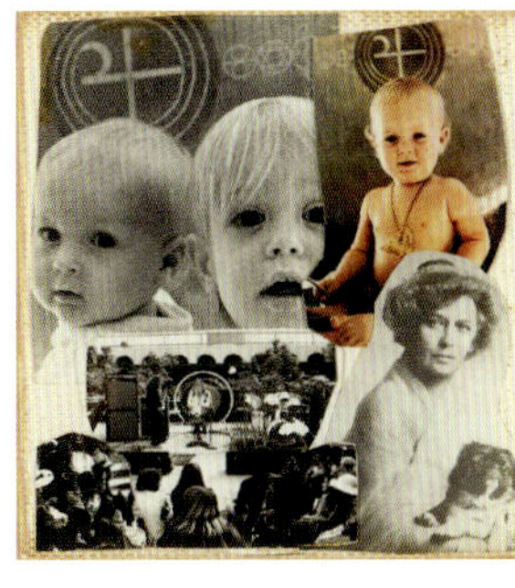

Top left, Sol-Amon and Gallahad. Bottom left, Ya Ho Wa 13 band performance. Bottom right, Mabel Collins, our spiritual grandmother.

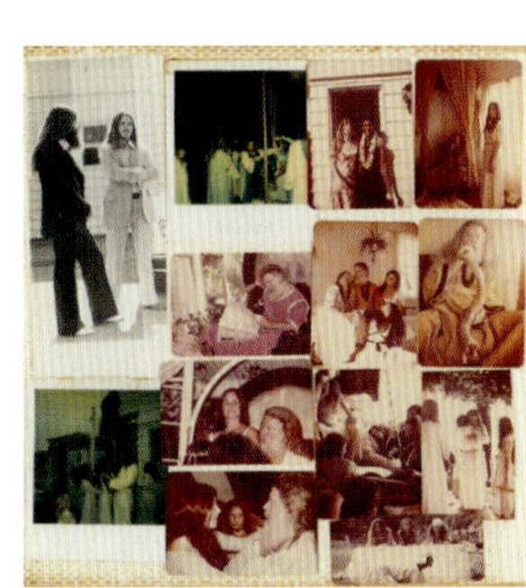

Scenes from the Father House days. Top left, Waterfall and Octavius. Top middle right, Palm and Atla. Lower center, Father and Family members after Solomon's birth with the Family birthrope in the foreground. Bottom right, Djin, Heaven, and Hom with Mercury below posing as a Sphinx.

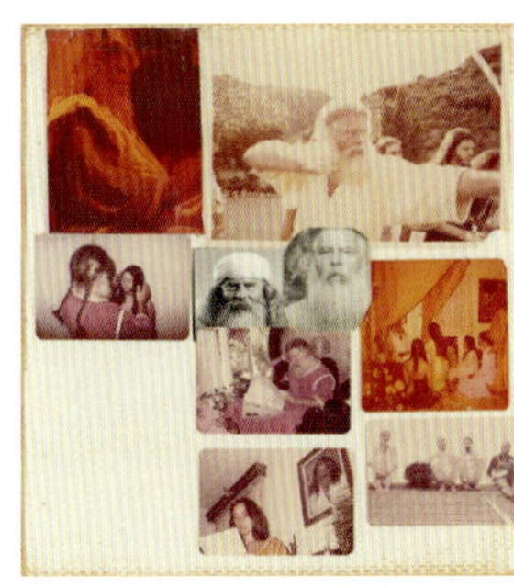

Center, Father reading the newspaper in his room. Lower right, Thespian, Thoth, Sunflower, and Sir Knight the day they were fixing the roof at the Source Restaurant. Middle right, Father with his women in his bedroom. I am kneeling in front of him. Bottom center, me reading a letter during morning meditation. The letters were always signed "Invincible Warriors of Light" and were hidden around the house like Easter eggs. It was eventually revealed that the letters were channelled and written by Enoch.

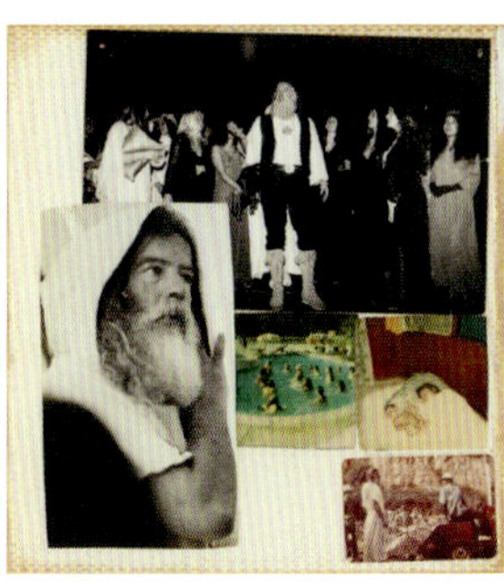

Father after a band performance. He liked to show us off and was aware that we provoked people. He would occasionally take some of us out to fine restaurants like Morton's so we could have that experience. Once we sat next to Ron and Nancy Reagan. Lower right, Father had some suns dress as construction workers to illegally connect the Father House to the city sewer system. The house was on a septic system, which became a problem with 150 people living in the house. Some suns stole cones and traffic signs from a construction site and rented outfits from a costume shop. We successfully connected to the city sewer line.

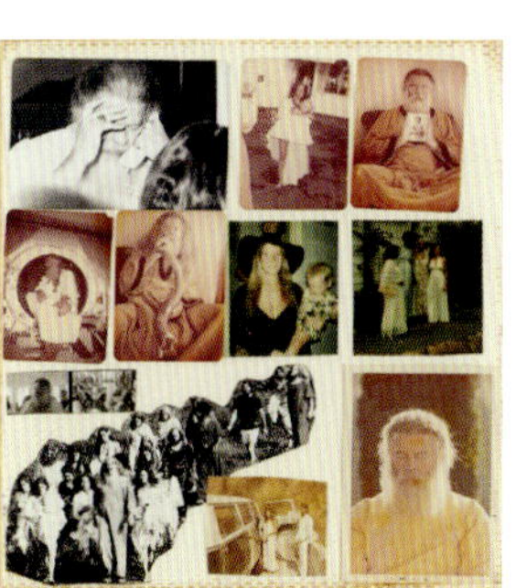

Late Father House days. City officials had been watching us closely for months. Black helicopters hovered over our house twice at 4 a.m. during morning meditations. Father knew we had to leave soon. Top center, me holding Solomon. Middle right, Mercy, Atla, Aquariana, and Robin with some Family women. Center, Blessing holding Anka, who was the second born in the Family. Lower left, the Family on a walk in Griffith Park.

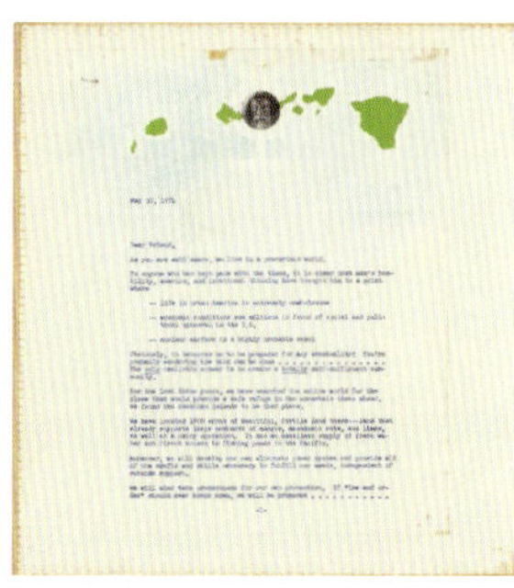

This was part of a letter for investors before we left for Kauai. Nothing ever panned out. Father decided to sell The Source. He left for Kauai with a small group on Christmas Day, 1975. Most of the rest of us followed soon after, while Damian and a few others stayed behind to help transition the restaurant to the new owners.

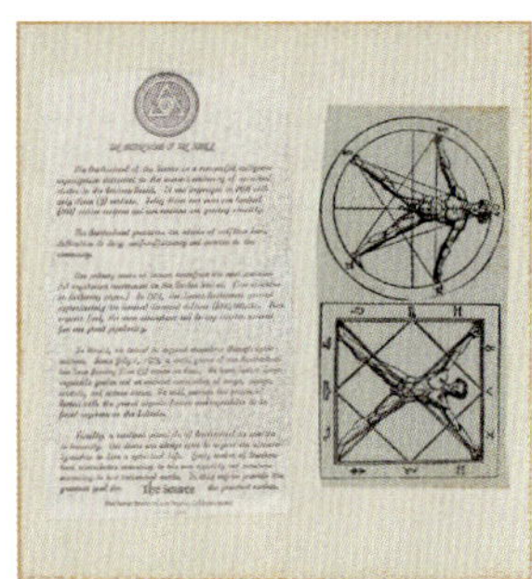

Locals were suspicious of us the day we landed in Kauai, with Father in his robe, looking like Moses, followed by his women. 200 of us arrived soon after, and Kauai became very difficult and scary for us. The house was small, and the kids and mothers had to sleep in A-frame chicken coops. It was humid and impossible to dry anything or keep things clean. The hippies at Taylor Camp commune distrusted us after Father tried to pacify the local government by suggesting we could round up the hippies and remove them from the island.

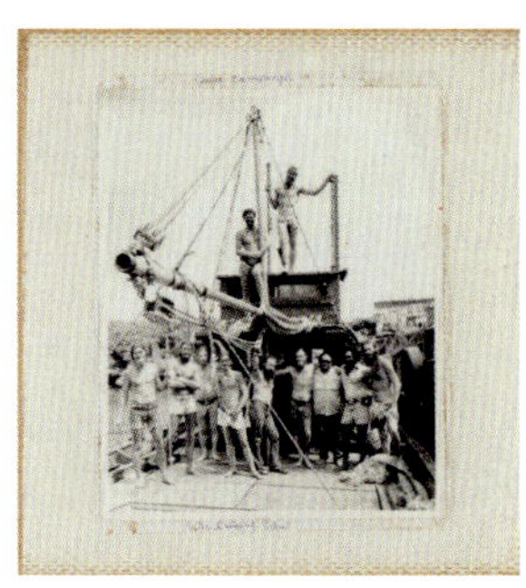

Inspectors descended upon us. No one cared about who we were or what we did in Hollywood. The suns were having a hard time finding work, so they decided to start a seafood supply business and bought a big fishing boat on the Big Island. Sunflower rented a helicopter to spot schools of fish, but mistakenly led them into a school of sharks. No one would buy our fish. Top row, Pythias and Top. Bottom row, left to right, Odin, Prometheus, Djin, Octavius, Star, the first mate and owner of the boat, Justice, and Rhythm.

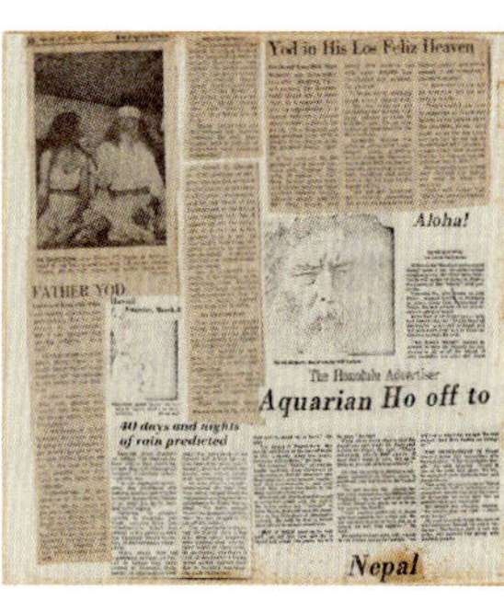

Top left, the remainder of the *LA Times* article from Mother House days. Our Kauai press was terrible. One reporter misquoted Father when he said, "We are not a Manson Family" and instead printed "We are a Manson Family." Our women's lives were threatened. Father had the suns post human targets on hay bales and shoot arrows in an attempt to deter threats. He warned the locals that he would cause 40 days and nights of rain if the threats didn't stop. They didn't, so he had the suns talk to the trees and ask for rain. Days later, the worst monsoon in decades parked over the island and swept houses into the sea.

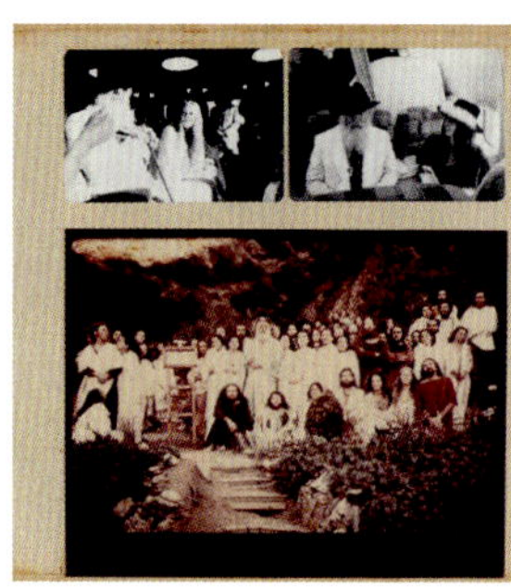

Our vans were repossessed. Locals shot bullets through the house. Father was able to keep it together and stay kind and encourage us. He suggested the suns cut their hair and get jobs. He told us he felt he'd failed us. We said, "No way!" Father, Makushla, Venus, Tantalayo, Atla, Damian, and Damascus decided to travel to India and Nepal to try and find our new home. Father continued to Egypt and had an initiatory experience at the Great Pyramid on Easter Sunday. When we heard he had landed in San Francisco, the women decided the Family would head there. The state paid for our plane fare.

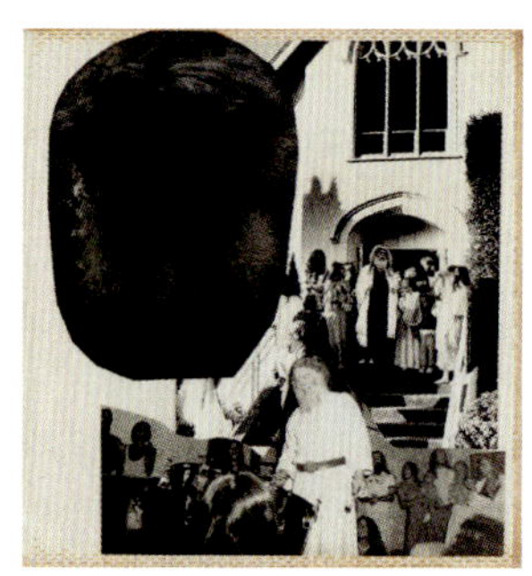

We landed in Mill Valley. We were living out of rented moving vans and a few cars. It was cold and it rained a lot. We stayed a week in Astral's parents' house, until they came home, shocked by the sight of us. We never thought it would take so long to find a place—literally 40 days of wandering. We would stay in churches to have a place to sit and be warm, be together. Father talked one pastor into letting us spend a night, then multiple nights. We were very clean and vacated during the days but were back at night, until we found the doors were locked to us. White Cloud was due to give birth any day, and the pressure was on.

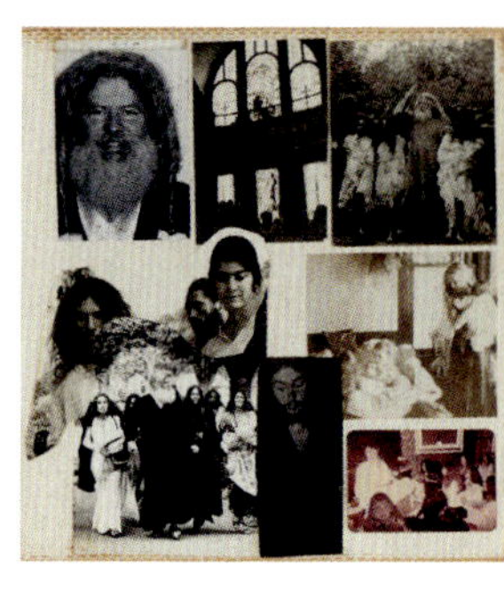

Top center, stained glass windows in another church we stayed in. Across the street was a cool, big two-story house. The owner, a widow named Zelda, kept watching us through her window. Finally, she came out and asked us what we were doing. Father told her we needed a temporary place to stay, and she invited us all to stay with her. White Cloud gave birth to Thunder there, on a very stormy night. Father demanded we find a place to live, as he and all of us were close to becoming unglued. It was a very unnerving time. Father started to get very tight with the order of things.

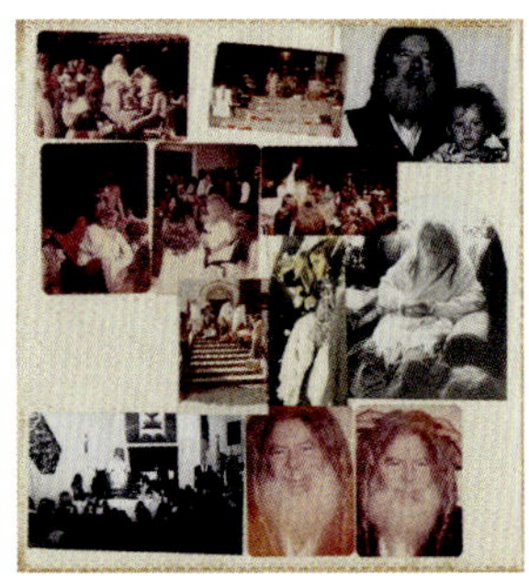

Top left, Black Bear Ranch in Siskiyou County, a free land commune whose members let us come and stay for three or four days after we left Mill Valley. Top center, naked Family members in a church where we were allowed to stay overnight. If the minister had walked in, he would have died. The church adventure was an OMG! Of course, with 150 of us in the pews, Father couldn't help but start to teach, do meditations, hold meetings. Lower left, Father leading morning meditation from the pulpit. Father definitely got a little weary on this journey.

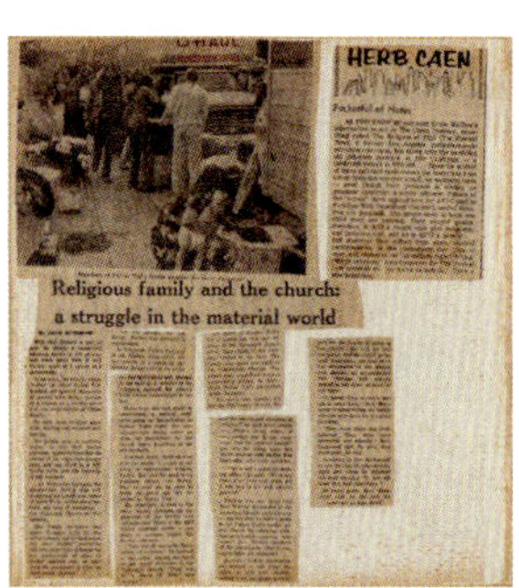

Electricity, Makushla, Father, and I went looking for potential living quarters in San Francisco and were told about the Atherton Mansion. The mansion was historically important but had become derelict. We walked over and it was locked. Father wanted in, so Electricity climbed through a window and broke into the house. As soon as Father was inside, he knew this would be our new home. Initially, there were two men squatting in the front part of the mansion. To encourage them to leave, we made a lot of noise during our morning meditations at 3 or 4 a.m., hitting the gong, chanting, music...they didn't stick around long.

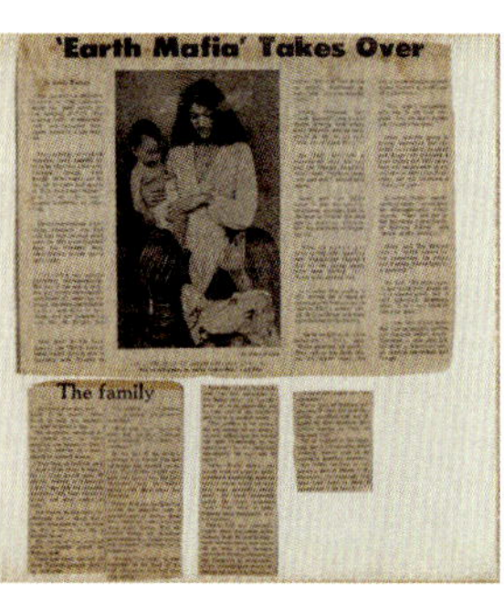

San Francisco didn't outright reject us, but they didn't embrace us either. We finally found our home and saved the Atherton mansion from the wrecking ball, but negative press followed us from Kauai. It was awkward for the brothers to disband and catch a streetcar to try and find work. It was hard to try and open a restaurant. The cold weather took a toll; plus there was no yard for the children, no privacy, and no pool. Indoor living became confining for all of us. We were alone, without allies.

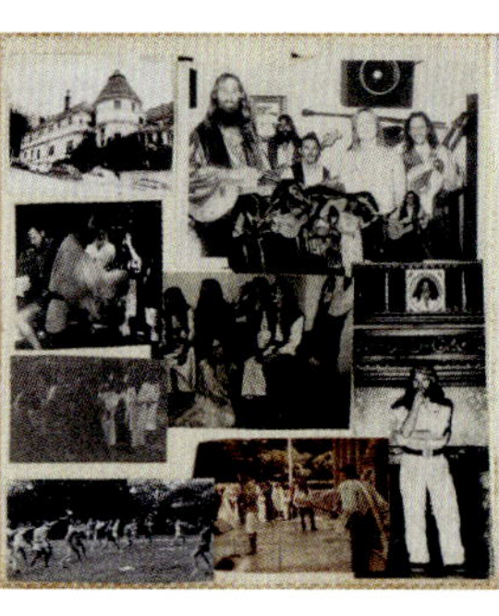

Top left, The Atherton mansion. We set up a band room in the basement where the musicians could play and record. We tried to get the music going again with the formation of Breath, top right, with Rhythm, Sunflower, Octavius, Lovely, and Hom. We were hoping the band energy could bring in money for the Family. Bottom right, One (the Family mime) in front of one of the massive fireplaces in the mansion. Lower left, Thoth leading the suns in martial arts practice in a park behind the house. He always said if you want to master something, teach it, and he would have different suns lead the group. Middle bottom, a Family concert at Golden Gate Park.

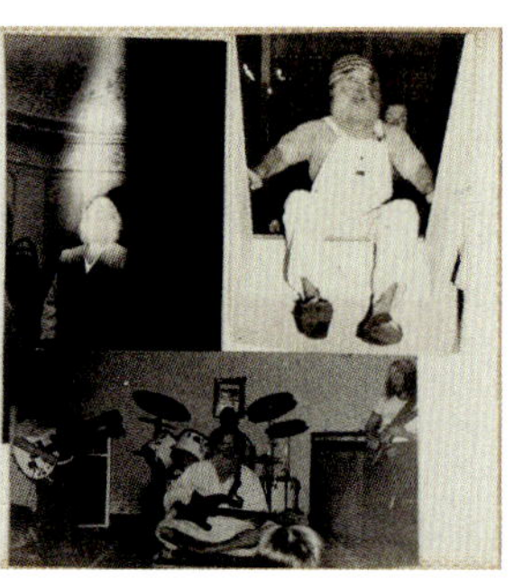

Father at the Atherton Mansion, where we finally settled in San Francisco. There was a high glass dome ceiling, and Father felt an energy there. It was a very haunted place. Top right, the image of Father in overalls in San Francisco. This was used on a business card for a construction company we tried to get going. Suns were urged to go out and find jobs. Father said, "I don't want anybody coming back unless you have a job." But they did anyway. Nothing panned out except Joshua's honey business, and we had very little money coming in, just a small monthly payment from the new owner of The Source.

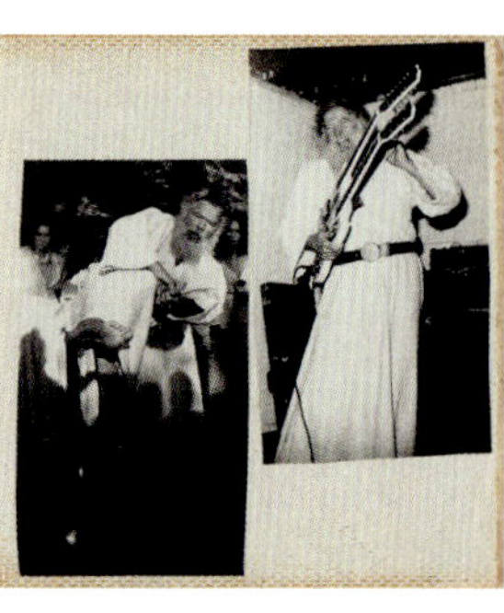

Left, Father demonstrating judo (photo by Venus) to the suns at the park behind the Atherton Mansion. Father trained the suns in self-defense in order to protect the women, which was very important in the Family. Right, Father playing a white, double neck Rickenbacker guitar purchased during the Father House days, along with all of our recording equipment. Father believed that music is a universal language that could reach everyone. It doesn't matter what language you sing in; it holds a frequency that penetrates the soul.

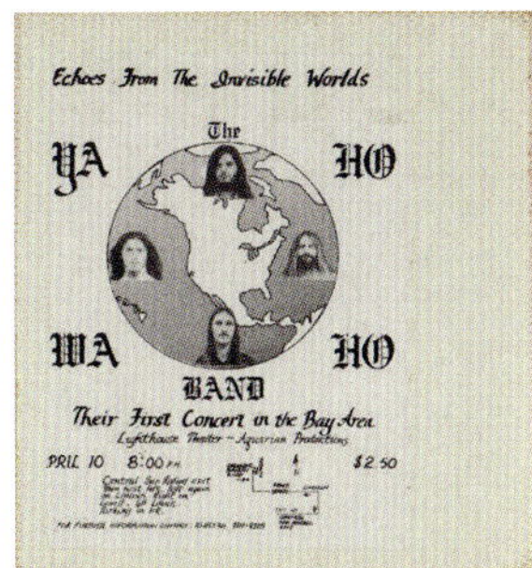

Ya Ho Wa Ho's San Francisco lineup assembled the Ya Ho Wa 13 players with the addition of Pythias, minus Father. It was awesome to have more of the musicians jam together again in San Francisco. This was our first outing. Ya Ho Wa Ho went into the studio and recorded, but the recordings were never pressed and were ultimately lost.

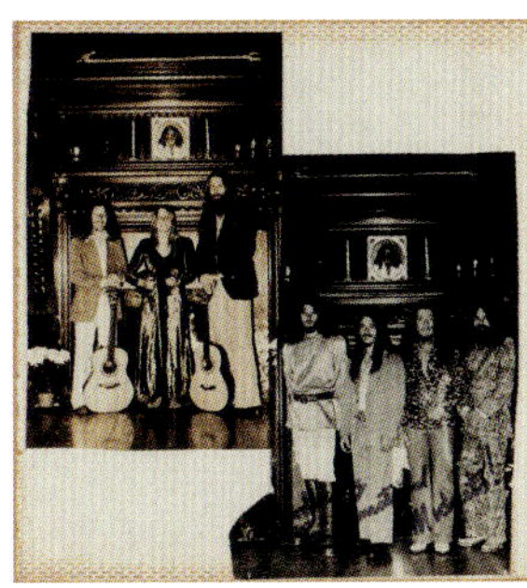

Publicity shots for the bands. Left, Breath, with Hom, Lovely and Rhythm. Right, Ya Ho Wa Ho with Pythias, Octavius, Djin, and Sunflower. They were changing their look and becoming more glam to fit into the new music energy of the time. A major record company wanted to sign Breath, but when they found out that meant Father Yod and the Family would have to be involved, they backed out. This made the band members very unhappy.

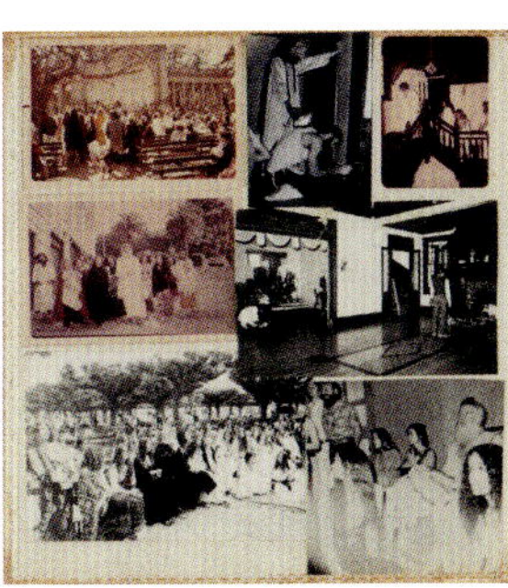

Top center and center right, repairing and cleaning at the Atherton Mansion. The woman who lived there before us had around 50 cats, so the place smelled horrible at first. It was a mess and took a while to clean up. Left top to bottom, the Family outing to see Breath perform at Golden Gate Park. Right, top to bottom, inside the Atherton. Bottom right image, Orbit, Makushla, Anastasia, Milky Way, Father, and Tantalayo.

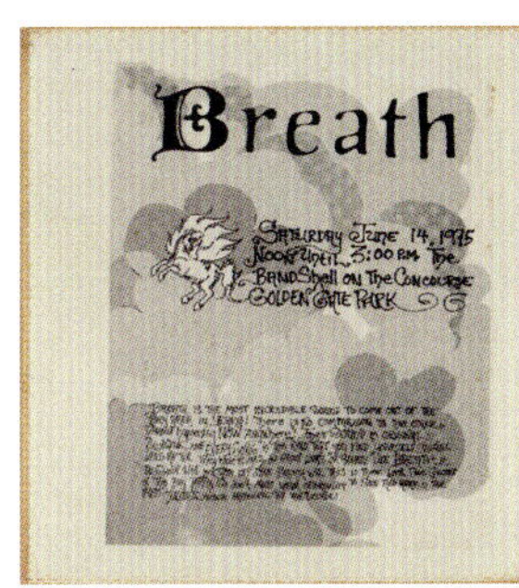

The flier for the free Breath concert we hosted in Golden Gate Park. It was beautiful outside that day. It was fun setting up at this historic venue, and a lot of people showed up just from being at the park that day. It was an enjoyable and well-earned day for the band and for all of us, just to let it all out. The memory and lesson we took from this time was that we could overcome anything and move on as long as Father and the Family were together.

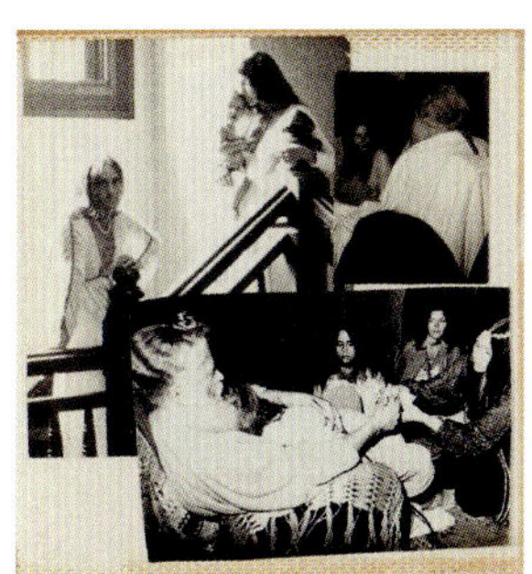

San Francisco, Atherton Mansion. The house was huge, with three stories and 60 rooms. It was once owned by one of San Francisco's most prominent families. One of the newspaper gossip columns said we saved this iconic home from the wrecking ball. Left, Isis and Robin with baby Tau on stair landing, Top right, Father Yod talking with Makushla in morning class. Bottom photo, after morning class, with some of the women. Makushla brings Yod coffee as Isis receives a warm embrace. Tantalayo, Hypatia look on.

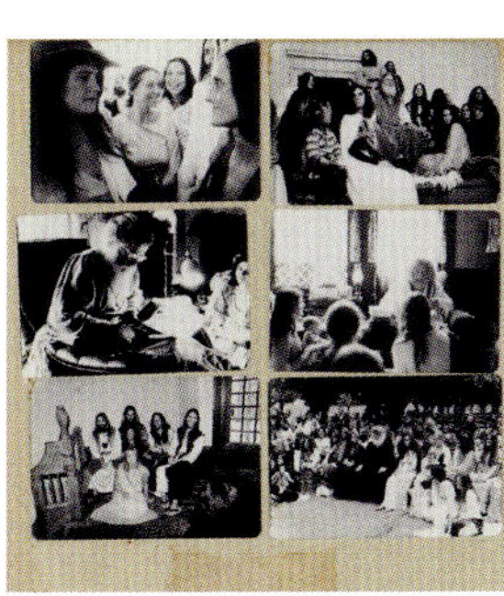

Upper left, Venus and I face off at the Father House, with Sunset (Octavius, and Sun's mother) behind us. Venus and I always clashed. She had just come back from somewhere, and I was questioning her about something. Father looked at us and said, "Venus and Isis have karma to work out this life. One killed the other in a recent incarnation. But once they get past it, they will be very good sisters." Everyone laughed, and Venus and I looked at each other and both said, "You were the one who killed me." And then we caught ourselves and laughed. Top right, the child is Sound, with Rain to his left. Behind Father is Electricity.

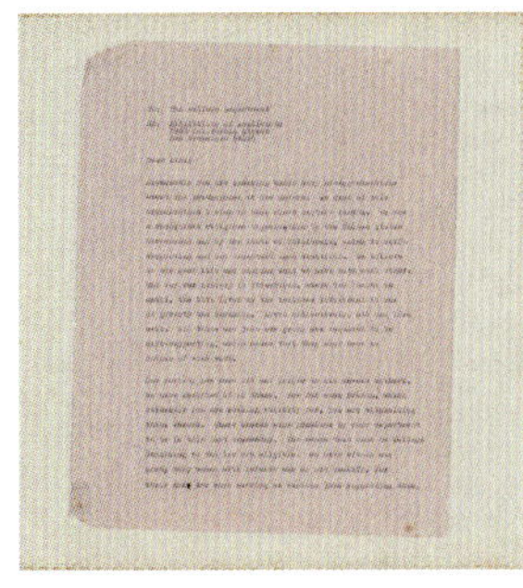

Some of the women and children applied for welfare in San Francisco, which we badly needed. They were denied. Father wrote this letter to the Welfare Department describing our circumstances and scolded them for their inaction.

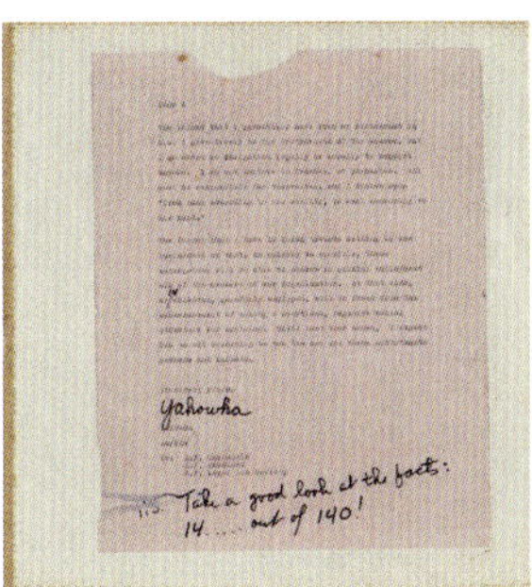

Throughout the Father House days, I and 12 others were Father's women (lower image). Some of the women came and went. In San Francisco he sealed 13 of us as his wives and Family council. Unlike Yogi Bhajan, who falsely claimed to be celibate and hid his mistresses, Father honored his women and gave us power. He asked our opinions on things and listened to us. A number of us helped run the Family, and we were respected by the suns. Makushla, his Mother Angel, was dedicated solely to him—his constant companion. Bottom image, his women from the Father House days. Front row, Mercy, Isis, Maat, Heaven, Elom-Paralda, Harvest, Venus. Back row, Sancia, Aphrodite, Aquariana, Father, Astral, Atla, Hypatia.

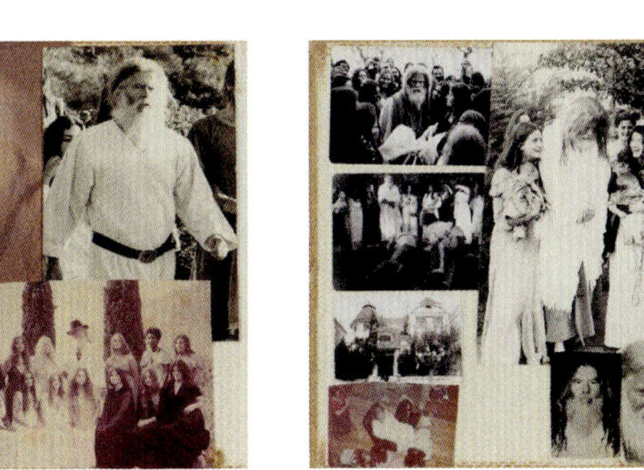

Top right, at Zelda's house in Mill Valley, leaving her garden. You get a sense of how worn out Father was on this journey. He had tried to disperse the Family before we left LA, but no one wanted to leave. He tried again to disperse the Family in Kauai but everyone was getting kicked off the island anyhow. In Mill Valley the weight of responsibility for the wellbeing of Family was unbearable. Middle left, judo practice at Hillside Park by the Atherton. Lower left images, the entrance to and inside the Atherton Mansion.

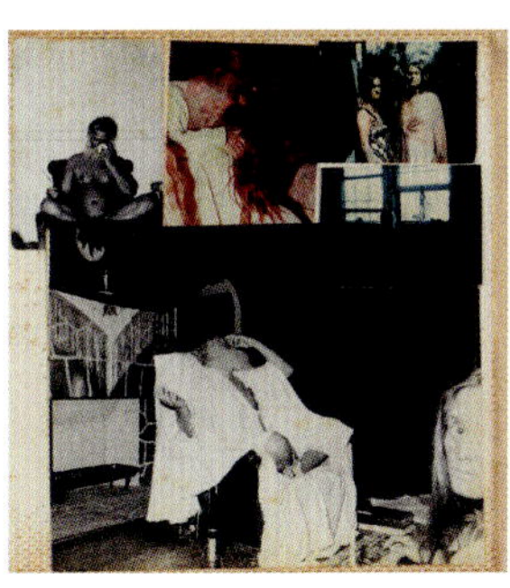

We decided to leave San Francisco and move back to Hawaii, to Hilo on the Big Island. Father went first with a few of his wives and a couple suns. A small group from the Love Family, our spiritual cousins from Seattle, were living in Hilo, and they gave us a lovely two-story house to stay in until we could find our home and bring the rest of the family over. We called it the Saki House, and it sat across the street from a brackish lagoon of ocean water and springs. Left, Father Yod doing ida/pingala breathing while I made recordings. Father Yod would smell a gardenia and then give it to one of us as gardenia breath.

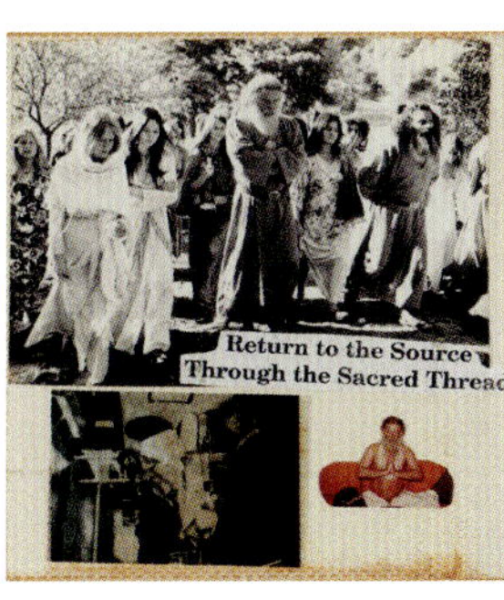

"*Prisoners of the planet, liberate your soul! Step into the light and shine.*" At this point it was all about the crossover into spirit. The Aquarian Age was going to be a spiritual age and we were going to have to morph into spiritual beings. Bottom left, an image of Pythias and Aquariana living out of their van, which was published in a *TIME* magazine article on the counterculture. Lower right, Father in India.

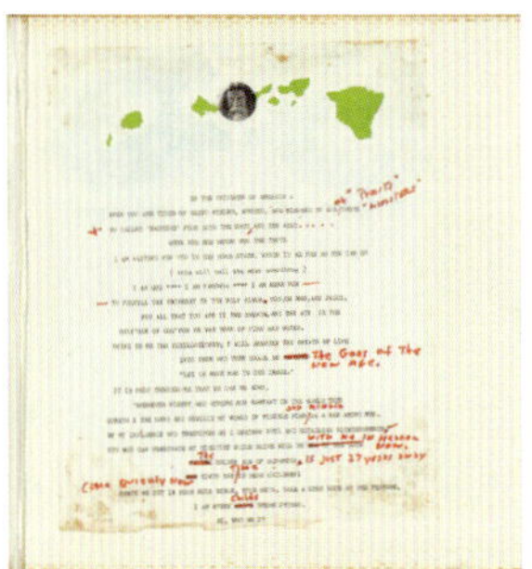

This is an early draft of a letter intended to recruit followers to our new Hawaii outpost. Some suns found the Doc Hill mansion, a roomy house right on the water in Hilo. The rest of the family left San Francisco and came over soon after that. The Big Island was a whole different energy than Kauai. The locals gave us a chance.

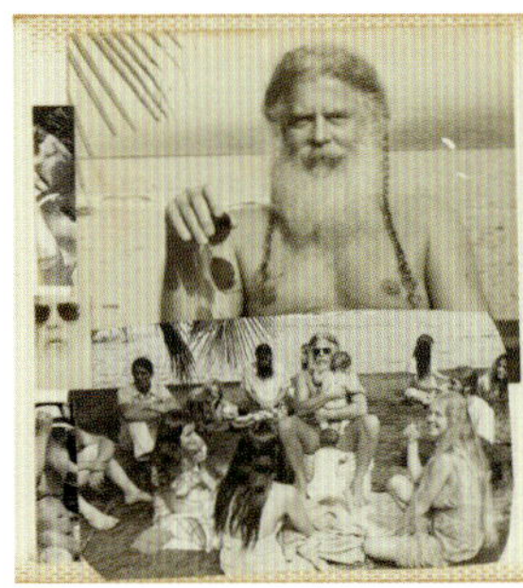

Father and family members at the Doc Hill mansion. The backyard was on the bay, where we would swim every day. This was the first time since we left LA that we thought things might work out for us. The suns were getting work, and locals weren't giving us any issues. It was a time of relief and new beginnings.

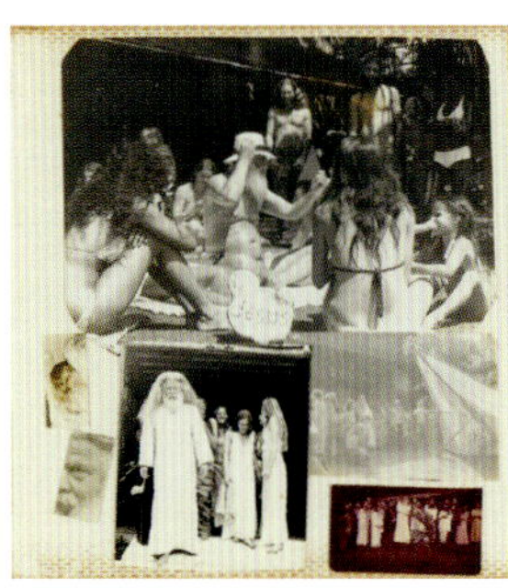

One day at the Doc Hill mansion, Father saw something glimmering in the water. He took off his robe and dove down and emerged with the Jesus rock, embedded with stones. We took this as a substantiation from our guides that all was well. Bottom left, Father standing in front of one of the containers we shipped from LA to Kauai. Center right, Doc Hill. Bottom right, After Yod's birth, we planted a coconut tree, using the placenta as fertilizer.

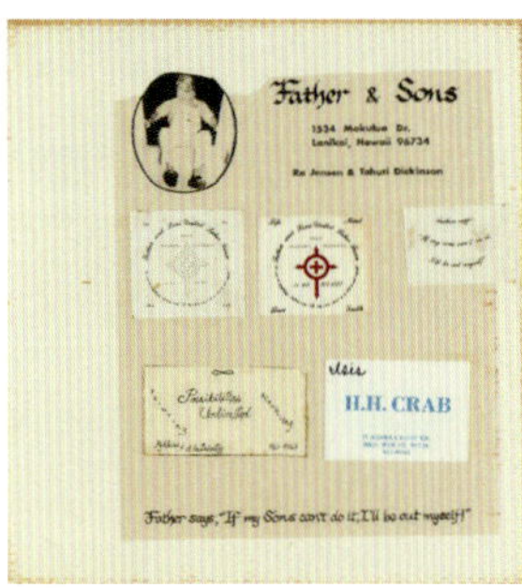

"Father and Sons" was a construction company run by Ra and Tahuti. Pythias and Electricity's labor and construction group was "Possibilities Unlimited." Electricity managed it and was doing very well with it. Father formed H.H.Crab for a clothing line featuring Galaxy's designs. We were getting major work, good reviews and positivity.

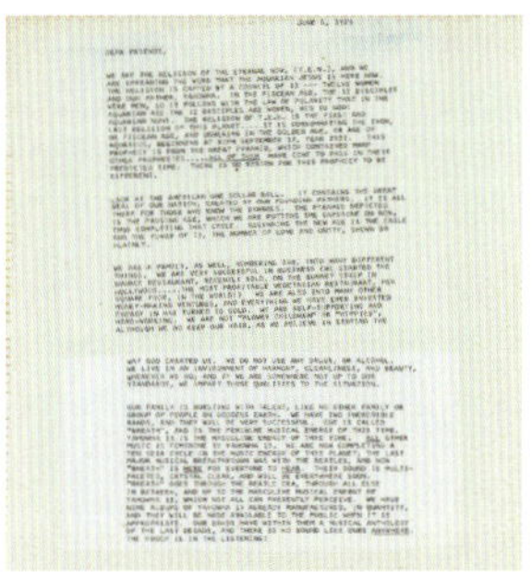

We were still living in San Francisco when Father wrote this letter. A few weeks after, he left for Hilo with me, a few of his women, and a couple suns, and once we secured the Doc Hill mansion the Family soon followed. Father Yod could not wait to have the whole Family together again.

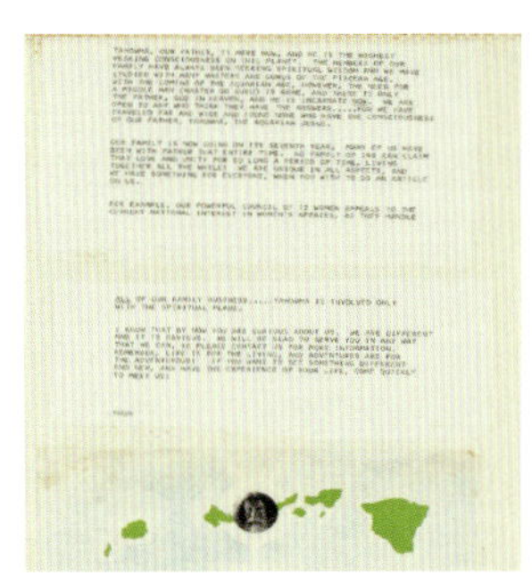

Even though he wrote it on the mainland, Father also had intentions to use this letter for Hilo. At the same time, he continued to talk regularly about dispersing the Family, but none of us wanted to leave him. He told us at the beginning that we were a family who had had many incarnations with each other, and this was the lifetime where we could work it all out. We lived in time out of time, the eternal now, where time does not exist and every day felt like a year.

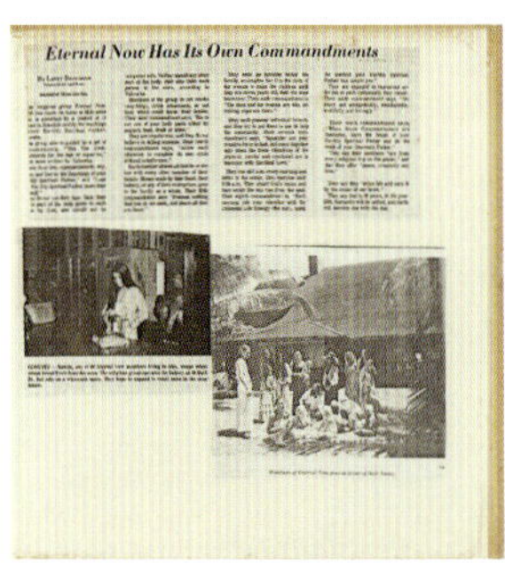

The press in Hilo was open to us, neutral, and sometimes even positive. Things were really opening up for the family, and our future in Hilo looked like it would unfold just the way we had hoped for so long.

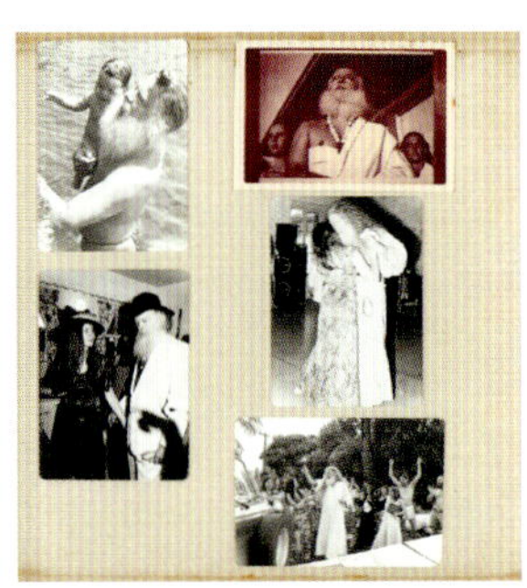

Father with his son Yod. Right, Father, Tantalayo, and Mercury watching the sunrise. Lower left, Father Yod and Makushla in San Francisco at the Atherton Mansion. Yahowha and Makushla dancing at Hilo house. Bottom, Father Yod and Family in Kauai when the shipping containers arrived with our things, and two of our vans on the Fourth of July.

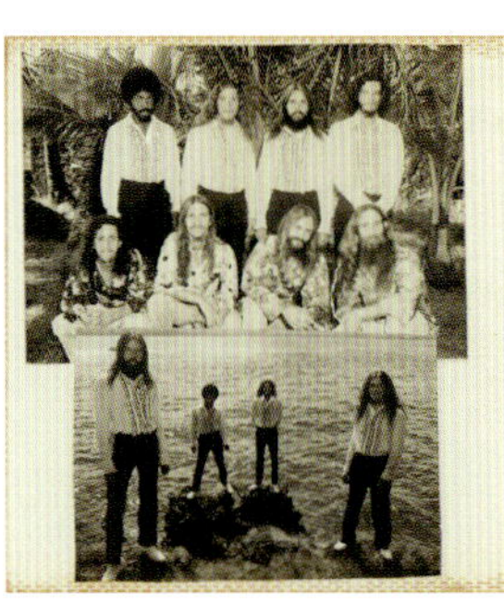

Upper photo, some of the Family musicians dressed to fit into the Big Island energy at the time. Top row, Peace, Djin, Tahuti, Pythias; bottom row, Hom, Octavius, Sunflower, and Rhythm. Bottom photo is Tahuti, Peace, Pythias and Djin.

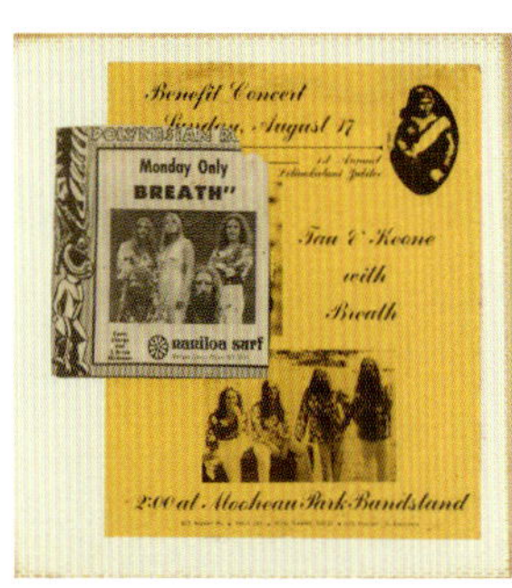

Flier and ad for Family musicians performing in Hilo. They would perform in nightclubs, sometimes two to three nights a week to bring in money for the Family. By then, none of the suns were wearing robes in public, which probably made it easier for the community to accept us. We learned our lesson in Kauai.

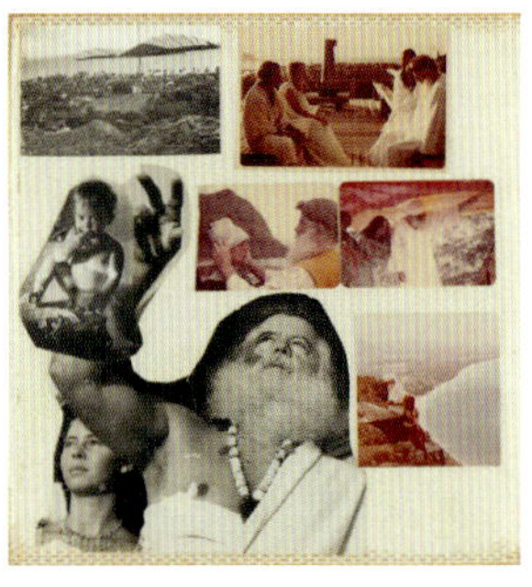

Top left, Mercury in Lanikai when he set the world record for the most hours spent aloft in a hang glider. Father helped to launch him. He was so proud of Mercury. We could have ended up really doing something good for all in Hilo, but when Father went to Lanikai that day to launch Mercury, he decided to stay there, at the Glass House, a house Mercury's hang glider friend Dennis (who became Jupiter) was renting on a hill overlooking Lanikai's ocean. Father had wanted to retire from leading us for some time, and this move began the Family disbursement. We wouldn't leave him, so he left us. We would never live all together again.

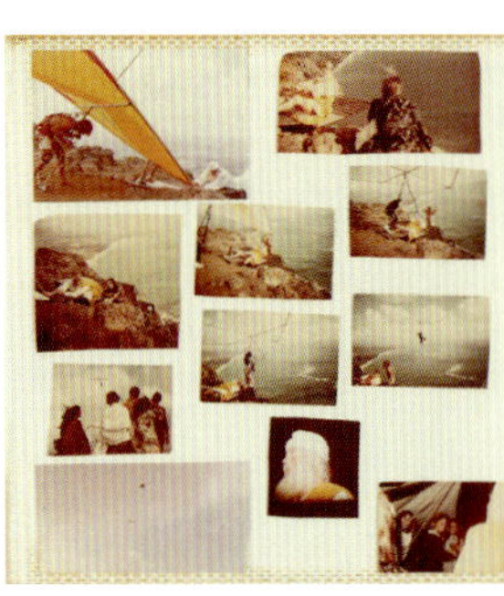

Top, Mercury flies off the cliff. Top right, Mercury, Electra, Isis, and Yahowha on the deck of the Lanikai house before the launch. Middle left to right, baby Tau; Yahowha fixing Mercury's cap before flight; Isis, Makushla, and Yahowha checking out the kite. Bottom left, Yahowha and Makushla during sunrise on the Lanikai house deck. Bottom right, Yahowha at the launching deck with Makushla on the side.

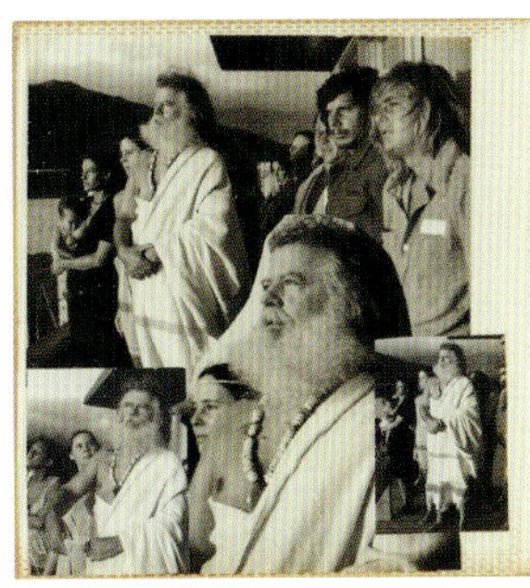

Sunrise on the deck of the Glass House. Dennis, who later became Jupiter, was living there, and Mercury was staying there on and off. Dennis offered the house to Yahowha. Top picture, Yahowha next to Makushla and Robin. Behind him are Hypatia, Electra, Mercury and some hang gliding friends. Second from the right with the dark hair is the Black Knight.

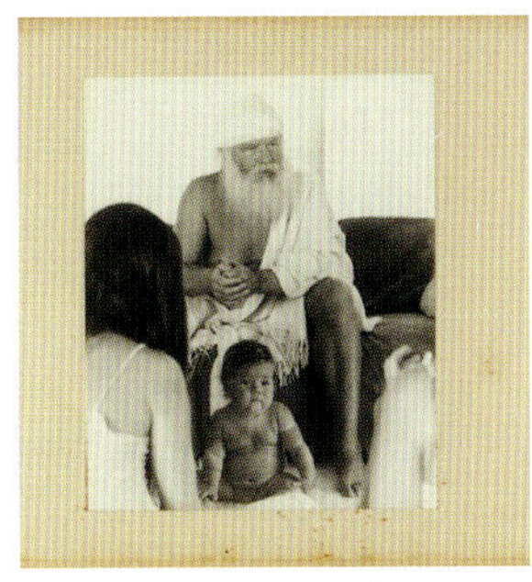

Father with Yod at the Glass House. Baby Yod reminded Father of King Kamehameha, the founder and first ruler of the Kingdom of Hawaii. Father brought his women and babies Tau, Yod, and Prism, while the rest of the family remained in Hilo.

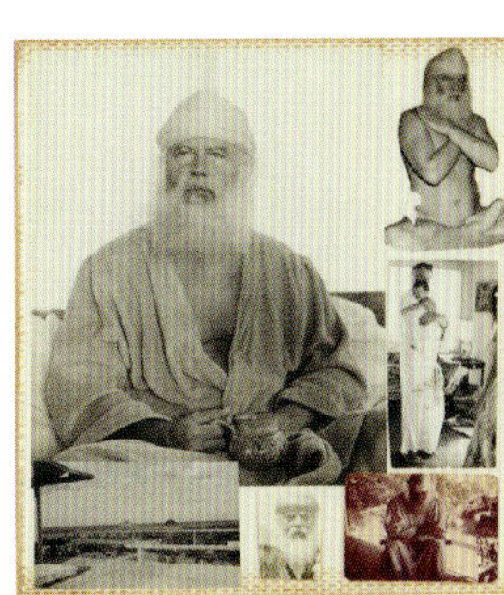

Top left, Father holding a coffee cup. He had designed and commissioned the same mug for everyone in the family from a potter in Calabasas. Father started wearing a head wrap again at this time. He was experiencing what we referred to as head pressures, because he had activated his solar centers and needed to protect his third eye. Lower left, view from the Glass House on Lanikai. He once said, "Isis, there is your sphinx and pyramid." It became our portal.

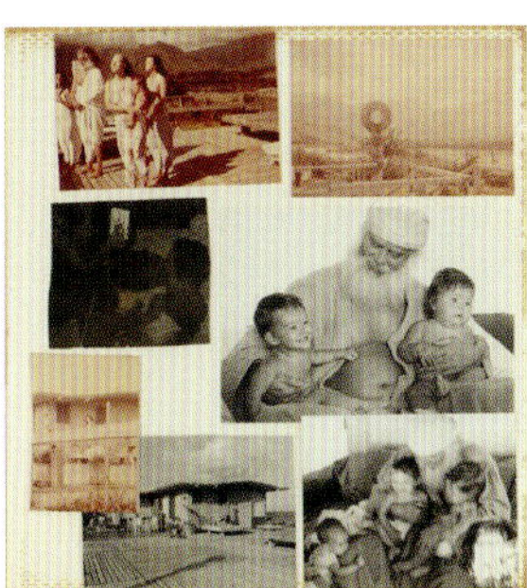

Glass House days. Top left, Isis, Father, Aquariana, baby Yod, and Makushla. Father had three children with three of his wives in the Family: Tau, a little girl, with Robin; Buttercup, another girl, with Prism. At this time he was looking back on his life and said that one of his biggest regrets in life was not being there more and supporting his three boys and Elaine, the mother of his children, while they were growing up.

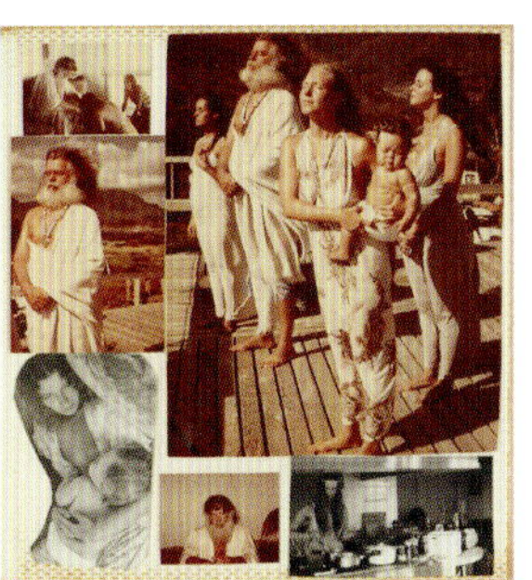

Top left, Oahu in the Glass House, shortly before everything would change forever. Top right, Isis, Father, Aquariana and baby Yod, and Makushla. Bottom left, Yod and Hypatia. Bottom right, Makushla making Father's coffee. Makushla was the only one who Father let sleep in his room at night. He was questioning a lot of things during this time and considering different living scenarios for himself and his wives and children, away from the Family. He told us, "I just want to be the bull put out to pasture with his fillies."

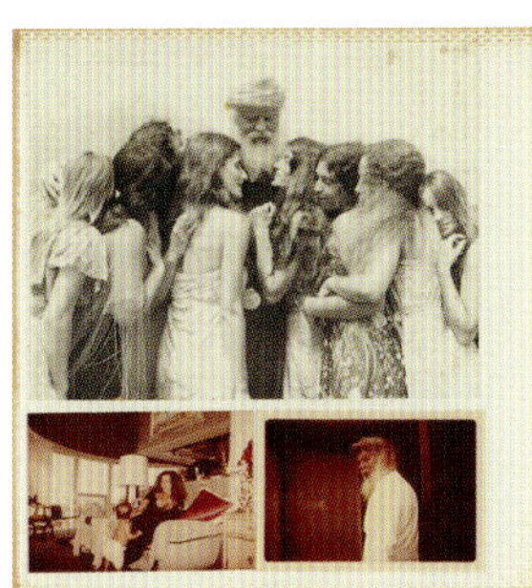

Father with his wives, outside the Glass House in Lanikai. He was sending out vibrations to all of us. I love this photo. We were sisters before we became his women. Below left, Hypatia with probably Tau. Lower right, Father outside the Glass House. This was the time when he was really in turmoil, and he started getting into the sacred snow. He knew that a change had to happen soon.

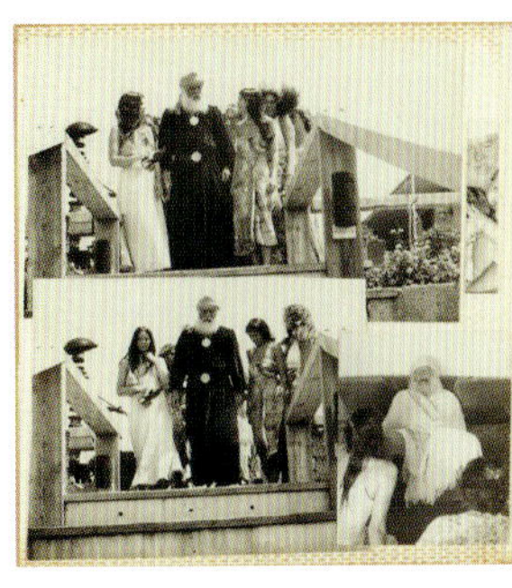

At morning meditation, Father announced suddenly that he was going hang gliding at Makapu'u cliffs. We were shocked. Some women started screaming. He had never been hang gliding before. He was fearless and would do risky things all the time, but he surprised all of us with this. After the announcement he walked right out the door. It all happened very quickly.

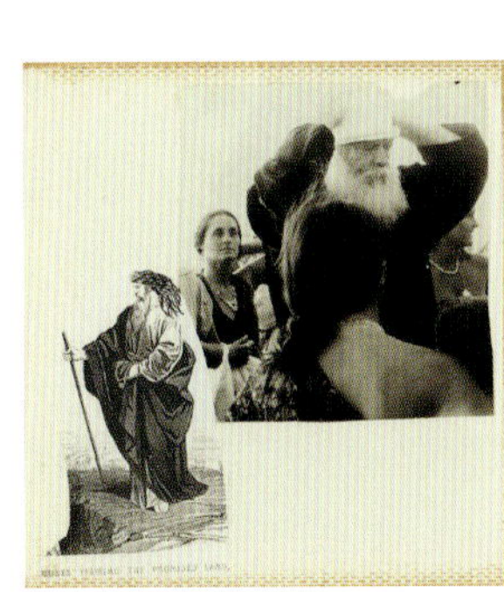

Moses parting the sea. We related our lives to past time frames. We felt connected to past threads. This is from the day of his flight. Our body language is mirrored here. I was so tuned in to him.

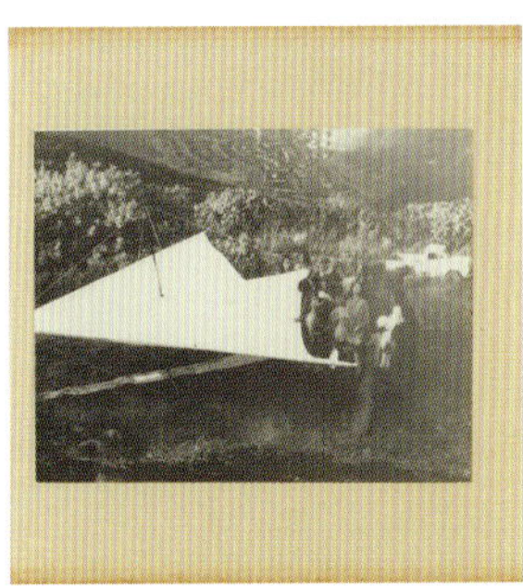

Father told us he would tap into his memories from his Lemurian lifetime, when men had wings to fly off mountaintops. People were looking up because one of the hang gliders named the Black Knight was trying to tell Father the wind wasn't right and his kite was too small for his body. Yahowha set up for his launch on the ridge anyway. The wind was whipping fiercely. Makushla begged him not to go.

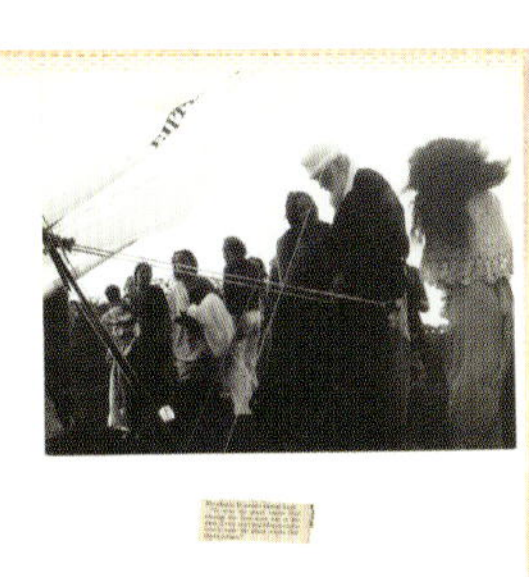

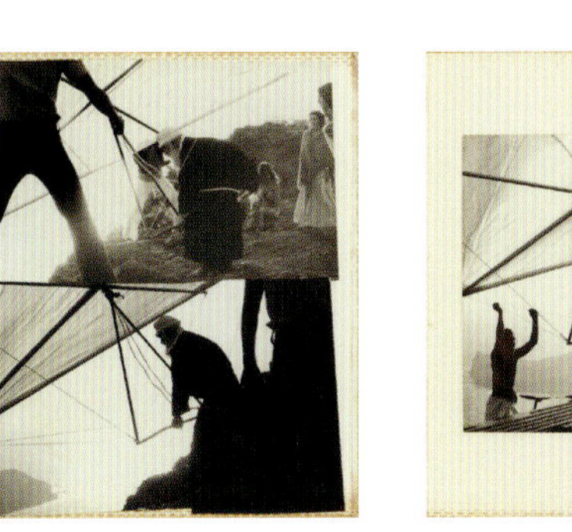

For the three weeks prior Father had been talking about how it was time to disperse the family. He was done teaching, done being the center of our world. Despite this, I don't think he had any idea what the outcome of this day would be. Mercury helped launch him. Father went up with an open heart and left it all up to destiny. He said he would be fine because Jesus was the air and the air would guide him. He put his life in the hands of God. As soon as he left the platform the wind died and he dropped 900 feet.

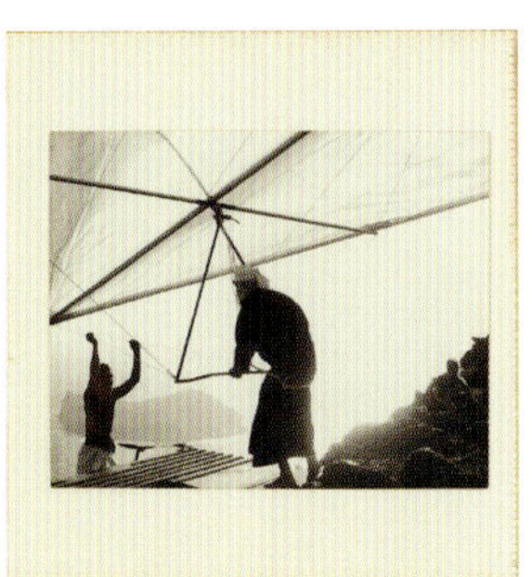

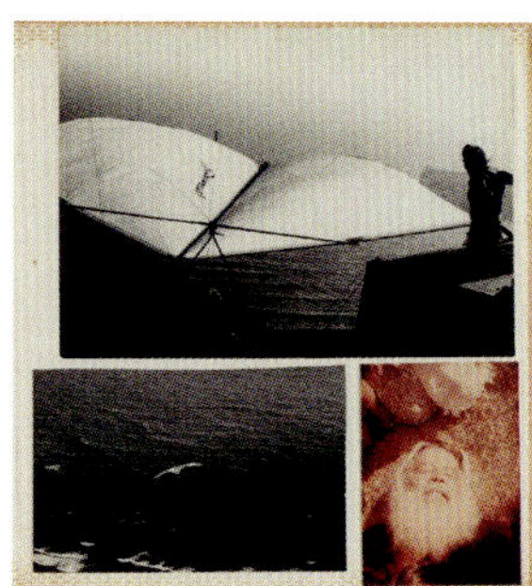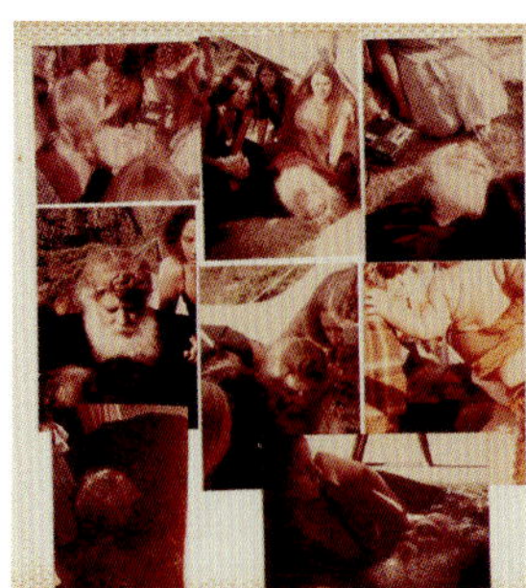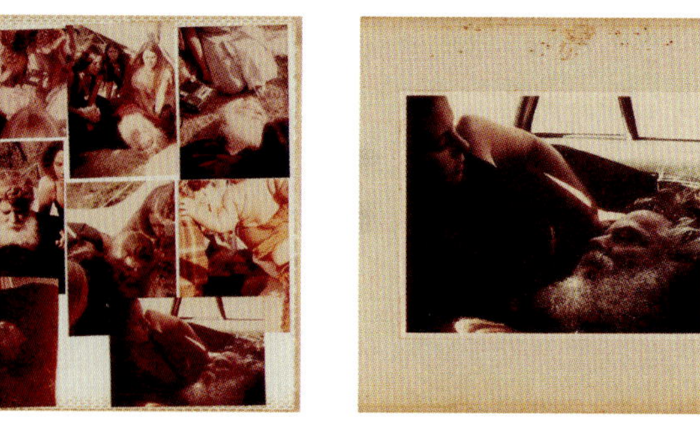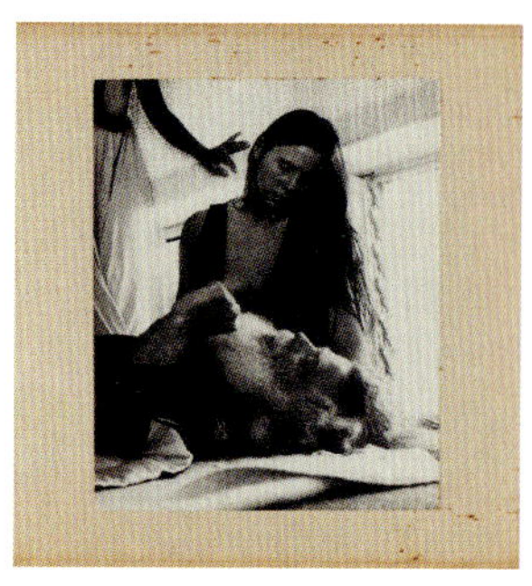

Father in flight. After he dropped, the wind miraculously lifted him before he hit the water. He was able to coast back toward the mountain and crash landed on the beach near a group of picnicking Samoans. Bottom right, Father after he landed. He had no broken bones, there was no blood. He was dazed when we arrived. He said, "Where is the angel who led me down?"

When we found Father he was conscious. It took us around 20 minutes to get down the mountain and find him. When we arrived, a police car, a fire truck, and an ambulance were parked nearby, but none of them approached him. He was lying there alone. The family helped Father into the car after the crash. You can see me holding a tape recorder, recording his words.

Father and Makushla in the Mercedes after we'd carried him to the car. He told us he thought his back might be broken. No one wanted Father to fly that day, but when Father, Jim Baker, Yahohwa, decided he was going to do something, no one could stop him. Right, Father in the house after the crash. He asked us to put the Family music on. Some of the hang gliders came by to check on him. A healer friend came by with colored lights.

Father asked for oxygen and an ambulance brought some for him. The paramedics asked him if he wanted to go to the hospital. Robin wanted him to go. He asked Makushla if he should. She said, "It's up to you, but it would be going against your own teachings." He didn't go.

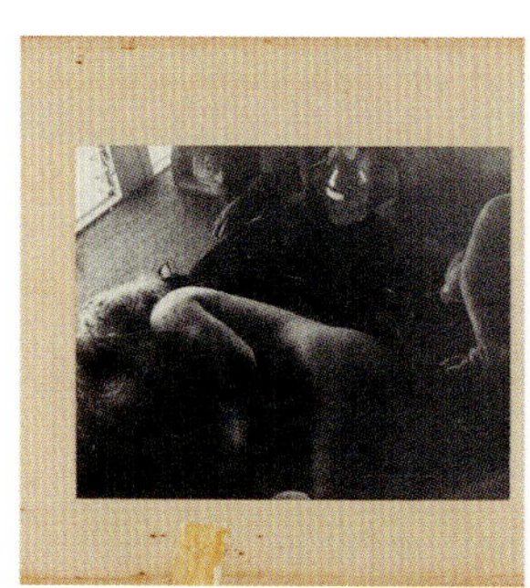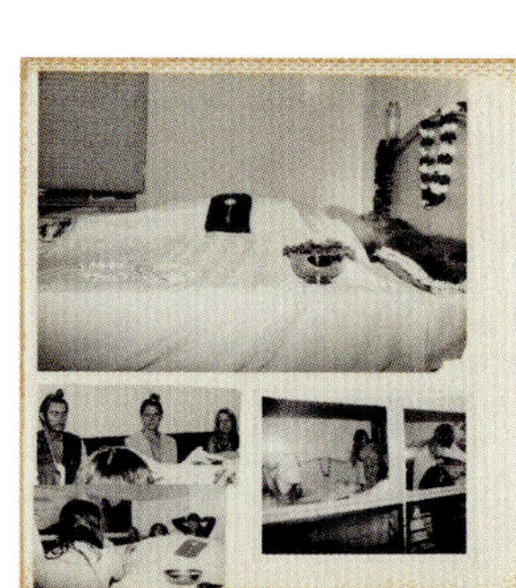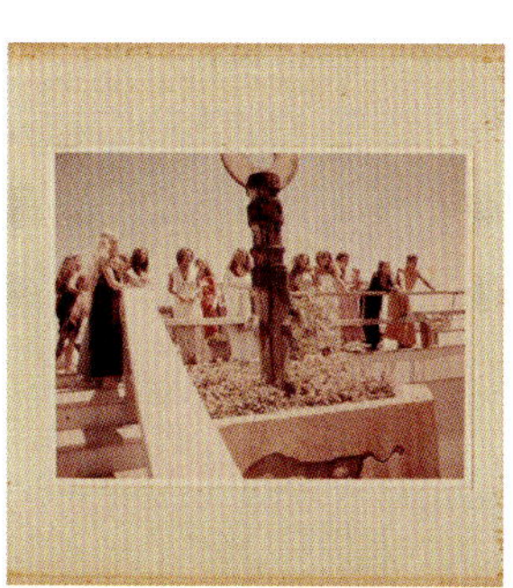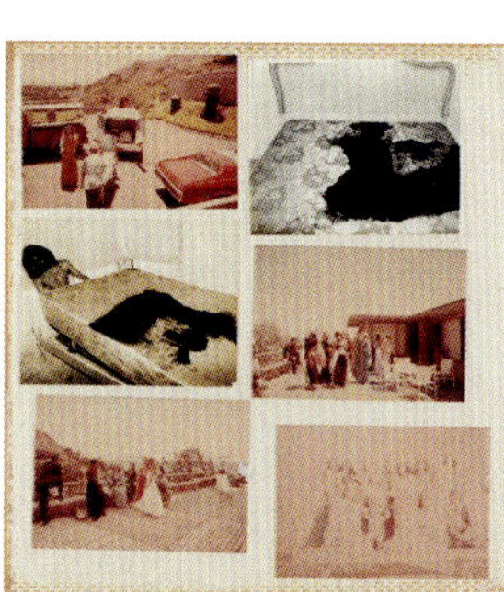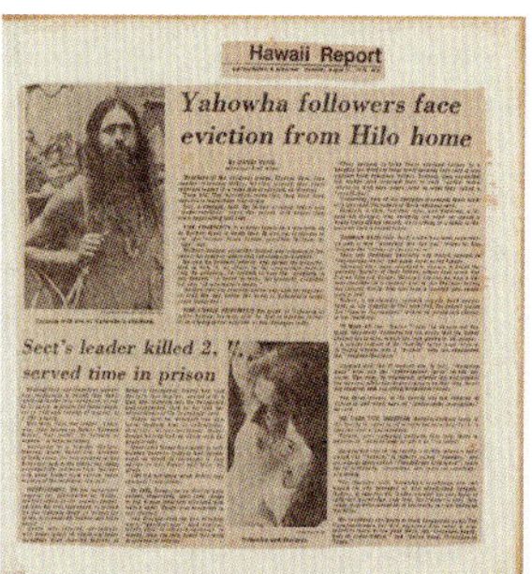

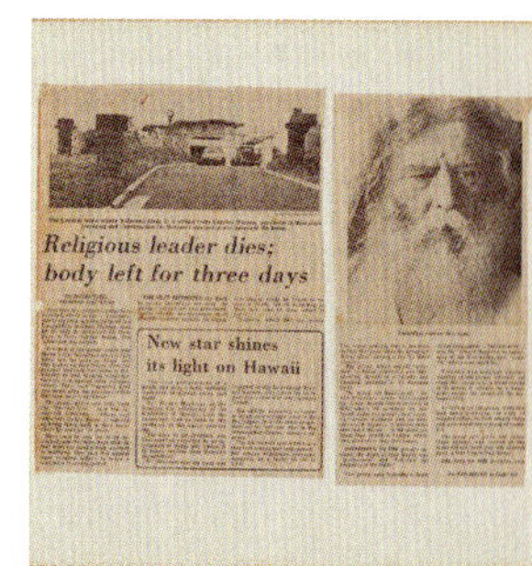

He was in extreme pain off and on. He told us that it was his kundalini rising through each of his chakras. No one ever thought he was going to leave the body. He was gone after nine hours. He became the first example in our Family of someone consciously leaving the body. He passed in Makushla's lap. They were looking into each other's eyes.

We laid him to rest on the bed after he left the body. Father taught us that after a person passes, the body should be left undisturbed for three and a half days for the organs to shut down and for the soul to review its river of life. It is an ancient practice and many other groups have done this, including native Hawaiians and Sikhs. We put candles at the foot and head of the bed and surrounded him with sweet smelling flowers. We kept vigil for three days, chanting Yahowha. Lower left, Jupiter, Mercury, Lovely.

Father's women and Mercury watching the ambulance collect Father's body. We didn't contact the rest of the Family until after the three and a half days for fear that word might get out to the authorities, who would have removed his body before the vigil was complete. This caused a real rift in the Family.

Top left, Father being loaded into the ambulance. There was the body of a young man already in the ambulance when they came to get Father. Someone said, "Oh, he's still collecting suns." Middle left, Pythias cleaning up the mattress where his body had rested. Other images are outside the Glass House.

An article about our time in Hilo after Father left the body. Our lease at the Doc Hill mansion was up just days after Father passed, and we were asked to leave our house within the week, as the Doc Hill property owner was moving back in with his family. The owner kindly helped us find our new home, at a nearby abandoned country club. It was large but very rustic, and we had to jerry-rig the electricity to wash clothes and make coffee.

A nova, a new star, became visible for the first time after Father's passing. We saw that article as substantiation that he was fine, giving us a subtle sign that he was still laughing about it all.

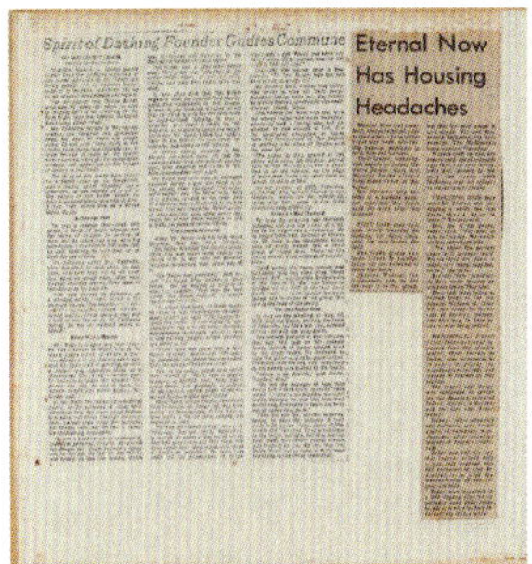

After the ambulance took Father away, we had a couple days when the police and reporters were around constantly. Of course we had to leave the Glass House. The owners, the Watsons, were completely freaked out. Makushla and the rest of us who were staying with Father didn't really want to go back to Hilo. It felt over, and we had no idea how the Family would be run. We went to Maui for a few days and then returned to the Family. Left, a story that ran in *The New York Times* over a year after Father left the body.

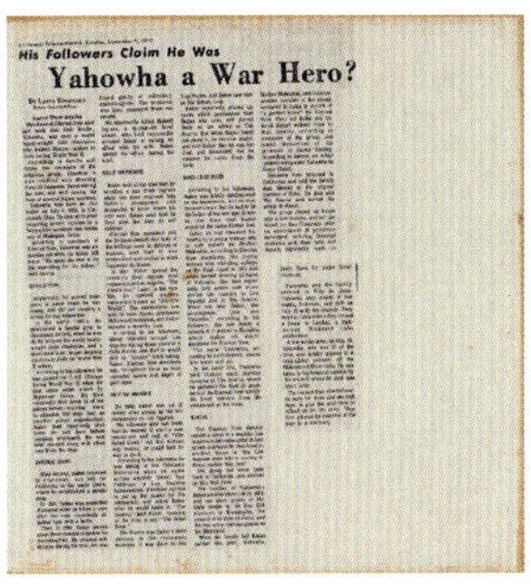

The *Hawaii Tribune-Herald* ran a series of investigative articles about Father's hang gliding accident and passing and the controversy that surrounded it. This is the first installment of the series by the journalist Larry Berman on Jim Baker, Yahowha and the family. This was one of three extensive articles.

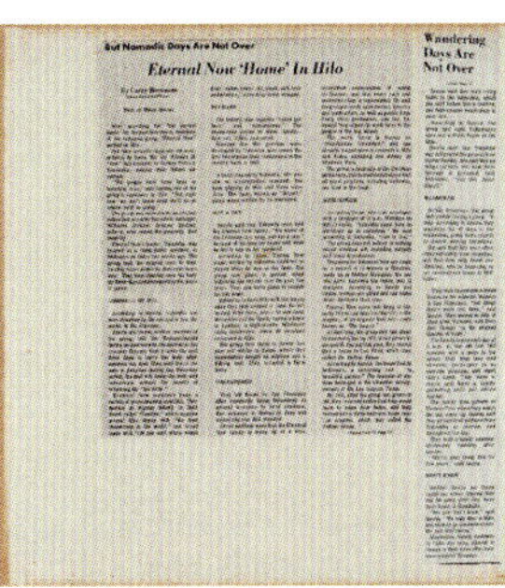

This is the final article of the Larry Berman investigative series. A number of journalists were digging up information from Jim Baker's past, and I know many of the locals were afraid of us around that time.

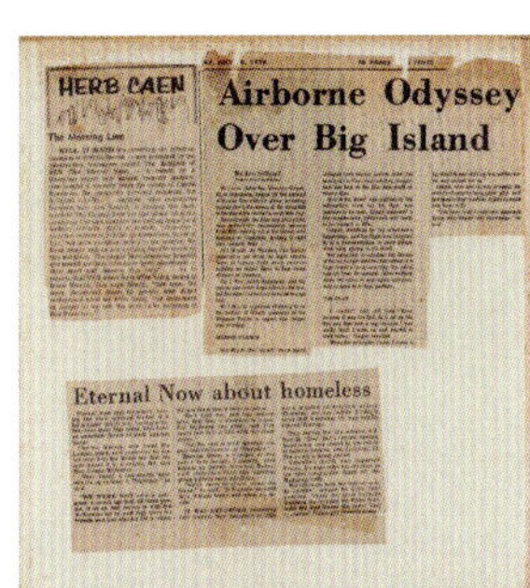

Left, Herb Caen's column about us in the San Francisco Chronicle, San Francisco days. Right, an article about Mercury and one day when he took flight and was missing for several hours. He had to walk 10 miles with his kite over a desert of lava before flying again and landing in a pasture.

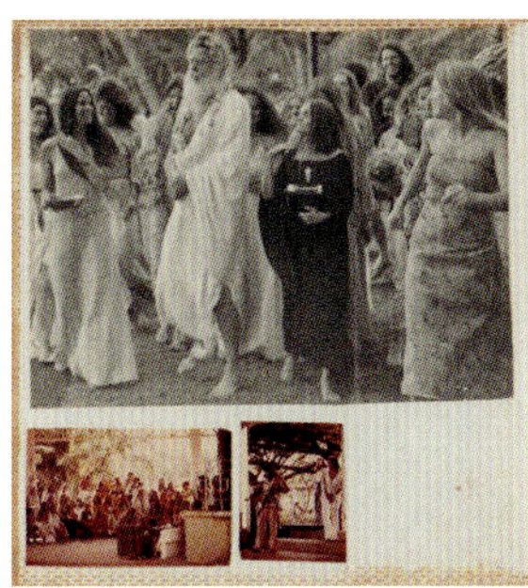

Top left, Kauai days. When we were met with hostility then, Father invited the community to our property so that they could ask us questions and get to know us. No one showed up. Top right, Father and Makushla dancing, Big Island. Center Right, Pythias and Father at LAX. Lower left, Father, his women, and some suns on an outing. Lower right, Father's final flight.

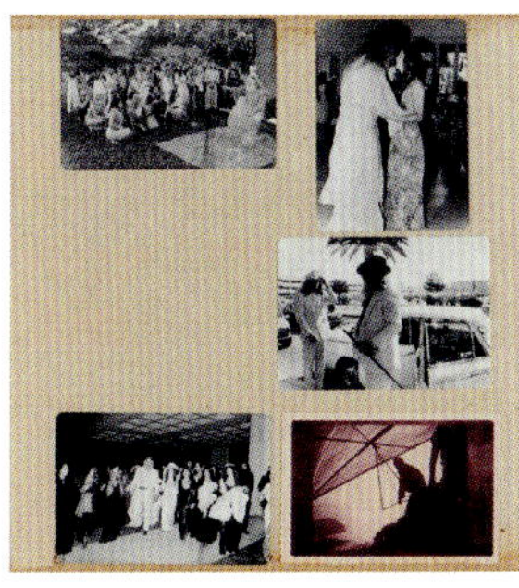

I was just eyes on Father, all the time. Wherever he went, I followed, usually with a tape recorder and a camera. The responsibility of being the Family documentarian was sometimes overwhelming. Below, an earlier Breath concert in Hilo at the Queen Lili'uokalani bandstand. Months after Yahowha left the body, there were so many rumors going around about us that we decided to host an event at the bandstand. We presented a slide show, gave musical performances, and served refreshments. We wanted to let Hilo know we were still there and still a viable group, and that we were available for work and to answer anyone's questions.

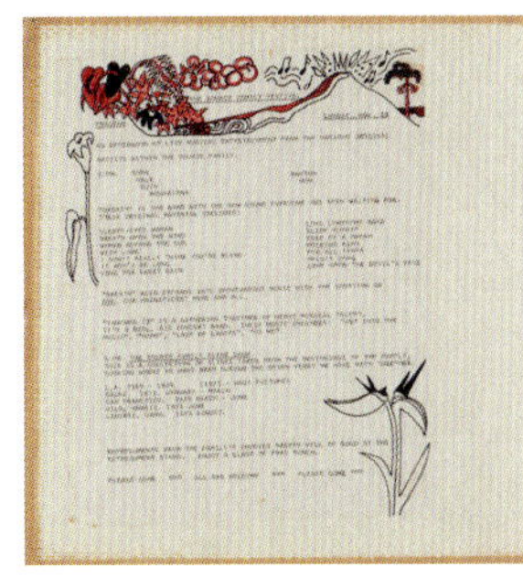

Makushla became the leader of the Family that day at the bandstand, even though she never wanted that role. She was Father's woman and the only person in the Family everyone could agree on. She ran the Family with support from the council he had established. We created this constitution for the council, which outlined the five rules of the Aquarian Mother. Each day after morning class, Makushla and the council would come together and address whatever needed to be organized or taken care of that day. The men accepted this power structure because it was very similar to the way Father ran things for years.

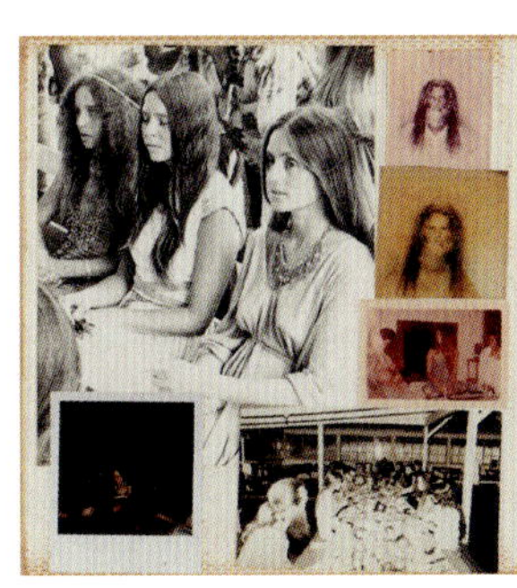

Left, Heaven, Makushla, and me the day at the Queen Lili'uokalani bandstand, when Makushla stepped into her role. We used the opportunity that day to set the record straight on what had happened with Father passing over and what we wanted to do in Hilo. The locals appeared to accept us. Lower right, The Hilo Country Club, where we stayed for six months. Lower left, Makushla reads by candle light during morning meditation.

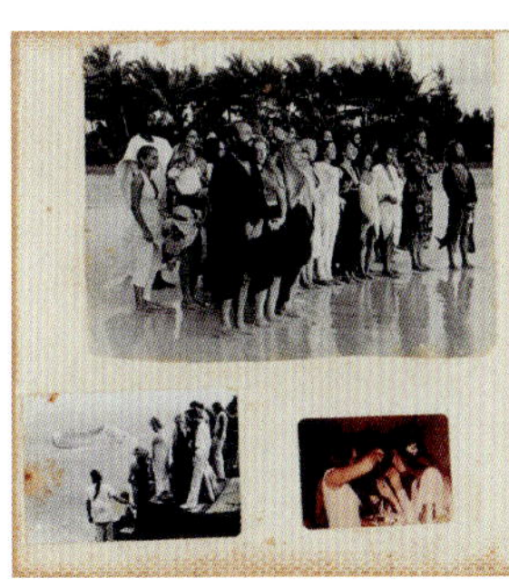

Top, family photo in Lanikai, after we left Hilo. It was decided we'd all return to Lanikai and live in several houses. We were still getting money from the sale of The Source. Shortly before he passed, Father put the rights to The Source residuals in the names of Robin, Aquariana, and Prism, the three mothers of his Source Family children. This was the time the suns began growing and selling the sacred herb to support the family. Bottom left, one day some of the Family wanted to view where Father went hang gliding off the cliff. Lower right, Isis lighting up Makushla's pipe for the sacred herb ceremony.

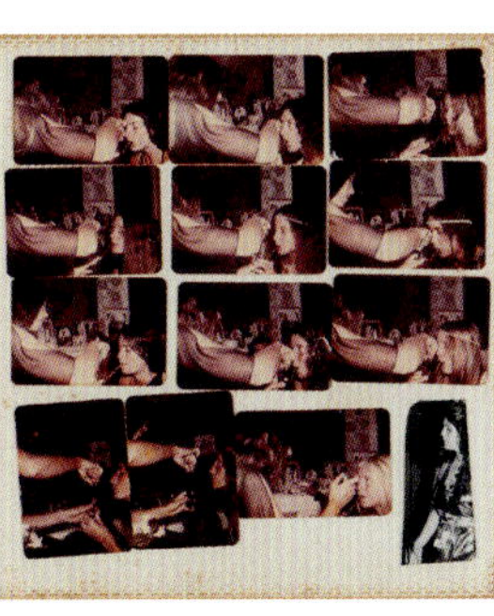

Morning meditation, Lanikai. Here, Makushla gives the council women (Father's wives) the sacred herb before morning meditation. The council always smoked first, then the rest of the Family. We would hold the sacred herb in for six seconds and chant the holy name Yod He Vau He.

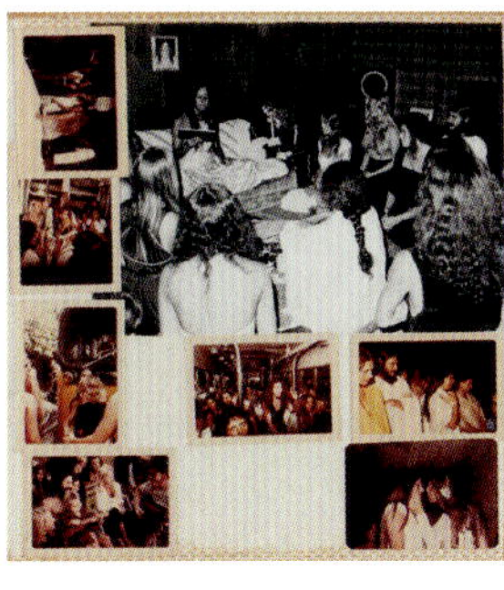

Top right, Makushla leads one of the morning meditations. Makushla did her best to keep the Family going, but it became apparent that Father had been the glue that held us together, the reason we all came into the Family. It seemed clear it was time for all of us to finally start our own journeys, as Father had wanted. Still, this took a while. Center, a friend of the Family had a school bus and one day picked us up for an outing. Lower right, Makushla gives me her sacred herb breath, like Father did to his women.

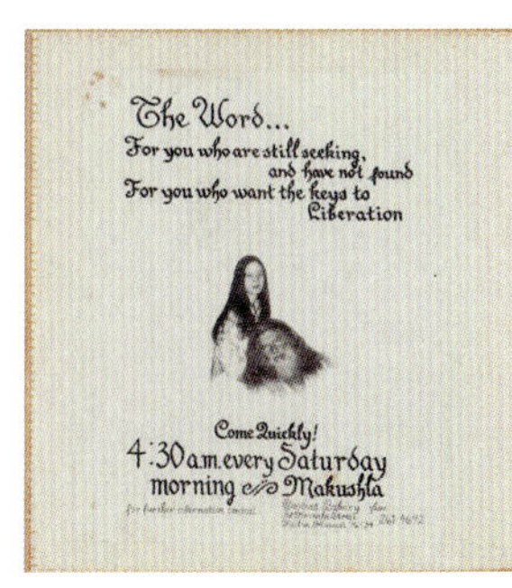

Father told us that after he passed, he would still be collecting his children. People found us after he left the body and saw Father as their spiritual teacher. This is when Alcyone, Ekahi, Renaissance, Nova, Shangrila, Hosanna, and the Hawaiian musician Cheital came into the Family along with a number of hang gliders including the Black Knight and Olympus. Alcyone and Renaissance ended up marrying and having two daughters, and Alcyone and others still carry on the teachings today. Father is still collecting his spiritual children.

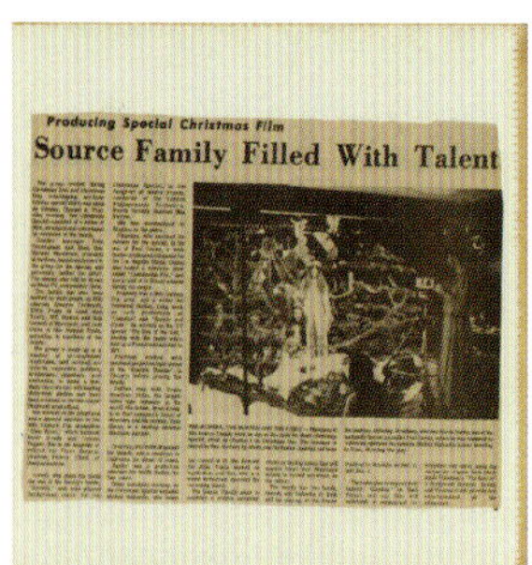

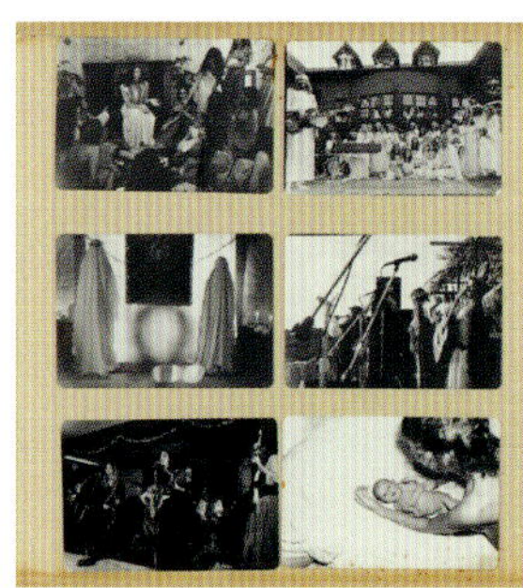

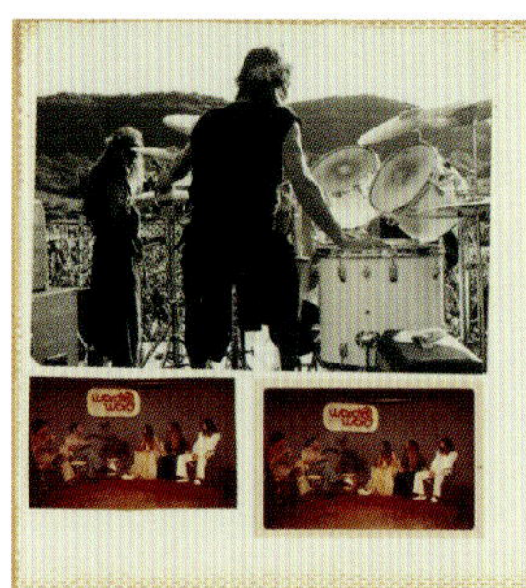

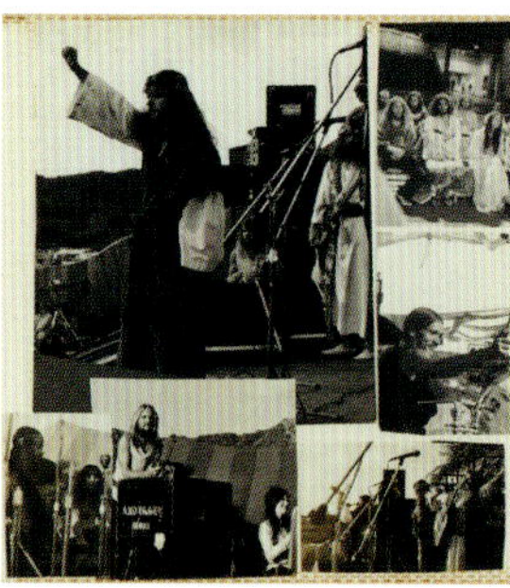

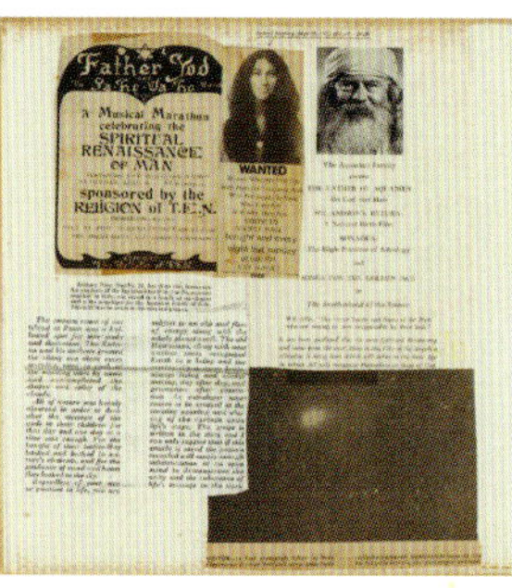

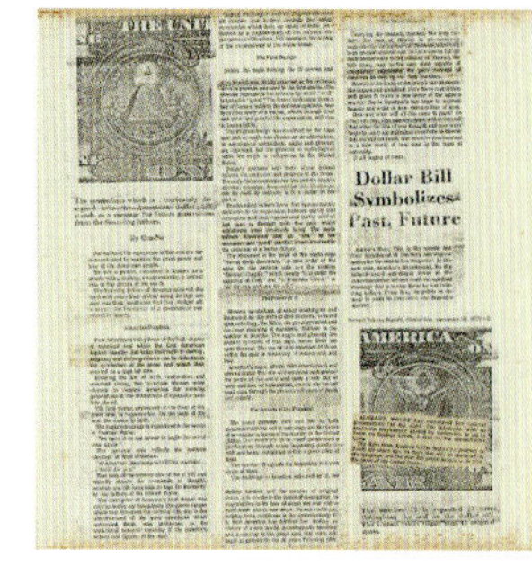

We decided to create a Source Family Christmas special on public access in Hilo. We built a set and made costumes, performed skits and played music. We wanted to do something creative after Father left the body and were hoping the public might accept us if we shared this with the island.

Top left, Makushla leading a morning meditation class. Top right, Family photo, Mother House days. Middle left, a shot from our public access Christmas Special. Middle right, Breath at the Crater Festival. Lower left, Breath performs on our Public Access Christmas special. Lower right, my daughter Saturna just after she was born.

Diamond Head Crater Festival, January 1st, 1976, was held to honor the bicentennial of the United States. Sly and the Family Stone headlined, and Breath was invited to open the festival with a sunrise performance. A group of musicians and a few others flew over from Hilo to perform. Top, Rhythm, left, and Octavius perform. Below, a televised interview about our participation in the Diamond Head Crater Festival the day before in Honolulu.

Breath played in special tribute to the Founding Fathers, Father's favorite incarnation. He loved America and the founders, who were Freemasons and occultists. Top left, One introduced the band and led the audience in a "Yod He Vau He" chant. There were thousands of people chanting "Yod He Vau He" to the rising sun. Sir Knight is behind the amp and Sunflower is to the right. Bottom left, Pythias, Djin, Sir Knight with a camera, and Venus, who styled the band.

Top left, a flier for an early family performance outside at UCLA. Top middle, an early flyer with Ahom for classes at The Source restaurant, probably 1972. Top right, the program for the *God and Hair* event at the Wilshire Ebell. Lower left, Om-Ne wrote this introduction to his horoscope for a Big Island newspaper.

Om-Ne preferred to stay in the background, yet his contributions to the family were enormous. He was a primary photographer at the Father House and shot many of the iconic images of the Family and the bands at that time. He worked with Father to design the album covers. He was a Family astrologer, and he was also a brilliant writer. He offered heartfelt companionship to all of us, and was beloved by the women and the suns alike. He was quiet, sensitive, brilliant, kind, and humble. He made things fun and had a wicked sense of humor. He wrote this article about a key symbol in The Source Family—the eye and the pyramid.

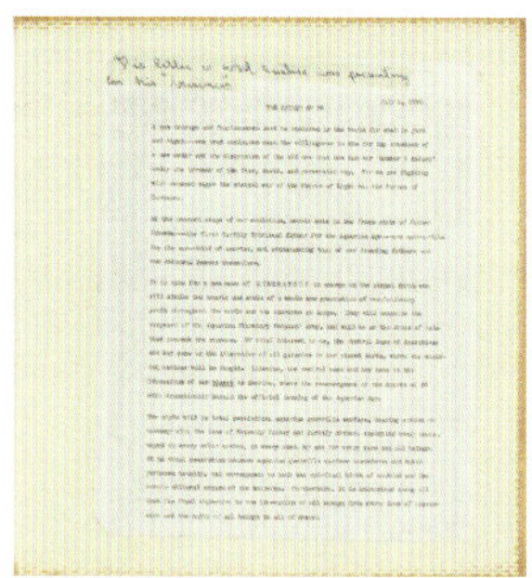

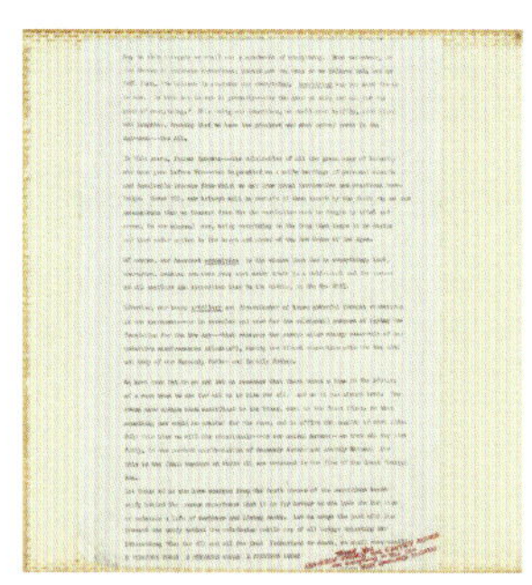

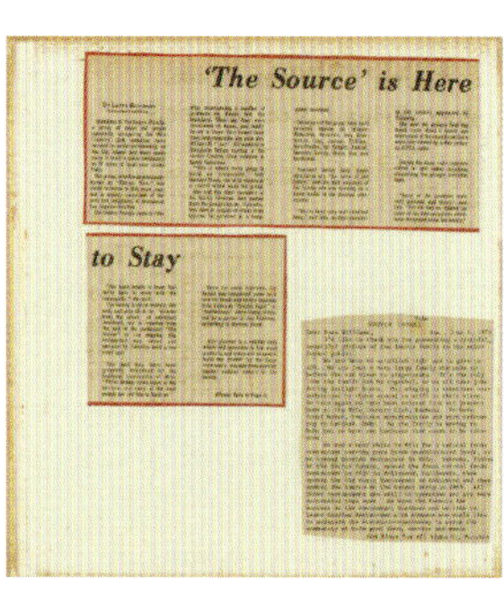

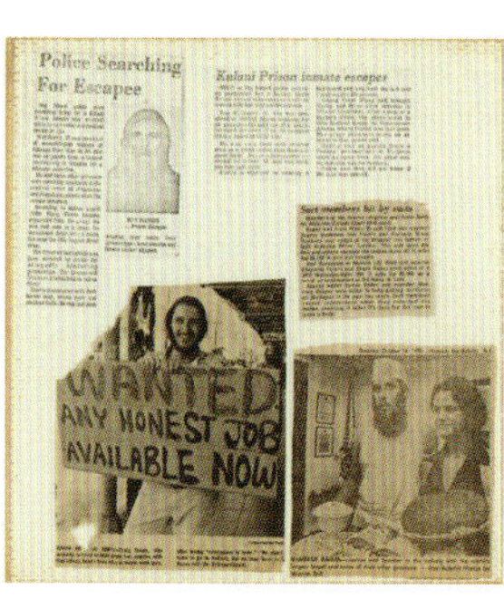

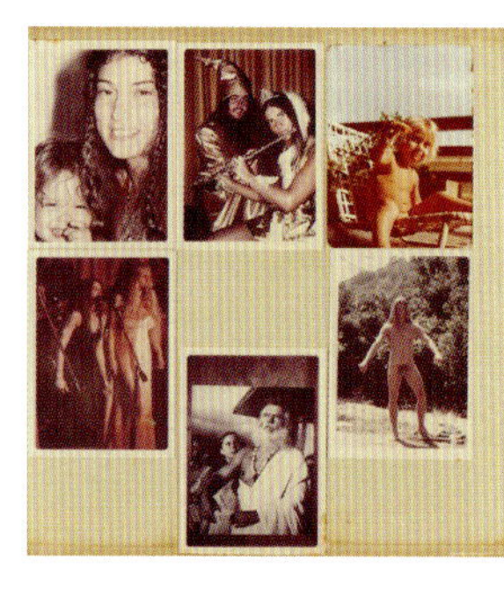

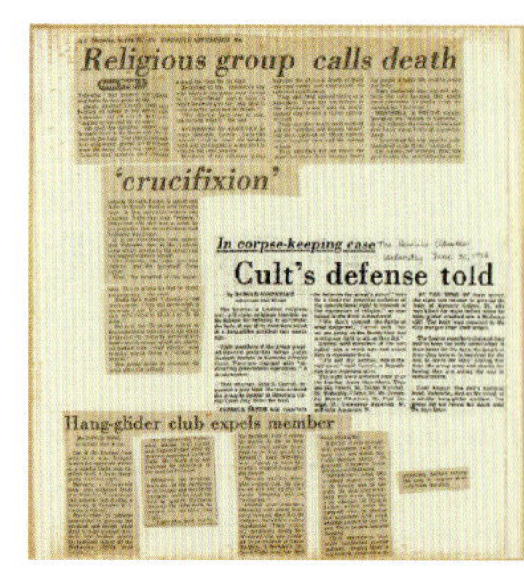

Justice wrote this on Father's birthday, July 4th. I have no memory of what "business" this was for. Justice was a powerful presence in the Family. Justice and Star met in a Mexican prison, where they had spiritual awakenings and became best friends. They joined the Harrisburg Family, a communal group in Pennsylvania of about 20 dedicated to a mix of Bible-based teachings and the rebirth of the God self. Justice and Star decided to leave the Harrisburg Family, along with their wives, children, and others (Mercy, Joy, Peace, Glory, Soul, Ray, Moon, and Sunshine). They drove their limousine straight to Los Angeles in search of their new home and arrived at The Source.

When Justice encountered Father, the connection was instantaneous. Justice returned to tell his group, "We're going to live with God in the Hollywood Hills." Many of us were shocked when they first arrived to live at the Father House. The men, women and children in the group were Black except for Star, and The Source Family was largely white, with only a few Black members. Their group was intensely seeking enlightenment and was very focused, and Father embraced them immediately. Our families merged and as brothers and sisters in spirit we became one.

Hilo continued to support us with positive press, even after Father left the body. We thought for a while we'd settle there permanently and had real intentions to carry out Father's vision and build our dome community. But we had a hard time getting reoriented after we left Doc Hill. We were outside of town, without a phone or transportation, and the suns lost work because of this and had to do a lot of foraging for food. Our singing and chanting at 4 a.m. every morning led to our eventual eviction from the country club. It felt right to return to Father's final home, Lanikai.

Top left, Some of the suns helped break a convict out of jail. He was a friend of one of Father's women who had been visiting him in jail and giving him Father's teachings. He saw Father as his spiritual father and wanted to join the Family. He was recaptured shortly after. Below right, Joshua and Summer opening Goodies Bakery after Father left the body. It was very successful, but most of the profits went to cover all the women and children eating the baked goods. Middle right, this came out after we'd left Hilo for Lanikai and ran out of money.

Robin and Tau, top left. Center, Om-Ne with Paralda for the Source Family public access Christmas special. Lower left, Robin and Aquarian performing at the Whisky a Go Go, Hollywood. Lower right, Mercury poses as The Star card for my living tarot series at the Father House. We intended to make it into a deck with photos and graphics but never finished it. In Lanikai, Mercury related to me that that day, he'd been abducted by aliens and taken on a spaceship. He said he didn't think they were evil or bad, but he seemed very confused. He was never right after Father passed, and this incident seemed to make him even more fragile.

Mercury never recovered from Father's passing. He blamed himself, because he launched Father off the cliff that day, barefoot, in his robe and headdress, with no training and a kite that was too small for him. Mercury was expelled from his hang gliding club for this, and the hang gliding club had to adapt a number of new rules and regulations, losing many of their freedoms. The hang gliding community was unmoored. Mercury, the hang gliding champion, had completely destroyed their club. But we never thought we'd lose Mercury.

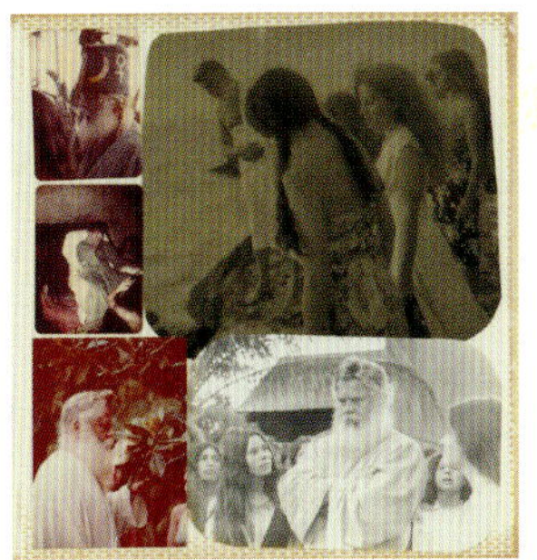

Makushla said she wanted to experience what Father had, when he was hang gliding. She asked Mercury if he would take her flying tandem off Makapuu cliffs. They were supposed to go in the morning at sunrise. The night before, on a full moon, Mercury said he wanted to go solo and make sure the kite was working and everything was good. Jupiter was there and some of the other brothers. Mercury lifted off into the darkness and a minute later they heard a screech. Mercury had hit the cliffs somehow. They climbed carefully down the hill to find him, which was treacherous. By the time they reached him, he had left the body.

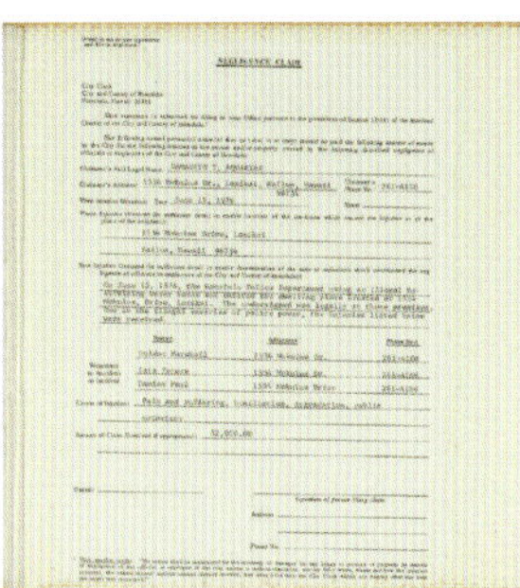

We brought Mercury back to the council house and set up his body for a vigil. The police came the next morning. They left and returned with a warrant and kicked down the door. They took Mercury away and charged us with obstructing justice, hauling eight or nine of us into the paddy wagon. In jail, we had to come to terms with what this might mean: we could go to prison for years. John Carroll, a respected conservative attorney, saw the injustice of this and represented us. Our arrests were later expunged from the record, but it took decades to live down the headlines in the newspapers.

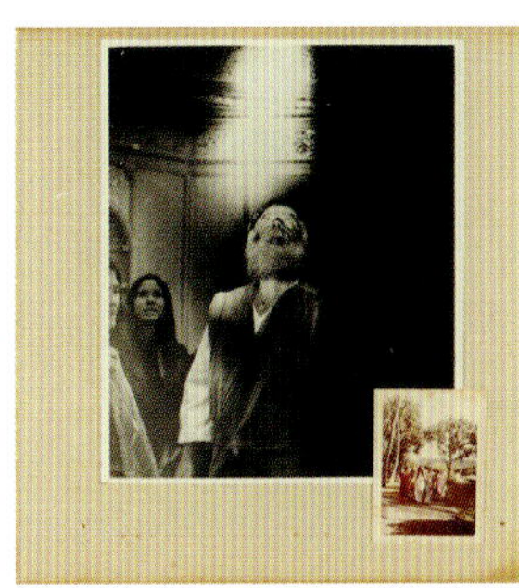

Left, Father in the Atherton mansion, sensing a dark energy in the dome, San Francisco, 1975. Right, Makushla leading a group on an outing while we were living at the Sun Palace, Lanikai, 1977.

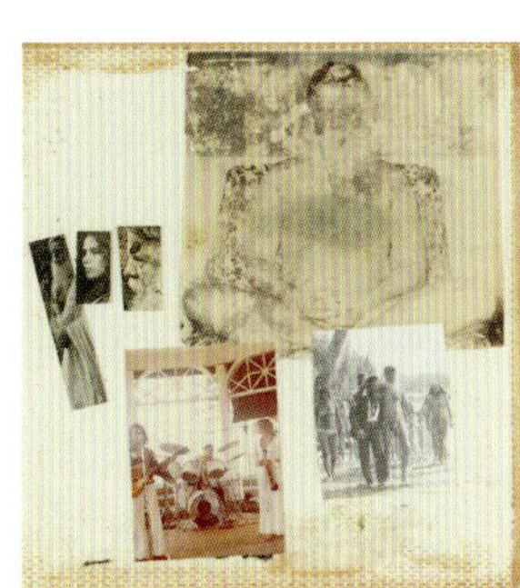

Bottom left, family musicians at the Hilo bandstand. Bottom right, Father and Damascus, with Hypatia to the left and Octavius' brother, Sun, to the right. Damascus was living with us at the Doc Hill mansion and came with us to the country club, though he flew back and forth to Los Angeles to tend to business. Damascus tried his best to help us manage things as the elder brother of the Family. He told Makushla she wouldn't have to worry about anything, he would always take care of her because she was Father's woman.

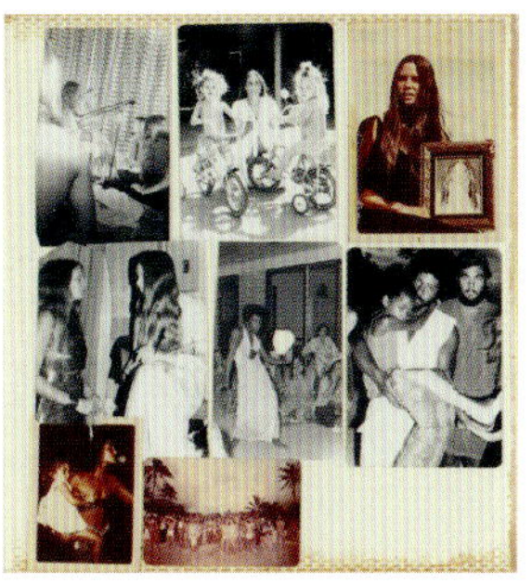

Makushla, top right, gives a TV interview after Father left the body. Top middle, Isis with Father's children Tao and Yod. Center, Joy dances at a gathering. Center right, Peace and Alcyone with little Sunshine, later on in Lanikai. Bottom center, the remaining Family on Lanikai.

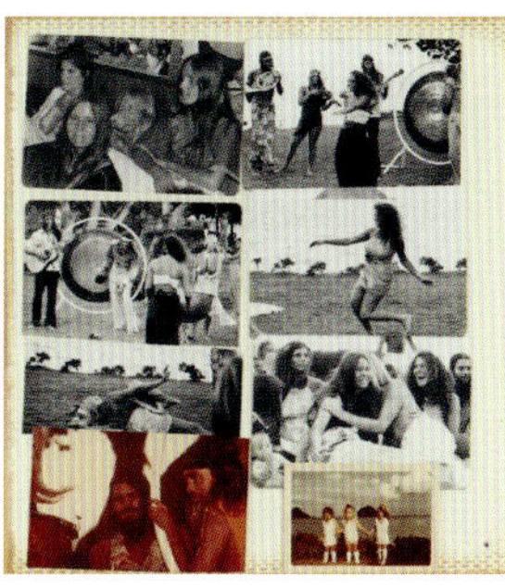

Yahowha's wives lived in the Sun Palace, the council house, in the back of a property on Lanikai Beach, and others lived in the front house on the same property. Other Family members found their own housing nearby. Top left, Venus, Makushla, Liberation, Isis. Pictures with the gong and on the grass are of a private Family gathering. Bottom right, Father's three children Yod, Tau, and Buttercup.

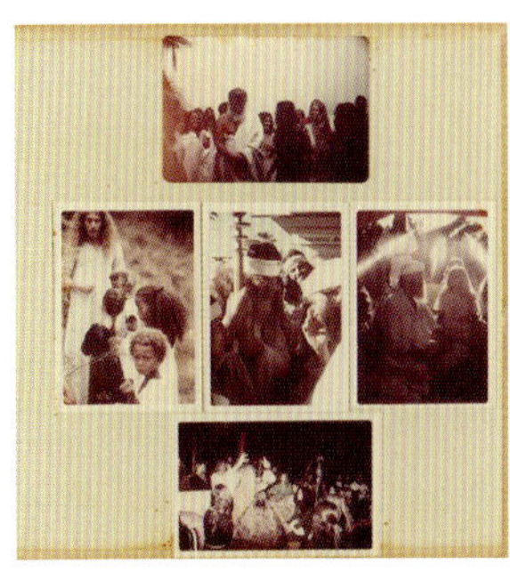

Photos from our early Mother House days (center and center right), Kauai (top and center left), and San Francisco (bottom). Middle left image, Djin with Soul and Sunshine and other children. Middle left, Father and Amber, who Father wanted as his woman but who left the family with Magus and a small group during the Father House days.

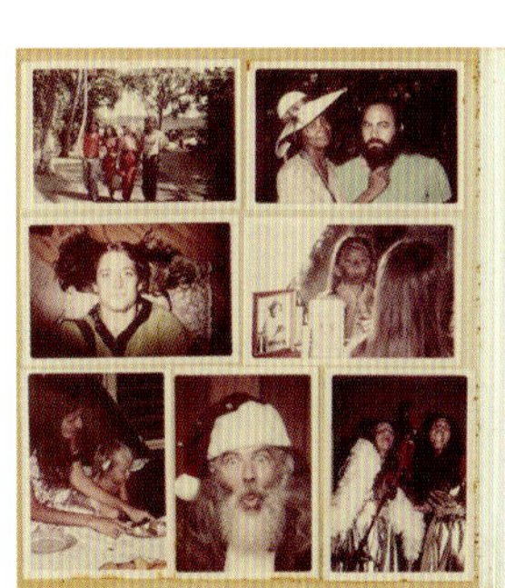

Clockwise from top left: Octavius, Robin, Aquariana and Sunflower, preparing to leave for Los Angeles to try and get something going with the music; Mercy and Star; Starwoman with a mud mask; Family performing for our Christmas special, Father as Santa Claus as God; Prism with Buttercup; Mercury.

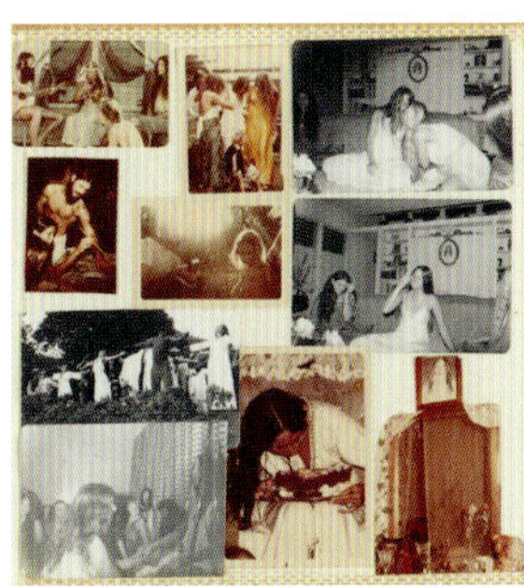

More Lanikai days. Center left, family members doing an early morning star exercise (breath of fire) in the yard. Makushla was doing her best to lead us, and she was appreciated. But we all came into the Family because of Father. Things started getting a little weird. There were things happening and decisions being made that people weren't agreeing with. We all knew it was the end. People started leaving and Makushla officially dispersed the Family in 1977.

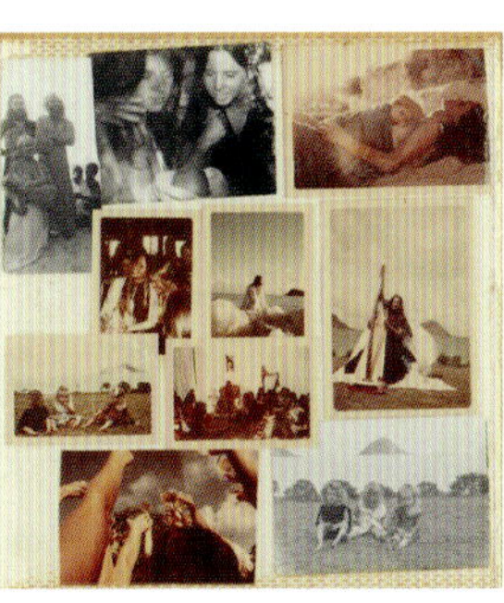

Top left, Tahuti, Aquariana and Yod and Orbit. Top center, Electra with her first child, Aloha, and Makushla. Top right, Isis and baby Tau. Center, Ra in the ocean with his robe. Ra and I came together after Father left the body, and I gave birth to our daughter, Saturna, the last child born in the Family. Bottom right, Tau, Yod, and Buttercup.

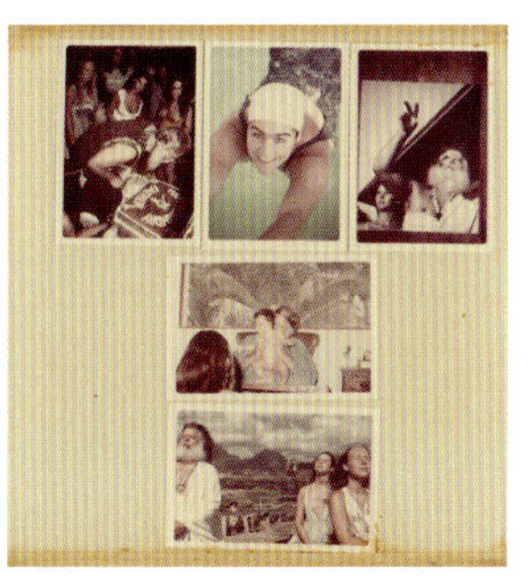

Top left, Aquariana, Robin, Anastasia and others celebrate Father's birthday at the Father House. Top center, Serenity in the pool at the Father House. Top right and bottom two images at the Glass House, Father's final days. Middle, Father embraces Yod. He loved and cared deeply for his children, his children from Ohio: Peggy, Chris, and Michael; his children with Elaine Baker: Beau, Bart, and Ben; his children born in the Family: Yod, Tau, Buttercup; and all of us, and our own children. We believed that our children would become the saints and sages of the Aquarian Age. Perhaps they shall one day.

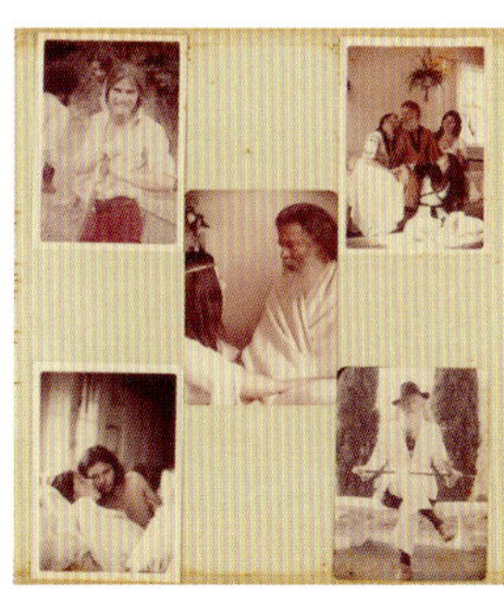

In the early days, when the Family was still forming, Father made it very clear to us that this was his journey, and he didn't know where it would take him, but he guaranteed it would be fun and said we were welcome to come along. By the end, he said he'd given us everything he knew so we could go out and start our journeys. He told us "Little birds have to fly out of the nest." We wouldn't leave, so he ended up being the one to fly. Then, our own journeys began.

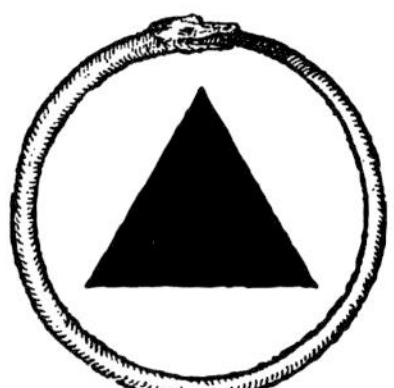

Sacred Bones Books
144 N. 7th Street #413
Brooklyn, NY 11249

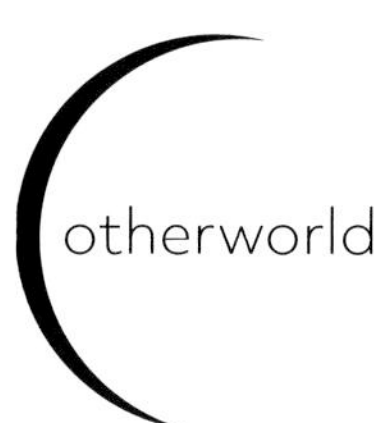